W9-BWO-964

COPY NOT FOR RESALE FREE COPY NOT FOR RESALE FREE COPY NOT FOR RESALE FREE COPY NOT

Social Problems
in a Diverse Society

FREE COPY NOT FOR RESALE FREE COPY NOT FOR RESALE FREE COPY NOT

Social Problems
in a Diverse Society

Diana Kendall

BAYLOR UNIVERSITY

ALLYN AND BACON
Boston   London   Toronto   Sydney   Tokyo   Singapore

Series Editor: Sarah L. Kelbaugh
Editor in Chief, Social Sciences: Karen Hanson
Editorial Assistant: Jennifer Muroff
Developmental Editor: Harriett Prentiss
Executive Marketing Manager: Suzy Spivey
Editorial-Production Administrator: Annette Joseph
Text Designer/Electronic Composition: Karen Mason
Copyeditor: Barbara Willette
Composition and Prepress Buyer: Linda Cox
Photo Researcher: Laurie Frankenthaler
Art Studio: LMY Studio, Inc.
Manufacturing Buyer: Megan Cochran
Cover Administrator: Linda Knowles
Cover Designer: Susan Paradise

Copyright © 1998 by Allyn & Bacon
A Viacom Company
Needham Heights, MA 02194

Internet: www.abacon.com
America Online: keyword: College Online

All rights reserved. No part of the material protected by this copyright notice may be reproduced or utilized in any form or by any means, electronic or mechanical, including photocopying, recording, or by any information storage and retrieval system, without the written permission of the copyright holder.

LIBRARY OF CONGRESS CATALOGING-IN-PUBLICATION DATA
Kendall, Diana Elizabeth.
  Social problems in a diverse society / Diana Kendall.
     p.   cm.
  Includes bibliographical references and index.
  ISBN 0–205–19835-X
  1. Social problems.   I. Title.
  HN17.5.K457   1997   97–42356
  361.1--dc21   CIP

Printed in the United States of America
10 9 8 7 6 5 4 3 2 1   RRDW   02 01 00 99 98 97

PHOTO CREDITS
PHOTO CREDITS appear on page 478, which constitutes a continuation of the copyright page.

Contents

FREE COPY NOT FOR RESALE FREE COPY NOT FOR RESALE FREE COPY NOT

FREE COPY NOT FOR RESALE FREE COPY NOT FOR RESALE FREE COPY NOT

▲ Chapter Ten
Violence   204

▲ Chapter Eleven
Health Care: Problems of
Physical and Mental Illness 226

▲ Chapter Twelve
The Changing Family   250

FREE COPY NOT FOR RESALE FREE COPY NOT FOR RESALE FREE COPY NOT

▲ **Chapter Thirteen**

Problems in Education 274

▲ **Chapter Fourteen**

Problems in Politics and the Economy 298

COPY NOT FOR RESALE FREE COPY NOT FOR RESALE FREE COPY NOT

▲ Chapter Fifteen

Problems in the Workplace   320

▲ Chapter Sixteen

Population and the Environmental Crisis   346

FREE COPY NOT FOR RESALE FREE COPY NOT FOR RESALE FREE COPY NOT

Preface

COPY NOT FOR RESALE FREE COPY NOT FOR RESALE FREE COPY NOT

[A social problems course] can provide a mind-opening . . . overview of a field of study, providing a method of perceiving and understanding the social realities we construct, playing a central role in leading students through the cognitive developmental processes that turn unchallenged dualism and other oversimplifications about everyday life into the complex formulations that better represent the social world in which we live.

—Sociologists Michael Brooks and Kendall Broad explain how they view the social problems course in their introduction to the *Resource Manual for Teaching Social Problems* (ASA Teaching Resources Center, 1997:1)

This statement sums up the main reasons why I enjoy teaching the social problems course and why I wrote *Social Problems in a Diverse Society*. Teaching and learning about social problems can be highly rewarding experiences for both instructors and students. Although we live in difficult and challenging times, the social problems course provides an excellent avenue for developing patterns of critical thinking and learning how to use sociological concepts and perspectives to analyze specific social concerns ranging from drug addiction and violence to inequalities of race, class, and gender.

My first and foremost goal in writing this book is to make sociology *interesting* and *relevant* for students. Consequently, I have focused on topics and issues that my students—along with well-informed sociologists and reviewers around the country—have found to be of particular importance. To stimulate interest in reading the chapters and participating in class discussions, I have used lived experiences (personal narratives of *real* people) throughout all chapters to show how social problems affect people at the individual, group, and societal levels. Moreover, I have applied the sociological imagination and relevant sociological concepts and perspectives to all the topics in a systematic manner.

Social Problems in a Diverse Society is unique in that it focuses on the centrality of race, class, and gender in understanding people's life experiences and social problems in the United States and other nations. Throughout the text, an inclusive approach has been

used that focuses on *all* people, including people of color and white women. Unlike some books, however, people—especially people of color and white women—are shown not merely as victims of social problems, but also as seeking to bring about change in families, schools, workplaces, and the larger society. To facilitate the inclusion of previously excluded perspectives, Chapters 2 through 6 examine wealth and poverty, racial and ethnic inequality, gender inequality, and inequalities based on age and sexual orientation. Thereafter, concepts and perspectives related to race, class, and gender are intertwined in the discussion of specific social problems such as prostitution, lack of access to adequate health care, and problems in the workplace.

Social Problems in a Diverse Society is theoretically balanced in its approach to examining social problems. However, it includes a more comprehensive view of feminist and postmodern perspectives on a vast array of subjects—such as the effect of new technologies and how the media depict social issues—than any other social problems textbook. As a sociologist who specializes in social theory, I was disheartened by the minimal use of sociological theory in most social problems texts. Those that discuss theory typically do so in early chapters but do not use them as a systematic framework for examining specific social issues in subsequent chapters. Similarly, many texts give the impression that social problems can be solved if people reach a consensus on what should be done. However, *Social Problems in a Di-*

verse Society emphasizes that how people view a social problem is related to how they believe the problem should be reduced or solved. Consider poverty, for example. People who focus on individual causes of poverty typically believe that individual solutions (such as teaching people the work ethic and reforming welfare) are necessary to reduce the problem, whereas those who focus on structural causes of poverty (such as chronic unemployment and inadequate educational opportunities) typically believe that solutions must come from the larger society. Moreover, what some people see as a *problem,* others see as a *solution* for a problem (e.g., the sex industry as a source of income or abortion to terminate a problematic pregnancy).

Finally, I wrote *Social Problems in a Diverse Society* in hopes of providing students and instructors with a text that covered all the major social concerns of our day but did not leave them believing that the text—and perhaps the course as well—was a "depressing litany of social problems that nobody can do anything about anyway," as one of my students stated about a different text. I have written this book in hopes of resolving that student's problem, along with many others, because I believe that the sociological perspective has much to add to our national and global dialogues about a host of issues such as environmental degradation; domestic and international terrorism; discrimination based on race, class, gender, age, sexual orientation, or other attributes; and problems in education. Welcome to an innovative examination of social problems—one of the most stimulating and engrossing fields of study in sociology!

ORGANIZATION OF THIS TEXT

As I noted previously, the text has been organized with the specific plan in mind of introducing disparities in wealth and poverty, race and ethnicity, gender, age, and sexual orientation early on so that the concepts and perspectives developed in these chapters can be applied throughout the text. Chapter 1 highlights the advantages and disadvantages associated with new information technologies to draw students into an examination of highly relevant social problems, including job deskilling and invasion of privacy, at the end of the twentieth century.

Chapter 2 looks at *wealth and poverty* in the United States and in global perspective. It provides concrete examples of how sociologists use social research methods to gain new insights into how people become wealthy and into problems such as homelessness, low-income and poverty-level neighborhoods, and the relationship between teen pregnancies and school dropout rates. The chapter concludes with a thematic question, which is applied to various topics throughout the text: "Can class-based inequality be reduced?" Chapter 3 integrates the previous discussion of class-based inequalities with an insightful examination of *racial and ethnic inequality.* The chapter ends on the optimistic note that perhaps the future of racial and ethnic relations will be better than the past as the children of today become the leaders of tomorrow. Chapter 4, *gender inequality,* highlights factors such as mainstream gender socialization and social structural barriers that contribute to the unequal treatment of women in the workplace, school, family, and other social institutions. Ageism and *inequality based on age* are discussed in Chapter 5, and Chapter 6 examines *inequality based on sexual orientation,* placing these important topics in a context similar to the studies of prejudice and discrimination rooted in racism and sexism in contemporary societies.

Chapter 7 links previous discussions of race, class, and gender to an analysis of *prostitution, pornography, and the sex industry.* The chapter provides up-to-date information on the globalization of prostitution and gives students insights into how sex workers view themselves, why they engage in this line of work, and why some other people view sex workers as a social problem. In Chapter 8, *alcohol and other drugs* are discussed in depth, and students are provided with information about the so-called "date rape drug" and about abuse of prescription drugs, over-the-counter drugs, and caffeine. Chapter 9 discusses *crime and criminal justice,* and Chapter 10 takes an incisive look at *violence,* particularly crimes such as murder, domestic violence, and hate crimes.

Beginning with Chapter 11, we examine some of the major social institutions in our society, such as *health care, particularly problems of physical and mental illness,* and note aspects of each that constitute a social problem for large numbers of people. Chapter 12 explores *the changing family,* with special emphasis on diversity in intimate relationships and families and child-related family issues. Chapter

13 presents contemporary *problems in education,* tracing the problems to issues such as what schools are supposed to accomplish, how they are financed, and why higher education is not widely accessible. Chapter 14 focuses on *problems in politics and the economy* and provides a variety of perspectives on political power and the role of the military–industrial complex in U.S. politics and the economy. Chapter 15 examines *problems in the workplace,* looking not only at workers' problems and workplace discrimination, but also at worker activism and how the global workplace is changing the United States and other nations. Chapter 16 provides a survey of problems associated with *population and the environmental crisis,* focusing particularly on the causes and consequences of overpopulation and high rates of global migration. Chapter 17 discusses *urban problems,* showing the powerful impact of urbanization on both the developed and developing nations of the world. Chapter 18 concludes the text with a look at *global social problems related to war and terrorism.* After examining such topics as militarism, military technology and war, and domestic and international terrorism, the text concludes with the hopeful idea that large-scale war and terrorism can be averted in the twenty-first century.

DISTINCTIVE FEATURES

A number of special features have been designed to incorporate race, class, and gender into our analysis of social problems and to provide students with new insights into social problems that they hear about on the evening news. These distinctive features include the following.

Lived Experiences throughout Each Chapter

Authentic first-person accounts are used as vignettes—"real words from real people"—to create interest and show how the problems being discussed affect people as they go about their daily lives. Lived experiences provide opportunities for students to examine social life beyond their own experiences ("to live vicariously," as one student noted) and for instructors to systematically incorporate into lectures

and class discussions examples of relevant, contemporary issues that, more likely than not, have recently been on the evening news and in newspaper headlines. Some examples of lived experiences include the following:

◆ Lawrence Otis Graham, a Harvard-educated corporate lawyer and author, describes how much trouble he and many other middle- and upper-middle-class African Americans have getting taxis in cities such as New York and working in corporate America in the 1990s (Chapter 3, "Racial and Ethnic Inequality").

◆ Hazel Wolf, age ninety-five, of Seattle, Washington, discusses her trip to Decatur, Alabama, to visit with a group of elementary students who had seen her picture in *USA Today* and wrote letters to her (Chapter 5, "Inequality Based on Age").

◆ Nadia, a nineteen-year-old prostitute in New York City, explains how she went from being a minister's daughter to working in the sex industry (Chapter 7, "Prostitution, Pornography, and the Sex Industry").

◆ Cesille Hyde, age twenty-three, describes the night her car struck and killed a police officer who was directing traffic at an accident site and how she was subsequently charged with driving under the influence of alcohol (Chapter 8, "Alcohol and Other Drugs").

◆ Ruben Navarette, Jr., a Harvard graduate, recalls the day when his second-grade teacher divided the class into ability groups and notes how he believes that this process has a harmful effect on students, especially Latinos/as, African Americans, and Native Americans who attend racially integrated schools (Chapter 13, "Problems in Education").

Interesting and Highly Relevant Boxed Inserts

Three different boxed features—Social Problems in the Media, Social Problems in Global Perspective, and Social Problems and Social Policy—highlight current hot topics involving various long-term social problems, such as the following:

◆ *Social Problems in the Media:* "Downsizing in the Comic Strips" shows how cartoons such as *Dilbert* have portrayed the impact of information technology and corporate downsizing on people's lives (Chapter 1, "Taking a New Look at Social Problems").

◆ *Social Problems in Global Perspective:* "Organized Crime: The Global Empire" describes international money laundering that includes U.S. cities such as New York, Los Angeles, Dallas, and Miami as points of entry or exit to destinations such as Moscow (Chapter 9, "Crime and Criminal Justice").

◆ *Social Problems and Social Policy:* "Is Affirmative Action a Problem or a Solution?" examines the continuing debate over affirmative action, citing advocates and critics ranging from newspaper columnist William Raspberry to critic Linda Chavez (Chapter 3, "Racial and Ethnic Inequality").

▲ Built-In Study Features

These pedagogical aids promote students' mastery of sociological concepts and perspectives:

◆ *Chapter Outlines.* A concise outline at the beginning of each chapter gives students an overview of major topics.

◆ *Key Terms.* Major concepts and key terms are defined and highlighted in bold print within the text. Definitions are provided the first time a concept is introduced; they are also available in the Glossary at the back of the text.

◆ *Summary in Question-and-Answer Format.* Each chapter concludes with a concise summary in a convenient question-and-answer format to help students master the key concepts and main ideas in the chapter.

STUDY GUIDE

Because I believe that the study guide is one of the most important study tools available to students, I prepared a comprehensive *Study Guide for Social Problems in a Diverse Society.* The guide provides the following for each chapter: a chapter summary, learning objectives, a detailed chapter outline, a glossary of key terms, and a practice test composed of multiple-choice, true-false, matching, and fill-in-the-blank questions.

ACKNOWLEDGMENTS

I wish to personally thank the many people who made *Social Problems in a Diverse Society* a reality. First, I offer my profound thanks to the following reviewers who provided valuable comments and suggestions on how to make this text outstanding. Whenever possible, I incorporated their suggestions into the text. The reviewers are:

Allan Bramson, Wayne County Community College
Scott Burcham, University of Memphis
Keith Crew, University of Northern Iowa
Mike Hoover, Western Missouri State College
Mary Riege Laner, Arizona State University
Patricia Larson, Cleveland State University
Kathleen Lowney, Valdosta State College
Edward Morse, Tulane University
Charles Norman, Indiana State University
James Payne, St. Edward's University
Anne Peterson, Columbus State Community College
Margaret Preble, Thomas Nelson Community College
Dale Spady, Northern Michigan University
John Stratton, University of Iowa

Social Problems in a Diverse Society has involved the cooperative efforts of many people who have gone above and beyond the call of duty to make the book possible. I am extremely grateful to Karen Hanson, Editor in Chief, Social Sciences, for encouraging me to write the book. I wish to thank Sarah Kelbaugh, Series Editor, for her understanding and support throughout the entire process. Likewise, the gentle reminders and words of encouragement from Jennifer Muroff, Editorial Assistant, kept me on the right track. The production of *Social Problems in a Diverse Society* was supervised by Annette Joseph, who made everything run smoothly. The copyediting of Barbara A. Willette, Book Production Services, was outstanding and is greatly appreciated: Barbara does not let anything slip past her thoughtful gaze!

My most profound thanks go to editorial cartoonist Ben Sargent for his insight and for his generous contribution of cartoons for this text.

When I say that I could not have written this book without the assistance of two people, I am not exaggerating. Without the fine work of Developmental Editor Harriett Prentiss, this book would not be in your hands at this moment. Harriett has the unique ability to get inside someone's head and help them to convey in writing what they are thinking. Throughout this project, especially in its final stages, Harriett's energy, insights, and writing skills made this book what it is today. Despite looming deadlines, she was always optimistic that everything would turn out just fine, and indeed it did. Finally, my husband, Terrence Kendall, has done so much outstanding advising, and editing—and sometimes consoling—on this and other texts I have written

that I have declared him to be not only a lawyer but also an "Honorary Sociologist."

To each of you reading this preface, I wish you the best in teaching or studying social problems and hope that you will share with me any comments or suggestions you have about *Social Problems in a Diverse Society*. This text was written with you in mind, and your suggestions (with appropriate attribution) will be included whenever possible in future editions. Let's hope that our enthusiasm for taking a new look at social problems will spread to others so that we—together—may help to reduce or solve some of the pressing social problems we encounter during our lifetime.

Diana Kendall
Division of Sociology
Baylor University
P.O. Box 97326
Waco, TX 76798-7326

e-mail: Diana_Kendall@Baylor.edu

Chapter One

Taking a New Look at Social Problems

Here we are, all having been in the same boat. We've all lost jobs, and we're not even 30, an age when you're supposed to be highly desirable at corporations. I'll never forget the day my roommate came home with her boxes. The same day she was notified, she had to clear out. She was 25. . . .

I think there is going to be a backlash. Maybe not this year, maybe not next year, but there's going to be one. People aren't going to give 100 percent anymore. I see this with a lot of my friends. I'm not going to be like my dad and work till 10 o'clock at night and never see the kids. What for? So I'll be thanked with a pink slip?

I wish corporate executives could see all the faces of these people they're downsizing. I wish they could see them shopping for food and putting their kids to bed. All they seem to care about is the bottom line. And therefore all of us are nothing but Social Security numbers.

—*From an interview with "Laura," a twenty-nine-year-old vice president at New York's Chase Bank, who—along with her three roommates—has experienced corporate downsizing*
(Kleinfield, 1996:A9–10)

When I graduated from high school in the Washington, D.C., area in 1972, I went to college, but my old boyfriend Ricky didn't. He looked for a good, unionized factory job. He knew he could make good money and maybe buy a little house in the same neighborhood his parents and sister Sara lived in. His sister didn't go to college, either. She had a job as a typist in a big office building outside the Beltway, in the Maryland suburbs. . . .

Now, the factory is gone, and Ricky is trying to figure out how he can keep paying his mortgage on one third of his old salary. The factory moved to Mexico and now employs young Mexican women. The home office is still in Bethesda, Maryland, but it employs only half the number of men it did 20 years ago. Most of the jobs have been taken over by computers or are done on a consulting basis. The only job Ricky could find was as a security guard for one of the new hotels. . . .

The typewriter Sara used is also gone. When her office switched to computers, Sara had to learn how to use the new system. She thought that when she did, perhaps she could move into a better paying job, but that didn't happen. She still spends all her time typing, but now, instead of getting together with the other "girls in the pool" between typing letters, she sits alone all day in an office with a computer. During her breaks, she sometimes logs onto a computer bulletin board on the Internet. There, she pretends that she is a famous artist with an international reputation. Nobody knows differently; nobody will ever meet the face behind the computer identity.

— *Beth Rubin, a sociologist, describing the impact of changes in the U.S. economy on her friends*
(Rubin, 1996:25–26)

The everyday concerns of people provide us with important insights into pressing social problems in the United States. Job loss and the deskilling of work (downgrading a job so that less proficiency is required) as a result of new technology not only create personal problems for people like Laura and her roommates and Ricky and Sara, but also generate social problems.

Technology **refers to the knowledge, techniques, and tools that allow people to transform resources into usable form and the knowledge and skills required to use what is developed.** The pace of technological change has increased phenomenally in the past century. It may have taken 4,000 years for humans to advance from digging sticks and hoes to the plow, but in the past 150 years, we have moved from the steam engine and cotton gin to computers, laser surgery, organ transplants, industrial robots, and genetic engineering. These technological changes have vastly improved the quality of life for many people, especially in industrialized nations such as the United States, Germany, Japan, and the United Kingdom.

At the same time, technological innovation has had its downside, worsening existing social problems and producing new ones. Consider, for example, the positive and negative effects of some of the technology mentioned above: Organ transplants may save lives, but social class, celebrity, or some other factor often determines who receives one. Similarly, industrial robots reduce manufacturing costs, but they eliminate jobs. So the question is: At what point does

a new technology become a social problem? Or, more generally, what is a social problem?

WHAT IS A SOCIAL PROBLEM?

Although not all sociologists agree on what constitutes a social problem, a general definition might be that a *social problem* **is a social condition (such as poverty) or a pattern of behavior (such as substance abuse) that people believe warrants public concern and collective action to bring about change.** Social phenomena, such as new technologies, typically become redefined as social problems when they systematically disadvantage or harm a significant number of people or when they are seen as harmful by many of the people who wield power, wealth, and influence in a group or society. To put it still another way, social problems are social in their causes, consequences, and sources of possible resolution. A sociological examination of social problems focuses primarily on *society*—**a large social grouping that shares the same geographical territory and is subject to the same political authority and dominant cultural expectations**—not on individual attitudes and behavior.

Sociologists apply theoretical perspectives and use a variety of research methods to examine social problems. The study of social problems is one area of inquiry within *sociology*—**the academic and scholarly discipline that engages in systematic study** of human society and social interactions. Some social problems—such as crime and environmental pollution—are commonly viewed as conditions that affect all members of a population. Other social problems—including racial discrimination and sexual harassment—may be viewed (correctly or incorrectly) as conditions that affect some members of a population more than others. However, all social problems may be harmful to all members in a society whether they realize it or not, as is the case with racial discrimination. Sociological research has documented the extent to which white racism wastes the energies and resources of people who engage in racist actions as well as those of the intended targets (see Feagin and Sikes, 1994; Feagin and Vera, 1995).

Social problems often involve significant discrepancies between the ideals of society and their actual achievement. For example, the United States was founded on basic democratic principles that include the right to "Life, Liberty, and the pursuit of Happiness," as set forth in the Declaration of Independence. The rights of individuals are guaranteed by the U.S. Constitution, which also provides the legal basis for remedying injustices. Significant discrepancies exist, however, between the democratic ideal and its achievement. One example is *discrimination*—**actions or practices of dominant group members that have a harmful impact on members of subordinate groups.** Discrimination heightens existing inequalities along class, racial, gender, and age lines. It also may be directed against subordinate group members whose sexual orientation, religion, nationality, or other attributes or characteristics are devalued by those who discriminate against them.

Most people think of discrimination as being based on race, gender, or age, but class-based discrimination is also a daily occurrence. Consider, for example, fifty-three-year-old Marcos Muñoz, a first-generation immigrant from Mexico, who became a high school Spanish teacher after many years as a high school janitor. While supporting his family, Muñoz attended a community college and a four-year university where he received his college degree. After he was hired as a teacher, Muñoz explained how his change in class-based status—from being a janitor to being a high school teacher—affected his life: "It has changed for me, for my family, for my neighborhood, and many people now see me as an example for other people. . . . Oh, yes, I like it because now they call me MISTER Muñoz, teacher.

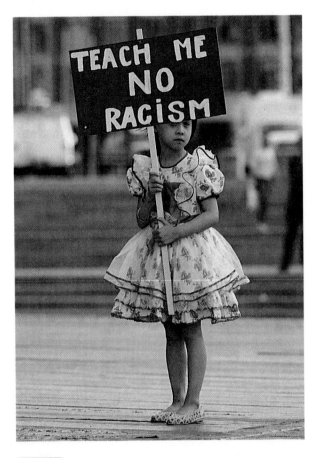

What does this photo show us about the discrepancies that exist between the democratic ideals and the social realities of our society? Does discrimination against subordinate group members take place in other societies as well?

[When I was a janitor] they didn't even call me by my name, they would just say, 'Come here, go there, do this, do that'" (quoted in Guerra, 1996:A11).

Marcos Muñoz's case reflects a strongly held, but unspoken, belief of many people that an individual's worth is based on characteristics that are ascribed (from birth) or achieved (acquired during the person's lifetime), rather than basic humanity. For Muñoz, these characteristics included the circumstances of his immigration (although he entered the country illegally, he is now a U.S. citizen), lack of educational opportunities (family poverty and few alternatives to traditional educational settings), low-paying jobs (which were, until recently, believed to be associated with limited years of formal education), and discrimination based on class, race, or other devalued characteristics or attributes.

Subjective Awareness and Objective Reality

The subjective awareness that a social problem exists usually emerges before the objective reality of the problem is acknowledged. The subjective awareness tends to be expressed as an uneasiness or skepticism about something, but it is not founded on any concrete evidence that a problem actually exists. When people fly in airplanes, for example, they may subjectively be aware that something bad can happen while they are traveling through the air at 30,000 feet in a metal canister; however, when they see an engine catch fire, they quickly experience the objective reality that a major—perhaps life-threatening—problem is at hand.

Similarly, the subjective awareness of information technology as a social problem occurred before the objective reality. (*Information technology* refers to the convergence of several streams of technical developments, including microelectronics, computer science, telecommunications, software engineering, and system analysis.) Information technology was developed for the U.S. military during World War II and gradually spread to business, industry, government, and education. With the introduction of the microchip, however, the rate of change accelerated in the workplace. Room-sized mainframe computers were replaced by much smaller, cheaper, and more powerful microcomputers. For corporate managers and owners, introduction of this new technology meant greater productivity and a higher profit margin (Pursell, 1994). Some workers were equally enthusiastic, believing that the new technologies would positively transform the nature of their work by consigning routine tasks such as typing or operating a cash register to machines and opening up creative new opportunities (Zuboff, 1988).

The risks of the new technologies for workers, families, and communities did not become apparent until decades later, during the 1980s. Many U.S. workers realized that they were being permanently displaced by the new information technologies. Just as automation had dramatically changed the nature of farming and manufacturing in previous decades, the computer and other information technologies dramatically changed—or eliminated—jobs in a wide array of employment sectors, including banking, insurance, and the telecommunications industry. As more people were affected, more became concerned, and an objective reality emerged that the advanced technologies were heightening existing social problems and bringing about new ones. The media, especially journalists and cartoonists, further increased people's awareness of the downside of these new technologies, as discussed in Box 1.1.

Measuring or Experiencing a Social Problem

A social problem is generally considered an objective reality—or condition—when it is possible to measure or experience its effects. For example, social problems posed by information technologies can be measured or experienced as surveillance, job deskilling, and intrusion on personal privacy. *Surveillance* is the direct and physical monitoring of a worker's behavior and communications by supervisors (Bennett, 1996). Work settings with linked or integrated computer networks allow supervisors and managers to measure productivity and oversee employees' daily activities without workers knowing when they are being observed (Zuboff, 1988; Perrolle, 1996; Rule, 1996). For many workers, surveillance is similar to working at a "glass desk," as Ceal Paoli, a word processing clerk, explains:

> With computers they can always look. And I hate for anyone to see something full of typos. You can type so fast now, you fly with these new machines. But what it looks like before you correct it! And what a table looks like before you format it! My boss would get scared if he saw it on the screen. . . . So what I do, if I'm halfway through something, let's say I did a rough draft but I didn't have a chance to edit it or run the spell check . . . if I'd be embarrassed to have somebody see it half done, I change the document's title to something like XMASMEMO. . . . If I couldn't hide my unfinished files, I would be working at a glass desk. Would you want everyone to be able to see right into your drawers? (quoted in Garson, 1989:213–214)

In addition to workplace monitoring, many workers have experienced *job deskilling*—the pro-

SOCIAL PROBLEMS
IN THE MEDIA

BOX 1.1

Downsizing in the Comic Strips

From *Doonesbury* and *Cathy* to *Dilbert*, dozens of syndicated comics regularly portray the impact of information technology and corporate downsizing on people's lives (see Rifkin, 1996). Take Dilbert as an example. He works in an office that is composed mainly of small cubicles where the nonmanagerial employees work. What are their jobs? To the employees, their jobs are meaningless parts of a "larger picture" that they do not understand. Decisions are made on high by people who appear to know almost nothing about the product they are creating. Whether it works or doesn't work is an ongoing discussion between management and Dilbert's coworkers. The bottom line—profit—is management's primary concern. From time to time, the employees' cubicle space (already quite limited) is made smaller—a form of downsizing. The very jobs that Dilbert and his colleagues perform also are periodically downsized or "sent offshore" to the "Elbonians," who work for less money. At any time, therefore, Dilbert and his coworkers may be replaced.

How true to life is *Dilbert*? To the readers of over 1,000 newspapers, Scott Adams's cartoon strikes a meaningful chord. Cartoonist Adams, who worked in a Pacific Bell cubicle for seventeen years, now receives 200 to 300 e-mail messages a day from readers who send comments and suggestions for future strips. Because so many people have been affected by corporate downsizing, it is the subject of numerous *Dilbert* strips. Some—like the one reprinted here—show how management thinks employees should respond to downsizing: They should be happy—it's good for the company. According to Adams (1996:1), "No matter how absurd I try to make the comic strip I can't stay ahead of what people are experiencing in their own workplaces."

DILBERT reprinted by permission of United Features Syndicate, Inc.

cess by which technological innovations reduce the proficiency needed to perform a specific job, leading to correspondingly lower wages for that job.

Job deskilling is not a twentieth-century U.S. phenomenon. When the power loom was invented in Britain in the nineteenth century, it greatly enhanced productivity and profitability for owners. It also devalued the weavers' skills and seriously reduced their wages. Some weavers rebelled against the negative effects of machine technology by smashing the power looms and burning the factories (Johnson, 1996).

Today, deskilling often involves the computerization of as many tasks as possible and the routinization of any tasks that cannot be computerized. Deskilling thus decreases workers' power, their wages, and any job security they may have possessed. For many supervisors and managers, however, deskilling increases their control over workers and heightens profitability. In highly routinized jobs, workers need to know only one basic routine; most decisions about how the work should be done are made in advance (Leidner, 1993). Jason Pratt describes his job as a McDonald's griddle operator:

"They called us the Green Machine 'cause the crew had green uniforms then. And that's what it is, a machine. You don't have to know how to cook, you don't have to know how to think. There's a procedure for everything and you just follow the procedures" (quoted in Garson, 1989:1).

Owners of McDonald's franchises probably would not agree with Jason that his job was deskilled, but franchisees have very different values and interests—such as increasing the profitability of their franchise—from those of their workers. Sociologist George A. Ritzer (1996:1) suggests that deskilling is a characteristic of "McDonaldization"—"the process by which the principles of fast-food restaurants are coming to dominate more and more sectors of American society as well as of the rest of the world." According to Ritzer, McDonaldization enhances efficiency (e.g., the ability to serve a hamburger, fries, and milkshake in fifty seconds), calculability (e.g., a McDonald's slice of cheese always weighs one-half ounce), predictability (e.g., the Big Mac burger is the same no matter where it is in the world), and control through automation, which minimizes human responsibility. The result, however, is that workers tend to be frustrated and demoralized (Garson, 1989, 1994; Leidner, 1993). In fact, Ritzer suggests that McDonaldization results in overwhelming problems across all areas of social life, especially by dehumanizing people and limiting our potential to be thoughtful, skillful, creative, and well-rounded human beings.

Finally, social analysts can measure information technologies as social problems by the way they intrude on personal privacy (see Lyon, 1994; Lyon and Zureik, 1996). Today, computerized data banks provide bureaucrats in government, education, health care, and other organizations with personal information about each of us (see Gandy, 1996; Gotlieb, 1996; Poster, 1996). Credit ratings, school records, housing information, medical histories, military status, automobile and driving records, welfare records, tax data, and other information are easily accessible. Beyond our right to privacy, what if the information is incorrect? Inaccurate records may harm people who have no knowledge that they cannot get jobs, credit cards, or insurance because of misinformation (Kling and Allen, 1996). In the future, information that is even more personal may become available through sources such as genetic profiles. Prospective employers and insurers would then have information about individuals' predisposition to certain diseases or behavioral traits. Given the impact of information

technologies on emerging social problems, some social thinkers refer to computerization as the "cursor" of our time (Nelkin, 1994:7).

WHY STUDY SOCIAL PROBLEMS?

Studying social problems helps us to understand the social forces that shape our lives on both the personal and societal levels. We learn to take a sociological approach instead of a commonsense approach. In our daily lives, we rely on common sense—"what everybody knows"—to guide our ordinary conduct and make sense out of human behavior: Why do people behave the way they do? Who makes the rules? Why do some people break rules and others follow the rules? But many commonsense notions about human behavior are myths—beliefs that persist even when the actual truth is different. Myths about social problems—ranging from crime and poverty to educational inequality—garner widespread acceptance and sometimes extensive media coverage.

A sociological examination of social problems enables us not only to move beyond commonsense notions but also to gain new insights into ourselves and to develop an awareness of the connection between our own world and the worlds of other people. According to sociologist Peter Berger (1963:23), we come to realize that "things are not what they seem." We can therefore approach pressing national and global concerns in new ways and make better decisions about those problems. In particular, taking a global perspective reveals our global interdependence: The lives of all people are closely intertwined, and any one nation's problems are part of a larger global problem.

Finally, a sociological analysis of social problems shows that social problems are multifaceted. People usually have strong opinions about what is "good" and "bad" in society and what might be done to improve conditions. This is true of sociologists no less than others. So sociologists use systematic research techniques and report their findings to other social scientists for their consideration. Sociologists strive to be *objective*, free from subjective (personal or emotional) biases. At the same time, complete objectivity may not be an attainable—or desirable—goal in studying human behavior. Max Weber, an early German sociologist, acknowledged that complete objectivity might be impossible and pointed out that *verstehen* ("understanding" or "insight") was critical to any analysis of social problems. According to Weber, *verstehen* enables individuals to see the world as others see it and to empathize with them. *Verstehen*, in turn, enables us to develop what is called the sociological imagination.

THE SOCIOLOGICAL IMAGINATION AND SOCIAL PROBLEMS

According to sociologist C. Wright Mills, the *sociological imagination* is the ability to see the relationship between individual experiences and the larger society. The sociological imagination enables us to connect personal troubles to public issues. Personal troubles are private problems of individuals and the networks of people with whom they associate regularly (Mills, 1959b). For example, one person's unemployment is a personal trouble facing the individual, other family members, and friends. Public issues (or social problems) are matters beyond a person's control that originate at the regional or national level and can be resolved only by collective action. Widespread unemployment resulting from economic changes, corporate decisions (downsizing or relocating a plant abroad), or technological innovations (computers and advanced telecommunications systems displacing workers) is a public issue. The sociological imagination helps us to place seemingly personal troubles, such as being unemployed, into a larger social context. In other words, we shift our focus to see how personal troubles may be related to public issues.

Ask yourself, "What is my most pressing personal trouble?" When I ask students in my sociology classes this question, they often respond, "MONEY!" Many students (perhaps you too) are concerned about how to pay for college and how to get a well-paying job after graduation. One student's worrying about paying tuition or finding a job is an example of a personal trouble. But personal troubles are shaped by larger social forces, so applying the sociological imagination, we might ask, "What factors in U.S. society contribute to students' money problems?" We also might ask, "Are getting an education and finding a job problems that affect students differently according to race, class, or gender? What about age, ability/disability, and sexual orien-

tation?" In fact, factors such as race, class, and gender link most private troubles and social problems in the United States today.

Sociologists make connections between personal and public issues in society through microlevel and macrolevel analysis. *Microlevel analysis* focuses on small-group relations and social interaction among individuals. Using microlevel analysis, a sociologist might investigate how fear of unemployment affects workers and their immediate families. In contrast, *macrolevel analysis* focuses on social processes occurring at the societal level, especially in large-scale organizations and major social institutions such as politics, government, and the economy.

Using macrolevel analysis, a sociologist might examine how the loss of more than 43 million U.S. jobs over the past two decades has affected the U.S. economy. The interconnectedness of microlevel and macrolevel economic issues is the point of this *New York Times* report on downsizing in the workplace:

> What companies do to make themselves secure is precisely what makes their workers feel insecure. . . . The job apprehension has intruded everywhere, diluting self-worth, splintering families, fragmenting communities, altering the chemistry of workplaces. . . . Dispossessed workers are finding themselves on anguished journeys they never imagined, as if being forced to live the American dream of higher possibilities in reverse. (Uchitelle and Kleinfield, 1996:1)

On one hand, large-scale corporate decisions are made to maximize profits in a growing global marketplace; on the other, individual lives are shattered. Through a systematic study of social problems such as unemployment, we gain a clearer picture of the relationship between macrolevel structures such as the U.S. economy and microlevel social interactions among people in their homes, workplaces, and communities.

SOCIOLOGICAL PERSPECTIVES ON SOCIAL PROBLEMS

Sociologists view society in a variety of ways. Some describe society as basically a stable and orderly entity; others view it as an arena of competition and conflict; still others focus on the everyday, routine interactions among individuals. Regardless of their basic approach, sociologists develop theories and conduct research to determine how social life is organized. A *theory* **is a set of logically related statements that attempt to describe, explain, or predict social events.** Theories are useful for explaining relationships between social concepts or phenomena, such as age and unemployment. They also help us to interpret social reality in a distinct way by giving us a framework for organizing our observations. Sociologists refer to this theoretical framework as a *perspective*—**an overall approach or viewpoint toward some subject.** Three major theoretical perspectives have emerged in sociology: the functionalist, conflict, and interactionist perspectives. The functionalist and conflict perspectives are based on macrolevel analysis because they focus on social processes occurring at the societal level. The interactionist perspective is based on microlevel analysis because it focuses on small-group relations and social interaction.

The Functionalist Perspective

The functionalist perspective grew out of the works of early social thinkers such as Auguste Comte (1798–1857), the founder of sociology, who compared society to a living organism such as the human body. Just as muscles, tissues, and organs perform specific functions that maintain the body as a whole, the various parts of society contribute to its maintenance and preservation. According to the *functionalist perspective*, **society is a stable, orderly system composed of a number of interrelated parts, each of which performs a function that contributes to the overall stability of society** (Parsons, 1951). These interrelated parts are social institutions (such as families, the economy, education, and the government) that a society develops to organize its main concerns and activities so that social needs are met. Each institution performs a unique function, contributing to the overall stability of society and the well-being of individuals (Merton, 1968). For example, the functions of the economy are producing and distributing goods (such as food, clothing, and shelter) and services (such as health care and dry cleaning), whereas the government is responsible for coordinating activities of other institutions, maintaining law and order, dealing with unmet social needs, and handling international relations and warfare.

MANIFEST AND LATENT FUNCTIONS

Though the functions of the economy and the government seem fairly clear-cut, functionalists suggest that not all functions of social institutions are intended and overtly recognized. In fact, social institutions perform two different types of societal functions: manifest and latent. *Manifest functions* are intended and recognized consequences of an activity or social process. A manifest function of education, for example, is to provide students with knowledge, skills, and cultural values. In contrast, *latent functions* are unintended consequences of an activity or social process that are hidden and remain unacknowledged by participants (Merton, 1968). Latent functions of education include the babysitter function of keeping young people off the street and out of the full-time job market and the matchmaking function whereby schools provide opportunities for students to meet and socialize with potential marriage partners. These functions are latent because schools were not created for babysitting or matchmaking, and most organizational participants do not recognize that these activities take place.

DYSFUNCTIONS AND SOCIAL DISORGANIZATION

From the functionalist perspective, social problems arise when social institutions do not fulfill the functions they are supposed to perform or when dysfunctions occur. *Dysfunctions* are undesirable consequences of an activity or social process that inhibit a society's ability to adapt or adjust (Merton, 1968). Dysfunctions can occur in society as a whole or in a part of society (a social institution). For example, a function of education is to prepare students for jobs, but if schools fail to do so, then students have problems finding jobs, employers have to spend millions of dollars on employee training programs, and consumers have to pay higher prices for goods and services to offset worker training costs. In other words, when education does not fulfill its function, other social institutions, especially families and the economy, are threatened.

According to functionalists, dysfunctions in social institutions create social disorganization in the entire society. Early in the twentieth century, sociologists Robert E. Park (1864–1944) and Ernest W. Burgess (1886–1966) developed social disorganization theory to explain why some areas of Chicago had higher rates of *social deviance*, which they defined as a pattern of rule violation, than other areas had. *Social dis-*

organization refers to the conditions in society that undermine the ability of traditional social institutions to govern human behavior. Social disorganization causes a breakdown in traditional values and norms that serve as the social control mechanisms that, under normal circumstances, keep people from engaging in nonconforming behavior. *Values* are collective ideas about what is right or wrong, good or bad, and desirable or undesirable in a specific society (Williams, 1970). Although values provide ideas about behavior, they do not state explicitly how we should behave. Norms, on the other hand, have specific behavioral expectations. *Norms* are established rules of behavior or standards of conduct. French sociologist Emile Durkheim (1858–1917) suggested that social problems arise when people no longer agree on societal values and norms. According to Durkheim, periods of rapid social change produce *anomie*—a loss of shared values and sense of purpose in society. Social bonds grow weaker, social control also is diminished, and people are more likely to engage in nonconforming patterns of behavior such as crime.

Social disorganization is intensified by rapid social change that disrupts the stability of society. Early sociologists examined the relationship between social problems and rapid industrialization and urbanization in Britain, Western Europe, and the United States in the late nineteenth and early twentieth centuries. *Industrialization* is the process by which societies are transformed from a dependence on agriculture and handmade products to an emphasis on manufacturing and related industries. At the beginning of the Industrial Revolution, thousands of people migrated from rural communities to large urban centers to find employment in factories and offices. New social problems emerged as a result of industrialization and *urbanization*, the process by which an increasing proportion of a population lives in cities rather than in rural areas. During this period of rapid technological and social change, a sharp increase occurred in urban social problems such as poverty, crime, child labor, inadequate housing, unsanitary conditions, overcrowding, and environmental pollution.

APPLYING THE FUNCTIONALIST PERSPECTIVE TO PROBLEMS OF TECHNOLOGY

How might the functionalist perspective analyze social problems associated with rapid scientific and technological change? Functionalists note that science and technology produce both functional and dysfunctional consequences. As was previously discussed, positive functional consequences of technology include a greatly enhanced quality of life for many people in industrialized nations. Science and technology also can result in *cultural lag,* a situation in which changes in ideas, values, and moral and legal institutions trail behind changes in material technology. Sociologist William F. Ogburn (1886–1959) was among the first to identify the gap between the introduction of new technology and its acceptance in society. According to Ogburn (1966/1922), change in one part of society typically leads to change in another part, but only after some delay. When social institutions cannot keep pace with technological innovations, social problems can arise.

Consider, for example, the Internet, which provides instant access to a wide array of information for millions of computer users worldwide. The technological capabilities of the Internet are virtually unlimited, but questions remain about what kind of information is permissible in cyberspace and what norms and values should be used to monitor the new technology. In 1996, the U.S. Congress enacted a law intended to prohibit Internet users from sending "indecent" or "patently offensive" material to minors or from making such material available in any way that children could access (see Box 1.2). Cultural lag often comes from a discrepancy between the availability of technology and its acceptance by moral and legal institutions. The Internet is only one example of such technology.

From the functionalist perspective, scientific and technological innovations bring about social change in other parts of society, resulting in social disorganization when social institutions fail to keep pace with these changes and the stability of society is threatened. Proponents of functionalism suggest that this perspective makes us aware of the important functions that social institutions perform in maintaining stability in society and the well-being of individuals. Critics of this perspective note that it downplays the fact that social practices may be beneficial to one group at the expense of another, an issue that the conflict perspective addresses.

The Conflict Perspective

The *conflict perspective* is based on the assumption that groups in society are engaged in a continuous

SOCIAL PROBLEMS
AND SOCIAL POLICY

BOX 1.2

Freedom of Speech versus "Indecency" on the Internet

Do you have access to the Internet through your college or university? If so, should you have unrestricted freedom to post anything on the Internet that you wish? Should your school be held responsible for its students' Internet communications? Questions such as these have arisen in recent controversies:

A university linguistics major with a 3.2 average made national headlines and was suspended from school after he posted violent, sadistic sexual fantasies that were perpetrated against a "fictional" victim, whom he named after a female student in one of his classes. (Elmer-Dewitt, 1995:69)

A student at another university posted centerfolds of nude women on his World Wide Web home page and attracted such an enormous volume of traffic—up to 250 requests at a time—that college officials removed his page because it was slowing down the entire campus network. The student argued that "I definitely feel censored. . . . [it] doesn't offer anything you can't find on HBO or Cinemax after 10 at night." (Young, 1996a:A21, A25)

Information technology allows us to access mail, documents, books, pictures and photographs, voice and music, video and television images and programs, and films quickly and inexpensively over the Internet (see Petersen, 1994). The possible benefits to individuals and groups from this flow of information are almost unlimited, but many questions remain about whether or not there should be limits to free speech in cyberspace, just as there are questions about the limits on any other type of free speech.

U.S. social policy regarding the Internet is just beginning to develop. In 1996, Congress passed the Communications Decency Act, prohibiting users from sending "indecent" or "patently offensive" material to minors or from making such material available in such a way that children could access it (Wallace and Mangan, 1996). Although the law was enacted primarily to crack down on commercial pornography providers, four student Web sites containing images of nude women were submitted among the examples of data that needed monitoring on the Internet. The law was challenged in the courts, and the U.S. Supreme Court held that it was unconstitutional.

The Court agreed with civil liberties groups that the law violated the constitutional right to freedom of speech. If the government reviews student and scholarly activities on line, freedom of expression on college campuses would be limited. Defenders of the new law argued that the restrictions were no different from those governing the distribution of printed pornography (Young, 1996a).

Sociological research often is used to formulate contemporary *social policy*—formally enacted procedures or programs set up by local, state, or federal governmental agencies for the purpose of remedying some social issue. Although nonprofit organizations such as the American Civil Liberties Union and for-profit corporations may participate in the development of social policy, the vast majority of social policy debates are based on the extent to which various levels of government can or should be involved in attempts to produce solutions to various social problems. What do you think about restricting what can be distributed over the Internet?

power struggle for control of scarce resources. Unlike functionalist theorists, who emphasize the degree to which society is held together by a consensus on values, conflict theorists emphasize the degree to which society is characterized by conflict and discrimination. According to conflict theorists, certain groups of people are privileged while others are disadvantaged through the unjust use of political, economic, or social power. The conflict perspective consists of a variety of related approaches that hold differing views regarding what constitutes the most important form of conflict. We will examine two principal approaches: the value conflict and critical-conflict perspectives.

VALUE CONFLICT APPROACH

According to value conflict theorists, social problems are conditions that are incompatible with group values. From this perspective, value clashes are ordinary occurrences in families, communities, and the larger society, in which people commonly hold many divergent values. Although individuals may share certain core values, they do not share all values or a common culture. Culture refers to the knowledge, language, values, customs, and material objects that are passed from person to person and from one generation to the next in a human group or society.

Discrepancies between ideal and real culture are a source of social problems in all societies. *Ideal culture* refers to the values and beliefs that people claim they hold; *real culture* refers to the values and beliefs that they actually follow. In the United States, for example, members of the National Association for the Advancement of Colored People (NAACP), La Raza, the Ku Klux Klan, and the White Aryan Resistance all claim to adhere to ideal cultural values of equality, freedom, and liberty; however, these ideal values come into direct conflict when issues of racial-ethnic relations arise. Urban marches and protest rallies held by members of the NAACP and the Ku Klux Klan on Martin Luther King Day, which celebrates the birthday of the African American minister and civil rights activist who was murdered in 1968, are a concrete example of the clash between ideal and real cultural values.

The value conflict approach has been criticized by critical-conflict theorists, who argue that it overlooks the deeper social problems of inequality and oppression based on class, race, and gender.

CRITICAL-CONFLICT PERSPECTIVES

Unlike the value conflict approach, critical-conflict theorists suggest that social problems arise out of major contradictions inherent in the way societies are organized. Some of these approaches focus on class inequalities in the capitalist economic system; others focus on inequalities based on race/ethnicity or gender.

Most class perspectives on inequality have been strongly influenced by Karl Marx (1818–1883), a German economist and activist, who recognized that the emergence of the capitalist economic system produced dramatic and irreversible changes in social life. *Capitalism* **is an economic system characterized by private ownership of the means of production, from which personal profits can be derived through market competition and without government intervention.** According to Marx, members of the *capitalist class* (the *bourgeoisie*), who own and control the means of production (e.g., the land, tools, factories, and money for investment), are at the top of a system of social stratification that affords them different lifestyles and life chances from those of the members of the *working class* (the *proletariat*), who must sell their labor power (their potential ability to work) to capitalists. In the process, the workers forfeit control over their work, and the capitalists derive excessive profit from the workers' labor.

Marx believed that capitalism led workers to experience increased levels of impoverishment and alienation—a feeling of powerlessness and estrangement from other people and from oneself (Marx and Engels, 1971:96). He predicted that the workers would eventually overthrow the capitalist economic system. Although his forecast has not proven true, his analysis of class relations remains valid.

Some critical-conflict approaches focus on racial and gender subordination instead of class-based inequalities. Critical-conflict theorists who emphasize discrimination and inequality based on race or ethnicity note that many social problems are rooted in the continuing exploitation and subordination of people of color by white people. For example, scholars suggest that Native Americans have the highest rates of poverty in the United States because of extended periods of racial subordination and exploitation throughout this country's history (see Feagin and Feagin, 1996).

Critical-conflict theorists who use a feminist approach focus on *patriarchy,* a system of male domi-

Feminist critical-conflict theorists believe that African American women face a system of the interlocking oppression of race, class, and gender.

nance in which males are privileged and women are oppressed. From this perspective, male domination in society contributes not only to domestic violence, child abuse, and rape, but also to poverty and crimes such as prostitution. Feminist scholars state that gender inequality will not be eliminated in the home, school, and workplace until patriarchy is abolished and women and men are treated equally.

Finally, some critical-conflict theorists emphasize that race, class, and gender are interlocking systems of privilege and oppression that result in social problems in society. For example, black feminist scholar Patricia Hill Collins (1990) has pointed out that race, class, and gender are simultaneous forces of oppression for women of color, especially African American women. Critical-conflict analysts focusing on these intersections believe that equality can come about only when women across lines of race and class receive equal treatment (Andersen and Collins, 1995; Collins, 1995).

Regardless of their specific focus, most critical-conflict theorists highlight the power relations that result in social problems.

APPLYING THE CONFLICT PERSPECTIVE TO PROBLEMS OF TECHNOLOGY

How might conflict theorists analyze social problems associated with scientific and technological change? Karl Marx suggested that private ownership of technology—not the technology itself—

was the primary source of social problems such as poverty and crime. Technological advances that have the potential to enhance all people's lives by providing improved food, shelter, clothing, and other resources instead benefit only the people in the wealthy capitalist class who own virtually all of the income-producing assets. The solution, according to Marx, would be a change in the ownership and control of technology from the capitalist class to the whole society (Westrum, 1991).

Using Marx's ideas as a springboard for analyzing late twentieth-century social problems, philosopher Douglas Kellner (1989:181) suggests that *techno-capitalism* (characterized by a new synthesis of technology and capitalist social relations) plays an increasingly important role in structuring and organizing not only economic production but also everyday life. According to Kellner, techno-capitalism, which occurs under capitalist directives and control, contributes to the exploitation of the working class by the better-off members of society. Marx's capitalist class of individual owners of the means of production has been replaced by the increased concentration and centralization of capital in the hands of major shareholders and chief executive officers of transnational corporations, which operate on a global basis but have instantaneous information and communications networks. As a result, the working class has grown increasingly "fragmented, disorganized and brutalized" (Kellner, 1989:180).

Some contemporary feminist scholars have examined how technological change results in increased social problems for women. According to Australian sociologist Judy Wajcman (1991), the people who control the latest technology are able to direct the future and derive political, economic, and social benefit from it. She notes that the high value of technology, in terms of the material rewards that expertise in this area brings, is bestowed more on men than on women. As Wajcman (1991:150) notes:

> Computing is a crucial example, because as a completely new type of technology it had the potential to break the mold. In terms of sexual divisions . . . computing could have been gender-neutral with no basic differentiation between female and male users. . . . Yet recent evidence on the gender gap in access to computers at school, at play, and at home, supports the idea that our culture has already defined computers as preeminently male machines.

Some social analysts believe that computers are seen as preeminently "male machines" in the United States. Do you think this assessment will prove true in the future? Why or why not?

According to communications scholar Herbert I. Schiller (1996), new and advanced information technologies tend to widen the gap between information "haves" and "have nots" across lines of class and race/ethnicity. In 1993, wealthy and upper-middle-class families accounted for more than half of the 30 percent of U.S. families that owned computers (see Figure 1.1). Access to computers and the Internet also varies widely between and within nations (see Box 1.3).

Conflict theorists point out that access to information technology affects what kinds of jobs people are able to get. Recent studies have found that employees who have computer skills typically earn 15 percent more than employees without those skills do (Ratan, 1995). In sum, the conflict perspective suggests that scientific and technological innovations do not necessarily benefit everyone equally but, in many instances, result in greater disparity between rich and poor, men and women, and whites and peo-

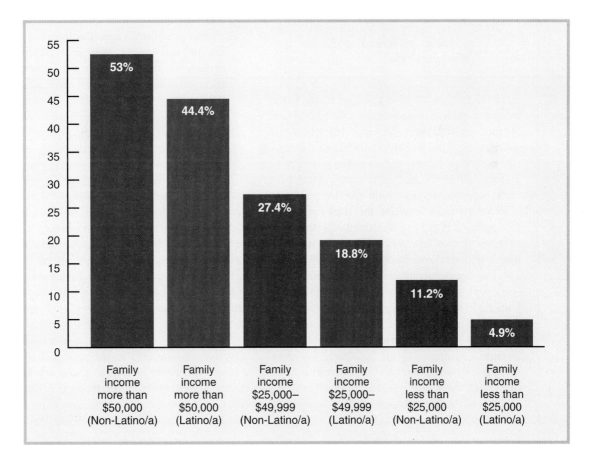

FIGURE 1.1   *U.S. Computer Gap by Household Income, 1993*
(SOURCE: Data from Wilhelm, 1996.)

SOCIAL PROBLEMS

IN GLOBAL PERSPECTIVE

BOX 1.3

The Internet: Information Haves and Have-Nots?

A survey of recent news articles provides interesting insights on the extent to which people in various countries have access to information technologies such as the Internet:

Item: Cyberia Cafe in London sells not only cappuccino but also access to one-half hour on the Internet for $2.85 (Jackson, 1995).

Item: Mountain climbers scaling Mount Everest communicated to a worldwide audience over the Internet before eight died during a ferocious storm (Egan, 1996).

Item: Only twelve of Africa's fifty-four countries are linked to the Internet (French, 1995).

As these news items reflect, access to the Internet varies widely across nations. While it is becoming an electronic highway for people in some areas of the world, others have no access.

Initially, the Internet was not intended to be a global electronic highway; it was created for military purposes. In 1969, the U.S. Department of Defense provided the start-up money to develop a bombproof wartime communication system that would link U.S. bases and military personnel worldwide (Thurow, 1996).

The electronic highway is now doubling in size every year (*The Economist,* 1995). Even with rapid growth, however, access to computer networks and the Internet varies widely between and within countries. The United States, Canada, Australia, New Zealand, Norway, Sweden, Finland, and Iceland currently lead the rest of the world in direct Internet connections, while many African nations have none (see Map 1.1).

Why is North America relatively well wired in comparison to Africa, Europe, and parts of Asia? Some economic analysts suggest that officials in some nations fear that the Internet will have a negative impact on current revenues derived from well-developed telephone networks (French, 1995). Similar problems seem to exist in Europe and parts of Asia:

[M]onopolistic telephone systems erect a bewildering array of speed limits and tollgates that make traveling the Infobahn a costly and often frustrating experience. High long-distance fees and connection surcharges levied by monopolistic government communications ministries can make the use of the Internet and [on-line] services . . . unduly expensive for ordinary users. . . . Even after they get connected, users need access to good-quality telephone lines [for modem connections], which are neither as ubiquitous nor cheap as in the U.S. Waiting lists for phone connections range from mere weeks in France to years—or never—in the communications-deprived nations of the former Soviet Union. (Jackson, 1995:81)

What impact—if any—will being "wired" or "not wired" have on nations in the future? One scenario suggests that unless the current have-nots such as countries in Africa get online quickly, the poorest nations in the world will probably become even more economically marginalized and information deprived. Compare, for example, all current sources of rapid information available to the residents of Côte d'Ivoire (formerly known as the Ivory Coast), the most prosperous of the tropical African nations, with those of U.S. residents (*The World Almanac and Book of Facts,* 1996: 755, 831):

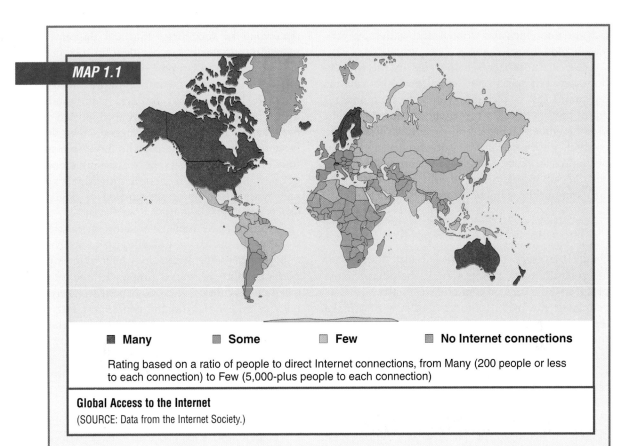

MAP 1.1

■ Many ■ Some ■ Few ■ No Internet connections

Rating based on a ratio of people to direct Internet connections, from Many (200 people or less to each connection) to Few (5,000-plus people to each connection)

Global Access to the Internet
(SOURCE: Data from the Internet Society.)

	Côte d'Ivoire	United States
Television sets	1 per 17 people	1 per 1.2 people
Radios	1 per 8.9 people	1 per 0.5 person
Telephones	1 per 62 people	1 per 1.3 people

Is the future bleak for nations such as Côte d'Ivoire because they lack access to the Internet? Scholars and social analysts offer different opinions. Some suggest that Africa may move to the leading edge of twenty-first-century fiber optics and wireless communications because it is not encumbered with outdated technologies, such as huge investments in copper wiring and existing information systems. When African countries come on line, their economies will benefit greatly, and teachers, students, scientists, and businesspeople will be able to communicate directly with each other for the first time.

Other analysts say that the Internet has been greatly overrated as a source of communication and information. From this point of view, the Internet—like television and satellite communications systems—is gradually coming under the control of transnational corporations that will use the advanced technology mainly for corporate advantage, especially to enhance global consumerism (Schiller, 1996).

Do the Internet and other information technologies have the potential to improve people's quality of life? Are wealthy national or global elites most likely to benefit from new information technologies? Or will middle- and lower-income people benefit most? What do you think?

rich and poor, men and women, and whites and people of color.

Conflict approaches help to clarify the connections between society and social problems such as unequal access to technology and the economic rewards that it affords to those who are able to exploit its inherent advantages and profits. Critics of the conflict approach point out, however, that it overemphasizes the domination of powerful groups and the subordination of all others without taking into account the stability afforded by society.

The Interactionist Perspective

Unlike the conflict perspective, which focuses on macrolevel inequalities in society, the interactionist perspective focuses on a microlevel analysis of how people act toward one another and how they make sense of their daily lives. The **interactionist perspective views society as the sum of the interactions of individuals and groups.** Most interactionists study social problems by analyzing the process whereby certain behavior is defined as a social problem and how individuals and groups come to engage in activities that a significant number of people and/or a number of significant people view as a major social concern.

As a founder of the interactionist approach, German sociologist Georg Simmel (1858–1918) investigated the impact of industrialization and urbanization on people's values and behavior within small social units. Simmel (1950/1902) noted that rapid changes in technology and dramatic growth of cities produced new social problems by breaking up the "geometry of social life," which he described as the web of patterned social interactions among people that constitute a society. According to Simmel, alienation is brought about by a decline in personal and emotional contacts. How people *interpret* subjective messages that they receive from others, as well as the situations that they encounter in their daily life, strongly influences their behavior and their perceptions of what constitutes a social problem.

LABELING THEORY AND THE SOCIAL CONSTRUCTION OF REALITY

While Simmel focused on how people interpret their own situations, other interactionists examine how people impose their shared meanings on others.

According to sociologist Howard Becker (1963), *moral entrepreneurs* are people who use their own views of right and wrong to establish rules and label others as deviant (nonconforming). From this perspective, behavior that deviates from established norms is deviant because it has been labeled as such by others. *Labeling theory* suggests that deviants (nonconformists) are people who have been successfully labeled as such by others. Labeling theory raises questions about why certain individuals and certain types of behavior are labeled as deviant but others are not.

According to some interaction theorists, many social problems can be linked to the *social construction of reality*—the process by which people's perception of reality is shaped largely by the subjective meaning that they give to an experience (Berger and Luckmann, 1967). From this perspective, little shared reality exists beyond that which people socially create. However, the social construction of reality still influences people's beliefs and actions. English and law scholar Stanley Fish (1996:A11) illustrates the social construction of reality with this example:

It is no contradiction to say that something is socially constructed and also real. Perhaps a humble example from the world of baseball will help make the point. Consider the following little catechism:

Are there balls and strikes in the world? Yes.

Are there balls and strikes in nature (if by nature you understand physical reality independent of human actors)? No.

Are balls and strikes socially constructed? Yes.

Are balls and strikes real? Yes.

Do some people get $3.5 million either for producing balls and strikes or for preventing their production? Yes.

So balls and strikes are both socially constructed and real, socially constructed and consequential. The facts about balls and strikes are also real but they can change, as they would, for example, if baseball's rule makers were to vote tomorrow that from now on it's four strikes and you're out.

Interactionists suggest that how we initially define a situation affects our future actions. According to sociologist W. I. Thomas (1863–1947), when people define situations as real, the situations become real in their consequences. Elaborating on Thomas's idea, sociologist Robert Merton (1968) suggested that when people view a situation in a certain way and act according to their perceptions, the end result may be a *self-fulfilling prophecy*—**a false definition of the situation that evokes a new behavior that makes the originally false conception come true.** For example, a teenager who is labeled a "juvenile delinquent" may accept the label and adopt the full-blown image of a gang member as portrayed in television programs and films: wearing gang colors, dropping out of school, and participating in gang violence or other behavior that is labeled as deviant. If this person subsequently is arrested, the initial label becomes a self-fulfilling prophecy.

APPLYING INTERACTIONIST PERSPECTIVES TO PROBLEMS OF TECHNOLOGY

The interactionist approach makes us aware of how social problems affect our daily lives and influence our perceptions about reality. For example, so-

Computers and the Internet have the potential for dramatically changing people's lives around the globe. What social forces do you think might limit change in settings such as this? What social forces might create pressures for change?

ciologist George Ritzer (1996) found that technological innovations often increase people's feelings of dehumanization and social alienation. Workers in high-tech, fast-food restaurants, for instance, tend to feel like the Burger King worker who said, "Any trained monkey could do this job" (quoted in Ritzer, 1996:130). Customers often feel dehumanized by technology that minimizes their contact with other human beings, such as automated teller machines for banking and telephones answered by prerecorded voices that give callers an elaborate array of instructions.

Social alienation and dehumanization intensify as humans interact by computer because this type of interaction has few emotional and social cues. Some analysts suggest that extended replacement of in-person interaction by virtual interaction decreases a person's ability to socialize comfortably with other people when in their physical presence (Neill, 1995). Sociologist Sherry Turkle (1995:9–10) paints a more positive picture of virtual interactions on the Internet:

> In cyberspace, we can talk, exchange ideas, and assume personae of our own creation. We have the opportunity to build new communities, virtual communities, in which we participate with people from all over the world, people with whom we converse daily, people with whom we may have fairly intimate relationships but whom we may never physically meet. . . . In the real-time communities of cyberspace, we are dwellers on the threshold between the real and virtual, unsure of our footing, inventing ourselves as we go along.

How will the Internet affect existing communities and people's daily interactions with others? Some analysts believe that computer networks can draw people together; others think that we will "scatter ourselves into a million mediated communities" (Bill Gates, quoted in Atlas, 1995:E1).

Proponents of the interactionist perspective suggest that this approach makes us aware of how social change and social problems affect individuals and small groups. However, this approach has been criticized for focusing primarily on microlevel interactions and ignoring macrolevel social structures and their consequences.

TABLE 1.1   SOCIOLOGICAL PERSPECTIVES ON SOCIAL PROBLEMS

Perspective	Analysis Level	Nature of Society and Origins of Social Problems	Application to New Technologies
FUNCTIONALISM	Macrolevel	Society is composed of interrelated parts that work together to maintain stability within society. Social problems result from dysfunctional acts and institutions.	Rapid technological changes produce disorganization in society and erode social institutions. Cultural lag exists between new technologies and their acceptance by moral and legal institutions.
CONFLICT THEORY	Macrolevel	Society is characterized by conflict and inequality. Value conflict theory attributes social problems to lack of agreement on values. Critical-conflict theory focuses on oppression due to class, race, gender, and other social divisions.	Technological changes in society benefit some categories of people at the expense of others. Some innovations may contribute to oppression and greater inequalities. People's access to technology varies widely across lines of race, class, and gender.
SYMBOLIC INTERACTIONISM	Microlevel	Society is the sum of the interactions of people and groups. Social problems are based on the behavior people learn from others; how people define a social problem is based on subjective factors.	Technological innovations, especially in communications, dramatically change people's daily interactions and their perceptions of many situations.

In Sum

Interactionist, conflict, and functionalist perspectives involve different assumptions and provide different lenses for viewing social problems. Functionalists, who emphasize social cohesion and order in society, commonly view social problems as the result of institutional and societal dysfunctions, social disorganization, or cultural lag, among other things. Conflict theorists, who focus on value conflict or on structural inequalities based on class, race, gender, or other socially constructed attributes, suggest that social problems arise either from disputes over divergent values or from exploitative relations in society, such as those between capitalists and workers or between women and men. In contrast, interactionists focus on individuals' interactions and on the social construction of reality. For interactionists, social problems occur when social interaction is disrupted and people are dehumanized, when people are labeled deviant, or when the individual's definition of a situation causes him or her to act in a way that produces a detrimental outcome. Table 1.1 summarizes these perspectives, which we will use throughout the book.

In this chapter, we have posed many questions about information technology, and these remain unanswered: Will advanced information technologies and the networks of cyberspace improve or worsen social inequality (see Schiller, 1996)? Is the Information Age the beginning of a caring society, or is it a source of surveillance and tightening of control over people (see Lyon, 1994)? Does advanced information technology produce highly educated people who have ready access to knowledge, or does it result in a deluge of trivia, sensationalism, and misleading propaganda (see Webster, 1995)? Please join me in exploring these and other pressing social issues as we examine a wide variety of social problems in the coming chapters.

SUMMARY

➡ *How do sociologists define a social problem?*

According to sociologists, a social problem is a social condition (such as poverty) or a pattern of behavior (such as substance abuse) that people believe warrants public concern and collective action to bring about change.

➡ *When do we become aware that a social problem exists?*

We develop a subjective awareness that a social problem exists before we gain an objective awareness about the reality of the problem. The subjective awareness tends to be expressed as an uneasiness or skepticism about something but is not founded on any concrete evidence that a problem actually exists. A social problem is generally considered an objective reality—or condition—when it is possible to measure or experience its effects.

➡ *Why should we study social problems?*

Studying social problems helps us to understand the social forces that shape our lives on both the personal and societal levels and makes it possible for us to examine national and global concerns in new ways and make better decisions about those problems.

➡ *What is the sociological imagination?*

The sociological imagination is the ability to recognize the relationship between personal troubles (such as being unemployed) and public issues (for example, sweeping changes in the economy such as downsizing or technological innovations that displace workers).

➡ *How do sociologists examine social life?*

Sociologists use both microlevel and macrolevel analyses to examine social life. Microlevel analysis focuses on small-group relations and social interaction among individuals; macrolevel analysis focuses on social processes occurring at the societal level, especially in large-scale organizations and major social institutions.

➡ *How does the functionalist perspective view society and social problems?*

In the functionalist perspective, society is a stable, orderly system composed of interrelated parts, each of which performs a function contributing to the overall stability of society. According to functionalists, social problems arise when social institutions do not fulfill the functions that they are supposed to perform or when dysfunctions occur.

➡ *What is social disorganization theory?*

Social disorganization theory suggests that new social problems arise during times of rapid technological and social change.

➡ *Why does the introduction of new technologies often lead to social problems?*

According to cultural lag theory, social problems emerge when changes in ideas, values, and moral and legal institutions in society trail behind changes in material technology.

➡ *How does the conflict perspective view society and social problems?*

The conflict perspective asserts that groups in society are engaged in a continuous power struggle for control of scarce resources. This perspective consists of a variety of related approaches, including the value conflict and critical-conflict perspectives.

➡ *How does the value conflict approach differ from the critical-conflict approach?*

According to value conflict theorists, social problems are conditions that are incompatible with group values. From this perspective, value clashes are ordinary occurrences in families, communities, and the larger society, in which people commonly hold many divergent values. In contrast, critical-conflict theorists suggest that social problems arise out of major contradictions inherent in the way societies are organized.

➡ *Why are there so many different approaches in the critical-conflict perspective?*

Different critical-conflict theorists focus on different aspects of power relations and inequality in society. Perspectives based on the works of Karl Marx emphasize class-based inequalities arising from the capitalist economic system. Feminist approaches focus on patriarchy—a system of male dominance in which males are privileged and women are oppressed. Others emphasize that race, class, and gender are interlocking systems of privilege and oppression that result in social problems in society. However, all of these approaches are based on the assumption that inequality and exploitation, rather than social harmony and stability, characterize contemporary societies.

➡ *How does the interactionist perspective view society and social problems?*

Unlike the functionalist and conflict perspectives that focus on society at the macrolevel, the interactionist perspective views society as the sum of the interactions of individuals and groups. For interactionists, social problems occur when social interaction is disrupted and people are dehumanized, when people are labeled deviant, or when the individual's definition of a situation causes him or her to act in a way that produces a detrimental outcome.

KEY TERMS

capitalism, p. 11
conflict perspective, pp. 9, 11
cultural lag, p. 9
discrimination, p. 3
functionalist perspective, p. 8
industrialization, p. 9
interactionist perspective, p. 16
job deskilling, pp. 4–5
macrolevel analysis, p. 7
microlevel analysis, p. 7
norms, p. 9

perspective, p. 8
self-fulfilling prophecy, p. 17
social disorganization, pp. 8–9
social problem, p. 2
society, p. 2
sociological imagination, p. 7
sociology, p. 2
technology, p. 2
theory, p. 8
urbanization, p. 9
values, p. 9

QUESTIONS FOR CRITICAL THINKING

1. If many U.S. workers' jobs have disappeared because of technological advances or the movement of factories to other nations, why do many people blame themselves for being unemployed or for earning low wages? As a sociologist, how would you explain social problems such as unemployment and low wages?

2. The functionalist perspective is concerned about stability in times of rapid change. In a global world linked by the Internet, fax machines, telephones, airplanes, and other forms of rapid communication and transportation, is the stability of U.S. society still a primary goal? Is global stability now a primary goal?

3. Value conflict theorists suggest that social problems are conditions that are incompatible with group values. In contrast, critical-conflict theorists suggest that social problems arise out of major contradictions that are inherent in the way societies are organized. Use both approaches to explain why workers often clash with managers or owners over wages, working conditions, and benefits.

4. Some people think that girls and women are not as interested as boys and men are in playing computer games and working with computers in the classroom and workplace. How does this commonsense notion compare with feminist and interactionist perspectives on the relationship between gender and technology? How does this notion compare with your own observations about computer use among women and men at your school?

Chapter Two

Wealth and Poverty

Doing Sociological Research

I'd like to be able to fix the kids' rooms up nice and I haven't been able to. And if I do have the money, it's always something else that comes up. . . . It's so frustrating when you're trying to lead a normal life, but you can't do it. And then I was trying to think, "Well, if I get this in this month. If I can take so much out of this from the savings account. . . ." There was a time where I could have done that, but now I'm down so low that I didn't have anything. I got paid and that week it was gone. It was all gone. So it was hard. I had to resort to borrowing.

—Joyce Mills
Quoted in Rank (1994:53)

In a recent study of poverty in the United States, sociologist Mark Robert Rank interviewed welfare recipients to determine their most pressing day-to-day problems. Joyce Mills, who was separated from her husband, told Rank that she was having a hard time taking care of herself and her three children even though she was working full-time in a clerical position and receiving eighty-one dollars a month from the food stamp program.

What kinds of opportunities exist today for families such as Joyce's? For decades, the United States has been described as the "land of opportunity"—the land of the "American Dream." Simply stated, the American Dream is the belief that each generation can have a higher standard of living than that of its parents (Danziger and Gottschalk, 1995). Implicit in the American Dream is the assumption of equality of opportunity, as recently described by President Bill Clinton: "The American Dream that we were all raised on is a simple but powerful one—if you work hard and play by the rules you should be given a chance to go as far as your God-given ability will take you" (quoted in Hochschild, 1995:18). The American Dream is the belief that all people—regardless of race, creed, color, national origin, sex, sexual orientation, or religion—should have an equal opportunity for success.

AN OVERVIEW OF WEALTH AND POVERTY

Despite the American Dream, one of this country's most persistent social problems is that the United States is a highly stratified society. *Social stratification* **is the hierarchical arrangement of large social groups on the basis of their control over basic resources** (Feagin and Feagin, 1994). Today, the gap between the rich and the poor in this nation is wider than it has been in half a century.

Stratification in the United States is linked with global systems of stratification. Throughout the world, the wealthiest and poorest people are living in increasingly separate worlds (Crossette, 1996b). This widening gap between rich and poor has a dramatic impact on everyone's life chances and opportunities. *Life chances* **are the extent to which individuals have access to important societal resources such as food, clothing, shelter, education, and health care.** Affluent people typically have better life chances than do the less affluent because the affluent have greater access to quality education, safe neighborhoods, high-quality nutrition and health care, police and private security protection, and an extensive array of other goods and services. In contrast, people who have low and poverty-level incomes tend to have limited access to these resources.

In this chapter, we look at how sociologists study inequality and poverty in the U.S. class system and worldwide. **A** *class system* **is a system of social inequality based on the ownership and control of resources and on the type of work people do** (Rothman, 1993). A primary characteristic of the class system is social mobility. *Social mobility* refers to the upward or downward movement in the class structure that occurs during a person's lifetime and from one generation to another.

How are social classes determined in the United States? Most contemporary research on class is influenced by either Karl Marx's means of production model or Max Weber's multidimensional model. For Marx, class position is determined by people's relationship to the means of production. Chapter 1 described Marx's division of capitalist societies into two classes: the bourgeoisie, or capitalist class, which owns the means of production, and the proletariat, or working class, which sells its labor power to the capitalists to survive. According to Marx, in-equality and poverty are inevitable by-products of the exploitation of workers by capitalists (Vanneman and Cannon, 1987:39).

Like Marx, early German sociologist Max Weber (1864–1920) believed that economic factors are important in determining class location and studying social inequality, but he also believed that other factors are important. Weber developed a multidimensional class model that focused on the interplay of wealth, power, and prestige as determinants of people's class position. **Wealth is the value of all economic assets, including income, personal property, and income-producing property.** While some people have great wealth and are able to live off their investments, others must work for wages. **Power is the ability of people to achieve their goals despite opposition from others.** People who hold positions of power can achieve their goals because they can control other people; on the other hand, people who hold positions that lack power must carry out the wishes of others. **Prestige is the respect, esteem, or regard accorded to an individual or group by others.** Individuals who have high levels of prestige tend to receive deferential and respectful treatment from those with lower levels of prestige.

Sociologists measure wealth, power, and prestige by conducting research into various social issues. They conduct their research using scientific research methods.

SOCIAL RESEARCH METHODS

Research methods are strategies or techniques for systematically collecting data about social life and social problems. Some methods produce quantitative data that can be measured numerically and lends itself to statistical analysis. For example, quantitative data such as gross national product (GNP), gross domestic product (GDP), per capita income, or other indicators of overall economic development can be used to compare stratification and inequality among specific countries. Other methods produce qualitative data that are reported in the form of interpretive descriptions (words) rather than numbers. For example, qualitative data on poverty in the United States might provide us with new insights on intangible aspects of inequality such as how it feels to be homeless.

Sociologists use four major types of research methods: field research, survey research, secondary analysis of existing data, and experiments. Although our discussion focuses on each separately, many researchers use a combination of methods to enhance their understanding of social issues.

Field Research

Field research is the study of social life in its natural setting: observing and interviewing people where they live, work, and play. When sociologists want firsthand information about a social problem, they often use *participant observation*—field research in which researchers collect systematic observations while being part of the activities of the group they are studying. Some kinds of behavior and social problems can be studied best by being there; a fuller understanding can be developed through observations, face-to-face discussions, and participation in events. For example, sociologists David A. Snow and Leon Anderson (1993) used participant observation to gain a better understanding of the problems homeless people face in their daily lives. By living on the streets and in a shelter with homeless men, the researchers could learn firsthand what it is like to be homeless, how other people treat those who are homeless, and how homeless people perceive themselves.

As part of their participant observation, Snow and Anderson used a research technique known as *unstructured interviews*—extended, open-ended interactions in which researchers pursue avenues of inquiry as they emerge—and found that one of the greatest problems facing homeless people is how to continually salvage their self-esteem. As Sonny McCallister, a respondent, noted, "The hardest thing's been getting used to the way people look down on street people. It's real hard to feel good about yourself when almost everyone you see is looking down on you" (Snow and Anderson, 1993:202).

Field research on social problems can take place in almost any setting, from neighborhoods and communities to Salvation Army shelters, battered women's centers, mental hospitals, and prisons. In fact, the world is the laboratory for field researchers.

Sociologists using field research must have good interpersonal skills. They must be able to gain and keep the trust of the people they want to observe or interview. They also must be skilled interviewers who can keep systematic notes on their observations and conversations. Above all, they must treat research subjects fairly and ethically. The Code of Ethics of the American Sociological Association provides professional standards for sociologists to follow in conducting social science research.

Survey Research

Survey research is probably the method that social scientists use most frequently. *Survey research* is a poll in which researchers ask respondents a series of questions about a specific topic and record their responses. Survey research is based on a sample of people who represent the attributes of the larger population from which they are selected. Survey data are collected by using self-administered questionnaires or by interviewers who ask questions of people in person or by mail, telephone, or Internet.

An example of survey research is the large-scale Urban Poverty and Family Life Study (UPFLS) conducted by the National Opinion Research Center at the University of Chicago in 1987 and 1988. This survey included more than 2,400 African American, non-Hispanic white, Mexican, and Puerto Rican parents ages eighteen to forty-four who resided in poor neighborhoods (at least 20 percent of residents had family incomes below the federal poverty level) in Chicago. From this research, sociologist William Julius Wilson (1996) and others have shown the devastating effects that high jobless rates and lower employment growth have had on individual, family, and neighborhood life in the impoverished inner city.

Survey research such as the UPFLS allows sociologists to study a large population without having to interview everyone in that population. It also yields numerical data that can be compared between groups and over periods of time. However, survey research does have certain limitations. Using standardized questions puts limitations on the types of information researchers gain from respondents. Also, since data can be reported numerically, survey research may be misused to overestimate or underestimate the extent of a specific problem such as homelessness.

Secondary Analysis of Existing Data

Whereas the UPFLS is primary data that researchers collected specifically for that study, sociologists often rely on *secondary analysis of existing data*—a research design in which investigators analyze data that originally were collected by others for some other purpose. This method is also known as unobtrusive research because data can be gathered without the researcher having to interview or observe research subjects. Secondary data include public records such as birth and death records, official reports of organizations or governmental agencies such as the U.S. Bureau of the Census, and information from large databases such as the General Social Surveys, which also are administered by the National Opinion Research Center (see Davis and Robinson, 1988).

Secondary analysis often consists of *content analysis*—a systematic examination of cultural artifacts or written documents to extract thematic data and draw conclusions about some aspect of social life. For example, sociologist Michael Allen (1987) wanted to examine the U.S. corporate rich (or capitalist class) but was turned down for interviews by members of that class. Allen therefore designed a study in which he analyzed existing documents, such as reports filed with the Securities and Exchange Commission and newspaper articles, to gain insight into how members of the capitalist class enter the upper class and how upper-class families maintain their wealth and social position over time. Allen concluded that a "clear majority" of the wealthiest people in the United States are inheritors who go to great lengths to preserve their family fortunes.

A strength of secondary analysis is its unobtrusive nature and the fact that it can be used when subjects refuse to be interviewed or the researcher does not have the opportunity to observe research subjects firsthand. However, secondary analysis also has inherent problems. Because the data originally were gathered for some other purpose, they may not fit the exact needs of the researcher, and they may be incomplete or inaccurate.

Experiments

Perhaps the least used sociological research method is the experiment because it often is difficult to simulate real-life social problems under controlled circumstances to discover how subjects respond. **An experiment is a carefully designed situation in which**

the researcher studies the impact of certain factors on subjects' attitudes or behavior. In conventional experiments, subjects are divided into two groups: an experimental group and a control group. The researcher applies an experimental condition to the members of the experimental group to study its effect on them. The control group is matched to the experimental group on relevant characteristics so that comparisons can be made between the groups; however, the people in the control group are not exposed to the experimental condition. When the researcher compares the experiences of members of the experimental and control groups, differences between the groups are assumed to be due to the effects of the experimental condition. For example, sociologists Arline Geronimus and Sanders Korenman used a quasi-experimental technique to study the following question: Are teen mothers more likely than teens without children to drop out of school, depend on public assistance, and remain in poverty after their teenage years? To conduct their experiment, Geronimus and Korenman decided to use pairs of sisters, of whom one had become pregnant as a teenager and the other had not, as their subjects. Interestingly, becoming pregnant as a teenager did not seem to have significant bearing on whether a young woman drops out of school and becomes a welfare recipient (Geronimus and Korenman, 1992). Other researchers have suggested that factors such as emotional and psychological discouragement must be taken into account in explanations of dropout rates and welfare recipiency (Luker, 1996).

Because experiments help us to determine cause-and-effect relationships and can be conducted with a limited number of subjects, they offer some advantages to sociologists. However, experiments present major problems for researchers in that they often are artificial and do not provide meaningful results when they are conducted in a laboratory setting. For this reason, some sociologists conduct field experiments in real-life settings.

In sum, all research methods have certain strengths and weaknesses, but taken together, they provide us with valuable insights that go beyond commonsense knowledge about social problems and stereotypes of people. Using multiple methods and approaches provides an even wider scope of information about social problems such as inequality and poverty in the United States and other nations.

WEALTH AND POVERTY AS A SOCIAL PROBLEM

Let's return to the idea of the American Dream that began this chapter. If some people work harder than others, shouldn't they be entitled to more wealth, power, and prestige? How do people differ in life chances and opportunities on the basis of their class location? To answer these questions, let's look first at the U.S. class structure.

▲ Analyzing U.S. Class Inequality

A variety of social problems are associated with the growing gap between the rich and the poor in the United States. Over the past decade, wealth has been increasingly concentrated in the hands of the richest families. (Remember that wealth is the value of all economic assets, including income, personal property, and income-producing property.) The richest 10 percent of U.S. households held 66.8 percent of the nation's net wealth in 1994, up from 61.9 percent in 1984. The picture becomes more startling when we consider that the richest 20 percent of households controls about 80 percent of the wealth in this country, while all other households (80 percent) control only 20 percent of the wealth (Bradsher, 1996).

WEALTH VERSUS INCOME INEQUALITY

How is the unequal distribution of wealth a social problem? According to sociologists Melvin L. Oliver and Thomas M. Shapiro (1995:2), wealth is a particularly important indicator of individual and family access to life chances:

Wealth signifies the command over financial resources that a family has accumulated over its lifetime along with those resources that have been inherited across generations. Such resources, when combined with income, can create the opportunity to secure the "good life" in whatever form is needed—education, business, training, justice, health, comfort, and so on. Wealth is a special form of money not used to purchase milk and shoes and other life necessities. More often it is used to create opportunities, secure a desired stature and standard of living, or pass class status along to one's children.

Using secondary analysis of existing data and in-depth interviews with African American and white American families, Oliver and Shapiro found that African Americans have accumulated much less wealth than white Americans because whites, especially well-off whites, have had the opportunity to amass assets and pass them on from generation to generation, whereas African Americans have not. According to Oliver and Shapiro, African Americans have experienced the cumulative effects of racial discrimination as evidenced by poor schooling, high unemployment rates, and low wages. It has therefore been difficult, if not impossible, for multiple generations of African Americans to acquire wealth, keeping them cemented to the bottom of the U.S. economic hierarchy.

Like wealth, income is extremely unevenly divided in the United States. ***Income* is the economic gain derived from wages, salaries, income transfers (governmental aid such as Aid to Families with Dependent Children), or ownership of property** (Beeghley, 1989). The income gap between the richest and poorest U.S. households has been wide for many years (U.S. Bureau of the Census, 1996a). The top 20 percent of households earned almost half of the nation's aggregate income in 1994, and the top 5 percent alone received over 21 percent of aggregate income (see Figure 2.1). As is shown in Figure 2.2, median income for households across racial and ethnic lines has remained relatively constant over the last decade. Although African Americans have made some gains in income in recent years, median income of both African American and Latina/o households remains far behind median income for white households (Rawlings, 1995).

DIVISIONS IN THE U.S. CLASS STRUCTURE

The United States has a number of class divisions, ranging from upper to lower, that are characterized by a wide diversity in lifestyles and life chances. The upper or capitalist class is the wealthiest and most powerful class of investors, heirs, and executives. Some members of the capitalist class derive profits from investments in income-producing property such as media conglomerates, high-rise hotels, apartment buildings, and office parks; others earn their wealth as entrepreneurs, presidents of major corporations, sports or entertainment celebrities, or top-level professionals. For example, the top ten corporate executives in a recent Forbes survey of

FIGURE 2.1 *Median U.S. Income, 1984 and 1994*

(SOURCE: U.S. Bureau of the Census, 1995a.)

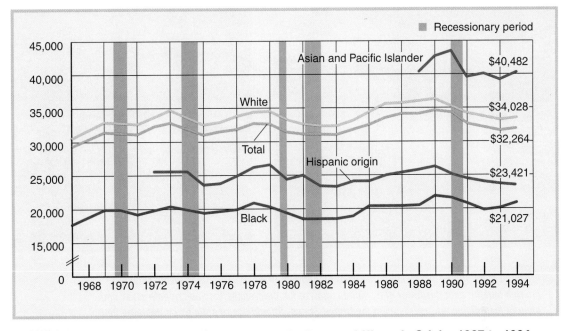

FIGURE 2.2   *Median U.S. Household Income by Race and Hispanic Origin, 1967 to 1994 (median income in 1994 dollars)*

NOTE: People of Hispanic origin may be of any race. Data for Hispanic-origin households are not available prior to 1972. Data for Asian and Pacific Islander households are not available prior to 1988. Data points represent the midpoints of the respective years.

(SOURCE: U.S. Bureau of the Census, 1995a.)

executive compensation had 1995 salaries and bonuses ranging from about $17.4 million to over $65.5 million. The upper-middle class is composed of professionals, including physicians, attorneys, business analysts, stockbrokers, and corporate managers who generally do not own the means of production but have substantial control over production and other workers (Wright, 1979, 1985). The middle class includes white-collar office workers, middle-management personnel, and people in support positions such as medical technologists, nurses, legal and medical secretaries, semiprofessionals, and nonretail salesworkers.

The working class is composed of people in occupations such as semiskilled machine operators in industrial settings and those in nonmanual, semiskilled positions such as day-care workers, checkout clerks, cashiers, and counter help in fast-food restaurants. The working poor are those who work full-time in unskilled positions such as seasonal or migrant agricultural jobs or the lowest-paid service sector jobs but still remain at the edge of poverty. In research by sociologist Mark Robert Rank, Jack Collins, a married fa-

ther with six children, described the transitory nature of work for the working poor:

> You name it, I've done it. I started out cooking. I've been a janitor. I've been an auto mechanic. I drove a school bus for five years. I drove a semi [truck] coast to coast. I've worked in a foundry. I've worked in a shoe factory. I've worked in other factories, warehouses. I'll do just about anything. . . . The main problem was findin' [a job] with starting pay that's enough to really get by on. (Rank, 1994:43)

Jack Collins and his family may be only one paycheck away from the chronically poor, the bottom category in the U.S. class system.

The chronically poor constitute about 20 percent of the U.S. population but receive only 3.6 percent of the overall U.S. income. People in this category have an average net worth of –$7,075 (i.e., they owe more than they own). In 1994, over 38 million people (14.5 percent of the U.S. population) fell below the poverty threshold, which ranged from

Although most people are aware of the wide disparity in lifestyles and life chances between the rich and the poor, far fewer of us stop to analyze the differences between middle-class and poverty-level living arrangements in the United States. Should social policies be implemented to equalize opportunities for the young people shown in these photos? Why or why not?

$7,547 for a single-person household to $15,141 for a family of four. Individuals who are chronically poor include people of working age who are unemployed or outside the labor force and children who live in poor families caught in long-term deprivation. Also overrepresented among low-income and poverty-level individuals are those who are unable to work because of age or disability and single mothers who are heads of households. The term *underclass* is sometimes used to refer to people who are chronically poor, but this term not only negatively labels poor people, it also puts them outside the mainstream of society.

A Global View of Wealth and Poverty

Just as the United States is divided into classes, the world is divided into unequal segments characterized by extreme differences in wealth and poverty. When sociologists conduct research on global stratification and inequality, they frequently analyze secondary data that originally were collected by the World Bank and the United Nations. These data focus on quality-of-life indicators such as wealth, income, life expectancy, health, sanitation, the treat-

ment of women, and education for developed and developing nations. *Developed nations* **are countries with highly industrialized economies; technologically advanced industrial, administrative, and service occupations; and relatively high levels of national and per capita (per person) income.** Examples include Australia, New Zealand, Japan, the European nations, Canada, and the United States. *Developing nations* **are countries undergoing transformation from agrarian to industrial economies.** These nations still have many people who work the land, and national and per capita incomes remain relatively low. Generalizations are difficult to make about developing nations because they vary widely in levels of development and life chances. For example, nations such as South Korea, Brazil, and Mexico are industrializing rapidly, while some nations in Africa remain much less developed.

Comparisons between the developed and the developing nations reflect the growing gap between the rich and the poor, both within and among nations. As shown in Figure 2.3, average per capita income varies widely between developed and developing nations. As the figure also shows, the per capita income of the poorest 20 percent of the population in some nations—including the United States—is only a small fraction of the average per capita income.

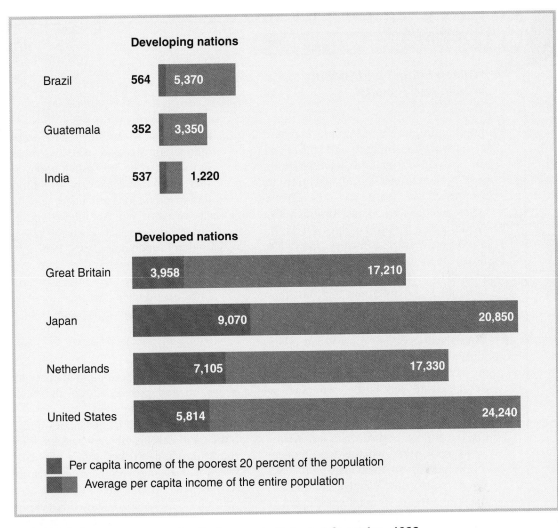

Developing nations

Brazil	**564**	5,370
Guatemala	**352**	3,350
India	**537**	1,220

Developed nations

Great Britain	3,958	17,210
Japan	9,070	20,850
Netherlands	7,105	17,330
United States	5,814	24,240

■ Per capita income of the poorest 20 percent of the population
■ Average per capita income of the entire population

FIGURE 2.3 *Average per Capita Income in Selected Countries, 1993*
(SOURCE: United Nations, 1996.)

Disparity in life chances between the developed and the developing nations also is apparent. Poverty, food shortages, hunger, and rapidly growing populations are pressing problems in many developing nations. Today, more than 1.3 billion people live in *absolute poverty,* **a condition that exists when people do not have the means to secure the most basic necessities of life.** Absolute poverty is often life-threatening, as when people suffer from chronic malnutrition or die from hunger-related diseases. Current estimates suggest that over 600 million people suffer from chronic malnutrition, and over 40 million people die each year from hunger-related diseases. To put this figure in perspective, the number of people worldwide dying from hunger-related diseases is the equivalent of over 300 jumbo jet crashes a day with no survivors and half the passengers being children (Kidron and Segal, 1995).

Despite these current conditions, experts project that the populations of developing nations will increase by almost 60 percent by the year 2025 compared to an increase of about 11 percent in developed nations. Because half of the world's population of about 5,500 million people already lives in developing nations, this rapid increase in population can only compound existing problems and increase inequality on a global basis.

SOCIAL PROBLEMS
IN GLOBAL PERSPECTIVE

BOX 2.1

"Cheap Labor" and Global Wealth and Poverty

◆ Jakarta, Indonesia. "I think maybe I could work for a month and still not be able to buy one pair [of Reebok sneakers]"—Tini Heyun Alwi, an assembly line worker at the Dong Joe shoe factory where Reeboks are made. Although Tini works ten-hour shifts six days a week (in a poorly ventilated factory in stifling heat), she earns only 2,600 Indonesian rupiah ($1.28) a day. With overtime, her monthly wages are about $39, less than half of the $110 retail price of a pair of the Reeboks (Goodman, 1996:F1, F6).

◆ San Salvador, El Salvador. When a U.S. journalist asked a woman who works in an assembly plant (located behind cinderblock walls and barbed wire and patrolled by armed guards) whether her three-year-old daughter had enough to eat, the woman replied, "Oh no. We are very poor." Asked whether her daughter drinks milk, the woman answered, "No. We can't afford it. We give her coffee." According to the woman, her daughter's diet is an egg for breakfast and boiled or fried beans for dinner. Meals with meat or vegetables are extremely rare. "My daughter is very thin and also weak, sometimes she falls down," the woman said (Herbert, 1995:A11).

◆ The United States of America. Labor activists recently alleged that television entertainer Kathie Lee Gifford's line of Wal-Mart clothing, which made a reported $9 million profit in 1995, is made by young Honduran girls earning 31 cents an hour.

◆ The United States of America. Professional basketball player Michael Jordan earns $20 million a year endorsing Nike sneakers, a sum that is greater than the total annual payroll for the thousands of Indonesian workers who assemble the shoes. When he was asked about recent allegations that Nike exploits its Indonesian workers, Jordan replied, "I'm not really aware of that. My job with Nike is to endorse the product. Their job is to be up on that" (quoted in Gibbs, 1996:29). According to a spokesperson, Nike owns no plants in Indonesia; it hires Korean- and Taiwanese-owned factories to make its products, which earned profits of more than $397 million in 1995 alone (*Time*, 1996a:79).

What do these examples tell us about global wealth and poverty? Over the past three decades, many companies have closed plants and factories in the United States and set up business in nations where wages are low, environmental and worker safety standards are weak, and local government officials offer assurances that strikes and independent unions will not be tolerated. Today, U.S.-based multinational corporations employ more than 8 million workers in other nations, and many executives believe that the use of cheap labor is a survival strategy that they must use to be competitive in the global marketplace. Although some labor activists and social analysts call for a shutdown of global sweatshops, one analyst suggests a crucial irony exists in the exploitation of workers in developing nations: Demanding that corporations either shut down plants or pay higher wages could mean that people who currently live in near poverty will have no wages at all in the future (Gibbs, 1996). What do you think will happen when corporations run out of nations where labor is cheap? What part will technology play in the global factory of the twenty-first century?

How do social scientists explain the disparity between wealth and poverty in developed and developing nations? According to the "new international division of labor" perspective, the answer lies in the global organization of manufacturing production (Bluestone and Harrison, 1982). Today, workers in a number of developing nations primarily produce goods such as clothing, electrical machinery, and consumer electronics for export to the United States and other developed nations (see Box 2.1). This global assembly line provides multinational corporations with low-cost (primarily female) labor, no corporate taxes, and no labor unions or strikes (Petras, 1983). Owners and shareholders of multinational corporations, along with subcontractors and managers in developing nations, thus benefit while workers remain in poverty despite long hours in sweatshop conditions.

POVERTY IN THE UNITED STATES

When sociologist Mark Robert Rank asked Denise Turner, an African American mother of four living in poverty, to describe her daily life, Denise replied,

> . . . it can be summarized in one word, and that's survival. That's what we're tryin' to do. We're tryin' to survive. And . . . I talk to a lot of people, and they say, "Well, hey, if you went to Ethiopia, you know, survival would be one thing. And that's . . . eating." But, damn it, I'm not in Ethiopia! You know. So I want a little bit more than just . . . having some food. Having a coupla meals. So, if I can just summarize it, in one word, it would be we're tryin' to survive. We're tryin' to stay together. That's my major concern, keepin' all my family together, my children together. And to survive. (quoted in Rank, 1994:88)

Sociologists refer to the distinction that Denise makes between poverty in Ethiopia and poverty in the United States as the difference between absolute poverty and relative poverty. Absolute poverty exists when people do not have the means to secure the most basic necessities of life. *Relative poverty* exists when people may be able to afford basic necessities such as food, clothing, and shelter but cannot maintain an average standard of living in comparison to that of other members of their society or group (Ropers, 1991). Denise does not suffer from absolute poverty, but she does experience relative poverty on the basis of what is available to other people in the United States.

The United States has the highest poverty rate of any advanced industrial nation (Rothchild, 1995). The *poverty rate* is the proportion of the population whose income falls below the government's official poverty line—the level of income below which a family of a given size is considered to be poor. As is shown in Figure 2.4, the U.S. poverty rate has remained relatively constant over the past two decades, although the total number of people living in poverty has increased because of growth in the total population. The official poverty rate is based on money income and cash government assistance programs such as Social Security payments; however, it does not reflect the value of in-kind benefits such as public housing subsidies, food stamps, Medicare, or Medicaid.

The Poverty Line

How is the U.S. poverty line determined? The official poverty line is based on a minimum family *market basket*—a low-cost food budget that contains a minimum level of nutrition for a family—multiplied by 3 to allow for nonfood costs. Established in 1965 by the Social Security Administration, the poverty line is based on an assumption that the average family must spend about one-third of its total income on food. By multiplying this amount by 3, nonfood costs such as rent and utilities are factored in. Although the poverty line is adjusted for the number of people in the household and is corrected at least annually for changes in the cost of living, essentially the same poverty test has been used since the 1960s.

Today, many social analysts argue that the official poverty line is too low. According to economist Patricia Ruggles (1990, 1992), the poverty line is based on outdated (pre-1960) standards, and poverty thresholds should be increased by at least 50 percent. When the poverty formula was originally developed, fewer households were composed of two working parents or of single parents who faced employment-related expenses such as work clothes, transportation, child care, and quick and convenient foods.

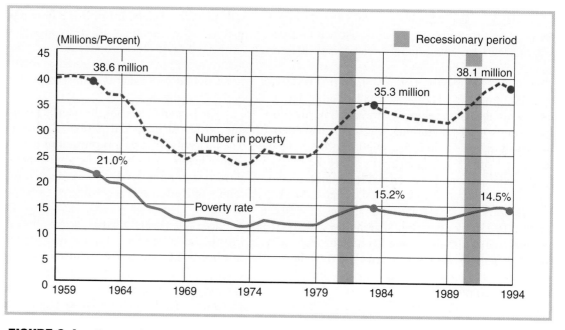

FIGURE 2.4   *Poverty in the United States, 1959 to 1994*
(SOURCE: U.S. Bureau of the Census, 1995a.)

▲ Who Are the Poor?

If poverty were equally distributed among all social groups in the United States, all people regardless of their age, race or ethnicity, sex, household composition, or other attributes statistically would have an equal chance of being among the poor in any given year. However, poverty is not distributed equally: People in some categories are at greater risk for poverty than are people in other categories.

AGE, GENDER, HOUSEHOLD COMPOSITION, AND POVERTY

The vast majority of poor people in the United States are women and children. Children under age eighteen, who make up 25 percent of the U.S. population, account for over 40 percent of the poor. About one in five children age eighteen and under lives in poverty (see Table 2.1). The percentage of children under six years of age who live in poverty-level households is even higher: In 1994, about one in four was considered poor. When children under age six live in households headed by women with no adult male present, almost two-thirds are poor. Children of working-poor parents are the fastest grow-

ing segment of children living in poverty (Holmes, 1996b). More than half of all poor children live in families in which one or both parents work outside the home (U.S. Bureau of Census, 1996a).

About two-thirds of all adults living in poverty are women; households headed by women are the fastest-growing segment of the overall poverty population. Researchers have discovered a number of reasons why single-parent families headed by women are at such a great risk of poverty. Single-parent families typically have fewer employed adults in them and therefore a lower annual income than most two-parent households, and women generally earn less money than men, even for comparable work. Women bear the major economic burden for their children, and contributions from absent fathers in the form of child support and alimony payments account for less than 10 percent of family income. About 43 percent of unmarried mothers with incomes above poverty level receive child support from the fathers; however, only 25 percent of unmarried mothers at or below the poverty line receive such support (U.S. House of Representatives, 1994). Sociologist Diana Pearce (1978) refers to the association between gender and poverty as the *feminization of*

	PERCENTAGE BELOW POVERTY LEVEL			
YEAR	All Races	White	Black	Hispanic Origin
1990	19.9	15.1	44.2	37.7
1993	22.0	17.0	45.9	39.9

TABLE 2.1 CHILDREN (Under 18 Years Old) BELOW THE U.S. POVERTY LEVEL, 1990 AND 1993

SOURCE: U.S. Bureau of the Census, 1995a.

poverty—the trend whereby women are disproportionately represented among individuals living in poverty. On the basis of research on the feminization of poverty, some sociologists suggest that high rates of female poverty are related to women's unique vulnerability to event-driven poverty—poverty resulting from the loss of a job, disability, desertion by a spouse, separation, divorce, or widowhood (Weitzman, 1985; Bane, 1986; Kurz, 1995).

RACE, ETHNICITY, AND POVERTY

African Americans, Latinos/as, and Native Americans are overrepresented among people living in poverty (see Figure 2.5). Across racial-ethnic categories, about three times as many African American families and Latina/o families lived in poverty in 1994 as non-Latina/o white families (U.S. Bureau of the Census, 1995a). Within racial-ethnic categories, fewer than one in ten (non-Latino/a) whites fell below the official poverty level in 1994, in contrast to 14.6 percent of all Asian and Pacific Islanders, 30.6 percent of all African Americans, and 30.7 percent of all Latinos/as.

Differences in household composition show a stark contrast in poverty rates. In households headed by women with no husband present, about half of all Latina/o families (52.1 percent) and African American families (46.2 percent) had incomes below the official poverty level in 1994, in contrast to 29 percent of white (non-Latino/a) families. Recent research suggests that two out of three African American families headed by women were poor before the family event that made the woman a single mother (Bane and Ellwood, 1994). According to sociologist Demie Kurz (1995), the feminization of poverty is intensified by the racialization of poverty—the process by which the effects of low income are made even worse by racial discrimination, which is experienced by all people of color but particularly by women who are single heads of household.

Consequences of Poverty

Although poverty statistics provide some insight into who is poor, such statistics are more than just a snapshot of how people live: They tend to predict a grim future for individuals who live below the poverty line and for the entire nation (Gleick, 1996). As one social analyst suggested, "Poverty narrows and closes life chances. . . . Being poor not only means economic insecurity, it also wreaks havoc on one's mental and physical health" (Ropers, 1991:25).

HEALTH AND NUTRITION

Although the United States has some of the best high-tech medical facilities in the world, not all people have access to them. Although about half of all people below the poverty line receive Medicaid, which provides limited access to certain types of medical care, coverage often is inadequate and begins only after a deductible has been paid. For the working poor and unemployed, lack of health insurance is a major problem. About 35 percent of all people under age sixty-five with a family income of less than $16,000 have no health insurance. The highest rates of uninsured persons are among African Americans and Latinas/os.

Good nutrition is essential to good health, and when people are poor, they are more likely to go without food or to purchase cheap but filling foods such as beans, rice, and potatoes that may not meet all daily nutritional requirements. Poor children particularly are at risk for inadequate nutrition and hunger (Community Childhood Hunger Identification Project, 1995). It

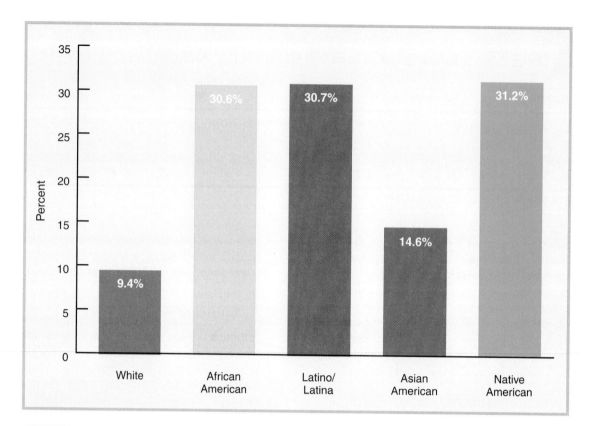

FIGURE 2.5   *People below U.S. Poverty Level, 1994, by Race*

NOTE: Data on Native Americans are based on 1990 figures.
(SOURCE: U.S. Bureau of the Census, 1995a.)

is estimated that about 4 million U.S. children under age twelve are hungry during some part of any twelve-month period. Prolonged malnutrition may result in such medical problems as rickets, scurvy, parasitic worms, and mental retardation. Between one-third and one-half of all children living in poverty consume significantly less than the federally recommended guidelines for caloric and nutritional intake (Children's Defense Fund, 1995). Problems associated with food and shelter are intricately linked. When parents have to decide between paying the rent and putting food on the table, many choose to pay the rent in hopes of keeping a roof over their children's head. Sometimes, however, they cannot afford to do either.

HOUSING

Many regions of the United States lack affordable housing for low-income families. The problem is even greater for individuals and families living in poverty because the number of low-cost housing units has decreased in recent years. Some low-cost units have been replaced by expensive condominiums or single-family residences for affluent residents. Some low-income housing is located in racially segregated areas plagued by high crime rates and overcrowded conditions, inadequate heating and plumbing facilities, cockroach and rodent infestation, and dangerous structural problems due to faulty construction or lack of adequate maintenance. Although much substandard housing exists in central cities, rural areas have more than 50 percent of all inadequate housing units (*1994 Green Book*, 1994).

In recent years, increasing rates of homelessness reflect one of the most devastating effects of poverty. Today, homeless people include single men, single women, increasing numbers of teenage runaways, older people, and entire families (see studies by Rossi, 1989; Liebow, 1993; Lundy, 1995). Families with children accounted for almost 40 percent of all homeless people in 1994, up from about 27 percent a

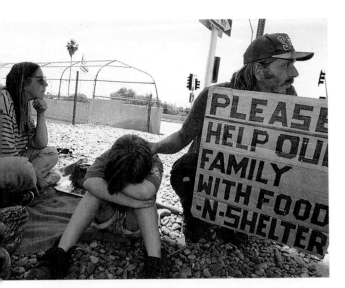

The sight of homeless individuals and families has become all too familiar in both cities and rural areas of the United States. What social factors do you think have caused an increase in homeless families in recent years?

decade earlier (Children's Defense Fund, 1995). Regardless of age or marital status, homeless people are among the poorest of the poor, and people of color are overrepresented in the homeless population.

EDUCATION

A crucial relationship exists between educational opportunities and life chances. Children from low-income families tend to have inadequate educational opportunities that keep them at the bottom of the class system (Bowles and Gintis, 1976). They get fewer years of schooling and are less likely to graduate from high school or college than are children from more affluent families. The schools that poor children attend are more likely to be in areas with lower property values and more limited funding bases for education than are the schools in property-rich suburbs attended by more affluent students. Schools located in high-poverty rural areas or central cities often are dilapidated, have underpaid and overworked teachers, and must rely on outdated equipment and teaching materials.

Lack of educational opportunity results in lower levels of educational attainment among peo-

ple from lower-income and poverty-level families and tends to perpetuate poverty by making it significantly more difficult for these individuals to acquire well-paying jobs or a more secure economic future.

SOCIAL WELFARE IN THE UNITED STATES

The initial wave of U.S. welfare programs was established by Roosevelt's New Deal during the Great Depression of the 1930s and marked the beginning of the *welfare state*—**a program under which the government takes responsibility for specific categories of people by offering them certain services and benefits, such as employment, housing, health, education, or income.** From their inception, government assistance programs have been viewed as "good" if recipients were thought to be deserving of assistance and "bad" if recipients were considered undeserving (see Box 2.2).

Following the New Deal programs, the second wave of welfare programs began with passage of the Economic Opportunity Act of 1964 and implementation of the War on Poverty programs that focused on education and vocational training for low-income children and adults to help them escape poverty. These programs included preschool education (Head Start), compensatory education, and vocational training programs such as the Job Corps, Neighborhood Youth Corps, and Manpower Development (Kelso, 1994). These antipoverty programs steadily reduced the percentage of people living in poverty from 22 percent in 1960 to 12 percent in 1976 (see Coleman, 1966; Jencks et al., 1972). However, the Reagan and Bush administrations in the 1980s and early 1990s greatly reduced or eliminated funding for Aid to Families with Dependent Children (AFDC), food stamps, subsidized housing, child-nutrition programs, maternal and child health programs, family planning, and job training (see Danziger and Gottschalk, 1995).

During the 1990s, the Clinton administration expanded the Earned Income Tax Credit (EITC), which had been enacted in 1975 to provide a reimbursement for the working poor if their income falls below the poverty line. EITC is available to both one-parent and two-parent families and does not require recipients to apply for welfare to receive the credit.

SOCIAL PROBLEMS
AND SOCIAL POLICY

BOX 2.2

The Welfare Battle in the United States

It is hard to imagine a less popular word than welfare. Its two simple syllables conjure a mental mural of poverty, failure and futility. Welfare mother, welfare cheat, welfare state—the associations steamroll to the conclusion . . . Cut Welfare. (DeParle, 1994:E5)

Why is welfare for the needy stigmatized more than other government assistance programs? The answer partially lies in the history of the U.S. welfare system. For many years, a distinction has been made between people who are deserving of government assistance—such as widows, orphans, farmers hit by droughts or other natural disasters, the permanently disabled, workers who experience unemployment through no fault of their own, and older workers who retired after many years of employment—and those who are considered undeserving of assistance. The undeserving are believed to be able-bodied individuals who are lazy and unwilling to work (Katz, 1989).

The distinction between deserving and undeserving recipients of government largess can be traced back to the Great Depression of the 1930s when the New Deal was implemented and the Social Security Act of 1935 established income transfer programs. Among these programs were federal pensions for older people (Social Security), unemployment relief for workers, aid for people with disabilities, and

Aid to Dependent Children (ADC), which was changed to Aid to Families with Dependent Children (AFDC) in 1950. From the outset, however, important distinctions were made between Social Security and AFDC. Social Security is age-tested—individuals who have paid money into the program are entitled to receive benefits on reaching retirement age. By contrast, AFDC has been a *means-tested* program—recipients have to show proof of poverty to receive benefits. This distinction between the two programs contributed to the stigmatization of poverty and of single motherhood. As a result, the 1996 welfare reform law primarily targeted single mothers with young children, especially unmarried mothers under age eighteen.

As President Clinton signed the law, he stated, "Today we are ending welfare as we know it. But I hope this day will be remembered not for what it ended, but for what it began: a new day that offers hope, honors responsibility, rewards work and changes the terms of the debate so that no one in America ever feels again the need to criticize people who are poor or on welfare" (Kilborn, 1996:A10). Do you think the president's hope will prove true? Why or why not?

ADDITIONAL SOURCES: Trattner, 1989; L. Gordon, 1994; Quadagno, 1994; Danziger and Gottschalk, 1995; Borosage, 1996.

Perhaps the most dramatic shift in welfare policy in recent decades came with passage of the 1996 welfare bill that abolished the federal guarantee of welfare benefits, principally AFDC, and gave states block grants to use as they wished to aid the poor. The law also established a work requirement (referred to as *workfare*) for most people seeking welfare and allowed states to set limits on how long recipients can receive benefits (Langford, 1996; Arenson, 1996). Wide diversity exists in programs from state to state. Some states have established job training programs to assist welfare recipients in finding a job with a living

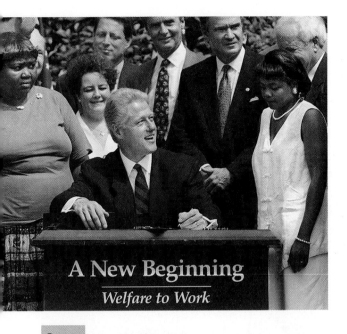

Signing the welfare reform bill of 1996, President Bill Clinton stated that he hoped the nation was entering a new era when government-funded welfare payments would no longer be necessary in this country. Do you think we are closer to reaching this goal today than we were when he signed the bill?

wage; others have employed welfare recipients to clean subways and parks. Regardless of its exact implementation, this law dramatically affects single mothers and their children, legal immigrant families, children with disabilities in low-income families, and many food stamp recipients.

Is welfare a problem or a solution? The answer to this question depends on how poverty itself is explained.

EXPLANATIONS FOR POVERTY

Poverty can be explained in individualistic, cultural, or structural terms. Whichever framework is applied influences people's beliefs about how poverty might be reduced. Individual explanations for poverty are based on one of two issues: (1) attitudinal and motivational problems of individuals that cause them to be poor and (2) the amount of human capital that a person possesses (Rank, 1994). Attitudinal and

motivational explanations focus on the United States as the "land of opportunity," suggesting that people who do not succeed have no one to blame but themselves for their lack of motivation, laziness, or other flaws (Feagin, 1975). In contrast, human capital explanations of poverty highlight the individual's lack of *human capital*—the assets that a person brings to the labor market such as education, job training, experience, and specialized knowledge or skills (Becker, 1964). For example, the introduction of new workplace technologies has resulted in many people having limited human capital to bring to the job market. The 1996 workfare program for welfare recipients appears to be based on individual explanations for poverty and welfare dependency. To many sociologists, however, individual explanations of poverty amount to *blaming the victim*—a **practice used by people who view a social problem as emanating from within the individual who exhibits the problem** (Ryan, 1976).

Cultural explanations for poverty focus on how people's cultural background affects their values and behavior. Among the earliest of these explanations is the culture of poverty thesis. According to anthropologist Oscar Lewis (1966), some—but not all—poor people develop a separate and self-perpetuating system of beliefs and values that keeps them trapped in poverty. Among these attitudes and behaviors are an inability to defer gratification or plan for the future; feelings of apathy, hostility, and suspicion toward others; and deficient speech and communication patterns. The culture of poverty thesis has provided political leaders and social analysts with a rationale for labeling the poor as lazy and perpetually dependent on "government handouts."

More recent cultural explanations of poverty have focused on the lack of *cultural capital*—the **values, beliefs, attitudes, and competencies in language and culture that are required for success and social advancement** (Bourdieu and Passeron, 1990). From this perspective, low-income people do not have adequate cultural capital to function in a competitive global economy. According to some sociologists, cultural explanations deflect attention from the true sources of poverty and shift blame from the affluent and powerful to the poor and powerless (Sidel, 1996:xvii–xviii).

In comparison to individual and cultural explanations of poverty, which operate at the microlevel, structural explanations focus on the macrolevel orga-

Reprinted by permission.

nization of society that is beyond an individual's ability to change. Functionalist explanations for poverty point to structural changes in the economy that have dramatically altered employment opportunities for people, particularly those who have the least wealth, power, and prestige (see Wilson, 1996). According to functionalists, social inequality serves an important function in society because it motivates people to work hard to acquire these scarce resources.

Another structural explanation for poverty is based on the conflict perspective that suggests poverty is a side effect of the capitalist system. Workers are increasingly impoverished by the wage squeeze and high rates of unemployment and underemployment. The wage squeeze refers to the steady downward pressure on the real take-home pay of workers that has occurred over the past two decades, while shareholders in major corporations have had substantial increases in profits and chief executive officers have received extremely lucrative salaries and compensation packages (D. M. Gordon, 1996). Corporate downsizing and new technologies that take the place of workers have further enhanced capitalists' profits and contributed to the impoverishment of middle- and low-income workers by creating a reserve army—unemployed people whom

the capitalists use as a source of cheap labor and a means to keep other workers' wages low. In sum, corporations' intense quest for profit results in low wages for workers, a wide disparity in the life chances of affluent people and poor people, and the unemployment and impoverishment of many people. Although some analysts suggest that high rates of poverty will always exist in advanced capitalist societies, others believe that inequality and poverty can be reduced if not eliminated.

CAN CLASS-BASED INEQUALITY BE REDUCED?

Chapter 1 made the point that how people view a social problem is related to how they believe the problem should be reduced or solved. Poverty and social inequality are no exceptions. Analysts who focus on individual causes for poverty typically suggest individual solutions: Low-income and poverty-level people should change their attitudes, beliefs, and work habits. For example, economist George Gilder (1981) has stated that "The only dependable route from poverty is always work. . . . The poor must not only work, they must work harder than the classes above them."

Similarly, people who believe poverty is culturally based seek cultural solutions, suggesting that poverty can be reduced by enhancing people's cultural capital. We should develop more job training and school enrichment programs to enhance people's cultural capital and counteract negative familial and neighborhood influences. For example, the federal government developed Head Start programs and the Job Corps to provide children and adolescents from low-income families, especially families of color, with the cultural capital (e.g., white middle-class values) that they needed to succeed (see Quadagno and Fobes, 1995).

Although some structural solutions suggest that poverty can be eliminated only if capitalism is abolished and a new means of distributing valued goods and services is established, others state that poverty can be reduced by the creation of "a truly open society—a society where the life chances of those at the bottom are not radically different from those at the top and where wealth is distributed more equitably" (MacLeod, 1995:260). From this perspective, federal and state governments should play a vital role in reducing poverty and lessening people's dependency on welfare. Recent proposals include the following:

◆ Establishing a coordinated employment policy that emphasizes the creation of jobs with livable wages and benefits
◆ Building individual assets through government policies that provide incentives and resources for low-income families to acquire and build economic assets
◆ Providing tax benefits such as EITC to assist low-income workers

◆ Giving economic assistance to help families deal with divorce, unwanted teenage pregnancy, and child-care problems
◆ Providing universal medical coverage for low-income families, older people, and individuals with serious health problems without qualifying deductibles that reduce assets and income
◆ Investing in lower-income areas of communities and empowering residents to organize and address problems such as affordable housing and better schools (Rank, 1994)

Although these changes would not "solve" the problem of poverty, they might temper and reduce the price poor people pay for living in the "land of opportunity" (Rank, 1994). In the meantime, amazingly, many people living in poverty have not given up on the American Dream. Sara, a woman struggling to find opportunities for herself and her children, said,

I got my vision, I got my dreams. . . . I have goals—I want to be something different from what I have right now. . . . I guess to be somebody in poverty, to see that generation that's coming behind us—it's sad, it's real sad, what do they have to strive for? . . . I just got to believe I only can make the difference. . . . even though obviously the system doesn't really want you to succeed. . . . I can become what statistics has designed me to be, a nothing, or I can make statistics a lie. . . . Today, I am making statistics a lie. (Polakow, 1993:73)

SUMMARY

➡ *Why is social stratification a social problem?*

Social stratification refers to the hierarchical arrangement of large social groups based on their control over basic resources. In highly stratified societies, low-income and poor people have limited access to food, clothing, shelter, education, health care, and other necessities of life.

➡ *How do sociological research methods differ?*

Field research takes place in a natural setting in which sociologists can observe and interview people where they live, work, and play. In survey research, sociologists use written questionnaires or structured interviews to ask respondents a series of questions about a specific topic. In secondary analysis of existing data, sociologists analyze data that originally were collected by others for some other purpose. An experiment is a carefully designed situation in which the researcher studies the impact of certain factors on subjects' attitudes or behavior.

➤ *How is the U.S. class structure divided?*

The U.S. population is divided into a number of classes. The upper or capitalist class is the wealthiest and most powerful class of investors, heirs, and executives. The upper-middle class is composed of professionals and owners of small businesses. The middle class includes white-collar office workers, middle-management personnel, and people in technical support positions. Members of the working class hold occupations such as semiskilled machine operators and counter help in fast-food restaurants. The chronically poor include individuals of working age who are outside the labor force and children who live in poor families.

➤ *What are the major problems of the developing nations?*

Studies of global inequality distinguish between developed nations—countries with highly industrialized economies and relatively high levels of national and per capita (per person) income—and developing nations—countries that are undergoing transformation from agrarian to industrial economies. Poverty, food shortages, hunger, and rapidly growing populations are pressing problems in many developing nations.

➤ *How does the new international division of labor perspective explain global inequality?*

The new international division of labor refers to the global organization of production set up by multinational corporations whereby workers, earning extremely low wages in developing nations, produce goods for export to the developed nations such as the United States and Japan.

➤ *Who are the poor in the United States?*

The major categories of poor people in the United States are women, children under age eighteen, and people of color, especially African Americans, Latinas/os, and Native Americans.

➤ *What are individual and cultural explanations of poverty?*

Individual explanations for poverty focus on attitudinal and motivational problems of individuals or the amount of human capital a person possesses. Cultural explanations for poverty focus on how people's cultural background affects their values and behavior.

➤ *Why do sociologists prefer structural explanations of poverty?*

Sociologists believe that an analysis of how social organizations and institutions contribute to poverty and inequality provides a more adequate explanation of these phenomena than do the attributes of individuals or their cultural background. Therefore sociologists prefer to examine the structural features of society such as how changes in the economy alter employment opportunities or how inequality and exploitation are inherent in the structure of class relations in a capitalist economy.

➤ *What solutions have been suggested for poverty?*

Most solutions focus on the importance of work. Individual perspectives suggest that people should work harder. Structural perspectives are based on the assumption that society can reduce poverty by creating job and training programs and investing in people through provision of child care, health care, and affordable housing.

KEY TERMS

absolute poverty, p. 31
blaming the victim, p. 39
class system, p. 24
cultural capital, p. 39
developed nations, p. 30
developing nations, p. 30
experiment, p. 26
feminization of poverty, pp. 34–35
field research, p. 25
income, p. 27

life chances, p. 24
poverty rate, p. 33
power, p. 24
prestige, p. 24
relative poverty, p. 33
secondary analysis of existing data, p. 26
social stratification, p. 24
survey research, p. 25
wealth, p. 24
welfare state, p. 37

QUESTIONS FOR CRITICAL THINKING

1. You have decided to study wealth and poverty in your community. What research method(s) would provide the best data for analysis? What secondary sources might provide useful data? What kinds of information would be easiest to acquire? What kinds of information would be most difficult to acquire?

2. What would happen if all the wealth in the United States were redistributed so that all adults had the same amount? Some analysts suggest that within five years, most of the wealth would be back in the possession of the people who hold it today. What arguments can you give to support this idea? What arguments can you give to disprove this idea?

3. How do the lives of assembly line workers in developing nations compare with the lives of people who live in poverty in central cities and rural areas of the United States? Should U.S. foreign policy include provisions for reducing the problems of people in developing nations? Should it be U.S. government policy to help disadvantaged people in our own country? Why or why not?

4. Pretend that cost is no object and develop a plan for solving the problem of poverty in the United States. What are your priorities and goals? How long will your plan take to implement? Who will be the primary beneficiaries of your plan? Will the plan have any effect on you?

Chapter Three

Racial and Ethnic Inequality

We are unable to get taxis to pick us up in front of office buildings. We are frisked and detained on suburban commuter trains. We are watched in department stores and mistaken for coat-check clerks and restroom attendants while lunching in the best restaurants. We are directed to freight elevators and delivery windows by receptionists who fail to recognize us in our own company offices.

We are black professionals in corporate America in the 1990s.

Although I am at my desk each morning facing the same corporate challenges as my white co-workers, a great deal of my job-related stress comes from sources totally unrelated to my job. . . . The amount of subtle bias I face as a lawyer continues to dismay me. For example, I have worked with clients or co-counsel who have become comfortable with me through phone conversations and correspondence. But upon meeting me, they are suddenly fidgety and wary of my competence.

"Where did you go to law school?" they ask almost immediately.

Unable to focus on anything else until they hear "Harvard," these clients rarely say, "I pay that firm a lot of money. How come they gave me the black lawyer?" But they do practice more subtle, and ultimately more damaging, discrimination. The client, for example, may phrase his immediate dissatisfaction at being assigned to a black as a complaint that is vague yet incriminating ("I don't feel very comfortable working with Larry") or, worse, may complain about my skills ("I don't think Larry is up to the job, so assign me another lawyer").

In both cases, the forthright employer is left thinking there is no bias, and the black employee is left without a client, but with an abiding sense of failure and anger.

—*Lawrence Otis Graham, a corporate lawyer and author, describing the experiences of many middle- and upper-middle-class African Americans in corporate America*
(Graham, 1995:F13)

As Graham suggests, African Americans and other people of color often experience overt and subtle discrimination in their daily lives, regardless of their educational background and level of income. As described in Chapter 1, *discrimination* is the actions or practices of dominant group members that have a harmful impact on members of subordinate groups (Feagin and Feagin, 1996). Like many other social problems, racial and ethnic discrimination signals that there is a discrepancy between the ideals of U.S. society and the actual achievement of these ideals. While equality and freedom for all—regardless of race, color, creed, or national origin—are stated ideals of this country, many subordinate group members experience subordination and racial discrimination regardless of their class, gender, or age.

RACIAL AND ETHNIC INEQUALITY AS A SOCIAL PROBLEM

As we reach the end of the twentieth century, race is among the most divisive social problems facing the United States. At the same time, sociologists such as William J. Wilson (1996) suggest that we all—regardless of racial or ethnic background—share certain common interests and concerns that cross racial and class boundaries. Some of the problems are unemployment and job insecurity, declining real wages, escalating medical and housing costs, a scarcity of good-quality child-care programs, a sharp decline in the quality of public education, and the toll of crime and drug trafficking in all neighborhoods. From this perspective, racial and ethnic inequality is a problem for everyone, not just for people of color.

What Are Race and Ethnicity?

Many sociologists view race as a social construct—a classification of people based on social and political values—rather than something objective and fixed, a biological given (see Omi and Winant, 1994). How, then, does a sociological definition of race differ from a biological one? A biological definition of a race is a population that differs from other populations in the incidence of some genes. In the past, some anthropologists classified diverse categories of peoples into races on the basis of skin color (pig-

mentation) and features and build (morphology). However, contemporary anthropologists classify races in terms of genetically determined immunological and biochemical differences. In the process, they have concluded that, because of multiple generations of interbreeding, no "pure" races exist.

In contrast with the biological definition of race, sociologists define a *racial group* as a category of **people who have been singled out, by others or themselves, as inferior or superior, on the basis of subjectively selected physical characteristics such as skin color, hair texture, and eye shape.** African American, Native American, and Asian American are examples of categories of people that have been designated racial groups.

Racial groups typically are defined on the basis of real or alleged physical characteristics; ethnic groups are defined on the basis of cultural or nationality characteristics. An *ethnic group* is a category of **people who are distinguished, by others or by themselves, as inferior or superior primarily on the basis of cultural or nationality characteristics** (Feagin and Feagin, 1996). Briefly stated, members of an ethnic group share five main characteristics: (1) unique cultural traits, (2) a sense of community, (3) a feeling that one's own group is the best, (4) membership from birth, and (5) a tendency, at least initially, to occupy a distinct geographic area (such as Chinatown, Little Italy, or Little Havana). "White ethnics" such as Irish Americans, Italian Americans, and Jewish Americans are examples of ethnic groups.

"Official" Racial and Ethnic Classifications

Racial and ethnic classifications have been used for political, economic, and social purposes for many years. During the sixteenth century, northern Europeans used the concept of race to rationalize the enslavement of Africans, who were deemed an "inferior race" (Feagin and Feagin, 1996).

Before the Civil War, race was used to justify the subordination of African Americans—whether they were "slaves" in the South or "freemen" in the North. In some southern states, people were classified on the basis of the "one-drop rule"—a person with any trace of African blood was considered "black" and treated as inferior (Davis, 1991). Other states traced "black blood" by fractions, such as one-sixteenth African American ancestry, or used an "eyeball test" based on physical features such as hair texture, eye color, and shape of nose, ears, lips, and skull (Funderburg, 1994). Being classified as "Negro," "black," or "colored" had a profound effect on people's life chances and opportunities during slavery and the subsequent era of legally sanctioned segregation. Gregory Howard Williams describes how he felt when he learned from his father in the 1950s that he was "colored" rather than white, as he previously had been led to believe:

[My father said,] "Life is going to be different from now on. In Virginia you were white boys. In Indiana, you're going to be colored boys. I want you to remember that you're the same today that you were yesterday. But people in Indiana will treat you differently. . . ."

No, I answered, still refusing to believe. I'm not colored, I'm white! I look white! I've always been white! I go to "whites only" schools, "whites only" movie theaters, and "whites only" swimming pools! I never had heard anything crazier in my life! How could Dad tell us such a mean lie? I glanced across the aisle [of the bus] to where he sat grim-faced and erect, staring straight ahead. I saw my father as I never had seen him before. . . . My father was a Negro! We were colored! After ten years in Virginia on the white side of the color line, I knew what that meant. (Williams, 1996:33–34)

When Williams and his younger brother went to live with their African American grandmother in Muncie, Indiana, they quickly saw the sharp contrast between the "white" and "black" worlds: The first was one of privilege, opportunity, and comfort, and the second was one of deprivation, repression, and struggle. Since that time, Williams has become a lawyer and then a law school dean; however, his memories of the prejudice and discrimination he experienced in Muncie because of the change in his racial classification still remain with him (Williams, 1996).

Government racial classifications are based primarily on skin color. One category exists for "whites" (who vary considerably in actual skin color and physical appearance); all the remaining categories are considered "non-white." The Bureau of the Census requires respondents to choose from the categories of White, Black, Asian or Pacific Islander, American Indian, Eskimo or Aleut, or "Other" in designating their racial classification. To overcome inadequacies in the existing classification system, a multiracial category may be added to the census conducted in the year 2000 (Morganthau, 1995). Although racial classifications initially may seem unimportant, they affect people's access to employment, housing, social services, federal aid, and many other publicly and privately valued goods and services (Omi and Winant, 1994).

The Meaning of Majority and Minority Groups

When sociologists use the terms *majority group* and *minority group,* they are referring to power differentials among groups, not to the numerical sense in which the words *majority* and *minority* are generally used. A *majority* (or *dominant*) *group* is one that is advantaged and has superior resources and rights in a society (Feagin and Feagin, 1996). Majority groups often are determined on the basis of race or ethnicity, but they can also be determined on the basis of factors such as gender, sexual orientation (homosexuality, heterosexuality, or bisexuality), and physical ability. A *minority* (or *subordinate*) *group* is one whose members, because of physical or cultural characteristics, are disadvantaged and subjected to unequal treatment by the dominant group and regard themselves as objects of collective discrimination (Wirth, 1945). In the United States, people of color, all women, people with disabilities, and gay men and lesbian women tend to be considered minority group members regardless of their proportion in the overall U.S. population.

The racial and ethnic majority group in the United States typically is associated with the *white-skin privilege* that accrues to people who trace their ancestry to Northern Europe and think of themselves as European Americans or WASPs (white Anglo-Saxon Protestants). Women's studies scholar Peggy McIntosh describes the white-skin privilege of the majority group this way:

I have come to see white privilege as an invisible package of unearned assets that I can count on cashing in each day, but about which I was "meant" to remain oblivious. White privilege is like an invisible weightless knapsack of special provisions, assurances, maps, guides, codebooks, passports, visas, clothes, compass, emergency gear, and blank checks. (McIntosh, 1995:76–77)

Most white Americans are not aware of the benefits that they derive from the white-skin privilege (see Frankenberg, 1993; Wellman, 1993; Hacker, 1995; McIntosh, 1995). Nevertheless, the advantage/disadvantage and power/exploitation relationships of majority and minority groups are deeply rooted in patterns of prejudice and discrimination in the United States.

RACISM, PREJUDICE, AND DISCRIMINATION

Racism is a set of attitudes, beliefs, and practices that are used to justify the superior treatment of one racial or ethnic group and the inferior treatment of another racial or ethnic group. In the United States, racism is sometimes referred to as white racism because it favors white Americans over people of color. The term *white racism* refers to socially organized attitudes, ideas, and practices that deny people of color the dignity, opportunities, freedoms, and rewards that are typically available to white Americans (Feagin and Vera, 1995:7). From this perspective, people of color pay a *direct, heavy, and immediately painful price* for racism, while white discriminators pay an *indirect and seldom recognized price.*

Prejudice is a negative attitude based on faulty generalizations about members of selected racial and ethnic groups (Allport, 1958). If we think of prejudice as a set of negative attitudes toward members of another group simply because they belong to that group, we quickly realize that all people have prejudices, whether or not they acknowledge them. Prejudice is rooted in *ethnocentrism*—the assumption that one's own group and way of life are superior to all others. For example, most schoolchildren are taught that their own school and country are the best. The school song, the pledge to the flag, and the national anthem are forms of *positive ethnocentrism.* However, *negative ethnocentrism* also can result from constant emphasis on the superiority of one's own group or nation if individuals come to believe that other groups or nations are inferior and should be treated accordingly (Feagin and Feagin, 1996). Negative ethnocentrism is manifested in stereotypes that adversely affect many people.

Stereotypes are overgeneralizations about the appearance, behavior, or other characteristics of all members of a group. For example, second-generation Filipino American Steven De Castro and his friends were the objects of stereotyping during their school years:

> The young Filipinos I know don't have to do any heavy analysis to understand racism. We understand racism through our eyes and our ears. . . .
> "What's up, monkey?" "Hey Ching Chong! Hey eggroll!" "Here comes the gook!" If you are Filipino in America, that is what you grow up hearing in the schoolyard. All you want to do is belong, but white and black classmates never let you forget that you will never belong in their America. (De Castro, 1994:303–304)

As shown in Box 3.1 in the example of Canada, stereotyping and discrimination occur in most nations that have diverse populations. Discrimination may be carried out by individuals acting on their own or by people operating within the context of large-scale organizations or institutions such as schools, corporations, and government agencies. *Individual discrimination* consists of one-on-one acts by members of the dominant group that harm members of the subordinate group or their property (Carmichael and Hamilton, 1967). Individual dis-

In 1996, several black churches in the South were burned, including historic Matthews-Murkland Presbyterian Church in Charlotte, North Carolina. Rev. Larry Hill, the pastor, is shown here looking at the charred wreckage.

SOCIAL PROBLEMS
IN GLOBAL PERSPECTIVE

BOX 3.1

Racism in Canada

You feel it every day, but there is no concrete evidence. You see it when you walk into stores, you see that the security is heightened. You see it on the subway. When I get on in the morning to go to work, there aren't too many people. Gradually, the car fills up, but often nobody sits next to me. Sometimes, people are rushing and you may bump into someone and they'll say, "You . . . nigger, why don't you go back where you came from," stuff like that. (quoted in Corelli, 1995:42–43)

Recent studies show that racism directed against African Canadians and recent immigrants is a major social problem. Many African Canadians, who make up only 3 percent of the Canadian population, trace their ancestry to the 3,500 former U.S. slaves who were relocated to Canada after they won their freedom by fighting for the British during the American Revolution. Throughout their tenure in Canada, African Canadians have been largely excluded from churches, schools, and jobs (Blount, 1996). Some social analysts predict that racial discrimination in Canada will become an even larger issue because recent immigration has increased

the size of Canada's black population and many newcomers have higher levels of education and better-paying jobs than do native-born African Canadians (Blount, 1996).

Racism in Canada is not limited to African Canadians. Canada has experienced a high level of immigration by Chinese, Arab, East Indian, and Caribbean peoples as well (Cannon, 1995). Immigrants are blamed for growing unemployment, high welfare costs, problems in the schools, and increasing crime. Discrimination and racially motivated violence are reinforced by negative stereotypes. Asian Canadians, for example, are viewed as the "new criminal class" that steals, terrorizes, and settles disputes with guns, and Arabs are stereotyped as "sneaky and sly" and "oppressors of women" (Cannon, 1995).

How do the experiences of dominant group members in Canada compare with those of dominant group members in the United States? Are the experiences of subordinate racial-ethnic group members in Canada similar to those in the United States? Do you think recent immigration to the United States has affected how African Americans and other people of color are treated in the United States?

crimination results from the prejudices and discriminatory actions of bigoted people who target one or more subordinate group members. For example, a taxi driver who refuses to pick up African American passengers is practicing individual discrimination.

In contrast, *institutional discrimination* consists of the day-to-day practices of organizations and institutions that have a harmful impact on members of subordinate groups. For example, many mortgage companies are more likely to make loans to whites than to people of color (see Squires, 1994). Institu-

tional discrimination is carried out by the individuals who implement policies and procedures that result in the negative and differential treatment of subordinate group members. For example, Jewish immigrants in the late 1800s experienced institutionalized discrimination in accommodations and employment. Signs in hotel windows often read "No Jews Allowed," and many "help wanted" advertisements stated "Christians Only" (Levine, 1992:55). Such practices are referred to as *anti-Semitism*—prejudice and discriminatory behavior directed at Jews.

PERSPECTIVES ON RACIAL AND ETHNIC INEQUALITY

Over the course of the twentieth century, sociologists have developed perspectives to explain why racial and ethnic inequality occurs and why it persists. Some perspectives are social-psychological; others focus on sociological factors such as migration, assimilation, conflict, and exploitation.

Social-Psychological Perspectives

Are some people more prejudiced than others? Social-psychological perspectives on prejudice emphasize psychological characteristics or personality traits. We'll look at the frustration-aggression hypothesis and the authoritarian personality.

According to the *frustration-aggression hypothesis,* individuals who are frustrated in their efforts to achieve a highly desired goal tend to develop a pattern of aggression toward others (Dollard et al., 1939). If they have a very high level of frustration and are unable to strike out at the source of their anger and hostility, they instead may take out their hostility and aggression on a *scapegoat*—a person or group that is incapable of offering resistance to the hostility or aggression of others (Marger, 1994). For example, "illegal aliens" (people who have entered the United States without permission) are blamed for a wide variety of societal woes such as high rates of unemployment, an economic recession over which they have no control, or high taxes to provide them with services such as health care.

Another major social-psychological perspective suggests that people who have an authoritarian personality are most likely to be highly prejudiced. According to psychologist Theodore W. Adorno and his colleagues (1950), the *authoritarian personality* is characterized by excessive conformity, submissiveness to authority, intolerance, insecurity, a high level of superstition, and rigid, stereotypic thinking. Individuals with this type of personality typically view the world as a threatening place and are highly intolerant of members of subordinate racial, ethnic, or religious groups.

Interactionist Perspectives

Somewhat related to social-psychological explanations of prejudice and discrimination are theories based on the interactionist perspective in sociology. One interactionist approach emphasizes how racial socialization contributes to feelings of solidarity with one's own racial-ethnic group and hostility toward all others. *Racial socialization* is a process of social interaction that contains specific messages and practices concerning the nature of one's racial-ethnic status as it relates to (1) personal and group identity, (2) intergroup and interindividual relationships, and (3) one's position in the social stratification system. Racial socialization is made up of direct statements made by parents, peers, teachers, and others about race; it also includes indirect behaviors such as modeling, whereby children imitate the words and actions of parents and other caregivers (M. C. Thornton et al., 1990). Racial socialization affects how people view themselves, other people, and the world. Here, for example, racial relations scholar and historian Manning Marable (1995:1) describes how race is a prism through which African Americans and other people of color view their daily lives:

> Black and white. As long as I can remember, the fundamentally defining feature of my life, and the lives of my family, was the stark reality of race. . . . It was the social gravity which set into motion our expectations and emotions, our language and dreams. . . . Race seemed granite-like, fixed and permanent, as the center of the social universe. The reality of racial discrimination constantly fed the pessimism and doubts that we as black people felt about the apparent natural order of the world, the inherent unfairness of it all, as well as limiting our hopes for a better life somewhere in the distant future.

Though all groups practice racial socialization, white racial socialization emphasizes white racial bonding, which perpetuates racism and discrimination. According to Christine E. Sleeter (1996), white racial bonding occurs when white people act in ways that reaffirm the common stance on race-related issues and draw we–they boundaries. Such people choose to live near other whites, to socialize with other whites, and to vote for other whites, thus maintaining racial solidarity. Although many whites do not support racist beliefs, actions, or policies, they fear breaking bonds with other whites and may simply remain silent in the face of prejudice and discrimination (Sleeter, 1996).

Functionalist Perspectives

To functionalists, social order and stability are extremely important for the smooth functioning of society. Consequently, racial and ethnic discord, urban unrest, and riots are dysfunctional and must be eliminated or contained. One functionalist perspective focuses on *assimilation*—**the process by which members of subordinate racial and ethnic groups become absorbed into the dominant culture.** Assimilation has been viewed as a stabilizing force that minimizes differences that otherwise might result in hostility and violence (M. M. Gordon, 1964). Its most complete form is *amalgamation,* also referred to as the **melting pot model—a process whereby the cultural attributes of diverse racial-ethnic groups are blended together to form a new society incorporating the unique contributions of each group.** Amalgamation occurs when members of dominant and subordinate racial-ethnic groups intermarry and procreate so-called mixed-race children.

However, early assimilation in the United States focused primarily on the Anglo-conformity model, not the melting pot model. The *Anglo-conformity model* **refers to a pattern of assimilation whereby members of subordinate racial-ethnic groups are expected to conform to the culture of the dominant (white) Anglo-Saxon population.** Assimilation does not always lead to full social acceptance. For example, many successful African Americans and Jewish Americans have been excluded from membership in elite private clubs and parties in the homes of coworkers.

Recently, political conservatives have focused on assimilation and, particularly, adopting English as the country's official language. In her recent influential book *Out of the Barrio* (1991), social analyst Linda Chavez says Latinas/os must learn English and adopt the dominant culture if they want economic success and social acceptance in the United States. According to Chavez, Latinos/as should forget about entitlement programs such as affirmative action and focus on assimilating into the U.S. economic mainstream (see Box 3.2).

Another functionalist perspective emphasizes *ethnic pluralism*—**a situation in which diverse racial-ethnic groups coexist in society but have separate identities and cultures.** In a pluralistic society, political and economic systems link diverse groups, but members of some racial-ethnic groups maintain enough separation from the dominant group to guarantee that their group and ethnic cultural traditions continue (M. M. Gordon, 1964). Ethnic pluralism in the United States typically has been based on *segregation* because subordinate racial-ethnic groups have less power and privilege than do members of the dominant group (Marger, 1994). *Segregation* **is the spatial and social separation of categories of people by race/ethnicity, class, gender, religion, or other social characteristics.** Recent sociological studies have found that when high levels of racial segregation are followed by interracial contact, racial competition may ensue, tending to increase ethnic and racial unrest and the potential for urban riots (Olzak et al., 1996).

Conflict Perspectives

Conflict theorists explain racial and ethnic inequality in terms of economic stratification and access to power. Conflict explanations include class perspectives, split-labor market theory, gendered racism, internal colonialism, and the theory of racial formation.

Class perspectives on racial and ethnic inequality highlight the role of the capitalist class in racial exploitation. For example, according to sociologist Oliver C. Cox (1948), the primary cause of slavery was the profit motive of capitalists, not racial prejudice. African Americans were enslaved because they were the cheapest and best workers that owners of plantations and mines could find to do the heavy labor. Contemporary class perspectives suggest that members of the capitalist class benefit from a split-labor market that fosters racial divisions among workers and suppresses wages. *Split-labor market theory* states that the U.S. economy is divided into two employment sectors: a primary sector composed of higher-paid workers in more secure jobs and a secondary sector composed of lower-paid workers in jobs that often involve hazardous working conditions and little job security (Bonacich, 1972, 1976). Dominant group members are more likely to be employed in primary sector positions; subordinate group members most often are employed in the secondary sector. Workers in the two job sectors tend to have divergent interests and goals; therefore worker solidarity is unlikely (Bonacich, 1972, 1976). Members of the capitalist class benefit from these divisions because workers are less likely to bind together and demand pay increases or other changes in the workplace. White workers in the primary sector attempt to exclude

SOCIAL PROBLEMS
AND SOCIAL POLICY

BOX 3.2

Is Affirmative Action a Problem or a Solution?

Newspaper columnist William Raspberry compares U.S. racial inequality with a basketball game in which it is discovered at halftime that the referees cheated during the first half of the game. If one team was allowed to gain 16 undeserved points, does expelling the referees make the rest of the game fair? According to Raspberry, past injustices—whether in sports or daily life—do not remedy themselves just because former referees have been removed from the game: Remedial steps such as affirmative action are necessary to equalize the game (L. Chavez, 1991).

The Civil Rights Commission defines affirmative action as any measure that permits the consideration of race, national origin, sex, or disability to provide opportunities to a class of qualified individuals who have been denied those opportunities. Advocates of affirmative action agree with Raspberry that programs must be kept in place if we want to dismantle discrimination and reduce inequality. It is not only people of color who have benefited from affirmative action programs, but also white women and men, people with disabilities, and poor and working class people. However, critics argue that affirmative action should be abolished.

According to critic Linda Chavez (1991), affirmative action should be dismantled because it merely installed a new system of racial rights that benefits people of color—regardless of their qualifications or class location—over whites. To Chavez, affirmative action was supposed to provide training programs to help minorities compete with whites; instead, it created programs that excluded whites from participation altogether (e.g., minority scholarships and government contract set-asides). From this perspective, affirmative action is ineffective, stigmatizes minorities, and results in reverse discrimination.

Other social analysts disagree with this assessment, noting that affirmative action results in better economic and employment outcomes for people of color and white women. A recent study by sociologists Cedric Herring and Sharon M. Collins (1995) showed that firms with affirmative action policies are much more likely to employ African Americans than are companies without such policies. For example, only 7 percent of affirmative action companies employed no African Americans, compared to 33 percent of firms that did not have affirmative action programs. Moreover, according to Herring and Collins, people of color and white women employed in affirmative action companies also have greater access to higher-level jobs and higher income than do those in non–affirmative action firms.

Proponents also point out that affirmative action programs are necessary because we have not gone far enough in our efforts to remedy racial injustice. Little has been done to transform the actual power relations between persons of color and whites in our society (Marable, 1995). Because of continuing racial inequality and discrimination, according to African American scholar Manning Marable (1995), we have not reached the point at which a color-blind society is possible, so affirmative action is necessary to eliminate race and gender inequality, uproot prejudice and discrimination, and begin to establish a truly democratic nation.

How are students, faculty, and staff recruited at your school? If you are employed, how are workplace hiring and promotion decisions made? What would your school or workplace look like if it reflected the gender distribution and racial-ethnic diversity of your community or state?

Reprinted by permission.

subordinate group members from higher-paying jobs by barring them from labor unions, supporting discriminatory laws, and opposing immigration.

A second conflict perspective links racial inequality and gender oppression. *Gendered racism is* **the interactive effect of racism and sexism in exploiting women of color.** According to social psychologist Philomena Essed (1991), not all workers are exploited equally by capitalists. For many years, jobs in the primary sector of the labor market were held primarily by white men, while most people of color and many white women were employed in secondary sector jobs. Below that tier, in the underground sector of the economy, many women of color worked in sweatshops or the sex trade to survive. Work in this sector is unregulated, and people who earn their income in it are vulnerable to exploitation by many people, including unscrupulous employers, greedy pimps, and corrupt police officers (Amott and Matthaei, 1991).

A third conflict perspective examines *internal colonialism*—**a process that occurs when members of a racial-ethnic group are conquered or colonized and forcibly placed under the economic and political control of the dominant group.** According to sociol-

ogist Robert Blauner (1972), people in groups that have been subjected to internal colonialism remain in subordinate positions in society much longer than do people in groups that voluntarily migrated to this country. For example, Native Americans and Mexican Americans were forced into subordination when they were colonized by European Americans. These indigenous groups lost property, political rights, components of their culture, and often their lives. Meanwhile, the capitalist class acquired cheap labor and land, frequently through government-sanctioned racial exploitation (Blauner, 1972). Vestiges of internal colonialism remain visible today in the number of Native Americans who live in poverty on government reservations, as well as Mexican Americans in *colonias*—poor subdivisions that usually lack essential services such as water, electricity, and sewage disposal—located along the U.S.-Mexico border (see Valdez, 1993).

The last conflict perspective we will look at is the *theory of racial formation,* **which is based on the assumption that the government substantially defines racial and ethnic relations.** From this perspective, racial bias and discrimination tend to be rooted in government actions ranging from passage of race-related legislation to imprisonment of members of groups that are believed to be a threat to society. According to sociologists Michael Omi and Howard Winant (1994), the U.S. government has shaped the politics of racial inequality in this country through actions and policies that have resulted in the unequal treatment of people of color. For example, much immigration legislation reflects specific racial biases. The Naturalization Law of 1790 permitted only white immigrants to qualify for naturalization, and the Immigration Act of 1924 favored northern Europeans and excluded Asians and southern and eastern Europeans.

INEQUALITIES AMONG RACIAL AND ETHNIC GROUPS

Although all subordinate racial and ethnic groups have been the objects of prejudice and discrimination and share many problems, each has its own unique identity and concerns. In our examination of Native Americans, African Americans, Latinos/as, and Asian Americans we will note commonalities and differences in the discriminatory practices each group has experienced in contact with members of the dominant group.

Native Americans (American Indians)

Perhaps because they are often somewhat invisible in daily life, Native Americans tend to be viewed not as real people so much as artifacts of "Indian culture" such as turquoise jewelry and deerskin clothing, "Indian" Barbie dolls, vehicles such as the Jeep "Cherokee," and sports teams' stereotypical images of "Braves," "Redskins," "Chiefs," and "Seminoles" (Churchill, 1992, 1994; Hilden, 1995; Oxendine, 1995). To some extent, movies such as *Dances with Wolves, The Last of the Mohicans, Pocahontas,* and *The Indian in the Cupboard* have increased public awareness of Native Americans, but some of the movies also have perpetuated myths and stereotypes.

COLONIZED MIGRATION AND GENOCIDE

When Christopher Columbus arrived in 1492, approximately 15 million indigenous people lived on this continent. They had many distinct cultures, languages, social organizations, technologies, and economies (R. Thornton, 1987; Sale, 1990; Mohawk, 1992). The arrival of the white Europeans changed the native inhabitants' way of life forever as they became the victims of *colonization migration*—a process whereby a new immigrant group conquers and dominates an existing group in a given geographical area (Lauber, 1913; Feagin and Feagin, 1996). During this period of conquest, white European immigrants engaged in *genocide,* killing hundreds of thousands of Native Americans with firearms and other weaponry. **Genocide is the deliberate, systematic killing of an entire people or nation.** This widespread murder was rationalized by stereotypes depicting Native Americans as subhuman "savages" and "heathens" (Takaki, 1993).

FORCED MIGRATION AND "AMERICANIZATION"

After the Revolutionary War the newly founded federal government negotiated treaties with various Native American nations to acquire additional land for the rapidly growing white population. Nevertheless, federal officials gradually displaced Native Americans from their lands by ignoring boundary rights. When the demand for land escalated, Congress passed the Indian Removal Act of 1830, forcing entire nations to move to accommodate white "settlers" (Green, 1977; Churchill, 1994). During the "Trail of Tears," perhaps the most disastrous of the forced migrations, over half the Cherokee nation died while being relocated from the southeastern United States to the Indian Territory in Oklahoma in the bitter cold winter of 1832 (R. Thornton, 1984). After the forced relocation, Native Americans were made wards of the government—a legal status akin to that of a minor or a mental incompetent—and by 1920, about 98 percent of all native lands were controlled by the U.S. government (McDonnell, 1991).

Because Native Americans were less "civilized" than whites, Native American children were subjected to an extensive Americanization process. Boarding schools and mission schools, cosponsored by the government and churches, were located some distance from the reservations to facilitate assimilation. White teachers cut Native American boys' braids, eliminated the children's traditional clothing, handed out new names, and substituted new religious customs for old ones (Oxendine, 1995).

CONTEMPORARY NATIVE AMERICANS

Today, Native Americans number slightly over 2 million, less than 1 percent of the U.S. population. Most Native Americans live in Oklahoma, California, Arizona, and New Mexico (U.S. Bureau of the Census, 1995b). Although the majority of Native Americans live in cities, 38 percent live on reservations or other officially designated areas.

At the end of the twentieth century, Native Americans are the most disadvantaged racial or ethnic group in the United States. They have the highest unemployment and school dropout rates in the country. The average family income of Native Americans is $21,750, compared with a national average of more than $35,000 (U.S. Bureau of the Census, 1995b). The average life expectancy on reservations is less than forty-five years for men and less than forty-eight years for women (Churchill, 1994). Infant mortality rates and adult death rates from alcoholism, diabetes, tuberculosis, and suicide are much higher than the national averages (Bachman, 1992).

Many Native Americans have organized to resist discrimination and oppression. They actively oppose mining, logging, hunting, and real estate development on native lands without permission or compensation (Serrill, 1992). Groups such as the American Indian Movement and Women of All Red Nations have struggled to regain control of native lands, to end centuries of colonization, and to stop cultural exploitation.

African Americans

The term *African American* does not reflect the diversity of the more than 33 million African Americans who currently make up about 13 percent of the U.S. population. Although some are descendants of families that have been in this country for many generations, others are recent immigrants from the West Indies, South America, Africa, and the Caribbean. Many have Native American, white, or Latino/a ancestors (Feagin and Feagin, 1996; Kivel, 1996).

Although media coverage has improved somewhat over the past decade, stereotypic depictions of African Americans continue to "demonize blackness" (Gray, 1995). Television and films frequently depict African American women as "welfare mothers," drug addicts, sex objects, prostitutes, and elderly, overweight, aggressive family matriarchs who are made the object of derision by their families and others (see Gray, 1995). African American men are depicted as "menacing black male criminals" who murder, rape, pimp, and sell drugs (Feagin and Feagin, 1996; Kivel, 1996).

SLAVERY AND THE RACIAL DIVISION OF LABOR

Beginning with the importation of Africans to North America in 1619 for forced labor, slavery created a rigid, castelike division of labor between white slave owners and overseers and African slave labor. Southern plantation owners derived large profits from selling raw materials harvested by the slaves. Northern capitalists were enriched by profits from converting those raw materials into finished products that could be sold at market (e.g., the cotton fiber used in textile manufacturing). White immigrants benefited from slavery because it provided the abundant raw materials needed for their factory jobs.

SEGREGATION AND LYNCHING

After slavery was abolished in 1863, the racial division of labor was maintained through *de jure segregation*, laws that were passed to systematically enforce the physical and social separation of African Americans in all areas of public life, including schools, churches, hospitals, cemeteries, buses, restaurants, water fountains, and restrooms. (These laws were referred to as Jim Crow laws after a derogatory song about a black man.) African Americans who did not stay "in their place" were subjected to violence by secret organizations such as the Ku Klux Klan and by lynch mobs (Franklin, 1980).

While African Americans in the South experienced de jure segregation, those who migrated to the North experienced *de facto segregation*—racial separation and inequality enforced by custom. African Americans seeking northern factory jobs encountered *job ceilings*—specific limits on the upward job mobility of targeted groups—set up by white workers and their unions to maintain occupational segregation (see Baron, 1969; Allen, 1974). Because African American men were barred from many industrial jobs, African American women frequently become their families' primary breadwinners. Most African American women were employed as domestic workers in private households or as personal service workers such as hotel chambermaids (Higginbotham, 1994).

Dr. Martin Luther King, Jr., was perhaps the most influential person in obtaining passage of the Civil Rights Acts in the 1960s that have profoundly affected the lives of many African Americans.

PROTESTS AND CIVIL DISOBEDIENCE

During World War II, new job opportunities opened up for African Americans in northern defense plants, especially after a presidential order was issued prohibiting racial discrimination in federal jobs. After the war, increasing numbers of African Americans demanded an end to racial segregation. Between the mid-1950s and 1964, boycotts, nonviolent protests, and *civil disobedience*—nonviolent action seeking to change a policy or law by refusing to comply with it—called attention to racial inequality. The civil rights movement culminated in passage of the Civil Rights Acts of 1964 and 1965, which signified the end of *de jure* segregation; however, *de facto* segregation was far from over.

CONTEMPORARY AFRICAN AMERICANS

Since the 1960s, African Americans have made significant political gains. Between 1964 and 1994, the number of African American elected officials increased from about 100 to almost 8,000. African Americans won mayoral elections in many major cities that had large African American populations such as Los Angeles, New York, Atlanta, and Washington, D.C. Nevertheless, African Americans represent less than 3 percent of all elected officials in this country.

The proportion of African Americans in professional, managerial, sales, clerical, crafts, and operative jobs increased between 1955 and 1972, but this growth slowed dramatically in the late 1970s and 1980s. In the 1990s the job ceiling and racial division of labor are still evident in many corporations, including the Fortune 500 companies (the 500 highest revenue-producing companies), which had no African American executives (vice presidents or above) (Glass Ceiling Commission, 1995). Approximately one-fourth of the African American work force is employed in the public sector, including federal, state, city, and county governments (Higginbotham, 1994).

The unemployment rate for African Americans (11 percent in 1994) has remained twice as high as that for white Americans (5 percent in 1994) for over three decades. As new technology has been introduced in the workplace and more jobs have moved to suburban areas and other countries, employment opportunities for African Americans in central cities have declined (see Neckerman and Kirschenman, 1991; Tienda and Stier, 1996; Wilson, 1996).

As is shown in Figure 3.1, a wide disparity exists between the median income of white Americans and that of African Americans. Whereas African American married-couple families with children had median earnings of $36,670 in 1993, the median earnings of white non-Latino married-couple families with children were 33 percent higher ($48,630). However, fewer than half (47 percent) of all African American families were married-couple families. Households headed by African American women with children had median earnings of $10,380, or 28 percent of the median for married-couple African American families with children (U. S. Bureau of the Census, 1995b).

Contemporary scholars suggest that the legacy of slavery, segregation, and individual and institutionalized discrimination is evident in the high percentage of racially segregated schools and residential areas; persistent—though informal—racial discrimination by banks, real estate agents, mortgage lenders, and other businesses; and the daily bias that many African Americans face in the workplace and other public spaces (see Feagin and Sikes, 1994; Feagin and Feagin, 1996). Residential discrimination is one of the more persistent inequalities experienced by African Americans; in the 1990s, African Americans and whites are no more likely to be neighbors than they were 30

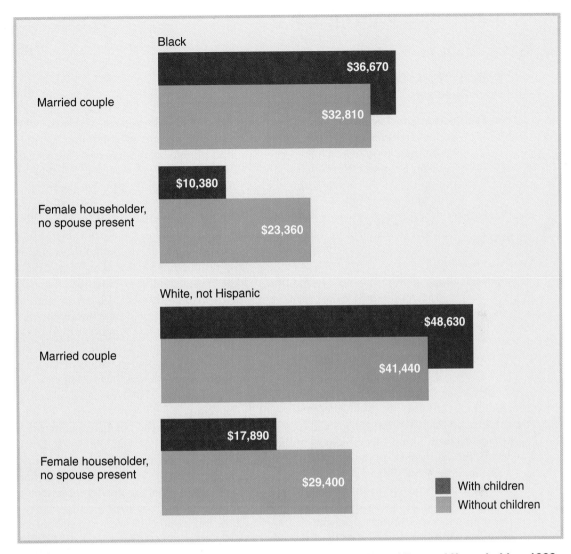

FIGURE 3.1   *Median U.S. Family Income, by Type of Family and Race of Householder, 1993*
(SOURCE: U.S. Bureau of the Census, 1995b.)

years ago (O'Hare and Usdansky, 1992). Residential segregation produces a ripple effect on all other areas of social life, including the schools that children attend, the quality of education they receive, the types of jobs people have access to, and the availability and quality of public facilities such as hospitals and transportation systems (Massey and Denton, 1992).

Latinos/as (Hispanic Americans)

Of the nearly 24 million Latinos/as who make up about 9 percent of the U.S. population today, near-

ly two-thirds are of Mexican origin. After Mexican Americans, the largest groups of Latinos/as are Puerto Ricans and Cuban Americans. The remainder trace their ancestry to Central and South America or the Dominican Republic.

Latinas/os have been the objects of stereotyping based on skin color and perceived cultural differences such as food preferences ("beaner") or language ("foreigner"). The media often depict Latinos/as as rich drug lords or illegal aliens (McWilliams, 1968; Morales, 1996). Box 3.3 examines stereotypical images of Latinas/os and Asian Americans in the media.

SOCIAL PROBLEMS

IN THE MEDIA

BOX 3.3

Don't Blink: Latinas and Latinos in Television

Fact: Although Latinos/as constitute about 10 percent of the U.S. population, they represented only 2 percent of all prime-time characters during the 1995–96 television season (Morales, 1996).

Fact: Only 11 percent of prime-time network series had a continuing Latina/o character in 1996 (Morales, 1996).

Fact: When Latinos/as are prime-time characters (defined as all speaking parts, regardless of the importance of the role), they are among the most likely to kill, get killed, or both (Gerbner, 1995).

How they are depicted on television is one issue for Latinos/as, because representation of subordinate racial-ethnic groups affects viewers' perceptions about racial inequality (Gray, 1995). But Latinos/as also have a second issue: They are largely invisible as characters and actors on prime-time television (Dawes, 1995).

In 1996, for the first time in two decades, a situation comedy (sitcom) featured Latina/o characters and actors in four of the six leading roles. In *Common Law,* Greg Giraldo plays a Harvard Law School graduate working in a prestigious Manhattan law firm (Dougherty, 1996). The last prime-time sitcom that featured a Latino, *Chico and the Man,* went off the air in 1978 when Freddie Prinze, who played Chico Rodriguez, committed suicide. In that show, white garage owner Ed Brown made Chico, his young assistant, the butt of sarcastic barbs, while Chico tempered Ed's closed-minded attitudes and kept the garage from going out of business (Lichter et al., 1991).

Given that Latinas/os are the fastest-growing segment of the U.S. population and a ripe market for television advertisers, why don't television executives develop programs featuring Latino/a story lines and characters? Aside from Jimmy Smits in *L.A. Law* and in *N.Y.P.D. Blue,* roles in prime-time series are few and far between for Latinos and virtually nonexistent for Latinas (Mendoza, 1995).

According to actor Jeff Valdez, Hollywood television executives hold socioeconomic and/or racial-ethnic biases that keep Latinos/as in the background, if not invisible. Gabriel Reyes, a creative affairs director, agrees with Valdez's assessment: "Any time you submit a Latino script, the knee-jerk reaction of the studios and the networks is to Anglicize it, to whitewash it. They don't think the Latino experience sells" (quoted in Mendoza, 1995:B13).

As a result, Latino/a activists have formed the National Hispanic Media Coalition to protest the absence of Latino/a actors in television and film. Through boycotts, demonstrations, and letter-writing campaigns to television networks and major advertisers, the coalition is seeking greater representation of Latinas/os both in front of the camera as actors and behind the scenes as producers, writers, and directors (Mendoza, 1995). Will they be successful? That remains to be seen.

For a discussion of film and video representations of Latinos/as, see the work of Norieg (1992), Noriega and Lopez (1996), and Morales (1996).

Do the television shows and films that you watch have Latinos/as, African Americans, Asian Americans, Native Americans, or other people of color as characters and actors? Does it matter if some subordinate racial and ethnic groups are largely invisible on television? Why or why not?

INTERNAL COLONIALISM AND LOSS OF LAND

Beginning in the late 1400s and continuing into the early 1500s, Spanish soldiers took over the island of Puerto Rico, Central America, and the area now known as the U.S. Southwest. Mexico gained its independence from Spain in 1810 but then lost Texas and most of the Southwest to the United States in 1848. Under the treaty ending the war, Texans of Mexican descent were granted U.S. citizenship; however, their rights were violated when Anglo Americans took possession of their lands, transforming the *Tejanos/as* into a landless and economically dependent laboring class.

When Spain lost the Spanish-American War, it gave Puerto Rico to the United States. U.S.-owned corporations gradually took over the sugarcane plantations, leaving the peasant farmers and their families with no means of earning a living other than as seasonal sugarcane laborers. Gradually, nearly one-third of the Puerto Rican population migrated to the U. S. mainland, where they settled primarily in the Northeast and found work in garment factories or other light manufacturing.

MIGRATION

In the late 1950s and early 1960s, waves of immigrants escaping from Fidel Castro's Communist takeover of Cuba were admitted to the United States as political refugees (Rogg, 1974). Puerto Ricans, by contrast, have been allowed unrestricted migration between the mainland and the island since Puerto Rico became a U.S. possession in 1917 (Melendez, 1993). Mexicans have been allowed to migrate to the United States whenever there has been a need here for agricultural workers. However, during times of economic depression or recession in this country, they have been excluded, detained, or deported (see Moore, 1976; Acuna, 1984).

Over the past decade, many Latinos/as have experienced discrimination as a result of the Immigration Reform and Control Act (IRCA) of 1986. Although IRCA was passed to restrict illegal immigration into the United States, it has adversely affected many Mexican Americans. To avoid being penalized for hiring undocumented workers, some employers discriminate against Latinas/os who "look foreign" on the basis of facial features, skin color, or clothing (see L. R. Chavez and Martinez, 1996).

CONTEMPORARY LATINOS/AS

Currently, slightly over 200 Latinos are top executives in Fortune 1000 corporations, most often in industries such as beverages, entertainment, and soaps and cosmetics that actively pursue Latina/o consumers; however, Latinos/as still hold only 1.4 percent of the senior executive positions at these companies (Zate, 1996). At the other end of the employment spectrum, low wages, hazardous workplaces, and unemployment are pressing problems for Latinos/as in secondary sector employment. The unemployment rate for Latinos/as is about 12 percent, almost twice the rate for white non-Latinos/as. Almost one-third (30 percent) of Latinas/os lived below the poverty level in 1992. Although Latino/a children accounted for almost 12 percent of all U.S. children, they made up 21.3 percent of all children in poverty.

Many Latinas/os continue to experience high levels of segregation in housing and education. According to a recent study by anthropologist Martha Menchaca (1995), landlords, realtors, and bankers in many communities have colluded to keep Mexican Americans in barrios and out of predominantly Anglo neighborhoods. Segregated schools are a major problem for many Latino/a children and their

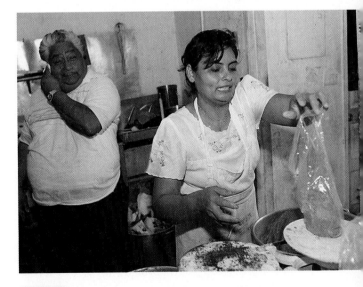

Despite recent gains by some Latinas and Latinos in the workplace, many are still employed in secondary sector jobs, where the wages are low and working conditions are difficult. Many parents work hard to provide better educational opportunities for their children in hopes that they can share the American Dream.

parents. In the mid-1990s, 80 percent or more of all Latina/o students in New York, Illinois, Texas, New Jersey, and California attended schools where students of color made up between 50 and 100 percent of the school population (DeWitt, 1992).

Asian Americans and Pacific Islanders

Asian Americans and Pacific Islanders are one of the fastest-growing racial-ethnic groups; their numbers have risen from one million in 1960 to nine million today. In the 1990s, about half of all legal immigrants to this country have had Asian or Pacific Island ancestry. Constituting about 3 percent of the U.S. population, most of them reside in California, New York, and Hawaii (U. S. Bureau of the Census, 1995b).

Asian Americans have been stereotyped as "Orientals," and advertisements often depict Asian American women as exotic beauties with silky black hair, heavy eye makeup, and seductive clothing (Shah, 1994). Asian Americans also have been stereotyped as the model minority because many are college-educated and have middle- or upper-income occupations. However, the model minority stereotype ignores the reality that many Asian Americans, especially recent immigrants, are employed in low-paying service jobs or sweatshops.

IMMIGRATION AND OPPRESSION

Among the first Asians to arrive in this country were Chinese immigrants, who came between 1850 and 1880. Some were fleeing political oppression and harsh economic conditions in China; others were recruited to build the transcontinental railroad. Employers paid the Chinese laborers far less than white workers (Takaki, 1993). Almost immediately, anti-Asian stereotypes developed, such as "the yellow peril," a nineteenth-century belief that Asians constituted a threat to Western Civilization. In response to demands from white workers who were concerned about cheap labor, Congress passed the Chinese Exclusion Act of 1882, bringing all Chinese immigration to an abrupt halt. This law wasn't repealed until World War II, when Chinese American workers contributed to the U.S. war effort by working in defense plants (see Chan, 1991).

Facing high levels of overt discrimination, many Chinese Americans opened laundries, stores, and restaurants where they did business primarily with each other (Takaki, 1993). However, young second- and third-generation Chinese Americans have left these ethnic niches to live and interact with people from diverse racial-ethnic groups (see Chen, 1992).

INTERNMENT

From their initial arrival in this country, Japanese Americans experienced high levels of prejudice and discrimination, but their internment in U.S. concentration camps during World War II remains the central event of the Japanese American experience (Kitano and Daniels, 1995). After Japan bombed Pearl Harbor in 1941, anti-Japanese sentiment soared in this country. Japanese Americans were forcibly removed to concentration camps on remote military bases with barbed wire fences and guard towers, where they were confined for more than two years. During their internment, most Japanese Americans lost their residences, businesses, and anything else they had owned. Four decades later, the U.S. government issued an apology for its actions and agreed to pay $20,000 to each Japanese American who had been detained in a camp (Kitano and Daniels, 1995).

COLONIZATION

After Spain lost the Spanish-American War, it surrendered the Philippine Islands to the United States. This action led to a bloody guerilla war between Filipino Islanders and U.S. soldiers. When the battle ended in 1902, the United States established colonial rule over the islands, and Filipinos were "Americanized" by schools that the U.S. government established (Espiritu, 1995).

Most early Filipino migrants were recruited to provide cheap labor for the sugar plantations in Hawaii, agriculture in California, and fish canneries in Seattle and Alaska. Like members of other racial-ethnic groups, Filipino Americans were accused of stealing jobs and suppressing wages during the Great Depression, and Congress restricted Filipino immigration to fifty people per year until after World War II.

NEWER WAVES OF ASIAN IMMIGRATION

Today, many Asian immigrants arriving from the Republic of India and Pakistan are highly educated professionals. Some immigrants from Korea are also professionals, but many have few years of formal schooling. They have been able to acquire an ethnic niche in "Koreatowns," which are similar to the communities of earlier generations of Chinese Americans (Kim and Yu, 1996).

Since the 1970s, many Indochinese American refugees have arrived in the United States from Vietnam, Cambodia, Thailand, and Laos. About half of them live in western states, especially California. Although many early Vietnamese refugees were able to reenter their professions as physicians, pharmacists, and engineers in the United States, more recent immigrants typically have had less formal education, fewer job skills, and much higher rates of unemployment. Recent immigrants are more likely to live in poverty and rely on assistance from others (Du Phuoc Long, 1996).

PACIFIC ISLANDERS

Today, over 1.6 million people live on the Hawaiian Islands. About 13 percent are native or part-native Hawaiians who trace their ancestry to the original Polynesian inhabitants of the islands. Having originally been a monarchy and then a republic, the Hawaiian Islands were annexed by the United States in 1898. In 1959, Congress passed legislation that made Hawaii the fiftieth state. Because of widespread immigration to Hawaii and high rates of intermarriage, contemporary Hawaiians include people of Chinese, Japanese, Filipino, Korean, Puerto Rican, and Portuguese ancestry.

CONTEMPORARY ASIAN AMERICANS AND PACIFIC ISLANDERS

Asian Americans and Pacific Islanders have high educational levels compared to the overall U.S. population. In 1994, among Asian Americans and Pacific Islanders age 25 and over, nearly nine out of ten males and eight out of ten females had at least a high school diploma. They are more than $1\frac{1}{2}$ times as likely to have a bachelor's degree than are white non-Latinas/os. In 1994, 40 percent of Asian Americans and Pacific Islanders age twenty-five and over held at least a bachelor's degree (Applebome, 1996a).

The median income of people in this category is not far below that of non-Latino/a whites: $23,490 in 1993 for male high school graduates, compared to $28,370 for whites in the same category. The median family income of Japanese Americans is more

People from diverse racial and ethnic backgrounds often find an understanding and solidarity within their families that helps them cope with the daily struggles of life in the larger society, particularly with problems of racism and discrimination.

than 30 percent above the national average, and fewer than 4 percent of Japanese American families live below the official poverty line, compared to nearly 14 percent of all Asian Americans and Pacific Islanders.

Summary

As we end our discussion of the experiences of various subordinate racial and ethnic groups in the United States, let's look at the commonalities in their experience: (1) Each has been the object of negative stereotypes and discrimination, (2) each has resisted oppression and continued to strive for a better life for its members and their children, and (3) each has been the object of some government policy that shaped its place (or lack thereof) in U.S. race and ethnic relations over the past two centuries. However, members of each group also have had unique experiences based on the time and circumstances of their original arrival in this country and how they were viewed by the dominant members of the racial-ethnic groups.

CAN RACIAL AND ETHNIC INEQUALITIES BE REDUCED?

How do functionalists suggest reducing racial-ethnic inequality? In their view, a stable society requires smoothly functioning social institutions and people who have common cultural values and attitudes. They would say, therefore, that social institutions should be restructured to reduce discrimination and diffuse racial-ethnic conflict. According to sociologist Arnold Rose (1951), discrimination robs society of the talents and leadership abilities of many individuals, especially people of color. Rose suggests that societies invest time and money to foster racial-ethnic inclusion and eliminate institutionalized discrimination in education, housing, employment, and the criminal justice system. From a global perspective, U.S. racial discrimination should be reduced because it negatively affects diplomatic and economic relations with other nations made up of diverse racial-ethnic groups (Feagin and Vera, 1995).

From a conflict perspective, racial and ethnic inequality can be reduced only through struggle and political action. If inequality is based on the exploitation of subordinate groups by the dominant group, political intervention is necessary to bring about economic and social change. People should mobilize to put pressure on public officials. According to social activist Paul Kivel (1996), racial inequality will not be reduced until the United States has significant national public support and leadership for addressing social problems directly and forcefully.

According to interactionists, prejudice and discrimination are learned, and what is learned can be unlearned. As sociologist Gale E. Thomas (1995:339) notes, "In the areas of race, ethnic, and human relations, we must learn compassion and also to accept and truly embrace, rather than merely tolerate, differences . . . through honest and open dialogue and through the formation of genuine friendships and personal experiential . . . exchanges and interactions with different individuals and groups across cultures." In other words, only individuals and groups at the grass-roots level, not government and political leaders or academic elites, can bring about greater racial equality.

Whether or not the United States works for greater equality for people of all racial-ethnic groups, one thing is certain: The U.S. population is growing increasingly diverse at a rapid rate. Today, African Americans, Latinos/as, Asian Americans, Native Americans, and people who trace their ancestry to other regions of the world make up more than 25 percent of the U.S. population, while white non-Latinas/os are a shrinking percentage of the population. By the year 2000, white Americans will make up 70 percent or less of the U.S. population (see Figure 3.2); and by the year 2050, most U.S. residents will trace their roots to Africa, Asia, the Hispanic countries, the Pacific Islands, and the Middle East—not white Europe (Henry, 1990). If we fail to recognize the challenges posed by increasing racial-ethnic and cultural diversity and we do not develop a more visionary and inclusive perspective, the Los Angeles fires that occurred in the 1960s and the 1990s may spread across the nation, as African American activist James Baldwin (1963) suggested in the phrase "the fire next time" (Thomas, 1995).

On a more optimistic note, perhaps the future of racial-ethnic relations in the United States is forecast by this newspaper reporter's recent description of a Chicago kindergarten class:

They stand with arms outstretched, touching fingertip to fingertip on a yellow circle inscribed on the floor of a kindergarten classroom.

A girl with braids who describes herself as a light-skinned black stands next to a boy who has a white mother and a black father. Just a few feet away is a boy whose mother is black and whose father is white. He is flanked by a classmate born in Sweden of Chinese parents.

He stretches his fingertips to touch the hand of a close friend, a blond girl whose parents are from Idaho. She stands next to two girls with dark ponytails who whisper their secrets in

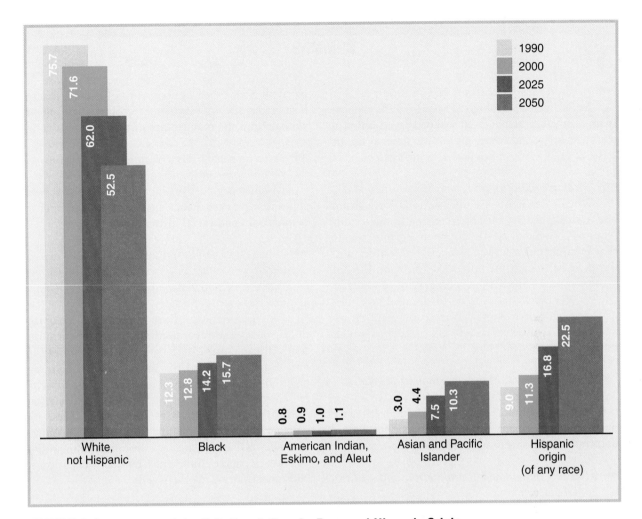

FIGURE 3.2 *Percent of the U.S. Population, by Race and Hispanic Origin, 1990, 2000, 2025, and 2050 (middle-series projections)*
(SOURCE: U.S. Bureau of the Census, 1995b.)

Spanish. They smile at their neighbor, a shy and tiny girl most comfortable speaking Polish.

They are the pupils in Mary Sigman's kindergarten at Ogden Elementary School in Chicago. To much of America, having all these diverse backgrounds in a kindergarten class remains atypical. But that may be changing: These children already are experiencing a multiracial, multiethnic world that increasingly will come to characterize this country by 2008, the year they graduate from high school. (Schreuder, 1996:F1)

SUMMARY

➤ *How do racial and ethnic groups differ?*

According to sociologists, racial groups typically are defined on the basis of real or alleged physical characteristics, and ethnic groups are defined on the basis of cultural or nationality characteristics.

➤ *What are majority and minority groups?*

When sociologists use the terms *majority group* and *minority group,* they are referring to power differentials. A majority (or dominant) group is one that is advantaged and has superior resources and rights in a society. A minority (or subordinate) group is one whose members, because of physical or cultural characteristics, are disadvantaged and subjected to unequal treatment by the dominant group and regard themselves as objects of collective discrimination.

➤ *How are prejudice and discrimination related?*

Prejudice is a negative attitude that may or may not lead to discrimination, which is an action or practice of dominant group members that has a harmful impact on subordinate group members.

➤ *How do individual discrimination and institutional discrimination differ?*

Although individual discrimination and institutional discrimination are carried out by individuals, individual discrimination consists of one-on-one acts by members of the dominant group; institutional discrimination refers to actions and practices that are built into the day-to-day operations of large-scale organizations and social institutions.

➤ *How do the interactionist and functionalist perspectives view racial and ethnic relations?*

Interactionists focus on microlevel issues such as how people develop a racial-ethnic identity and how individuals from diverse racial-ethnic groups interact with each other. Functionalists focus on macrolevel issues such as how entire groups of people assimilate into the mainstream of the society.

➤ *What are the major conflict explanations for racial-ethnic inequality?*

Conflict perspectives include class perspectives, split-labor market theory, gendered racism, internal colonialism, and racial formation theory.

➤ *What types of discrimination have been experienced by Native Americans, African Americans, Latinos/as, and Asian Americans in the United States?*

Native Americans have experienced colonization, genocide, forced migration, and Americanization. African Americans have experienced slavery, *de jure* segregation (Jim Crow laws), and *de facto* segregation—racial separation and inequality enforced by custom. Latinos/as have experienced internal colonialism, exclusionary immigration policies, and segregation in housing and education. Asian Americans also have experienced exclusionary immigration policies; Japanese Americans uniquely experienced internment during World War II.

➤ *What commonalities can be seen in the experiences of all subordinate racial-ethnic groups?*

Members of most subordinate racial-ethnic groups have had these commonalities in their experiences in the United States: (1) Each has been the object of negative stereotypes and discrimination, (2) each has resisted oppression and continued to strive for a better life for its members and their children, and (3) each has been the object of some government policy that has shaped its place (or lack thereof) in U.S. race and ethnic relations over the past two centuries.

KEY TERMS

amalgamation, p. 51
Anglo-conformity model, p. 51
anti-Semitism, p. 49
assimilation, p. 51
ethnic group, p. 46
ethnic pluralism, p. 51
ethnocentrism, p. 48
gendered racism, p. 53
genocide, p. 54
individual discrimination, p. 48
institutional discrimination, p. 49

internal colonialism, p. 53
majority (dominant) group, p. 47
melting pot model, p. 51
minority (subordinate) group, p. 47
prejudice, p. 48
racial group, p. 46
racism, p. 48
scapegoat, p. 50
segregation, p. 51
stereotypes, p. 48
theory of racial formation, p. 53

QUESTIONS FOR CRITICAL THINKING

1. Do you consider yourself part of the majority or dominant racial-ethnic group or of a minority or subordinate racial-ethnic group in the United States? In what specific ways might your life be different if you were in the opposite group?

2. Sociologists suggest that we acquire beliefs about ourselves and others through socialization. What specific messages have you received about your racial-ethnic identity? What specific messages have you received about dealing with people from other racial-ethnic groups?

3. Have all white Americans, regardless of class, gender, or other characteristics, benefited from racial prejudice and discrimination in the United States? Why or why not?

4. Compare recent depictions of Native Americans, African Americans, Latinos/as, and Asian Americans in films, television shows, and advertisements. To what extent have we moved beyond the traditional stereotypes discussed in the chapter? To what extent have the stereotypes remained strong?

Chapter Four

Gender Inequality

The prevailing attitude toward women was demonstrated on the first day of classes by my anatomy instructor, who remarked that our elderly cadaver "must have been a Playboy bunny" before instructing us to cut off her large breasts and toss them into the thirty-gallon trash can marked "cadaver waste." Barely hours into our training, we were already being taught that there was nothing to be learned from examining breasts. Given the fact that one out of nine American women will develop breast cancer in her lifetime, to treat breasts as extraneous tissue seemed an appalling waste of an educational opportunity, as well as a not-so-subtle message about the relative importance of body parts. . . . My classmates learned their lesson of disrespect well. Later in the year one carved a tick-tack-toe on a female cadaver and challenged others to play.

▲ *—Adriane Fugh-Berman, a graduate of the Georgetown University School of Medicine, describing how medical students often learn demeaning attitudes toward women*
(Fugh-Berman, 1992)

When sociologists conduct research on organizational environments such as medical schools, women students and professors often report experiences like Fugh-Berman's. What conclusions can we draw from jokes and behavior such as this? Is it merely humor in which the speaker intends no harm? Or is it a form of *sexism*—the subordination of one sex, usually female, based on the assumed superiority of the other sex? According to some social analysts, problems of sexism have been overblown: Sexism was a problem in the *past* when women were underrepresented in organizations such as medical schools; however, *today* women have made significant inroads in education and professions such as medicine and law. For example, in the late 1970s, women represented slightly more than 20 percent of all medical students, but in the 1990s they make up more than 40 percent of all first-year medical students (Women's International Network, 1995b). Similarly, women make up about 44 percent of today's law students and 31 percent of all lawyers. With increases such as these, some analysts suggest that women should learn to take an occasional "joke" on themselves. As one male student suggested, "If women can't take the heat in medicine, they ought to get out of the kitchen. . . . Taking care of sick and dying people isn't for the thin-skinned" (author's files).

However, most sociologists do not believe that derogatory jokes or sexist comments in organizational settings should be ignored. They argue that such humor creates in-group solidarity among men, particularly in male-dominated occupations, while marginalizing women and perpetuating gender inequality (Benokraitis and Feagin, 1995). From this perspective, pervasive sexism (along with racism and class-based inequality) is deeply rooted in many organizational environments and has a negative impact on all organizational participants (see Benokraitis and Feagin, 1995; Myers and Dugan, 1996).

GENDER INEQUALITY AS A SOCIAL PROBLEM

Just as subordinate racial-ethnic group members experience discrimination based on innate characteristics, women are the targets of sex-based discrimination. Since 51 percent of the people in the United States are female, women constitute the numerical majority. However, they sometimes are referred to as the largest minority group because they typically do not possess as much wealth, power, or prestige as men do.

Defining Sex and Gender

How do sex and gender differ? Although many people use these terms interchangeably, sociologists believe that there are significant differences in their meanings. *Sex is the biological differences between females and males.* Our sex is the first label we receive in life. Before birth or at the time of birth we are identified as male or female on the basis of our sex organs and genes. In comparison, *gender is culturally and socially constructed differences between females and males that are based on meanings, beliefs, and practices that a group or society associates with "femininity" or "masculinity."* For many people, being *masculine* means being aggressive, independent, and not showing emotions, and being *feminine* means the opposite—not being aggressive,

being dependent, and being very emotional. Understanding the difference between sex and gender is important, according to sociologists, because what many people think of as *sex differences* such as attributes of masculinity and femininity are actually socially constructed *gender differences* based on widely held assumptions about men's and women's attributes (Gailey, 1987). In other words, males are supposed to be aggressive and independent not because they have male sex organs but because that's how people in society think males should act, and the converse is true for females.

Biological and Social Bases for Gender Roles

To study gender inequality, sociologists begin with an examination of the biological and social bases for *gender roles,* which are the rights, responsibilities, expectations, and relationships of women and men in a society (Benokraitis and Feagin, 1995). The biological basis for gender roles is rooted in chromosomal and hormonal differences in men and women. When a child is conceived, the mother contributes an X chromosome, and the father contributes either an X chromosome (which produces a female embryo) or a Y chromosome (which produces a male embryo). As the embryo's male or female sex glands develop, they secrete the appropriate male hormones (androgens) or female hormones (estrogens) that circulate through the bloodstream, producing sexual differentiation in bodily organs such as the external genitalia, the internal reproductive tract, and possibly some areas of the brain. At birth, medical personnel and family members distinguish male from female infants by their *primary sex characteristics:* the genitalia used in the reproductive process. At puberty, hormonal differences in females and males produce *secondary sex characteristics,* the physical traits that, along with the reproductive organs, identify a person's sex. Females develop secondary sex characteristics such as menstruation, more prominent breasts, wider hips and narrower shoulders, and a layer of fatty tissue throughout the body. In males, secondary sex characteristics include the development of larger genitals, a more muscular build, a deeper voice, more body and facial hair, and greater height. Although both males and females have androgens and estrogens, it is the relative proportion of each hormone that triggers masculine or feminine physical traits.

Are boys naturally more boisterous because of their biological and genetic makeup? As sociologist Judith Lorber (1994:39) notes, "When little boys run around noisily, we say 'Boys will be boys,' meaning that physical assertiveness has to be in the Y chromosome because it is manifest so early and so commonly in boys." However, Lorber questions this widely held assumption: "But are boys universally, the world over, in every social group, a vociferous, active presence? Or just where they are encouraged to use their bodies freely, to cover space, take risks, and play outdoors at all kinds of games and sports?"

Similarly, what do we mean when we say, "She throws like a girl"? According to Lorber, we mean that "she throws like a female child, a carrier of XX chromosomes." Actually, the girl is probably a product of her culture and time: She has had more limited experience than many boys at throwing the ball and engaging in competitive games at an early age. According to Lorber, boys and girls who are given tennis rackets at the age of three and encouraged to become champions tend to use their bodies similarly. Even though boys gradually gain more shoulder and arm strength and are able to sustain more concentrated bursts of energy, after puberty girls acquire more stamina, flexibility, and lower-body strength, that—coupled with training and physical exercise—enhance, compensate for, or override different physical capabilities (Lorber, 1994).

The social basis for gender roles is known as the *gender belief system*—ideas regarding masculinity and femininity that are held to be valid in a society (Lorber, 1994). The gender belief system is reflected in what sociologists refer to as the **gendered division of labor**—the process whereby productive tasks are separated on the basis of gender. How do people determine what constitutes "women's work" or "men's work"? Evidence from cross-cultural studies shows that social factors, more than biological ones, influence the gendered division of labor in societies. In poor agricultural societies, for example, women work in the fields as well as tend to their families' daily needs; the men typically produce and market cash crops but spend no time in household work. In developed nations, an increasing proportion of women are in paid employment but still have heavy household and family responsibilities (see Box 4.1). Across cultures, women's domain is the private and domestic, and men's domain is the public, economic, and political. This difference in how labor is divided

and how workers are rewarded in turn affects access to scarce resources such as wealth, power, and prestige. Men therefore have greater access to wealth, power, and prestige, a situation that leads to gender inequality in other areas.

To explain gender inequality, some sociologists use a *gender role approach,* focusing on how the socialization process contributes to male domination and female subordination. Other sociologists use a *structural approach,* focusing on how large-scale, interacting, and enduring social structures determine the boundaries of individual behavior. Let's look first at how socialization can perpetuate gender stereotyping and inequality.

GENDER INEQUALITY AND SOCIALIZATION

Numerous sociological studies have found that gender-role stereotyping is one of the enduring consequences of childhood socialization of girls and boys into mutually exclusive gender roles. Socialization into appropriate "feminine" behavior makes women less likely than men to pursue male-dominated activities, and socialization into appropriate "masculine" behavior makes men more likely than women to pursue leadership roles in education, religion, business, politics, and other spheres of public life (Peterson and Runyan, 1993). We learn our earliest and often most lasting beliefs about gender roles from a variety of *socializing agents*—people, groups, or institutions that teach us what we need to know to participate in society. Among the most significant socializing agents are parents, peers, teachers and schools, sports, and the media.

▲ Gender Socialization by Parents

From birth, parents create and maintain gender distinctions between girls and boys by differential treatment of daughters and sons. Because parents typically believe that boys are less fragile than girls, they are more likely to bounce an infant son, hold him up in the air, and generally play with him more vigorously than they would with a girl (MacDonald and Parke, 1986). Parents tend to cuddle girls, treat them gently, and provide them with verbal stimulation through cooing, talking, and singing to them (Basow, 1992).

SOCIAL PROBLEMS
IN GLOBAL PERSPECTIVE

BOX 4.1

"Shall I Serve Tea at Home, the Office, or Both?": The Dilemma of Women in Japan

My father almost never steps inside the kitchen. If Mom is around, he wouldn't even serve tea. He'd just yell, "Tea!" But of course, if my mother isn't around, he has to do it by himself. Would I marry someone like my dad? No way!

> —Chie Suzuki, a twenty-three-year-old systems engineer in Tokyo (quoted in WuDunn, 1995c:6)

I pour tea for my boss, there's no question about that. Even when we are far away from them and from the teapot, they come running over to us to tell us that we have to make tea for them. I'm too afraid to say no.

> —Emi Omasa, a thirty-year-old office worker in Tokyo (quoted in WuDunn, 1995a:6)

As these statements suggest, many women in Japan feel constrained by traditions, such as serving tea, that they believe perpetuate male dominance and female subordination. According to journalist Sheryl WuDunn (1995a:E3), Japanese women have historically been thought of as "accessories to men." Despite some recent changes in women's roles and women's greater presence in the Japanese workplace since World War II, gender stereotyping of women as passive and subservient remains strong. As twenty-three-year-old graduate student Sachiko Nonaka says, "Women in Japan are very changed, but men don't change" (quoted in Deans, 1995: E4).

In the workplace, women are expected to accept routine jobs with much lower pay and less job stability than male workers have. As a result, women's income potential and career

At birth and in early childhood, parents reinforce gender distinctions through their selection of infants' and children's clothing. Most parents dress boys in boldly colored "rough and tough" clothing and girls in softly colored "feminine" clothing. Parents purchase girls' sweatshirts that are decorated with hearts and flowers or female characters such as Minnie Mouse, Tweety Bird, or Pocahontas; they

Across cultures, parents tend to socialize daughters and sons differently, including the assignment of household chores. What gender-specific chores were you assigned as a child? What messages about gender did you receive from your parents? Do you wish to convey the same messages to your children?

opportunities are limited. Over 90 percent of career-track workers are men, who typically are prepared for jobs as salarymen (white-collar workers), while women primarily are offered jobs as clerks and secretaries (see Brinton, 1988, 1989). Women, on average, earn about 60 percent of what men earn (Landers, 1996). Women college graduates who are hired by major Japanese corporations are responsible for making tea and performing other chores for their male superiors (Deans, 1995). Many women experience sexual harassment, and employers automatically assume that women will leave their jobs when they get married or have their first child. If women keep their jobs after marriage, they often are criticized by both their bosses and their husbands, who believe that married women should be full-time homemakers.

Now, in the late 1990s, more Japanese women are rebelling against making tea and taking orders from men. They are setting up hotlines, organizing pressure groups, and holding nationwide rallies. Some women are choosing to marry later, have fewer children, and challenge sex discrimination in the work-

place. However, other women are either remaining at home to serve their husbands and children or pursuing careers in such female-dominated fields as flight attendant—soochoowadesu—that reward youth and beauty. As journalist Peter Landers (1996:G5) explains, "In Japan, where female office workers are often expected to make tea and tidy up after their male colleagues, becoming a flight attendant offers women a greater payoff in prestige for the kind of subservience that would probably be expected of them anyway." But the ingrained nature of gender stereotyping is reflected in the alternative explanation given by Kaori Umezawa, a former flight attendant who now trains flight attendants: "The desire to give good service is something that's inherent in women" (quoted in Landers, 1996:G5).

Do you think Japanese women and men will experience greater gender role equality in the twenty-first century? Why or why not? Do the global media contribute to people's changing perceptions of gender-appropriate behavior? Why or why not?

purchase boys' sweatshirts that feature male superheroes, athletic motifs, or characters such as Mickey Mouse, Elmer Fudd, or the Lion King.

Parents further reinforce gender stereotyping and gender distinctions by the toys they buy and the chores they assign to sons and daughters. Besides providing fun and entertainment, toys and games develop different types of skills and can encourage boys and girls to participate in gender-typed activities. For example, parents buy blocks and building sets, vehicles, sporting equipment, and action toys such as guns, tanks, and soldiers for boys. In contrast, parents buy dolls, doll clothing, dollhouses, play cosmetics, and homemaking items such as dishes and miniature ovens for girls (Leaper, 1994). Boys are assigned maintenance chores such as carrying out the garbage, cleaning up the yard, or helping dad or an older brother; girls are given domestic

chores such as shopping, cooking, clearing the table, and doing laundry (Weisner et al., 1994). When parents purchase gender-specific toys and give children gender-specific household assignments, they send a powerful message about the gendered division of labor. Most research confirms that parents use toys and chores as a means to encourage their sons toward greater independence than their daughters (Basow, 1992). However, gender socialization varies widely, and the extent of peer group involvement is an important factor.

Peers and Gender Socialization

Peer groups are among the most powerful socializing agents, reinforcing existing gender stereotypes and pressuring individuals to engage in gender-appropriate behavior. *Peer groups* are social groups linked by common interests and generally by similar age. Children are more widely accepted by their peers when they conform to the group's notion of gender-appropriate behavior (Maccoby and Jacklin, 1987; Martin, 1989). Male peer groups place more pressure on boys to do "masculine" things than female peer groups place on girls to do "feminine" things (Fagot, 1984). Today, for example, most girls wear jeans and many play soccer and softball, but boys who wear dresses or play hopscotch with girls are banished from most male peer groups.

During preadolescence, male peers also reinforce gender-appropriate emotions in boys. In a study of a Little League baseball team, for example, sociologist Gary Fine (1987) found that the boys were encouraged by peers to engage in proper "masculine" behavior, such as acting tough even when they were hurt or intimidated, controlling their emotions, being competitive and wanting to win, and showing group unity and loyalty. When a boy failed to display these characteristics, he received instantaneous feedback from the other boys.

Peers are important in both women's and men's development of gender identity and their aspirations for the future (Maccoby and Jacklin, 1987). Among college students, for example, peers play an important part in career choices and the establishment of long-term, intimate relationships (Huston, 1985; Martin, 1989). Even in kindergarten and the early grades, peers influence how we do in school and our perceptions of ourselves and others.

Education and Gender Socialization

Like parents and peers, teachers reinforce existing gender stereotypes by communicating to students that males and male-dominated activities are more important than females and female-dominated activities are. Research on education continues to show the effects in schools of *gender bias*—a situation in which favoritism is shown toward one gender. For example, education scholars Myra Sadker and David Sadker (1994) found that teachers subtly convey the message to students that boys are more important by devoting more time, effort, and attention to boys than to girls. In day-to-day interactions, teachers are more likely to allow boys to interrupt them and give boys more praise, criticism, and suggestions for remediation than girls. Boys are more likely to be called on in class, whether they volunteer

or not. When boys make comments, teachers often follow up with additional questions or suggestions; but when girls make comments, teachers often respond with a superficial "OK" and move on to the next student. Teachers praise girls for their appearance or for having a neat paper, but boys are praised for their accomplishments.

Gender-segregated activities are encouraged by teachers when they organize classroom and playground activities by sex ("Boys line up on the left; girls on the right") and when they set up unnecessary competition between the sexes. One teacher divided her class into the "Beastly Boys" and the "Gossipy Girls" for a math game and allowed students to do the "giving five" handslapping ritual when one group outscored the other (Thorne, 1995).

In some schools, teachers take a "boys will be boys" attitude about derogatory remarks and aggressive behavior that constitute sexual harassment against girls. Teachers and school administrators frequently overlook *sexual harassment—unwanted sexual advances, requests for sexual favors, or other verbal or physical conduct of a sexual nature.* In some cases, real, humiliating sexual harassment is trivialized by media stories such as when a first-grade boy was suspended from school for kissing a female classmate on the cheek (see Orenstein, 1996). Stories such as this tend to undermine efforts to reduce gender bias and sexual harassment, which for many girls and young women create a hostile environment that makes it more difficult for them to learn and accomplish as much as their male counterparts (Sadker and Sadker, 1994). For example, researchers have found that in some schools, male students regularly refer to girls as "slut," "bitch," and "ho" without fear of reprimand from teachers, and the girls' fear of reprisal keeps them from speaking out against their harassers (Orenstein, 1996). In an American Association of University Women survey, 76 percent of 1,600 middle school and high school girls indicated that they had experienced unwanted sexual comments, jokes, gestures, or looks at school. Sixty-five percent had been grabbed or pinched. More than one in ten had been forced to perform a sexual act other than kissing. Girls respond to the hostile environment by not speaking in class, letting their grades drop, or saying that they do not want to go to school at all (AAUW Educational Foundation, 1992). A high school student describes her experience in a shop class: "The boys literally pushed me around, right into tables and chairs. They pulled my hair, made sexual comments, touched me, told sexist jokes. And the thing was that I was better in the shop class than almost any guy. This only caused the boys to get more aggressive and troublesome"(Sadker and Sadker, 1994:127).

Although it may seem that boys benefit from sexual harassment and teachers' gender bias (or at least are not harmed by it), that is not the case. Boys are limited by stereotypical notions about masculinity and gender-appropriate behavior. According to Sadker and Sadker (1994:220), boys confront "frozen boundaries" of the male role at every turn in their school life. They are taught to "Be cool, don't show emotion, repress feelings, be aggressive, compete, and win"—the same messages that sociologist Gary Fine (1987) found Little Leaguers using in reinforcing each other. Such beliefs not only limit the range of emotions boys are allowed to feel but also encourage boys to see themselves—and other males—as better than girls and to distance themselves from any activity that is considered "feminine," even though it may be an activity they enjoy.

Male gender norms such as being active, aggressive, and independent often come in conflict with school norms requiring students to be quiet, passive, and conforming. Although many boys walk a tightrope between compliance and rebellion, they tend to receive lower grades than girls do and are more likely to drop out of school (Sadker and Sadker, 1994). Similarly, sociologist Michelle Fine (1991) found in a recent study that for many girls, the price of academic success is being compliant and muting their own voice.

Inequities that constitute gender bias against women also occur at the college level. Research consistently shows that more educational resources, ranging from athletics and dormitories to course offerings and career advising, are targeted primarily at men even though women constitute more than half of all U.S. college students. In the classroom, many professors give more attention to men than to women (Hall and Sandler, 1982; Hall, 1984). Women tend to be called on less frequently and to receive less encouragement. When they speak out in class, women are more likely to be interrupted, ignored, or devalued than men are (Fox, 1995). Women often experience a drop in self-esteem while in college, yet they tend to have higher grade-point averages and they earn a higher percentage of bachelor's and master's

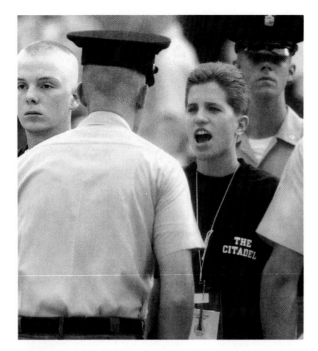

In recent years, the media have made people in the United States more aware of sexual harassment at the college level. For example, many stories focused on the problems experienced by women cadets at the Citadel, a formerly all-male military school in Charleston, South Carolina. According to media reports, although all first-year cadets go through a rigorous military training program at the Citadel, some female cadets were the objects of discriminatory actions ranging from overt ridicule to having their hair set afire by male cadets.

degrees than men do. However, women are underrepresented in fields such as engineering, computer and information sciences, and physical sciences and are overrepresented in the number of degrees awarded in education, psychology, and nursing and allied health (Women's Research and Educational Institute, 1996). Some analysts attribute the underrepresentation of women in math, science, and engineering to the way these courses are taught: "The traditions are based on military applications. The programs started out in military schools and colleges" (Jane Daniels, Women in Engineering, Purdue University, quoted in Urschel, 1996:2D). However, by the doctoral (Ph.D.) level, men outnumber women as recipients of degrees in all fields.

Sports and Gender Socialization

Although girls' participation in athletics has increased dramatically since the 1972 passage of Title IX, which mandates equal opportunities in academic and athletic programs, boys' participation is still almost twice that of girls. When students in a recent study in Michigan were asked about sports participation, most students listed all sports as male domains with the exception of figure skating, gymnastics, and jumping rope, which were identified as female activities (Michigan Department of Education, 1990). Obviously, gender socialization has a profound effect on how girls and boys perceive themselves in relation to sports.

While young boys are socialized to participate in highly competitive, rule-oriented games with a larger number of participants, girls are socialized to play in small groups with other girls of their own age and to engage in largely noncompetitive activities such as hopscotch or jump rope (Lever, 1978; Ignico and Mead, 1990). From elementary school through high school, boys are encouraged to play football and other competitive sports while girls are encouraged to become cheerleaders, drill team members, or homecoming queens. For males, competitive sports become a means of developing a masculine identity and a legitimate outlet for feelings of violence and aggression (Lorber, 1994).

Across lines of race or ethnicity and gender, extracurricular activities and sports provide important opportunities for leadership, teamwork, and personal contact with adult role models. Girls' participation in sports is consistently lower than that of boys despite research indicating that girls, especially those from minority backgrounds, benefit from participation in athletic programs and sporting events. For example, one study found that Latinas who participate in sports are more likely than nonparticipants to improve their academic standing, to graduate from high school, and to attend college (Women's Sports Foundation, 1989).

The Media and Gender Socialization

The media, including newspapers, magazines, television, and movies, are powerful sources of gender stereotyping. While some critics argue that the media simply reflect existing gender roles in society, others point out that the media have a unique ability to shape ideas. From children's cartoons to adult shows, more male than female roles are shown on television, and male characters act strikingly different from female ones. Educational programs such as *Sesame Street* may perpetuate gender stereotypes because most characters have male names and masculine voices and participate in "boys' activities." In children's and adult's programming, male characters are typically more aggressive, constructive, and direct, while female characters defer to others or manipulate them by acting helpless, seductive, or deceitful (Basow, 1992).

Daytime soap operas exemplify gender stereotyping. As media scholar Deborah D. Rogers (1995) suggests, although more contemporary soaps feature career women, the cumulative effect of these programs is to reconcile women to traditional feminine roles and relationships. Whether female characters are shown at home or in the workplace, they typically are gossiping about romances or personal problems or competing for a man. Meanwhile, male characters are shown as superior beings who give orders and advice to others and do almost anything. In a hospital soap, for example, the same male doctor delivers babies, handles AIDS patients, and treats trauma victims while female nurses gossip about hospital romances and their personal lives (Rogers, 1995).

Recent studies of music videos on MTV have found that these videos often show stereotyped gender roles and condone harassment of and discrimination against women. Most female characters were dressed in revealing clothing, made sexual advances toward men, and generally were presented as sex objects. In contrast, male characters routinely pursued fantasy adventures or engaged in aggression and violence (Seidman, 1992).

Changes have occurred in the roles men and women play in movies, but they are still powerfully slanted toward stereotypes. Even though there are many women movie stars, few notable roles exist for women, and even fewer films examine women's lives and issues from their own perspectives. (Exceptions include *Fried Green Tomatoes*, *A League of Their Own*, and *Thelma and Louise*.) In recent years, little boys and young men have played a wider range of roles than have little girls and young women in movies. For example, in *Free Willy*, *Home Alone*, *Last Action Hero*, and *The Mighty Ducks*, boys tame a killer whale, outwit burglars, help police solve crimes, and become hockey champions, respectively. Meanwhile, girls and young women in films such as *Clueless* are depicted as "bimbos," shopaholics, and strictly uninterested in school. According to social psychologist Hilary Lips (1993:19), "We are surrounded with the message that masculine males can be powerful, but feminine females cannot, or that women's only effective source of feminine influence is beauty and sex appeal."

Why is awareness of gender socialization important for understanding sex discrimination and gender inequality? Examining gender role socialization reveals how parents, peers, teachers, and the media influence our perceptions of who we are and what our occupational preferences should be. From this perspective, gender role socialization contributes to a gendered division of labor, creates a *wage gap* between women and men workers, and limits the occupational choices of men and women. Some social analysts say, however, that no direct evidence links gender role socialization and social inequality and that it is therefore important to use social structural analysis to examine gender inequality (see Reskin and Hartmann, 1986). In other words, decisions that people make (such as the schools they attend and the occupation they pursue) are linked not only to how they were socialized but also to how society is structured. We now examine structural features that contribute to gender inequality.

CONTEMPORARY GENDER INEQUALITY

How do tasks in a society come to be defined as "men's work" or "women's work" and to be differentially rewarded? Many sociologists believe that social institutions and structures assign different roles and responsibilities to women and men and, in the process, restrict women's opportunities. According to feminist scholars, gender inequality is maintained and reinforced through individual and institutionalized sexism. The term *individual sexism* refers to individuals' beliefs and actions that are rooted in antifemale prejudice and stereotypic beliefs. The term *institutionalized sexism* refers to the power that men have to engage in sex discrimination at organizational and institutional levels of society. The pattern of male domination and female subordination is known as *patriarchy*—a hierarchical system of social organization in which cultural, political, and economic structures are controlled by men. According to some analysts, the primary evidence of patriarchy in the United States is the location of women in the workplace and on the economic pyramid (Epstein, 1988). In this section we focus on five structural forms that contribute to contemporary gender inequality: the gendered division of labor, the wage gap, sexual harassment, the glass ceiling and the glass escalator, and the double shift.

The Gendered Division of Paid Work

Many people are optimistic about the gains U.S. women have made in employment in recent decades, especially during the last few years. These gains often are attributed to an overall increase in the number of employed women in this country. Whether by choice or economic necessity, women have entered the paid labor force in unprecedented numbers. In 1940, about 30 percent of working-age women in the United States were employed. Today, women represent over 45 percent of the work force. Among women age twenty-five to fifty-four, the increase is even more dramatic: 75 percent currently are either employed or looking for a job. In fact, a higher proportion of women of all races, ages, and marital status groups are employed or seeking work than ever before. At the same time the proportion of male employees has gradually declined because of layoffs in the industrial sector and the long-term trend toward early retirement.

Despite changes in the overall proportion of employed women, women's position as a social category in the labor force is lower than men's in terms of status, opportunities, and salaries. Today, most women and men remain concentrated in occupations that are segregated by gender (see Table 4.1). The term *gender-segregated work* refers to the extent to which men and women are concentrated in different occupations and places of work (Reskin and Padavic, 1994). For example, some individuals are employed in settings where workers of one sex predominate (e.g., women in word-processing pools and child-care centers, men in the construction trades). Other individuals are employed in settings where both men and women are present but women are employed predominantly in clerical or other support positions while men hold supervisory, managerial, or other

TABLE 4.1 EMPLOYMENT PERCENTAGES BY OCCUPATION AND SEX, 1994

Occupation	Men	Women
Total percentage[1]	100.00	100.00
Managerial and professional specialty	26.5	28.7
Executive, administrative, managerial	14.0	12.4
Professional specialty	12.5	16.3
Technical, sales, and administrative support	20.0	42.4
Technical and related support	2.8	3.6
Sales occupations	11.4	12.8
Administrative support, including clerical	5.9	26.0
Service occupations	10.3	17.8
Private household	0.04	1.4
Protective service	2.8	0.7
Service, except private household and protective	7.4	15.7
Precision production, craft, and repair	18.4	2.2
Operators, fabricators, and laborers	20.4	7.7
Farming, forestry, and fishing	4.2	1.2

[1]Percentages may not add to 100 because of rounding.

SOURCE: U.S. Bureau of Labor Statistics, 1994.

professional positions that afford greater authority and economic rewards than do positions held by the average woman employee. Despite the increasing number of women entering the legal profession, for example, most attorneys are men, and most support-staff workers, such as legal secretaries and paralegals, are women (see Epstein, 1993; Pierce, 1995). Gender-segregated work is most visible in occupations that remain more than 90 percent female (such as secretary, registered nurse, kindergarten or elementary school teacher, and bookkeeper/auditing clerk) or more than 90 percent male (such as carpenter, construction worker, mechanic, truck driver, and electrical engineer) (U.S. Bureau of Labor Statistics, 1995). In fact, to eliminate gender-segregated jobs in the United States, more than half of all employed men or women would have to change occupations (Reskin and Hartmann, 1986).

Observers who are optimistic about women's gains point out that government statistics show women employed in a wide variety of organizations and holding nearly every kind of job. It is important to note, however, that the types of work women and men do still vary significantly. For example, the large occupational categories shown in Table 4.1 mask significant underlying differences in employment by gender. The data show that the occupational group in which women and men are most equally represented is *managerial and professional specialty*; however, when we look at specific occupations *within* this category, a different picture emerges. Lumped together are such diverse occupations as prekindergarten, kindergarten, and elementary school teachers (92 percent female); computer systems analysts (70 percent male); and engineers (90 percent male). Therefore 60 percent of all em-

CATHY © 1992 Cathy Guisewite. Reprinted with permission of UNIVERSAL PRESS SYNDICATE. All rights reserved.

ployed women in the United States today are concentrated in *pink-collar occupations*—**the relatively low-paying, nonmanual, semiskilled positions that are held primarily by women**—such as clerical work, counter help in fast-food restaurants, medical assistance, and child-care work.

Women are overrepresented in the contingent work force as well. **Contingent work is part-time work, temporary work, and subcontracted work.** Many employers stress that having more contingent workers and fewer permanent, full-time employees keeps corporations competitive in the global marketplace. However, this type of employment actually makes it possible for employers to avoid providing contingent workers with job security and benefits such as health insurance and pension plan coverage. Women are overrepresented in contingent

work because it often provides greater flexibility to meet family responsibilities. However, nearly 2 million women who accepted part-time or temporary work in 1995 did so because they were unable to find permanent jobs (Costello et al., 1996). Although all contingent workers experience problems related to this type of work, women especially are affected by the fact that contingent workers are unlikely to qualify for unemployment compensation if they lose their jobs (see Bassi and Chasanov, 1996), and most of them do not qualify for pension coverage (see Hounsell, 1996; Patterson, 1996).

Although the degree of gender segregation in the workplace and in professions such as accounting, law, and medicine has declined in the last three decades, occupational segregation by race and ethnicity persists. Today, a larger percentage of white women (30 percent) than African American women (21 percent) or Latinas (17 percent) hold managerial and professional specialty jobs. When African American women become professionals, they often find their employment opportunities more limited than those of white women and men. For example, sociologist Elizabeth Higginbotham (1994) found that most African American professional women are concentrated in public sector employment (as public school teachers, welfare workers, librarians, public defenders, or faculty members at public colleges) rather than in the private sector (e.g., large corporations, major law firms, and elite private universities).

Both Latinas and African American women are more likely than white women to work in service occupations such as private household workers. Although private household work became less common among African American women during the last two decades, Latinas remain heavily represented among the 800,000 women who are employed as private household workers. Across racial and ethnic lines, women continue to be concentrated in jobs where they receive lower wages and fewer benefits on average than men do.

The Wage Gap

The *wage gap*—the disparity between women's and men's earnings—is the best-documented consequence of gender-segregated work (Reskin and Padavic, 1994). No matter what their race, men earn more than women of the same racial or ethnic group. For example, the median earnings for women who worked full time in 1994 were $399 per week compared to $522 for men. This means that a woman who works full time makes about 76 cents for every dollar that a man makes.

The wage gap varies by age: The older the worker, the larger the gap. Between the ages of twenty and twenty-four, women earn an average of 95 cents for every dollar that men earn. Younger workers tend to have about the same amount of work experience and to be concentrated in entry-level jobs. However, women between the ages of twenty-five and thirty-four earn only 83 cents for every dollar that men earn. Women of age thirty-five to forty-four, in sharp contrast, earn only 73 cents per dollar; and by ages forty-five to fifty-four the amount has dropped to only 67 cents for each dollar men earn (U.S. Bureau of Labor Statistics, 1995).

Social analysts suggest that the higher wage gap for older workers probably reflects a number of factors, including the fact that women in those age groups tend to have, on average, less overall work experience and less time with their present employer than do men of the same age (Herz and Wootton, 1996). As Figure 4.1 shows, the wage gap has narrowed somewhat between women and men over the last three decades, but much of the decrease in wage disparity can be attributed to a decline in men's average earnings since 1973 rather than to a significant increase in women's earnings (Roos and Reskin, 1992).

For pay equity to occur between men and women, there has to be a broad-based commitment to *comparable worth*—the belief that wages ought to reflect the worth of a job, not the gender or race of the worker (Kemp, 1994). To determine the comparable worth of different kinds of jobs, researchers break a specific job into components to determine (1) how much education, training, and skills are required; (2) how much responsibility a person in that position has for others' work; and (3) what the working conditions are. Points are then allocated for each component to determine whether or not men and women are being paid equitably for their work (Lorber, 1994). For pay equity to exist, men and women in occupations that receive the same number of points should be paid the same. However, pay equity exists for very few jobs. (See Figure 4.2 for a comparison of men's and women's earnings in selected occupations.)

Comparable worth is an important issue for men as well as women. Male workers in female-dominated jobs such as nurse, secretary, and elementary teacher pay an economic penalty. Also, if women were compensated fairly, an employer could not undercut men's wages by hiring women at a cheaper rate (Kessler-Harris, 1990).

Sexual Harassment

Millions of men never harass women in the workplace or elsewhere, but so many do that it is almost impossible for women to avoid the experience (Langelan, 1993). Sexual harassment is a form of intentional, institutionalized gender discrimination that includes all unwelcome sexual attention affecting an

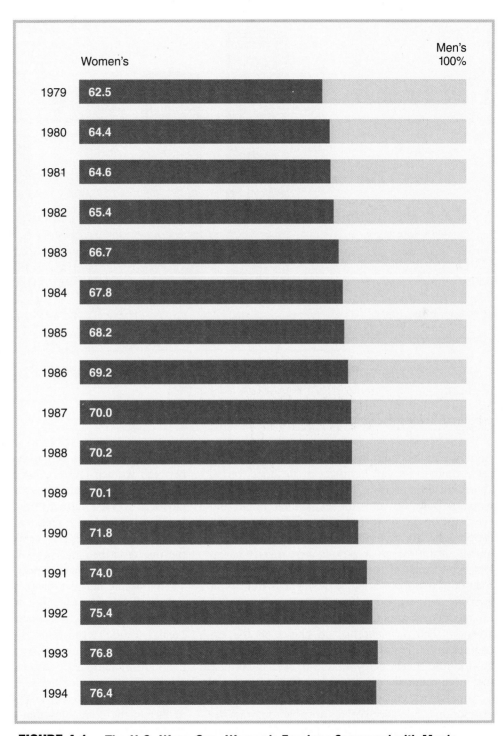

FIGURE 4.1   *The U.S. Wage Gap: Women's Earnings Compared with Men's Earnings, 1979–1994*

(SOURCE: U.S. Bureau of Labor Statistics, 1994.)

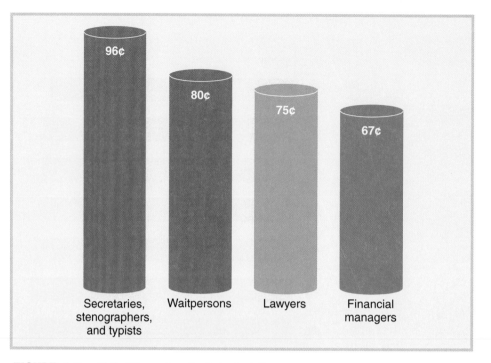

FIGURE 4.2   *U.S. Wage Gap in Selected Occupations*
(SOURCE: U.S. Bureau of Labor Statistics, 1994.)

employee's job conditions or creating a hostile work environment. Sexual harassment includes verbal abuse, touching, staring at or making jokes about a woman's body, demands for sexual intercourse, and even rape on the job (Benokraitis and Feagin, 1995). People who are accused of sexual harassment frequently claim that their actions were merely harmless expressions of (supposedly) mutual sexual attraction. However, sexual harassment is not about attraction; it is about *abuse of power.* Sexual harassment constitutes a form of intimidation and aggression: The recipient has no choice in the encounter or has reason to fear repercussions if she or he declines. Some men are able to harass because they hold economic power over women (e.g., bosses, supervisors, colleagues who have some say over promotions and raises); others are able to harass because they hold gender-based power (e.g., power rooted in cultural patterns of male dominance and backed up by the threat of violence and the ability to rape) (Langelan, 1993). In either case, sexual harassment serves as a means of boundary heightening between men and women in the workplace. For ex-

ample, male lawyers may exaggerate the differences between women lawyers and themselves by directing unwanted sexual invitations, attention, and behavior at women in their firm. In her recent study of law firms, sociologist Jennifer L. Pierce interviewed many female lawyers who reported incidents such as the one described by Gabriella, a twenty-six-year-old associate who had slapped a male partner who was harassing her at a firm cocktail party: "Everyone else knew about George, but I was new, I didn't know to avoid him. So, when he tried to grab my breasts, I didn't even think, I just came out swinging. . . . It was so humiliating. Then, afterwards . . . the snide remarks, the knowing glances, the comments, 'How's your left hook?' It was the second public humiliation." (Pierce, 1995:108–109). According to Pierce, the comments that male attorneys made about Gabriella's reaction (slapping George) show that they considered her behavior (not George's actions) inappropriate and worthy of derision.

Sexual harassment is a costly problem for women who may lose employment opportunities and for their employers, who lose more than $7 million a year in low productivity, absenteeism, and employee turnover related to harassment (Basow, 1992). Sexual harassment and other forms of blatant and subtle discrimination in the workplace also contribute to the glass ceiling that limits women's opportunities to rise to the top positions in corporations and other occupational settings (see MacCorquodale and Jensen, 1993; Rosenberg et al., 1993).

The Glass Ceiling and the Glass Escalator

Recently, feminist researchers have used the advancement (or lack of advancement) of women into top tier management jobs as a litmus test for how well women are faring in the labor force as a whole. They have found that although women are inching their way up the corporate ladder, they hold only a handful of top positions. In nearly every occupation, women encounter barriers when they try to enter lucrative and prestigious specialties. This is because of the *glass ceiling*—an invisible institutional barrier constructed by male management that prevents women from reaching top positions in major corporations and other large-scale organizations. For example, male executives may believe that male workers will not work under women supervisors and that women workers are supposed to be in support roles (Benokraitis and Feagin, 1995).

The glass ceiling is evident in the nation's 500 largest companies, in which men still get virtually all of the top jobs and the largest paychecks. In 1996, fewer than 3 percent of the 2,400 people having titles such as chairman, chief executive, vice chairman, president, chief operations officer, or executive vice president were women. Women of color occupy fewer than 1 percent of top management positions. According to a recent study by Catalyst (Dobrzynski, 1996a), a nonprofit research group that studies women in upper-level management, fourteen of the top hundred companies do not have a woman among their top officers (see Table 4.2).

TABLE 4.2   TOP 100 CORPORATIONS WITH NO WOMEN AMONG TOP OFFICERS

Fortune 500 Rank	Corporation	Number of Officers
3	Exxon	20
8	Mobil	9
27	Kroger	12
33	Merrill Lynch	17
44	Loews	17
49	Bellsouth	22
59	NationsBank	6
72	Compaq Computer	14
82	Lehman Brothers	18
85	Nynex	27
89	Texas Instruments	12
90	Rockwell International	19
92	Archer Daniels Midland	23
94	IBP	59

Source: Based on Dobrzynski, 1996a.

Overall, women are most likely to reach top positions in the service sector, in which they have traditionally been employed in greater numbers. Examples include savings and diversified finance, publishing, retailing, food services, and entertainment. Women fare the worst in male-dominated businesses such as mining, crude oil, brokerages, and manufacturing. In its research, Catalyst found that women who continue to bump into glass ceilings tend to leave large corporations and start their own businesses (Dobrzynski, 1996a).

Women who enter male-dominated occupations often have a more difficult time rising to the top than do men who enter female-dominated occupations. In recent research on men in "women's professions" such as registered nurses, elementary teachers, librarians, and social workers, sociologist Christine L. Williams (1995) found that men tend to rise in disproportionate numbers to administrative jobs at the top of these occupations. Williams (1995:12) refers to men's upward movement in "women's professions" as the *glass escalator effect* because, "like being on an invisible 'up' escalator, men must struggle to remain in the lower (i.e., 'feminine') levels of their professions." Men also move into more "masculine" specialties within traditionally female-dominated occupations, such as male librarians who concentrate in the high-technology computer information specialties and administration. In contrast, women in male-dominated occupations typically find no such escalator to the top, and they often work a double shift: paid work and family work.

The Double Shift

Even with recent dramatic changes in women's labor force participation, the division of labor by sex in many families has remained essentially unchanged. Although more married women share responsibility for earning part—or all—of the family income, many men do not participate in routine domestic chores (Reskin and Padavic, 1994). Consequently, many employed women have a double work load. In the words of sociologist Arlie Hochschild (1989), women with dual responsibilities as wage earners and unpaid household workers work "the second shift."

Not only does the relative number of hours spent on housework differ widely between women and men, but the kinds of chores men and women

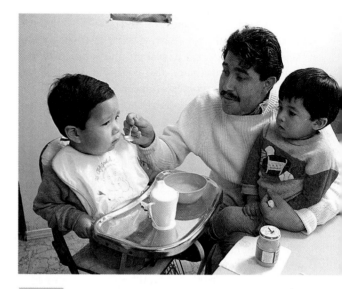

As more women have entered the paid workforce, they have encountered a double shift at home. According to researchers, employed women still do most of the daily household chores such as taking care of the children. Is this photo a hopeful sign for the future?

do also varies significantly. Women do most of the *daily* chores such as taking care of the children, making the beds, and cooking and cleaning up after meals. Men are more likely to do chores that do not have to be done on a fixed schedule. For example, men typically mow the lawn, repair cars or other equipment, and do home improvements (Shelton, 1992). Although some kinds of housework can be put off, young children's needs cannot be ignored or delayed, so in families with young children, daily domestic duties consume a great deal of time and energy. A sick child or a school event that cannot be scheduled around work causes additional stress for parents, especially mothers. Increasingly, women also find themselves in "the sandwich generation," caught between the needs of their young children and those of older relatives, for whom they are often the primary caregivers. To try to keep up with family obligations while being employed full-time or part-time, many women spend a large portion of their earnings on family maintenance, such as day-care and elder-care centers, prepared foods and meals from fast-food restaurants, and laundry and dry cleaning (Bergmann, 1986).

When sociologists conduct research on participation in household work, both men and women state that working couples should share household responsibilities. However, when it gets down to who actually does family household tasks, most studies find that women, even those who hold full-time employment, do most of the work. According to Arlie Hochschild (1989), many women try to solve their time crunch by forgoing leisure activities and sleep.

PERSPECTIVES ON GENDER INEQUALITY

Unlike functionalist and conflict perspectives, which focus on macrolevel sources of gender inequality, interactionist perspectives typically focus on social constructs such as language, which structures our thinking and discourse about domination and subordination.

The Interactionist Perspective

Interactionists examine social problems through a microlevel analysis, viewing society as the sum of all people's interactions. From this approach, language is extremely significant in defining social realities because it provides us with shared meanings and social realities. Historically, what men have thought, written, and concluded have been the givens of our discourse (Peterson and Runyan, 1993). Today, English and other languages are being criticized for *linguistic sexism,* words and patterns of communication that ignore, devalue, or make sex objects of one sex or the other, most often women.

Linguistic sexism perpetuates traditional gender role stereotypes and reinforces male dominance. For example, embedded in the English language is the idea that women are secondary to men in importance: The masculine form ("he") is used to refer to human beings generally, and words such as *chairman* and *mankind* are considered to include both men and women (Miller and Swift, 1991). When a woman enters a profession such as medicine or law, she is frequently referred to as a "female doctor" or "woman lawyer"; such terms linguistically protect these male-dominated professions from invasion by females (Lindsey, 1994).

Language can also be used to devalue women by referring to them in terms that reinforce the notion that they are sex objects. For example, women are described with terms such as *fox, broad, bitch, babe,* or *doll,* which ascribe childlike, toylike, or petlike attributes to them (Adams and Ware, 1995). According to one analyst, at least 220 terms exist for sexually promiscuous women, but only 22 terms exist for promiscuous men (Stanley, 1972).

Research by scholars in a variety of disciplines has demonstrated the importance of language in patterning our thoughts and how gender—and the hierarchy it constructs—is built into the English language (Peterson and Runyan, 1993). According to sociologists Claire M. Renzetti and Daniel J. Curran (1995:151), "Given that women are denigrated, unequally defined, and often ignored by the English language, it serves not only to reflect their secondary status relative to men in our society, but also to reinforce it."

Linguist Deborah Tannen (1990, 1994) has examined how power differentials between women and men at home and in the workplace are reflected in their communication styles. According to Tannen (1990), men and women speak different *genderlects:* Women speak and hear a language of intimacy and connection, while men speak and hear a language of status and independence. For example, women's conversations tend to focus more on relationships with others and include "rapport talk." Men's conversations are more likely to include "information talk" and to convey messages about their position in workplace or social hierarchies.

Similarly, men's and women's communication styles differ: Men have a more direct style of communication and are more likely to dominate conversations than women are. Men tend to seek immediate solutions for problems, while women may ponder alternatives before reaching a decision. From this perspective, communication not only reflects women's and men's relative power in society but also perpetuates male domination and female subordination.

According to interactionists, male dominance is also perpetuated through nonverbal communication such as bodily movement, posture, eye contact, use of personal space, and touching. Men typically control more space than women do, whether they are sitting or standing. Men tend to invade women's personal space by standing close to them, touching them, or staring at them. Such actions are not necessarily sexual in connotation; however, when a man nudges and fondles a flight attendant or a coworker in the office, these actions do have sexual overtones that cannot be dismissed. Recent sexual harassment cases show that women do not appreciate such acts and feel threatened by them, especially if the toucher is the employer (Lindsey, 1994:79).

Although the interactionist perspective has been criticized for ignoring larger, structural factors that perpetuate gender inequality, it is important to note that language and communication patterns are embedded in the structure of society and pass from generation to generation through the socialization process.

The Functionalist Perspective

In contrast to the interactionist perspective, the functionalist perspective focuses on macrolevel issues affecting gender inequality. In particular, functionalists are interested in employment opportunities and the wage gap between men and women.

According to early functionalist theorists, gender inequality is inevitable because of the biological division of labor: Men generally are physically stronger and have certain abilities and interests, whereas women, as the only sex able to bear and nurse children, have their own abilities and interests. Therefore, according to sociologist Talcott Parsons (1955), given their biological attributes, men find themselves more suited to *instrumental* (goal-oriented) *tasks* and women to *expressive* (emotionally oriented) *tasks*. In the home, husbands perform such instrumental tasks as providing economic support and making the most important decisions for the family, while wives perform such expressive tasks as nurturing children and providing emotional support for all family members. The division of labor by gender ensures that important societal tasks—such as procreation and the socialization of children—are fulfilled and that the family is socially and economically stable.

Similarly, according to Parsons, in the workplace, women do expressive work and men do instrumental work. Women cluster in occupations that require expressive work, such as elementary school teacher, nurse, and secretary because of their interests and abilities. Women also are concentrated in specific specialties within professions such as law and medicine because of their aptitude for expressive work and their desire to spend more time with their families than men in the more lucrative specialties are able to spend. For example, many women in law specialize in family law, and many women in medicine specialize in pediatrics (infants and children), obstetrics and gynecology (women), or family practice. In corporations, women are thought to be more adept at public relations and human resources; men are viewed as more adept at financial management. Critics, however, reject the dichotomy between men's instrumental work and women's expressive work as set forth by functionalists (see Scott, 1996). The functionalist explanation of gender inequality does not take into account sex discrimination and other structural barriers in society that make some educational and occupational opportunities more available to men than to women. It also fails to examine the underlying power relations between women and men and does not consider the fact that society places unequal value on tasks assigned to men and to women (Kemp, 1994).

Other functionalist explanations of gender inequality focus on the human capital that men and women bring to the workplace. According to this model, what individuals earn is based on choices they have made, including the kinds of training and experience they have accumulated. For example, human capital analysts argue that women diminish their human capital when they leave the labor force to engage in childbearing and child-care activities. While women are out of the labor force, their human capital deteriorates from nonuse. When they return to work, women earn lower wages than men do because women have fewer years of work experience and "atrophied human capital" because their education and training may have become obsolete (Kemp, 1994: 70).

Critics of the human capital model note that it is based on the false assumption that all people, regardless of gender, race, or other attributes, are evaluated and paid fairly on the basis of their education, training, and other job-enhancing characteristics. It fails to acknowledge that white women and people of color tend to be paid less even when they are employed in male-dominated occupations and take no time off for family duties (Lorber, 1994).

▲ Conflict and Feminist Perspectives

Conflict perspectives on gender inequality are based on the assumption that social life is a continuous struggle in which members of powerful groups (males, in this case) seek to maintain control of scarce resources such as social, economic, and political superiority. By dominating individual women and commanding social institutions, men maintain positions of privilege and power. However, not all men are equally privileged: Men in the upper classes have greater economic power because they control elite positions in corporations, universities, the mass media, and government (Richardson, 1993).

Conflict theorists using a Marxist approach believe that gender inequality primarily results from capitalism and private ownership of the means of production. Under capitalism, men gain control over property and over women. Basing their work on this Marxist approach, *socialist feminists* combine the exploitation of women by *capitalism* in the workplace with women's exploitation by *patriarchy* at home (Kemp, 1994). According to this perspective, capitalists benefit from the gendered division of labor in the workplace because they can pay women lower wages and derive higher profits. At home, women do unpaid work that benefits individual men and also maintains the capitalist economic system. For example, women reproduce the next generation of workers while maintaining current employees (often including themselves) by providing food, clean clothes, and other goods and services necessary for those who must show up at the workplace each day (Hartmann, 1976).

Unlike socialist feminists, *radical feminists* focus exclusively on *patriarchy* as the primary source of gender inequality. From this perspective, men's oppression of women is deliberate, with ideological justification provided by other institutions such as the media and religion. *Liberal feminists* believe that gender inequality is rooted in *gender-role socialization* that perpetuates women's lack of equal civil rights and educational opportunities. *Black feminists* believe that women of color face inequalities based on the multiplicative effect of race, class, and gender as simultaneous forces of oppression (Andersen and Collins, 1995).

Conflict and feminist perspectives have been criticized for their emphasis on male dominance without a corresponding analysis of how men also may be oppressed by capitalism and/or patriarchy.

CAN GENDER INEQUALITY BE REDUCED?

Although improvements have been made in the rights and working conditions of women during the past thirty years, much remains to be done before gender inequality is significantly reduced. As for how, specifically, to go about reducing gender inequality, a point that was made in previous chapters bears repeating: How people view social problems directly affects how they think the problem should be solved. Interactionists, for example, think gender inequality can be reduced only when people redefine social realities such as linguistic sexism. Language should be modified so that it no longer conveys no-

Carol Mosely-Braun, Democrat from Illinois, is the first African American woman elected to the Senate, an almost exclusively male body even though women outnumber men in the general U.S. population.

SOCIAL PROBLEMS
AND SOCIAL POLICY

BOX 4.2

The Women's Movement and Social Policy: "If You Want the Job Done, Do It Yourself"

Throughout history women—individually, collectively, and sometimes with men—have struggled against direct and indirect barriers to their self-development and their full social, political, and economic participation. (Peterson and Runyan, 1993:116)

From the time the Founding *Fathers* wrote that "All *men* are created equal," some women have realized that they would have to take action to bring about greater equality for women. Early feminists began the first wave of the U.S. women's movement at the Women's Rights Convention in Seneca Falls, New York, in 1848 when they drafted the Declaration of Sentiments calling for social equality with men, particularly the right to vote and to own property. However, women did not gain the right to vote until 1920, when the suffragist movement continued to press for passage of the Nineteenth Amendment guaranteeing women the right to vote.

With the civil rights movement of the 1950s and 1960, women activists advocated voting rights for people of color and an end to racial segregation. This movement culminated in passage of the Civil Rights Act of 1964, which included Title VII, which makes it illegal to discriminate against women in hiring and promotion.

During the 1970s and 1980s, women made some gains in political representation, and more social legislation was passed that benefited women and children, though divisions among women based on race, class, and sexual orientation also became apparent. The National

tions of male superiority and female inferiority, which are then transmitted intergenerationally through the socialization process.

Some functionalists believe that traditional gender roles should be redefined for the well-being of individuals and society, but other functionalists suggest that women should become more aware of how their human capital is diminished by decisions they make. From this perspective, to be competitive in the workplace, women must have the same educational background and qualifications for positions that men have. Some functionalists also suggest that overt sex discrimination could be reduced by enforcing existing legislation such as Title VII of the Civil Rights Act of 1964, which forbids discrimination on the basis of sex. However, this approach typically does not affect covert or institutionalized discrimination, which also has a negative and differential impact on white women and people of color.

While some conflict theorists view elimination of sex discrimination as the primary solution for gender inequality, those using a Marxist approach believe that gender equality will occur only when capitalism is abolished. Socialist feminists agree that capitalism should be eliminated and a new economy that eliminates the gendered division of labor and the wage gap between women and men should be developed. Liberal feminists say that we could make a good start in reducing gender inequality by dramatically changing gender socialization and what children learn from their families, teachers, and the media about appropriate masculine and feminine attitudes and

Women's Political Caucus encouraged women to run for public office, and more women received political appointments, including a position on the U.S. Supreme Court. However, a significant setback for women's rights occurred when the Equal Rights Amendment was not ratified by the required number of states, and pressing issues such as affirmative action, child care, and abortion became highly contested political terrain (Faludi, 1991).

Despite slight political gains in recent decades, the percentage of women holding public office remains low. Although women constitute over 50 percent of the population, they constitute only 11 percent of Congress with 48 women in the House and 8 women in the Senate (1995). At the state level, women make up about 25 percent of statewide elected officials and 20 percent of state legislators (Women's Research and Education Institute, 1996).

Why are women underrepresented in Congress and other high elected positions? Some social analysts suggest that few women with sufficient experience and credentials choose to run; others believe that the answer lies in the structure of patriarchy, especially the unequal division of labor at home and in the workplace. As a result of this inequality, women have difficulty in finding necessary resources—such as time, money, and energy—to run for office (Berg, 1994). Female candidates also are targets of sexist assumptions and public scrutiny of their families. A statement sent out by the Newt Gingrich Congressional Campaign several decades ago is typical of the treatment received by many female candidates (such as his then-opponent, Democrat Virginia Shapard): "The Gingriches have two daughters. . . . When elected, Newt will keep his family together. . . . The Shapards have four children. . . . If elected Virginia will move to Washington, but her children and husband will remain in Georgia" (quoted in Mandel, 1981:90). Do such attitudes persist today? What macrolevel and microlevel changes must occur to increase the proportional representation of women in elective offices? Do you think these changes are possible?

behavior. Radical feminists suggest that gender inequality can be reduced only when patriarchy is abolished. To achieve this goal, the legal system must continue to provide relief for sex discrimination, especially sexual harassment in schools and the workplace, and alternative institutions must be developed to replace existing gendered social institutions. For example, women's health care centers would replace male-dominated medicine, and child-care and eldercare centers would assume some of women's caregiving burdens. Finally, black feminists believe that equality will occur only when all women—regardless of race, class, gender, age, religion, sexual orientation, and ability or disability—are treated more equitably (Andersen and Collins, 1995).

Clearly, many gender issues remain unresolved. Gender-segregated jobs may increase, rather than decrease, as a result of technological changes discussed in Chapter 1 and the proliferation of service jobs such as information clerk, nurses' aide, and fast-food restaurant worker, which often are equated with "women's work." Moreover, if the number and quality of "men's jobs" shrink, many men at all class levels may become more resistant to women entering traditionally male-dominated occupations and professions (Reskin and Padavic, 1994). Many analysts suggest that for a significant reduction in gender inequality to occur, women have to become more involved in the political arena and take action themselves (see Box 4.2).

SUMMARY

➤ *How does sex differ from gender?*

Sex is the biological aspects of being male or female; gender is the socially constructed differences between females and males. In short, sex is what we (generally) are born with; gender is what we acquire through socialization.

➤ *How are sexism and patriarchy related?*

Individual and institutional sexism are maintained and reinforced by patriarchy, a hierarchical system in which cultural, political, and economic structures are dominated by males.

➤ *What are the primary socializing agents?*

The key socializing agents are parents, peers, teachers and schools, sports, and the media, all of which may reinforce gender stereotypes and gender-based inequalities as they attempt to teach gender-appropriate behavior.

➤ *What are some of the primary causes of gender inequality?*

Gender inequality results from economic, political, and educational discrimination against women as evidenced in gender-segregated work, which in turn results in a disparity—or wage gap—between women's and men's earnings. Even when women are employed in the same job as men, on average they do not receive the same (or comparable) pay.

➤ *What is the second shift and why is it a problem for women?*

Many women have a second shift because of their dual responsibilities for paid and unpaid work. The typical woman in the United States who combines paid work in the labor force and family work as a homemaker does not have enough hours in the average day to fulfill all her responsibilities, and many men have been unwilling or unable to pick up some of the slack at home.

➤ *How do functionalist and conflict analysts explain the gendered division of labor?*

According to functionalist analysts, women's caregiver roles in contemporary industrialized societies are crucial in ensuring that key societal tasks are fulfilled. While the husband performs the instrumental tasks of economic support and decision making, the wife assumes the expressive tasks of providing affection and emotional support for the family. According to conflict analysts, the gendered division of labor within families and the workplace results from male control and dominance over women and resources.

➤ *What are the major feminist perspectives and how do they explain gender inequality?*

In liberal feminism, gender equality is connected to equality of opportunity. In radical feminism, male dominance is seen as the cause of oppression. According to socialist feminists, women's oppression results from capitalism and patriarchy and women's dual roles as paid and unpaid workers. Black feminism focuses on race and class in analyzing gender inequality.

KEY TERMS

comparable worth, p. 78
contingent work, p. 77
gender, p. 68
gender bias, p. 72
gendered division of labor, p. 69
glass ceiling, p. 81

patriarchy, p. 75
pink-collar occupations, p. 77
sex, p. 68
sexism, p. 67
sexual harassment, p. 72
wage gap, p. 78

QUESTIONS FOR CRITICAL THINKING

1. Examine the various administrative and academic departments at your college. What is the gender breakdown of administrators and faculty in selected departments? Can you identify a gender-related pattern associated with women's and men's majors at your school? What conclusions can you draw about the relationship between gender and education based on your observations?

2. Will the increasing numbers of women in higher education, the workplace, and the military tip the balance of power between men and women and result in greater gender equality in the future? Explain your answer.

3. What kind of study might you develop to examine the effects of children's clothing and toys on the socialization of children? How could you isolate the clothing or toy variable from other variables that influence children's socialization?

4. What steps do you think should be taken to reduce sexism and bring about greater gender inequality in the United States? What resources would you need to implement your plan?

Chapter Five

Inequality Based on Age

A teacher saw my picture [in a newspaper article about ninety-year-olds] in *USA Today* and had her class write to me. I got thirty lovely letters. . . . I've never been to the South, so I flew [to Decatur, Alabama]. . . . I answer any of their questions. Do you still have your own teeth? Do you have a boyfriend? I say, "No, but I'm looking for one who can cook. If you find somebody like that, let me know." They think it's funny.

They want to know how it feels to be ninety. I tell them I feel like myself. Don't you all feel like yourself? Okay, there's a difference. When I was your age, I loved to play basketball and climb mountains and slide down the other side. One thing I didn't want to do was make speeches. It was scary. Now I don't want to climb mountains and play basketball. I love to make speeches. So you see, when you're ninety, you'll do what you feel like doing. In a way, I'm telling them to value old age and respect it.

—Hazel Wolf, age 95, Seattle, Washington, in an interview with author Studs Terkel (1996:140)

As Hazel Wolf's statement indicates, how people of one age view people in another age category is relative. Young people may view older people as "over the hill" while older people consider the young as lacking experience. Throughout one's lifetime, age is a very important ascribed characteristic. Just consider how many times you have been asked, "How old are you?" Most of us answer this question in terms of *chronological age*—age based on date of birth. Although chronological age constitutes our "official" age, most of us view other people in terms of their *functional age*—observable individual attributes such as physical appearance, mobility, strength, coordination, and mental capacity that are used to assign people to age categories (Atchley, 1994). People may appear to be younger or older than their chronological age; their functional age can be influenced by a wide range of physical, psychological, and intellectual factors (Chudacoff, 1989). Driving is an area of life in which we often distinguish

"My mom and dad are still very sharp."

Drawing by M. Twohy; © 1994 The New Yorker Magazine, Inc.

between chronological and functional age. Children—regardless of ability—are not allowed to drive an automobile and therefore eagerly look forward to the time when they will be "old enough" to drive. However, as some people reach old age, they begin to lose some of the functional abilities such as vision or hearing that are necessary for driving. For the younger person, changes in chronological and functional age are positive; the older person may view such changes negatively. Although age-based restrictions are placed on young drivers, restrictions on older drivers are widely viewed as a form of ageism (Stock, 1995).

AGEISM AS A SOCIAL PROBLEM

Ageism—prejudice and discrimination against people on the basis of age—is a social problem that particularly stigmatizes and marginalizes older people. Gerontologist Robert Butler (1969) introduced the term *ageism* to describe how myths and misconceptions about older people produce age-based discrimination. According to Butler, just as racism and sexism perpetuate stereotyping and discrimination against people of color and all women, ageism perpetuates stereotyping of older people and age-based discrimination. Most research has therefore focused on the negative and differential impact ageism has on older people.

Age-Based Stereotypes

There are more stereotypes about the physical and mental abilities of older people than about those of people in any other age category; however, children and adolescents are not exempt from age-based stereotypes. For example, comedians often refer to very young children as "crumb crunchers," "curtain climbers," and "little hellions." Stereotypic depictions of children and young adolescents are found in animated television characters such as Bart and Lisa Simpson (*The Simpsons*), Beavis and Butthead (*Nick at Night* on Nickelodeon), and young characters in many situation comedies and movies.

Older people are stereotyped in numerous ways. Some stereotypes depict older people as slow in their thinking and movement; as living in the past and unable to change; and as cranky, sickly, and lacking in social value (Atchley, 1994). Other stereotypes suggest that older people are "greedy geezers," living an affluent lifestyle and ignoring the needs of future generations (Toner, 1995). Age-based stereotypes can affect how people vote and what types of social policies legislators enact for older people. The media perhaps unwittingly contribute to distorted perceptions about older people (see Box 5.1). Negative stereotypes of older people reinforce ageism and influence how younger people interact with older people.

Although most of us do not believe that we engage in stereotypical thinking about older people, researcher William C. Levin (1988) found that college students in one study evaluated people differently on the basis of their assumed age. When Levin showed photographs of the same man, who had been made up to appear as twenty-five, fifty-two, and seventy-three years old in various photos, to the students and asked them to evaluate these (apparently different) men for employment purposes, many students described the "seventy-three-year-old" as less competent, less intelligent, and less reliable than the "twenty-five-year-old" and the "fifty-two-year-old." But our place in the social structure changes during our life course, and if we live long enough, any of us may become the target of stereotyping and discrimination directed at older people (Hooyman and Kiyak, 1996).

Social Inequality and the Life Course

To study age and social inequality, many sociologists and social gerontologists focus on the *life course*—the age-based categories through which people pass as they grow older. In the United States the life course tends to be divided into infancy and childhood, adolescence and young adulthood, middle age, later maturity, and old age. The field of *gerontology* examines the biological, physical, and social aspects of the aging process. We will focus primarily on *social gerontology—the study of the social (nonphysical) aspects of aging* as we examine age classifications in the United States.

CHILDHOOD

Infants (birth to age two) and children (ages three to twelve) are among the most powerless individuals in society. Historically, children were seen as the property of their parents, who could do with the children as they chose (Tower, 1996). Although we have a more liberal attitude today, children remain vulnerable to problems such as family instability, poverty, maltreatment by relatives and other caregivers, and sexual exploitation. For example, the Children's Defense Fund (1995) reports that *every day* in the United States:

◆ 2,699 infants are born into poverty
◆ 95 infants die before their first birthday
◆ 8,189 children are reported abused or neglected
◆ 1,200,000 latchkey children (children who receive no supervision at home after school because their parents are at work) come home to residences in which there is a gun
◆ 15 children die from gun wounds

Many children face a complex array of problems and social relationships in their families because of relatively high rates of single parenthood, a significant increase in the divorce rate in recent decades, and the fact that many parents work several jobs in an attempt to make ends meet. A large number of children believe that they do not receive enough attention from their parents. Raoul, an eleven-year-old Cuban American, is an example:

I live with my mom. My dad moved to Miami when they broke up and I was about two. So I have a stepdad and a stepbrother. . . . My stepbrother and my mom get along, but not too good. He misses his mom. My stepdad took him because his mom was bad. And then my mom and his dad got married and we became a family. I think he would like to get his mom and dad back together 'cause he gets in trouble a lot. . . .

I've had a nice life so far, for eleven years, but I wish everybody would pay more attention to kids. That's something we really need. Sometimes grown-ups pay attention, but not a lot. They're kind of all wrapped up in their jobs and they don't really pay attention to little children. I think I wouldn't be so violent [in society] if

SOCIAL PROBLEMS
IN THE MEDIA

BOX 5.1

Ageism in the Media

Bob Dole is calling himself an optimist. I understand this because a lot of people would look at a glass as half empty. Bob Dole looks at the glass and says, "What a great place to put my teeth."

—David Letterman in a TV monologue

Bob Dole's senior aides are urging him to hurry up and make his list of potential choices for Vice President. Searching for a Vice President doesn't bother me. What bothers me is that Bob Dole has senior aides? How old are they—90, 100? I mean, senior aides?

—Jay Leno in a TV monologue

Oscar is 68, younger than Bob Dole.

—Whoopi Goldberg at the 1996
Academy Awards

During the 1996 Presidential election, Republican candidate Bob Dole, age seventy-two, was repeatedly the object of jokes and comments by television talk show hosts and comedians because of his age. Although racism and sexism have long been taboo topics in the mainstream media, many entertainers and journalists still consider ageism fair game. Does the way the media depicts older political candidates influence people's attitudes toward political candidates? It would seem so. According to recent polls, many people in the United States form their impressions of political candidates primarily from entertainers' jokes and comedians' political satire on television (Klein, 1996).

Of course, jokes about age may reflect people's deep-seated denial about their own aging. But are most media depictions of older people negative? Despite the age-bashing in the 1996 presidential election, the media have begun to view older people as *consumers*. In recent ads for Clinique skin care products, for example, a woman who gives her age as seventy-nine says, "Age to me is nothing. This nonsense about being old is nothing." A Compaq Computer ad shows two sixty-plus "grandmothers" who fax their recipes back and forth, and an IBM ad features two male actors, one with a gray wispy beard and the other with an age-lined face, to advertise virus-spotting software. (Note the gender differences in these two high-tech ads!)

In some ways these ads are an improvement over television's previous pattern of neglecting or trivializing older people. Characters age sixty and older made up fewer than 8 percent of all major prime-time roles from 1981 to 1992 on network television programs. During the 1991–92 season, depiction of "visibly old" characters in *any* role dropped to a new record low of 0.4 percent of all prime-time characters. When older characters are depicted, they typically have bit parts such as the older medical personnel on *E.R.* or the older man victimized by thugs on *NYPD Blue* (Littlefield, 1995).

What media depictions of older people have you seen recently on television or in the movies or newspapers? As the eighteen- to thirty-four-year-old segment of the U.S. population shrinks and the fifty-plus generation grows by about 12 million people in this decade, do you think changes will occur in media presentations of older people? Why or why not?

ADDITIONAL SOURCES: Darling, 1994; Berke, 1996; Gubernick, 1996.

people paid attention. (quoted in Children's Express, 1993:43–45)

ADOLESCENCE

The line between childhood and adolescence has not always existed, and today it remains blurred. While some researchers define adolescence as the teenage years (ages thirteen to nineteen), others place the lower and upper ages at fifteen and twenty-four, respectively (Corr et al., 1994). Before the twentieth century, the concept of adolescence did not exist. When children grew big enough to do adult work, they were expected to fulfill adult responsibilities such as making money to support their family (Chudacoff, 1989).

Today, adolescents are not treated as children, but they are not afforded the full status of adulthood. Early teens are considered too young to drive, to drink alcohol, to stay out late, and to do other things that are considered adult behavior by the media, particularly television and movies, and by members of some peer groups. Adolescents face an identity crisis in which they must figure out who they are and what they want to become. They also face difficult decisions pertaining to their sexuality and their relationships with people of the same sex and the opposite sex. Teen pregnancy and parenthood are major concerns for many adolescents.

Many adolescents face conflicting demands for money and school attendance. Most states have compulsory school attendance laws that require young people to attend school from about ages six through sixteen or eighteen. However, some students balk at this requirement; they cannot see what school is doing for them and would prefer to find employment. In fact, many teenagers live in families that are trapped in poverty, and young people may hold jobs to supplement the family income or support themselves. These adolescents may view being required to remain in school as a form of discrimination.

Although child labor laws allegedly control the amount of work and working conditions of young employees, recent studies show that many adolescents are employed in hazardous working conditions and work longer than the allowable number of hours per day. For example, few restrictions are placed on farm labor, and teenagers who harvest crops such as strawberries for thirteen hours a day, earning $2.80 per hour or less, may be exposed to harmful pesticides (Lantos, 1992). Teenagers employed in fast-food restaurants have been injured by electric knives that cut off fingers. In one case a fifteen-year-old boy employed by a bakery died when he was pulled into a dough-mixing machine.

Many teens, especially males, join gangs because they perceive a lack of opportunity for them in the adult world. For example, unemployment rates among adolescents, particularly African American males, is extremely high, and the available jobs are in the service sector, such as fast-food restaurants, paying minimum wage or slightly above. Some social analysts suggest that we should not be surprised that individuals between the ages of fifteen and twenty-four account for almost half of all property crime arrests in the United States.

YOUNG ADULTHOOD

Typically beginning in one's early to mid-twenties and lasting to about age thirty-nine, young adulthood is a period in which people acquire new roles and have a feeling of new freedom. However, many also experience problems finding their niche, particularly when it appears doubtful that they will have as high a standard of living as their parents had. Subsequent chapters examine a variety of issues affecting young adults, including alcohol and drug abuse, divorce, and employment instability. Many of these issues also concern people older than age forty.

MIDDLE AGE

Because life expectancy—the average length of time a group of individuals will live—was lower in the past, the concept of middle age, from age forty to sixty or sixty-five, did not exist until fairly recently. As people progress through middle age, they experience *senescence (primary aging)*, which results from molecular and cellular changes in the body. Some signs of senescence are visible (e.g., wrinkles and gray hair); others are not (e.g., arthritis or stiffness in connective tissue joints; a gradual dulling of senses such as taste, touch, and vision; and slower reflexes). Vital systems also undergo gradual change; lung capacity diminishes, and the digestive, circulatory, and reproductive systems gradually decline in efficiency (Atchley, 1994). In addition to primary aging, people also experience *secondary aging* related to environmental factors and lifestyle choices. For example, a recent MacArthur Foundation study on aging identified several factors that contribute to "successful aging," including regular physical activity, continued social connections, resiliency—the ability to bounce back readily after suffering a loss—and self-efficacy, a feeling of control over one's life. According to one gerontologist, "Only about 30 percent of the characteristics of aging are genetically based; the rest—70 percent—is not" (Brody, 1996:B9).

Some people fight the aging process by spending billions of dollars on products such as Oil of Olay, Clairol or Grecian Formula, and Buster's Magic Tummy Tightener. Others have cosmetic surgery. In a recent study, one interviewee explained that she had decided to undergo liposuction (a surgical procedure in which fat is removed) because she had started to get a lot of "crepeyness" in her neck and her jowls were "coming down" owing to aging (Dull and West, 1991:57). As this woman suggests, the United States is a youth-oriented society that tends to equate beauty, stamina, and good health with being young. Because of this belief system, many changes associated with growing older are viewed as something to be avoided at all costs.

While women in middle age may believe that they are now less sexually attractive, men tend to begin to realize that their physical strength and social power over others are limited. Women and men also may have to face the fact that their children have grown and left home. However, for some people, middle age is the time when their income and prestige are greatest, the problems of raising their children are behind them, they are content with their spouse of many years, and they may have grandchildren who give them another tie to the future. Even so, middle-aged people know that their status will change significantly as they grow older.

LATER MATURITY AND OLD AGE

Later maturity is usually considered to begin in the sixties. The major changes associated with this stage are social. As friends and relatives die, the peer groups of people over age sixty shrink noticeably. Many people in later maturity increasingly find themselves caring for people of their own age and older people. However, they retain sufficient physical strength to be able to carry on an active social life.

Old age is usually considered to begin in the late sixties or in the seventies. Although some people continue to work past age seventy, most have left paid employment by the time they reach their seventieth birthday. Problems are not just social, but also increasingly biological. Some changes, such as arteriosclerosis (the loss of elasticity in the walls of the arteries), are potentially life-threatening (Belsky, 1990). As bones become more porous, they also become more brittle; a simple fall may result in broken bones that take longer to heal than those of a younger person. Strength, mobility, and height may decline; and the abilities to see, hear, taste, touch, and smell may diminish. Because taste and smell work together to allow us to enjoy food, the effects of aging on these senses may make eating less pleasurable and so contribute to poor nutrition in some older adults (Belsky, 1990). Although it is not true of all elderly people, the average person over age sixty-five does not react as rapidly (physically or mentally) as does the average person who is younger than sixty-five (Lefrançois, 1993).

The chances of heart attacks, strokes, and cancer increase along with the likelihood of some diseases that primarily affect the elderly. Alzheimer's, a degenerative disease that attacks the brain and severely impairs memory, thinking, and behavior, may be the best-known example. People who have this disease have an impaired ability to function in everyday social roles; eventually, they cease to be able to recognize people they have always known, and they lose all sense of their own identity. Finally, they may revert to a speechless childishness, at which point others must feed them, dress them, sit them on the toilet, and lead them around by the hand. Alzheimer's strikes one in ten people over age sixty-five and nearly half of those over eighty-five. The disease can last eight to twenty years, ending only with death (Lefrançois, 1993).

Life expectancy has increased dramatically during the twentieth century. Today, life expectancy at birth is approximately seventy-six years, compared to only forty-seven years in 1900. Moreover, it is predicted that life expectancy will increase to about seventy-eight years by 2005 and about eighty-two years by 2050. Sociologists use an age pyramid to show the distribution of a given population by age and sex groupings at various points in time. As Figure 5.1 shows, the United States is undergoing what some social analysts refer to as the *graying of Amer-*

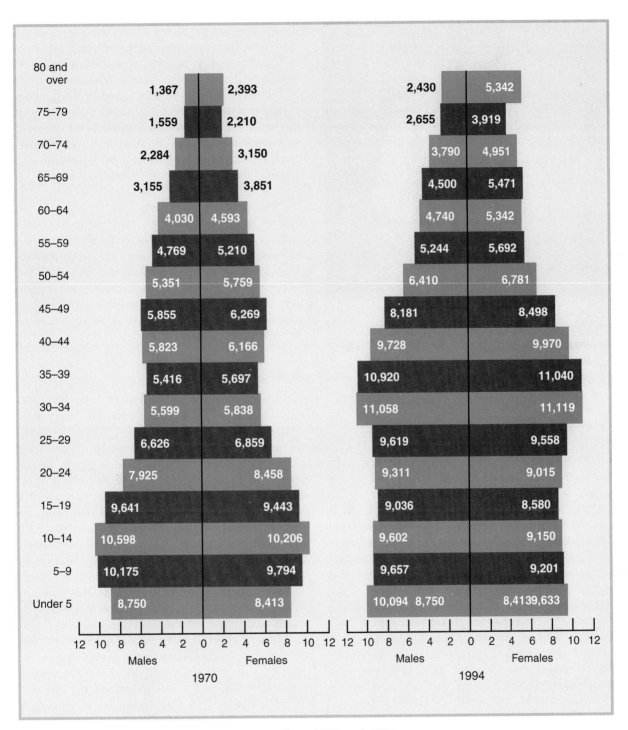

FIGURE 5.1   *U.S. Age Pyramid by Age and Sex, 1970 and 1994*

(SOURCE: U.S. Bureau of the Census, 1995c.)

Gerontologists stress that it is hard to generalize about older individuals. The stereotypes don't fit. This couple, for example, in their eighties, apparently enjoy good health—and each other.

ica, the aging of the population due to an increase in life expectancy combined with a decrease in the birth rate (Atchley, 1994).

As older people began to live longer, gerontologists recognized that there are significant differences among the "young-old" (ages sixty-five to seventy-four), the "old-old" (ages seventy-five to eighty-four), and the "oldest-old" (ages eighty-five and older). Although more than half of all people age sixty-five and older are in the young-old category, the oldest-old category has grown more rapidly over the past three decades than has any other age group in the United States (Angier, 1995b). As with other age categories, it is difficult to make generalizations about older people, as gerontologists Nancy R. Hooyman and H. Asuman Kiyak (1996:5) note:

> Older people vary greatly in their health status, their social and work activities, and their family situations. Some are still employed full- or part-time; most are retired. Most are healthy; some are frail, confused, or home-bound. Most still live in a house or apartment; a small percentage

are in nursing homes. Some receive large incomes from pensions and investments; many depend primarily on Social Security and have little discretionary income. Most men over age 65 are married, whereas women are more likely to become widowed and live alone as they age. . . . It is . . . impossible to define aging only in chronological terms, since chronological age only partially reflects the biological, psychological, and sociological processes that define life stages.

As a spokesperson for the American Association of Retired Persons suggests, "Age is simply not a measure of competence in any way, shape or form and people need to be judged on their own individual characteristics" (quoted in Berke, 1996:E1). Or, in the words of Virginia McCalmont, age eighty-five, "I feel like I'm about 30 or 40—until I look in a mirror. So I try not to look in the mirror" (quoted in Kolata, 1996b:B10).

Death and Dying

In previous generations, death was a common occurrence at all stages in the life course, but today most deaths occur among older people. Because of medical advances and the increase in life expectancy, death is now viewed as the final stage of the life course—one that occurs in old age. According to social gerontologists, the increased association of *death* with the process of *aging* has caused many people to deny the aging process and engage in ageism as a means of denying the reality of death, particularly their own (Atchley, 1994). For example, many people use euphemisms such as "pass away" or "sleep" to refer to death. Researchers have found, however, that many people do not actually fear death itself as much as they fear the possibility of pain and suffering, loss of control, and the consequences of their death for survivors (Marshall and Levy, 1990). Most people greatly prefer a painless death over prolonged physical and mental deterioration and the prospect of being a burden on one's family. Some researchers have also found that older people have less fear of death than younger people do; others have found that education and religious beliefs are important factors in how people view death and dying (Kalish, 1985). However, little research has focused on attitudes toward death among African Americans, Latinas/os, and other people of color, so it is important to be wary of overgeneralizations about fear of death (see Kalish and Reynolds, 1981).

There are three widely known frameworks for explaining how people cope with the process of dying: the *stage-based approach,* the *dying trajectory,* and the *task-based approach.* The *stage-based approach* was popularized by Elisabeth Kübler-Ross (1969), who proposed five stages in the dying process: (1) denial ("Not me"), (2) anger ("Why me?"), (3) bargaining and asking for divine intervention to postpone death ("Yes me, but . . ."), (4) depression and sense of loss, and (5) acceptance. According to some social scientists, Kübler-Ross's study is limited because she focused primarily on the attitudes of younger people who had terminal illnesses: The same stages might not apply to older people who believe that they have already lived a full life (Marshall, 1980; Kalish, 1985).

In contrast, the concept of the *dying trajectory* focuses on the perceived course of dying and the expected time of death. From this perspective, not all people move toward death at the same speed and in the same way. A dying trajectory may be sudden (e.g., a heart attack) or slow (e.g., lung cancer) and is usually shaped by the condition causing death. A dying trajectory involves three phases: the acute phase, in which maximum anxiety or fear is expressed; the chronic phase, in which anxiety declines as the person confronts reality; and the terminal phase, in which the dying person withdraws from others (Glaser and Strauss, 1968).

The *task-based approach* suggests that daily activities can still be enjoyed during the dying process and that fulfilling certain tasks makes the process of death easier on everyone involved (not just the dying person). *Physical tasks* are performed to satisfy bodily needs and to minimize physical distress. *Psychological tasks* help to maximize psychological security, autonomy, and richness of experience. *Social tasks* sustain and enhance interpersonal attachments and address the social implications of dying. *Spiritual tasks* are performed to identify, develop, or reaffirm sources of spiritual energy and to foster hope (Corr et al., 1994). Most important in any approach are the rights of the dying person and how care is provided to them.

In recent years, greater attention has been paid to the needs of dying patients and their families. More people are choosing to sign a *living will*—a document stating their wishes about the medical circumstances under which their life should be allowed to end. Some people reject the idea of being kept alive by elaborate life-support systems and other forms of high-tech medicine, choosing to die at home rather than in a hospital or nursing home. The hospice movement has provided additional options for caring for the terminally ill. **Hospices are organizations that provide a homelike facility or home-based care (or both) for people who are terminally ill.** Some hospices have facilities where care is provided, but hospice is primarily a philosophy that affirms life, not death, and offers holistic and continuing care to the patient and family through a team of visiting nurses, on-call physicians, and counselors. Home care enables many people to remain in familiar surroundings and maintain dignity and control over the dying process (Corr et al., 1994). Sophia Mumford summarizes the feeling of many older people about death:

> I'm afraid of one thing. I want my death to be dignified. My fear is that something will cause me to live past the point where my life has value. I don't want to live on. . . . From now on, if life says it's leaving, I'm not doing anything about it. If I get a bad pain and it's diagnosed as cancer, then I won't wait, I'll go. I'm ready, because I feel I've had a good life. (Terkel, 1996:429)

For reasons such as Mumford's, as well as a variety of others, it is not altogether surprising that older people around the world have a relatively high rate of suicide (see Box 5.2).

PROBLEMS ASSOCIATED WITH AGING

As we have seen, age stratification occurs throughout the life course. *Age stratification* refers to the inequalities, differences, segregation, or conflict between age groups (Atchley, 1994). Age stratification is a determinant of how education, jobs, and other scarce resources and opportunities are allocated in society. But age stratification limits roles and opportunities. Many people automatically assume that at age fourteen, a person should be in school and at age sixty-five, the person should retire from full-time employment. Such perceptions about age may create

SOCIAL PROBLEMS
IN GLOBAL PERSPECTIVE

BOX 5.2

Quantity versus Quality of Life: Suicide and the Graying of the Globe

Ironically, as the number of people age sixty-five and older continues to grow rapidly in both industrialized and developing nations, suicide rates among older people also seem to be increasing significantly. About 360 million people worldwide are age sixty-five and older, and this population is growing by about *800,000 people a month*. At the same time, in many nations the highest suicide rates also are found among older people, particularly men (Kristof, 1996a).

Worldwide, suicide rates tend to (1) increase with age, (2) increase slightly in young adulthood and increase dramatically in old age, or (3) peak in middle age (ages forty-five to fifty-four or fifty-five to sixty-five). The first pattern is found in nations such as Austria, Italy, Japan, and West Germany, where suicide rates for both women and men increase regularly with age. The second pattern is characteristic of *male* suicides in countries such as Australia, Canada, England, and the United States. The third pattern is characteristic of *female* suicides in the United States, Canada, and France (Lester, 1992).

Although suicide rates among older people are significantly higher than those among other age groups in most countries, older men are up to *twelve times* more likely to commit suicide than older women are. Figure 5.2 shows dramatic differences between suicide rates for men age seventy-five and older per 100,000 people in European countries compared to rates for men of all ages in the same countries. Some analysts suggest that higher rates of suicide among males can be explained by the disparity between images of masculinity, such as being independent and productive, and the realities of growing old, such as dependence on others, loss of occupational and social status, and perhaps chronic illness or disability. Social isolation also may contribute to higher rates of suicide among unmarried older men (Lester, 1992). In the United States, for example, the highest suicide rates are found among older white men who do not have a spouse, children, or other support systems. In recent years, the suicide rate also has increased among African American older people who lack support systems that traditionally were provided by families and who lack role models for successfully adapting to the aging process (Alston et al., 1995).

How is quantity of life related to quality of life? Do you think advances in medical technology might bring unintended consequences such as high rates of suicide among older people in industrialized nations worldwide? Why or why not?

ADDITIONAL SOURCES: Albert and Cattell, 1994; Andrews and Fonseca, 1995.

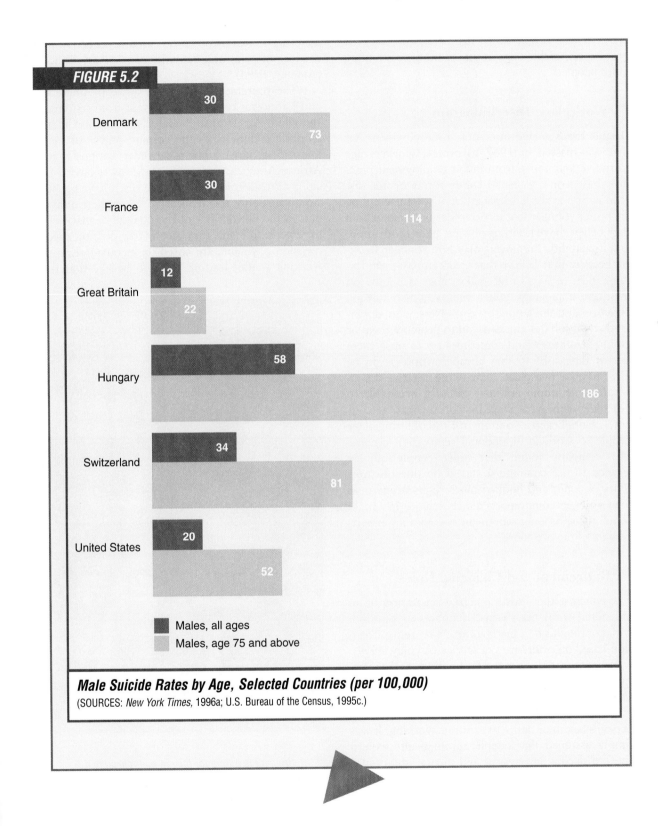

FIGURE 5.2

Denmark — 30 / 73
France — 30 / 114
Great Britain — 12 / 22
Hungary — 58 / 186
Switzerland — 34 / 81
United States — 20 / 52

■ Males, all ages
▨ Males, age 75 and above

Male Suicide Rates by Age, Selected Countries (per 100,000)
(SOURCES: *New York Times,* 1996a; U.S. Bureau of the Census, 1995c.)

problems for people in all age categories, but the problems typically are most pronounced among older people.

Workplace Discrimination

Despite the Age Discrimination in Employment Act that was passed in 1967 to protect workers age forty-five and above from unfair employment practices based on age, many subtle forms of age discrimination in the workplace remain. Some employers prefer younger workers to older workers, whom they believe have health problems, poor motivation, and low ability. Employers may hire younger workers because they believe that they can pay them less than older workers and make more demands on their time and energy. Older employees also may experience discrimination by employers who downgrade their job descriptions, fail to promote them or grant them raises, and sometimes try to push them out of their jobs so that cheaper workers can be hired to take their place. Despite the negative stereotypes, some employers have found it profitable to hire older employees. Days Inns of America, a major hotel chain, began a program in 1986 of hiring older people to work in its national reservation centers. The company found that older people quickly learned to use computers, stayed on the job three times as long, and booked more reservations than their younger counterparts did (Foreman, 1993). At some point, though, retirement becomes an expected part of the life course.

Retirement and Changing Roles

Retirement is the institutionalized separation of an individual from her or his occupational position, with continuation of income from a retirement pension based on prior years of service (Atchley, 1994). In the past, people in many occupations and professions (including tenured faculty members at universities, police officers, and fire fighters) faced mandatory retirement at age sixty-five regardless of the person's health or desire to continue working. It was simply assumed that people automatically experienced a decline in physical and mental ability at a specific age. With changes in compulsory retirement laws, many people still retire but see this time as a newfound period of leisure and an opportunity for adaptation and reflection. For some, however,

adapting to less income, increased dependency, and the loss of roles and activities can be very difficult (Atchley, 1994).

The retirement process for African Americans and Latinos/as typically is different from retirement for white Americans. Racial discrimination in the workplace diminishes the earning power of many minority group members, so older Latinos/as and African Americans who have held lower-paying positions throughout their lifetime often have no pension plans, only Social Security. When these individuals in the bottom tier of the dual labor market do have pension plans, they receive low pension checks (pension payments are based on income during the working years), leading some to believe that they

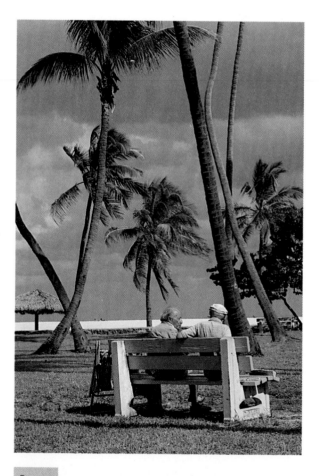

Retirement is a time for leisure and reflection if it comes by choice and the individual is healthy and financially prepared. But for others, adapting to less income, increased dependency, and the loss of roles can be difficult.

have no choice but to work into their seventies (Uchitelle, 1995).

Women who are over sixty-five today are less likely to have access to pension and Social Security income in their own name than are younger women who are currently employed. However, women—as well as many men—are losing out on traditional pension coverage because of changes in the economy and the workplace. Many unionized industrial jobs that provided pension coverage have virtually disappeared, and more women than men are employed as part-time workers, who are less likely to have pension coverage than full-time workers. People in part-time, contingent, and temporary jobs also are unlikely to have health insurance.

Health, Illness, and Health Care

At age ninety-three, Malcolm Clarke plays doubles tennis four times a week and sails his boat; he shops and cooks for himself (Brody, 1996). Although Clarke attributes his longevity and good health to "luck," studies show that many older people are not developing disabling diseases, and the vast majority are functioning quite well. Improvement in the health status of older people has been attributed, at least in part, to better education (knowing what to do and not do to stay healthy), nutrition, and health insurance through Medicare and sometimes Medicaid (see Box 5.3). Because most people over age sixty-five are covered by Medicare, health care coverage is essentially a problem of the young and middle-aged. Lack of health insurance affects substantial portions of all age groups below age sixty-five, as discussed in Chapter 11.

For some older people, malnutrition and disease are life-threatening problems. Although malnutrition is sometimes related to poverty, nutritionists suggest that the condition is pervasive even among older people who are not poor. Today, malnutrition is a problem for 25 percent of people over age sixty-five, and recent studies have found that 16 percent of all older people consume less than 1,000 calories per day (New York Times, 1995a).

About seven of every ten deaths among older people are due to heart disease, cancer, or stroke. By far, the leading killer of persons over age sixty-five is heart disease. Cancer has overtaken heart disease as the leading cause of death among white women; breast cancer and lung cancer are responsible for nearly half of all cancer deaths in women. African American women are more likely than white women to die from a stroke or diabetes. Men, particularly African Americans, are highly vulnerable to cancer of the prostate, a reproductive gland. Many people over age eighty-five die of multiple organ failure or pneumonia, which has been referred to as the "old folk's friend" (Angier, 1995b). Recently, the number of AIDS cases has risen at a faster rate among older people than among other age groups, and AIDS educators are seeking to make older people aware of the risk of becoming infected with HIV, the virus that causes AIDS (New York Times, 1994b).

People age sixty-five and older account for about one-third of all dollars spent on health care, and this figure is expected to rise dramatically with the aging of the U.S. population. The problem will be intensified by the feminization of aging, the increasing proportion of older women. The feminization of aging has important consequences for health care and medical costs because older women, on average, have a greater likelihood of being poor and having no spouse to care for them (Weitz, 1996). Chapter 11 discusses health care issues in greater detail.

Victimization

Although older people are in fact less likely than younger people to be victims of violent crime, they have a higher fear of this type of crime than do people in other age categories. However, older people are the victims of other types of crime. Older people often are targeted by con artists who contact them by mail or telephone to perpetrate a scam, which often promises prizes or involves a "stockbroker" selling a "hot" stock or commodity (Hays, 1995a). In a recent scam, older people received a message to call a number beginning with the area code 809 for important information about a family member who had become ill or died or about a prize they had won. The older people were charged $25 per minute for the call and often were kept on the line for an extended period of time. Some people received phone bills for more than $100.00 per call, not knowing that the 809 area code is located in the British Virgin Islands (the Bahamas) and is a pay-per-call number that is not covered by U.S. regulations regarding 900 numbers (City of Austin, 1996).

Another form of victimization is elder abuse. The National Center on Elderly Abuse estimates

SOCIAL PROBLEMS
AND SOCIAL POLICY

BOX 5.3

Government-Funded Health Care for Older People: Medicare

Are people entitled to health care regardless of their ability to pay? For years this has been a disputed question in the United States. The issue of health care for older people was partially addressed in 1965 when Congress enacted the Medicare program, a federal program for people age sixty-five and over who are covered by Social Security or railroad retirement insurance or who have been permanently and totally disabled for two years or more. Funded primarily through Social Security taxes paid by current workers, Medicare is an *entitlement program*. Those who receive benefits must have paid something to be covered. Medicare Part A provides coverage for some inpatient hospital expenses (for up to about 90 days) and limited coverage for skilled nursing care at home; Part B, which covers some outpatient expenses, may be purchased for an additional premium that amounts to about $50 per month.

Clearly, Medicare has created greater access to health care services for many older people, but it has serious limitations. Medicare primarily provides for acute, short-term care and is limited to partial payment for ninety days of hospital care and for a restricted amount of skilled nursing care and home health services. It also has a deductible and co-payments (fees paid by people each time they see a health care provider), and it pays only 80 percent of *allowable* charges, not the *actual amount* charged by health care providers. Furthermore, Medicare does not include prescription drugs, dental care, hearing aids, eyeglasses, mental health services, long-term care such as nursing homes, or custodial or nonmedical service such as adult day care or homemaker services (Atchley, 1994). Because of these serious gaps in coverage, older people who can afford it often purchase *medigap policies*, supplementary private insurance (Weitz, 1996).

Some low-income older people are eligible for Medicaid, a joint federal-state *means-tested welfare program* that provides health care insurance for poor people of any age who meet specific eligibility requirements. Today, people over age sixty-five constitute about 13 percent of Medicaid recipients but account for more than 40 percent of the program's total expenditures (Hooyman and Kiyak, 1996). However, Medicaid recipients have been stigmatized because Medicaid is a "welfare program." Because the administrative paperwork is burdensome and reimbursements are so low—typically less than one-half of what private insurance companies pay for the same services—many physicians refuse to take Medicaid patients.

In sum, Medicare and Medicaid provide broad coverage for older people, but both programs have major flaws: (1) they are extremely expensive, (2) they are highly vulnerable to costly fraud by health care providers and some recipients, and (3) they typically provide higher-quality health care to older people who are white and more affluent than to African Americans, Latinos/as, people with disabilities, and individuals living in rural areas (Pear, 1994). Chapter 11 discusses U.S. health care in greater detail.

What impact do you think the aging of the U.S. population will have on governmentally funded programs such as Medicare and Medicaid? What solutions can you suggest for providing more adequate health care for older people at less cost?

ADDITIONAL SOURCES: Harvard Medical Project, 1986; Women's Research and Education Institute, 1994.

that 818,000 older people were victims of domestic abuse in 1994. Elder abuse, according to the Center, includes physical, emotional, sexual, and financial abuse as well as neglect (*Austin American-Statesman*, 1995). Many analysts believe that elder abuse is underreported because other people are unwilling to report the abuse and the older people who are the victims are ashamed or afraid to notify authorities. As a government official noted, "Seniors are . . . embarrassed to admit that a relative, a loved one, a child is abusing them, either physically or financially, or neglecting or exploiting them" (*Austin American-Statesman*, 1995:A6). Although some analysts initially believed that younger people might exploit older people who were psychologically and economically dependent on them, just the opposite often proves true: Younger people are more likely to exploit elders on whom they themselves are dependent (Atchley, 1994).

Family Problems and Social Isolation

Older people can easily become socially isolated from their families. Younger members who once asked for advice stop asking, perhaps because they think that their older relatives are out of touch or perhaps because of some miscommunication. Sometimes, younger members feel unduly burdened by the concerns of their elders that don't seem truly important. For one reason or another, older people come to believe (rightly or wrongly) that they are isolated from the rest of the family.

Older people are more likely to live apart from other family members than are younger people. In 1994, 30 percent of people age sixty-five and above lived alone (U.S. Bureau of the Census, 1995c). Many older people live alone voluntarily, but others live by themselves because they are divorced, widowed, or single. Living alone is not the equivalent of social isolation. Many older people have networks of friends with whom they engage in activities. To a large degree, the extent to which they associate with others has to do with social class: People with more money are able to pursue a wider array of activities and take more trips than are those with more limited resources.

Perhaps one of the saddest developments in contemporary society is the growing number of older people who are homeless. Some older homeless people have lived on the streets for many years. Others have arrived more recently after being displaced from low-income housing such as single room occupancy (SRO) hotels. In recent years, many SROs in cities such as New York and San Francisco have been replaced by high-rise office buildings, retail space, and luxury condominiums. Older people who are homeless typically lack nutritious food, appropriate clothing, adequate medical care, and a social support network. They tend to die prematurely of disease, crime victimization, accidents, and weather-related crises such as freezing to death on a park bench in a winter blizzard. Fortunately, the picture is not this bleak for many older people who remain in residences they have occupied for many years.

Housing Patterns and Long-Term Care Facilities

Many people mistakenly assume that most older people live in long-term care facilities such as nursing homes, but only about 5 percent of older people live in any kind of institution. In fact, older people are more likely than people of any other age catego-

Although only about 5 percent of older people live in nursing homes or other long-term care facilities in the United States, living in an institutional setting remains the only option for some older individuals. What alternative living arrangements can you suggest for older people in the future?

ry to reside in housing where they have lived for a number of years and own free and clear of debt. White Americans are significantly more likely than African Americans and Latinas/os to own their home, and married couples are more likely to own their homes than are single people. Older women, who are more likely to live alone than are older men, are at a distinct disadvantage due to the high costs of utilities, insurance, taxes, and repairs and maintenance if they attempt to maintain their own homes (Hooyman and Kiyak, 1996).

Some low-income older people live in planned housing projects that are funded by federal and local government agencies or private organizations such as religious groups. Older people with middle and upper incomes are more likely to live in retirement communities such as Sun City or in *congregate housing* that provides amenities such as housekeeping, dining facilities, and transportation services (Hooyman and Kiyak, 1996). In recent years, religious organizations and for-profit corporations have developed *multilevel* facilities that provide services ranging from independent living to skilled nursing care at the same site. These facilities often are quite expensive, requiring that housing units be purchased or that residents pay a substantial initial entry fee and/or sign life care contracts, which provide for nursing home care if it becomes necessary.

Today, only 1.2 percent of people age sixty-five to seventy-four live in nursing homes; however, the percentage increases to almost 24 percent among people age eighty-five and over. Because of their greater life expectancy, higher rates of chronic illness, and higher rates of being unmarried, women are disproportionately represented among the 1.7 million people who reside in nursing homes (U.S. Bureau of the Census, 1995c). According to social gerontologists, the primary factors related to living in a nursing home are age (eighty-five and over), being female, having been in the hospital recently, living in retirement housing rather than being a homeowner, having no spouse at home, and having some cognitive or physical impairment that interferes with the activities of daily living (Greene and Ondrich, 1990).

White Americans constitute over 90 percent of nursing home residents, compared to 7 percent who are African American, 2.5 percent who are Latino/a, and fewer than 0.5 percent who are Native American or Asian American. Ethnic minorities may be underrepresented because their families are less willing to institutionalize older people or because more caregivers exist to help meet the needs of older relatives. Racial discrimination and a lack of consideration of residents' ethnic backgrounds also may contribute to the perception among many minority group members that nursing homes are no place for their older family members. For example, sociologists have found that many nursing home assistants, who often are recent immigrants to the United States, do not speak the same language as the residents (Diamond, 1992). While some nursing home facilities may be excellent, others have undergone extensive media scrutiny and public criticism for violations of regulations and harmful practices such as elder abuse and neglect, causing many people to select home care, adult day care, or assisted living for older relatives rather than an institutional setting that tends to depersonalize individuals and "reify the image of age as inevitable decline and deterioration" (Friedan, 1993:516).

PERSPECTIVES ON AGING AND SOCIAL INEQUALITY

Although each of the major sociological perspectives focuses on different aspects of aging and social inequality, they all provide insights into how people view the aging process and how ageism contributes to social inequality in society.

The Functionalist Perspective

According to functionalists, dramatic changes in social institutions such as the family and religion have influenced how people look at the process of growing old. From this perspective, both the stability of society and the normal and healthy adjustment of older people require that they detach themselves from their social roles and prepare for their eventual death (Cumming and Henry, 1961). Referred to as *disengagement theory*, this perspective suggests that older people want to be released from societal expectations that they continue to be productive and competitive. Disengagement also facilitates a gradual and orderly transfer of statuses and roles from one generation to the next instead of an abrupt change, which might result in chaos. Retirement policies, then, are a means of ensuring that younger people can move into occupational roles while ensuring that older workers are recognized for years of service (Williamson et al., 1992). Younger workers who move into vacated positions have more up-to-date training, such as the computer skills that most younger people learn in school today.

Critics of this perspective object to the assumption that disengagement is functional for society and that all older people want to disengage even though they are still productive and gain satisfaction from their work. In fact, according to some social analysts, disengagement as evidenced by early retirement policies has been dysfunctional for society. Social Security and other pension systems are strained by the proportionately fewer workers who are paying into the plan to support an increasing number of retired workers. Contrary to disengagement theory, older people may disengage not by choice but because of a lack of opportunity for continued activity.

▲ The Interactionist Perspective

Interactionist perspectives on aging and inequality focus on the relationship between life satisfaction and levels of activity. *Activity theory* is based on the assumption that older people who are active are happier and better adjusted than are less active older persons. From this perspective, older people shift gears in late middle age and find meaningful substitutes for previous statuses, roles, and activities (Havighurst et al., 1968). Those who remain active have a higher level of life satisfaction than do those who are inactive or in ill health (Havighurst et al., 1968). In contrast to disengagement theory, activity theory suggests that older people must deny the existence of old age by maintaining middle-age lifestyles as long as possible. However, an eight-year study found that death rates among older Mexican Americans and whites were not significantly reduced by engaging in such activities as going hunting or fishing, or attending movies and sporting events (Lee and Markides, 1990).

Other interactionist perspectives focus on role and exchange theories. Role theory poses the question "What roles are available for older people?" Some theorists note that industrialized, urbanized societies typically do not have roles for older people (Cowgill, 1986). However, many older people find active roles within their own ethnic group. Although

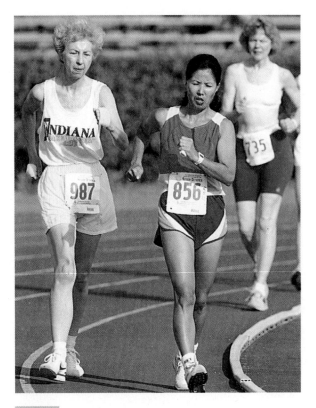

Does this photo of participants in the U.S. Senior Sports Classic better represent disengagement theory (a functionalist perspective) or activity theory (an interactionist perspective)?

their experiences may not be valued in the larger society, they are esteemed within their ethnic subculture because they provide a rich source of knowledge of ethnic lore and history. According to sociologist Donald E. Gelfand (1994), older people can exchange their knowledge for deference and respect from younger people.

▲ The Conflict Perspective

Conflict theorists focus on the political economy of aging in analyzing the problems of older people in contemporary capitalist societies. From this perspective, class constitutes a structural barrier to older people's access to valued resources, and dominant groups attempt to maintain their own interests by perpetuating class inequalities. According to conflict theorists, aging itself is not the social problem.

The problem is rooted in societal conditions that older people often face without adequate resources such as income and housing. People who were poor and disadvantaged in their younger years become even more so in late adulthood. Women age seventy-five and over are among the most disadvantaged because they often must rely solely on Social Security, having outlived their spouses and sometimes their children (Harrington Meyer, 1990).

In the capitalist system, many older people are set apart as a group that depends on special policies and programs. However, to minimize demands for governmental assistance, some services are made punitive and stigmatizing to those who need them (Atchley, 1994). Class-based theories suggest that social and economic policies such as Social Security, Medicare, and Medicaid are a means of social control designed to meet the dominant needs of the economy (Hooyman and Kiyak, 1996). Feminist explanations of age-based inequality suggest that social control policies perpetuate inequality based on gender, class, race, and ethnicity (Harrington Meyer, 1990).

Although Social Security and Medicare do benefit some older people, they primarily benefit upper- and middle-income groups and thus perpetuate class inequalities. Conflict analysis draws attention to how class, gender, and race divide older people just as they do everyone else. The conflict perspective adds to our understanding of aging by focusing on how capitalism devalues older people, especially women. Critics assert, however, that this approach ignores the fact that industrialization and capitalism have been positive forces in society, greatly enhancing the longevity and quality of life for many older people.

CAN AGE-BASED INEQUALITY BE REDUCED?

As we have seen, technological innovations and advances in medicine have contributed to the steady increase in life expectancy in the United States. Technological advances in the diagnosis, prevention, and treatment of diseases associated with old age, such as Alzheimer's, may revolutionize people's feelings about growing older (Atchley, 1994). Technology also may bring about greater equality and freedom for older people. Home-based computer services such as banking and shopping make it possible for older people to conduct their daily lives without having to leave home to obtain services. Computerized controls on appliances and lighting and air conditioning make it possible for people who have limited mobility to control their environment. Technology brings recreation and education into the home. For example, Senior Net is a nationwide computer network that encourages discussion of diverse topics and provides hands-on classes in computer use. Robotics and computer systems may eventually be used by frail older people who otherwise would have to rely on family or paid caregivers to meet their needs or move to a nursing home. However, class once again is a factor: More than 75 percent of home accessibility features currently are paid for by users or their families (Hooyman and Kiyak, 1996).

Economic concerns loom large in the future as baby boomers, who were born between 1946 and 1964, begin to retire in about 2010, bringing about a dramatic shift in the *dependency ratio*—the number of workers necessary to support people under age fifteen and over age sixty-three. Instead of *five* workers supporting one retiree by paying Social Security taxes, *three* workers will be providing support for each retiree. Some social analysts suggest that increased age-based inequality may bring about a "war" between the generations (Toner, 1995). However, advocates of *productive aging* suggest that instead of pitting young and old against each other, we should change our national policies and attitudes. Older people should be encouraged to continue or create their own roles in society, not to disengage from it. Real value should be placed on unpaid volunteer and caregiving activism, and settings should be provided where older people can use their talents more productively (Hooyman and Kiyak, 1996).

Changes must occur in the workplace so that time for family responsibilities and leisure are more evenly distributed throughout the life course. Today, younger workers struggle with caring for their families, without the support of employers in many cases (see Chapter 12), and leisure typically is associated with old age and "being put out to pasture." But in the future, people who have had no opportunity to engage in leisure activities earlier in their life are unlikely to suddenly become leisure oriented. Employment, family responsibilities, and leisure must become less compartmentalized, and changes in technology and employment (as discussed in Chapter 1) may make this more possible. For most people, however, it is difficult to have *free time* and *money* at the same time.

Functionalists suggest that change must occur in families and other social institutions to resolve problems brought about by high rates of divorce, single-parent households, and cohabitation by unmarried couples, which tend to reduce the individual's commitment to meet the needs of other family members. As a result, individuals must be socialized to care for an increasing number of living generations in their family and given economic incentives such as tax breaks for fulfilling their responsibility to children and older relatives. Because adult children may have to provide economic and emotional support for aging parents and grandparents at the same time that they are caring for their own children, more community services are needed, particularly to assist adult children who are "suitcase caregivers" for frail, elderly relatives who live many miles away (Foreman, 1996). Communities could create or expand existing facilities such as day-care centers for children and seniors, provide affordable housing, and build low-cost, community-based health facilities.

Other social analysts suggest that people need to rely more on themselves for their retirement and old age. Younger workers should be encouraged to save money for retirement and not assume that Social Security, Medicare, and other entitlement programs will be available to take care of them when they reach old age. As conflict theorists point out, however, many young people do not have jobs or adequate income to meet their current economic needs, much less to save for the future. A 1995 Gallup poll found that people with children under age eighteen indicated that they were saving primarily for their children's education and did not have adequate resources to put aside money for retirement (Golay and Rollyson, 1996).

From the conflict perspective, age-based inequality is rooted in power differentials, and short of dramatic changes in the structure of political and economic power in society, the only way for older people to hold onto previous gains is through continued activism. However, this approach does not take into account the fact that some older people have benefited more than others from social programs such as Medicare, Social Security, and the Older Americans Act (the federal law that authorizes and funds direct services such as senior centers, nutrition programs, and referral services). Groups such as the Gray Panthers and the American Association of Retired Persons work for passage of specific legislation that has benefited many older people. Nevertheless, older people as a category are devalued in a society that prizes youth over old age and in a social structure that defines productivity primarily in terms of paid employment.

According to interactionists, however, individuals who maintain strong relationships with others and remain actively involved throughout their lifetime have reason to be optimistic about life when they reach old age. An example is Victor Reuther, age 81, a founder—with his brother Walter—of the United Auto Workers:

> I still have hope. When you lose hope, you bury yourself. I'm not ready for that. I have too much work to do yet. I never did find it comfortable to sit in a rocking chair complaining about my aches and pains. I think society has a lot of aches and pains. We shouldn't become obsessed with them. We've got to be pragmatic and say: There's a challenge. Let's change. Let's turn things over. (Terkel, 1996:96)

SUMMARY

➤ *What is ageism and why is it considered a social problem?*

Ageism is prejudice and discrimination against people on the basis of age. Ageism is a social problem because it perpetuates negative stereotypes and age-based discrimination, particularly against older people.

➤ *What is the life course and why are different stages problematic for some people?*

The life course is generally divided into infancy and childhood, adolescence and young adulthood, middle age, later maturity, and old age. During infancy and childhood we are dependent on other people and so relatively powerless in society. Adolescence is a stage in which we are not treated as children but also are not afforded the full status of adulthood. In young adulthood, people acquire new roles and have a feeling of new freedom but also may have problems ranging from alcohol and drug abuse to employment instability that may make life complicated. During middle age, people begin to show such visible signs of aging as wrinkles and gray hair, and roles begin to change in the workplace and family as children leave home. In later maturity, people increasingly find themselves involved in caring for people of their own age and older people. Problems of older adults vary widely because of the diverse needs of the "young-old" (ages sixty-five to seventy-four), the "old-old" (ages seventy-five to eighty-four), and the "oldest-old" (ages eighty-five and older).

➤ *What types of problems do older people face today?*

Despite laws to the contrary, older workers may experience overt or covert discrimination in the workplace. Retirement also brings about changing roles and a loss of status for many older people whose identity primarily has been based on their oc-

cupation. For some older people, malnutrition, disease, and lack of health care are life-threatening problems. Older people may become the victims of scams by con artists and elder abuse by family members or nursing home personnel. For most older people, moving into a nursing home represents a loss of autonomy.

➤ *How do people cope with the process of dying?*

Three explanations have been given for how people cope with dying. Kübler-Ross identified five stages in the process: (1) denial, (2) anger, (3) bargaining, (4) depression, and (5) acceptance. However, the dying trajectory suggests that individuals do not move toward death at the same speed and in the same way. The task-based approach suggests that daily activities can still be enjoyed during the dying process and that fulfilling certain tasks makes the process of death easier on everyone involved (not just the dying person).

➤ *How do functionalist and interactionist explanations of age-based inequality differ?*

According to functionalists, disengagement of older people from their jobs and other social positions may be functional for society because it allows the smooth transfer of roles from one generation to the next. However, interactionists suggest that activity is important for older people because it provides new sources of identity and satisfaction later in life.

➤ *How do conflict theorists explain inequality based on age?*

According to conflict theorists, aging itself is not a social problem. The problem is rooted in societal conditions that older people often face when they have inadequate resources in a capitalist society. In the capitalist system, older people are set apart as a group that depends on special policies and programs.

KEY TERMS

ageism, p. 92
dependency ratio, p. 108

hospices, p. 99
social gerontology, p. 93

QUESTIONS FOR CRITICAL THINKING

1. If you were responsible for reducing ageism, what measures would you suggest to bring about greater equality? What resources would be required to fulfill your plan?
2. Should retirement be compulsory for neurosurgeons (brain surgeons), airline pilots, police officers, and fire fighters? Explain your answer.
3. Does disengagement theory or activity theory more closely reflect how you plan to spend your later years? What other approaches to aging can you suggest?
4. Will future technological advances change how people view growing old? Explain your answer.

Chapter Six

Inequality Based on Sexual Orientation

I've been punched, kicked; I've been urinated on; I've been spit on; I've had things thrown at me. . . . Being urinated on, I think, is one of the most humiliating experiences that I've ever had happen in my life, and I felt worse than an animal. I mean, it was just so degrading and so humiliating.

—*Jamie Nabozny describing harassment he received from other students because of his sexual orientation*
(Terry, 1996:A8)

Jamie Nabozny won a federal lawsuit against the Ashland, Wisconsin, school system for failing to protect him from other students' verbal and physical abuse. Some students called Nabozny "sissy," "queer," and "faggot," and on at least one occasion, male students surrounded him and performed a mock rape. However, no student was ever disciplined for harassing Nabozny. Ruth Harlow, an attorney for the Lambda Legal Defense and Education Fund—the national gay legal group that represented Nabozny—explains that many gays and lesbians experience similar treatment in their schools:

Unfortunately this is not an isolated incident at all. The types of harassment—both verbal and physical—that Jamie had to suffer for four years are suffered by all kinds of lesbian and gay teenagers across the country, and they need their school officials to respond appropriately to that kind of harassment and physical abuse. So we're hoping that this [case] will have a profound deterrent effect. . . . that school officials will learn that they need to take this type of problem seriously. (Court TV, 1996)

The Nabozny case is an example of the high level of prejudice and discrimination that some people experience because of their *sexual orientation*—a preference for emotional-sexual relationships with persons of the same sex (homosexuality), the opposite sex (heterosexuality), or both (bisexuality) (Lips, 1993). The terms *homosexual* and *gay* are most often used in association with males who prefer same-sex relationships; the term *lesbian* is used in association with females who prefer same-sex relationships. Heterosexual individuals, who prefer opposite-sex relationships, are sometimes referred to as *straight* (e.g., "What's it like to be straight?"). It is important to note, however, that heterosexual people are much less likely to be labeled by their sexual orientation than are people who are gay, lesbian, or bisexual.

What criteria do social scientists use to classify individuals as gay, lesbian, or bisexual? In a definitive study of sexuality in the mid-1990s, researchers at the University of Chicago established three criteria for identifying people as homosexual or bisexual: (1) *sexual attraction* to persons of one's own gender, (2) *sexual involvement* with one or more persons of one's own gender, and (3) *self-identification* as a gay man, lesbian, or bisexual (Michael et al., 1994). According to these criteria, then, having engaged in a homosexual act does not necessarily classify a person as homosexual. In fact, many respondents in the Chicago study indicated that although they had at least one homosexual encounter when they were younger, they no longer were involved in homosexual conduct and never identified themselves as lesbians, bisexuals, or gay.

NATURE AND EXTENT OF INEQUALITY BASED ON SEXUAL ORIENTATION

How many homosexuals and bisexuals are there in the United States? Although the Bureau of the Census keeps track of numbers in sex, age, and racial-ethnic categories, it does not specifically count people on the basis of their sexual orientation. Estimates of the homosexual population range from 2 percent to 7 percent of all U.S. men and from 3 percent to 5 percent of all U.S. women. However, lesbian and gay advocates say that these estimates are too low—that more than 10 percent of the population primarily engages in same-sex relationships and an even higher percentage is bisexual (Weinberg et al., 1994).

From a global perspective, homosexuality has existed in most societies throughout human history. Nevertheless, for most of the last two thousand years, there have been groups—sometimes entire societies—that considered homosexuality "a crime against nature," "an abomination," or "a sin" (Doyle, 1995: 224). Most societies have norms pertaining to *sexuality*—attitudes, beliefs, and practices related to **sexual attraction and intimate relationships with others.** The norms are based on the assumption that some forms of attraction and sexual relationships are *normal* and *appropriate* while others are *abnormal* and

inappropriate. Thus in many societies, homosexual conduct is classified as a form of *deviance*—**a behavior, belief, or condition that violates social norms.** This classification may make people targets of prejudice, discrimination, and even death. Extreme prejudice directed at gay men and lesbians is known as *homophobia*—**excessive fear or intolerance of homosexuality.** According to sociologists, homophobia is a *socially determined prejudice,* not a medically recognized *phobia* (Lehne, 1995). Homophobia is intensified by the ideology of *compulsory heterosexism,* a belief system that denies, denigrates, and stigmatizes any gay, lesbian, or bisexual behavior, identity, relationship, or community. Somewhat like institutional racism and sexism, compulsory heterosexism is embedded in the society's social structure and maintained by ideologies that are rooted in religion and law (Herek, 1995).

IDEOLOGICAL BASES OF INEQUALITY BASED ON SEXUAL ORIENTATION

Social analysts such as Bruce Bawer (1994:81), an author and cultural critic, believe that homophobia differs significantly from other forms of bigotry:

> In a world of prejudice, there is no other prejudice quite like [homophobia]. Mainstream writers, politicians, and cultural leaders who hate Jews or blacks or Asians but who have long since accepted the unwritten rules that forbid public expression of those prejudices still denounce gays with impunity. For such people, gays are the Other in a way that Jews or blacks or Asians are not. After all, they can look at Jewish or black or Asian family life and see something that, in its chief components—husband, wife, children, workplace, school, house of worship—is essentially a variation of their own lives; yet when they look at gays—or, rather, at the image of gays that has been fostered both by the mainstream culture and by the gay subculture—they see creatures whose lives seem to be different from theirs in every possible way.

According to Bawer, other people cannot identify with the daily lives of lesbians and gay men, who—unlike heterosexuals—exist as identifiable categories primarily because there is such strong antigay prejudice in the United States. In fact, the stereotypic beliefs that dominant (heterosexual) group members hold about gay men and lesbians are a major impediment to achieving gay rights and reducing inequalities based on sexual orientation (Nava and Dawidoff, 1994).

Stereotypic beliefs about lesbians and gay men often equate people's sexual *orientation* with sexual *practice*. For example, all gay men and lesbians—regardless of the nature and extent of their sexual activity—are stereotyped as being "sex obsessed, sexually compulsive, and sexually predatory" (Nava and Dawidoff, 1994:32). Media depictions tend to reinforce stereotypes of gay men as sexual exploiters or "limp-wristed sissies," while lesbians are "stomping macho soldiers" (Nava and Dawidoff, 1994:32). Recently, daytime television talk shows have focused on gays, lesbians, bisexuals, and transsexuals (people who believe they were born with the body of the wrong sex). Although some shows have given voice to gay rights issues, most reinforce negative stereotypes and present show participants and viewers with excuses for ridiculing, bashing, and even killing gay people (see Box 6.1).

◢ Religion and Sexual Orientation

Most of the major religions of the world—including Judaism, Christianity, Islam, Hinduism, and Confucianism—historically have regarded homosexuality as a sin. Buddhism is the only major world religion that does not condemn homosexuality (Dynes, 1990). Religious fundamentalists in particular denounce homosexual conduct as a sign of great moral decay and societal chaos. In the Judeo-Christian tradition, religious condemnation of homosexuality derives from both the Hebrew Scriptures (e.g., Genesis 19 and Leviticus 18:33) and the New Testament (e.g., Romans 1:26-27 and I Corinthians 6:9) (Kosmin and Lachman, 1993).

During the 1990s, same-sex marriages and the ordination of "practicing" lesbians and gay men have been vigorously debated. For example, the Vatican directed Roman Catholic bishops in the United States to oppose laws that protect homosexuals, promote public acceptance of homosexual conduct, or give gay relationships equal footing with traditional, heterosexual marriage. However, many Roman Catholics disagreed with the directive, stating that it

is based on the faulty assumption that lesbians and gay men seek to influence the sexual orientation of children or youths with whom they live or work; that gay people are erotically attracted to every person of their own gender; and that they cannot control their sexual impulses in same-sex environments (cited in Bawer, 1994). Roman Catholics are not the only religious group debating this controversial issue: The Southern Baptist Convention voted to expel two congregations—one for blessing the union of two gay men and the other for licensing a gay divinity student to preach. Although Baptist congregations typically are allowed to be autonomous, religious leaders determined that this autonomy did not extend to "acts to affirm, approve or endorse homosexual behavior" because they are deemed to be "contrary to the Bible on human sexuality and the sanctity of the family" (cited in Kosmin and Lachman, 1993:230). Episcopalians have been debating for two decades whether or not "practicing homosexuals" should be ordained. In 1996, an Episcopal bishop was accused of heresy for ordaining a gay deacon (Niebuhr, 1996; Dunlap, 1996).

Increasing numbers of lesbians and gay men are carving out their own niches in religious organizations. Some gay and lesbian people have sought to bring about changes in established religious denominations; others have formed religious bodies, such as the Metropolitan Community Church, that focus on the spiritual needs of the gay community. However, many gay men and lesbians believe that they should not have to choose between full participation in their church and committed same-sex relationships (Dunlap, 1996).

◢ Law and Sexual Orientation

Throughout U.S. history, moral and religious teachings have been intertwined with laws that criminalize homosexual conduct. It is important to note that law deals with homosexual *conduct* differently from the way it deals with *homosexuality*. To be a homosexual is not a crime, but to engage in homosexual conduct is a crime in some states. Although fewer states today have *sodomy laws* that criminalize oral or anal intercourse between persons of the same sex, about twenty states have laws pertaining to "deviant sexual conduct," "crimes against nature," or "unnatural intercourse" whereby people can still be imprisoned for oral or anal intercourse. According to lesbian and gay

SOCIAL PROBLEMS

IN THE MEDIA

BOX 6.1

Do Tell: Sexual Orientation and Daytime TV Talk Shows

Recently, sociologist Joshua Gamson (1996) suggested that TV talk shows give voice to people who have been silenced by social norms and public policy, including gay men, lesbians, bisexuals, and transsexuals. However, TV talk shows also may subject people to ridicule, harassment, and even violence. For example, the taping of a *Jenny Jones* episode about "Secret Crushes on People of the Same Sex" ended in a killing, as Gamson (1996:81–82) explains:

When Scott Amedure appeared on a "secret admirer" episode of the Jenny Jones Show, the admired Jon Schmitz was apparently expecting a female admirer. Schmitz, not warming to Amedure's fantasy of tying him up in a hammock and spraying whipping cream and champagne on his body, declared himself "100 percent heterosexual." Later, back in Michigan, he punctuated this claim by shooting Amedure with a 12-gauge shotgun, telling police that the embarrassment from the program had "eaten away" at him.

Media critics immediately blamed Amedure's killing on the show, calling it an ambush; however, Jenny Jones claims this was not true:

Getting the news was so shocking—I was devastated. But [it] had nothing to do with the show. We have no responsibility whatsoever because [Schmitz] was not misled. All the guests knew that [the secret admirer] could be a man or a woman—it's very clear [from phone logs and producer's notes] that he did know. This was not an ambush show. (cited in Green, 1995:42).

Why are real people willing to expose their private lives for public consumption? Why do talk shows often include on-camera surprises—such as the encounter between Amedure and Schmitz—that are calculated to embarrass guests? According to some analysts, guests and television audiences are victimized by the programs, which analysts say are "a case study in rot" (Dell'Angela and Anderson, 1995). However, other analysts believe that most guests are savvy about what they are

---

rights advocates, these laws are unconstitutional or indefensible for two reasons: (1) If the acts are conducted between consenting adults in *private,* they should not be subject to criminal sanction because any reported violation invades the privacy of their relationship; and (2) some states criminalize this conduct only if it is between persons of the same sex. However, in 1986, in *Bowers* v. *Hardwick,* the U.S. Supreme Court ruled that people do not have a constitutionally protected right to engage in private homosexual conduct. On a legal level, the decision upheld state laws banning sodomy whether or not the conduct is between persons of the same sex. But as a

matter of practicality, the court's decision has very different consequences for heterosexuals and homosexuals—for whom it virtually eliminates protection for sexual activities and creates the impression that gay or lesbian couples have *no* privacy rights (Aday, 1990). In fact, Justice Harry A. Blackmun's dissenting opinion in this case stated that the Supreme Court had invited the state to "invade the houses, hearts and minds of citizens who choose to live their life differently" (cited in Nagourney, 1996:E4).

In several decisions since *Bowers* v. *Hardwick,* the Supreme Court has been called on to rule on civil rights issues pertaining to lesbians and gay men.

doing when they appear on a show. Some have a grievance they want to air or a cause they want to push; others want a free trip to the taping or hope to be "discovered" for a television or movie career (Kolbert, 1995).

From the standpoint of the shows' producers, directors, and stars, it is no secret why the episodes are planned as they are: ratings and profits. Successful talk shows such as *Jenny Jones* and *Ricki Lake* generate profits of $50 million to $60 million a year, primarily from advertising revenue, because the shows attract the younger viewing audiences that advertisers want to reach (Carter, 1995). The way to high advertising revenue is high ratings; the way to high ratings is large viewing audiences. Apparently, many audiences like to watch guests who talk about forbidden topics, get into embarrassing situations, and cause audience members to take sides.

From this viewpoint, the show taped with Amedure and Schmitz fits the criteria for a top-notch episode. In fact, after the taping, but before the killing, the producers decided to delay broadcasting "Secret Crushes on People of the Same Sex" until "sweeps week" so they could get high audience ratings (Carter, 1995). After the killing, of course, they did not air the show at all. Nevertheless, the story that began

on a television show ended up on television as viewers of *Court TV* watched live broadcasts of the trial, conviction, and sentencing of Schmitz to twenty-five to fifty years in prison for the murder of Amedure.

The attorneys defending Schmitz claimed that he had been so "humiliated" by Amedure's advances that he had snapped and shot his admirer. Many viewers took a similar stance. According to sociologist Verta Taylor, the fact that so many people identified with Schmitz's "humiliation" at the thought that people might think he is gay indicates that accusing someone of being gay "is still the worst thing you could say to someone" (cited in Moss, 1996:39). Gay rights advocate Jeffrey Montgomery suggests that people should rethink this assumption: "What is so humiliating about being thought of as gay? It's a deep question that gets into how schools educate students, how religious institutions talk about homosexuality, what gets said around the water cooler, and what gets discussed at the dinner table" (cited in Moss, 1996:39).

Do television talk shows such as *Jenny Jones* give voice to people who have been silenced by social norms and public policy, or do they tend to exploit the powerless? What do you think?

For example, in 1996, the Court struck down an initiative that Colorado voters had passed, which banned all measures protecting gay men and lesbians against discrimination (Nagourney, 1996). The initiative was a reaction to ordinances passed by Colorado municipalities such as Boulder, Denver, and Aspen that barred discrimination against lesbians and gay men (N. A. Lewis, 1995a). Many gay rights issues—including those pertaining to same-sex marriages—appear to be won or lost on a case-by-case or state-by-state basis, and some gay rights advocates believe that the fight for equality is far from over (Bawer, 1994).

DISCRIMINATION BASED ON SEXUAL ORIENTATION

As campaigns are waged for equal rights and an end to antigay discrimination, more people have come forward to declare that they are gay, lesbian, or bisexual and to indicate their support for gay organizations. Many lesbian or gay couples have sought the statutory right to marry, to obtain custody of their children if they are fit parents, to adopt, and to have their property pass to one another at death—in sum, to do all the things that people in heterosexual

Reprinted by permission.

marriages are permitted to do. However, because ideas about marriage and the family are at the core of many people's moral or religious objections to homosexuality, gay marriage is among the most controversial social issues as we approach the twenty-first century.

Lack of Marital Rights

In the United States, many gay or lesbian couples cohabit because they cannot enter into a legally recognized marital relationship. In *cohabitation*, partners live together without being legally married. Although some gay men and lesbians take part in social or religious ceremonies of marriage (for example, in 1993, more than 3,000 couples participated in a mass wedding at a national gay rights march in Washington, D.C.), their unions are not legally sanctioned.

Over the past few years, some cities and states have given legal recognition to *domestic partnerships*—household partnerships in which an unmarried couple lives together in a committed, sexually intimate relationship and is granted the same rights and benefits accorded to heterosexual couples (Aulette, 1994). Many gay rights advocates consider recognition of domestic partnerships a major step

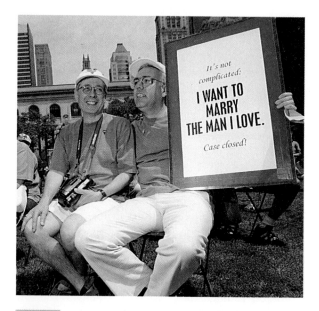

Legal analysts suggest that the U.S. Supreme Court eventually will be called on to determine the issue of same-sex marriages. In the meantime, gay rights advocates continue to fight for legal recognition of such marriages, while opponents wage an ongoing battle against legalized marriage for lesbians or gay men.

forward because employment benefits—including health insurance coverage—that are offered to legal spouses (in heterosexual marriages) also are offered to partners of unmarried employees. In this way, domestic partnership agreements benefit all unmarried cohabiting couples, gay and straight. However, certain rights come only with a marriage license and cannot be exercised by unmarried couples. These rights include "the right to joint parenting, through birth or adoption; the right to file joint income tax returns; legal immigration and residency for partners from other countries; benefits such as annuities, pensions, and Social Security for surviving spouses; wrongful death benefits for surviving partners; and immunity from having to testify in court against a spouse" (Findlen, 1995:90).

Gay rights advocates continue to fight for legal recognition of same-sex marriages and recently declared a major victory. The State of Hawaii made the first move toward issuing marriage licenses to same-sex couples after a long series of political and legal battles during the mid- to late-1990s. Realizing that the Hawaiian courts might recognize same-sex marriages, Congress enacted the 1996 Defense of Marriage Act that allows states to deny recognition of same-sex marriages that might be accorded full legal status in other states (Tribe, 1996). But the Defense of Marriage Act will no doubt be challenged on the basis of the U.S. Constitution's "full faith and credit" clause, which provides that laws enacted in one state must be recognized by other states. For example, every state recognizes heterosexual marriages performed in other states. Nevertheless, many people apparently are not ready to support legally sanctioned gay marriages. In a 1996 *New York Times* poll, for instance, fewer than 40 percent of respondents said they supported gay marriage, in contrast to 85 percent—a wide majority—who said they supported equal rights for gays in the workplace (Gover, 1996a).

Parental Rights

There are as many as 5 million lesbian mothers and 3 million gay fathers in the United States. An estimated 6 million to 14 million children have a gay or lesbian parent (Patterson, 1992). Some gay fathers and lesbian mothers have children from relationships with opposite-sex partners, and sometimes the other biological parent seeks custody of the children on the grounds that the lesbian or gay parent is "unfit" be-

cause of sexual orientation. In several widely publicized cases, lesbian mothers have lost custody of their children when their fitness was challenged in court by ex-spouses or the children's grandparents (Gover, 1996a). Gay fathers sometimes face double jeopardy in child custody struggles: Both their sexual orientation and the widespread belief that women make better parents may work against them (Gover, 1996a).

Parental rights are a pressing concern for gay or lesbian partners who are raising children together, particularly when only one partner is legally recognized as the parent or guardian. Many couples rely on legal documents such as special powers of attorney, wills, and guardianship agreements to protect both partners' rights, but these documents do not have the legal force of formal adoption (Bruni, 1996). As more lesbian couples choose donor insemination to become parents, new issues arise about the rights of nonbiological gay parents, whose claims often are the least recognized (Gover, 1996c). In recent court custody cases, nonbiological parents have had no standing because they have neither biological nor legal ties to the child. Some lesbian and gay couples draft their own parenting contracts, but these agreements generally are not enforceable in court and can be revoked by the biological parent at any time (Gover, 1996c). As more states allow unmarried partners—whether gay or straight—to adopt children, more same-sex couples will probably seek joint legal custody of their children. However, the process is extremely time consuming and expensive as well as a great invasion of personal privacy (Bruni, 1996).

Many gay men and lesbians experience discrimination when they seek to become foster parents or to adopt a child. Widespread myths about the "homosexual lifestyle" lead to the notion that children living with lesbian or gay parents may witness immoral conduct or be recruited into homosexuality (Singer and Deschamps, 1994). In fact, research shows that children raised by lesbian or gay parents typically are well adjusted, and the parents often serve as role models for equal sharing in the family (Sullivan, 1996).

Gay rights advocates are cautiously optimistic that social norms and laws are gradually changing so that sexual orientation alone will no longer be grounds for denying parental custody or visitation rights to lesbian or gay parents and that courts will rule solely on the basis of which parent can provide a better home for the child (Goldberg, 1996a).

Housing Discrimination

In recent years, opponents of gay rights have worked to pass state constitutional amendments removing existing protection afforded to gay men, lesbians, and bisexuals against discrimination in housing, public accommodations, and other areas of life. Carrying signs that say "God Made Adam and Eve, NOT Adam and Steve," for example, opponents of gay rights maintain that they are not "bashing gays" but rather are upholding the family (Dunlap, 1995:10).

Some lesbian and gay people are denied housing because they are gay; others are evicted from apartments where they have lived for some period of time. Even those who successfully rent or purchase property tend to remain targets of discrimination from some heterosexual residents, building managers, and custodial personnel, as Bruce Bawer explains:

> When two gay people decide to move in together, they commit themselves to insult and discrimination and attack. At one apartment building in which [a male partner] and I lived, the superintendent spit on me one day without provocation; at our next address, members of the building staff, not knowing that I understood Spanish, joked with one another in my presence about the maricones (faggots). Living alone, most gay people can conceal their sexuality; living together, a gay couple advertise theirs every time they step out of the house together. (Bawer, 1994:254)

Discrimination in Medical Care

Like housing, medical care is not exempt from discrimination based on sexual orientation. Recent studies by the American Medical Association have found that some physicians do not ask about patients' sexual orientation, and many lesbians and gay men do not tell (*JAMA*, 1996). Consequently, in making diagnoses, physicians may overlook diseases that gay men or lesbians are more prone to contract. For example, gay men's risk of developing anal cancer is 25 to 84 times higher than that of heterosexual men (*JAMA*, 1996). Gay men also have a greater

likelihood than heterosexual men of acquiring gastrointestinal and rectal diseases.

Some physicians and nurses adopt a judgmental stance when dealing with gay and lesbian patients. For example, one study of 100 nurses teaching in nursing programs found that 34 percent believed that lesbians are "disgusting" and 17 percent believed that lesbians molest children (Stevens, 1992). Other physicians and nurses may provide reduced care to gays and lesbians or deny them medical care altogether (*JAMA*, 1996). For example, lesbians have a greater risk for terminal breast or ovarian cancer because doctors may not provide adequate information about the importance of early cancer detection through routine gynecological examinations and mammography screening (Gessen, 1993).

Probably the most controversial topic in health care for gay men, lesbians, and bisexuals is HIV/AIDS. Although physicians, dentists, nurses, and other health professionals may learn about treating patients who are HIV-positive, many feel inadequate to deal with these patients' psychological and social needs. Today, HIV/AIDS is the eighth leading cause of death in the United States. It is the top cause of death among men between the ages of twenty-five and forty-four and the fourth leading cause of death among women in the same age group (U.S. Bureau of the Census, 1996b). Despite the prevalence of HIV/AIDS among gay men and bisexuals in certain age groups, many medical professionals do not inform their patients about risks associated with various types of sexual conduct and intravenous drug use or about measures that could be taken to prevent exposure to sexually transmitted diseases and the HIV virus. Although HIV/AIDS has been referred to as "the gay disease," social analysts suggest that it should be viewed as *everyone's* problem (see Chapter 11).

Occupational Discrimination

Fearing that they might be stigmatized or discriminated against in the workplace, many gay and lesbian people do not reveal their sexual orientation (Woods, 1993). Their fears have some ground in reality. Despite laws in many states prohibiting discrimination in employment on the basis of sexual orientation, openly lesbian and gay people often experience bias in hiring, retention, and promotion in private and public sector employment. More than 100 major companies have stated that they do not discriminate on the basis of sexual orientation. Nevertheless, studies show that about two-thirds of gay employees in private sector employment such as small businesses and large corporations have witnessed some type of hostility, harassment, or discrimination toward lesbians or gay men at their place of employment (Singer and Deschamps, 1994). Many chief executive officers are reluctant to put a lesbian or gay man at the top of the corporate hierarchy, and some employees express concern about working around gay men and lesbians (Woods, 1993). Many who do not reveal their sexual orientation to coworkers are nonetheless subjected to a general disparagement of gays, as Brian, a gay executive in a large New York corporation, explains:

> I was in an office with the boss and another person who is my same level, and we were talking about another professional that we should probably get involved in this transaction. The person who was at the same level as me said, "Oh, he's really good, but he's a flaming faggot." What was very shocking to me was that it was an attack on this person in a professional context. You are sort of used to the way straight men sort of banter around, calling each other queer, on a social level. But it's really strange when they talk about it in a professional setting. But this person thought it was okay. I assume that he thought there were three straight men there, so he could still say these things that in mixed company he would never say. (quoted in Mead, 1994:40)

Worse than derogatory office banter about gay men and lesbians is the fact that supervisors do not take same-sex sexual harassment seriously. Victims of harassment may be blamed for causing the incident, and many fear they will lose their job if they file a grievance. The Equal Employment Opportunity Commission, a federal agency, acknowledges that same-sex sexual harassment occurs in the workplace; but to prove sexual harassment, victims must show that the harasser targeted a specific category of people such as gay men. As a result, charges of same-sex sexual harassment reflect the victim's sexual orientation, which gay rights advocates believe should be irrelevant in determining whether harassment has occurred (Gover, 1996b).

Same-sex sexual harassment and blatant discrimination in hiring and promotion are also prob-

lems in public sector positions in the federal and state government and local law enforcement agencies. Consider the blatant discrimination of an executive order signed in 1953 by President Dwight D. Eisenhower mandating that "sexual perverts" be fired from federal jobs. For many years, most law enforcement agencies and police departments did not employ lesbian or gay people. For example, until 1993, the Dallas police department refused to hire gay men or lesbians because of Texas sodomy laws criminalizing same-sex conduct. Today, many more gay and lesbian people are employed in law enforcement agencies throughout the country because of antibias policies that preclude the agencies from asking job applicants questions about their sexual orientation. Despite such provisions, sociologist Stephen Leinen (who is a former lieutenant in the New York City police department) found in his study of "gay cops" that many remain "totally closeted" for fear of how other police officers and other gay people will treat them. The total secrecy among lesbians and gay men in many large police departments was illustrated by one gay police officer's surprise on learning that his partner, with whom he had worked for some time, also was gay: "I was deeply shocked when he told me. We had worked together for over three years and neither of us knew about the other. He said, 'How the hell could we have worked together for so long and neither one of us knew it?'" (Leinen, 1993:3)

In recent years, some gay advocates have encouraged people to "come out" (identify their sexual orientation) at work and to make the biases against people based on their sexual orientation known to the media and the general public so that demands for change will be met. The assumption is that, as long as people remain "in the closet," workplace discrimination will not be eliminated (Nava and Dawidoff, 1994). However, extensive media coverage about openly lesbian and gay soldiers in the U.S. armed forces has not led to lifting the ban against gays and lesbians in the military.

Discrimination in the Military

According to the U.S. military—the nation's largest employer—lesbians and gay men are unfit to serve their country, especially if they make their sexual orientation known to others. Although many closeted gay men and lesbians have served in various branches of the military over the years, the official government policy was one of exclusion, based on the assumption that homosexuals are a security risk because they might be blackmailed by someone who found out about their sexual orientation. Accordingly, tens of thousands of gay and lesbian military service personnel have sought to appear as conventional as possible and behave exactly like heterosexual people in order to keep their positions. This course of action often has devastating personal consequences for closeted soldiers and sailors (see Shilts, 1993).

After an attempt by the Clinton administration to lift the ban on gays in the military led to an outcry by many military and religious leaders, a compromise policy known as "don't ask, don't tell" was implemented. Essentially, the policy states that commanders may no longer ask about a serviceperson's sexual orientation, and gay men and lesbians can serve in the military as long as they do not reveal their sexual orientation. While some social analysts believe this policy provides gay men and lesbians with the same opportunity to serve their country as heterosexual people, others believe that this compromise is a form of institutionalized discrimination: "while heterosexuals would continue to enjoy their right to lead private lives and to discuss those lives freely, gays would be allowed to remain in the armed forces only so long as they did not mention that they were gay or lesbian or have relationships on or off base" (Bawer, 1994:61).

A recent study by the Servicemembers Legal Defense Network appears to support the belief that the "don't ask, don't tell" policy has led to differential treatment of some gay men and lesbians in the military. Some commanders continue to ask about sexual orientation, and the number of soldiers, sailors, Marines, and Air Force personnel discharged for homosexuality increased by 17 percent between 1994 and 1995, the latest years for which figures are available. Internal Navy documents show, for example, that the Navy sought evidence of homosexual conduct if sailors acknowledged being gay or were reported to have told friends or others that they were gay. In some cases, heterosexual women indicated that they were falsely accused of being lesbians after they filed sexual assault or sexual harassment charges against male military personnel (Shenon, 1996c). In other cases, gay men have been victims of hate crimes, perhaps because of the government's

highly equivocal position on lesbians and gay men in the armed services.

Victimization and Hate Crimes

Before the early 1990s, hate crimes against gays and lesbians were not acknowledged as such, even though civil rights groups had been tracking growing violence motivated by group prejudice for over a decade. Few acts of violence against gays and lesbians were ever reported in the media.

Hate crimes appear to be most prevalent where homophobic attitudes and behaviors are tolerated or at least overlooked. For example, the military's "don't ask, don't tell" policy may have exacerbated the problem of hate crimes in the military. In one case, a sailor who killed a gay shipmate because he hated homosexuals stated, "I regret that this incident happened and I feel like it could have been averted had homosexuals not been allowed in the military" (Sterngold, 1993:A11). Shortly before the attack, the victim had informed the ship's commander that he was homosexual. While the Navy was in the process of discharging him, the victim's killer stalked him through a park and into a public toilet, then punched and kicked him until he was dead. The injuries inflicted were as severe as if the victim had been killed in "a high-speed auto accident or low-speed airplane crash" (Jameson, 1993:A6). Documents later released by the Navy indicated that hostile attitudes toward gay and lesbian people were tolerated—if not condoned—by officers and sailors on the victim's ship (Sterngold, 1993).

In other incidents around the country, pipe-wielding youths yelling "kill the faggot" beat a gay man unconscious in Laguna Beach, California; a gay man was so seriously injured in an act of "gay bashing" in Boston that doctors initially believed he might not survive; and another gay man was killed by an antigay cruiser who had "picked up" his victim on the Internet (Meers, 1996). Lesbians also have been assaulted, raped, and sometimes killed when they have been seen in public with their partners (Dunlap, 1995).

Before enactment of the Hate Crimes Statistics Act of 1990, hate crimes were classified as such only on the basis of race, ethnicity, or religion. Gay rights advocates argued that not including sexual orientation in the law created a double standard in the United States: Crimes against gays and lesbians

SOCIAL PROBLEMS
AND SOCIAL POLICY

BOX 6.2

School's Out: Closing the Books on Homophobia

History, as taught, is devoid of gays or lesbians. Without knowing that history, it's no surprise that many consider their present-day presence strange or unnatural.
> —Kevin Jennings, founder of the Gay Lesbian Straight Teachers Network (cited in Seavor, 1996:E11)

Recently, some U.S. schools modified their curricula to incorporate information on lesbians, gays, and bisexuals. However, journalist Dan Woog (1995), author of a recent book on the impact of gay and lesbian issues in schools, suggests that much remains to be done. According to Woog, there should be at least one advocate within the administration of each school to address gay issues—a person who is available to gay, lesbian, and bisexual students; who makes sure that schools comply with their responsibility to all students; and who helps with referrals to outside support groups, counseling agencies, hot lines, and organizations for family members. Woog also suggests that schools define harassment on the basis of sexual orientation and make clear that inappropriate use of language, jokes, graffiti, and vandalism based on sexual orientation is unfair, offensive, and harmful to everyone in the school community. He argues that the contributions of lesbians, gay men, and bisexuals should be discussed routinely in all classes, including history, literature, art, music, science, and athletics. Gay and lesbian materials should be included on reading lists and as possible topics for written assignments and class presentations. School libraries should include openly bisexual, lesbian, and gay books; and all students should be encouraged to read them to obtain a greater understanding and a higher level of tolerance—or acceptance—of those whose sexual orientation differs from their own.

Woog believes that if every school in this nation followed these suggestions, homophobic attitudes and hate crimes would be reduced, and students would learn the importance of treating other people with the same dignity and respect that they want to receive themselves.

Thinking about your own educational experiences, have you been provided with information about the contributions of gay men, lesbians, and bisexuals to U.S. history, the social sciences, literature, and other areas of study? Do you agree with Woog that including bisexuals, gay men, and lesbians throughout the curriculum would bring about greater tolerance and perhaps eventual acceptance of people regardless of their sexual orientation? Why or why not?

---

would be classified as "less significant, less pervasive, and less reprehensible" than crimes motivated by racial, religious, or ethnic prejudice. In contrast, some senators argued that the law gave undue protection and respectability to gays and lesbians (Fernandez, 1991). Information gathered since passage of the Hate Crimes Act shows that over 50 percent of all reported antigay harassment and violence is perpetrated by young males age twenty-one or under (Comstock, 1991). In some situations, police officers and judges may not take hate crimes against lesbians and gay men seriously. According to a former Dallas judge, "I put prostitutes and queers at the same level . . . and I'd be hard-put to give somebody life for killing a prostitute" (quoted in Singer and Deschamps, 1994:68). One way (see Box 6.2) to decrease homophobia and hate crimes, say some social analysts, is to change school curricula.

PERSPECTIVES ON SEXUAL ORIENTATION AND SOCIAL INEQUALITY

Sexual orientation and social inequality can be understood from various perspectives. Biologists take one approach, and psychologists take another. Sociological explanations focus primarily on how sexual orientation and homophobia are associated with social learning and/or social structural factors in society. We'll look at each perspective separately.

Biological and Psychological Perspectives

If biologists determined that sexual orientation is genetic in origin and that gay men and lesbians do not choose to be homosexuals, would homophobia decrease? There is no simple answer to this question, but some gay advocates applaud recent studies that suggest sexual orientation may be determined by a person's genetic inheritance. According to this view, gay men and lesbians cannot be blamed for their sexual orientation because homosexuality—like heterosexuality—is an ascribed characteristic, present from birth, that cannot be changed through counseling or therapy.

Research over the past decade has produced evidence that sexual orientation may be partially linked to genetic inheritance. For example, some researchers believe they have isolated a specific marker on the sex chromosome that may increase the likelihood of homosexuality among members of the same family (LeVay and Hamer, 1994). Other researchers are searching for a "gay gene" in studies of twins. So far, they have found some support for the presence of a gay gene in their studies of identical twins (who have the same genetic material) and fraternal twins (who share some, but not all, genetic material) by documenting that identical twins are much more likely to both be gay (if one is gay) than are fraternal twins (see Bailey and Pillard, 1991; Bailey and Benishay, 1993). Researchers have also identified an area on the X chromosome (but not the specific gene) that might carry the predisposition for

homosexuality (see Angier, 1993; Travis, 1995). Although these studies may be promising, critics suggest that biological explanations alone cannot account for sexual orientation (Doyle, 1995).

Unlike biologists, who typically focus on genetic determinants of sexual orientation, psychologists associate homosexuality with mental processes and childhood experiences. Early psychological approaches considered homosexuality a form of *maladjustment*. Sigmund Freud, founder of the psychoanalytic approach, believed that humans are constitutionally bisexual—meaning that masculine and feminine currents coexist in everyone—but children over time move toward adult heterosexuality. According to Freud, not everyone makes it down the difficult path to heterosexuality because it is fraught with dangers and problems. For example, sons whose mothers are domineering and overprotective have more difficulty achieving heterosexuality. Following in Freud's footsteps, later psychologists generally equated heterosexuality with good mental health and homosexuality with mental illness (see Bieber et al., 1962).

In 1942, the American Psychiatric Association formally classified homosexuality as a form of mental illness and suggested that treatments ranging from castration to electroshock therapy might remedy the problem (Marcus, 1992). However, the Association's classification did not go undisputed. By administering standard personality tests to two groups of men—one heterosexual and the other homosexual—and asking a panel of psychiatrists and psychologists to tell her the sexual orientation of each subject on the basis of those tests, psychologist Evelyn Hooker (1957; 1958) showed that not all homosexuals are maladjusted or mentally ill. The judges were unable to differentiate between the heterosexuals and homosexuals. In 1973, the American Psychiatric Association removed homosexuality from its list of mental disorders.

Today, many psychologists believe that biological and psychosocial factors interact in the formation of sexual orientation. Psychologist Daryl J. Bem, for example, thinks that genetic factors and gender roles in childhood interact to produce sexual orientation. According to Bem, "In most societies, including our own, most boys and girls are raised so that they tend to feel more similar to children of their own sex and different from children of the opposite sex" (cited in Shea, 1996:A11). These feelings of similarity and difference are often formed on the playground, where boys are more aggressive than girls. Over time, children's belief that people of the opposite gender are different—and somewhat mysterious—translates into heterosexual desire. However, some children see themselves as more similar to children of the opposite gender. For example, boys who do not like rough-and-tumble play or sports but like to play with dolls or other "girls' toys" may grow up feeling different from other boys. Similarly, girls who prefer "boys' sports" frequently feel awkward around other girls. According to Bem, the best predictor of sexual orientation is the degree to which children are gender-conforming or nonconforming; children who fit in sometimes but not others are likely to become bisexual.

Advocates of Bem's theory point out that it is supported by earlier studies showing that 66 percent of gay men (compared to 10 percent of heterosexual men) did not enjoy activities typical of their own gender. Critics point out that Bem's theory does not take into account the fact that what is defined as gender-appropriate behavior differs widely across cultures and over time. For example, girls who wanted to play soccer thirty years ago might have been viewed as tomboys with few female friends, but today, many girls—and boys—play soccer, and their sports participation does not single them out as different from others of their gender. Nor does Bem's theory explain the stages in the process of taking on a homosexual identity or how labeling by others may influence people's perceptions of themselves as homosexual, heterosexual, or bisexual.

▲ Interactionist Perspectives

In contrast with the biological and psychological perspectives, interactionist perspectives focus on heterosexual and homosexual conduct as learned behavior and on the process by which individuals come to identify themselves as gay, lesbian, bisexual, or straight. According to interactionists, most people acquire the status of *heterosexual* without being consciously aware of it because heterosexuality is the established norm and they do not have to struggle over their identity. But the same is not true of people who identify themselves as *homosexual* or *bisexual*. In fact, some sociologists suggest that sexual orientation is a master status for many gay men, lesbians, and bisexuals (Schur, 1965). **A *master status* is the most significant status a person possesses**

because it largely determines how individuals view themselves and how they are treated by others. Master status based on sexual orientation is particularly significant when it is linked to other subordinate racial-ethnic group statuses. For example, working-class gay Latinos are more hesitant than white, middle-class gay men to come out to their families because of cultural norms pertaining to *machismo* (masculinity) and fear that relatives will withdraw the support that is essential for surviving at the subordinate end of race and class hierarchies (see Almaguer, 1995).

Interactionists have identified several stages in the process of accepting the identity of lesbian, gay, or bisexual (Weinberg et al., 1994). First, people experience identity confusion—a situation in which they feel different from other people and struggle with admitting that they are attracted to individuals of the same sex. For example, someone who identified himself as a fourteen-year-old boy posted the following note on an Internet newsgroup:

> I feel like my life is over. Am I gay? God, I hope not. I walk around going, "God, I hope not." I walk around going, "Do I like him?" "Do I like her?" "How would it feel to do it with him/her?" WHY DOES THIS HAVE TO HAPPEN TO ME!! The funny thing is, I absolutely detest everything about sex with men, and relationships with men. But somehow, I feel attracted to them anyway!! (Gabriel, 1995b:1)

In the past, many gay and lesbian people had nowhere to turn in their quest for answers and support from others; today, many use the Internet and other forms of global communication to connect with others who share their concerns (Gabriel, 1995b).

The second stage in establishing a lesbian or gay identity is seeking out others who are openly lesbian or gay and perhaps engaging in sexual experimentation or making other forays into the homosexual subculture. In the third stage, people attempt to integrate their self-concept and acceptance of a label such as "homosexual," "gay," or "lesbian" by pursuing a way of life that conforms to their definition of what those labels mean (Cass, 1984; Coleman, 1981/2; Ponse, 1978). Like most "stage" theories, however, not all people go through these stages. Even those who do may not go through each stage

Individuals seem to accept their identities as lesbian, gay, or bisexual in stages. Initially there is identity confusion. But seeking out others who are open about their sexual orientation and experimenting sexually can eventually lead to acceptance.

in the same way, and some may move back and forth between stages (Weinberg et al., 1994).

Research on how people come to accept their sexual identity as a gay man, bisexual, or lesbian shows the significance of labeling and how it can create barriers to full participation in U.S. society. However, these studies are typically based on a relatively narrow selection of people, which makes it difficult to generalize the findings to larger populations. That is, respondents who openly identify themselves as gay or bisexual may not be characteristic of the larger homosexual or bisexual population (Weinberg et al., 1994).

Functionalist and Conflict Perspectives

Unlike the interactionist approach, which focuses primarily on how individuals come to identify themselves as homosexual, bisexual, or heterosexual, functionalist perspectives focus on the relationship between social structure and sexual orientation. To functionalists, social norms and laws are established to preserve social institutions and maintain stability in society. Many societies punish homosexual con-

duct because it violates social norms that prohibit both nonmarital sex and same-sex sexual relations. Sociologist David P. Aday, Jr., provides an overview of this perspective:

> Marriage and family are structural arrangements that contribute to the continuity of our contemporary society. . . . [Homosexuality undermines] arrangements that currently operate to replace societal members in an orderly way—that is, the arrangement has survival value. . . . If homosexual conduct were allowed to exist unchallenged and unpunished, then it might in time undermine norms and laws that underpin monogamous marital sex, at least some of which results in the production of offspring to repopulate the society. . . . The punishment of homosexual conduct, from ridicule and discrimination to imprisonment, reinforces expectations about heterosexual and marital sex and defines the boundaries of society. (Aday, 1990:25)

The functionalist perspective explains why some people do not believe homosexual conduct or marriages between lesbian or gay couples should be protected legally. It also explains the call by some reli-

Does this photo tend to support or reject some functionalist analysts' assumption that gay or lesbian families destroy "family values" in this country? Why or why not?

gious and political leaders for a renewal of "family values" in this country. According to this approach, homosexuality undermines social institutions and jeopardizes the stability of society (Aday, 1990).

Critics suggest that the functionalist approach supports the status quo and ignores a need for new definitions of marriage and family. If marriage is understood to be the decision of two people to live together in a partnership—be a family—then the intention or the capacity to have children should not be a condition. Today, nothing but custom mandates that marital partners must be of different genders (Nava and Dawidoff, 1994).

Whereas the functionalist approach focuses on how existing social arrangements create a balance in society, the conflict approach focuses on *tensions* in society and *differences* in interests and power among opposing groups. From this perspective, people who hold the greatest power are able to have their own attitudes, beliefs, and values—about sexual orientation, in this case—represented and enforced while others are not (Aday, 1990). Therefore norms pertaining to *compulsory heterosexuality* reflect the beliefs of dominant group members who hold high-level positions in the federal and state government, the military, and other social institutions. However, critics assert that the conflict approach fails to recognize that some people who have wealth and power are gay or lesbian yet take no action to reduce discrimination based on sexual orientation.

According to Karl Marx, conflicts over values are an essential element of social life, and less-powerful people often challenge the laws imposed upon them by those in positions of power. For example, adverse decisions by state courts and the U.S. Supreme Court often result in increased political activism by gay and lesbian rights groups. In recent years, more openly lesbian and gay people can be found in public office as elected or appointed officials, in the medical and legal professions, as educators and business leaders, and in all walks of life. However, regardless of their location in the power structure, most gay men, lesbians, and bisexuals remain acutely aware that many social barriers have not been lifted and there has not been a major shift in people's attitudes toward homosexuality and bisexuality.

With rapid Internet communications, lesbian and gay people around the world keep informed about political decisions that may adversely affect gay men and lesbians. Many coalitions have been formed to organize gay pride marches and protests around the world. For example, the International Lesbian and Gay Association reports that more than three hundred lesbian and gay groups exist in over fifty nations today (Hendriks et al., 1993).

CAN INEQUALITIES BASED ON SEXUAL ORIENTATION BE REDUCED?

As we emphasized in previous chapters, how people view a social problem is related to how they believe the problem should be reduced or solved. Inequality based on sexual orientation is no exception. From an interactionist perspective, homosexual conduct is learned behavior, and people go through stages in establishing a lesbian or gay identity. Society should therefore be more tolerant of people as they come to accept their sexual identity. Legal and social barriers that block gay and lesbian people from fully participating in society should be removed, making it easier for those who choose to go through the complex psychological and social process of coming out to friends, family, and coworkers.

According to the functionalist perspective, social norms and laws exist to protect the family and maintain stability in society. Therefore gay activists' demands for equal rights, including the reversal of sodomy laws and legal recognition of same-sex marriage, is a major problem—not a solution—to the social issue of sexual orientation. For example, groups such as the Alliance for Traditional Marriage advocate passage of a constitutional amendment making marriage the legal union between a man and a woman. Same-sex marriage is considered part of a host of other moral issues; and if gay advocates were to succeed in getting legally sanctioned marriage redefined, there would be no stopping others who wish to strike down what remains of "foundational truths once thought to be self-evident" (Thomas, 1996:A15). Some advocates of this position believe that lesbians and gay men can change their sexual orientation:

Homosexuals can and do change. My files bulge with stories of those who once engaged in sex with people of the same gender, but no longer do. They testify to the possibility of change for those who want to.

The struggle to maintain what remains of the social fabric will ultimately determine whether we will continue to follow ancient Rome on the road to destruction, or come to our senses, turn around and re-enter a harbor of safety ordained by God for our own protection. (Thomas, 1996: A15)

Whether gay, lesbian, and bisexual individuals can or should change their sexual orientation is the subject of widespread disagreement. However, most functionalists agree that homosexuality may be dysfunctional for society if it does not contribute to society's need for new members or if it undermines social norms and laws that preserve the family unit and maintain stability in society.

Conflict theorists believe that prejudice and discrimination against lesbians, gay men, and bisexuals are embedded in the social structure of society and are reinforced by people who hold the greatest power and thus are able to perpetuate their own attitudes, beliefs, and values about what constitutes "normal" sexual conduct. From this perspective, homophobia is similar to racism, sexism, and ageism, and the overt and covert discrimination that gay men and lesbians experience is similar to the discrimination experienced by people of color, white women, and older people. According to the conflict approach, the best way to reduce inequality based on sexual orientation is to repeal laws prohibiting sexual acts between consenting adults and to pass laws that ban all forms of discrimination against gay men, lesbians, and bisexuals. However, to gain equal rights, activism is necessary: People must continue to demand social change.

In the late 1990s, gay advocacy is perhaps the most effective means of reducing homophobia and bringing about greater equality for gay and lesbian people. In fact, it took a small riot to make the general public aware of inequality based on sexual orientation and the need for social change. In 1969, police raided the Stonewall Inn, a bar patronized by gay men in New York City's Greenwich Village, for alleged liquor law violations. The angry response by militant gay activists caused police to stop raiding the Stonewall Inn and other gay bars and clubs on Christopher Street, and the Gay Liberation Movement was ushered into existence (Weinberg and Williams, 1975). However, by the late 1970s and the 1980s, the tide of change turned as groups such as

"Save Our Children" crusaded against gay rights, successfully defeating gay rights bills in a number of states. With the emergence of HIV/AIDS as a major problem in the 1980s, many gay advocates shifted the focus of their lobbying from civil rights to the need for medical research on HIV/AIDS (Shilts, 1988). Today, more than 2,500 organizations seek equal rights and protections for gay men, lesbians, and bisexuals; these groups represent a wide cross-section of the U.S. population. For example, the Association of Lesbian and Gay Asians focuses on the unique needs and concerns of gay and lesbian Asian Americans (Leong, 1996), and groups such as the Bisexual Resource Group, BiWomen of Color,

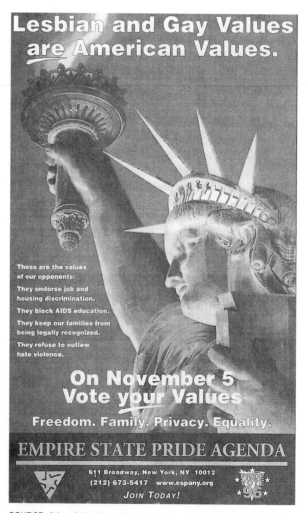

SOURCE: Advertising in the *New York Times* by the Empire State Pride Agenda, New York State's lesbian and gay political organization, as part of a "Lesbian and Gay Values Are American Values" public affairs campaign to get out the vote.

BiAdult Children of Alcoholics, and BiStar Trekkies focus on the needs of bisexual people (Gabriel, 1995a; Leland, 1995).

Despite some changes in attitudes and laws pertaining to homosexuality, however, discrimination remains strong. According to a recent study, even gay, lesbian, and bisexual sociologists who advocate gay rights are more likely than their heterosexual colleagues to encounter difficulty in obtaining academic positions, to experience bias in the tenure and promotion process, and to be excluded from social and professional networks (Taylor and Raeburn, 1995). But not all findings are negative; for some sociologists, being involved in gay rights issues brings professional visibility, recognition, and opportunities for advancement (Taylor and Raeburn, 1995).

Gay rights advocates suggest that gay men, lesbians, and bisexuals should not be the only ones responsible for reducing or eliminating inequality based on sexual orientation:

It all comes down to this: Are people equal in this society by virtue of their citizenship, or not? If the answer is no, then we will be saying that equality does not exist in America anymore but has been replaced by tiers of citizenship, and that what tier you occupy depends on whether people like you or not. And if we accept this, then we will have repudiated the constitutional principles of liberty and equality upon which America was founded and which have been its historic challenge to the world. . . . We believe that you will join in this cause because it is your cause, too, the cause of individual liberty and human equality. (Nava and Dawidoff, 1994:167)

Some analysts suggest that people in the future will ask, "What was all the fuss over gay men and lesbians (or sexual orientation) about?" What do you think?

SUMMARY

➤ *What criteria do sociologists use to study sexual orientation?*

Sociologists define sexual orientation as a preference for emotional-sexual relationships with persons of the same sex (homosexuality), the opposite sex (heterosexuality), or both (bisexuality). Recent studies use three criteria for classifying people as homosexual or bisexual: (1) sexual attraction to persons of one's own gender, (2) sexual involvement with one or more persons of one's own gender, and (3) self-identification as a gay man, lesbian, or bisexual.

➤ *How do religion and law influence people's beliefs about homosexuality?*

Most major religions regard homosexuality as a sin. Contemporary religious fundamentalists denounce homosexual conduct as a sign of great moral decay and societal chaos. Throughout U.S. history, moral and religious teachings have been intertwined with laws that criminalize homosexual conduct. Some states have sodomy laws or other laws pertaining to "deviant sexual conduct," "crimes against nature," or "unnatural intercourse" whereby people can still be imprisoned for oral or anal intercourse.

➤ *How does cohabitation differ from domestic partnership?*

In cohabitation, same-sex or opposite-sex partners live together without being legally married. Many gay or lesbian couples cohabit in this country because they cannot enter into a legally recognized marital relationship. However, some cities and states have given legal recognition to domestic partnerships—household partnerships in which an unmarried couple lives together in a committed, sexually intimate relationship and is granted the same rights and benefits as those accorded to heterosexual couples. Domestic partnership agreements benefit some couples by providing health insurance coverage and other benefits that were not previously afforded them.

➤ *What types of discrimination do gay and lesbian people experience?*

Although lesbians and gay men experience discrimination in most aspects of daily life, some of the principal areas are (1) child custody and adoption, (2) housing, (3) medical care, (4) occupations, and (5) the military. In each of these areas, gains have been made over the past three decades. However, discrimination against lesbians and gay men remains among the most blatant of all forms of prejudice and discrimination experienced by members of subordinate groups.

➤ *What are hate crimes and why are they a problem for lesbians and gay men?*

Hate crimes are acts of violence against people because of their sexual orientation, race-ethnicity, religion, or other characteristics that are devalued or "hated" by the perpetrator. Over 50 percent of all reported antigay harassment or violence is done by young males age twenty-one or under. Sometimes law enforcement officials do not take hate crimes seriously enough.

➤ *How do biologists and psychologists explain sexual orientation?*

Biologists suggest that sexual orientation may be determined by a person's genetic inheritance. Researchers have identified an area on the X chromosome (but not the specific gene) that might carry the predisposition for homosexuality. Until fairly recently, psychologists associated homosexuality with maladjustment or mental illness. Today, however, social psychologists believe that genetic and social factors combine to produce sexual orientation. According to Bem's theory, the best predictor of sexual orientation is the degree to which children are gender-conforming or nonconforming; children who fit in sometimes but not others are likely to become bisexual.

➤ *How do interactionists explain problems associated with sexual orientation?*

According to interactionists, most people acquire the status of heterosexual without being consciously aware of it. But for lesbians, gay men, and bisexuals, sexual orientation may be a master status because it largely determines how individuals view themselves and how they are treated by others. Interactionists identify several stages in the process of accepting the identity of lesbian, gay, or bisexual:

(1) experiencing identity confusion, (2) seeking out others who are openly lesbian or gay and sometimes engaging in sexual experimentation, and (3) attempting to integrate self-concept and acceptance of a label such as "homosexual," "gay," or "lesbian."

➤ *How do functionalists explain problems associated with sexual orientation?*

Functionalists focus on how social norms and laws are established to preserve social institutions such as the family and to maintain stability in society. They also analyze reasons why societies find it necessary to punish sexual conduct that violates social norms prohibiting nonmarital sex and same-sex sexual relations. According to functionalists, homosexual conduct is punished because it undermines social institutions and jeopardizes the society.

➤ *How do conflict theorists explain problems associated with sexual orientation?*

Conflict theorists believe that the group in power imposes its own attitudes, beliefs, and values about sexual orientation on everyone else. Thus norms enforcing compulsory heterosexuality reflect the beliefs of dominant group members in the federal and state government, the military, and other social institutions. According to conflict theorists, social change can occur only if people demand that laws be changed to bring about greater equality for gay men and lesbians.

➤ *How have gay rights advocates sought to reduce inequality based on sexual orientation?*

Beginning with the Gay Liberation movement in the 1960s, advocates have argued that lesbians and gay men are citizens and entitled to the same rights and protections other citizens enjoy, including the right to equal employment and housing, legally sanctioned same-sex marriage, and protection from harassment and hate crimes. Some analysts suggest that future social change depends on the continued vigilance of gay and lesbian advocacy organizations.

KEY TERMS

deviance, p. 114
domestic partnerships, p. 118
homophobia, p. 114

master status, p. 125
sexuality, p. 114
sexual orientation, p. 113

QUESTIONS FOR CRITICAL THINKING

1. How is homophobia similar to racism, sexism, and ageism? How is it different?
2. As a sociologist, how would you study the problem of discrimination against lesbians and gay men? What are the strengths and weaknesses of using survey research, interviews, observations, and experiments to study discrimination based on sexual orientation?
3. Some people think that state laws should be changed to give legal recognition to same-sex marriage. How would you find out what students at your college or university believe about this issue? If student organizations for gay men and lesbians exist on your campus, how might you find out about members' beliefs on this topic? Do you think their responses would differ from those of a cross-section of the student population? Why or why not?
4. In Chapters 2 through 6, we examined inequality and discrimination as it relates to class, race-ethnicity, gender, age, and sexual orientation. If you could do one thing to reduce these problems, what would it be? What resources would be needed to implement your plan?

Chapter Seven

Prostitution, Pornography, and the Sex Industry

I was a minister's daughter. As far as I was concerned, prostitution was the last thing in the entire world I would think of. . . . Then I met my man. That's how I got into it. . . . They meet you. They're nice to you. They take you out. It's like you think you're meeting a normal guy and falling in love . . . . Some of them, they tell you right up front that you have to work for them. My man told me after two weeks. He said he cared for me, he liked me, and he felt deeply, but this is what he does and the only way I could be with him is by coming out here and working. He drove me around here. He said, "See those girls? They have furs, diamonds, houses. They have everything." I fell for it. My first day, I made $100. One hundred dollars! I couldn't believe it! After a while, you're not thinking about the sex. There's no intimacy. You don't [care] about your date. If he dropped dead, fine. Just leave your wallet behind.

—*Nadia, a nineteen-year-old
prostitute in New York City*
(Kasindorf, 1988:56)

To some, like Nadia, sex work is a career choice and a purely economic exchange—with willing buyers and sellers—that is inherently no more or less degrading than any other profession (McWilliams, 1996). The thriving multibillion-dollar U.S. sex industry—including prostitution, the adult film and video trade, printed pornography, escort services, massage parlors, and strip and table dancing clubs—may appear to support that belief. However, prostitution and other types of sex work have always been controversial; not all social scientists even agree on whether or not the sex industry is a social problem. To better understand the controversy over prostitution, pornography, and other sex work, let's look at what constitutes deviant behavior.

DEVIANCE, THE SEX INDUSTRY, AND SOCIAL PROBLEMS

Chapter 6 defined *deviance* as a behavior, belief, or condition that violates social norms. To learn about deviance, sociologists ask such questions as the following: Why are some types of behavior considered deviant while others are not? Who determines what is deviant? Whose interests are served by stigmatizing some people as deviants but not others?

Sociologists generally take one of three approaches in studying deviance. The first approach assumes that deviance is *objectively given:* A deviant is any person who does not conform to established social norms—specifically, folkways, mores, and laws. *Folkways* are informal norms or everyday customs that may be violated without serious consequences. Contemporary U.S. folkways include eating certain foods with silverware and shaking hands when introduced to someone. In comparison, *mores* are strongly held norms with moral and ethical connotations. An example of unethical conduct is ticket scalping (selling tickets at inflated prices) by college football players who receive free game tickets from their school to give to family members and friends. *Laws* are formal, standardized norms enacted by legislatures and enforced by formal sanctions such as fines and imprisonment. Laws may be either civil or criminal. *Civil law* deals with disputes between people or groups, such as an argument between a landlord and a tenant over the provisions of an apartment lease. *Criminal law* deals with public safety and well-being and defines the behaviors that constitute a *crime*—a behavior that violates criminal law and is punishable by fine, a jail term, or other negative sanctions. Crimes range from relatively minor offenses such as traffic violations to major offenses such as murder.

If deviance is considered to be objectively given, then social problems such as prostitution and pornography are viewed as violations of deeply held convictions (folkways or mores) about good taste or morality or as significant departures from existing criminal laws (Smith and Pollack, 1994). Societies must therefore employ social control mechanisms to limit the amount of deviance and criminal behavior in society. *Social control* refers to the systematic practices developed by social groups to encourage conformity and discourage deviance. Social control

may be either internal or external. Internal social control occurs through socialization: People learn to adhere to the norms of social groups and the larger society. Internal social control mechanisms are strengthened by external mechanisms such as the criminal justice system, which enforces laws whether or not individuals choose to adhere to them.

The second approach to studying deviance considers it to be *socially constructed:* A behavior, belief, or condition is deviant because it is labeled as such (Goode, 1996; Rubington and Weinberg, 1996). Sociologist Howard S. Becker (1963:8) summed up this approach when he wrote, "Social groups create deviance by making rules whose infraction constitutes deviance, and by applying those rules to particular people and labeling them as *outsiders.*" According to Becker and other interactionists, deviance is not a quality of any act the person commits; rather, a deviant is one to whom the label of deviant has been successfully applied. For example, street prostitutes who openly solicit customers ("johns") are more likely to be labeled deviant than are women and men who work for high-priced escort services, even though their actions are essentially the same.

The third approach assumes that deviance is rooted in *the social structure of society,* particularly in power relations. In fact, deviance is defined—initially and disproportionately—by the most powerful members of the dominant class, racial, and gender groups (Feagin and Feagin, 1994). According to this approach, rule makers and rule enforcers protect the power and privilege of dominant group members, often at the expense of subordinate group members. For example, prostitutes are more likely than their customers or pimps to be apprehended and punished for their alleged sexual deviance. In the highly publicized Los Angeles case involving actor Hugh Grant and prostitute Divine Brown, for instance, Brown was fined $1,350 and given a 180-day jail sentence for performing a sex act in a car with the actor, who received probation (Buckley, 1995; *Facts on File,* 1995).

What is sexual deviance? Although all societies have social norms regulating sexual conduct, not all societies regulate it in the same way. In the United States alone, definitions of what is sexually deviant vary from time to time, from place to place, and from group to group. Traditionally, at least four types of sexual conduct between heterosexual partners have been regarded as deviant: (1) premarital sex or fornication—sexual relations between two people who are not married to each other; (2) extramarital sex or adultery—sexual relations between a married person and a partner other than her or his spouse; (3) promiscuous sex—casual sexual relations with many partners; and (4) underage sex or statutory rape—sexual relations with children below the age of consent as defined by state law, usually about age fourteen, fifteen, or sixteen. Prostitution crosses several lines of *proscribed* (prohibited) sexual conduct and is viewed as deviance because it involves promiscuous behavior between two (or more) people, who may be married to other people, and sometimes underage sex. Despite changes in proscribed rules of sexual conduct during the twentieth century, the United States is one of the few developed nations where prostitutes are defined as criminals today (Jolin, 1994).

PROSTITUTION IN GLOBAL PERSPECTIVE

Narrowly defined, *prostitution* is the sale of sexual services (of oneself or another) for money or goods and without emotional attachment. More broadly defined, systems of prostitution refer to any industry in which women's or children's—and sometimes men's—bodies are bought, sold, or traded for sexual use and abuse (Giobbe, 1994). According to this definition, systems of prostitution include pornography, live sex shows, peep shows, international sexual slavery, and prostitution as narrowly defined. The vast majority of prostitutes around the globe are women and children. A certain amount of male prostitution exists, though most boys and men in the sex industry engage in sexual encounters with other males (see McNamara, 1994; Browne and Minichiello, 1995; Snell, 1995).

The World's Oldest Profession?

Prostitution has been referred to as the "world's oldest profession" because references to it can be found throughout recorded history. However, over the past 4,000 years, prostitution has been neither totally accepted nor completely condemned. For example, prostitution was widely accepted in ancient Greece, where upper-class prostitutes were admired and frequently became the companions of powerful Greek citizens (see Bullough and Bullough, 1987; Roberts, 1992). Despite this acceptance, prostitutes were refused the status of wife—the ultimate affirmation of legitimacy for women in Greek society—and were negatively compared with so-called virtuous women in a "bad woman–good woman" dichotomy (Jolin, 1994).

In other eras, attitudes and beliefs about prostitution ranged from generally tolerant to strongly averse. For example, early Christian leaders such as St. Augustine and St. Thomas Aquinas argued that prostitution was evil but still encouraged tolerance toward it. According to Aquinas, prostitution served a basic need that, if left unmet, would result in greater harm than prostitution itself. Later Christian leaders such as Martin Luther in sixteenth-century Europe strenuously disagreed, believing that prostitution should be abolished on moral grounds (Otis, 1985; Jolin, 1994).

In the nineteenth-century feminist movement, women for the first time voiced their opinions about prostitution. Some believed that prostitution led to promiscuity and moral degeneracy in men and should therefore be eradicated. Others believed that prostitution should be legitimized as a valid expression of female sexuality outside of marriage. Recently, some advocates have suggested that prostitution should be viewed as a legitimate career choice for women (prostitute as sex worker), but others argue that prostitution is rooted in global gender inequality (prostitute as victim of oppression).

The Global Sex Industry

Over the past three decades, prostitution has been industrialized, normalized, and globalized. Although *industrialization* typically refers to mass production of manufactured goods and of services for exchange in the market, sociologist Kathleen Barry (1995:122) suggests that this term should apply as well to commercialized sex manufactured within the human self. Prostitution becomes *normalized* when sex work is treated as merely a form of entertainment and there are no legal impediments to promoting it as a commodity. The *globalization* of prostitution refers to the process by which the sex industry has increasingly become global in scope as people's political, economic, and cultural lives have become increasingly linked globally (e.g., international conglomerates of hotel chains, airlines, bars, sex clubs,

SOCIAL PROBLEMS
IN GLOBAL PERSPECTIVE

BOX 7.1

Economic Development or Childhood Sexual Slavery?

Tens of thousands of children in Asia . . . are slaves working in the plantations of the 1990s: the brothels of Cambodia, India, China, Thailand, the Philippines, Taiwan, and other countries. . . . Americans and other Westerners helped build the child prostitution trade in Asia, and many of the brothel districts date . . . from the Vietnam War, or surround former American military bases. Now they sustain it with an appetite for what at home would be child molestation and rape. A result is a partnership between local people, who run the brothels, and Westerners like the one who posted an item on the Internet informing sex tourists that in Cambodia "a six-year-old is available for US$3." (Kristof, 1996b:1,6)

Although it is impossible to know exactly how many child prostitutes there are in the world, recent estimates suggest that as many as a million girls and boys aged seventeen and younger engage in prostitution in Asia alone. Initially, social analysts believed that the end of the Vietnam War and economic development would end child prostitution in Asian cities such as Shanghai, Hong Kong, and Hanoi, where brothels have existed for many years. But this has not happened. Instead, sex tourism has emerged as a form of economic development, and the AIDS scare has dramatically increased child prostitution in some nations. Brothel owners purchase girls as young as twelve and force them to become house prostitutes. Girls who try to escape are caught, severely beaten, and sometimes starved. While imprisoned in the brothel, they are forced to have sex with many customers each night (Kristof, 1996b).

In Thailand, a large sex industry services Thai men and foreigners. Most of the prostitutes are younger than fifteen years old. Young girls from impoverished areas can no longer earn a living in agriculture, and their opportunities in the labor market are limited to extremely low-wage production and service jobs—often on an assembly line for a transnational corporation. In contrast, sex work offers a rate of pay that—though still very low—can be 25 times higher than the wages for seamstresses or domestics. Sex-based tourism in Thailand is estimated at $4 billion a year. In fact, because many foreign visitors consider sex the country's chief attraction, on the macroeconomic level sex is now part of the economy of international domination.

Some families sell their daughters into prostitution out of economic necessity. Indenturing a daughter to sex industry recruiters makes it possible for an entire rural family to survive. However, others simply do not want another mouth to feed or want to acquire material possessions. One woman in Manila periodically sells the sexual services of her two daughters, ages ten and twelve, to a Japanese man for cash so that she can purchase amenities such as a karaoke music system, which costs several hundred dollars, for her shack, where the stench of garbage and an open sewer waft into the room (Kristof, 1996b:6).

While some analysts believe that the values of one culture should not be imposed on another, others believe that activities such as child prostitution constitute a form of suffering that violates basic human rights. Should child prostitution in other nations be judged on the basis of U.S. values? What do you think?

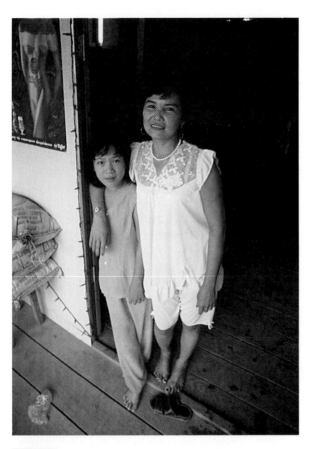

Do the two in this photo look like mother and daughter? Actually, both are employed in a Cambodian brothel. What global social and economic factors contribute to the growing number of young girls working in the sex industry?

massage parlors, brothels, and credit card companies that have an economic interest in the global sex industry) (Barry, 1995; Davidson, 1996). Recently, the use of child prostitutes in the sex tourism industry has been the focus of investigations by journalists and sociologists (see Box 7.1).

The demand for prostitution is greatest when large numbers of men are congregated for extended periods of time in the military or on business far from home. Similarly, war produces large populations of refugees and victims of rape and sexual violence, who tend to be exploited by networks of pimps and organized crime gangs such as the yakuza in Japan (Women's International Network, 1995a). The connection between wartime rape and increased prosti-

tution has been documented for the Vietnam War and more recently the wars in El Salvador and Bosnia.

Recent research suggests that the global sex industry, especially prostitution, contributes to the transmission of HIV, the virus that causes AIDS (Gil et al., 1996; Purvis, 1996). But many agencies and governments have not come to grips with the problem. For example, the Japanese Foundation for AIDS Prevention, an organization affiliated with the Japanese government, launched a poster campaign featuring a grinning, middle-aged man wearing a business suit and displaying his passport, with a caption reading, "Have a nice trip! But be careful of AIDS." The Japanese government is obviously aware that many businessmen participate in sex tourism abroad (Sachs, 1994), but the poster gives a mixed message rather than the strong warning merited by HIV/AIDS.

The global sex industry reflects the economic disparity between the poorest, developing regions of the world—where women and children tend to be bought, sold, or traded like any other commodity—and the richest, developed regions of the world, such as Europe and North America, where many of the global sex industry's consumers reside (see Bauerlein, 1995; Davidson, 1996).

PROSTITUTION IN THE UNITED STATES

In movies, prostitution is often depicted as a way in which a beautiful but poor woman can meet and marry a rich, handsome man (Michael et al., 1994). Consider, for example, *Pretty Woman* with Julia Roberts and Richard Gere. But sociological research reveals a different picture.

The Nature of Prostitution

Prostitutes in the United States are not all alike: Their life experiences, family backgrounds, years of formal education, locales of operation, types of customers, and general methods of doing business vary widely. Sociologists have identified levels of prostitution ranging from escort prostitutes to street prostitutes and women exchanging sex for drugs in crack houses.

Top-tier prostitutes typically are referred to as *escorts* or *call girls* and *call boys,* and most of them do not think of themselves as prostitutes. They are considered the upper echelon in prostitution because they tend to earn higher fees and have more selectivity in their working conditions and customers than do other prostitutes (see Macy, 1996). Escort prostitutes typically have more years of formal education than other types of prostitutes do. Many dress nicely—and often conservatively—so that they do not call undue attention to themselves at luxury hotels, clubs, and apartment buildings. Sydney Biddle Barrows (1986:69), the former owner of a well-known New York escort service, explains:

> While good looks were generally important [for escort prostitutes], I was more concerned with the *right* look. Men have always responded to the way I dress, and I decided that the elegant, classic look that worked for me would also work for the girls. . . . Quite a few of the new girls had no money and nothing appropriate to wear, so I would either lend them something of mine or take them to Saks and charge whatever they needed on my credit card. They would pay me back from their future earnings.

Escort prostitutes work "on call," going out to see customers who are referred to them by their escort service, pimp, or other procurers such as hotel concierges and taxi drivers who receive a percentage of the prostitute's fees. Although their work is not as visible as that of other prostitutes, they face some of the same hazards, including abusive customers and sexually transmitted diseases.

The second tier of prostitutes is comprised of hustlers, strippers, and table dancers who engage in prostitution on the side. People in this tier primarily work out of night clubs, bars, and strip joints. The hustlers are sometimes referred to as *bar girls* or *bar boys* because they are supposed to pressure (hustle) customers to buy drinks. Most hustlers are not paid by the bar but earn their livelihood by negotiating sexual favors with potential customers, who often are lonely and want someone to talk to as well as to have sex with (Devereaux, 1987).

The third tier in the prostitution hierarchy is made up of *house girls* who work in brothels (houses of prostitution) run by a madam or a pimp who collects up to half of the fees earned by the women. Customers choose "dates" from women lined up in a parlor or receiving room. House prostitutes are not allowed to engage in "dirty hustling"—such as

winking, running one's tongue over one's lips, or shaking a leg—or to turn down a customer (Devereaux, 1987). Since prostitution is illegal in most states, houses of prostitution typically operate as body-painting studios, massage parlors, or other businesses in the underground (illegal) economy. The only legal brothels in the United States are located in eleven Nevada counties where prostitution has been decriminalized. However, the state of Nevada requires house prostitutes to register, be fingerprinted, pay a state business fee, and provide up-to-date medical certification that they are free of sexually transmitted diseases.

Near the bottom tier of prostitution are *streetwalkers,* who publicly solicit customers and charge by the "trick." Most street prostitutes work a specific location and defend it from competition by other prostitutes, as Nadia (whom we met earlier) explains:

> I only work this corner, 'cause this is the first-class street. . . . Even here, you know there's always the chance you're going with someone who might want to kill you. My [pimp] drives around to make sure I'm okay, but not every day. So you're always alert. You watch your date's every move. You're sexy, you're smiling, you're teasing, everything, but you're watching their every move. You're always listening to their conversation so you can know what they're leading up to. Then you're okay. (quoted in Kasindorf, 1988:56)

Pimps are extremely important for Nadia and other streetwalkers, who derive status and some degree of protection from them. However, researchers have also documented the exploitative and sometimes violent nature of the pimp–prostitute relationship.

The very bottom rung of prostitution is occupied by women who are addicted to crack cocaine and engage in crack-for-sex exchanges (Fullilove et al., 1992). Researchers have found that many crack-addicted women perform unprotected oral sex on men in crack houses in exchange for hits of crack. According to one study,

> Some men will enter a crack house, purchase enough rocks for two people for several hours, and then make it clear to every woman in the house what he has in mind. . . . [There] seems to be an expectation [in the crack house] that if a

man wants to have sex with a woman, she will not oppose the offer. The expectations are implicit. Everyone involved—the house owner, the male user/customer, and the female user/prostitute are all aware of what is expected. (Inciardi et al., 1993b:74–75)

Although less research has been done on levels of male prostitution, it appears to follow patterns similar to those of female prostitution except that most customers are of the same gender as the prostitute. For example, in her report on escort services, journalist Marianna Macy (1996:249) found that some male escorts exist but that "Men normally go see men." Some male prostitutes work as hustlers in bars and night clubs, where they typically wear blue jeans, a leather jacket, and boots, seeking to project a strong heterosexual image. Sexual orientation is frequently an issue with male prostitutes, some of whom do not define themselves as gay and limit the types of sexual acts they are willing to perform. Others view sex strictly as an economic exchange by defining work-related sex as "not real sex" (Browne and Minichiello, 1995).

The Extent of Prostitution

Estimates of the number of working prostitutes in the United States range from 100,000 to more than 500,000, but accurate estimates are impossible for several reasons (Reynolds, 1986). First, there is the question of how prostitution is defined. Second, because of its illegal nature, much prostitution is not reported. Third, arrest records—which are about the only source of official information on prostitution—do not reflect the extent of prostitution. Streetwalkers who are visibly soliciting customers are more likely to be apprehended, tried, and convicted of prostitution than are prostitutes working for exclusive escort services. Finally, many people drift into and out of prostitution, considering it temporary work between full-time jobs or as part-time work while attending school (Potterat et al., 1990).

Prostitution and Age, Class, and Race

The vast majority of prostitutes are young women between the ages of seventeen and twenty-four. In contrast, the typical customer is a middle-aged, white, married male, although some teenage and college-age males also hire prostitutes (National Victims Resource Center, 1991). Some prostitutes are as young as fourteen or fifteen; the peak earning age appears to be about twenty-two (Clinard and Meier, 1989). Often, the age difference between teenage prostitutes and older customers is striking, as a woman forced into prostitution at age thirteen by a pimp explains:

> The men who bought me—the tricks—knew I was an adolescent. Most of them were in their 50s and 60s. They had daughters and granddaughters my age. They knew a child's face when they looked into it. . . . It was even clearer that I was sexually inexperienced. So they showed me pornography to teach me and ignored my tears as they positioned my body like the women in the pictures, and used me. (Giobbe, 1993:38)

Although a small percentage of teenagers enter prostitution through coercion, most are runaways who left home because of sexual abuse or other family problems. Some teen prostitutes are "throwaways"—thrown out of their homes by parents or other family members (Snell, 1995; Vissing, 1996). Regardless of their prior history, many teens become prostitutes because prostitution is the best—or only—job they can get.

Social class is directly linked to prostitution: Lower-income and poverty-level women and men are far more likely to become prostitutes than are more affluent people (Miller, 1986). Some people with little formal education and few job skills view prostitution as an economic necessity. As one woman stated, "I make good money [as a prostitute]. That's why I do it; if I worked at McDonald's for minimum wage, then I'd feel degraded" (quoted in McWilliams, 1996: 340). At the other end of the class spectrum, women working for exclusive escort services are more likely to have attended college and come from the middle or upper-middle class. For example, Heidi Fleiss—the so-called Hollywood madam—is the daughter of a prominent California physician.

Race is also an important factor in prostitution. Sociologist Patricia Hill Collins (1991) suggests that all African American women are affected by the widespread image of black women as sexually promiscuous and therefore potential prostitutes. Collins traces the roots of this stereotype to the era of slavery when black women—and black men and

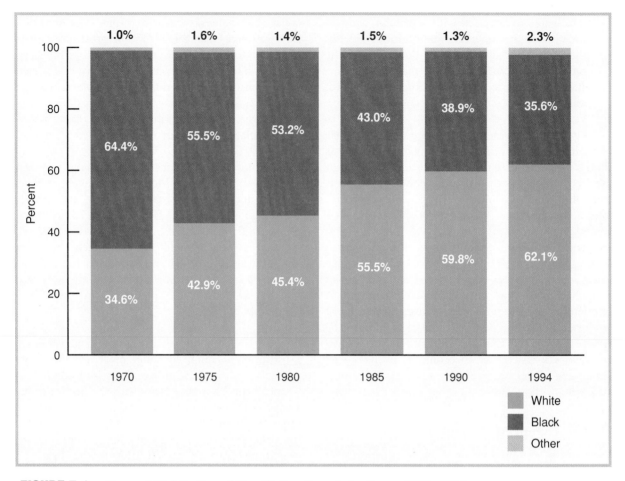

FIGURE 7.1   *Percent Distribution of Prostitution Arrests by Race, 1970–1994*
(SOURCE: Federal Bureau of Investigation, 1995b; U.S. Bureau of the Census, 1996b.)

children—were at the mercy of white male slave owners and their sexual desires. According to Collins (1991:175), prostitution exists within a "complex web of political and economic relationships whereby sexuality is conceptualized along intersecting axes of race and gender." Today, prostitution remains linked to the ongoing economic, political, and social exploitation of people of color, especially women. At the same time, since 1971, there has been a significant reversal in the racial composition of people arrested for prostitution and commercialized vice—which includes keeping a brothel, procuring (pimping), and transporting women for immoral purposes (see Figure 7.1).

SOCIOLOGICAL PERSPECTIVES ON PROSTITUTION

Sociologists use a variety of perspectives to examine prostitution as a social problem. Functionalists focus on how deviance—including prostitution—serves important functions in society. Interactionists investigate microlevel concerns, such as how and why people become prostitutes and how the stigmatization affects their self-esteem. Conflict perspectives seek to explain how the powerful enact their moral beliefs into law and how prostitution is related to capitalism and/or patriarchy.

▲ The Functionalist Perspective

Functionalists believe that the presence of a certain amount of deviance in society contributes to its overall stability. According to early sociologist Emile Durkheim, deviance clarifies social norms and helps societies to maintain social control over people's behavior. By punishing those who engage in deviant behavior such as prostitution, the society reaffirms its commitment to its sexual norms and creates loyalty to the society as people bind together to oppose deviant behavior.

According to sociologist Kingsley Davis (1937), prostitution will always exist because it serves important functions in societies that have restrictive norms governing sexual conduct, which includes the United States. First, prostitution provides quick, impersonal sexual gratification that does not require emotional attachment or a continuing relationship with another person (Freund et al., 1991). Second, prostitution provides a sexual outlet for men who otherwise do not have an ongoing sexual relationship because they are not married or have a heavy work schedule. Third, prostitution provides people with the opportunity to engage in sexual practices—such as multiple sex partners, fellatio (oral stimulation of the male genitalia), cunnilingus (oral stimulation of the female genitalia), anal intercourse, or sadomasochism (S&M), including the use of such devices as handcuffs, whips, and chains—that regular sex partners or spouses might view as immoral or distasteful. Fourth, prostitution protects the family as a social institution by making a distinction between "bad girls" or "bad boys"—with whom one engages in promiscuous sexual behavior—and "good girls" and "good boys"—with whom one establishes a family. Finally, prostitution benefits the economy by providing jobs for people who have limited formal education and job skills.

▲ The Interactionist Perspective

Why do people become prostitutes? Do some prostitutes like their work? Interactionists investigate questions such as these by using a social psychological framework, for example, by examining people's lived experiences. Here is an excerpt from an interview with a prostitute named Dolores:

I set my own schedule. I set my own limits and made my own rules, and I didn't have to answer to anyone. I learned a lot about myself: what I would and would not do for money, and what I was willing to do for the right amount of money. . . . I didn't have to see anyone I didn't want to see. If a man was too boring or too rough or too crude or took too much time, I didn't have to see him again. I loved it. (French, 1988:180)

Dolores suggests that some people become prostitutes because it provides them with greater autonomy and more career options than they otherwise would have. These reasons fit with sociologist Howard Becker's suggestion (1963) that entering a deviant career such as prostitution is similar in many ways to entering any other occupation. The primary difference is the labeling that goes with a deviant career. Public labeling of people as deviant and their acceptance or rejection of that label are crucial factors in determining whether or not a person stays in a deviant career. Some people are more willing than others to accept the "deviant" label or may believe they have no other option.

Why do men seek out prostitutes? Research by interactionists suggests that some young men seek out prostitutes to fulfill what they believe is a rite of passage from boyhood to manhood. Consider, for example, John's comments after several trips to a house of prostitution:

We went back to school, Mike and I, after going to that first whorehouse. We were probably the only two guys in the class that had done it. We were celebrities. We had crowds around us when we'd tell them all the details, how great it was, what studs we were. . . . My reaction to all this was it wasn't really very exciting. After all the talk you hear about it, all the writing, all the pictures, all the taboos about sex, I thought, "For this? This is what it was about?" . . . It wasn't something bad; it just wasn't nearly as exciting as I thought it would be. But we thought, "This is a good chance to learn," so we went back several times. . . . I can remember up to eleven. . . . I always thought I'd keep count all my life; that was part of what being a man was all about. (quoted in Raphael, 1988:74–75)

Social analysts suggest that an important factor in seeking out prostitutes is the need of men of all ages to validate their sexual prowess or reaffirm their masculinity (Raphael, 1988). Interactionist perspectives such as these highlight how people define social realities—such as the importance of sexual prowess or masculinity—in light of competing and often contradictory values they have learned through socialization.

The Conflict Perspective

Conflict perspectives on prostitution highlight the relationship between power in society and sex work: Laws making prostitution illegal are created by powerful dominant group members who seek to maintain cultural dominance by criminalizing sexual conduct that they consider immoral or in bad taste (Barry, 1995).

Conflict analysts using a liberal feminist framework believe that prostitution should be *decriminalized*—meaning that laws making it a crime should be repealed. Prostitution is a *victimless crime*—a **crime that many people believe has no real victim because it involves willing participants in an economic exchange.** Therefore sex workers should not be harassed by police and the courts. According to Margo St. James, a former prostitute and founder of an activist group called COYOTE (Call Off Your Old Tired Ethics), "The profession itself is not abusive; it's the illegality; it's the humiliation and degradation that is dealt to them at the hands of the police" (quoted in McWilliams, 1996:340). In other words, prostitution is sex work in the sex industry and should be treated as a labor issue.

Conflict perspectives using Marxist feminist and radical feminist frameworks suggest that women become prostitutes because of structural factors such as economic inequality between women and men and patriarchy, which gives men control over women's bodies (Jolin, 1994). Women's bodies are simply commodities under capitalism and patriarchy: "when a man has bought a woman's body for his use as if it were like any other commodity . . . the sex act itself provides acknowledgment of patriarchal right. When women's bodies are on sale as commodities in the capitalist market . . . men gain public acknowledgment as women's sexual masters" (Pateman, 1994:132).

According to Marxist feminists, the only way to eliminate prostitution is to reduce disparities in income levels between women and men and eliminate poverty. However, radical feminists believe that prostitution will not be eliminated until patriarchy is ended.

Conflict theorists who focus on the interrelationship of race, class, and gender in examining social problems suggest that criminalizing prostitution uniquely affects poor women, especially poor women of color, who are overrepresented among street prostitutes. According to these theorists, white male supremacy—which traditionally preserves the best-paying jobs for men—makes women of color particularly vulnerable to recruitment or coercion into prostitution. As one woman explains: "As a Black coming up in Indiana in the steel mill industry up there, they hired men. All the men got jobs in the mills there; very few women. . . . but there were lots of jobs for you in strip joints, dancing, or even down at some of the restaurants and bars outside of the steel mills for when the guys came in" (quoted in Giobbe, 1994:122).

Analysts using a race, class, and gender framework also suggest that discrimination in law enforcement uniquely affects women of color. For example, law enforcement officials target street prostitutes and other sex workers, particularly when political elites decide to crack down on "deviant" behavior such as prostitution and pornography (Barry, 1995).

PORNOGRAPHY

Nina Hartley, founder of the Pink Ladies club, a group of women in the pornography industry, wrote of herself (1994, 176–177):

"A feminist porno star?" Right, tell me another one, I can hear some feminists saying . . . why porno? Simple—I'm an exhibitionist with a cause: to make sexually graphic (hard core) erotica, and today's porno is the only game in town. . . . As I examine my life, I uncover the myriad influences that led me to conclude that it was perfectly natural for me to choose a career in adult films. . . . I stripped once a week while getting my bachelor's degree in nursing, magna cum laude. . . . I went into full time [adult] movie work immediately following graduation.

Although Hartley claims to be both a feminist *and* a porn star, many social analysts believe that this is a contradiction in terms because pornography is a pressing social problem. *Pornography* **is the graphic depiction of sexual behavior through pictures and/or words—including by electronic or other data retrieval systems—in a manner that is intended to be sexually arousing.** However, the specific nature of pornography as a social problem is not clear cut, as sociologist Wai-Teng Leong (1991:91) explains:

> Some religious groups preach that pornography propagates perverse sexualities and its proliferation portends the poverty of morality. Some women promulgate the view that pornography preserves and promotes patriarchal power. Some other women claim that pornography in popular music leads to all kinds of teenage pathology. On the other hand, producers of pornography argue that their products have the positive potential of catharsis, channeling off sexual desires into masturbatory fantasies. And many people who purchase pornography consume it in the privacy of their homes and cannot comprehend why a private matter should become a public problem.

For all these reasons, social scientists have difficulty determining what constitutes pornography. Moreover, public attitudes change over time regarding what should be tolerated and what should be banned because of *obscenity*—**the legal term for pornographic materials that are offensive by generally accepted standards of decency.** Whereas religious groups typically construe pornography as a social problem because of its obscenity, social analysts, particularly feminists, usually frame the problem in terms of patriarchy—male oppression of women (Leong, 1991).

Who decides what is obscene? According to what criteria? In *Miller* v. *California* (1973), the U.S. Supreme Court held that material can be considered legally obscene only if it meets three criteria: (1) The material as a whole appeals to prurient interests (lustful ideas or desires), (2) the material depicts sexual conduct in a patently offensive way as defined by state or federal law, and (3) the work as a whole lacks serious literary, artistic, political, or scientific value (Russell, 1993). But according to some analysts, including Leong (1991), the Court's decision contributes to the social construction of pornography as a social problem.

The Social Construction of Pornography as a Social Problem

The social construction of pornography as a social problem involves both a cognitive framework and a moral framework. The cognitive framework refers to the reality or factualness of the situation that constitutes the "problem." In regard to pornographic materials, the cognitive framework refers to the assumption that pornography *actually affects* people's actions or attitudes; an opposing cognitive framework would be that pornography is a fantasy mechanism that allows people to express the forbidden without actually engaging in forbidden behavior (Kipnis, 1996). The moral framework refers to arguments as to whether something is immoral or unjust. In the case of pornography, moral condemnation arises from the belief that graphic representations of sexuality are degrading, violent, and sinful. From this perspective, pornography is less about sex than about violating taboos in society. The moral framework often distinguishes between pornography and *erotica*—**materials that depict consensual sexual activities that are sought by and pleasurable to all parties involved.** According to sociologist Diana E. H. Russell (1993), materials can be considered erotic—rather than obscene—only if they show respect for all human beings and are free of sexism, racism, and homophobia. Contemporary erotica might include romance novels that describe two consenting adults participating in sexual intercourse (see Snitow, 1994). On the other hand, materials depicting violent assault or the sexual exploitation of children would be considered pornographic or obscene. However, the distinction appears to be highly subjective, as feminist scholar Ellen Willis (1981:222) notes: "Attempts to sort out good erotica from bad porn inevitably come down to 'What turns me on is erotic: what turns you on is pornographic.'"

SOCIAL PROBLEMS
IN THE MEDIA

BOX 7.2

The Faces behind Adult "Entertainment" Magazines for Men

If you are a man between 18 and 80, *Playboy* is meant for you. . . . We want to make it clear from the start, we aren't a family magazine. If you are somebody's sister, wife, or mother-in-law and picked us up by mistake, please pass us along to the man in your life and get back to *Ladies Home Companion*.
— Hugh Hefner's statement in the first issue of *Playboy*, published in 1953 (quoted in Dines, 1995:256)

I felt that if someone published a magazine more attuned to what the average Joe really liked, a whole new market could be created. To put it bluntly, if you got the models to spread their legs a little wider, you'd sell more magazines. I made a mental note of this.
— Larry Flynt, publisher of *Hustler* magazine (quoted in Merzer, 1997:C6)

I'm upset about this film [*The People vs. Larry Flynt*] because it supports my dad's argument that pornography does not harm. If you want to see a victim of pornography, just look at me.

— Tonya Flynt, age thirty-two, daughter of Larry Flynt, discussing the movie about his life (quoted in Steinem, 1997:A13)

I don't defend pornography so much as pornography's right to exist. Two things you will not find in the pages of *Screw* are animal sex and kiddie porn.
— Al Goldstein, publisher of *Screw* magazine (quoted in Holden, 1997:B22)

Since the introduction of *Playboy* in the 1950s, adult male "entertainment" magazines that can be purchased—by people over age eighteen—at local newsstands and convenience stores have thrived. According to media scholar Gail Dines (1995:254), Hefner's *Playboy* magazine played a major role in "bringing pornography out of the closet and onto the coffee table, and in the process it helped to pave the way for the now $10 billion-a-year pornography industry." Dines attributes the initial success of *Playboy* to the fact that the magazine turns sex into a *commodity*—an object or service that can be bought and sold in the marketplace—while at the same time, it takes commodities such as

The Nature and Extent of Pornography

Technological innovations such as digital media have greatly increased the variety of pornographic materials available as well as their methods of distribution. Although some people visit live peep shows and "X-rated" adult bookstores and video arcades, sexually explicit materials are available at home or

in the office through mail-order services, movies on "X-rated" cable television channels, dial-a-porn, digitized scans and striptease QuickTime movies, and private computer bulletin boards and Usenet newsgroups specializing in adult chat areas and graphics exchanges on the Internet.

As part of the multibillion-dollar sex industry, hard-core pornography is profitable to many people, including investors, film makers, and owners of stores that distribute such materials. *Hard-core* pornogracars, boats, clothes, alcohol, and food and *sexualizes* them. For example, the centerfold of the magazine depicting a nude or nearly nude woman—which Dines asserts is one of the keys to the success of *Playboy*—is surrounded by other objects of lust: advertisements featuring "overwhelmingly affluent (white) men in the prime of life who live in expensive homes outfitted with numerous gadgets, drive fast cars, take vacations on private yachts, and are nearly always accompanied by younger, glamorous big-breasted women who are willing and ready to have sex at any time" (Dines, 1995:256–257). Even *Playboy* cartoons routinely carry out this theme.

According to Dines (1995:254–255), *Playboy* offers an affluent lifestyle, whereas magazines like Flynt's *Hustler* and Goldstein's *Screw* offer hard-core pornography:

[Hard-core pornography] advertises the woman (via the codes and conventions of pornographic representation) as *the* commodity on offer whereas [soft-core pornography] offers a lifestyle that involves the consumption of numerous upmarket commodities as a way of capturing the ultimate prized commodity: lots and lots of attractive, young, big-breasted women.

Although adult male "entertainment" magazines have been accused of using increasingly explicit and sexually violent depictions in recent years, content analysis shows that this is generally untrue (Scott and Cuvelier, 1987; Scott, 1993). The emphasis in magazines such as *Hustler* and *Screw* remains on total nudity, hard-core pornography, and extensive coverage of the sex industry.

Many feminist scholars oppose pornography even if studies do not show that it causes violence against women. They believe that any image that associates sexual arousal with male domination and violence perpetuates sexist ideology and behavior. In response, other scholars suggest that women need to take a more active role in all forms of media production to improve the quality of women's images:

[Women] should produce, direct, and create not only pornography, but also a wider range of more popular cultural forms, such as advertisements, rock music, movies, theatre, and so on. This is necessary because if there is a link between representational practices and social action. . . . it is to be found in not just sexist pornography alone, but also in popular culture generally. (Leong, 1991:113)

What, if anything, do you think should be done about pornography?

phy is material that explicitly depicts sexual acts and/or genitals, in contrast with *soft-core* pornography, which is suggestive but does not depict actual intercourse or genitals (see Box 7.2).

Hard-core pornographic films gross over $400 million a year in the United States alone. It is not uncommon for a small production company that shoots, manufactures, and distributes such videos to gross more than one million dollars a year (*New York Times,* 1993). However, "Ron," who works in the pornography industry, suggests that these profits do not extend to most actors in the films:

You'd have to go a long way to find an industry with worse labor practices. They work people very hard; they pay them very little, really, for what they do. . . . As a porn performer, you're putting up with a couple of days of hard, even abusive, behavior that compromises your ability to do anything else in your life ever again, be-

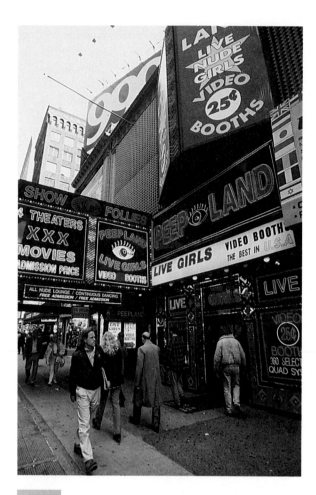

Why do you think public officials and some merchants in New York City are attempting to eliminate live peep shows and video arcades in Times Square and other areas of the city visited by hundreds of thousands of tourists each year? Do you think that scenes such as the one shown in this photo will be eliminated or just relocated?

cause the piece of evidence of your past misbehavior continues to exist. . . . But after you've done porn films, you can't do anything else. You can't even do commercials. . . . Another thing. There's an endless appetite for new faces and new bodies, which means they work [actors] to death for about six months or a year, put out twenty to thirty videos with them. And then they can't get work any more. New ones have come along. The audience is sick of looking at the old ones and wants to see new ones. (quoted in Stoller 1991:209–210)

According to some social analysts, pornography is a prime example of the principle of supply and demand. As long as demand is high, pornographers will continue to market their goods and services and find new ways to use technology. According to Walter Kendrick, a scholar whose research focuses on pornography:

> Pornographers have been the most inventive and resourceful users of whatever medium comes along because they and their audience have always wanted innovations. Pornographers are excluded from the mainstream channels, so they look around for something new, and the audience has a desire to try any innovation that gives them greater realism or immediacy. (quoted in Tierney, 1994:H18)

Each new development in technology changes the meaning of pornography and brings new demands for regulation or censorship. For example, interactive media presentations and pornography on the Internet are widely believed to be a far more powerful influence on people, especially children, than the printed word is.

Research on Pornography

During the past three decades, two presidential commissions have examined pornography and reached contradictory conclusions. The 1970 U.S. Commission on Pornography and Obscenity found no conclusive links between pornography and sex crimes or antisocial behavior. However, the 1986 Attorney General's Commission on Pornography (known as the Meese Commission) concluded that pornography is dangerous, causes sex crimes, increases aggression in males, inspires sexism against women, and encourages *pedophilia* (adults engaging in sexual intercourse with children). The Meese Commission concluded (although some members strongly disagreed) that sexually explicit materials should be further restricted and obscenity laws should be more stringently enforced.

Sociologists do not agree on the extent to which pornography that depicts excessive sex, violence, and domination of one person by another affects behavior. More than 80 percent of X-rated films in one study included scenes showing women dominated and exploited by men. The vast majority of these films portrayed physical aggression against women, and about half explicitly depicted rape (Cowan et al., 1988; Cowan and O'Brien, 1990). Explicit violence is also part of many videos in the adult section of video stores (see Duncan, 1991). Nevertheless, studies have not established that watching such films and videos contributes to aggressive or violent behavior in viewers, and most people therefore do not support efforts to censor adults' access to pornographic material.

Pornography and Age, Gender, Class, and Race

Because viewing pornography is a secretive activity, the data on consumers of various forms are limited. Some studies have found that the typical customer of an adult bookstore is a white, relatively well-educated, married middle-class man between the ages of twenty-five and sixty-six. Other studies have found that younger and more educated adults express more accepting attitudes toward pornography than do older, less educated adults (Lottes, 1993).

Overall, men watch more sexually explicit material and hold more favorable attitudes toward it than women do. Some analysts attribute this difference to gender role socialization. In a society in which men are socialized to be sexual initiators and often fear rejection, pornography is satisfying because it typically shows a willing female partner. In contrast, women have been socialized to respond negatively to material showing nude bodies and male pleasure that may occur at the expense of a woman's sense of safety and dignity (see Reiss, 1986). However, in recent years, more women have become consumers of *Playgirl* magazine, erotic novels, and videos such as those made specifically for women by Candida Royalle, a former porn star (see Lottes, 1993; Macy, 1996).

In general, though, women are more vocal than men in opposing pornography. According to sociologist Michael Kimmel (1990), men are relatively silent for several reasons: embarrassment or guilt for having enjoyed pornography, anger at women's interference in male privilege, lack of interest in what they perceive to be a nonissue, fear that speaking out will lead to questions about their masculinity, reluctance to talk openly about their sexual feelings, and confusion about "what it means to be a 'real man' in contemporary society" (Kimmel, 1987:121).

Also, according to film scholar Laura Kipnis (1996), much sentiment against pornography is rooted in class-based elitism: Opposition to pornography is a form of snobbery related to maintaining class distinctions in society. From this perspective, rejecting pornography amounts to rejecting all that is vulgar, trashy, and lower class. Although Kipnis does not suggest that all consumers of pornography are lower class, she believes that members of the upper classes typically view pornography consumers as lower-class people who may imitate the images they see. Similarly, women who appear in pornography or consume it are seen as brainwashed or unenlightened people who lack "class."

In another class analysis of pornography, philosopher Alan Soble (1986) links men's use of pornography with their feelings of boredom and powerlessness, which result from capitalist work relations, the nature of labor, and the centralization of economics and politics. In other words, pornography is a diversion—a means of escaping from the dull, predictable world of work. Soble suggests that consumers of pornography use the material to construct fantasies and gain a sense of control; it gives men the opportunity—otherwise rarely available—to organize the world and conduct its events according to their own wishes and tastes. In fact, pornography consumption is not an expression of men's power as much as it is an expression of their lack of power (Soble, 1986).

In other research, sociologists Alice Mayall and Diana E. H. Russell (1993) have shown how different racial-ethnic groups are portrayed in pornography. Examining materials in a heterosexual pornography store, the researchers found that skin color is a highly salient issue: White women were featured in 92 percent of the pornography, perhaps because they fulfill traditional stereotypes equating female beauty with white skin and Caucasian features (Mayall and Russell, 1993).

People of color were more likely to be found in materials featuring rape, bondage and sadomasochism, anal sex, sex with children, and sex between women. Among women of color, African American women were most frequently featured, followed by

Asian or Asian American women, and Latinas. African American men who consume pornography have a choice of buying magazines portraying only whites, white men with African American women, or African American men with white women. The researchers were unable to determine whether these options were based on the preferences of consumers or those of the makers of pornography (Mayall and Russell, 1993). Sociologist Patricia Hill Collins (1991) suggests that racism in pornography can be traced to the oppression of black women in slavery: African American women were depicted as animals and used as sex objects for the pleasure of white men. At the same time that the white man was exploiting the black woman, he was obsessive about protecting the white woman from the black man (Gardner, 1994).

Sexually explicit sites on the Internet are available to many students through their university computer accounts. Should colleges and universities be able to restrict students' access to computer pornography? Why or why not?

THE FUTURE OF PORNOGRAPHY AND THE SEX INDUSTRY

Public opinion polls show that people in the United States are ambivalent about pornography and other aspects of the sex industry. While they acknowledge that the sex industry may produce goods and services that serve as a "safety valve" for some, many believe that the same goods and services can be a "trigger" for others. There does seem to be consensus in regard to children: Children should be shielded from some materials. But who should do the shielding and what materials should be banned?

The controversy over sexually explicit materials is particularly strong in schools, and some school boards have banned books and audiovisual materials they considered obscene. For example, *Our Bodies, Ourselves,* a women's health manual, has been banned in some schools because of its written material and pictures. Many adults would also like to see children shielded from sexually explicit movies, television shows, and rock music videos—to say nothing of the sophisticated adult entertainment on child-oriented gaming platforms such as the CD-equipped Sega Genesis (Stefanac, 1993).

Children may also have access to sexually explicit materials on the Internet. Although Congress passed the Communications Decency Act in 1996, making it a crime for a person to knowingly circulate "patently offensive" sexual material to on-line sites that are accessible to users under age eighteen, the law was held to be unconstitutional (see Chapter One). The censorship wars—both on line and in real life—continue to pose serious social policy questions.

All of the issues pertaining to pornography and censorship that we've discussed bring us to a point we've made in previous chapters: How people view social problems affects how they believe such problems should be solved. People seem to view pornography in one of four ways: liberal, religious conservative, antipornography feminist, and anticensorship feminist (Segal, 1990; Berger et al., 1991). Each point of view espouses a different solution to the problem of pornography.

According to the *liberal* point of view, pornography may offend some people but brings harmless pleasure to others. It may even serve as a safety valve for those who have no other sexual outlet. Moreover, no scientific evidence links pornography to actual sexual violence or degradation of women. Therefore the social problem is not really pornography but censorship—people attempting to impose their morals on others and thereby violating First Amendment rights (Cottle et al., 1989).

In contrast, from a *religious conservative* point of view, pornography is a threat to the moral values of society, especially family values. Pornography encourages people to have sexual intercourse outside marriage and to engage in deviant sexual behavior. Therefore sexually explicit and violent materials should be censored to protect families and societal values.

Feminist analysts are generally critical of pornography because it is sexist in its portrayal of women, emphasizes male dominance and female submission, and encourages the valuing of women according to their ability to please men. However, not all feminists agree on what—if anything—should be done about pornography. *Antipornography feminists* believe that pornography is a primary source of male oppression of, and violence against, women. Pornography should therefore be restricted or eliminated as a form of sexual discrimination that diminishes women's opportunities in all areas of life including employment, education, and freedom of movement (see MacKinnon, 1987; Dworkin, 1988). Antipornography feminists typically view pornography as a civil rights issue and believe that communities should pass antipornography ordinances that would enable people who have been victimized by pornography to sue pornographers for damages (see Russell, 1993).

In contrast, *anticensorship feminists* do not believe that women's subordination is caused by a single factor such as pornography. Focusing on pornography as the primary source of sexual oppression "downplays the sexism and misogyny at work within all of our most respectable social institutions and practices, whether judicial, legal, familial, occupational, religious, scientific, or cultural" (Segal, 1990:32). Therefore pornography should not be censored because open discussions about sexuality and sexual practices promote women's sexual freedom and their right to express themselves (Willis, 1983; Kaminer, 1990).

The controversy over censorship may be rapidly becoming an obsolete concept in a world linked by the Internet and other rapid sources of communication. For example, whose community standards should be applied in determining whether on-line materials are obscene? Should we use the standards of Berkeley, California, or those of Tokyo, Japan? Should we use the standards of the community where the image is posted, the community where it is viewed, or both? Censorship is a very complicated proposition in the global marketplace. To restrict local access to a picture, story, or idea on the Internet, access must be blocked to computer users all over the world. This situation poses problems for Internet service providers such as CompuServe and America Online. For instance, German authorities asked CompuServe, a U.S.-based corporation, not to let German subscribers access 200 discussion groups and picture databases that allegedly violated German pornography laws. To meet this request, CompuServe had to block worldwide access to those sites. Although the ban was only temporary, it sent shock waves through the community of Internet users who became concerned that material deemed pornographic or obscene by people anywhere in the world could become unavailable everywhere. Some of the materials Germany sought to ban were sexuality support groups for the handicapped and a bulletin board for gay men and lesbians that provided a network for gay youths (*Time*, 1996b).

In this chapter, we have focused on prostitution and materials that are defined as pornographic, obscene, and erotic. However, it is important to note that mainstream media—including magazines, movies, videos, television programming, and specifically music videos shown on MTV and other channels—also may contribute to negative images of women and the exploitation of children. Furthermore, the mainstream media can desensitize people to sexual assault, rape, violence, and murder through repeated exposure to depictions of women as victims and sex objects and men as aggressors, rapists, and killers.

SUMMARY

➤ *How do sociologists view deviance?*

Some sociologists view deviance as objectively given: Social problems such as prostitution and pornography are violations of folkways, mores, or laws. Others view deviance as socially constructed: A behavior, belief, or condition is deviant because it is labeled as such. Still others believe that deviance is rooted in the social structure of society: People in positions of power maintain their cultural dominance by defining as deviant the behaviors they consider immoral, distasteful, or threatening to them.

➤ *What kinds of behavior have traditionally been defined as sexual deviance in the United States?*

Four types of sexual conduct among heterosexual partners have traditionally been regarded as deviant: premarital sex (fornication), extramarital sex (adultery), promiscuous sex (casual sexual relations with many partners), and underage sex (statutory rape).

➤ *What is prostitution and how has it changed in recent years?*

Prostitution is the sale of sexual services (one's own or another's) for money or goods and without emotional attachment. According to some social analysts, prostitution has recently become industrialized, normalized, and globalized. The industrialization of prostitution refers to commercialized sex as a product manufactured within the human self. Normalization is the process whereby sex work comes to be treated as a form of entertainment with no legal impediments to promoting it as a commodity. The globalization of prostitution refers to the process by which the sex industry has increasingly become global in scope.

➤ *What categories of prostitution have sociologists identified?*

Sociologists have identified several categories: Escort prostitutes (call girls or call boys) earn higher fees and can be more selective in their working conditions and customers than other prostitutes. Hustlers (bar girls or bar boys) work out of night clubs, bars, and strip joints, where they solicit their customers. House prostitutes (house girls) work in brothels, and a substantial portion of their earnings

goes to the house madam or pimp. Street prostitutes (streetwalkers) publicly solicit customers and charge by the "trick."

➤ *How do functionalists view prostitution?*

Functionalists point out that prostitution—like other forms of deviance—is functional for society. Prostitution continues because it provides people with (1) quick, impersonal sexual gratification without emotional attachment; (2) a sexual outlet for those who have no ongoing sexual relationships; (3) the opportunity to engage in nontraditional sexual practices; (4) protection for the family as a social institution; and (5) jobs for low-skilled people.

➤ *How do interactionists view prostitution?*

Interactionists believe that prostitution—like other forms of deviance—is socially constructed. Entering a deviant career such as prostitution is like entering any other occupation, but public labeling—and the individual's acceptance or rejection of that label—determines whether a person stays in a deviant career.

➤ *How do conflict theorists view prostitution?*

There are several conflict perspectives on prostitution. Liberal feminists consider prostitution a victimless crime—involving a willing buyer and a willing seller—that should be decriminalized. Marxist feminists see prostitution as linked to the capitalist economy. Radical feminists trace the roots of prostitution to patriarchy in society. Conflict theorists who focus on the intersection of race, class, and gender believe that the criminalization of prostitution is a form of discrimination against poor women, particularly poor women of color.

➤ *Does pornography differ from obscenity and erotica?*

Sometimes it is difficult to distinguish among these categories, but pornography generally refers to the graphic depiction of sexual behavior through pictures and/or words—including delivery by electronic or other data retrieval systems—in a manner that is intended to be sexually arousing. Obscenity is the legal term for pornographic materials that are offensive by generally accepted standards of decency. Erotica refers to material depicting consensual sexual activities that are sought by and pleasurable to all parties involved.

➤ *Has pornography changed in recent years?*

Yes, technological innovations have greatly increased the variety of pornographic materials available as well as their methods of distribution. According to some analysts, as long as the desire for such materials is high, the multibillion-dollar pornography industry will continue to produce and market goods and services, adapting to new technologies as they become available.

➤ *Does research indicate that pornography contributes to sexual violence?*

No conclusive answer has been found to this question. Some studies have found that hard-core pornography is associated with aggression in males and sexual violence in society, but other studies have found no conclusive evidence that pornography contributes to sexual violence. However, most feminist scholars suggest that pornography exploits all women—and sometimes men and children.

➤ *How do people react to the censorship of pornography?*

Reactions to the censorship of pornography are varied. People with a liberal view of pornography believe that it is a safety valve for society, and censorship—not pornography—is the social problem. Religious conservatives consider pornography a threat to moral values and encourage censorship of some materials. Antipornography feminists view pornography as a primary source of male oppression and violence against women and argue for its restriction or elimination. Anticensorship feminists believe that some pornography is bad but censorship is worse because it suppresses free speech.

KEY TERMS

crime, p. 134
erotica, p. 143
obscenity, p. 143
pornography, p. 143

prostitution, p. 135
social control, p. 134
victimless crime, p. 142

QUESTIONS FOR CRITICAL THINKING

1. Suppose you are going to participate in a class debate on decriminalizing prostitution. What arguments would you present in favor of decriminalization? What arguments would you present against decriminalization?
2. Are prostitution and pornography the result of sexism, racism, homophobia, and class-based inequality? Why or why not?
3. On the basis of the text discussion of pornography, obscenity, and erotica, find examples from the mainstream media (including films, music videos, talk shows, and fashion ads in magazines) that might fit each category.
4. Peter McWilliams suggests that the problem with censorship can be summed up in two words: Who decides? Who do you think should decide what materials—if any—should be censored as pornographic or obscene? Besides deciding what's acceptable and what isn't, who should decide on the punishment for violating these standards?

Chapter Eight

Alcohol and
Other Drugs

I knew I had hit a person. . . . You don't have to be legally intoxicated to be dangerous. I used to think drunk drivers were guys who were alcoholics and staggered into their car. I know now that they are kids and adults like myself. . . . When I got into my car [after leaving the bar] . . . it never occurred to me at any time that I was intoxicated. I didn't stumble. I wasn't sick. I started the car easily. Nothing indicated to me that I was not in control. . . . That's the danger of so-called social drinking. How can you judge that you are intoxicated when your judgment is already impaired? Just a little alcohol can do it.

—Cesilee Hyde, age 23, describes the night in 1995 that her car struck and killed a police officer directing traffic at an accident site (quoted in Banta, 1996:A1)

When most people think of alcohol abuse as a social problem, they picture someone who is mentally slow, with slurred speech and a flushed face. As Hyde's situation shows, however, not all alcohol-related problems involve alcoholics. Even occasional overconsumption of alcoholic beverages can have dire consequences, especially when combined with driving an automobile. For example, there were 17,274 alcohol-related deaths on U.S. streets and highways in 1995 (Wald, 1996a). In this chapter, we'll examine this and other issues pertaining to alcohol and other drug abuse.

DRUG USE AND ABUSE

What is a drug? There are many answers to this question, so the definition is not always consistent or clear. For our purposes, a **drug** is **any substance—other than food or water—that, when taken into the body, alters its functioning in some way.** Drugs are used for either therapeutic or recreational purposes. *Therapeutic* use occurs when a person takes a drug for a specific purpose such as reducing a fever or controlling an epileptic seizure. Sometimes, individuals who take prescription drugs for therapeutic purposes cross the line to drug abuse. In contrast, *recreational* drug use occurs when a person takes a drug for no other purpose than achieving some pleasurable feeling or psychological state. Alcohol and tobacco (nicotine) are licit drugs that are used for recreational purposes; heroin and cocaine are illicit recreational drugs (Levinthal, 1996). *Illicit* (illegal) drugs such as marijuana, cocaine, heroin, and LSD (lysergic acid diethylamide) are socially defined as deviant, and using them is criminal behavior and hence a social problem. *Licit* (legal) drugs, which include such substances as vitamins, aspirin, alcohol, tobacco, and prescription drugs, are legal to manufacture, sell, possess, and use. We live in a society that is saturated with both licit and illicit drugs, some of which are difficult to obtain, though others are as handy as the local drugstore (Akers, 1992).

Defining Drug Abuse

What is drug abuse? *Drug abuse* is the excessive or inappropriate use of a drug that results in some form of physical, mental, or social impairment. Drug abuse has both objective and subjective components. The *objective component* of drug abuse is physical, psychological, or social evidence that harm has been done to individuals, families, communities, or the entire society. The *subjective component* of drug abuse refers to people's perceptions about the consequences of drug abuse and what social action they believe should be taken to remedy the problem.

Let's take marijuana as our example. The subjective component of marijuana use is the general belief that marijuana is harmful and therefore should not be legal—even though little evidence has been found that marijuana use is detrimental to health—while alcohol use, which is legal, continues to impair more people and produce greater costs to individuals and society. As this example shows, not all people agree on what constitutes drug abuse.

Drug Addiction

The term *drug addiction (or drug dependency)* refers to a psychological and/or physical need for a drug to maintain a sense of well-being and avoid withdrawal symptoms. Drug dependency has two essential characteristics: tolerance and withdrawal. *Tolerance* occurs when larger doses of a drug are required over time to produce the same physical or psychological effect that was originally achieved by a smaller dose. Tolerance is a matter of degree: Some drugs produce immediate and profound levels of tolerance, whereas others produce only mild tolerance. For example, when a person first drinks coffee, the stimulant effect of a five-ounce cup of coffee, containing about 100 milligrams of caffeine, is usually quite pronounced. After that person drinks the same amount of coffee over a period of several days or weeks, the effect is greatly diminished, and a second or third cup of coffee (for a total of 200 to 300 milligrams of caffeine) becomes necessary to duplicate the earlier feeling (Levinthal, 1996). *Withdrawal refers to a variety of physical and/or psychological symptoms that habitual users experience when they discontinue drug use.* For example, people who suddenly terminate their alcohol intake after long-term, heavy drinking experience various physical symptoms ranging from insomnia to DTs (short for *delirium tremens,* or mental confusion often accompanied by sweating and tremor) and psychological symptoms such as a reduced sense of self-worth.

ALCOHOL USE AND ABUSE

The use of alcohol—ranging from communion wine in religious ceremonies to beer, wine, and liquor at business and social gatherings—is considered an accepted part of the dominant culture in the United States. *Alcohol* and *alcoholic beverages* are terms that refer to three major forms in which ethyl alcohol (ethanol) is consumed: *wine,* which is made from fermentation of fruits and contains between 12 and 14 percent ethyl alcohol; *beer,* which is brewed from grains and hops and usually contains 3 to 6 percent; and *liquor,* which includes whiskey, gin, vodka, and other distilled spirits and usually contains 40 percent (80 proof) to 50 percent (100 proof) alcohol. In the United States, adults consume an average of 2.5 gallons of wine, 32 gallons of beer, and 1.8 gallons of liquor a year. In fact, adults consume more beer on average than milk (24.7 gallons) or coffee (21.1 gallons) (U.S. Bureau of the Census, 1996b). But statistics on average alcohol consumption do not indicate how much *each* person drinks during a given year. Some people do not drink at all, and others drink heavily. Among those who drink, 10 percent account for roughly half the total alcohol consumption in this country (Levinthal, 1996).

DRUG-FREE AMERICA

AGE 0-4	4-12	12-18	18-24	24-38	38-65	65 —
AMOXICILLIN	RITALIN	APPETITE SUPPRESSANTS	NO-DOZ	PROZAC	ZANTAC	EVERYTHING ELSE

Signe Wilkinson/Cartoonists & Writers Syndicate

Many people do not think of alcohol as a drug because it can be purchased legally—and without a prescription—by adults. But it is a psychoactive drug that is classified as a *depressant* because it lowers the activity level of the central nervous system. The impairment of judgment and thinking associated with being drunk is the result of alcohol's depressing brain functions. Alcohol also affects mood and behavior. One to two drinks often bring a release from tensions and inhibitions. Three to four drinks affect self-control—including reaction time and coordination of the hands, arms, and legs—and judgment, muddling the person's reasoning ability. Five to six drinks affect sensory perception, and the person may show signs of intoxication such as staggering, belligerence, or depression. At seven to eight drinks, the drinker is obviously intoxicated and may go into a stupor. Nine or more drinks affect vital centers, and the drinker may become comatose or even die. Of course, factors such as body weight,

physical build, and recent food and fluid consumption must be taken into account in estimating the rate of alcohol absorption in the body.

Although negative short-term effects of alcohol are usually overcome, chronic heavy drinking or alcoholism can cause permanent damage to the brain or other parts of the body (Fishbein and Pease, 1996). Social scientists divide long-term drinking patterns into four general categories. *Social drinkers* consume alcoholic beverages primarily on social occasions; they drink occasionally or even relatively frequently. *Heavy drinkers* are more frequent drinkers who typically consume greater quantities of alcohol when they drink and are more likely to become intoxicated. *Acute alcoholics* have trouble controlling their use of alcohol and plan their schedule around drinking. *Chronic alcoholics* have lost control over their drinking and tend to engage in compulsive behavior such as hiding liquor bottles and sneaking drinks when they are not being observed.

▲ Alcohol Consumption and Class, Gender, Age, and Race

Although people in all social classes consume alcohol, income and class differences are associated with alcohol use. For example, studies show that people who earn more than $50,000 a year tend to drink expensive special or imported beers and more wine than liquor, whereas those who earn less than $20,000 tend to consume less expensive domestic beers and drink more beer than wine or liquor (Levinthal, 1996). The relationship between social class and rates of alcohol abuse is not as clear. Some studies show that people in the middle and upper classes are *less* likely to be heavy drinkers or have high rates of alcoholism, but other studies show that alcohol consumption and abuse tend to be *higher* in the middle and upper classes than in the lower class (Akers, 1992). In any case, more affluent people typically have greater resources and more privacy than lower-income individuals have and can often protect themselves from being labeled "drunk" or "alcoholic." A member of the upper-middle or upper class who drinks to excess at the country club is less visible to the public and less likely to be negatively sanctioned by law enforcement officials—unless the person drives while under the influence—than a lower-income or poverty-level person who sits on a public sidewalk drinking beer or wine.

Gender, age, and race are also associated with drinking behavior. More men than women drink, and men are more likely than women to be labeled as problem drinkers or alcoholics. Women who drink alcoholic beverages tend to be lighter drinkers than men, who are more likely to consume alcohol daily and experience negative personal and social consequences from drinking. However, drinking patterns in the teen years are similar for males and females.

In a recent national survey, about half of all respondents between the ages of twelve and seventeen reported that they had tried alcohol at least once, and slightly more than 15 percent reported that they were current users. Among respondents in the eighteen to twenty-five age category, the vast majority (86.8 percent) reported that they had tried alcohol at least once, and over 60 percent indicated that they were current users (U.S. Bureau of the Census, 1996b). Among first-year college students, about half the respondents in a national survey reported that they consume alcohol frequently or occasionally (see Figure 8.1). Young adults—particularly men—between the ages of twenty-one and thirty are at greater risk of alcohol abuse if they remain single or become divorced rather than making the transition into marriage and parenthood (Chilcoat and Breslau, 1996).

Most research on race and alcohol consumption has focused on male drinking patterns; studies show that young African American males as a category are less likely than their white counterparts to abuse alcohol, but the pattern reverses later in life. After age thirty, African American men have higher rates of heavy drinking and alcoholism than do white males. Some analysts attribute this difference to structural inequalities that uniquely affect men of color such as high rates of unemployment in central cities, racial discrimination in employment practices, and inadequate housing conditions (Herd, 1988). Low-income Native American men living on government-controlled reservations are especially vulnerable to chronic alcohol abuse and alcoholism. Our knowledge of alcohol consumption among Latinas and African American women is limited, but studies show that such factors as physical health, marital status, religious orientation, and previous life experiences apparently play a role (Taylor and Jackson, 1990). For example, Latinas and African American women who have higher levels of income and education typically consume alcohol more frequently than do their counterparts with lower incomes and education levels (Parker et al., 1995).

▲ Alcohol-Related Social Problems

Alcohol consumption in the United States has been declining across lines of class, gender, race, and age over the past two decades, but chronic alcohol abuse and alcoholism are nevertheless linked to many social problems. Here we will examine health problems, workplace and driving accidents, and family problems.

HEALTH PROBLEMS

Although not all heavy drinkers and chronic alcohol abusers exhibit the physical problems that are typically associated with alcoholism, their risk of major health problems is greatly increased. For alcoholics, the long-term health effects include *nutritional deficiencies* resulting from poor eating habits. Chronic heavy drinking contributes to high caloric

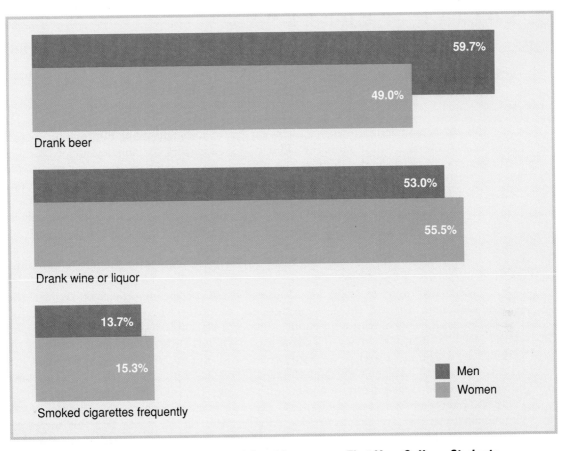

Drank beer

59.7%

49.0%

Drank wine or liquor

53.0%

55.5%

Smoked cigarettes frequently

13.7%

15.3%

Men
Women

FIGURE 8.1 *Alcohol Consumption and Smoking among First Year College Students. Based on survey responses of 240,082 freshmen entering two-year and four-year institutions in the fall of 1995.*

(SOURCE: Chronicle of Higher Education, 1996.)

consumption but low nutritional intake. Alcoholism is also associated with fluctuations in blood sugar levels that can cause adult-onset diabetes. Structural loss of brain tissue may produce *alcoholic dementia,* which is characterized by difficulties in problem solving, remembering information, and organizing facts about one's identity and surroundings (Levinthal, 1996).

Chronic alcohol abuse is also linked to *cardiovascular problems* such as inflammation and enlargement of the heart muscle, poor blood circulation, reduced heart contractions, fatty accumulations in the heart and arteries, high blood pressure, and cerebrovascular disorders such as stroke (Levinthal, 1996). However, studies show that moderate alcohol consumption—such as a glass of wine

a day—may improve body circulation, lower cholesterol levels, and reduce the risk of certain forms of heart disease.

Over time, chronic alcohol abuse also contributes to irreversible changes in the liver that are associated with *alcoholic cirrhosis*—a progressive development of scar tissue that chokes off blood vessels in the liver and destroys liver cells by interfering with their use of oxygen. Alcoholic cirrhosis is the ninth most frequent cause of death in the United States, most deaths occurring between ages forty and sixty-five (U.S. Bureau of the Census, 1996b). Alcoholics typically have a shorter life expectancy— often by as much as ten to twelve years—than that of nondrinkers or occasional drinkers who consume moderate amounts of alcohol.

SOCIAL PROBLEMS

IN THE MEDIA   **BOX 8.1**

A Fading Drumbeat against Drunken Driving?

It's harder and harder for us to get major media coverage. . . . If anyone would have told me 15 years ago that this many people, 17,000 people, would still be dying on the road, I would not have believed it.
— Katerine Prescott, National President, Mothers Against Drunk Driving (quoted in Wald, 1996a)

Like many other members of Mothers Against Drunk Driving (MADD), Katerine Prescott has a personal reason for confronting the problem of drunk driving: Her son was killed by a drunken driver in an automobile crash, as was the daughter of Candace Lightner, who founded the organization in the early 1980s. Over the past decade, MADD has campaigned for stricter laws against drunk driving and mounted a media campaign against driving and drinking.

Through public information messages in newspapers and on television, MADD continues to put human faces on the problem of drunk driving and encourage people to mobilize for action. Two periods of unusually high media attention are credited with reducing the number of people killed in drunk-driving accidents: Between 1983 and 1984, the campaign focused on making the public more aware of the problem; between 1989 and 1992, it focused on the importance of having a designated driver when people have been drinking. MADD also originated the "Friends Don't Let Friends Drive Drunk" ad campaign.

But in 1995—the same year that the mass media ran fewer public service ads on drinking—the number of people killed in drunk-driving accidents rose by 4 percent, the first increase in 10 years. Did this increase occur because people are tired of the campaign and "the sermon seems to be wearing off" (Wald,

---

Abuse of alcohol and other drugs by a pregnant woman can damage the unborn fetus. The greatest risk of *fetal alcohol syndrome (FAS)*—**characterized by mental retardation and craniofacial malformations in the child of an alcoholic mother**—occurs during the first three months of pregnancy. Binge drinking during the third week of gestation has particularly been linked with this syndrome because that is when crucial craniofacial formation and brain growth take place in the fetus.

ALCOHOL IN THE WORKPLACE

A recent study by the National Institute on Alcohol Abuse and Alcoholism found that lost productivity and time spent in treatment programs in the United States cost about $100 billion annually (Pedersen-Pietersen, 1997). But a person does not have to be a chronic drinker or alcoholic to have job-related problems such as absenteeism, tardiness, and workplace accidents associated with drinking. Excessive alcohol consumption impairs the sensorimotor skills necessary to operate machinery, heavy equipment, and motor vehicles, and numerous studies show a relationship between alcohol—and other drugs—and many workplace injuries or fatalities (Macdonald, 1995). On the basis of Bureau of Labor Statistics reports of more than 1,300 fatal occupational accidents, researchers concluded that alcohol, cocaine, and marijuana are the three leading substances involved in workplace injuries and deaths (Marine and Jack, 1994).

1996a:E5)? Or is it possible that strong messages backfired by increasing young people's motivation to drink (Bensley and Wu, 1991)? Or could it be that the number of drunken driving fatalities has not risen any faster than the number of highway fatalities not related to alcohol and that both numbers are rising because we travel more by car and many speed limits are higher (Wald, 1996b)? Although each of these viewpoints probably has validity, some social analysts partially attribute the increase to the media's greater concern with generating advertising dollars from the alcohol industry than with promoting public health and safety (Wald, 1996a). Over $1 billion is spent each year on alcoholic beverage advertising in the United States; about $626 million is spent annually on television advertising by the beer industry alone. In the future, these revenues may increase dramatically if liquor manufacturers decide to ease a decades-old voluntary restraint on television liquor ads (Jung, 1994). So far, most major broadcast television networks have refused to accept liquor ads; however, some lobbyists for the liquor industry have increased their contributions to members of Congress and argue that all they want is a level playing field with their competitors, particularly beer manufacturers (Seelye, 1997b).

At the same time, some politicians want a reassessment of even beer and wine advertising in sports programming, which has a huge percentage of viewers younger than the legal drinking age (Seelye, 1997b). In one study, researchers found that beer commercials appear more frequently than commercials for any other beverage during televised sports events (Madden and Grube, 1994).

Some beer commercials appear to address the problem of excessive drinking with slogans such as "Know When to Say When," but the ads themselves undermine the message. The images and fantasies associated with drinking make it seem far more exciting, romantic, and adventurous to drink than to abstain. Do you think that alcoholic beverage manufacturers have a responsibility to inform the public about the potential consequences of their products? Why or why not?

DRIVING AND DRINKING

Alcohol-related driving accidents occur when drivers lose control of their vehicles or fail to see a red traffic light, for example, or a car or pedestrian in the street, or a sharp curve in the road (Gross, 1983). Drivers who have been drinking often do not realize how much alcohol they have consumed or what effects it has on their driving ability. As a result, many people drive dangerously even when they are not legally drunk, which in most states requires a minimum blood alcohol level of 0.08 or 0.10 and is referred to as driving while intoxicated (DWI) or driving under the influence (DUI). Alcohol is implicated in about 41 percent of all fatal motor vehicle accidents in the United States; among people sixteen to twenty-four years of age, alcohol is involved in 30.8 percent of all motor vehicle fatalities (U.S. Bureau of the Census, 1996b). As high as these figures are, the exact size of the problem is unknown because only 68 percent of the drivers killed in automobile crashes are tested for alcohol, and only 24 percent of the drivers who survive accidents in which someone else dies are tested (Wald, 1996b). Moreover, despite some alcoholic beverage advertising and public service announcements by groups such as Mothers Against Drunk Driving to educate people about the hazards of drinking and driving, public interest in the issue appears to be declining (see Box 8.1).

FAMILY PROBLEMS

Chronic alcohol abuse or alcoholism makes it difficult for a person to maintain social relationships

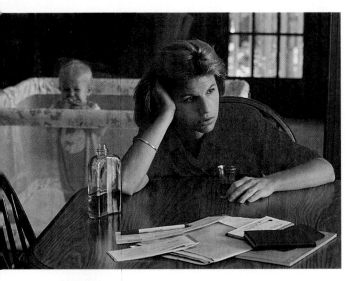

The relationship between alcohol abuse and family problems is extremely complex. Does this young mother view alcohol use as the **cause** *of her problems or a* **solution** *to them? What might be the long-term effects of her drinking on her child?*

and have a stable family life. The social effects of alcoholism are felt not only by the alcoholics themselves, but also by other family members. For every person who has a problem with alcohol, an average of at least four other people are directly affected on a daily basis (Levinthal, 1996). Domestic abuse and violence in families are frequently associated with heavy drinking and alcohol abuse by one or more family members. Similarly, growing up in a family that is affected by alcohol can have a profound impact on children. The extent to which alcohol abuse affects other family members depends on the degree of alcoholism and the type of alcoholic. Some alcoholic parents are violent and abusive; others are quiet and sullen or withdrawn. Many alcoholic families appear to be normal to outsiders, but family members may feel as though they have an "elephant in the living room," as journalist Joyce Maynard (1994:80–81) explains:

> I grew up in an alcoholic household. But as difficult as it was dealing with my father's drinking, the greater pain for me was the secret keeping. Adult children of alcoholics refer to the phe-

nomenon as "the elephant in the living room": You have a huge, inescapable fact about your life that affects everything in your home, but nobody mentions it, although everybody's behavior is altered to accommodate or deal with it. . . . Our family squeezed past the elephant in the living room, felt his breath on our faces, and rearranged furniture to make room for him. I hid liquor bottles if a friend was coming over. To prevent my father from driving, I even stashed away the keys to his car. But I never uttered a word, and neither did the rest of my family, about what was behind those actions. . . . It wasn't until I became an adult myself that I recognized the unhealthiness of our family's conspiracy of silence.

As Maynard suggests, she and many other members of alcoholic families take on the role of *enablers*—people who adjust their behavior to accommodate an alcoholic. Enabling often takes the form of lying to cover up the alcoholic's drinking, absenteeism from work, and/or discourteous treatment of others. Enabling leads many alcoholic families to develop a pattern of *codependency*—a reciprocal relationship between the alcoholic and one or more nonalcoholics who unwittingly aid and abet the alcoholic's excessive drinking and resulting behavior (Jung, 1994). When codependency occurs, the spouse or another family member takes on many of the alcoholic's responsibilities and keeps the alcoholic person from experiencing the full impact of his or her actions. Children who grow up in alcoholic families tend to have higher than normal rates of hyperactivity, antisocial behavior, low academic achievement, and cognitive impairment (Fishbein and Pease, 1996). However, although the statistical risks of becoming an alcoholic increase if one's parent has been an alcoholic, most children of alcoholics (as many as 59 percent) do not become alcoholics themselves (Sher, 1991).

TOBACCO (NICOTINE) USE AS A SOCIAL PROBLEM

The nicotine in tobacco is a toxic, dependency-producing psychoactive drug that is more addictive than heroin. It is categorized as a *stimulant* because it stimulates central nervous system receptors and activates them to release adrenaline, which raises blood pressure, speeds up the heartbeat, and gives the user a sense of alertness. Some people claim that nicotine reduces their appetite, helps them to lose weight, and produces a sense of calmness and relaxation (Akers, 1992). Perhaps these physical and psychological effects of tobacco dependency help to explain why about one in every four U.S. adults over the age of seventeen smokes, and about 70 percent of all smokers have more than fifteen cigarettes a day.

Although the overall proportion of smokers in the general population has declined somewhat since the 1964 Surgeon General's warning that smoking is linked to cancer and other serious diseases, tobacco is still responsible for about one in every five deaths in this country (Akers, 1992). Compared to nonsmokers, people who smoke cigarettes, cigars, or pipes have a greater likelihood of developing lung cancer and cancer of the larynx, mouth, and esophagus because nicotine is ingested into the bloodstream through the lungs and soft tissues of the mouth (Akers, 1992). In fact, smokers are ten times more likely than nonsmokers to contract lung cancer. Nearly 90 percent of the more than 140,000 lung cancer deaths annually are attributed to cigarette smoking (Fishbein and Pease, 1996; Levinthal, 1996). Many cases of bronchitis, emphysema, ulcers, and heart and circulatory disorders can also be traced to nicotine consumption. When tobacco burns, it forms carbon monoxide, which disrupts the transport of oxygen from the lungs to the rest of the body and hence contributes to cardiovascular disease (Levinthal, 1996).

Smoking typically shortens life expectancy. It is estimated that about a half a pack (ten cigarettes) a day on average reduces a person's life expectancy by four years, and smoking more than two packs a day (forty cigarettes) reduces life expectancy by eight years. When a person uses both tobacco and alcohol, the cancer-causing effects of tobacco are exacerbated (Fishbein and Pease, 1996).

Even people who never light up a cigarette are harmed by *environmental tobacco smoke*—**the smoke in the air inhaled by nonsmokers as a result of other people's tobacco smoking** (Levinthal, 1996). Researchers have found that environmental smoke is especially hazardous for nonsmokers who carpool or work with heavy smokers. When someone smokes a cigarette, about 75 percent of the nicotine ends up in the air. Therefore smoking has been banned in many public and private facilities throughout the country.

Not surprisingly, cigarette smoking adversely affects infants and children. Infants born to women who smoke typically have lower than average birth weight and sometimes slower rates of physical and mental growth. When a pregnant woman smokes, blood vessels constrict, reducing the amount of oxygen reaching the fetus. Furthermore, carbon monoxide is transmitted from the mother's blood to the fetus and interferes with the distribution of oxygen that does reach the fetus (DiFranza and Lew, 1995). Children who grow up in households where one or both parents smoke have increased likelihood of suffering from frequent ear infections, upper respiratory infections such as bronchitis and sinusitis, allergies, asthma, and other health problems.

Today, at least 3 million teenagers smoke, and many report that they started in the sixth or seventh grade (Johnston et al., 1994). The National Institute on Drug Abuse reports that almost 20 percent of eighth-graders say they smoke—an increase of nearly one-third since the early 1990s (Hostetler, 1995). About 19 percent of high school seniors report that they smoke on a daily basis, and about 11 percent indicate that they smoke as much as half a pack of cigarettes a day. Like smokers of all ages, high-school-age smokers differ from nonsmokers on the basis of educational level and socioeconomic status. High school seniors who are not planning to attend college are three times more likely to smoke half a pack a day than college-bound seniors. Those who drop out of high school are four times more likely to smoke cigarettes daily than are those who remain in high school through graduation. College students have lower rates of smoking than do individuals of the same age who are not attending college (Levinthal, 1996).

In recent years, young people have been targeted for smokeless tobacco products such as chewing tobacco and moist snuff, which is placed between the cheek and the gum. White teenage boys and young adult males, particularly in the South and West, are the primary consumers of these products. However, since oral smokeless tobacco is absorbed through the membranes of the mouth into the bloodstream, it increases the risk of cancer of the tongue, cheeks, gums, and esophagus. Most habitual snuff users have *leukoplakia*—a white, thick precancerous patch that is visible on tissues in the mouth—and *erythro-plakia*—a red precancerous spot inside the mouth and nasal cavity (Akers, 1992).

Why do so many people use nicotine if it is so dangerous? Several reasons have been suggested. First, nicotine creates a high level of dependency, so once a person has begun to use tobacco regularly, the withdrawal symptoms may be strong enough to make the person light up another cigarette. Some researchers have found that the majority of people who smoke recognize that smoking is bad for them and would like to quit but cannot (Fishbein and Pease, 1996:213). Second, sophisticated marketing campaigns associate smoking with desirable cultural attributes such as achieving maturity, gaining wealth and happiness, or being thin and sexy. Although cigarette manufacturers are no longer allowed to advertise their products on radio or television, they have other venues. More than $4 billion dollars is spent annually on magazine and newspaper advertising, billboards, sponsorship of sports events, and other forms of cigarette promotions (Hostetler, 1995). Some cigarette ad campaigns appear to specifically target young people, and they appear to work. Researchers have found that 86 percent of all children who smoke prefer heavily advertised brands such as Marlboro, Camel, or Newport.

In August 1997, it appeared that the U.S. government and the tobacco industry were close to reaching an agreement under which tobacco products would become more regulated, less readily available to the public, and taxed at a higher level. Under the proposed agreement, the tobacco companies would pay billions of dollars to the government over a period of years to help compensate for increased health care costs the government will incur as a result of tobacco-related illnesses and diseases such as lung cancer. However, the benefits tobacco companies may receive from the agreement (such as limited monetary liability) are less clear. Also uncertain is the issue of whether the number of people who smoke will actually decrease as a result of the agreement.

PRESCRIPTION DRUGS, OVER-THE-COUNTER DRUGS, AND CAFFEINE

When most people think of drug abuse, they picture unscrupulous drug dealers in dark alleys selling ille-gal drugs. But two categories of drugs that are sold legally in the United States are also abused: *prescription drugs,* which are dispensed only by a registered pharmacist on the authority of a licensed physician or dentist, and *over the counter (OTC) drugs,* which are available off the shelf and are restricted only by the customer's ability to pay.

Prescription Drugs

Pain medication is probably the most abused prescription drug. Though millions of people benefit from *narcotics*—natural or synthetic opiates such as morphine (brand names Duramorph and Roxanol), propoxyphene (Darvon), and codeine—that relieve pain, suppress coughing, control chronic diarrhea, and reduce heroin withdrawal symptoms, there are risks of short-term abuse and long-term psychological and physical dependence. Over time, users develop tolerance for the drug and must continue to increase dosages to obtain the same effect that was previously derived from a lower dose. Drug dependency that results from physician-supervised treatment for a recognized medical disorder is called *iatrogenic addiction.* Iatrogenic addiction is most likely to occur with long-term use and/or high dosages of a prescription drug; it most often affects people from the middle or upper class who have no previous history of drug abuse or addiction (Fishbein and Pease, 1996).

Two widely prescribed drugs that have been the subject of controversy regarding their use and abuse are methylphenidate (Ritalin) and fluoxetine (Prozac). Ritalin is a stimulant that is prescribed for children who are diagnosed with *attention-deficit hyperactivity disorder* (ADHD). According to the American Psychiatric Association, ADHD is characterized by "emotionality, behavioral hyperactivity, short attention span, distractibility, impulsiveness, and perceptual and learning disabilities" (Fishbein and Pease, 1996). Although some children are probably correctly diagnosed with this disorder, one survey concluded that Ritalin is being overprescribed; in the United States, it has been prescribed for 3 to 5 percent of all schoolchildren. Boys are three times more likely than girls to be diagnosed with ADHD, and it is estimated that 10 percent to 12 percent of boys between the ages of six and fourteen take or have taken the drug (Crossette, 1996a). Advocates believe that children with normal to above average intelligence who are performing poorly in school can benefit from Ritalin, which has proven to be safe for more than 40 years. But critics argue that many parents, doctors, and teachers see Ritalin as a quick fix for dealing with troublesome children and note that the drug typically is prescribed to be taken *only* during the school year (Crossette, 1996a).

One of the most abused prescription drugs for adults is Prozac, an antidepressant. Introduced in 1987 as a breakthrough medication for major depression, Prozac has become a "cure-all for the blues" for many people who do not meet the medical criteria for clinical depression. Advocates believe that the more than 4.5 million prescriptions for Prozac that are filled annually enhance the quality of life for many people, freeing them from depression and suicidal thoughts. But the long-term side effects of the drug are unknown, and there is some evidence that Prozac is associated with intense, violent suicidal thoughts in some patients. Both Prozac and Ritalin are approved by the U.S. Food and Drug Administration (FDA) and are considered safe and effective if taken as directed (Angier, 1990; Kramer, 1993).

Over-the-Counter Drugs

A fine line exists between prescription and over-the-counter (OTC) drugs. Today, both types of drugs are advertised directly to the consumer in the electronic and print media with suggestions to "ask your doctor or pharmacist about [our product] on your next visit." Some drugs are available both by prescription and over the counter, depending on their strength and dosage. For example, medication for stomach ulcers (e.g, Zantac and Tagamet) are sold over the counter in lower doses and by prescription in higher doses. Some drugs that are now sold over the counter were previously available only by prescription.

Widely used OTC drugs include analgesics, sleep aids, and cough and cold remedies. Abuse of aspirin and other analgesics can cause gastric bleeding, problems with blood clotting, complications in surgery patients and pregnant women in labor and delivery, and Reye's syndrome (a potentially life-threatening condition that arises when children with flu, chicken pox, or other viral infections are given aspirin). Overdoses of analgesics such as acetaminophen (e.g., Tylenol and Anacin-3), aspirin, and ibuprofen (e.g., Motrin, Advil, and Midol) have been linked to cases of attempted suicide, especially by white females between the ages of six and seventeen years. Few of these suicide attempts resulted in death except when the analgesics were combined with alcohol or other drugs (Levinthal, 1996). Like analgesics, sleep aids are dangerous when combined with alcohol or some cough and cold remedies because they are depressants that slow down the central nervous system. Even cough and cold medications alone have side effects such as drowsiness that can be hazardous if users attempt to drive a car or operate heavy machinery. To counteract drowsiness, some drug companies add caffeine to their product.

Caffeine

Although caffeine is a relatively safe drug, it is a dependency-producing psychoactive stimulant (Gilbert, 1986). Caffeine is an ingredient in coffee, tea, chocolate, soft drinks, and stimulants such as NoDoz and Vivarin. Generally speaking, people ingest caffeine because they like the feeling of mental alertness and reduced fatigue it produces. However, the extent to which caffeine actually improves human performance is widely debated. Caffeine may improve concentration when a person is performing boring or repetitive tasks but has little effect on the performance of complex tasks such as critical thinking and decision making (Curatolo and Robertson, 1983; Dews, 1984). Short-term effects of caffeine include dilated peripheral blood vessels, constricted blood vessels in the head, and a slightly elevated heart rate (Levinthal, 1996). Long-term effects of heavy caffeine use (more than three cups of coffee or five cups of tea per day) include increased risk of heart attack and osteoporosis—the loss of bone density and increased brittleness associated with fractures and broken bones (Kiel et al., 1990). Overall, abuse of caffeine and prescription and OTC drugs is relatively minor when compared with the social problems associated with illegal drugs.

ILLEGAL DRUG USE AND ABUSE

Are some drugs inherently bad and hence classified as illegal? What constitutes an illegal drug is a matter of social and legal definitions and is subject to change over time. During the nineteenth and early twentieth centuries, people in the United States had fairly easy access to drugs that are currently illegal for general use. In the 1800s, there were no licensed doctors or pharmacists, and people referring to

SOCIAL PROBLEMS
AND SOCIAL POLICY

BOX 8.2

The Battle over Marijuana: Medicalization or Legalization?

Perhaps the most persuasive argument for medicinal marijuana I've encountered came two years ago, when the California Assembly was debating a medical-marijuana bill. One GOP assemblyman said he had had a great deal of trouble with the issue. But when a relative was dying a few years before, the family had used marijuana to help her nausea. That story helped the bill pass. Wouldn't it be awful if people changed their minds only after someone close to them had died?
—Marcus Conant (1997:26), a doctor at the University of California, San Francisco, who has treated more than 5,000 HIV-positive patients in his private practice

[Until adequate testing is done on marijuana] . . . it is inconceivable to allow anyone of any age to have uncontrolled use of marijuana for any alleged illness—without a doctor's

examination or even a prescription. But that is precisely what the California law lets people do. Can you think of any other untested, home-made, mind-altering medicine that you self-dose, and that uses a burning carcinogen as a delivery vehicle? I think it's clear that a lot of people arguing for the California proposition and others like it are pushing the legalization of drugs, plain and simple.
—Barry R. McCaffrey (1997:27), a retired army general who is director of the Office of National Drug Control Policy, Washington, D.C.

As these statements suggest, the controversy over marijuana is far from resolved. Advocates of *legalization* suggest that marijuana use should no longer be subject to legal control. Some states have adopted some form of decriminalization laws for the possession of small amounts—usually less than one ounce or so—of

themselves as "doctors" sold *patent medicines* that contained such ingredients as opium, morphine, heroin, cocaine, and alcohol. Patent medicines could be purchased in stores, through mail-order advertisements, and from medicine wagons that used free entertainment to attract crowds (Young, 1961). Over time, prescriptions became required for some drugs because of the rapidly growing number of narcotics addicts. Some forms of drug use were criminalized because of their association with specific minority groups. For example, opium could legally be consumed in cough syrup, but smoking the same amount of opium was declared illegal in 1908 because opium smoking was a favorite pastime of the Chinese workers building railroads in the western

United States (James and Johnson, 1996). Other forms of opium use were regulated when Congress passed the Harrison Narcotics Act in 1914.

The Harrison Act required anyone who produced or distributed drugs to register with the federal government, keep a record of all transactions, and pay a tax on habit-forming drugs such as heroin, opium, and morphine; it also required that certain drugs be purchased only from physicians (James and Johnson, 1996). However, the Harrison Act and drug-related legislation that followed it have not been able to eliminate illegal drug use in this country (Bertram et al., 1996). Today, the most widely used illegal drugs are marijuana, stimulants such as cocaine and amphetamines, depressants such as bar-marijuana. About twenty-six states and the District of Columbia have passed medical-marijuana laws that permit use of the drug under specific medical circumstances. Advocates of these laws believe doctors should be allowed to prescribe marijuana or that the federal government should lift the ban on medical use of this drug altogether. Advocates of medical legalization believe marijuana's benefits in treating certain medical conditions far outweigh its possible adverse consequences. For example, marijuana can help to control glaucoma, an eye disease that eventually produces blindness. It also can forestall AIDS-related complications, ease the nausea brought on by cancer chemotherapy, and counter some of the symptoms of epilepsy and multiple sclerosis (Cowley, 1997). Advocates envision a physician-controlled, prescription-based system or a legalized regulatory system something like that in place now for alcohol and tobacco. If marijuana were treated as a legal substance, it could be subject to restrictions on advertising, content, purchase age, and other regulations for production, distribution, and sale (Akers, 1992).

In sharp contrast, federal drug enforcement officials and other opponents of medical-marijuana laws or legalization argue that the medical benefits of marijuana are modest at best and the drug is useless or dangerous at worst. Opponents believe that medical-marijuana laws or legalization would increase the general level of use and open the door for legalization of drugs such as cocaine, heroin, amphetamines, and hallucinogens, which are far more dangerous. Although problems associated with the criminalization of drugs, such as drug smuggling and global drug trafficking, might be lessened by legalization, the costs to society would be too great. According to sociologist Ronald L. Akers (1992:160), marijuana use "has the potential to grow to the same level as tobacco and alcohol use with basically the same magnitude of threat to health and life. . . . The benefits of legalization . . . are no more certain than are the harmful consequences of legalization."

Do you think marijuana for medical use should be treated differently than for recreational use? What pros and cons would you give in a debate over the legalization of marijuana?

---

biturates, narcotics such as heroin, and hallucinogens such as LSD.

Marijuana

Marijuana is the most extensively used illicit drug in the United States: About one in three people over the age of twelve has tried marijuana at least once. It is ingested by smoking a hand-rolled cigarette known as a *reefer* or a *joint* or through a pipe or other smoking implement. Potent marijuana, with high levels of the plant's primary psychoactive chemical, delta-9 tetrahydrocannabinol (THC), has existed for many years, but potency has increased in recent years because more marijuana plants are now grown in indoor gardens in the United States. Indoor crops have levels of THC up to four times as high as plants grown outdoors and in other nations (Navarro, 1996).

Although most marijuana users are between the ages of eighteen and twenty-five, use by teens between the ages of twelve and seventeen has more than doubled over the past decade (Substance Abuse and Mental Health Services Administration, 1996). Many teenage users report that marijuana is as easy to acquire as alcohol or cigarettes. According to one teenager, "It is so popular, so well known, it is around everywhere. Nobody is afraid of the consequences of selling it or buying it. . . . It is really easy to get" (quoted in Friend, 1996: 2A). Many young people buy the drug from friends who grow their own plants.

Marijuana is both a central nervous system depressant and a stimulant. In low to moderate doses, the drug produces mild sedation; in high doses, it produces a sense of well-being, euphoria, and sometimes hallucinations. Marijuana slightly increases blood pressure and heart rate and greatly lowers blood glucose levels, causing extreme hunger. The human body manufactures a chemical that closely resembles THC, and specific receptors in the brain are designed to receive it. Marijuana use disrupts these receptors, impairing motor activity, concentration, and short-term memory (Cowley, 1997). As a result, complex motor tasks such as driving a car or operating heavy machinery are dangerous for a person who is under the influence of marijuana. Some studies show that heavy marijuana use can impair concentration and recall in high school and college students (Wren, 1996b). Users become apathetic and lose their motivation to perform competently or achieve long-range goals such as completing their education. Overall, the short-term effects of marijuana are typically milder than the short-term effects of drugs such as cocaine (Fishbein and Pease, 1996).

High doses of marijuana smoked during pregnancy can disrupt the development of a fetus and result in lower than average birth weight, congenital abnormalities, premature delivery, and neurological disturbances (Fishbein and Pease, 1996). Furthermore, some studies have found an increased risk of cancer and other lung problems associated with inhaling because marijuana smokers are believed to inhale more deeply than tobacco users.

Over the past decade, medical uses of marijuana have been widely debated. In 1985, the Food and Drug Administration approved a synthetic version of THC, called Marinol, for prescription use to ease the nausea and vomiting that are common side effects of chemotherapy in cancer patients. Marinol is now also used to help AIDS patients regain their appetites (Cowley, 1997). Voters in some states have sought passage of laws establishing therapeutic research programs, allowing doctors to prescribe marijuana, and seeking to lift the ban on medical use of marijuana. Debates over these initiatives are far from over (see Box 8.2 on pages 164–165).

◣ Stimulants

Cocaine and amphetamines are among the major stimulants that are abused in the United States. Co-caine is an extremely potent and dependency-producing drug derived from the small leaves of the coca plant that grows in several Latin American countries. In the nineteenth century, cocaine was introduced in the United States as a local anesthetic in medical practice and a mood-enhancer in patent medicines (Akers, 1992). It was a major ingredient in Coca-Cola from the 1880s to the early 1900s (Miller, 1994). Today, cocaine is the third most widely used psychoactive drug after alcohol and marijuana. Users typically sniff, or "snort," the drug into their nostrils, inject it intravenously, or smoke it in the form of crack—a potent form that is specially processed for smoking.

About 23 million people over the age of twelve in this country report that they have used cocaine at least once, and about one million acknowledge having used it during the past month (Substance Abuse and Mental Health Services Administration, 1996). According to recent research, more males than females use cocaine, and the majority of users are in their twenties (Fishbein and Pease, 1996). In the mid-1980s, extensive media coverage of the hazards of cocaine use resulted in decreased usage by middle-class white high school and college-age students; however, an upswing in use occurred among young minority group members living in central cities (Fishbein and Pease, 1996). For some central city residents living in poverty, with no hope of gainful employment, cocaine became a major source of revenue and an entry point for other drug-related crime. Here's how one fourteen-year-old male in Miami, Florida, described his involvement in the drug business (quoted in Inciardi et al., 1993a:86–87):

I was sort of a scout, a lookout, for Mr. George. That was the name of the man who delivered the stuff [cocaine] to the places that sold it. . . . I was 11, an' Mr. George had a kid like me probably on every block. . . . I'd be in my front yard, see, watchin' for the cops. Mr. George would drive by my house . . . a few times. I'd watch and see if he was being followed. If everything looked OK, I'd go over to his car an' he'd give me the stuff, and tell me where to take it, or who to give it to. Sometimes he'd just give me a key an' say somethin' like "blue Pontiac 75/25." That would mean that near the corner of 75th Street and 25th Avenue there'd be a blue Pontiac. The stuff, and instructions, or maybe something else,

Many people were shocked and saddened to learn of the death of actor River Phoenix from a drug overdose. Do you believe the death of a celebrity such as this sends a message to young people about the problem of illicit drug use? Or do you think most people believe such things will never happen to them?

would be in the trunk. Mr. George was real careful. When I'd drop it off I'd collect the money too. . . . For each job I'd get $10.

This young man's experience is not unique; studies point out how selling drugs such as cocaine, crack, and heroin are the fastest-growing means of economic survival for men in locations ranging from Miami to Harlem (New York City) and Los Angeles (Bourgeois, 1995).

The effects of cocaine on the human body depend on how pure the dose is and what effect the user expects from the drug. Most cocaine users experience a powerful high or "rush" in which the blood pressure rises and the heart rate and respiration increase dramatically. Reactions vary in length and intensity depending on whether the drug is injected, smoked,

or snorted. When the drug wears off, the user becomes increasingly agitated and depressed. Some users become extremely depressed and suicidal; others develop such a powerful craving that they easily become addicted to the drug (Gawin and Ellinwood, 1988). Occasionally, cocaine use results in sudden death by triggering an irregular heart rhythm.

People who use cocaine over extended periods of time have higher rates of infection, heart disturbance, internal bleeding, hypertension, cardiac arrest, stroke, hemorrhaging, and other neurological and cardiovascular disorders than do nonusers. Although these problems may develop gradually as cocaine use continues, some users experience these problems after a single dose of the drug. Intravenous cocaine users who share contaminated needles and syringes are also at risk for AIDS. As was discussed in Chapter 7, the risk of contracting AIDS is especially high in crack houses, where women addicts often engage in prostitution to acquire drugs.

Cocaine use is extremely hazardous during pregnancy. Children born to crack-addicted mothers typically suffer painful withdrawal symptoms at birth and later show deficits in cognitive skills, judgment, and behavior controls. "Crack babies" must often be cared for at public expense in hospitals and other facilities because their mothers cannot meet their basic needs or provide nurturance. But social scientist Philippe Bourgeois suggests that blame for the problem cannot be placed on the women alone. Many mothers of crack babies desperately seek meaning in their lives and refuse to sacrifice themselves to the impossible task of raising healthy children in the inner city. They are not cruel and unfeeling but rather self-destructive rebels who have given up fighting the odds that history has structured against them (Bourgeois, 1995). Instead, Bourgeois blames the problem on patriarchal definitions of "family" and the dysfunctional public sector that relegates the responsibility for nurturing and supporting children almost exclusively to women. For change to occur, fathers and the larger society must share the women's burden (Bourgeois, 1995).

Like cocaine, amphetamines ("uppers") stimulate the central nervous system. Amphetamines in the form of diet pills and pep formulas are legal substances when they are prescribed by a physician, but many people, believing that they cannot lose weight or have enough energy without the pills, become physically and/or psychologically dependent on the drugs. Speed freaks—heavy users who inject massive doses of amphetamines several times a day—often do a "run," staying awake for extended periods of time, eating very little, and engaging in bizarre behavior such as counting cornflakes in a cereal box or pasting postage stamps on the wall before "crashing" and sleeping for several days (Goode, 1989). Chronic amphetamine abuse can result in *amphetamine psychosis,* which is characterized by paranoia, hallucinations, and violent tendencies that may persist for weeks after use of the drug has been discontinued. Overdosing on amphetamines can produce coma, brain damage, and even death. Recent concern about amphetamine abuse has focused on a smokable form called ICE that contains a high percentage of the pure drug and produces effects that last longer, from four to twenty-four hours (Lauderback and Waldorf, 1993).

Depressants

Many people who abuse stimulants also abuse depressants—alcohol and other drugs that depress the central nervous system and may have some pain-killing properties. The most commonly used depressants are barbiturates (e.g., Nembutal and Seconal) and antianxiety drugs or tranquilizers (e.g., Librium, Valium, and Miltown). Relatively low oral doses of depressants produce a relaxing and mildly disinhibiting effect; higher doses result in sedation. Users may develop both physical addiction to, and psychological dependency on, these depressants. Depressants are also used for *potentiation*—the interaction that takes place when two drugs are mixed together to produce a far greater effect than the effect of either drug administered separately. For example, when users combine heroin and barbiturates in hopes of prolonging a high and extending the heroin supply, they are seeking potentiation (Fishbein and Pease, 1996).

Recently, there has been much discussion on college campuses about Rohypnol and GHB (short for gamma-hydroxybutyrate), also known as "Grievous Bodily Harm" or "Liquid X." Rohypnol is used as an anesthetic and sleep aid in other countries, but it is not approved for use in the United States. GHB was sold in health food stores and used by body builders to increase muscle growth before it was banned by the FDA in 1990. Currently, GHB is manufactured illegally, and some people acquire the recipe on the Internet. Rohypnol and GHB are popular among young people because they are inexpensive ("lunch money" drugs) and they produce a "floaty" state, a mild euphoria, increased sociability, and lowered inhibitions. For people such as Jenny Altick, who was a college student when she tried Rohypnol, the drug works like a powerful sleeping pill: "I'd just pass out. . . . it seemed like a very safe thing to take. It wasn't like acid or something that was totally chemical and bad. If you're thinking about trying coke [cocaine], you've heard how bad it is. There's that little thing in your head. But this one, no one had heard about it. It was one of those new things everyone was doing" (quoted in Bonnin, 1997: E1). Other users report more dire consequences, however. Rohypnol is known as the "date rape drug" because a number of women have reported that they were raped after an acquaintance secretly slipped the drug into their drink. The combination of alcohol and Rohypnol or GHB has also been linked to automobile accidents and deaths from overdoses because it is difficult to judge how much intoxication will occur when depressants are mixed with alcohol (Bonnin, 1997).

Narcotics

Narcotics or opiates are available in several forms: natural substances (e.g, opium, morphine, and codeine), opiate derivatives created by making slight changes in the chemical composition of morphine (e.g., heroin and Percodan), and synthetic drugs that produce opiatelike effects but are not chemically related to morphine (e.g., Darvon and Demerol). Because heroin is the most widely abused narcotic, we will focus primarily on its effects.

Who uses heroin? Young people are among the heaviest heroin users; however, only 1 percent of people between eighteen and twenty-nine years of age acknowledge that they have ever used the drug. Some people who try the drug have adverse side effects such as nausea and vomiting and never use it again. Current estimates of the number of U.S. heroin abusers range from 300,000 to 700,000. Most studies conclude that the typical heroin abuser is a young male, often a minority group member, under age thirty, who lives in a low-income area of a large urban center such as New York City (Fishbein and Pease, 1996).

What effect does heroin have on the body? Most heroin users inject the drug intravenously—a practice known as *mainlining* or *shooting*—so that they can experience an initial tingling sensation and feeling of euphoria, typically followed by a state of drowsiness or lethargy. Heroin users quickly develop a tolerance for the drug and must continually increase their dosage to achieve the same effect. Heroin and other opiates are highly addictive; users experience intense cravings for another fix and have physical symptoms such as diarrhea and dehydration if the drug is withdrawn.

What are the long-term effects of heroin? Although some users experience no long-term physical problems from the drug, other risk factors are extremely serious. In high doses, heroin produces extreme respiratory depression, coma, and even death. Because the potency of street heroin is unknown, overdosing is always a possibility. Street heroin also tends to be diluted with other ingredients that produce adverse reactions in some users. Shooting up with contaminated needles and syringes can lead to hepatitis or AIDS. Heroin use also has been more directly linked to crimes than have some other types of drug use. Because hard-core users have difficulty holding a job, yet need a continual supply of drugs, they often turn to robbery, burglary, shoplifting, pimping, prostitution, or working for the underground drug industry (Johnson et al., 1985).

Hallucinogens

Hallucinogens or psychedelics are drugs that produce illusions and hallucinations. Mescaline (peyote), lysergic acid diethylamide (LSD), phencyclidine (PCP), and MDMA (Ecstasy) produce mild to profound psychological effects, depending on the dosage. Mescaline or peyote was the earliest hallucinogen used in North America. Its consumption dates back to ancient Native American religious celebrations.

In the 1960s, LSD became a well-known hallucinogen because of Dr. Timothy Leary's widely publicized advice, "turn on, tune in, drop out." LSD is one of the most powerful psychoactive drugs; a tiny dose (10 micrograms) of the odorless, tasteless, and colorless drug can produce highly unpredictable, dramatic psychological effects for up to 12 hours. These effects are often referred to as a *psychedelic trip,* and users report experiences ranging from the beautiful (a good trip) to the frightening and extremely depressing (a bad trip). Consequently, some LSD users take the drug only with the companion-

ship of others who are familiar with the drug's effects. However, some studies have found that there is a possibility of *flashbacks* in which the user reexperiences the effect of the drug as much as a year after it was taken. Most long-term psychiatric problems associated with the drug typically involve people who are unaware that they have been given LSD, who show unstable personality characteristics before taking the drug, or who experience it under hostile or threatening circumstances (Levinthal, 1996).

Among the most recent hallucinogens are PCP ("angel dust") and MDMA ("Ecstasy"). PCP can be taken orally, intravenously, or by inhalation, but it is most often smoked. Initially, PCP was an anesthetic used in surgical procedures, but it was removed from production when patients showed signs of agitation, intense anxiety, hallucinations, and disorientation after receiving the drug. Then PCP became a relatively inexpensive street drug that some dealers pass off as a more expensive drug such as LSD to unknowing customers.

In the mid-1980s, MDMA ("Ecstasy") hit the street market. Manufactured in clandestine labs by inexperienced chemists, Ecstasy, or "E," is a "designer drug" derived from amphetamines that produces hallucinogenic effects. Users claim that it produces a state of relaxation, insight, euphoria, and heightened awareness without the side effects of LSD. Ecstasy has a high abuse potential and no recognized medical use (Milkman and Sunderwirth, 1987).

EXPLANATIONS OF DRUG ABUSE

Why do people abuse drugs? Various explanations have been given. Some focus on biological factors; others emphasize environmental influences. Social scientists believe that drug abuse is associated with continuous and cumulative influences from the time of conception and throughout the life course (Fishbein and Pease, 1996). To answer the question of why people abuse drugs, we must therefore examine the intertwining biological, psychological, and sociological factors that affect people's behavior.

Biological Explanations

Some biological explanations of alcohol and drug addiction focus on genetic factors. Some studies of alcoholism have found that children with an alcoholic parent have a higher than normal risk of becoming alcoholics themselves, even if they were adopted at birth and reared by nonalcoholic parents. According to the biological perspective, the child of an alcoholic parent inherits a biological predisposition (or vulnerability) to problem drinking or alcoholism. For example, the child may inherit increased sensitivity to alcohol as indicated by impaired enzyme production, brain function, and physiological responsivity during alcohol intake. The child also might inherit cognitive or learning impairments (e.g., hyperactivity, attention deficit disorder, or language delay) or psychological features (e.g., impulsivity, sensation seeking, anxiety, or aggressiveness) that increase the risk of alcohol abuse by exaggerating the rewarding biological and psychological properties of alcohol (Fishbein and Pease, 1996).

Other biological studies focus on the relationship between the brain and drug addiction and have found convincing evidence that drugs such as alcohol, heroin, and cocaine act directly on the brain mechanisms responsible for reward and punishment. As the drug stimulates the areas of the brain that create the sensation of pleasure and suppress the perception of pain, the user receives reinforcement to engage in further drug-taking behavior. According to these findings, then, drugs that provide an immediate rush or intense euphoria (e.g., cocaine and heroin) are more likely to be abused than are drugs that do not. Similarly, drugs that produce pleasant but rapidly dissipating effects (e.g., alcohol) tend to encourage users to take additional doses to maintain the pleasurable effects. Biological explanations provide some insights on drug abuse, but biological factors alone do not fully explain alcoholism and other drug dependency.

Psychological Explanations

Psychological explanations of drug abuse focus on either personality disorders or the effects of social learning and reinforcement on drug-taking behavior. Some studies have found that personality disorders—including antisocial personality, psychopathy, impulsivity, affective disorder, and anxiety—are more common among drug abusers than among nonabusers (Shedler and Block, 1990). Hyperactivity, learning disabilities, and behavioral disorders in childhood are also associated with a greater risk of substance abuse in adolescence or young adulthood. When people have low self-esteem or lack motivation, their desire to get away from problems is intensified, and drugs often provide the most available option for escape.

Social psychologists explain drug behavior in terms of social learning. According to *social learning theory*, drug and alcohol use and abuse are socially influenced behaviors that are acquired and sustained through a learning process. Learning takes place through instrumental conditioning (getting positive reinforcement or punishment) and modeling (imitation) of other people's behavior. Every person learns attitudes, orientations, and general information about drug use from family members, friends, and significant others, so he or she comes to associate positive consequences (positive reinforcement) and negative consequences (punishment) with drug use. Therefore whether the person abstains from or takes drugs, as well as whether he or she abuses drugs, depends on past, present, and anticipated rewards and punishments associated with abstinence, use, and abuse. In a nutshell, the more an individual defines drug behavior as good or at least excusable, the more that person is likely to use drugs (Akers, 1992).

Sociological Explanations

The social psychological perspective on drug abuse and the interactionist perspective overlap. In contrast, functionalists focus on how drug use and abuse fulfills a function in society, and conflict theorists emphasize the role of powerful elites in determining what constitutes legal or illegal drug use.

THE INTERACTIONIST PERSPECTIVE

Like social psychologists, sociologists who use an interactionist framework believe that drug behavior is learned behavior that is strongly influenced by families, peers, and other people. In other words, individuals are more likely to abuse drugs if they have frequent, intense, and long-lasting interactions with people who abuse drugs. Similarly, when there are more factors favoring drug use than there are opposing it, the person is likely to use drugs. For example, some children learn to abuse alcohol or other drugs by watching their parents drink excessively or use illegal drugs. Other young people learn about drug use from their peer group. In his classic study of marijuana users, sociologist Howard S. Becker (1963) concluded that drug users not only learn how to "do" drugs from other users, but they also learn what pleasurable reactions they should expect to have from drug use. It also follows that people are more prone to accept attitudes and behaviors favorable to drug use if they spend time with members of a *drug subculture*—**a group of people whose attitudes, beliefs, and behaviors pertaining to drug use differ significantly from those of most people in the larger society.** Over time, people in heavy drinking or drug subcultures tend to become closer to others within their subculture and more distant from people outside the subculture. In fact, participants in hard-core drug subcultures quit taking drugs or drinking excessively only when something brings about a dramatic change in their attitudes, beliefs, and values regarding drugs. According to *labeling theory,* it is particularly difficult for individuals to discontinue alcohol and other drug abuse once they have been labeled an "alcoholic" or a "drug addict." It is widely believed that most addicts could change their behavior if they chose to do so. Because of the prevailing ideology that alcoholism and drug addiction are personal problems rather than social problems, individuals tend to be held solely responsible for their behavior.

THE FUNCTIONALIST PERSPECTIVE

Why does the level of drug abuse remain high in the United States? Functionalists point out that social institutions such as the family, education, and religion that previously kept deviant behavior in check have become fragmented and somewhat disorganized. Hence it is now necessary to use formal mechanisms of social control to prohibit people from taking illegal drugs or driving under the influence of alcohol or other drugs. External controls in the form of law enforcement are also required to discourage people from growing, manufacturing, or importing illegal substances.

Functionalists believe that activities in society continue because they serve important societal functions. Prescription and over-the-counter drugs, for example, are functional for patients because they ease pain, cure illness, and sometimes enhance or extend life. They are functional for doctors because they provide a means for treating illness and help to justify the doctor's fee. They are functional for pharmacists because they provide a source of employ-

ment; without pills to dispense, there would be no need for pharmacists. But dysfunctions also occur with prescription drugs. Patients may experience adverse side effects or develop a psychological dependence on the drug; and doctors, pharmacists, and drug companies may be sued because they manufactured, prescribed, or sold a drug that is alleged to cause bodily harm to users.

Illicit drugs have both positive functions and dysfunctions as well. On the one hand, illicit drug use creates and perpetuates jobs at all levels of the criminal justice system, the federal government, and social service agencies that deal with problems of alcoholism and drug addiction. What, for example, would employees at the Drug Enforcement Administration (DEA)—the principal federal narcotics control agency—do if the United States did not have an array of illicit drugs that are defined as the "drug problem"? On the other hand, the dysfunctions of illicit drug use extend throughout society. At the individual level, addictive drugs such as heroin, cocaine, and barbiturates create severe physical and mental health problems as well as economic crises for addicts, their families, and acquaintances. At the societal level, drug abuse contributes to lost produc-

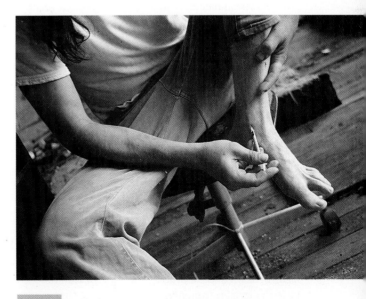

This man may be playing double jeopardy with his life. The purity of street drugs often is in doubt, and shooting up with contaminated needles is a significant source of new AIDS cases in the United States.

tivity, human potential and life, and money. Billions of dollars in taxpayers' money—that might be used for education or preventive health care—are spent making and enforcing drug laws and dealing with drug-related crime and the spread of AIDS by addicts who shoot up with contaminated needles. Addiction to illegal drugs, the abuse of legal drugs, and the abuse of alcohol and tobacco exacerbates the loss of human potential and undermines the stability of society.

THE CONFLICT PERSPECTIVE

According to conflict theorists, people in positions of economic and political power make the sale, use, and possession of some drugs illegal. Those in privileged positions criminalize the use of drugs such as marijuana, cocaine, and heroin because historically these are substances abused by the poor and the powerless. We mentioned earlier that opium smoking was outlawed because it was associated with the Chinese. Similarly, marijuana smoking—which was associated primarily with people in the Mexican working class brought to the United States during the 1920s to work in some fields and factories—was restricted by the Marijuana Tax Act of 1937. Although the name of this legislation suggests that its purpose was to raise tax revenues, the intent was to criminalize marijuana and provide a mechanism for driving Mexican workers back across the border so that they would not be a threat to U.S.-born workers who couldn't find jobs during the Great Depression. As middle- and upper-middle class, college-educated people took up marijuana smoking in the 1950s and 1960s, penalties for its use were reduced in many states. In sum, restricting the drugs that members of a subordinate racial-ethnic group use is one method of suppressing the group and limiting its ability to threaten dominant group members or gain upward mobility in society (Fishbein and Pease, 1996). Whether a drug is legal or illegal is determined by those who control the nation's political and legal apparatus.

Conflict theorists also point out that powerful corporate interests perpetuate the use and abuse of legal drugs. By contributing millions of dollars each year to election campaigns, corporations that manufacture, market, and sell alcohol, tobacco, and pharmaceuticals position themselves to manipulate political decisions that could affect them. Hence they reap huge profits from products that exact a heavy toll on the personal health and well-being of abusers, their families and communities, and the larger society. Recent Congressional hearings on the tobacco industry's alleged manipulation of nicotine levels to make cigarette smoking more addictive have highlighted the issue. Members of Congress who control most tobacco-related regulations typically receive large campaign contributions from tobacco industry–funded political action committees and often represent districts where tobacco companies are among the largest employers. Using their wealth and political clout, elites in tobacco companies have vigorously fought measures affecting the industry's more than $50 billion annual revenue, including attempts to classify and regulate tobacco as a drug for many years (Kluger, 1996). However, as noted previously, it appears that a settlement may be reached between the tobacco companies and the federal and state governments that would have the effect of requiring the tobacco companies to accept more responsibility for the effects of using tobacco products.

THE FUTURE OF ALCOHOL AND DRUG ABUSE

How to prevent abuse of alcohol and other drugs and how to treat drug-related problems after they arise are controversial issues in contemporary society. What kinds of drug abuse prevention programs are available? Will future treatment programs for alcoholics and drug addicts differ from the ones that are available today?

▲ Prevention Programs

Drug and alcohol prevention programs can be divided into three major categories: primary, secondary, and tertiary prevention. *Primary prevention* refers to **programs that seek to prevent drug problems before they begin.** Most primary prevention programs focus on people who have had little or no previous experience with drugs. In contrast, *secondary prevention* programs seek to limit the extent of drug abuse, prevent the spread of drug abuse to other substances beyond the drugs already experienced, and teach strategies for the responsible use of licit drugs such as alcohol (Levinthal, 1996). For example, a program directed at college students who already consume al-

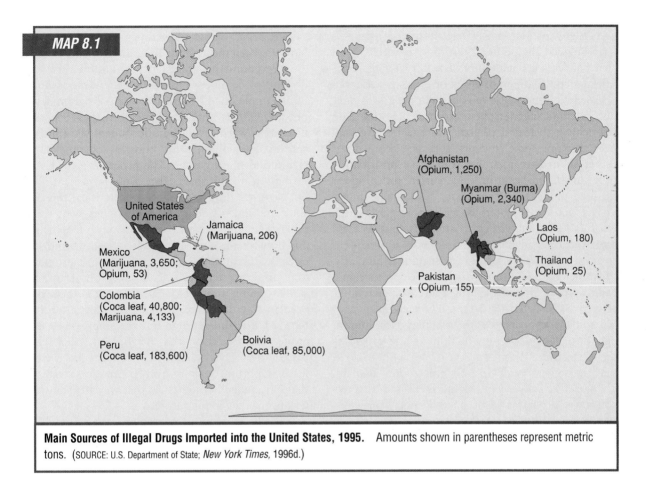

MAP 8.1

Main Sources of Illegal Drugs Imported into the United States, 1995.   Amounts shown in parentheses represent metric tons.   (SOURCE: U.S. Department of State; *New York Times*, 1996d.)

cohol might focus on how to drink responsibly by emphasizing the dangers of drinking and driving. Finally, *tertiary prevention* programs seek to limit relapses by individuals recovering from alcoholism or drug addiction. The purpose of tertiary prevention is to ensure that people who have entered treatment for some form of drug abuse become free of drugs and remain that way.

In the United States, a variety of primary and secondary prevention strategies have been employed, including (1) reduction in the availability of drugs, (2) punishment of drug addicts, (3) scare tactics and negative education, (4) objective-information approaches, (5) promotional campaigns, and (6) self-esteem enhancement and affective education (Levinthal, 1996). We'll look at each in more detail.

The United States has attempted to reduce the supply and availability of drugs. Law enforcement

agencies have expended vast resources to control the domestic production, sale, and consumption of illicit drugs, but their efforts have removed only a small fraction of drugs (Wren, 1996a). The U.S. government has also tried to reduce the influx of drugs from other countries. However, estimates of global retail sales of illicit drugs range from $180 billion to more than $300 billion annually, making the underground drug economy one of the most expansive commercial activities in the world. In North America and Europe alone, the combined sales of heroin, cocaine, and marijuana add up to about $122 billion annually (Stares, 1996). Despite drug laws and an array of sanctions against drug trafficking, drug use and abuse have not been significantly deterred in the United States or elsewhere. Map 8.1 shows the volume of drugs that continue to arrive in the United States from other nations.

Drug wars and other efforts to punish offenders have clogged the criminal justice system and overcrowded prisons without noticeably reducing the sale and consumption of illegal drugs in this country. Scare tactics and negative education programs have not fared much better; they turn students off and do not achieve their desired goal. Scare tactics even appear to pique some students' curiosity about drugs rather than deter their use. Objective information programs often begin in kindergarten and progress through grade 12. Using texts, curriculum guides, videos, and other materials, teachers impart factual information about drugs to students, but as with scare tactics, students sometimes become more—instead of less—interested in experimenting. Similarly, "Just Say No" and other magic bullet promotional campaigns for preventing drug abuse have had limited success in deterring drug use. An eighteen-year-old student who smoked his first marijuana joint at age thirteen explains why he thinks these programs are ineffective: "When someone tells you not to do it, that makes you want to do it even more" (Kolata, 1996a:A12). Self-esteem enhancement and affective education programs focus on the underlying emotional and attitudinal factors that are involved in drug abuse while building character through teaching positive social values and attitudes. These programs are most effective when they are incorporated into more comprehensive prevention programs.

If the purpose of prevention programs is to reduce actual drug-taking behavior, what types of programs have the greatest likelihood of success? Many social analysts suggest that families and schools are the best venues for primary and secondary prevention programs. Some prevention programs previously focused on high school students, but today elementary schools are among the first lines of attack because drug-taking behavior now starts at younger ages. Nearly 75 percent of U.S. public schools have a program known as DARE (Drug Abuse Resistance Education), which is taught by specially trained police officers who come into schools and teach children how to resist drugs. Critics suggest that police officers, whom many young people view as authority figures, are not the best people to teach adolescents that drug use is not cool. Also, one-shot programs that are forced on students may not prevent drug abuse. Children who have been through the DARE program are no less likely to smoke, drink, or use other drugs than children who have not been through the program (Kolata, 1996a).

Prevention programs for the future that look hopeful place more emphasis on *life skills training*. For example, the Life Skills Training Program developed by Gilbert Botvin at Cornell Medical School is directed toward seventh-grade students in a fifteen-session curriculum, with booster sessions in the eighth and ninth grades. The program provides information on the short-term consequences of alcohol or other drug use and teaches critical thinking skills and independent decision making, ways to reduce anxiety and resist peer pressure to take drugs, and how to gain a sense of personal control and self-esteem (Botvin and Tortu, 1988). Unlike programs that primarily tell students to stay off drugs, life skills training attempts to give them the tools they need to stay drug free. Although the short-term effects of life skills programs are impressive, they erode over time (Levinthal, 1996). But social scientist Charles F. Levinthal (1996) believes that we can learn important lessons from prevention strategies that have failed in the past so that we can create better approaches in the future.

The focus of future prevention programs will be family, school, and community based, providing alternative activities and outlets to drug use. These programs—like other drug abuse prevention efforts—will take into account issues that affect people differently depending on their race/ethnicity, religion, or other factors. Across lines of race, class, and gender, the next generation of drug abuse prevention programs will use cable television channels to make people aware of the effects of drugs on the human body and how to get help in dealing with alcoholism and drug addiction. The Internet will also become a vital source of information. Current World Wide Web sites include an array of information on drugs and unique features such as an on-line dictionary of street drug slang.

Future prevention programs provide cause for optimism, but only if social structural factors change. If illegal drugs continue to flow into the United States and television, other mass media, and advertising continue to glamorize smoking, drinking, and other drug use, the future of preventive programs is pretty bleak. Without social change, efforts will be directed toward apprehension and incarceration of drug offenders and treatment programs for drug addicts and alcoholics, not toward primary or secondary prevention strategies.

Treatment Programs

Treatment programs are a form of *tertiary prevention,* aiming to ensure that people who have sought help for some form of drug abuse remain drug free. *Alcohol and drug treatment* involves activities designed to eliminate physical and psychological addiction to alcohol and/or other drugs and to prevent relapse—returning to abuse and/or addiction (Fishbein and Pease, 1996). Most treatment programs are based on a medical model or therapeutic community.

THE MEDICAL TREATMENT MODEL

It follows from the biological and social learning explanations for substance abuse and alcohol addiction that treatment must deal with the body's physiological and psychological responses. This is the *medical treatment model,* which considers drug abuse and alcoholism to be medical problems that must be resolved by medical treatment by medical officials. Treatment may take the form of *aversion therapy* or *behavioral conditioning*. For example, drugs such as Cyclazocine and Nalozone are given to heroin and opiate addicts to prevent the euphoric feeling that they associate with taking the drugs. Supposedly, when the pleasure is gone from taking the drug, the person will no longer abuse the drug. Some heroin addicts also receive methadone detoxification to alleviate withdrawal symptoms associated with stopping heroin use. Over a one to three week period, the patient receives decreasing doses of methadone, a synthetic opium derivative that blocks the desire for heroin but does not have its negative side effects.

Antabuse is used in the treatment of alcoholism. After the person has been detoxified and no alcohol remains in the bloodstream, Antabuse is administered along with small quantities of alcohol for several consecutive days. Because this combination produces negative effects such as nausea and vomiting, the individual eventually develops an aversion to drinking, which becomes associated with uncomfortable physical symptoms. Although the medical treatment model works for some people, it is criticized for focusing on the physiological effects of alcohol and drug dependency and not dealing with the psychological and sociological aspects of the problem.

THE THERAPEUTIC COMMUNITY

When substance abusers are perceived to have an underlying psychological problem, treatment generally involves counseling, rehabilitation, and/or the therapeutic community. Counseling often employs rehabilitated alcoholics or addicts who encourage participants to take more responsibility for their lives so that they can function better in the community. Some counseling and rehabilitation programs take place on an outpatient basis or as day treatment; others involve residential treatment. *Outpatient programs* allow drug abusers to remain at home and keep working while attending regular group and individual meetings. *Day treatment* takes place in a hospital setting where the abuser participates in day-long treatment groups and individual counseling sessions and returns home in the evening. The *therapeutic community approach* is based on the idea that drug abuse is best treated by intensive individual and group counseling in either a residential or a nonresidential setting. Residential treatment takes place in a special house or dormitory where alcoholics or drug addicts remain for periods of time ranging from several months to several years. One of the most widely known residential treatment centers is the Betty Ford Clinic in California, but many others exist throughout the country. Residents in these programs receive therapy and try to establish new behavior patterns outside of their drinking or drug abuse environments (Bertram et al., 1996).

Perhaps the best known nonresidential therapeutic communities are Alcoholics Anonymous (AA), founded in 1935, and its offshoot, Narcotics Anonymous (NA). Both AA and NA provide members with support in their efforts to overcome drug dependence and addiction. AA was established in 1935 by two alcoholics who were seeking a way of returning to sober life (Fishbein and Pease, 1996). Today, the organization has more than 30,000 chapters with over 600,000 members. Members use only their first names to ensure anonymity, and recovering alcoholics serve as sponsors and counselors for others. AA and NA are based on a twelve-step program that requires members to acknowledge that they are alcoholics or drug addicts who must have the help of God and other people to remain sober or drug free. Group support is central to success in these programs, as journalist Caroline Knapp (1996:253–254) explains about her AA group:

> A few months after my one-year anniversary [of sobriety] I went to the meeting . . . on the ground floor of a church outside of Boston. . . . One person tells his or her story for the first half hour, and then the meeting opens up, first to those in their first month of sobriety, then to those with three months or less, then six months or less, and so on. . . . At the end of the meeting there was a presentation for a young guy named John, who was celebrating one year without a drink. . . . He was so happy that evening, so grateful to get that one-year medallion, and so moved by the amount of support he'd gotten over the year, that his eyes welled up and his voice kept cracking. "I can't thank you all enough," he said, and his face was the picture of hope. . . . Then I had an image of every person in that room . . . getting into our beds clean and sober, another day without a drink behind us. It was a simple image but it filled me with a range of complicated feelings: appreciation for the simple presence of all those people; admiration for their courage and strength; a tinge of melancholy for the amount of pain it must have taken each and every one of them to put down the drink; affection for their humanity. I didn't realize until hours later that there was a name for that feeling. It's called love.

Sociologists believe AA is successful because it gives former alcoholics the opportunity to be delabeled as a stigmatized deviant and relabeled as a former and repentant deviant. However, social class and personality factors affect people's ability to enter into the repentant role, which requires a public admission of guilt and repentance, and to successfully interact with others in the program (Trice and Roman, 1970).

All the approaches for reducing alcohol and drug abuse that we have discussed can help certain individuals, but none address what to do about social structural factors that contribute to the drug problem. Because drug- and alcohol-related problems and their solutions are part of deeper social issues and struggles, they cannot be dealt with in isolation, as social scientist Philippe Bourgeois (1995:319, 327) explains:

> Drugs are not the root of the problems . . . they are the expression of deeper, structural dilemmas. Self-destructive addiction is merely the medium for desperate people to internalize their frustrations, resistance, and powerlessness. In other words, we can safely ignore the drug hysterias that periodically sweep through the United States. Instead we should focus our ethical concerns and political energies on the contradictions posed by the persistence of inner-city poverty in the midst of extraordinary opulence. In the same vein, we need to recognize and dismantle the class- and ethnic-based apartheids that riddle the U.S. landscape. . . . The problem of substance abuse in the United States is worse in the 1990s than in the recent past because of a polarization of the structural roots that generate self-destructive behavior and criminal activity. The economic base of the traditional working class has eroded throughout the country. Greater proportions of the population are socially marginalized. The restructuring of the world economy by multinational corporations, finance capital, and digital electronic technology, as well as the exhaustion of social democratic models for public sector intervention [e.g., welfare programs] on behavior of the poor, has escalated inequalities around class, ethnicity, and gender. . . . There is no technocratic solution. Any long-term paths out of the quagmire will have to address the structural and political economic roots, as well as the ideological and cultural roots of social marginalization. The first step out of the impasse, however, requires a fundamental ethical and political reevaluation of basic socioeconomic models and human values.

If the United States sets out to reduce inequalities in all areas of social life, perhaps the drug problem will be alleviated as well. What do you think it would take to make this happen?

SUMMARY

➤ *What are the major patterns of drinking?*

Social scientists divide long-term drinking patterns into four categories: (1) *social drinkers* consume alcoholic beverages primarily on social occasions and may drink either occasionally or relatively frequently; (2) *heavy drinkers* are more frequent drinkers who typically consume greater quantities of alcohol when they drink and are more likely to become intoxicated; (3) *acute alcoholics* have trouble controlling their use of alcohol and plan their schedule around drinking; and (4) *chronic alcoholics* have lost control over their drinking and tend to engage in compulsive behavior such as hiding liquor bottles.

➤ *What are the major hazards associated with tobacco use?*

Nicotine is a toxic, dependency-producing drug that is responsible for about one in every five deaths in the United States. People who smoke have a greater likelihood of developing cardiovascular disease, lung cancer, and/or cancer of the larynx, mouth, and esophagus. Even those who do not smoke may be subjected to the hazard of environmental tobacco smoke—the smoke in the air inhaled by nonsmokers as a result of other people's tobacco smoking. Infants born to women who smoke typically have lower than average birth weights and sometimes have slower rates of physical and mental growth.

➤ *What problems are associated with use of prescription and over-the-counter drugs?*

Some prescription drugs have the potential for short-term abuse and long-term psychological and physical dependence. This form of dependency is known as *iatrogenic addiction*—drug dependency that results from physician-supervised treatment for a recognized medical disorder. Over-the-counter drugs, which are widely advertised and readily available, may be dangerous when combined with alcohol or other drugs.

➤ *What categories of people are most likely to use marijuana?*

Most marijuana users are between the ages of eighteen and twenty-five; however, use by twelve- to seventeen-year-olds more than doubled in the 1990s. More men than women smoke marijuana; however, teenage girls are slightly more likely than boys to have used marijuana at least once.

➤ *What are the major stimulant drugs in the United States?*

Cocaine and amphetamines are the major stimulant drugs abused in the United States. Cocaine is an extremely potent and dependency-producing stimulant drug. Amphetamines can be obtained legally in the form of diet pills and pep formulas when they are prescribed by a physician.

➤ *What are depressants and what health-related risk do they pose?*

As the name indicates, depressants depress the central nervous system; they also may have some pain-killing properties. The most common depressants are barbiturates and antianxiety drugs or tranquilizers. Users may develop both physical addiction and psychological dependency on these drugs. There is also the risk of *potentiation*—the drug interaction that takes place when two drugs are mixed together and the combination produces a far greater effect than that of either drug administered separately.

➤ *What other drugs are widely abused in the United States?*

Other widely abused drugs include narcotics or opiates, including natural substances (e.g, opium, morphine, and codeine), opiate derivatives (e.g., heroin and Percodan), and synthetic drugs with opiatelike effects (e.g., Darvon and Demerol). Hallucinogens or psychedelics such as mescaline (peyote), lysergic acid diethylamide (LSD), phencyclidine (PCP), and MDMA (Ecstasy) are also widely abused.

➡ *How do biological and psychological perspectives view alcohol and drug addiction?*

Biological explanations of alcohol and drug addiction focus on inherited biological factors and on the effects of drugs on the human brain. Psychological explanations of drug abuse focus on personality disorders and the effects of social learning and reinforcement on people's drug-taking behavior.

➡ *How do sociological perspectives view alcohol and drug addiction?*

Interactionists believe that drug use and abuse are learned behaviors that are strongly influenced by families, peers, and others who serve as role models. People are more prone to accept attitudes and behaviors that are favorable to drug use if they spend time with members of a drug subculture. Functionalists believe that drug-related problems have increased as social institutions such as the family, education, and religion have become fragmented and somewhat disorganized. However, use of alcohol and other drugs serves important functions even though some aspects of their use are dysfunctional for society. According to conflict theorists, people in positions of economic and political power are responsible for making the sale, use, and possession of some drugs illegal. Conflict theorists also point out that powerful corporate interests perpetuate the use and abuse of alcohol, tobacco, and other legal drugs.

➡ *What is the purpose of prevention and treatment programs?*

Primary prevention seeks to prevent drug problems before they begin. Secondary prevention seeks to limit the extent of drug abuse, prevent the spread of drug abuse to other substances beyond the drugs already experienced, and teach strategies for the responsible use of licit drugs such as alcohol. Tertiary prevention refers to programs such as the therapeutic community that seek to limit relapses by individuals recovering from alcoholism or drug addiction. The best-known therapeutic community is Alcoholics Anonymous (AA).

➡ *What other factors must be taken into account in efforts to reduce the drug problem?*

Alcoholism and drug abuse are deeply intertwined with other social problems such as dramatic changes in the economic and technological bases of the society, the growing gap between the rich and the poor, and inequalities based on race/ethnicity and gender.

KEY TERMS

codependency, p. 160
drug, p. 153
drug addiction, p. 154
drug dependency, p. 154
drug subculture, p. 171

environmental tobacco smoke, p. 161
fetal alcohol syndrome (FAS), p. 158
primary prevention, p. 172
tolerance, p. 154
withdrawal, p. 154

QUESTIONS FOR CRITICAL THINKING

1. Does public tolerance of alcohol and tobacco lead to increased use of these drugs? Why do many people view use of alcohol and tobacco differently from use of illicit drugs?

2. If stimulants, depressants, and hallucinogens have such potentially hazardous side effects, why do so many people use these drugs? If drug enforcement policies were more stringently enforced, would there be less drug abuse in this country?

3. As a sociologist, how would you propose to deal with the drug problem in the United States? If you were called upon to revamp existing drug laws and policies, what—if any—changes would you make in them?

4. How have changes in technology affected the problem of alcohol and drug abuse over the past century? How have changes in the global economy affected drug-related problems in this country and others?

Chapter Nine

Crime and Criminal Justice

A bunch of us were sitting on the curb on our block, shooting the breeze, when the ice cream man drove up the street. . . . The ice cream man rang his bell and stopped a half block from us as excited young children ran outdoors, flailing their arms. . . .

There was no special plan. We just got up, drifted on over, and studied the scene. The ice cream man was so busy serving children that he didn't notice us surrounding him. While the fellas stood in back, watching the man go in and out of the freezer, I walked to the front of the truck and peeked inside the cab. . . . I noticed he'd left the engine running. I quietly opened the door and slid inside, then stomped the accelerator and pulled away. As I drove down the street, I glanced into the big rearview mirror and saw the shocked ice cream man standing in the middle of the street, holding Popsicles in each hand.

—Journalist Nathan McCall remembers the day that he and other members of his gang stole an ice cream truck (McCall, 1994: 87–88)

As McCall tells the story, what he did seems nothing more than a youthful escapade, but his theft of the ice cream truck is an example of opportunistic crime. Some sociologists believe that for crime to occur, people must have access to *illegitimate opportunity structures*—circumstances that allow people to acquire through illegitimate activities what they cannot achieve legitimately (Cloward and Ohlin, 1960). In this chapter, we examine types of crimes and explanations of crime, as well as the criminal justice system.

CRIME AS A SOCIAL PROBLEM

Many people in the United States fear crime and are somewhat obsessed with it even though they have no direct daily exposure to criminal behavior. Their information about crime comes from the media (Chermak, 1995). For example, the double-murder trial of O.J. Simpson in the mid-1990s and his subsequent civil trial generated more media coverage—and attracted more readers and viewers—than almost any other news story in recent decades. Many of us also watch real-crime dramas such as *America's Most Wanted* and fictionalized crime stories such as *N.Y.P.D. Blue* on television. Media coverage of crime is extensive and may in fact contribute to our widespread perception that crime has increased dramatically in this country. But in most categories, crime rates have remained relatively stable over the past two decades, and the rate of serious and violent crime has continued to fall during the last five years (Butterfield, 1997). That is not to say that crime isn't a significant social problem—but crime statistics tell only part of the story. Crime *is* a social problem because it endangers people's lives, property, and sense of well-being. About 35 million people annually are victims of crimes in the United States, and 100 billion tax dollars are spent annually on law enforcement and the administration of justice (Donziger, 1996). Even individuals who are not directly victimized by crime are harmed by having to pay increased taxes to fight it (Barlow, 1996).

Defining Crime and Delinquency

In Chapter 7, we defined *crime* as behavior that violates the criminal law and is punishable by fine, jail term, or other negative sanctions. In the United States, criminal laws can be enacted at the local, state, and federal levels. As a result, some laws apply uniformly throughout the United States while others vary from state to state or apply only in the local jurisdiction where they were passed. Regardless of jurisdiction, though, crime always has two components: the act itself and *criminal intent*, expressed in the concept of *mens rea*, meaning "guilty mind." An individual's intent in committing a crime may range from willful conduct (hiring someone to kill one's spouse) to an unintentional act of negligence that is defined as a crime (for example, leaving a small child unattended in a locked automobile in extremely hot weather, resulting in the child's death).

Criminal law is divided into two major categories: misdemeanors and felonies. **Misdemeanors are relatively minor crimes that are punishable by a fine or less than a year in jail.** Examples include public drunkenness, shoplifting, and traffic violations. *Felonies* **are more serious crimes such as murder, rape, and aggravated assault, that are punishable by more than a year's imprisonment or even death.**

Children and adolescents below a certain age (usually eighteen) who commit illegal or antisocial acts are normally not charged with criminal conduct but are adjudicated as *delinquent* by a juvenile court judge. It is becoming increasingly common, however, when older juveniles are charged with violent crimes, to *certify* or *waive* them to adult court.

Studying crime, criminals, and juvenile delinquency is difficult because the motivations are complex and people often hide their actions or involvement. For example, homicide is a relatively rare crime, but people are more likely to report it and police are more likely to investigate it than more frequent but less obvious crimes, such as rape, domestic violence, organized crime, and occupational crime.

Problems with Official Statistics

Over the past two decades, sophisticated computer-based information systems have not only improved rates of detection, apprehension, and conviction of offenders, but also provided immediate access to millions of bits of information about crime, suspects, and offenders (Barlow, 1996). The leading source of information on crimes reported in the United States is the *Uniform Crime Report* (UCR). It is published annually by the Federal Bureau of Investigation and based on data provided by federal, state, and local law enforcement agencies. The UCR tracks two categories of crimes: index crimes and nonindex crimes. There are eight *index crimes*: murder, rape, robbery, assault, burglary (breaking into private property to commit a serious crime), motor vehicle theft, arson, and larceny (theft of property worth $50 or more). All other reported crimes (including arrests for prostitution and drug- and alcohol-related offenses) are considered *nonindex crimes*. The UCR also includes a "Crime Clock" (see Figure 9.1), showing how often (on average) the index crimes are committed in this country. In 1995, for example, a murder occurred in the United States an average of once every 24 minutes, a robbery every 54 seconds, and a forcible rape occurred every five minutes (FBI, 1996). During the same year, there were about 14.6 million arrests for all criminal offenses (excluding traffic violations). Because these statistics are highly publicized, it is easy to see why people are concerned for their personal safety, their property, and their very lives.

How accurate are the UCR crime statistics? Any answer to this question must take into account that

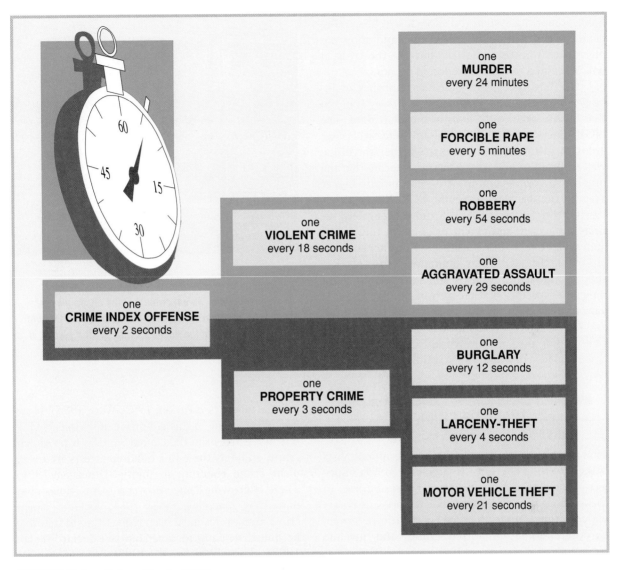

FIGURE 9.1 *Crime Clock, 1995*
The crime clock should be viewed with care. Being the most aggregate representation of UCR data, it is designed to convey the annual reported crime experience by showing the relative frequency of occurrence of the Index Offenses. This mode of display should not be taken to imply a regularity in the commission of the Part I Offenses; rather, it represents the annual ratio of crime to fixed time intervals.
(SOURCE: FBI, 1996.)

legal definitions of some offenses vary from jurisdiction to jurisdiction and that UCR statistics reflect only crimes that are reported to law enforcement agencies or that police officers see occur. (The number of crimes *reported* is not necessarily the number of crimes *committed*.) One trend is clear, though: According to the UCR, overall rates of crime (number of crimes per 100,000 people) increased sharply between 1987 and 1991 but have decreased annually since then. The recent downward trend probably reflects several factors, including a shift in population. The percentage of the U.S. population under age twenty-six—the age group most likely to commit crimes—began to decline in 1992. The FBI is in the process of replacing the UCR with a more comprehensive system called the National Incident-

Based Reporting System (NIBRS). It will keep more detailed information about offenders and allow sophisticated statistical analysis, but like the UCR, it will be limited to data on reported crimes.

The Bureau of Justice Statistics publishes an annual *National Crime Victimization Survey* (NCVS) that fills in some of the gaps in the UCR data. The NCVS interviews 100,000 randomly selected households to identify crime victims, whether the crime was reported or not. These surveys indicate that the number of crimes committed is substantially higher than the number reported in the UCR. Many sociologists believe that the NCVS more accurately reflects the nature and extent of crime in the United States because it uses scientific polling techniques. However, the NCVS has limitations, too: (1) Responses are based on recall, and some people don't remember specifically when a crime occurred; (2) for various reasons, respondents may not be truthful; and (3) the surveys focus on crimes of theft and assault and do not measure workplace crimes such as embezzlement or bribery (Vito and Holmes, 1994).

Property crimes such as this one occur far more frequently than violent crime, yet the media give far greater coverage to violence than to acts such as auto burglary. Should the media's motto be "If it bleeds, it leads"? Why or why not?

TYPES OF CRIMES

One way in which sociologists and criminologists make the study of crime—a large and complex subject—manageable is to categorize types of crime. In this section, we will look at six categories of crime: violent crime, property crime, occupational crime, corporate crime, organized crime, and juvenile delinquency.

▲ Violent and Property Crime

In the United States, a violent crime occurs an average of once every 18 seconds; a property crime occurs an average of once every 3 seconds (FBI, 1996). All eight of the Uniform Crime Report's index crimes are violent and property crimes. Violent crimes are committed against people; nonviolent crimes are usually committed against property.

Violent crime consists of actions involving force or the threat of force against others and includes murder, rape, robbery, and aggravated assault. People tend to fear violent crime more than other kinds because victims are often physically injured or even killed and because violent crime receives the most sustained attention from law enforcement officials

and the media (see Parker, 1995; Warr, 1995). However, most crime in this country is not violent. Only one in ten arrests in the United States is for a violent crime, and only three in a hundred arrests are for violent crime resulting in injury (Donziger, 1996). There is growing concern over violent crimes committed by juveniles. Since 1988, juvenile violent crime arrest rates have been rising, a trend that may be linked to gang membership (see Inciardi et al., 1993a; Thornberry et al., 1993). Violent crime is discussed in detail in Chapter 10.

Property crime consists of taking money or property from another without force, the threat of force, or the destruction of property. Burglary, larceny-theft, motor vehicle theft, and arson are examples of property crimes. According to victimization surveys, the most frequent property crime is *burglary*—unlawful or forcible entry or attempted entry of a residence or business with the intent to commit a serious crime. Burglaries usually involve theft: The burglar illegally enters by force—such as breaking a window or slashing a screen—or through an open window or unlocked door. Actually, burglary falls somewhere between a property crime and a violent crime. Although burglary is normally a crime against property, it carries the possibility of violent confrontation and the psychological sense of intrusion associated with violent crime and is therefore more serious than most nonviolent crimes. In their own words, burglars explain the pressures—both internal and external—that motivate them to commit burglary:

> Usually what I'll do is a burglary, maybe two or three if I have to, and then this will help me get over the rough spot. . . . Once I get it straightened out, I just go with the flow . . . the only time I would go and commit a burglary is if I needed the money at that point in time. That would be strictly to pay the light bill, gas bill, rent. (Dan Whiting, quoted in Wright and Decker, 1994:37)

> You ever had an urge before? Maybe a cigarette urge or a food urge, where you eat that and you got to have more and more? That's how that crack is. You smoke it and it hits you [in the back of the throat] and you got to have more. I'll smoke that sixteenth up and get through, it's like I never had none. I got to have more. Therefore, I gots to go do another burglary and gets some more money. (Richard Jackson, quoted in Wright and Decker, 1994:39)

> I started getting tickets and it was, like, I got four tickets for improper registration plates. Then it was like, "Hey, I need some money, this stuff is calculating up." So I just did [a burglary]. (Wild Will, quoted in Wright and Decker, 1994:46)

According to victimization surveys, African Americans and Latinos/as have a higher than average risk of being burglarized than whites. Risk of victimization is also much higher for families with incomes under $7,500 living in rental property or in central city areas. In contrast, people who live in well-maintained residences with security systems on well-lit streets or cul-de-sacs are less likely to be victimized (Vito and Holmes, 1994). The UCR does not accurately represent the number of burglaries committed because people tend to report only when very valuable goods are taken.

The most frequently reported index crime is *larceny-theft*—unlawfully taking or attempting to take property (with the exception of motor vehicles) from another person—which includes purse snatching and pickpocketing. Most people arrested for larceny-theft are white, but African Americans are overrepresented in arrests for this type of crime considering the proportion of the total population that

is African American. The average age of arrest for larceny-theft is twenty-five, and many offenders are under the influence of alcohol or other drugs at the time of their arrest (Gentry, 1995).

Statistics on auto theft are more accurate than those for many other crimes because insurance companies require that claimants report the theft to police. Analysts have identified four basic motives for auto theft: (1) joyriding—the vehicle is stolen for the fun of riding around in it and perhaps showing off to friends; (2) transportation—the vehicle is stolen for personal use; (3) to help commit another crime; and (4) profit—the vehicle is sold or is taken to a "chop shop," where it is dismantled for parts, which are sold separately (Barlow, 1996). Middle-class youths tend to steal cars for fun and joyriding; urban lower-class minority youths are responsible for most auto thefts for economic profit. Recent armed carjackings by young men under twenty-one years of age have generated considerable fear in large urban areas such as Miami, where tourists were murdered during carjackings, and Houston (Bynum and Thompson, 1996).

Shoplifting accounts for billions of dollars in losses to retail business each year. For some stores, the annual loss can be as high as 2 to 5 percent of the total value of inventory (Vito and Holmes, 1994). Early criminologists thought that shoplifters fell into three categories: the *snitch*—someone with no criminal record who systematically pilfers goods for personal use or to sell; the *booster* or *heel*—the professional criminal who steals goods to sell to fences or pawnshops; and the *kleptomaniac*—someone who steals for reasons other than monetary gain (e.g., for sexual arousal) (Holmes, 1983). Today, though, most experts think that shoplifting is committed primarily by amateurs across lines of race, class, gender, and age (Barlow, 1996).

The last type of nonviolent property crime that we will examine is *credit card fraud*—using a credit card or account number to obtain property, services, or money under false pretenses. Despite security measures taken by banks and other credit card issuers, credit card fraud is perpetrated in many ways. Credit cards are obtained by pickpockets, purse snatchers, robbers, burglars, and sometimes prostitutes who go through their customers' pockets. A lost or stolen wallet or purse can provide a potential offender with all the identification necessary to open up charge accounts in the other person's name and run up large bills before the individual becomes aware of what has happened. There are companies using the Internet to sell personal information—such as a person's Social Security number and mother's maiden name—that is required to apply for and activate some credit cards (Hansell, 1996). At this writing, such trade in information is legal. Credit card information can also be stolen by people with legitimate access to personal data (e.g., airline or hotel reservationists or department or grocery store personnel) or by computer hackers. Recently, two computer hackers downloaded a file containing 1,700 credit card numbers from the security network of Tower Records. Under federal law, each "access device," as credit cards are referred to, is worth $100, so the total theft amounted to $17,000, which is a felony. Even though the hackers did not do anything with the cards, they were found guilty and sentenced to prison (Weise, 1996).

Occupational (White-Collar) Crime

Occupational (white-collar) crime **refers to illegal activities committed by people in the course of their employment or normal business activity.** When sociologist Edwin H. Sutherland (1949) introduced the term *white-collar crime,* he was referring to such acts as employee theft, fraud (obtaining money or property under false pretenses), embezzlement (theft from an employer), and soliciting bribes or kickbacks. With computers, some white-collar crime is easier to commit, and some criminals have developed new types of crime based on computer technology. One type of white-collar crime that has been in the news lately is insider trading of securities: An offender buys or sells stocks on the basis of information that isn't publicly known and that he or she obtained only as a corporate insider. For individual investors, losses may be in the thousands of dollars, but for institutional investors such as pension funds, losses may be in the millions (Friedrichs, 1996), and the effect on retired people who depend on pensions is devastating.

Corporate Crime

Some white-collar offenders engage in *corporate crime*—**illegal acts committed by corporate employees on behalf of the corporation and with its support.** Examples include antitrust violations (seeking an illegal advantage over competitors); deceptive advertising; infringements on patents, copyrights, and trademarks; unlawful labor practices involving the

exploitation or surveillance of employees; price fixing; and financial fraud. These crimes arise from deliberate decisions by corporate personnel to profit at the expense of competitors, consumers, employees, and the general public. As in the case of white-collar crime, computers have changed the nature of some corporate crime. According to a recent study by the Computer Security Institute and the FBI, the biggest threat to a U.S. company's trade secrets, research and development plans, pricing lists, and customer information is a competing company that engages in electronic snooping. As a criminal lawyer who works with high-tech companies explained, "People do things in the computer environment that they would never do outside. An attorney in a courtroom would never look in the briefcase of another who stepped out of the room. And yet I have a case in which one attorney looked at the computer files of another. There is something [alluring] about the anonymity" (quoted in Young, 1996b:71).

Direct economic losses from corporate crime are immense in comparison to the money lost in street crime. For example, losses from twenty years of street property crime are estimated at less than half the losses from savings and loan (S&L) failures alone (Friedrichs, 1996). In one of the most publicized S&L scandals, Charles Keating, owner of a major S&L association, was convicted of bank fraud and other crimes, including paying five U.S. Senators more than $1.4 million to keep his institution open. His convictions were reversed on appeal, even though some depositors had lost their life savings and his institution was one of the ones that taxpayers had to bail out. Failed S&Ls cost U.S. taxpayers hundreds of billions of dollars (Pizzo et al., 1991).

The indirect costs of corporate crime include higher taxes, increased cost of goods and services, and higher insurance rates. Although personal injury and loss of life are typically associated with homicides and other conventional street crimes, deaths resulting from corporate crimes such as polluting the air and water, manufacturing defective products, and selling unsafe foods and drugs far exceed the number of homicides each year. Not least is the effect of corporate crime on the moral climate of society (Friedrichs, 1996; Simon, 1996).

Organized Crime

Organized crime **is a business operation that supplies illegal goods and services for profit.** These illegal enterprises include drug trafficking, prostitution, gambling, loan-sharking, money laundering, and large-scale theft such as truck hijackings (Simon, 1996). Organized crime thrives because there is great demand for illegal goods and services. But no single entity controls the entire range of corrupt and illegal enterprises in the United States (Chambliss, 1988). Organized crime consists of many groups—syndicated crime networks—sometimes with alliances among businesspeople, law enforcement officials, and politicians. These groups operate at all levels of society and even globally (see Box 9.1 on page 188). Some law enforcement and government officials are corrupted through bribery, campaign contributions, and favors that are intended to buy them off. Known linkages between legitimate businesses and organized crime exist in banking, hotels and motels, real estate, garbage collection, vending machines, construction, delivery and long-distance hauling, garment manufacture, insurance, stocks and bonds, vacation resorts, and funeral parlors (National Council on Crime and Delinquency, 1969).

▲ Juvenile Delinquency

Juvenile delinquency **involves a violation of law or the commission of a status offense by young people under a specific age.** Many behaviors that are identified as juvenile delinquency are not criminal acts per se but *status offenses*—acts that are illegal because of the age of the offender—such as cutting school, buying and consuming alcoholic beverages, or running away from home. In most states, the age range for juvenile delinquency is from seven to seventeen. Older offenders are considered adults and tried in the criminal court with older adult offenders.

The statistics for juvenile delinquency are astounding. People under age eighteen account for almost one-fifth of all arrests in the United States. People in the under-twenty-five age category account for nearly half (46 percent) of arrests in cities and 41 percent in suburban and rural areas. For the eight index crimes, 31 percent of people arrested were under the age of eighteen in 1994; 44 percent were under age twenty-one; and 56 percent were under age twenty-five. People in the under-twenty-five age group were also responsible for 47 percent of the violent crime arrests and 59 percent of the property crime arrests in 1994. Over 28 percent of all people arrested for robbery and over 31 percent of all people arrested for larceny-theft were under

Although juvenile gangs provide a sense of belonging and may be a source of identity for some young people, many community members and law enforcement officials view gangs as a constant threat to property, life, and community stability. What factors do you think are most significant in determining whether or not a person joins a gang?

age eighteen (FBI, 1995a). Note that these are arrest figures and do not necessarily reflect the true nature and extent of crime and status violations among juvenile offenders.

Juveniles who are apprehended are processed by the juvenile justice system, which is based on the assumption that young people can do better if they are placed in the right setting and receive guidance. Unlike adult offenders, whose cases are heard in criminal courts, most juveniles' cases are heard in juvenile courts or by specially designated juvenile judges. Unfortunately, most juvenile correction facilities or "training schools" hold large numbers of young people in overcrowded conditions and provide only limited counseling and educational opportunities for rehabilitation (Donziger, 1996).

WHO COMMITS CRIMES?

Although age is an important factor associated with delinquency and crime arrest rates, the most signifi-

Organized Crime: The Global Empire

Five nights a week, at least $100 million in crisp new $100 bills is flown from JFK [International Airport] nonstop to Moscow, where it is used to finance the Russian mob's vast and growing international crime syndicate. State and federal officials believe it is part of a multimillion-dollar money-laundering operation. When the money arrives in Moscow, it is transported by armored trucks to Russian banks, which have purchased the $100 bills on behalf of clients, who typically pay for the cash with wire transfers from London bank accounts. (Friedman, 1996:24)

This is one of many recent reports of international organized crime, in this instance allegedly involving the Russian mob and U.S. banks. The mob supposedly uses a steady supply of freshly minted U.S. currency to finance its vast and growing international crime syndicate and to invest in legitimate businesses across Europe and in the United States.

The "dirty" money allegedly comes from Russian *Mafiya* alliances with other crime syndicates such as the Sicilian Mafia, the Brighton Beach gang (a criminal gang of Russian immigrants living in Brooklyn, New York), and Colombian drug lords. Today, the Russian banking system is considered one of the world's leading money-laundering centers (Friedman, 1996).

Despite a 1992 law requiring U.S. banks to verify that they are not knowingly doing business with criminals or their agents, money laundering continues to flourish in the United States as well. Combating money laundering is difficult because there are about 700,000 wire transfers a day, totaling $2 trillion. About $300 million of that—less than one-sixtieth of 1 percent—is believed to be laundered funds. Because existing technology can identify only the most obvious money trading irregularities, a great deal of money laundering goes undetected (Friedman, 1996). Major U.S. cities such as New York, Los Angeles, Dallas, and Miami have become primary points of international entry or exit for money-laundering operations, as well as drug-trafficking operations.

Globally, seven or eight crime syndicates often operate in collusion. In addition to the Russian syndicate and the Sicilian Mafia, other organized crime groups allegedly include the Colombian cocaine cartels, which have operations in Spain, and ethnic Chinese from East and Southeast Asia, who have overseas bases in Rotterdam and London. At a lower level, the transport and marketing of drugs and other contraband is managed by syndicates of Nigerians, Moroccans, Pakistanis, Lebanese, Albanians, and others (Viviano, 1995).

What can the United States do about global organized crime? Can any one nation or organization—such as the United Nations—reduce international money laundering and drug trafficking? What do you think?

cant factor is gender. Men are more likely than women to commit major property crimes (such as robbery and larceny-theft), whereas women are more likely to be involved in minor property crimes such as larceny and fraud and in prostitution-type offenses (Steffensmeier and Allan, 1995). Men have higher arrest rates for violent crimes such as homicide, aggravated assault, robbery, and burglary; women are most often arrested for such nonviolent crimes as shoplifting, passing bad checks, credit card fraud, and employee pilferage. Although a considerable number of arrests and convictions of women are for larceny and theft, men still account for the vast majority of these arrests and convictions. Criminologists estimate that 15 to 20 percent of all homicides in this country are committed by women. Most of these are linked to domestic violence and self-defense (Harlow, 1991; Belknap, 1996).

Although there are significant gender differences in crimes committed, there are also commonalities. First, the most common offenses for both sexes are driving under the influence of alcohol or drugs (DUI), larceny, and minor or criminal mischief offenses. These three categories account for about 47 percent of all male arrests and about 49 percent of all female arrests. Second, liquor law violations (such as underage drinking), simple assault, and disorderly conduct are middle-range offenses for both men and women. Third, the rate of arrests for murder, arson, and embezzlement are relatively low for both men and women (Steffensmeier and Allan, 1995).

As our discussion of juvenile delinquency pointed out, the proportion of the population involved in serious crimes such as homicide, rape, and robbery tends to peak during the teenage years or early adulthood and then decline with age. Several reasons have been advanced for age-crime patterns including differential access to legitimate or illegitimate opportunity structures at various ages; differences in social factors such as peer influences; physiological factors such as the effects of aging on strength, speed, and aggression; and building up deviant networks that make it possible for people such as bookies or fences to commit less visible crimes (Steffensmeier and Allan, 1995).

Although individuals from all social classes commit crimes, some kinds of crimes are more associated with lower or upper socioeconomic status. People from lower socioeconomic backgrounds are more likely to be arrested for violent and property crimes; people from the upper classes generally commit white-collar or corporate crimes. Moreover, the majority of crimes committed by doctors, lawyers, accountants,

"My client pleads great wealth."

Drawing by C. Barsotti; © 1996 The New Yorker Magazine, Inc.

and other professionals are ignored because of the prestige associated with these professions. Friends and neighbors assume that these people are law-abiding citizens, and law enforcement officials are not likely to scrutinize their behavior, looking to street crime offenders instead (Coleman, 1995).

When we examine the intersection of race and class in arrest data, we see that low-income African Americans are overrepresented. In 1994, whites accounted for 64 percent of all property crime arrests and 53 percent of violent crime arrests; African Americans accounted for 33 percent of property crime arrests and 33 percent of property crime arrests (FBI, 1995a). However, African Americans comprise a little over 12 percent of the U.S. population. Compared with those for African Americans, arrest rates for whites are higher for nonviolent property crimes such as fraud and larceny-theft but lower for violent crimes such as robbery and murder. It is important to remember, however, that the Crime Index focuses on crimes that are more likely to be committed by low-income people, among whom African Americans and other people of color are overrepresented:

The present UCR Index opens a certain kind of window onto crime, a window onto "the streets." Undoubtedly, this crime window is of great importance to all Americans. However, the window is defined not just by what it allows us to see; it is at least as much defined by what it *excludes* from our sight, namely, much white collar and probably most silk-collar [female executive] crime. Because blacks are underrepresented and whites overrepresented in white and silk collar occupations, we must conclude that the set of crimes called Index crimes is skewed *away* from criminal opportunities where whites are overrepresented. This does not imply that the Index is biased *against* lower-class black street crime per se but rather that it is biased *away from* middle class and elite whites' "suite" crime. (Harris and Meidlinger, 1995: 118)

Having considered who commits crimes, let's look at who the victims are. Most people fear the violent stranger, but the vast majority of murders are committed by family members, friends, neighbors, or coworkers. In nearly half the cases, the murderers are members of the victim's family or an acquaintance. In 1995, 26 percent of female murder victims were killed by husbands or boyfriends; 3 percent of male victims were slain by wives or girlfriends (FBI, 1996). Most murder is intraracial. That is, whites most often murder whites (85 percent of the time), and African Americans most often murder African Americans (95 percent of the time) (see Table 9.1).

According to the NCVS, men are the most frequent victims of crimes of violence and theft, although women are more fearful of crime, particularly crime directed toward them, such as forcible rape (Warr, 1985). An estimated 89 percent of males who are now twelve years old will be the victim of a violent crime at least once during their lifetime compared to 73 percent of females. The elderly also tend to be more fearful of crime but are the least likely to be victimized. Young men of color between the ages of twelve and twenty-four have the highest rates of criminal victimization (Karmen, 1995).

The NCVS data on robbery victims indicates that males are robbed at more than twice the rate of females. African Americans are more than three times as likely to be robbed as whites. Young people

TABLE 9.1   RACE OF KILLERS AND VICTIMS, 1994

Victims	Killers		
	WHITE	BLACK	OTHER/UNKNOWN
WHITE	83%	15%	3%
BLACK	6%	92%	2%

Source: FBI, 1995a.

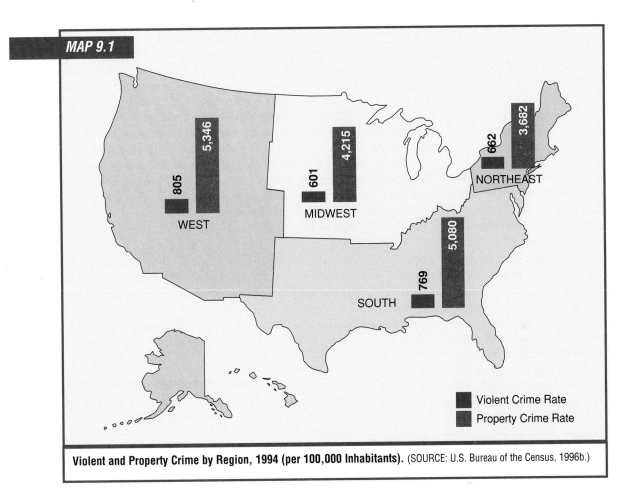

MAP 9.1

WEST
805
5,346

MIDWEST
601
4,215

NORTHEAST
662
3,682

SOUTH
769
5,080

Violent Crime Rate
Property Crime Rate

Violent and Property Crime by Region, 1994 (per 100,000 Inhabitants). (SOURCE: U.S. Bureau of the Census, 1996b.)

have a much greater likelihood of being robbed than middle-aged and older people do. People from lower-income families are more likely to be robbed than those from higher-income families (Karmen, 1995). Risk of being a crime victim varies by region of the country, too. Risk of violent crime or property crime is greatest in the western states and the South (see Map 9.1).

BIOLOGICAL AND PSYCHOLOGICAL EXPLANATIONS OF CRIME

As with other social problems, crime and delinquency have been explained in biological, psychological, and sociological terms. Most biological and psychological explanations are based on the assumption that criminal behavior is an inherent or acquired individual trait with genetic, biological, or psycholog-

ical roots. Sociological perspectives, in contrast, focus on external factors.

▲ Biological Explanations

One of the earliest biological explanations of criminality came from the *positivist school*, which created typologies to classify and study criminals. Some positivists also examined social structural factors involved in crime, but the biological approach of Cesare Lombroso, a nineteenth century Italian physicist, was probably the best known. According to Lombroso, some people are born criminals or *atavists*—biological throwbacks to an earlier stage of evolution—and can be recognized by their low foreheads and smaller than normal human cranial capacities. A later theory that received some attention for a time was proposed by physician William Sheldon (1949). According to Sheldon's *somatotype theory, mesomorphs*—people who are muscular, gregarious, aggressive, and assertive—are more prone to delinquency and criminal behavior than are *endomorphs*—people who are fat, soft, round, and extroverted—or *ectomorphs*—people who are thin, wiry, sensitive, and introverted.

Contemporary biological approaches based on genetics have attempted to link higher rates of aggression in men to levels of testosterone or chromosomal abnormality (an extra Y chromosome). But this research has produced no consistent findings, and social scientists argue that the differences in aggression may be due to gender role socialization of men and women, rather than to biological factors such as an extra chromosome (Katz and Chambliss, 1995).

Most biological researchers themselves acknowledge that genes alone do not determine how we behave. Instead, genes predispose individuals to act one way or another, but individual actions are also affected by the social environment. According to one medical geneticist, "My feeling is there is certainly no 'gene' for criminal behavior. There are genes which predispose people to an increased frequency of impulsive-compulsive behaviors and that put them at greater risk of being involved in criminal behavior" (quoted in Angier, 1995a:B9). However, sociologist Dorothy Nelkin (1995:A17) believes that we should stop looking for a "crime gene":

> At its core, the debate over crime has more to do with social than biological causes. We must deal with the real source of crime: the social conditions that are so strongly associated with violence. Biological predisposition is not necessary to explain why a child who suffers racism and violence, without much hope of escape, might become indifferent to human life.

Psychological Explanations

Like biological explanations of delinquency and crime, psychological explanations focus on individual characteristics. Some researchers have used personality inventories in hopes of identifying abnormal personality traits in individuals who have committed crimes or engaged in delinquent behavior. Other researchers have investigated the effects of social learning and positive reinforcement (e.g., rewards such as money or special attention) and negative reinforcement (e.g., the withdrawal of reward or lack of attention) on delinquent and criminal behavior.

The most enduring psychological explanations of delinquency and crime seem to be the ones that bridge the biological explanations by linking intelligence and crime. Since the introduction of IQ (intelligence quotient) tests in the early 1900s, some analysts have suggested that people with lower intelligence scores are more likely to commit crimes than are people with higher intelligence scores. However, the validity of IQ tests and the assertion that low intelligence causes delinquency or crime have both come under great scrutiny and much criticism (see Hirschi and Hindelang, 1977).

Of course, some social analysts do acknowledge that there may be some relationship between low intelligence and delinquency or crime. For example, low intelligence may indirectly promote delinquency because it affects school performance. Similarly, less intelligent offenders may commit more obvious crimes and be more likely to be apprehended by law enforcement officials (Vito and Holmes, 1994).

SOCIOLOGICAL EXPLANATIONS OF CRIME

Unlike biological and psychological explanations that focus on individual behavior, sociological explanations focus on aspects of society that may contribute to delinquent or criminal behavior.

The Functionalist Perspective

Why do people commit crimes? Although there are numerous functionalist perspectives on crime and delinquency, we will focus on three: strain theory, control theory, and social bond theory.

Functionalist explanations can be traced to Emile Durkheim, who believed that the macrolevel structure of a society produces social pressures that result in high rates of deviance and crime. He introduced the concept of *anomie* to describe a social condition that engenders feelings of futility in people because of weak, absent, or conflicting social norms. According to Durkheim (1964/1895), deviance and crime are most likely to occur when anomie is present in a society. On the basis of Durkheim's theory, sociologist Robert Merton (1938, 1968) developed strain theory to explain why some people conform to group norms while others do not. ***Strain theory*** states that people feel strain when they are exposed to cultural goals that they cannot reach because they do not have access to culturally approved means of achieving those goals. When they are denied legitimate access to goals such as success, money, or other material possessions, some people seek to acquire these things through deviant—and sometimes criminal—means.

Merton identified five ways in which people respond to cultural goals: conformity, innovation, ritualism, retreatism, and rebellion (see Table 9.2). *Conformity* occurs when people accept the culturally approved goals and pursue them through the approved means. People who want to achieve success through conformity work hard and save their money. Someone who is blocked from achieving a high level of education or a lucrative career typically conforms by taking a lower-paying job and attending school part-time, joining the military, or trying alternative (but legal) avenues, such as playing the lottery. People who choose *innovation* accept society's goals but use illegitimate means for achieving them. Innovations for acquiring material possessions include shoplifting, theft, burglary, cheating on income taxes, embezzling money, and other kinds of occupational crime. *Ritualism* occurs when people give up on societal goals but still adhere to the socially approved means for achieving them. People who can-

not obtain expensive material possessions or wealth seek to maintain the respect of others by being a "hard worker" or "good citizen" to an extreme degree. *Retreatism* occurs when people abandon both the approved goals and the approved means of achieving them. Retreatists include hard-core drug addicts and some middle- or upper-income people who reject conventional trappings of success and the means to acquire them, choosing to "drop out" instead. *Rebellion* occurs when people reject both the approved goals and the approved means for achieving them and advocate an alternative set of goals and means. Rebels may use violence (such as vandalism or rioting) or nonviolent tactics (such as civil disobedience) to change society and its cultural beliefs. Or they may withdraw from mainstream society, like the Amish, to live their own life.

Another functionalist perspective—control theory—seeks to answer the question: Why do people *not* engage in deviant behavior? According to control theory, people are constantly pulled and pushed toward deviant behavior. Environmental factors (pulls) such as adverse living conditions, poverty, and lack of educational opportunity draw people toward criminal behavior while, at the same time, internal pressures (pushes) such as feelings of hostility or aggressiveness make people not want to act according to dominant values and norms (Reckless,

TABLE 9.2   MERTON'S STRAIN THEORY

Mode of Adaptation	Method of Adaptation	Agrees with Cultural Goal	Follows Institutional Means
Conformity	Accepts culturally approved goals; pursues them through the culturally approved means	Yes	Yes
Innovation	Accepts culturally approved goals; adopts disapproved means of achieving them	Yes	No
Ritualism	Abandons society's goals but continues to conform to approved means	No	Yes
Retreatism	Abandons both approved goals and the approved means to achieve them	No	No
Rebellion	Challenges both the approved goals and the approved means to achieve them	No—seeks to replace	No—seeks to replace

Source: Adapted from Merton (1968).

1967). But why doesn't everyone who is poor or have a limited education commit crimes? According to control theorists, people who do not turn to crime or delinquent behavior have *outer containments*—such as supportive family and friends, reasonable social expectations, and supervision by others—or *inner containments*—such as self-control, a sense of responsibility, and resistance to diversions.

The best-known control theory is *social bond theory*—the proposition that criminal behavior is most likely to occur when a person's ties to society are weakened or broken—as proposed by sociologist Travis Hirschi (1969). According to Hirschi, social bonding consists of (1) *attachment* to other people, (2) *commitment* to conformity, (3) *involvement* in conventional activities, and (4) *belief* in the legitimacy of conventional values and norms. In sum, the probability of delinquency and crime increases when a person's social bonds are weak and when peers promote antisocial values and violent behavior (Massey and Krohn, 1986).

Functionalist explanations contribute to our understanding of crime by emphasizing that individuals who engage in such behavior are not biologically or psychologically impaired but responding to social and economic conditions in society. However, functionalists are not without their critics. Strain theory may point out that people from low-income and poverty-level backgrounds are prevented from achieving success goals through legitimate channels, but it is still criticized for focusing almost exclusively on crimes committed by the lower classes and ignoring crimes committed by people in the middle and upper classes. And social bond theory, say some researchers, is limited in its ability to explain more serious forms of delinquency and crime (Krohn, 1995).

The Conflict Perspective

Conflict theorists explain criminal behavior in terms of power differentials and/or economic inequality in society. One approach focuses on how authority and power relations can contribute to some people—but not others—becoming criminals. According to Austin Turk (1966, 1971), crime is not a *behavior* but a *status* that is acquired when people with the authority to create and enforce legal rules apply those rules to others. Consider, for example, the harsher penalties that were placed on the possession or use of crack cocaine after the cocaine-induced

death of University of Maryland basketball star Len Bias in 1986. Almost immediately after Bias died, Congress passed a law imposing strict mandatory sentencing for possessing or selling crack cocaine. As a result, penalties for the use of crack cocaine became much harsher than the penalties for use of cocaine in powder form. Before passage of this law, African Americans accounted for about 90 percent of crack arrests, while whites made up 75 percent of arrests for powder cocaine. Under the new law, African Americans—who still constitute the vast majority of crack users—were sent to prison in unprecedented numbers and were kept there for longer periods of time (Donziger, 1996).

A second conflict approach focuses on the relationship between economic inequality and crime. Having roots in the work of Karl Marx, the *radical-critical conflict approach* argues that social institutions (such as law, politics, and education) create a superstructure that legitimizes the class structure and maintains capitalists' superior position. In fact, say these theorists, the crimes people commit are based on their class position. Crimes committed by low-income people typically involve taking things by force or physical stealth, while corporate or white-collar crime is usually committed by nonphysical means such as paper transactions or computer fraud. Some critical theorists believe that affluent people commit crimes because they are greedy and continually want more than they have, whereas people commit street crimes such as robbery and theft to survive (Bonger, 1969/1916).

Finally, some conflict explanations are based on feminist scholarship and focus on why women commit crimes or engage in delinquent behavior. Scholars who use a *liberal feminist* framework believe that women's delinquency or crime is a rational response to gender discrimination in society. They attribute crimes such as prostitution and shoplifting to women's lack of educational and job opportunities and stereotypical expectations about roles women should have in society (Daly and Chesney-Lind, 1988). Scholars who espouse *radical feminism* believe that patriarchy (male domination over females) contributes to crimes such as prostitution, which reflects society's sexual double standard: It is acceptable for a man to pay for sex but unacceptable for a woman to accept money for such services. A third school of feminist thought, *socialist feminism,* believes that women are exploited by capitalism and

Some *feminist scholars believe that the exploitation of women contributes to female crime. Each year many women are arrested for crimes such as prostitution and shoplifting. Which sociological perspective do you think best explains why women commit crimes?*

patriarchy. Because most females have relatively low-wage jobs (if any) and few economic resources, crimes such as prostitution and shoplifting are a means of earning money and acquiring consumer products. Feminist scholars of color, however, point out that none of the feminist theories include race/ethnicity in their analyses. As a result, some recent studies have focused on the relationship between crime and the simultaneous effects of race, class, and gender (Arnold, 1990).

In sum, the conflict approach is useful for pointing out how inequalities of power, class, race, and gender can contribute to criminal or delinquent behavior. Nevertheless, critics say that conflict theorists have not shown that powerful political and econom-

ic elites manipulate law making and enforcement for their own benefit. Rather, say these critics, people of all classes share a consensus that acts such as murder, rape, and armed robbery are bad (Klockars, 1979).

The Interactionist Perspective

Interactionists emphasize that criminal behavior is learned through everyday interaction with others. We will examine two major interactionist theories: differential association theory and labeling theory. *Differential association theory* **states that individuals have a greater tendency to deviate from societal norms when they frequently associate with people who tend toward deviance rather than conformity.** According to sociologist Edwin Sutherland (1939), who formulated this theory, people learn not only the techniques of deviant behavior from people with whom they associate, but also the motives, drives, rationalizations, and attitudes. Former gang member Nathan McCall (1994:93–94) describes such a learning process in his own life:

> Sometimes I picked up hustling ideas at the 7-Eleven, which was like a criminal union hall: Crapshooters, shoplifters, stickup men, burglars, everybody stopped off at the store from time to time. While hanging up there one day, I ran into Holt. . . . He had a pocketful of cash, even though he had quit school and was unemployed. I asked him, "Yo, man, what you been into?" "Me and my partner kick in cribs and make a killin'. You oughta come go with us sometimes. . . . " I hooked school one day, went with them, and pulled my first B&E [breaking and entering]. . . . After I learned the ropes, Shell Shock [another gang member] and I branched out, doing B&Es on our own. We learned to get in and out of houses in no time flat.

As McCall's description indicates, criminal activity often occurs within the context of frequent, intense, and long-lasting interactions with people who violate the law. When more factors favor violating the law than not, the person is likely to become a criminal. Differential association theory contributes to our knowledge of how deviant behavior reflects the individual's learned techniques, values, attitudes, motives, and rationalizations. But critics question why many individuals who are regularly exposed to people who break the law still conform most of the time. Nor do critics think that the theory adequately takes into account possible connections between social inequality and criminal behavior.

Labeling theory takes quite a different approach from differential association theory. According to *labeling theory,* **delinquents and criminals are people who have been successfully labeled as such by others.** No behavior is inherently delinquent or criminal; it is defined as such by a social audience (Erikson, 1962). According to sociologist Howard Becker (1963), labeling is often done by *moral entrepreneurs*—people who use their own views of right and wrong to establish rules and label others "deviant." Furthermore, the process of labeling is directly related to the power and status of the people who do the labeling and those who are being labeled. For example, one study of juvenile offenders found that youths from lower-income families were more likely to be arrested and indicted than were middle-class juveniles who did the same things (Sampson, 1986). The criminal justice system generally considers such factors as the offender's family life, educational achievement (or lack thereof), and social class in determining how to deal with juvenile offenders. The individuals who are most likely to be apprehended, labeled delinquent, and prosecuted are people of color who are young, male, unemployed, and undereducated and who live in urban high-crime areas (Vito and Holmes, 1994).

Sociologist Edwin Lemert (1951) expanded labeling theory by distinguishing between primary and secondary deviance. *Primary deviance* **is the initial act of rule breaking** in which the individual does not internalize the delinquent or criminal self-concept. *Secondary deviance* **occurs when a person who has been labeled a deviant accepts that new identity and continues the deviant behavior.** The concept of secondary deviance is important to labeling theory because it suggests that when people accept a negative label or stigma that has been applied to them, the label may actually contribute to the behavior it was meant to control. In other words, secondary deviance occurs if a person is labeled a juvenile delinquent, accepts that label, and then continues to engage in delinquent behavior. Labeling theory is useful for making us aware of how social control and personal identity are intertwined: Labeling may contribute to the acceptance of deviant roles and self-images. Critics, however, do not think

that labeling theory explains what causes the original acts that constitute primary deviance. Nor do they think that it adequately explains why some people accept deviant labels and others do not (Cavender, 1995).

THE CRIMINAL JUSTICE SYSTEM

The term *criminal justice system* is misleading because it implies that law enforcement agencies and courts constitute one large, integrated system when actually they are a collection of somewhat interrelated, semiautonomous bureaucracies (Sheley, 1995). The *criminal justice system* **is the network of organizations involved in law enforcement and the administration of justice, including the police, courts, jails, and prisons** (Donziger, 1996). Originally, the criminal justice system was created to help solve the problem of social disorder and crime. Today, however, some social analysts wonder whether the criminal justice system is part of the crime *problem* in this country rather than the solution. Most cite two reasons for concern: (1) The criminal justice system fails in its mission to prevent, control, or rehabilitate offenders; and (2) unequal justice occurs because officials discriminate against people on the basis of race, class, gender, age, sexual orientation, or other devalued characteristics. We'll examine both issues in greater depth. First, though, let's look at each component of the justice system, starting with the police.

The Police

The police are the most visible link in the criminal justice system because they determine how to apply the law to control crime and maintain order. The police arrest and jail about 11 million people each year. Four factors seem to influence whether or not police make an arrest: (1) the nature of the alleged offense or problem; (2) the quality of available evidence; (3) the age, race, and sex of the alleged offender; and (4) the level of deference shown to police officers (Mastrofski, 1995). Law enforcement officials therefore have fairly wide *discretion*—use of personal judgment regarding whether and how to proceed in a given situation—in deciding who will be stopped and searched and which homes and businesses will be entered and for what purposes (Donziger, 1996). Because they must often make these decisions in a dangerous environment, sociologist Jerome Skolnick (1975) argues, police officers develop a sense of suspicion, social isolation, and solidarity. A New York City police officer describes this feeling:

> Guys . . . will eat you alive, even with the uniform on. They can sense fear, smell it like a dog smells it. Some of the mopes will come right out and tell you you're nothing, and you don't want that, oh no. If you're going to do this job, wear this uniform, you definitely don't want that. If it gets around that you're soft, that without your nightstick and gun you can't fight, that's bad. If you allow someone to smoke a joint in front of you or curse you out, word will spread throughout the neighborhood like a disease. You're a beat cop, out here every day, alone, so you set standards right away. (Norman, 1993:64)

Most officers feel that they must demand respect on the streets, but they also know that they must answer to their superiors, who expect them to handle situations "by the book."

The problem of discretion is most acute in the decision to use deadly force against an alleged offender. Generally, deadly force is allowed only when a suspect is engaged in a felony, is fleeing the scene of a felony, or is resisting arrest and has endangered someone's life (Barlow, 1996). But police officers' lives are often on the line in confrontations with suspects, and sometimes the officers have less firepower than the individuals they are attempting to apprehend. In a Los Angeles bank robbery, for example, the robbers were wielding AK-47 automatic rifles and using 100-round ammunition drums and 30-round clips from which they were firing steel-jacketed bullets capable of penetrating the police officers' body armor (Story, 1997). Rates of police shootings vary widely from one jurisdiction to another, but the percentage of shooting incidents involving African American suspects is disproportionately high. African Americans are from five to thirteen times more likely than whites to be killed by police officers (Mann, 1993).

People of color often have a negative image of police because they believe that they receive differential treatment (Anderson, 1990; Cose, 1993; Mann, 1993). Historically, criminal justice personnel at all levels have been white and male. The composition may be slowly changing, but white Americans still made up over 80 percent of all police officers in 1995 (U.S. Bureau of the Census, 1996b).

The Rodney King case in Los Angeles made people around the world aware of the potential that police have for excessive use of force. King, an African American, suffered nine skull fractures, a broken cheekbone, a shattered eye socket, a broken leg, partial paralysis of his face, internal bleeding, and broken teeth when Los Angeles police and California state troopers finally stopped him after a high-speed chase. A passing motorist with a camcorder captured the whole episode, which was later televised around the globe (Skolnick and Fyfe, 1993). The Rodney King beating and similar cases of police misconduct have seriously undermined confidence in U.S. law enforcement officials, particularly among people of color, who often perceive that they are both *overpoliced*—because of massive police intervention in central cities as part of the war on drugs—and *underprotected*—because police are often slow to respond to emergency calls from minority neighborhoods (Donziger, 1996).

In the past, women were largely excluded from law enforcement because of stereotypical beliefs that they were not physically and psychologically strong enough for the work. But by 1995, women accounted for slightly over 10 percent of all police officers (U.S. Bureau of the Census, 1996b). Even though more females have entered police work, research shows that they may still receive lower evaluations from male administrators even when objective measures show that they are equally effective on patrol (Reid, 1987).

How can police departments become more effective in reducing crime as a social problem? According to some analysts, police departments with entrenched problems must first reform their own agencies and win the respect of the communities they serve. One way to do this would be for police departments to reflect the racial and ethnic composition of the communities they serve. It is difficult for an all-white police force to build trust in a primarily African American neighborhood (Donziger, 1996). Greater representation of women in police departments might reduce complaints that domestic violence, child abuse, and other family-related problems are sometimes minimized or ignored by police officers.

Some police departments have begun *community policing* as a way of reducing crime. Community policing involves integrating officers into the communities they serve—getting them out of their patrol cars and into a proactive role, recognizing problems and working with neighborhood citizens to find solutions. In cities where community policing has been implemented, crime rates appear to have dropped; however, it should be noted that there has also been a general trend toward fewer crimes, especially violent crimes, in some cities where community policing is not employed (Donziger, 1996).

The Courts

Criminal courts are responsible for determining the guilt or innocence of people who have been accused of committing a crime. In theory, justice is determined in an adversarial process, with a prosecutor (an attorney who represents the state) arguing that the accused is guilty and a defense attorney arguing that the accused is innocent. In reality, judges have a great deal of discretion. Working with prosecutors, they decide who will be released, who will be held for further hearings, and—in many instances—what sentences will be imposed on people who are convicted.

Because courts have the capacity to try only a small fraction of criminal cases, prosecuting attorneys also have considerable discretion in deciding when to prosecute and when to negotiate a plea bargain with a defense attorney. About 90 percent of criminal cases are never tried in court; they are resolved by *plea bargaining*—a process whereby the prosecution negotiates a reduced sentence in exchange for a guilty plea. In other words, defendants (especially those who are poor and cannot afford to pay an attorney) plead guilty to a lesser crime in return for not being tried for the more serious crime for which they were arrested. As cases are sifted and sorted through the legal machinery, a steady attrition occurs. At each stage, various officials determine what alternatives will be available for the cases that remain in the system (Hills, 1971). Now that many jurisdictions specify mandatory minimum sentences, offenders typically spend a longer time in prison. In fact, mandatory sentencing guidelines have removed sentencing power from judges and transferred it to prosecutors, who determine what charges will be brought against the defendant. Then the judge must sentence the defendant according to the statutory prescription for the offense the accused is charged with, regardless of any facts that might

have led a different prosecutor to charge differently or any mitigating circumstances in the specific case.

Recently, the criminal and civil trials of O.J. Simpson made the general public more aware of the complexity of serving on a jury. Many people do not like to be called for jury duty and try any possible means to get out of serving. Some problems are the "cattle call" method of jury duty, which includes excessive waiting, little or no compensation, and the use of peremptory challenges that permit lawyers for either side to exclude a potential juror without stating a reason. Some analysts believe that peremptory challenges are used to remove jurors who will vote to convict or acquit a client because of race, ethnicity, gender, religion, or personal characteristics, and this is discriminatory (Donziger, 1996). Most judicial officers and laypeople agree that improvements are needed in the jury selection process and in the treatment of jurors during trials.

Punishment and the Prisons

Punishment **is any action designed to deprive a person of things of value (including liberty) because of an offense the person is thought to have committed** (Barlow, 1996). Punishment is seen as serving four functions:

1. *Retribution* imposes a penalty on the offender. Retribution is based on the premise that the punishment should fit the crime: The greater the degree of social harm, the more the offender should be punished. An individual who murders, for example, should be punished more severely than one who steals an automobile.
2. *Social protection* results from restricting offenders so that they cannot continue to commit crimes.
3. *Rehabilitation* seeks to return offenders to the community as law-abiding citizens. However, the few rehabilitation programs that exist in prisons are seriously understaffed and underfunded. Often, too, the job skills (such as agricultural work) that are taught in prison do not transfer to the outside world, and offenders are not given help in finding work that fits the skills they might have once they are released.
4. *Deterrence* seeks to reduce criminal activity by instilling a fear of punishment. Criminologists

debate, though, whether imprisonment has a deterrent effect, given that 30 to 50 percent of those who are released from prison commit further crimes.

Today, about 1.5 million people are behind bars in the United States. One million of these are in state and federal prisons; another half million are in local jails (U.S. Bureau of the Census, 1996b). This is the highest rate of incarceration in relation to population in any developed country. Moreover, another 11 million people are annually booked in jails at the city or county level, where they spend at least one night of incarceration. Most of these individuals are charged with disorderly conduct or misdemeanor offenses such as public drunkenness, traffic violations, shoplifting, and drug possession.

Disparate treatment of the poor and people of color is evident in the prison system, as in law enforcement. Although incarceration rates have risen steadily in recent years, the rate for minorities (with the exception of Asian Americans, who are the least likely to be incarcerated) was disproportionately higher than that for whites. For example, African Americans are incarcerated at a six times greater rate than whites: 1,947 per 100,000 African Americans compared to 306 per 100,000 white Americans. Nearly half of all prison admissions are African Americans, even though the majority of violent crime nationwide is committed by whites (FBI, 1996).

Jail and prison conditions often do little to rehabilitate offenders. In fact, three out of four inmates are housed in overcrowded facilities where two people often live in a space that is slightly larger than a walk-in closet. Some inmates suffer physical abuse by prison officials or other inmates. A videotape was recently shown on national television of an African American inmate restrained in a chair with a metal face mask over his head while a guard danced around, teasing him with a soft drink. The inmate was suffering from a drug overdose and begging for help; he eventually died.

Because of plea bargains, credit for "good time" served, and overcrowded prison conditions, most convicted criminals today do not serve their full sentences. They get out on either probation (close supervision of their everyday lives in lieu of serving time) or parole (early release from prison). About 3.6 million people are currently on probation or parole (U. S. Bureau of the Census, 1996). If offenders

According to the text, punishment serves four functions: retribution, social protection, rehabilitation, and deterrence. Which of these functions is shown in this photo?

violate the conditions of their probation or parole, they may be returned to prison to serve their full sentence. Some courts use *shaming penalties*—named for punishments such as the stocks used by the seventeenth century Puritans—with probationers or as alternatives to incarceration. Like the public stocks, these punishments typically take the form of a message to the community. For example, as a condition of his probation, one Illinois man had to put this sign at the end of his driveway: "Warning. A Violent Felon Lives Here. Travel At Your Own Risk" (Hoffman, 1997:A1). Drunk drivers may get special license plates; men who have been convicted of soliciting prostitutes may be identified in the media or on billboards; and shoplifters have been required to walk in front of the stores from which they stole, carrying signs admitting their guilt. Usually, these sentences are the result of a guilty plea, so they cannot be appealed except under very special circumstances (Hoffman, 1997).

Aside from their deterrent effect, shaming penalties are a way of avoiding the high cost of incarceration, another taxpayer burden. The average cost of building a new cell in a state prison is $54,000, and the cost per prisoner averages $22,000 per year, excluding food and medical services. Increasing numbers of older prisoners add to the costs because they often

TABLE 9.3   PRISONERS ON DEATH ROW, BY RACE, APRIL 1994

Race/Ethnicity	Number on Death Row	Percentage on Death Row	Percentage of U.S. Population
White	1445	49.9	74.8
African American	1155	39.9	11.9
Latino	209	7.2	9.5
Native American	52	1.8	0.7
Asian American	20	0.7	3.1
Not reported	9	0.3	0
Totals	2,890	100	100

Source: U.S. Bureau of the Census, 1996b.

have chronic health conditions that require long-term medical care. The $22,000 average per prisoner actually comes closer to $69,000 a year for elderly state prison inmates (Camp and Camp, 1994).

The Death Penalty

About 4,000 people have been executed in the United States since 1930, when the federal government began collecting data on executions (Smith, 1995). The death penalty—or *capital punishment*—is a highly controversial issue. Removal—not just expulsion—from the group is considered the ultimate form of punishment; and in the United States, capital punishment is considered an appropriate and justifiable response to very serious crimes.

In 1972, the U.S. Supreme Court ruled (in *Furman* v. *Georgia*) that *arbitrary* application of the death penalty violates the Eighth Amendment to the Constitution but that the death penalty itself is not unconstitutional. In other words, determining who receives the death penalty and who receives a prison term for similar offenses should not be done on a lotterylike basis (Bowers, 1984). To be constitutional, the death penalty must be imposed for reasons other than the race/ethnicity, gender, and social class of the offender.

Opponents of capital punishment argue that it is discriminatory because people of color, especially African Americans, and poor people are at greater risk of receiving a death sentence than are their white, more affluent counterparts (Smith, 1995). In fact, the former slave states are more likely to execute criminals than are other states, and African

Americans are eight to ten times more likely to be sentenced to death for crimes such as homicidal rape than are whites (non-Latinos/as) who commit the same offense (Marquart et al., 1994). Table 9.3 shows the number of prisoners on death row by racial-ethnic composition.

People who have lost relatives and friends because of a crime often see the death penalty as justifiable compensation—"an eye for an eye." But others fear that innocent individuals may be executed for crimes they did not commit. However controversial the death penalty is, it is likely to remain in place well into the twenty-first century because many political leaders and U.S. Supreme Court justices have expressed support for it. In fact, today, more people await execution than ever before. California, Florida, and Texas each have over 300 death row prisoners.

Is the solution to our "crime problem" to build more prisons and execute more people? If only about 20 percent of all crimes result in arrest, only half of those lead to a conviction, and fewer than 5 percent of convictions result in a jail term, the "lock 'em up and throw away the key" approach has little chance of succeeding. As for individuals who commit occupational and corporate crime, the percentage that enters the criminal justice system is so minimal that prison is relatively useless as a deterrent. Nor does the high rate of recidivism speak well for the rehabilitative efforts of our existing correctional facilities. One thing is clear: The existing criminal justice system cannot solve the crime problem. Some people believe that the way to reduce street crime, at least, is to short-circuit criminal behavior (see Box 9.2).

SOCIAL   PROBLEMS

AND SOCIAL POLICY   BOX 9.2

Crime Prevention or the Prison-Industrial Complex?

I know something serious has happened when I wake up well before dawn to discover two guards wearing armored vests and riot helmets taking a head count. . . . it's apparent that the prison is on "full lockdown status." At the minimum, we will be locked in our cells twenty-four hours a day for the next several days. . . . The experienced prisoner knows to be prepared for a few weeks of complete isolation. (Hopkins, 1997:66)

With these words, author Evans D. Hopkins describes the day at the Nottoway Correctional Center in Virginia when two correctional officers and two nurses were taken hostage by three prisoners after a botched escape attempt, and officials declared a lockdown that ultimately lasted four and a half months.

Although some politicians and social analysts believe that building more prisons and giving long sentences to offenders is the way to reduce the crime problem in the United States, others think that we should spend our money and energy on crime prevention instead. According to *prevention ideology,* the best way to reduce delinquency and crime is early intervention and prevention (Bynum and Thompson, 1996). Prevention typically takes three avenues: (1) early childhood and youth socialization that contributes to law-abiding behavior; (2) attacking the roots of delinquency and crime—poverty, unemployment, racism, sexism, drug abuse, and other problems discussed in this book; and (3) specific programs or services that intervene before individuals who have already engaged in delinquent or criminal behavior become immersed in deviant subcultures.

Current U.S. social policy is not based on prevention but consists of programs that include hiring more police officers, strengthen-

ing and enforcing gun control laws, and implementing the "three strikes" law, which requires a mandatory life sentence without parole for an individual who is convicted of a third felony. In fact, recent studies show that the government and private security companies spend nearly the same amount on crime control each year as the Pentagon spends on national defense (Donziger, 1996). The "war on crime" approach has contributed to the growth of a *prison-industrial complex*—a network of private companies, the government, and politicians—that greatly influences crime policy. In the past, most money spent on crime control went to public prisons; today, many state and local governments contract with private companies to build and operate correctional facilities, generating an annual revenue to these companies of more than $250 million. Other private enterprises also benefit from the prison-industrial complex, including investment houses that underwrite jail and prison construction and companies that provide food service, transportation, and health care for the facilities. Still other companies benefit from the sale of protective vests for guards, security systems, closed-circuit television systems, and other surveillance apparatus. Some analysts suggest that the prison-industrial complex, with its interlocking financial and political interests, has good reason to support the "war on crime" instead of developing social policies that prevent delinquency and crime before it happens (Donziger, 1996).

Does living in a prison environment with full lockdown status, as Hopkins describes, turn inmates into law-abiding citizens when they are released? What strategies can you suggest for rehabilitating prisoners? For preventing crime before it occurs?

Is equal justice under the law possible? As long as racism, sexism, classism, and ageism exist in our society, equal justice under the law may not be possible for all people; however, that does not keep it from being a goal that citizens and the criminal justice system can strive to reach.

SUMMARY

➤ *Why is it difficult to study crime and delinquency?*

Studying crime, criminals, and juvenile delinquency is difficult because it involves complex human behavior, and many criminals and victims hide their involvement. There also are problems inherent in using official sources of data such as the Uniform Crime Reports because they reflect crimes that are reported rather than crimes that are committed, and they do not provide detailed information about offenders.

➤ *How does violent crime differ from property crime?*

Violent crime consists of actions involving force or the threat of force against others and includes murder, rape, robbery, and aggravated assault. Property crime consists of taking money or property from another without force, the threat of force, or the destruction of property.

➤ *What is occupational crime?*

Occupational (white-collar) crime refers to illegal activities committed by people in the course of their employment or normal business activity. Occupational crime includes computer and other high-tech crimes, as well as more traditional crimes such as employee theft, fraud (obtaining money or property under false pretenses), embezzlement (theft from an employer), soliciting bribes or kickbacks, and insider trading of securities.

➤ *How does occupational crime differ from corporate crime?*

Occupational crimes are illegal activities committed by people in the course of their employment or normal business activity. Corporate crimes are illegal acts committed by corporate employees on behalf of the corporation and with its support.

➤ *What is organized crime and why does it flourish in the United States?*

Organized crime is a business operation that supplies illegal goods and services for profit. These illegal enterprises include drug trafficking, prostitution, gambling, loan-sharking, money laundering, and large-scale theft. Organized crime thrives because there is great demand for illegal goods and services.

➤ *How does juvenile delinquency differ from adult crime?*

Juvenile delinquency refers to a violation of law or the commission of a status offense by people who are younger than a specific age. Many behaviors that are identified as juvenile delinquency are not criminal acts per se but status offenses—acts that are illegal because of the age of the offender—such as cutting school or purchasing and consuming alcoholic beverages. Juvenile hearings take place in juvenile courts or before juvenile judges, whereas adult offenders are tried in criminal courts.

➤ *Who is most likely to be arrested for a crime in the United States?*

Men are more likely to be arrested than women. Teenagers and young adults are most likely to be arrested for serious crimes such as homicide, rape, and robbery. Although individuals from all social classes commit crimes, people from lower socioeconomic backgrounds are more likely to be arrested for violent and property crimes, whereas people from the upper classes generally commit white-collar or elite crimes. Low-income African Americans are overrepresented in arrest data.

➤ *How do functionalists explain crime?*

Functionalists use several theories to explain crime. According to strain theory, people are socialized to desire cultural goals, but many people do not have institutionalized means to achieve the goals and therefore engage in criminal activity. Control perspectives such as social bond theory suggest that delinquency and crime are most likely to occur when a person's ties to society are weakened or broken.

➤ *How do conflict theorists explain crime?*

Conflict theorists explain criminal behavior in terms of power differentials and/or economic inequality in society. One approach focuses on the relationship between authority and power and crime; another focuses on the relationship between economic inequality and crime. Feminist approaches offer several explanations of why women commit crimes: gender discrimination, patriarchy, and a combination of capitalism and patriarchy.

➡ *How do interactionists explain crime?*

Interactionists emphasize that criminal behavior is learned through everyday interaction with others. According to differential association theory, individuals have a greater tendency to deviate from societal norms when they frequently associate with people who are more likely to deviate than conform. Labeling theory says that delinquents and criminals are those people who have been successfully labeled by others as such.

➡ *What are the components of the criminal justice system?*

The criminal justice system is a network of or-

ganizations involved in law enforcement, including the police, the courts, and the prisons. The police are the most visible link in the criminal justice system because they are responsible for initially arresting and jailing people. Criminal courts are responsible for determining the guilt or innocence of people who have been accused of committing a crime. Imprisonment, probation, and parole are mechanisms of punishment based on retribution, social protection, rehabilitation, and deterrence.

➡ *Why is the death penalty controversial?*

The death penalty—or capital punishment—is a highly controversial issue. Some people believe that it is an appropriate and justifiable response to very serious crimes; others view this practice as discriminatory because people of color—especially African Americans—and poor people are at greater risk of receiving a death sentence than are their white, more affluent counterparts.

KEY TERMS

corporate crime, p. 186
criminal justice system, p. 196
differential association theory, p. 195
felony, p. 182
illegitimate opportunity structures, p. 181
juvenile delinquency, p. 187
labeling theory, p. 196
misdemeanor, p. 182
occupational (white-collar) crime, p. 186

organized crime, p. 186
plea bargaining, p. 198
primary deviance, p. 196
property crime, p. 184
punishment, p. 198
secondary deviance, p. 196
social bond theory, p. 194
strain theory, pp. 192–193
violent crime, p. 184

QUESTIONS FOR CRITICAL THINKING

1. Why doesn't the United States use all of its technological know-how to place known criminals and potential offenders under constant surveillance so that the crime rate can be really reduced?

2. If most of the crimes that are committed are property crimes, why do so many people fear that they will be the victims of violent crime?

3. Does the functionalist, conflict, or interactionist perspective best explain why people commit corporate crimes? Organized crimes? Explain your answer.

4. If money were no object, how would you reorganize the criminal justice system so that it would deal more equitably with all people in this country?

Chapter Ten

Violence

I relive my grief every time a child gets killed. It doesn't get a chance to heal. Your wounds. Your hurt. Your grief. It leaves a hole in your soul. . . . In their deaths there is sorrow, but there is also some unbelievable joy. If I had not had my three sons I would not be the type of person I am today. They help me be strong. They help me not to be selfish. It's not about me anymore. Society wants us to believe that our children died because they did something wrong. That's not true. There's single mothers who are single not by choice, but we still love our children.

—Frances Davis, describing the loss of three sons in six years to gunfire in Brooklyn, New York
(Gonzalez, 1995:A16)

—A university official on the death of Rex Chao, an exemplary student and gifted musician, who was shot and killed on campus by another student
(Janofsky, 1996b:A8)

This is clearly one of the most terrible occurrences in the history of the [Johns Hopkins] University. . . . This is absolutely devastating news for all of us here. It's horrible to think that his life has been cut so short.

Whether violence takes place in the central city or on an elite college campus, it leaves shock and anguish behind. *Violence* **is the use of physical force to cause pain, injury, or death to another, or damage to their property.** Frances Davis, the mother who lost her three sons to urban violence, and college student Rex Chao's parents know the grief of outliving their own children who died prematurely at the hands of others. After accidents, gunfire is the second-leading cause of death among U.S. children between the ages of ten and nineteen (U.S. Bureau of the Census, 1996b). Some victims are urban gang members, but others are four-year-olds outside skating or college students walking across campus. In this chapter, we examine violence against individuals—murder, rape, domestic violence, gang violence, and hate crimes.

VIOLENCE AS A SOCIAL PROBLEM

Many of us are ambivalent about violence. Although we condemn drive-by shootings and cold-blooded murders, we like to see a good action movie with lots of "blood and guts" or watch contact sports such as football, hockey, and boxing. However we explain this contradictory behavior, violence is a major social problem in this country. The United States has the highest homicide rates of any developed nation, and the deaths are concentrated in a particular segment of the population. Statistics show that African American males living in central cities of the United States have less chance of reaching their fortieth birthday than do people in the less developed nations of the world.

As a social problem, violence involves both an objective reality and a subjective awareness. Violence is an *objective reality* because we can measure and experience the effects of violent criminal behavior. For example, although the number of violent crimes reported to law enforcement officials has declined in recent years, a violent crime occurs, on average, every 17 seconds in this nation (FBI, 1996). We also have a *subjective awareness* that we should be fearful of violent personal crime because we might become victims. In a recent survey of U.S. teenagers, researchers found that fear of violence and crime affects the behavior, expectations, and school performance of 46 percent of today's teenagers (Applebome, 1996b). As a result, one in eight young people—and almost two in five from high-crime neighborhoods—carry a weapon for protection. According to one specialist in teen violence, "Crime has become this generation's Vietnam" (Applebome, 1996b:A6). The subjective awareness of violent crime may, in fact, be as strong as its objective reality. You don't have to live in a high-crime area of the central city to feel unsafe; localized violence reverberates nationally, making everyone *feel* less safe even though most people are actually safer than people were two decades ago (Donziger, 1996).

▲ Murder

The Uniform Crime Report defines **murder as the unlawful, intentional killing of one person by another.** (Killing in self-defense or during wartime is not murder.) By this definition, murder involves not only an unlawful act but also *malice aforethought*—the *intention* of doing a wrongful act. For example, a person who buys a gun, makes a plan to kill someone, and carries out the plan has probably committed murder. In contrast, *manslaughter* is the unlawful, *unintentional* killing of one person by another. For example, an intoxicated person who shoots a gun into the air probably holds no malice toward the bystander who is killed by a stray bullet. Sometimes a person's intentions are clear, but many times they are not, and the lines between intentional, unintentional, and accidental homicides are blurred. When one hunter accidentally shoots and kills another hunter, believing that the second is a deer moving in the distance, it's difficult to determine intention. In 1997, Thomas Richard Jones was found guilty of first-degree murder and sentenced to life without parole for killing two people in an automobile collision in North Carolina. Jones was under the influence of beer and painkillers at the time of the crash (Vick, 1997).

NATURE AND EXTENT OF THE PROBLEM

Statistics on murder are among the best official crime statistics available. Murders rarely go unreported, and suspects are usually apprehended and charged (FBI, 1996). Although annual rates vary slightly, murder follows certain patterns in terms of gender, age, race, and region of the country. Men make up the vast majority of murder victims and offenders. Of the 22,000 to 23,000 murders that are reported annually in this country, about 80 percent of the victims and 90 percent of the offenders are male. Males kill other males in about 86 percent of cases. Females kill 14 percent of the male victims, often because the females think they are in a life-threatening situation.

Age patterns are clearly evident in murder rates. Almost 90 percent of murder victims are eighteen or older; however, nearly half are between ages twenty and thirty-five. Interestingly, in 1995, the murder arrest rates per 100,000 for youths aged ten through seventeen decreased significantly for the second year in a row. According to one analyst, the decrease is due to "some of the glamour of being a thug, walking around with a gun . . . [being gone] . . . because people 13, 14, and 15 years old have seen so many of their friends or relatives being killed or going to prison" (Butterfield, 1996:A9).

Most murders are intraracial. More than half of all murder victims in the United States are African American, and over 90 percent of them are killed by other African Americans. Similarly, about 80 percent of white murder victims are killed by other white people (FBI, 1996). Murder takes a much greater toll on young African American males than on any other group in society. Race and class factors are often intertwined: Poor people are much more likely to kill than are members of the middle and upper classes, and a higher proportion of people of color live below the U.S. poverty level because of racial discrimination and generations of inequality in education and employment.

In the past, most murder victims knew their killers, but this pattern seems to be gradually changing. Today, slightly less than half of murder victims know their assailants. About 12 percent are related to their assailants, and 35 percent are acquainted with them well enough to at least engage in an argument. Of the remaining victims, 13 percent are murdered by strangers, and in about 40 percent of cases, the relationship between victim and offender is unknown. This pattern does differ somewhat when we look at gender differences in victimization. Among female murder victims, almost 30 percent are slain by a husband or boyfriend, whereas only 3 percent of male victims are killed by a wife or girlfriend (FBI, 1996).

Geographic differences exist in murder rates. Large metropolitan areas of the nation have a murder rate of about 10 victims per 100,000 residents; rural counties and cities outside metropolitan areas have a rate of about 5 per 100,000 (FBI, 1996). However, the incidence of murder is unevenly distributed within cities. Many suburbs have extremely low rates of murder compared to those of central cities. In the United States overall, murder is most likely to occur in the Southern states. Not only is the South the most populous region, it also views the possession and use of guns and other weapons more positively than other regions.

Across the nation, guns are used in approximately 70 percent of all murders annually—a fact that leads to ongoing political debate over gun control, especially of handguns (see Box 10.1). In 1996, the death rate from guns among African American males aged 15 to 19 was 153.1 per 100,000, as contrasted with 28.8 per 100,000 among their white peers. Cutting or stabbing instruments are used in slightly over 10 percent of murders, and hands, fists, and feet are used as weapons about 5 percent of the time (FBI, 1996).

MASS MURDER AND SERIAL MURDER

Mass murder is the killing of four or more people at one time and in one place by the same person. Unfortunately, there is no shortage of examples of mass murder in the United States. Among the most notorious "Texas killers" are George Hennard, who shot and killed twenty-two people at a Luby's Cafeteria in Killeen, Texas, in 1991, and Charles Whitman, who fatally shot fifteen people and wounded fourteen others from a tower on the campus of the University of Texas at Austin in 1965. Until Hennard's rampage, the record for the worst massacre by a single person in a single day was held by James Oliver Huberty, an unemployed man who killed twenty-one people and injured twenty others in a McDonald's restaurant in San Ysidro, California, in 1984.

According to criminologists, mass murderers tend to kill in the area where they live. They also are likely to be males, problem drinkers, and collectors of firearms and other weapons, often hiding them in a secret place (Dietz, 1986). Some recent mass murderers have been disgruntled workers or former employees who seek out supervisors and coworkers in the workplace; for some reason, these violent eruptions have occurred more than once in post offices (Holmes and Holmes, 1993).

Serial murder is the killing of three or more people over more than a month by the same person. Although serial murders account for fewer than 5,000 victims annually, extensive media coverage heightens public fear of killers like Ted Bundy, John Wayne Gacy, and Jeffrey Dahmer. Bundy, who was convicted of three murders and suspected in more than thirty-six other killings, was executed in Florida in 1989. Gacy was convicted of thirty-three murders of young men in Illinois, and Dahmer was convicted of fifteen counts of first-degree intentional homicide in Wisconsin, after he gruesomely killed many young males.

It's difficult to characterize serial killers, outside of the fact that the best-known ones are white males. Some travel extensively to locate their victims, but others kill near where they live. One study identified four basic types of serial killers: (1) *visionaries*, who kill because they hear a voice or have a vision that commands them to commit the murderous acts;

SOCIAL PROBLEMS
AND SOCIAL POLICY

BOX 10.1

Gun Control: The Whole Picture

In 1993, an American aged 10 to 19 died every 92 minutes from gunfire. . . . Gunfire is the leading cause of death among black men ages 15 to 19. . . . "What will it take for parents and religious, community, and political leaders to stand up and say enough?" (*New York Times*, 1996b)

> —Marian Wright Edelman, president of the Children's Defense Fund, on the increasing number of firearm deaths among young people

In 1993, 5,751 Americans under age twenty died from gunfire: 116 victims were under age five; 141 were five to nine years old; 700 were ten to fourteen years old; and 4,794 were fifteen to nineteen years old. Only vehicle accidents killed more children in the ten to nineteen age group. Some of these gun deaths were accidents, and a larger number were suicides, but the vast majority—3,661—were homicides (*New York Times,* 1996b). And the growing number of juveniles with guns are not just turning them on each other. In Los Angeles, for example, a twelve-year-old who shot and killed an eighty-two-year-old woman was turned over to police by his mother; days before, she had tried to physically force him to see his probation officer until she realized he was armed (Goldberg, 1996b).

The United States has a strong anti-gun-control lobby, and its slogan is taken from the Second Amendment: "The right of the people to bear arms shall not be infringed." But, say Americans who support gun control, let's hear the entire amendment, not just the second half. The whole Second Amendment to the Constitution reads as follows: "A well-regulated Militia, being necessary to the security of a free State, the right of the people to keep and bear Arms, shall not be infringed." In other words, the Second Amendment ensures an army, not private ownership (Lewis, 1995b). The Supreme Court ruled that this was the correct interpretation in 1939 and twice since, most recently in 1980. There is no constitutional right for individuals to bear arms.

Is the case closed? Hardly, says the National Rifle Association and other anti-gun-control lobbyists. If we passed laws controlling the sale of guns, criminals would still find a way to get them. Look, for example, at Japan, which has the strictest gun control laws in the world. Only about fifty Japanese citizens are allowed to own handguns, and they are expert marksmen who are required to leave their guns at the shooting range (Kristof, 1996c). Not even police officers are allowed to keep their guns at home in Japan. Illegal possession of a handgun is punishable by fifteen years in prison. Still, Japanese gangsters—the Yakuza—have guns, and it is possible to buy a handgun on the black market for $1,500. Granted, guns do find their way into Japan, but once again, let's look at the whole picture: In 1994, there were thirty-two gun murders in Japan, and twenty of these were gangsters killed by gangsters. In the same year, the United States had 15,456 gun deaths (Kristof, 1996c). We have twice the population of Japan but nearly 500 times as many gun deaths.

Should the U.S. pass stricter handgun controls? If private ownership of guns isn't constitutionally guaranteed, why haven't we ever passed strict gun control laws? Are there cultural—not legal—factors involved? Are there cultural differences that might contribute to Japan's lower violent crime rates as much as its strict laws? What do you think?

(2) *missionaries,* who take it on themselves to rid the community or the world of what they believe is an undesirable type of person; (3) *hedonists,* who obtain personal or sexual gratification from violence; and (4) *power/control seekers,* who achieve gratification from the complete possession of the victim (Holmes, 1988).

SOCIAL RESPONSES TO MURDER

Even though most violence is not random, many people have a deep and persistent fear of strangers. According to one analyst:

> We have responded [in various ways to the threat of violence]. Some of us by minimizing our time in public space for fear of encountering the random menace; many by purchasing a range of weapons, locks, bolts, alarms, and insurance; parents, by acting as virtual bodyguards for our children; governments, by dispensing crime prevention advice which promotes individual responsibility for keeping crime at bay. But has this reduced our fear? Or contributed to our greater security? Clearly not. (Stanko, 1990: viii)

Individual responses are intensified by media coverage of violent personal crimes, especially murder. The special newsworthiness of murder is discussed in Box 10.2 on pages 210–211.

At state and federal levels, the government has responded to the public's fear of violent crime by increasing expenditures on fear reduction programs and crime prevention programs that will supposedly help people to make their homes and neighborhoods safe from crime and violence. Lawmakers and enforcers continue to seek longer prison sentences—often without possibility of parole—for anyone convicted of murder (especially mass or serial murder) and other violent personal crimes.

Rape

Many people think that rape is a sexually motivated crime, but it is actually an act of violence with sex used as a weapon against a powerless victim (Vito and Holmes, 1994). Although both men and women can be victimized by rape, the legal definition of *forcible rape* is the act of forcing sexual intercourse on a woman against her will. Sexual assaults or attempts to commit rape by force or threat of force are included in FBI statistics on this crime. Unlike murder or other violent crimes, the age of the victim is a central issue in charging a person with rape. *Statutory rape* refers to sexual intercourse with a person who is under the legal age of consent as established by state law (some states now use the term *illegal intercourse* instead of *statutory rape*). In most states, the legal age of consent is between ages sixteen and eighteen. A few states have attempted to include male victims of sexual assault into definitions of rape, but criminologists estimate that (excluding men who are raped in prison) only about 1 percent of reported rape victims are men (Holmes, 1991).

NATURE AND EXTENT OF THE PROBLEM

Statistics on rape are misleading at best because rape is often not reported. National victimization studies, however, confirm trends since the 1950s: On average, one in five women in the United States is a victim of forced sex at some time during her life

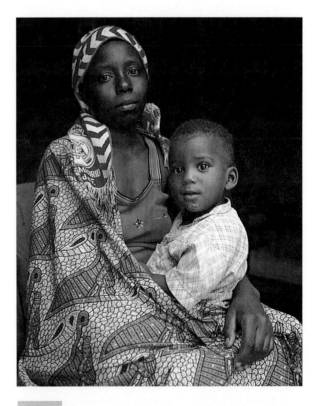

Rape in wartime is a global problem that has very personal ramifications for this Rwandan woman, whose son was born of rape.

What Makes Murder So Newsworthy?

"If it ain't a homicide, then I'm not interested."
— A newspaper reporter as he leafed through the morning police blotter reports (Chermak, 1995:55)

"Do you have any bodies for me?"
— A reporter making her daily calls to police divisions, hospitals, and the coroner's office (Chermak, 1995:55)

Crime is the fourth largest category of news reported in the media and, if we exclude sports and business, which take up so much space that they get their own newspaper sections and TV programs, the only topic that gets more news space and time is general interest (the arts, entertainment, people, etc.). Politics, foreign affairs, environmental issues, scientific discoveries, medical and health issues, natural disasters, plane crashes, power outages, chemical explosions, school strikes, accidents, ceremonies, parades—all get less coverage than crime. Moreover, almost 25 percent of the crime reported in

the news is murder (Chermak, 1995:53). What makes murder so newsworthy?

First, of course, there is the issue of seriousness. Reporters look for breaking stories on murder because the law says that murder is the most serious crime and society adds moral and humane reasons. At the same time, however, not every homicide is reported. As one television newsperson put it, "You can't cover every homicide—it's just not of interest. You need more unusualness" (Chermak, 1995:58). In other words, murder is newsworthy, but some murders are more newsworthy than others.

Certain characteristics of the victim make a murder more newsworthy. Age is very important. Children and the elderly are considered special groups within society and therefore get special media attention. Children are innocents, and the elderly are believed to deserve a peaceful life; when such people are murdered, the public thinks that the system has let them down. They should have been better protected.

(Sanday, 1996). Some women are victimized more than once. Despite the fact that some women do not report rape—perhaps believing that nothing will be done about it—arrests have been made in over half the forcible rapes reported to law enforcement officials in recent years (FBI, 1996). Map 10.1 on page 212 shows the rate of forcible rape by state.

Rape follows certain patterns in terms of gender, age, race, and region of the country. According to the definition that law enforcement officials use, rape is gender specific: That is, the victims of forcible rape are always female, and men make up the vast majority of offenders. Occasionally, women are charged as accomplices to male companions. Of the approximately 102,000 rapes reported annually in this country, almost 90 percent of the victims were raped by force, and the remaining 10 percent

were the victims of attempted rape or sexual assaults (FBI, 1996).

Most rapists tend to be under age twenty-five; their typical victims are also under twenty-five, white, divorced or separated, poor, and unemployed or in school (Vito and Holmes, 1994). In most reported rapes, the victim is under eighteen years of age. Although females of all ages are raped, the rate of victimization drops off sharply after age thirty-four.

Offenders and victims are usually of the same race and class. As with other violent personal crimes, women of color, particularly African Americans, are at greater risk of being rape victims than white women are (FBI, 1996). Moreover, in an intersection of class and race, young poor women of color who live in central cities are much more likely to be rape victims than other women are. Numeri-

The victim's occupation is also important. When a criminal justice professional—especially a police officer—is murdered, or someone in the helping professions (e.g., a nurse, doctor, teacher, or social worker), the case gets more attention. Again, the perception is that these people whose jobs are to protect and serve were somehow left unprotected themselves.

Murder victims from the suburbs are more newsworthy than residents of the inner city because educated, middle-class people are less often victimized, they may hold an important position, and more of the media audience can relate to them. Moreover, reporters get better human interest stories from the survivors: "[People] are so fatalistic in the inner city; it is almost like they expected it to happen" (Chermak, 1995:68). Sometimes reporters are afraid to go to inner city neighborhoods to interview friends and relatives of the victim. Murder in the suburbs, especially a wealthy suburb, also gets more attention because educated and affluent residents have contacts in the media and—just as important—because they give reporters more to report by posting flyers, offering rewards, and so forth.

It is not, of course, only the victim who can increase the newsworthiness of a murder. So can the defendant. Age is a factor if the defendant is very young (see Box 10.1, which mentions a twelve-year-old who killed an eighty-two-year-old woman). If the defendant is a politician or in the criminal justice system, the story immediately becomes more important because these people have betrayed a public trust. Occupation is also important if the defendant is a doctor, teacher, or priest—a guardian of life. In certain cases, it is the relationship between the victim and defendant that makes a murder exceptionally newsworthy, as when a parent murders a child.

Are you surprised by the way the media decide which murders are newsworthy and which are not? In one sense, the media are simply doing good business: "Murder is marketable . . . and the media respond to that market as would any entrepreneur" (Wilson, 1991:4–5). On the other hand, according to Steven Chermak (1995:80), "The public and reporters are desensitized to crimes that occur in certain parts of the city because they are automatically assumed to be 'normal.' Black-on-black killings are an example of this thinking." Do the media have a responsibility to present more balanced coverage? What is the effect of becoming desensitized to violence in our inner cities? Should *every* murder be reported? What do you think?

---

cally, more white women are raped than African American women, and more white men commit rape than African American men, but the probabilities of being a rape victim or an offender are significantly higher for African Americans than for whites (FBI, 1996). At the same time, there is no single profile of a rapist. Rape is committed by men of every class, race, ethnicity, and cultural background and across a wide range of age and educational levels (Fairstein, 1995).

The rate of reported rape varies geographically; the most populous Southern states account for almost 40 percent of the total each year, followed by states in the Midwest, the West, and the Northeast. In large metropolitan areas, the rate of rape is approximately 80 victims per 100,000 females, while it is 77 per 100,000 in cities outside metropolitan areas and 51 per 100,000 females in rural areas. Although most regions have experienced recent declines in reported rape (ranging from 2 percent in the South to 7 percent in the Northeast), the primary decrease has been in metropolitan areas. However, the rate of reported rape has increased by 88 percent in cities outside metropolitan areas and by 46 percent in rural areas over the past 10 years (FBI, 1996).

ACQUAINTANCE ("DATE") RAPE

Acquaintance rape is forcible sexual activity that meets the legal definition of rape and involves people who first meet in a social setting (Sanday, 1996). This definition is preferred by some scholars because it encompasses dates and casual acquaintances but excludes spouses (marital rape) and relatives (incest). The phrase was coined to distinguish

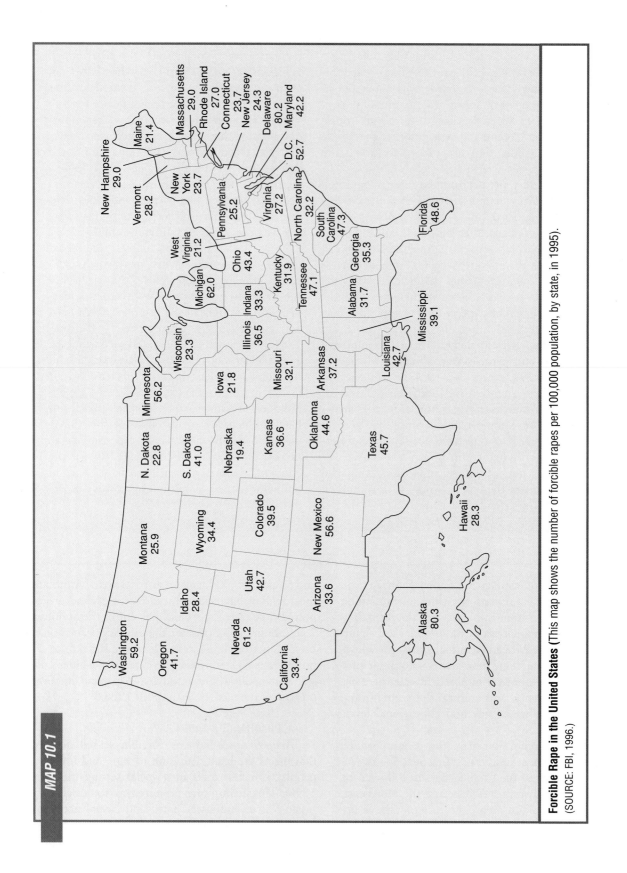

Forcible Rape in the United States (This map shows the number of forcible rapes per 100,000 population, by state, in 1995). (SOURCE: FBI, 1996.)

MAP 10.1

New Hampshire 29.0
Maine 21.4
Vermont 28.2
Massachusetts 29.0
Rhode Island 27.0
Connecticut 23.7
New Jersey 24.3
Delaware 80.2
Maryland 42.2
New York 23.7
Pennsylvania 25.2
D.C. 52.7
Virginia 27.2
North Carolina 32.2
South Carolina 47.3
West Virginia 21.2
Ohio 43.4
Kentucky 31.9
Tennessee 47.1
Alabama 31.7
Georgia 35.3
Florida 48.6
Michigan 62.0
Indiana 33.3
Wisconsin 23.3
Illinois 36.5
Missouri 32.1
Arkansas 37.2
Louisiana 42.7
Mississippi 39.1
Minnesota 56.2
Iowa 21.8
Kansas 36.6
Oklahoma 44.6
Texas 45.7
N. Dakota 22.8
S. Dakota 41.0
Nebraska 19.4
Colorado 39.5
New Mexico 56.6
Montana 25.9
Wyoming 34.4
Utah 42.7
Arizona 33.6
Idaho 28.4
Nevada 61.2
California 33.4
Washington 59.2
Oregon 41.7
Alaska 80.3
Hawaii 28.3

212

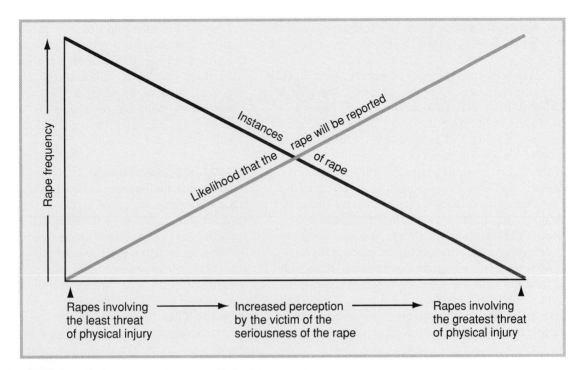

FIGURE 10.1 *The Likelihood That a Rape Will Be Reported*
Rapes involving the least threat of physical injury (e.g., most date rapes) are the most frequent but are much less likely to be reported to authorities than are rapes involving the greatest threat of physical injury. (SOURCE: Ellis, 1989:5.)

forced, nonconsensual sex between people who know one another from forced, nonconsensual sex between strangers—but both are rape. We probably know much less about the actual number of acquaintance rapes than stranger rapes because victims are less likely to report a sexual attack by someone they know. National studies in the 1980s concluded that one in every four women surveyed was a victim of rape or attempted rape, 84 percent of those who had been raped knew their attacker, and 57 percent of the rapes happened during a date (Koss, 1988). A study by the National Victim Center (1992) also found that most rape victims are attacked by someone they know. As Figure 10.1 shows, most rapes involve people who are at least acquaintances, and these rapes have the lowest probability of being reported to the police. It is estimated that fewer than 20 percent of the victims of acquaintance rape report the crime to the police, and 69 percent of the victims believe that they will be blamed by others for having caused the rape (Martin, 1992).

Acquaintance rape is often associated with alcohol or other drug consumption, especially among college students. As Robin Warshaw (1994), a journalist who has extensively studied acquaintance rape, explains:

Legal rape includes unwanted penetration when the victim is incapacitated by alcohol or drugs. Some men purposely give drinks to women in order to render them unable to object to sex. . . . Stating that women are sometimes "fed" alcohol intentionally doesn't mean that women don't have the ability to choose for themselves whether to drink or not. . . . when you drink and get drunk, you are responsible for what happens when you throw up or are too sick to go to work. In our society, though, responsibility for crime falls on those who commit it. Women don't "deserve" rape because they are intoxicated, but if they drive drunk and injure or kill someone, they *are* guilty of a crime. Likewise, men who are drunk when they rape are legally responsible for the crime of hurting someone else, even if she was drunk, too. (Warshaw, 1994:xxiv)

Acquaintance rape on college campuses often takes the form of gang or party rapes. Gang rape is different from individual acquaintance rape; it is used as a reinforcing mechanism for membership in the group of men (Warshaw, 1994). In fact, men who rape in groups might never commit rape alone. As they participate in gang rape, they experience a special bonding with each other, a unity of purpose that comes from the pride they feel in reducing their victim to an object or a property to be possessed by others. They use rape to prove their sexual ability to other group members and thereby enhance their status. Sometimes, the woman may have agreed to consensual sex with one member of the group, but the man invites his friends to take a turn. When such acts are committed by middle- and upper-income males, the behavior is overlooked with comments such as "They were just sowing their wild oats" or "Boys will be boys." But what is really being overlooked is the larger question of social responsibility and violent sexual crime—an issue that our society has been slow to address (Warshaw, 1994).

Many people believe that women are less traumatized by acquaintance rape because it usually involves little "real" violence, such as brutal beatings or use of weapons, but numerous researchers have found that this is not the case. Victims of acquaintance rape feel invaded and violated like any other rape victim. Georgette, an eighteen-year-old freshman at a state university in North Carolina who was raped by one of the resident assistants in her dormitory, described the emotional consequences of acquaintance rape this way (Warshaw, 1994:67–68):

I didn't tell anyone. In fact, I wouldn't even admit it to myself until about four months later when the guilt and fear that had been eating at me became too much to hide and I came very close to a complete nervous breakdown. I tried to kill myself, but fortunately I chickened out at the last minute.

There's no way to describe what was going on inside me. I was losing control and I'd never been so terrified or helpless in my life. I felt as if my whole world had been kicked out from under me and I had been left to drift all alone in the darkness. I had horrible nightmares in which I relived the rape and others which were even worse. I was terrified of being with people and terrified of being alone. I couldn't concentrate on anything and began failing several classes. Deciding on what to wear in the morning was enough to make me panic and cry uncontrollably. I was convinced I was going crazy, and I'm still convinced I almost did.

SOCIAL RESPONSES TO RAPE

Societal attitudes towards rape largely affect the female victims, as evidenced by the discrepancy between official statistics, such as the FBI's Uniform Crime Reports, and victimization studies. Many rapes are never reported. The extremely traumatic nature of the crime prevents some victims from coming forward. They may believe that if they don't think about it or talk about it, maybe the whole experience will just "go away." Often, the fear generated by the attack is carried over into fear that the attacker may try to get even with them or attack them again if they report the crime. This is a particularly significant issue for women who are still in proximity to their attacker. Suppose the attacker is in the same college class or works at the same place as the victim. How can the woman file a report without disrupting her whole life? Many women also fear how they will be treated by the police and by prosecutors and defense attorneys in the event of a criminal trial. Many victims also fear publicity for themselves and their families. Finally, if rape is attempted but not accomplished, the victim typically receives little legal or medical attention or help, even though researchers have found that victims of attempted rape experience short-term and long-term reactions similar to those of women who were raped (Sanday, 1996).

Some societal attitudes towards rape and rape victims have improved over the past three decades. Rape crisis centers and hotlines provide an avenue for reporting rape and getting medical and counseling help. Many urban police departments have specially trained personnel who work with victims from the time they call to report the crime and receive initial medical attention through the conclusion of any criminal trial that ensues. Remaining problematic, however, are situations in which the victim and the accused had a prior relationship. Some law enforcement officials and prosecutors view such cases as a private matter and take little action. Unlike rape perpetrated by a stranger, prior relationship cases are often considered less serious, and sometimes it is assumed that the woman contributed to her victimization by how she dressed, where she was, or other factors that are believed to indicate that she was "asking for it" (Estrich, 1987). Even more problematic from a legal and social standpoint is marital rape, a topic that we will examine later in the chapter.

◢ Domestic Violence

The term *domestic violence* obscures the fact that most victims of violence in the family are women and children. Women are more likely to be assaulted, injured, or raped by their male partners than by any other type of assailant. Children are extremely vulnerable to abuse and violence because of their age and economic and social dependence on their parents or other adult caregivers.

CHILD ABUSE

What do the words *child abuse* mean to you? When we first hear these terms, most of us think of cases involving physical injury or sexual abuse. But the most frequent form of child maltreatment is *child neglect*—not meeting children's basic needs for emotional warmth and security, adequate shelter, food, health care, education, clothing, and protection. According to the 1974 Federal Child Abuse Prevention and Treatment Act, child abuse and neglect refer to the physical or mental injury, sexual abuse, or negligent treatment of a child under the age of eighteen by a person who is responsible for the child's welfare. We will focus primarily on physical injury and sexual abuse of children because these actions are classified as violent personal crimes.

Historically, children in the United States were considered the property of their parents and could be punished or ignored as the parents wished. With passage of the Social Security Act in the 1930s, however, children became legally protected even from their own parents. But decades later, research established that many physical injuries to children are intentionally inflicted by parents and other caregivers. Parental violence can, in fact, lead to the *battered child syndrome,* a psychological disorder in which a child experiences low self-esteem and sometimes clinical depression associated with former or current abuse perpetrated by a biological or custodial parent (Kempe et al., 1962).

Physical abuse of children in the United States is a serious social problem that remains largely hidden. Some researchers have found that children are most likely to be assaulted in their own homes if their parents were abused, neglected, or deprived as children and if the parents are socially isolated as adults. Parents who lack a support network and suddenly face a crisis tend to make their children the targets of their frustration and sometimes their aggression (Kempe and Kempe, 1978). Other researchers have found that abusive parents characteristically feel unloved and unworthy and totally unprepared to cope with their circumstances (Tower, 1996).

Although we become most aware of child abuse when it results in death or serious injury to a child, there are many signs of physical abuse, including bruises, particularly on the backs of the legs, upper arms and chest, neck, head, or genitals. Fractures in infants under twelve months of age are a strong indication of abuse, as are head injuries and burns, especially cigarette burns. Most physicians and emergency room personnel are trained to identify signs of child abuse so that parents or guardians can be reported to the appropriate authorities. In fact, reporting of suspected child abuse has improved significantly in recent years because of increased training, awareness, and legislation, including the Federal Child Abuse Prevention and Treatment Act of 1974, which establishes that reports of suspected abuse will be investigated promptly and fully. In the past, even when physicians suspected abuse, they often chose to treat the child but not report the incident, believing that it would be too difficult to prove allegations against the aggressors (Tower, 1996).

One of the most disturbing forms of child maltreatment is sexual abuse; however, there is a lack of consensus about how sexual abuse should be defined. In one study, child sexual abuse was defined in terms of three actions: intrusion, molestation with genital contact or other forms of fondling, and inadequate supervision of a child's sexual activity (see Tower, 1996). Another study included all behaviors from "sexual overtures" to sexual intercourse that occurred between a child age thirteen and under and someone five or more years older or that involved adolescents aged thirteen to sixteen with someone ten or more years older (Finkelhor, 1984).

Although it is difficult to estimate the incidence and prevalence of sexual abuse, it appears that between 10 and 15 percent of girls and boys experience some form of sexual contact as children (Finkelhor, 1984). At all ages, females are more likely than males to be victims of sexual abuse as well as *incest,* or sexual relations between individuals so closely related that they are forbidden to marry by law. Males are more likely to experience assault in public places, by strangers or nonrelatives; girls are more likely to experience long-term victimization by relatives or family acquaintances in their own home. Both male and female victims are more likely to be abused by male offenders, and offenders are known to their victims in the vast majority of cases (Knudsen, 1992).

SPOUSE ABUSE

From the days of early Rome to current times, spouse abuse has been acknowledged to exist, but until recently, it was largely ignored or tolerated. Today, it is estimated that as many as 5 million spouses, primarily wives, are abused each year. Women are much more likely than men to be victims of domestic violence of all types. The U.S. Attorney General's office estimates that at least 94 percent of all cases of spouse abuse involve a man beating a woman. In fact, physical abuse by husbands or boyfriends is the single most common source of injury among women (Murphy-Milano, 1996). Injuries sustained by victims of spouse abuse are as serious as, or more serious than, injuries incurred in 90 percent of all rapes, robberies, and aggravated assaults. Spouse abuse ranges in intensity from slapping, kicking, and hitting with a closed fist to inflicting critical injuries or death (Straus et al., 1980). Spouse abuse is not restricted to members of any one class or race; it occurs across lines of race, class, region, religion, and other factors. Charlotte Fedders, for example, was abused by her husband, John Fedders, a powerful young lawyer in the Reagan administration:

I was in the bathroom sitting on a closed toilet, bathing two of the boys in the tub. John came home, went upstairs, and saw my note [that she had written a check for $80 to a marriage counselor]. He came into the bathroom and started beating me with his fists and pulling on my hair. I turned away to protect myself, and he beat me on my back. I managed to get out and run into Luke's [an older son] room, because I didn't think that he'd hit me in front of Luke. But he ran after me. I can remember crouching in the corner. He beat my neck and shoulder and back. Then he chased me into our bedroom. He yelled at one point, "I don't give a . . . if I kill you." It was one of the worst beatings John ever gave me. And I hadn't done anything but written a check. (Fedders and Elliott, 1987:158–159)

Although Charlotte Fedders had the financial means to divorce her husband and became an advocate for battered women, many abused women come from low-income backgrounds and have few options. Unfortunately, many end up the victims of homicide. Women are more than three times as likely to be killed by their spouses than men are. The only exception is African American husbands, who are at greater risk of being killed by their spouses than are African American wives or white spouses of either gender. Moreover, the risk of being killed by one's spouse is greater for individuals in interracial marriages (Mercy and Saltzman, 1989). When women kill their spouses, it is often because they have been physically and sexually abused by their husbands over a long period of time and see themselves as hopelessly trapped in a dangerous relationship.

Related to the issue of spouse abuse is marital rape. In *marital rape,* a husband forces sexual intercourse on his resisting wife. The federal criminal code and most state laws now identify marital rape as a crime. Three types of marital rape have been identified: (1) battering rape, in which sexual violence is part of a larger pattern of abuse; (2) nonbattering rape, in which the husband and wife do not agree over when, where, and whether or not to have sex; and (3) obsessive rape, which involves male sexual obsessions, sometimes related to use of pornography or force to become aroused (Finkelhor and Yllo, 1985). Many victims of spouse abuse and/or marital rape fear that if they try to leave the abusive husband, they will endanger themselves and their children. But in fact, women who have been severely assaulted sexually by their husbands and who do not have adequate support services for victims of domestic violence where they live are the most likely to kill their spouses (Browne and Williams, 1987).

SOCIAL RESPONSES TO DOMESTIC VIOLENCE

The civil and criminal trials of O.J. Simpson, the former professional football star, actor, and media celebrity who was accused of brutally slaying his ex-wife, Nicole Brown Simpson, and her friend, Ronald L. Goldman, put domestic violence in the forefront

Nicole Brown Simpson, the ex-wife of football legend O.J. Simpson, became the symbol for all victims of domestic violence after she was brutally killed. Does media coverage of celebrity violence make people more aware of problems in our society? Why or why not?

of public consciousness (Gross, 1994). Photographs of the battered and bruised face of Nicole Brown Simpson were splashed across the front of supermarket tabloids, daily newspapers, and television screens around the world. Despite cases such as this, many people who are aware of domestic abuse don't do anything about it, not wanting to become involved in a "private matter."

Historically, in the United States, an *ideology of nonintervention*—a strong reluctance on the part of outsiders to interfere in family matters—has led people and police officers to ignore or tolerate domestic violence (Lauer, 1995). Unfortunately, the pattern of violence that ultimately results in a homicide is eerily similar in many cases of domestic abuse, and in most of those cases, the deaths might have been prevented by much earlier intervention. Positive changes are now being made in how law enforcement officials handle domestic violence calls—changes that are long overdue.

Gang Violence and Hate Crimes

Like domestic violence, gang violence may be exacerbated by socialization of males for male domi-

nance and by patriarchal social structures. Throughout U.S. history, there have been gangs composed primarily of young males of the same race or ethnicity. Some gangs are basically peer groups that hang out together, but others are well organized and violent. In recent years, gang activity and gang-related violence have increased significantly not only in large metropolitan areas but also in smaller cities and suburbs. Incidents involving gang violence are among the most frequently mentioned memories of some students in Chicago's public high schools:

> One day in the halls the gangs came up to me and asked what I was doing. They said if I were in a gang they would kill me right there. . . . Another time a car came up to me and started shooting.
>
> The gangs killed one of my best friends. In high school, I always feel afraid because the gangs hang around the school and try to recruit the current students. (quoted in Hutchison and Kyle, 1993)

Sociologist Martín Sánchez Jankowski (1991) suggests that violence attributed to gangs is often committed by members of gangs acting as *individuals* rather than as agents of the organization. According to Jankowski, most gang members do not like violence and fear that they may be injured or killed in violent encounters. As a result, gang members engage in collective violence only to accomplish specific objectives such as asserting authority or punishing violations by their own members who are incompetent or who break the gang's code. Similarly, they engage in violence against other gangs primarily when they feel threatened or need to maintain or expand their operations in a certain area. In general, according to Jankowski, gang members use collective violence to achieve the goals of gang membership (proving their masculinity and toughness, providing excitement, and maintaining their reputation) mainly when they are provoked by others or when they are fearful.

INDIVIDUAL AND COLLECTIVE HATE CRIMES

Sociologists Jack Levin and Jack McDevitt (1993) suggest that gangs look for opportunities to violently attack "outgroup" members because they are seeking a thrill and view their victims as vulnerable. *Hate crimes* are attacks against people because of their race, religion, skin color, disability, sexual orientation, national origin, or ancestry (Levin and McDevitt, 1993).

Of course, not all hate crimes are committed by gang members. The case of Joseph Paul Franklin is a shocking example of attitudes that can result in hate crimes. Franklin believes that it is his mission to rid the United States of African Americans and Jews. He has been convicted of bombing a Jewish synagogue and killing several interracial couples. According to Franklin, these were not hate crimes, however, because "every murder is committed out of hate" (quoted in Gladwell, 1997). Moreover, Franklin expressed no remorse for his actions, as one journalist describes (Gladwell, 1997:132):

> In his confession to the police, after he detailed every step of the synagogue attack, Franklin was asked if there was anything he'd like to say. He stared thoughtfully over the top of his glasses. There was long silence. "I can't think of anything," he answered. Then he was asked if he felt any remorse. There was another silence. "I can't say that I do," he said. He paused again, then added, "The only thing I'm sorry about is that it's not legal."
>
> "What's not legal?"
>
> Franklin answered as if he'd just been asked the time of day: "Killing Jews."

When people with beliefs and attitudes like this join violent gangs or paramilitary groups, they can perpetrate devastating acts of violence, terrorism, and even war (see Chapter 18).

THE GANG-DRUGS-VIOLENCE CONNECTION

How strong is the gang-drugs-violence connection? Not all social analysts agree on the answer to this question. Some believe that drug trafficking is a major activity of most central city gangs and that a great deal of gang violence is linked to drug activity (see Hagedorn, 1988; Bourgeois, 1995). However, researchers studying street gangs in Chicago concluded that very few (8 out of 288) gang-motivated homicides were related to drugs. Murders were usually the result of intergang fights over turf (Block and Block, 1993). Sociologist Joan Moore (1993) suggests that the nature and extent of drug-related gang violence are directly linked to the economy in the city where the gang primarily operates. According to Moore, if a community's economy is not based on solid wages and salaries, illegal economies based on drug trafficking and other criminal activities emerge, and young people often see these activities as the only form of economic survival. Along the same lines, sociologist Felix M. Padilla (1993), who studied the Diamonds, a Chicago street gang, found that gangs get into drug activity as a rational response to the doors that are closed to them.

SOCIAL RESPONSES TO GANG VIOLENCE

The threat of gang violence—particularly such seemingly random events as drive-by shootings—has contributed to a climate of fear in low-income and poverty-level areas of central cities for many years now. But people living in smaller cities and suburban areas believed that they were immune. Gang violence was not their problem; it happened in big cities and involved people who were not like themselves. But as gangs have spread and become increasingly violent, more people are concerned and are demanding harsher penalties for youthful offenders, who often are under the jurisdiction of juvenile courts, not the adult criminal justice system (see Chapter 9).

Social responses based on intervention by law enforcement officials and the criminal justice system have had only limited success in dealing with the

Gang violence not only harms gang members but also innocent bystanders such as this three-year-old boy who was the victim of a drive-by shooting. Do you find it ironic that he is playing with a toy gun at the hospital?

structural problems—such as lack of educational opportunities and jobs, inadequate housing, and racial and ethnic discrimination—that accompany much gang behavior. The best solution seems to come from former gang members and former felons who band together to help break the cycle of crime and hopelessness that they believe produces gang violence. For example, the Alliance of Concerned Men of Washington, D.C., a collection of middle-aged former felons, substance abusers, and inmates, mediated a truce between two factions of a gang that had been terrorizing a Southeast Washington neighborhood. Members of the Alliance not only reduced gang violence in the city, they also helped gang members to find jobs, giving them hope that they would be able to reach their eighteenth birthday (Janofsky, 1997b).

As we have said about other social problems, how people view the problem in large measure determines what approach they believe should be used to reduce or eliminate the problem. Violence perpetrated by gang members and other people acting individually or collectively is no exception. The theoretical explanation that we believe best explains violence is likely to be the one we use to resolve the problem.

BIOLOGICAL AND PSYCHOLOGICAL EXPLANATIONS OF VIOLENCE

Because we have examined a number of biological, psychological, and sociological explanations of crime in Chapter 9, we will focus here primarily on how these approaches explain violence and what possible solutions might emerge from each perspective.

Biological Explanations

Most biological explanations are based on the assumption that violent behavior is an inherent individual trait. Therefore, say proponents of these explanations, violence is a natural and inevitable part of human behavior that only social organization can control. Some scientists, however, say that violence is neither natural nor inevitable but is nevertheless biologically based—or partly biologically based—in that it can result from traumatic brain injury or some combination of brain injury and other factors. Although most people with brain injuries are not violent, injuries to certain parts of the brain or injuries

in combination with an abusive childhood or psychotic symptoms (e.g., paranoia) can affect an individual's ability to conform to societal norms.

The cortex of the brain—particularly the frontal lobes—are most closely associated with violent behavior. It is the cortex that modifies impulses, allowing us to use good judgment, make decisions, and organize behavior; it also facilitates learning and adherence to rules of conduct (Gladwell, 1997). Using various neurological and psychiatric examinations, medical experts try to determine whether violent offenders have frontal lobe impairment, were abused as children, or have any psychological disorders. These factors, especially in combination, make people prone to violent behavior because they have fewer inhibitions. For example, a recent study of 279 veterans who suffered penetrating head injuries in the Vietnam War concluded that these veterans were from two to six times more aggressive and violent than were veterans who had not suffered such injuries (Gladwell, 1997). In another study, medical researchers examined brain scans of severely neglected children and found that the children's cortical regions were underdeveloped by 20 to 30 percent; such underdevelopment affects both their intelligence and their emotional health (Gladwell, 1997).

Psychological Explanations

One psychological explanation focuses on violence as a form of *aggression*—behavior intended to hurt someone, either physically or verbally—that results from frustration (Weiten and Lloyd, 1994). According to the *frustration-aggression hypothesis*, people who are frustrated in their efforts to achieve a highly desired goal become aggressive toward others (Dollard et al., 1939). The object of the aggression becomes a *scapegoat,* a substitute for the actual source of frustration who can be blamed, especially if that person or group is incapable of resisting the hostility or aggression (see Chapter 3). The amount of aggression is determined by the strength of the individual's unmet needs or wishes. Although the frustration-aggression hypothesis has been used to explain violent behavior ranging from individual acts of street violence to urban riots, it does provide insight into why frustration leads to aggression in some people but not others. As a result, psychologist Leonard Berkowitz (1969) has qualified the frustration-aggression hypothesis as follows: (1) Frustration does not necessarily lead to aggression, (2) many factors in addition to frustration—such as one's personality—influence the likelihood of aggression, and (3) frustration may produce responses other than aggression, such as apathy and depression.

Responses to Violence

Explaining violence in biological and/or psychological terms suggests responses based on psychiatric or other medical intervention. That is, if violent behavior is associated with specific neurological problems, it can be diagnosed and treated like any other neurological illness, and drugs such as anticonvulsants, antidepressants, and antihypertensive medications can act on the cortex to moderate violent behavior. However, biologically and psychologically based explanations of violence and medical interventions raise some important questions. Consider, for example, Joseph Paul Franklin, whom we discussed above (see Gladwell, 1997). What happens to society when violent offenders are turned into the objects of medical scrutiny? Does violent crime itself become somehow normalized and thus excused because the actions are beyond the individual's control?

SOCIOLOGICAL EXPLANATIONS OF VIOLENCE

Functionalist and conflict explanations of violence are based on the assumption that violence is in the structure of society. Interactionist explanations focus on how violent behavior is learned and under what conditions it is most likely to occur in social interactions.

The Functionalist Perspective

Some functionalists believe that violence arises from a sense of anomie (see Chapter 9), a feeling of helplessness, normlessness, or alienation. Others believe that violence increases when social institutions such as the family, schools, and religious organizations weaken and the main mechanisms of social control in people's everyday lives are external—law enforcement and the criminal justice system.

One functionalist perspective, known as the *subculture of violence hypothesis*, states that vio-

lence is part of the normative expectations governing everyday behavior among young males in the lower classes (Wolfgang and Ferracuti, 1967). Violent subcultures include violent juvenile gangs, neo-Nazi skinhead groups, and some organized crime groups. Violent subcultures are most likely to develop when young people, particularly males, have few legitimate opportunities available in their segment of society and when subcultural values accept and encourage violent behavior. In this context, young people come to consider aggression or violence a natural response to certain situations; violence is also considered a by-product of their culture, which idealizes toughness and even brutality in the name of masculinity (Wolfgang and Ferracuti, 1967). The subculture of violence hypothesis has been used to explain violence among lower-class young men in central cities (see Miller, 1958), as well as higher rates of violence in the South (see Gastil, 1971). However, many other studies have concluded that economic deprivation and poverty are more important factors in explaining high rates of violence than is subculture, race, or region of the country (Loftin and Hill, 1974; Parker, 1989).

Still other functionalist explanations of violence focus on how changes in social institutions put some people at greater risk of being victims of violent crime than others. According to the *lifestyle-routine activity approach*, the patterns and timing of people's daily movements and activities as they go about obtaining the necessities of life—such as food, shelter, companionship, and entertainment—are the keys to understanding violent personal crimes and other types of crime in our society (Cohen and Felson, 1979). Some of the changes over the past 50 years that have increased violent crime in the United States include more families in which both parents (or the sole parent) work outside the home, more people living by themselves, shopping hours extended into the night, and more people eating outside the home (Parker, 1995). Some people also occupy a status with role expectations that are riskier than others, such as young people out on a date at night. Social structure may also put constraints on behavior that make certain people more vulnerable to violent attack (e.g., people who are required to work at night). The lifestyle-routine activity approach suggests that people who willingly put themselves in situations that expose them to the potential for violent crime should modify their behavior, or society should provide greater protection for people who are out at night and have little recourse against attackers. The lifestyle-routine activity approach is good as far as it goes, but it does not address the issue of violence in the home and other supposedly safe havens in society.

How do functionalists explain violence perpetrated against women, such as rape and spouse abuse? Most functionalists emphasize shared moral values and social bonds. They believe that when rapid social change or other disruption occurs, moral values may erode, and problems such as rape and spouse abuse are more likely to occur. Functionalists believe that to reduce violence against women, the family, schools, religious organizations, and other social institutions should be strengthened, so that they, in turn, can regenerate shared values and morality. Most functionalists also believe the criminal justice system should get tough on rapists, spouse batterers, and others who engage in violent criminal behavior by making sure that justice is sure and swift.

▲ The Conflict Perspective

Conflict theorists who focus on class-based inequalities believe that the potential for violence is inherent in capitalist societies. In fact, say these theorists, the wealthy engage in one form of violence, and the poor engage in another. The wealthy often use third parties to protect themselves and their families from bodily harm as well as to secure their property and investments in this country and elsewhere in the world. The wealthy who live in the United States or other developed nations and own (or own stock in) factories in a Third World country would, for example, use the foreign government and police—third parties—to control workers who are threatening to strike. The wealthy also influence U.S. government policy. For instance, they are more likely to support U.S. military intervention—and thus violence—in nations such as Kuwait and Haiti where they have large investments at stake.

In contrast, violence among low-income and poverty-level people is typically committed by the individual and is a reaction against the unjust social and economic conditions they experience daily on the bottom rung of a capitalist society. The economic exploitation of the poor dramatically affects all aspects of a poor individual's life, including how the person reacts to daily injustices, stress, and other threatening

situations. The vast majority of victims—as well as offenders—in violent street crimes are poor, unemployed, or working in low-level, low-paying jobs. In fact, most violent street crime is an intraclass phenomenon: Poor and working-class people typically victimize others who are like themselves.

The conflict perspective emphasizes that the criminal justice system is biased in favor of the middle and upper classes and therefore defines violence differently, depending on how a person's race, class, and gender locate him or her in the system of stratification. In this way, violent crimes are one part of a larger system of inequality and oppression. Sexism and racism are reinforced by the overarching class structure that benefits the powerful at the expense of the powerless. Exploitation of people of color and the poor creates in them a sense of hopelessness, frustration, and hostility that may boil over into violent acts such as rape or murder. At the same time, it is important to note that rape, murder, and other violent acts occur across all class and racial-ethnic categories in the United States.

The branch of the conflict perspective that focuses on feminist issues specifically examines violence against women, such as rape and most spouse abuse. One feminist perspective suggests that violence against women is a means of reinforcing patriarchy. In a patriarchal system, the sexual marketplace is characterized by unequal bargaining power, making transactions between men and women potentially coercive in nature. Gender stratification is reinforced by powerful physical, psychological, and social mechanisms of control, including force or the threat of force. Rape and physical brutality are used by some men to degrade women who challenge their sense of superiority or to express their rage against the larger society. Fear of violence forces women to change their ways of living, acting, and dressing and thus deprives them of many basic freedoms (see Gardner, 1995).

The branch of the conflict perspective that focuses on racial-ethnic inequalities points out that racism is another important factor in explaining rape and other violence against women. Throughout U.S. history, African American men have been more likely to be executed for rape than white men. Since 1930, 89 percent of the men executed for rape in the United States have been African American (LaFree, 1980, 1989). Although an estimated 80 percent of all rapes and attempted rapes are intraracial (white on white or black on black), the myth persists that most rapes are interracial (between races) (Scully, 1990). Furthermore, the criminal justice system has been found to deal differently with African American women who report a rape than with white women. One study showed that prosecutors and investigating officers who are responsible for filing complaints against alleged rapists and bringing them to trial often try to discredit victims who are poor and/or African American or Latina (Frohmann, 1991).

According to any of these conflict approaches, violence against women is unlikely to diminish significantly unless inequalities based on class, gender, and race are reduced at the macrolevel in society. In the meantime, many feminists believe that women should receive help in getting away from domestic violence and protection against stalkers and rapists. National, state, and local coalitions against rape and domestic violence offer hotlines, shelters, and various kinds of support programs for women and their children to escape temporarily from their hazardous home environment and reevaluate their options (Murphy-Milano, 1996).

▲ The Interactionist Perspective

Interactionist explanations of violence focus on the microlevel of society and stress that violence is linked in several important ways to social interaction.

Violence is linked to social interaction because, first, human behavior is learned through social interaction, and violence is a learned response, not an inherent characteristic, in the individual. Some of the most interesting evidence of this point of view comes from studies done by social psychologist Albert Bandura on aggression in children (1973). Showing children a film of a person beating, kicking, and hacking an inflatable doll produced a violent response in the children, who, when placed in a room with a similar doll, duplicated the person's behavior and engaged in additional aggressive behavior. Also, people tend to repeat their behavior if they feel rewarded for it. When people learn that they can get their way by inflicting violence or the threat of violence on others, their aggressive behavior is reinforced.

Interactionists applying the social learning approach to rape suggest that the roots of the problem (and physical abuse of women in general) are societal beliefs about male and female roles in society. These beliefs are transmitted to children through such agents of socialization as families, peer groups, the media, schools, and sports. Boys may learn that part of the male role is sexual conquest of women and women are therefore more objects of a goal than equal human beings. For example, recent studies of rape on university campuses concluded that the organizational structure and membership of some fraternities encourages sexual violence. Rape-prone situations occur when fraternity members are pressed to show off their ability to consume large quantities of alcohol and prove their sexual prowess (Kalof and Cargill, 1991; Sanday, 1990, 1996).

In addition to studying violence in terms of learned behavior, interactionists look at types of social interactions that commonly lead to violence. According to the *situational approach,* **violence results from a specific interaction process, termed a "situational transaction."** Criminologist David Luckenbill (1977) identifies six stages in the situational transaction between victim and offender. In the first stage, the future victim does something behavioral or verbal that is considered an affront by the other (e.g., a glare or an insult). Next, the offended individual verifies that the action was directed at him or her personally. Third, the offended individual decides how to respond to the affront and may issue a verbal or behavioral challenge (e.g., a threat or a raised fist). If the problem escalates at this point, injury or death may occur in stage three; if not, the participants enter into the next stage. In stage four, the future victim further escalates the transaction, often prodded on by onlookers siding with one party or the other. In the fifth stage, actual violence occurs when neither party is able to back down without losing face. At this point, one or both parties produce weapons—ranging from guns and knives to bottles, pool cues, or other bludgeoning devices—if they have not already appeared, and the offender kills the victim. The sixth and final stage involves the offender's actions after the crime; some flee the scene, others are detained by onlookers, and still others call the police themselves.

The situational approach is based, first, on the assumption that many victims are active participants in the violence perpetrated against them and, second, on the idea that confrontation does not inevitably lead to violence or death. In the first four stages of the transaction, either the victim or the offender can decide to pursue another course of action (Parker, 1995).

According to interactionists, reducing violent personal crimes, including rape, requires changing societal values that encourage excessive competition and violence in the name of masculinity and rationalize male sexual aggression with an offhand comment such as "boys will be boys." In addition to changing sexual attitudes and building a national consensus about what is appropriate sexual behavior at the macrolevel, agents of socialization must make changes at the microlevel. They must transmit different attitudes and values towards violence. The next generation must learn that it is an individual's right—regardless of gender, race, class, age, religion, or other attributes or characteristics—to live free from violence and the devastating impact that violence has on individuals, groups, and the social fabric of society.

CAN VIOLENCE BE REDUCED?

Each of the theoretical explanations of violence has implicit within it possible ways to reduce violence in our society. But the question remains: Do we have the will as individuals and as a collectivity to do away with violence? Some means of reducing violence exist within the criminal justice system, but are there preventive steps we can take to reduce violence in our communities? According to some analysts, money that is now being spent on prisons should instead be spent on improving schools, libraries, and parks so that children will acquire the skills they need to succeed. Recent studies link lack of educational opportunities with violent crime rates; for example, fewer than 25 percent of state prison inmates have graduated from high school (Donziger, 1996).

Local- and state-level agencies try to prevent violence with early childhood development programs and parent-training programs, classes in conflict resolution, educational and recreational opportunities, drug treatment, counseling, job training, and improved street lighting. Some cities have reduced the rate of violent crime by providing young people with late-night activities such as the Midnight Basketball League (Donziger, 1996).

Unfortunately, these positive efforts to reduce the overall violence in our society are undermined by several alarming trends. First, an increasing number

Although some people initially laughed at the idea, there is some evidence that organized youth activities such as midnight basketball leagues keep some young people out of trouble. What other activities can you think of that might give adolescents opportunities they might otherwise not have?

of people own guns and other weapons in the United States. There are also growing numbers of militant individuals and groups who use violent means to serve their own ends, such as bombing abortion clinics and killing doctors who perform abortions, burning African American churches, sending mail bombs to university professors, setting fire to gay bars, and bombing the Alfred P. Murrah Federal Building in Oklahoma City. The number of paramilitary groups is also growing, and among their activities is teaching young children to use guns and to view certain other human beings as "the enemy." At the microlevel, violent personal crimes affect individuals, but at the macrolevel, terrorism has the potential to devastate not only individuals but our entire society—and perhaps even the world. Is this an unduly pessimistic outlook? What signs of hope do you see that our society can become less violent? We return to this question in Chapter 18, where we conclude our study of social problems.

SUMMARY

➡ *How do sociologists view violence?*

As a social problem, violence involves both an objective reality and a subjective awareness. Violence has an objective reality because we can measure and experience the effects of violent criminal behavior. We also have a subjective awareness that we should be fearful of violent personal crime because we might become victims.

➡ *What constitutes murder, and how do murder statistics differ according to gender, age, and race?*

Not only is murder an unlawful act, it involves malice aforethought—the intention of doing a wrongful act. Men make up the vast majority of murder victims and offenders. Nearly half of murder victims are between the ages of twenty and thirty-five. Most murders are intraracial; 90 percent of all African American murder victims are killed by other African Americans, and about 80 percent of white murder victims are killed by other white people. Murder takes a much greater toll on young African American males than on any other group in society.

➡ *Why is rape as a violent crime not well understood, and how is this lack of understanding reflected in our social response to rape?*

First, many people think that rape is a sexually motivated crime, but it is actually an act of violence in which sex is used as a weapon against a powerless victim. Moreover, statistics on rape are misleading at best because rape is often not reported. Many reasons keep victims from coming forward, but one major reason for not reporting rape—particularly acquaintance rape—is the societal response that the woman contributed to her victimization by how she dressed, where she was, or some other factor. Societal attitudes have improved (most noticeably toward stranger rape), as indicated by the establishment of rape crisis centers and training programs for police.

➡ *Why do parents abuse their children, and are we making any headway in helping these vulnerable victims?*

Researchers have found that children are most likely to be violently assaulted if their parents were abused, neglected, or deprived as children and are so-

cially isolated as adults. In a crisis, and without a support network, parents may make a child the target of their frustration. Other research has found that abusive parents characteristically feel unloved and unworthy and totally unprepared to cope with their circumstances. Reporting of suspected child abuse has improved significantly in recent years because of increased training, awareness, and legislation.

➡ *How widespread is spouse abuse, and why is it so often ignored or tolerated?*

An estimated 5 million spouses are abused each year, and in at least 94 percent of the cases, the abuse involves a man beating a woman. Related to spouse abuse is marital rape, when a husband forces sexual intercourse on his resisting wife. Historically, in the United States, an ideology of nonintervention—a strong reluctance on the part of outsiders to interfere in family matters—has contributed to citizens and police ignoring or tolerating domestic violence. Some positive and long overdue changes are now being made in how law enforcement officers handle domestic violence calls.

➡ *What are hate crimes?*

Hate crimes are attacks against people because of their race, religion, skin color, disability, sexual orientation, national origin, or ancestry. Some hate crimes are committed by gangs and paramilitary groups; others are committed by individuals.

➡ *How strong is the gang-drugs-violence connection, and how is society responding to the increasing spread of gangs and gang violence?*

According to sociologist Joan Moore, the nature and extent of drug-related gang violence are directly linked to the economy of the gang's city; some young people see drug trafficking and the accompanying violence as their only form of economic survival. Gang violence contributes to a climate of fear in low-income areas of central cities, and the spread of gangs to smaller cities causes more people to demand harsher penalties for offenders.

➡ *How do functionalists explain violence?*

One functionalist perspective, known as the subculture of violence hypothesis, states that violent subcultures arise when males have few legitimate opportunities and when they consider violence a natural response to certain situations or a by-product of a culture that idealizes brutality in the name of masculinity. According to the lifestyle-routine activity approach, the patterns and timing of people's daily movements as they go about obtaining the necessities of life—food, shelter, companionship, and entertainment—are the keys to understanding violent crime.

➤ *How does the conflict perspective explain violence?*

Conflict theorists who focus on class-based inequalities believe the potential for violence is inherent in capitalist societies. One feminist branch of conflict theory suggests that violence against women is a means of reinforcing patriarchy. Conflict theorists who focus on racial-ethnic inequalities point out that an estimated 80 percent of all rapes and attempted rapes are intraracial (white on white or black on black), but the myth persists that most rapes are interracial (between races).

➤ *What is the interactionist perspective on violence?*

Interactionists study violence in terms of learned behavior, and they look at types of social interactions that commonly lead to violence. According to the situational approach, violence results from a specific interaction process termed a "situational transaction." This approach emphasizes that many victims are active participants in the violence perpetrated against them and that confrontation does not inevitably lead to violence.

➤ *Can violence be reduced?*

Our society has made positive moves toward preventing violence, but several alarming trends are emerging. An increasing number of people own guns; militant individuals and groups increasingly use violent means to serve their own ends; and paramilitary groups are growing.

KEY TERMS

acquaintance rape, p. 211
forcible rape, p. 209
hate crimes, pp. 217–218
lifestyle-routine activity approach, p. 220
mass murder, p. 207
murder, p. 206

serial murder, p. 207
situational approach, p. 222
statutory rape, p. 209
subculture of violence hypothesis, p. 220
violence, p. 205

QUESTIONS FOR CRITICAL THINKING

1. Some victims of date rape not only don't report the crime, they continue to date the person, and some even go on to marry the rapist. How do you explain such behavior? How can date rape be prevented?

2. Explain how violence begets violence in regard to child abuse and spouse abuse in the home and, in turn, other violence in society.

3. The Midnight Basketball League is one creative and successful program for reducing gang activity; the Alliance of Concerned Men of Washington, D.C. is another. If you were called on to plan a new program for reducing the spread of gangs and gang violence in your community, what would you propose?

4. The Internet and World Wide Web are largely unregulated, so anyone can say anything there, including neo-Nazi and white supremacist groups. What is your reaction to hate groups on the Internet that spread racism, anti-Semitism, and homophobia and try to recruit new members? Should they be censored? Or does censorship carry the potential for even greater violence?

Chapter Eleven

Health Care

Problems of Physical and Mental Illness

I am a very different person now: more open, much more honest, and more self-knowing. . . . I turned it [cancer] into a possibility of opening up to myself, of discovering, and for exploring new areas. I've realized that I want to list the ways in which cancer can do that. You can get courage to take larger risks than you ever have before. I mean, you're already sick, so what can happen to you? You can have much more courage in saying things and in living than you ever had before. . . . And you can do the things you've always wanted to do. Cancer, by giving you the sense of your own mortality, can entice you into doing those things you've been postponing. . . . You have this sense of urgency. And you can turn this urgency—you can harness this energy that propels you—so that you go ahead and do these things and discover new parts of yourself. . . . Cancer has put me in touch with that. And then also, it has taught me to enjoy the tenderness and the preciousness of every moment. Moments are very important because there may not be any after that—or you may throw up. Cancer exquisitely places you in the moment. I have become very human to myself in a way that I would never have imagined. I've become a bigger person, a fuller person. This to me is one of the greatest lessons: just being human. Having cancer doesn't mean that you lose yourself at all. For me it meant that I discovered myself.

—*Sociologist Barbara Rosenblum explaining how cancer reshaped her thoughts about life sometime before her death at age forty-four of breast cancer*
(Butler and Rosenblum, 1991:160–161)

iseases, like Barbara Rosenblum's breast cancer, tend to be viewed as *personal problems,* but cancer—and some other diseases—are also *social problems.* For one thing, they affect large numbers of people; for another, these are problems that cannot be reduced or eliminated without a significant social response such as additional funding for research and programs for prevention and early detection. Consider that one out of every nine women in the United States will be diagnosed with breast cancer in her lifetime. Each year, nearly 200,000 new cases are reported, and about 50,000 women die from the disease. Even with early detection and treatment, breast cancer takes an average of nineteen years off a woman's life (Neuman, 1992). And breast cancer is only one of many diseases that affect individuals, families, and the health care industries in the United States and other countries. This chapter examines health care problems, including both physical and mental illness, and current problems in providing health services in this country.

HEALTH CARE AS A SOCIAL PROBLEM

According to the World Health Organization (1946:3), *health* is a state of complete physical, mental, and social well-being. In other words, health is not only a biological issue, it is also a social issue. Moreover, physical and mental health are intertwined. Physical illness can cause emotional problems, and mental illness can produce physical symptoms. Many people think there is a positive relationship between the amount of money a society spends on health care and the overall physical, mental, and social well-being of its people. But if this were the case, people in the United States would be among the healthiest and most fit in the world. We spend almost 950 billion dollars—the equivalent of $3,510 per person—on health care each year. The health service industry accounts for almost 14 percent of the gross domestic product, a proportion that has increased substantially since the 1960s (U.S. Bureau of the Census, 1996b). Table 11.1 shows the increase in health service expenditures between 1980 and 1994.

With such massive expenditures, how can health care be a social problem? For one thing, although

people in the United States pay more for health services than people in other developed nations do, our expenditures do not translate into improved life expectancy for everyone. *Life expectancy* **is an estimate of the average lifetime of people born in a specific year.** During this century, overall life expectancy has increased in the United States. For example, individuals born in 1996 can expect to live 76.3 years, compared to only 47.3 years for people born in 1900. But today's life expectancy statistics vary by sex and race. Overall, females born in 1996 can expect to live about 79.3 years, compared to 72.5 years for males. African American males born in 1996, however, have a life expectancy of only 64.8 years, compared to 74.5 years for African American females (U.S. Bureau of the Census, 1996b).

In developed nations, life expectancy has increased as the infant mortality rate has decreased. The *infant mortality rate* **is the number of deaths of infants under 1 year of age per 1,000 live births in a given year.** The infant mortality rate is an important indication of a society's level of preventive (prenatal) medical care, maternal nutrition, childbirth procedures, and care for infants. Infant mortality in the United States is considerably higher than that in a number of other developed nations (see Table 11.2). Perhaps the single most important cause of infant mortality is the lack of prenatal care. Drinking, smoking, taking drugs, and maternal malnutrition all contribute (Stewart, 1995). Divergent infant mortality rates for African Americans and whites indicate another kind of problem: unequal access to health care. Even with the high-tech medicine of the 1990s, the infant mortality rate for African American infants is twice as high as the rate for white infants. In 1993, for example, the U.S. mortality rate for African American infants was 19 per 1,000 live births compared to 8 per 1,000 live births for white infants (U.S. Bureau of the Census, 1996b).

Acute and Chronic Diseases and Disability

Life expectancy in the United States and other developed nations has increased largely because vaccinations and improved nutrition, sanitation, and personal hygiene have virtually eliminated many acute diseases, including measles, polio, cholera, tetanus, typhoid, and malaria. *Acute diseases* **are illnesses that strike suddenly and cause dramatic incapacita-**

TABLE 11.1 NATIONAL HEALTH EXPENDITURES, BY TYPE: 1980 TO 1994

[in millions of dollars, except percent. Includes Puerto Rico and outlying areas.]

Type of Expenditure	1980	1985	1989	1990	1991	1992	1993	1994
Totals	247,245	428,204	622,027	697,453	761,258	833,559	892,267	949,419
Annual percentage change[1]	14.9	9.9	11.2	12.1	9.1	9.5	7.0	6.4
Private expenditures	142,463	253,903	369,844	413,145	440,978	477,024	505,086	528,584
Health services and supplies	138,010	247,403	360,792	402,897	430,854	465,898	493,052	517,056
Out-of-pocket payments	60,254	100,595	136,186	148,390	155,098	164,382	169,376	174,879
Insurance premiums[2]	69,728	132,254	203,761	232,436	251,851	276,596	296,469	313,268
Other	8,028	14,554	20,846	22,071	23,905	24,920	27,207	28,909
Medical research	292	538	882	960	1,090	1,183	1,215	1,276
Medical facilities construction	4,161	5,962	8,170	9,288	9,034	9,942	10,819	10,252
Public expenditures	104,782	174,301	252,183	284,309	320,279	356,535	387,181	420,835
Percent Federal of public	68.7	70.7	69.3	68.9	70.1	71.5	71.9	72.1
Health services and supplies	97,599	164,430	239,012	270,033	305,469	340,100	370,036	402,163
Medicare[3]	37,519	72,186	102,484	112,091	122,986	138,723	151,717	169,246
Public assistance med. payments[4]	28,033	44,439	66,388	80,395	99,235	112,396	124,408	134,765
Temporary disability insurance	52	51	64	62	66	70	54	53
Workers' compensation (medical)[5]	5,141	7,971	14,298	16,067	17,163	18,983	18,910	18,903
Defense Dept. Hospital, medical	4,350	7,498	10,319	11,579	12,849	12,886	13,406	13,156
Maternal, child health programs	892	1,262	1,795	1,892	2,014	2,119	2,194	2,286
Public health activities	6,732	11,618	18,060	19,613	21,408	23,417	25,675	28,849
Veterans' hospital, medical care	5,934	8,713	10,640	11,424	12,366	13,205	14,267	15,140
Medical vocational rehabilitation	298	401	523	555	595	635	619	705
State and local hospitals[6]	5,589	7,030	10,583	11,346	11,030	11,134	11,841	11,784
Other[7]	3,059	3,263	3,859	5,009	5,758	6,531	6,944	7,277
Medical research	5,169	7,302	10,377	11,254	11,827	12,995	13,278	14,650
Medical facilities construction	2,014	2,569	2,793	3,022	2,983	3,440	3,866	4,021

1. Change from immediate prior year.
2. Covers insurance benefits and amount retained by insurance companies for expenses, additions to reserves, and profits (net cost of insurance).
3. Represents expenditures for benefits and administrative cost from federal hospital and medical insurance trust funds under old-age, survivors, disability, and health insurance programs.
4. Payments made directly to suppliers of medical care (primarily Medicaid).
5. Includes medical benefits paid under public law by private insurance carriers and self-insurers.
6. Expenditures not offset by other revenues.
7. Covers expenditures for Alcohol, Drug Abuse, and Mental Health Administration; Indian Health Service; school health; and other programs.

Source: U.S. Bureau of the Census, 1996b.

tion and sometimes death (Weitz, 1996). Acute diseases that are still common in the United States today are chicken pox and influenza. Recently, too, multi-drug-resistant strains of tuberculosis, Lyme disease, and HIV (the virus that causes AIDS) have become pressing health problems.

With the overall decline in death from acute illnesses in developed nations, however, has come a corresponding increase in *chronic diseases,* illnesses that are long-term or lifelong and that develop gradually or are present from birth (Weitz, 1996). Chronic diseases are caused by various biological,

TABLE 11.2   INFANT MORTALITY RATES IN SELECTED COUNTRIES

Country or Area	Infant Mortality Rate 1996	2000 proj.	Country or Area	Infant Mortality Rate 1996	2000 proj.
United States	6.7	6.2	India	71.1	63.5
Afghanistan	149.7	137.5	Indonesia	63.1	55.4
Angola	138.9	125.9	Iran	52.7	45.1
Argentina	28.3	26.1	Iraq	60.0	50.1
Australia	5.5	5.0	Israel	8.5	7.5
Bangladesh	102.3	93.0	Italy	6.9	6.4
Belgium	6.4	6.1	Japan	4.4	4.3
Brazil	55.3	47.7	Kenya	55.3	54.9
Bulgaria	15.7	14.8	Korea, North	25.9	22.2
Canada	6.1	5.5	Korea, South	8.2	7.4
Chad	120.4	113.6	Malawi	139.9	135.8
Chile	13.6	11.9	Mexico	25.0	20.7
China	39.6	32.6	Netherlands	4.9	4.7
Cuba	9.0	8.6	Pakistan	96.8	90.3
Czech Republic	8.4	8.0	Peru	52.2	44.4
Denmark	4.8	4.7	Philippines	35.9	33.2
Egypt	72.8	65.7	Poland	12.4	11.8
El Salvador	31.9	27.2	Portugal	7.6	7.1
Ethiopia	122.8	117.7	Russia	24.7	21.6
Finland	4.9	4.8	Rwanda	118.8	118.8
France	6.2	5.7	Somalia	121.1	111.6
Germany	6.0	5.7	Spain	6.3	5.7
Greece	7.4	6.6	Sweden	4.5	4.4
Guatemala	50.7	44.6	Switzerland	5.4	5.2
Haiti	103.8	98.4	Taiwan	7.0	6.3
Hong Kong	5.1	4.5	Thailand	33.4	28.3
Hungary	12.3	11.7	United Kingdom	6.4	6.0

1. Number of deaths of children under 1 year of age per 1,000 live births in a calendar year.

Source: U.S. Bureau of the Census, 1996b.

social, and environmental factors. In Chapter 8 we discussed two of the most common sources of chronic disease and premature death: tobacco use, which increases mortality among both smokers and people who breathe the tobacco smoke of others, and alcohol abuse. In fact, according to some social analysts, we have much more chronic disease in our society because of *manufacturers of illness*, groups that promote illness-causing behavior and social conditions, such as smoking (McKinlay, 1994). The effect of chronic diseases on life expectancy varies

because some chronic diseases are progressive (e.g., lung cancer worsens over time), whereas others are constant (e.g., paralysis after a stroke); also, some are fatal (lung cancer), but others are nonfatal (arthritis and sinusitis).

Some chronic diseases produce disabilities that significantly increase health care costs for individuals and for society. Disability can be defined in several ways. Medical professionals tend to define it in terms of organically based impairments—that is, the problem is entirely within the body (Albrecht,

1992). However, disability rights advocates believe that disability is a physical or health condition that stigmatizes or causes discrimination. According to medical sociologist Rose Weitz (1996:428), disability should be defined in terms of both physical and social factors: *Disability* **refers to a restricted or total lack of ability to perform certain activities as a result of physical limitations or the interplay of these limitations, social responses, and the social environment.** An estimated 48 million people in the United States have one or more physical or mental disabilities, and the number continues to increase for several reasons. First, with advances in medical technology, many people who once would have died from an accident or illness now survive with an impairment. Second, as more people live longer, they are more likely to experience chronic diseases (such as arthritis) that may have disabling consequences (Albrecht, 1992). Third, people born with serious disabilities are more likely to survive infancy because of medical technology. (However, fewer than 15 percent of people with a disability today were born with it; accidents, disease, violence, and war account for most disabilities in this country.) For many people with chronic illness and disability, life takes on a different meaning. Knowing that they probably will not live out the full life expectancy for people in their age category, they come to treasure each moment, as Barbara Rosenblum noted in the chapter opening vignette. Today, some of the most tragic instances of life cut short are because of AIDS.

The AIDS Crisis

AIDS—acquired immune deficiency syndrome—has reached crisis proportions in the United States and other nations as the number of cases rises annually. An estimated 200,000 people in this country have AIDS, and about 2 million are estimated to be infected with the human immunodeficiency virus (HIV); 40,000 new infections occur each year (Kolata, 1995). In the 25–44 age group, AIDS is the leading cause of death among men and the fourth leading cause among women. It is the eighth leading cause of death for the overall U.S. population (see Table 11.3). The U.S. Centers for Disease Control in Atlanta estimates that over 300,000 people in the United States have died from AIDS-related complications over the past two decades (U.S. Bureau of the Census, 1996b). We should note, however, that

people do not actually die of AIDS; they die because HIV gradually destroys their immune systems by attacking the white blood cells, making people with AIDS vulnerable to diseases such as pneumonia, tuberculosis, yeast infection, and Kaposi's sarcoma and other forms of cancer.

How is AIDS transmitted? AIDS is transmitted primarily through bodily fluids, such as semen (through oral, anal, or vaginal sex with someone who is infected with HIV) or blood (usually by sharing drug needles and syringes with an infected person). It can also be transmitted by blood transfusions and by infected mothers before or during birth or while breast-feeding. AIDS is *not* transmitted by routine contact such as a handshake or hugging a person who has the disease.

Who is most likely to become infected with the HIV virus? Initially, some people referred to AIDS as a "gay disease" because it was first identified in this country among gay men between the ages of twenty and forty. But according to the World Health Organization, about 75 percent of the people who are infected with AIDS worldwide were infected through heterosexual intercourse. In the United States, too, most new AIDS cases are linked to heterosexual relations and to sex with prostitutes (Kolata, 1995). Some women acquire the disease through sex with an infected male partner who may have contracted the disease from a prostitute, a homosexual en-

TABLE 11.3 TEN LEADING CAUSES OF DEATH IN THE UNITED STATES

Cause	Number of Deaths
Heart disease	743,460
Cancer	529,904
Cerebrovascular disease (stroke)	150,108
Chronic lung disease	101,077
Accidents	90,523
Pneumonia	82,820
Diabetes	53,894
HIV infection	37,267
Suicide	31,102
Homicide and legal intervention	26,009

Source: U.S. Bureau of the Census, 1996b.

SOCIAL PROBLEMS

IN GLOBAL PERSPECTIVE

BOX 11.1

AIDS in Thailand and India: Two Different Patterns

A ribbon of acrid, pale yellow smoke rose from the crematory as a Buddhist monk approached, clutching one end of his saffron robe in a bony, withered hand. . . . "I know that my body will end up here," said the AIDS-stricken monk. . . . "Of course I accept that." In a corner, set beneath a gilded statue of the Buddha, there was a pile of dozens of fist-sized white cotton bags, each containing the ashes from an earlier cremation. The 38-year old monk gently picked up some of the bags. "All of these people died of AIDS, and the ashes stay here because the families are afraid to claim them," he said. "They are afraid that they will get sick if they hold the ashes."

> —Phra Kamthorn Kitisalo, a Buddhist monk abandoned by his monastery, waiting with others to die at the temple crematory (Shenon, 1996a)

Phra Kamthorn was infected with the AIDS virus during "his playboy days," before he entered the monastery: "I would see prostitutes every day." His story is not unusual in Thailand, among the first countries in Asia hit by the AIDS epidemic because of its widespread sex industry. But Thailand confronted the problem in 1991 by distributing condoms and shutting down brothels that didn't use them and requiring radio stations to broadcast AIDS prevention information hourly, and the trend is reversing. In 1990 there were 215,000 new cases of HIV infection; by 2000 the number of new cases should be more than halved, down to about 90,000 (Shenon, 1996a).

The story is different in India, where AIDS appeared only in 1991, ten years after it was recognized as a new disease (Altman, 1996b). Today, AIDS is exploding in India, and the World Health Organization projects that by

---

counter, or an infected needle during intravenous drug use. In fact, a woman is 12 times as likely as a man to be infected with the HIV virus during heterosexual intercourse, and she is more likely to die quickly from the disease. Although not all people who carry HIV have developed AIDS, they still can transmit the disease to others. In some cases, ten years or more may elapse between the time of infection with HIV and the development of a full-blown case of AIDS.

Is there a cure for AIDS? No, thus far there is no cure for AIDS. Though drugs such as AZT in combination with protease inhibitors (which attack the virus during its reproductive process within the human body) have caused dramatic improvements in the health of many people with AIDS, once HIV develops into AIDS, it is fatal. The only way to re-

duce the rate of AIDS is to prevent the initial occurrence of AIDS. The U.S. health care industry was slow to respond to the emergence of AIDS as a life-threatening illness because of the stigma attached by its initial association with gay men and drug users. Like many other people, sociologist Philip Kayal (1993:xi, xii) realized that he had ambivalent feelings about the disease when a relative died from an AIDS-related illness:

When my cousin Paul died in his prime, nearly everyone knew his pneumonia was AIDS related. . . . There were so many people at Paul's wake, from so many disparate walks of life and so many distinct parts of his own life, that it was impossible to find a common way to symbolize the end of the century, India will be the world center of the disease, with one-fourth of all infected people (Burns, 1996). One immediate source of the problem is India's truck drivers, who often have long layovers with nothing to do and many available prostitutes along the roadsides, flying gaily colored scarves. Drivers who pick up the disease carry it to other prostitutes in previously uninfected regions as well as home to their wives and future children. The red-light districts of Bombay, Calcutta, and New Delhi are another source of the growing epidemic. An estimated 52 percent of the brothel "cage girls" (enslaved child prostitutes who are kept in cages during the day so they don't escape) in Bombay are infected with HIV (Burns, 1996).

Fighting AIDS in India means fighting more than the disease. It means fighting the caste system because prostitutes and AIDS victims are discriminated against. It means fighting social taboos against talking about sex. It means fighting poverty because prostitutes who use condoms lose clients and they starve. And it means fighting the denial of political leaders; only $35 million of a 5-year $100 million dollar AIDS prevention program has been spent in 4 years (Burns, 1996).

Though India may be the worst future case, Africa is still the hardest-hit continent, with 14 million cases, and AIDS is now sweeping Russia and Ukraine (Altman, 1996c). Each day, there are an estimated 8,500 new HIV infections in the world, and 1,000 are children; 42% of the adults are women (Altman, 1996c). "No country is free of HIV infection, nor is any province of India or China," according to Dr. Peter Piot, a United Nations official speaking at the eleventh international AIDS meeting in 1996 (Altman, 1996a). "Developed countries should act out of 'enlightened self-interest' to insure adequate treatment of AIDS in the third world."

Should the United States and other developed countries act to stop the global spread of AIDS? What should they do? What does Dr. Piot mean by "enlightened self-interest"? And another point: Could the United States, where the spread of AIDS has been stabilized, learn from Thailand, which has *reversed* the spread of AIDS in its country? What do you think?

---

our shared loss. . . . Were we, his mourners, ashamed of Paul? Did we blame him? Were we angry at him for dying? Did he disappoint us? Did we think deep down that something about his life and death should be hidden from the neighbors, from ourselves? Would Paul want us to bury him secretly? He lived his life openly and with pride. Why don't we accept why he, like all the others, really had to die? We need to accept that homophobia, like AIDS, also kills. I suppose that if Paul had died an ordinary death in ordinary times, it would not be as important to raise these questions. But he didn't, and his death remains as much a personal loss as a political issue.

Gradually, though, public attitudes are changing and people are coming to understand that AIDS is not an isolated problem that does not affect them. Public service advertising campaigns encouraging people to abstain from sex or to practice "safer sex" by using condoms have raised awareness, and many cities have started needle exchange programs for intravenous drug users in an effort to reduce the number of new AIDS cases. But even as efforts to control the spread of HIV continue, many moral and ethical questions have not been resolved. Should people be required to submit to testing for HIV? Should people who test positive for the virus be required to provide the names of sexual partners or people with whom they have shared hypodermic needles? Should schools distribute condoms to students? No doubt, politicians, educators, and religious leaders throughout the country will continue to debate these issues well into the twenty-first century.

Not all social scientists agree on how AIDS will ultimately affect life expectancy, mortality rates, or the health care industry in the United States. Perhaps even more than that for other chronic diseases, treatment for AIDS-related illnesses is complex and costly and typically requires lengthy stays in a hospital or hospice. The incidence of AIDS, the number of AIDS patients, and the cost of caring for AIDS patients are highest and most concentrated in central cities where clinics, hospitals, and other medical facilities are overcrowded, underfunded, and understaffed. Some analysts estimate that in the future, more people in the United States will die from AIDS-related illnesses than have died in all the wars fought by this nation (Petersen, 1994). Unfortunately, too, the AIDS problem in the United States is only a small part of the global picture of devastation caused by this disease (see Box 11.1 on pages 232–233).

MENTAL ILLNESS AS A SOCIAL PROBLEM

Why is mental illness a social problem? Mental illness is a social problem because of the number of people it affects, the difficulty of defining and identifying mental disorders, and the ways mental illness is treated. Although most social scientists use the terms interchangeably, many medical professionals distinguish between a *mental disorder*—a condition that makes it difficult or impossible for a person to cope with everyday life—and *mental illness*—a condition that requires extensive treatment with medication, psychotherapy, and sometimes hospitalization.

How many people are affected by mental illness? Some answers to this question come from the National Comorbidity Survey, a national study conducted by Ronald C. Kessler and his colleagues. The term *comorbidity* refers to the combination of physical and mental conditions—such as physical illness and depression—that compound each other and undermine an individual's overall well-being (Angel and Angel, 1993). The researchers found that 50 percent of respondents between the ages of fifteen and fifty-four years were diagnosed with a mental disorder at some time in their lives (Kessler, 1994). Severe mental illness—such as schizophrenia, bipolar affective disorder (manic-depression), and major depression—typically affected fewer than 15 percent

of U.S. adults at some time in their lives (Bourdon et al., 1992; Kessler, 1994). The National Comorbidity Survey showed that mental disorders in the United States were more prevalent than most analysts had thought. Moreover, the proportion of people who obtain treatment is low. Even among people with a lifetime history of three or more diagnosed mental disorders, fewer than 50 percent seek treatment (Kessler, 1994).

The most widely accepted classification of mental disorders is the American Psychiatric Association's (1994) *Diagnostic and Statistical Manual of Mental Disorders IV* (*DSM-IV*) (see Table 11.4). The *DSM* is now in its fourth edition, and with each revision the list of disorders has grown. Listings change partly because of new scientific findings but also because of changes in how we view mental disorders culturally (at one time, for example, homosexuality was considered a mental disorder). The number of categories has also grown because more precise descriptions are more useful than broad terms covering a wide range of behaviors. Despite the changes, some social analysts still question the extent to which mental health professionals can accurately detect and treat mental disorders.

▲ Treatment of Mental Illness

Although people with mental disorders typically do not receive professional treatment, it is also the case that the leading cause of hospitalization for men between the ages of fifteen and forty-four and the second leading cause (after childbirth) for women in that age group is mental disorders, particularly substance-related ones (due to alcohol and other drug abuse) (Kessler, 1994; U.S. Bureau of the Census, 1996b).

People who do seek professional help are treated with medication and psychotherapy, which is believed to help patients understand the underlying reasons for their problem. They are sometimes given treatment in psychiatric wards of local hospitals or in private psychiatric hospitals (Mechanic and Rochefort, 1990). Because medication is used so routinely today, we tend to forget that institutionalization used to be the most common treatment for severe mental illness. In fact, it was the development of psychoactive drugs that made possible the deinstitutionalization movement of the 1960s.

Deinstitutionalization is the practice of discharging patients from mental hospitals into the

TABLE 11.4   MENTAL DISORDERS IDENTIFIED BY THE AMERICAN PSYCHIATRIC ASSOCIATION

1. **Disorders first evident in infancy, childhood, or adolescence**
   These disorders include mental retardation, attention-deficit hyperactivity, anorexia nervosa, bulimia nervosa, and stuttering.

2. **Organic mental disorders**
   Psychological or behavioral disorders associated with dysfunctions of the brain caused by aging, disease, or brain damage.

3. **Substance-related disorders**
   Disorders resulting from abuse of alcohol and/or other drugs such as barbiturates, cocaine, or amphetamines.

4. **Schizophrenia and other psychotic disorders**
   Disorders with symptoms such as delusions or hallucinations.

5. **Mood disorders**
   Emotional disorders such as major depression and bipolar (manic-depressive) disorder.

6. **Anxiety disorders**
   Disorders characterized by anxiety that is manifest in phobias, panic attacks, or obsessive-compulsive disorder.

7. **Somatoform disorders**
   Psychological problems that present themselves as symptoms of physical disease, such as hypochondria.

8. **Dissociative disorders**
   Problems involving a splitting or dissociation of normal consciousness such as amnesia and multiple personality.

9. **Eating or sleeping disorders**
   Includes such problems as anorexia and bulimia or insomnia and other problems associated with sleep.

10. **Impulse control disorders**
    Symptoms include the inability to control undesirable impulses such as kleptomania, pyromania, and pathological gambling.

11. **Personality disorders**
    Maladaptive personality traits that are generally resistant to treatment such as paranoid and antisocial personality types.

Source: Adapted from American Psychiatric Association, 1994.

community. Originally devised as a solution for the problem of warehousing mentally ill patients in large, prisonlike mental hospitals in the first half of the twentieth century, deinstitutionalization is now viewed by many social scientists as the problem. The theory was that the civil rights of patients in state mental hospitals in the 1950s and 1960s were being violated because many were committed to psychiatric hospitals involuntarily (i.e., without their consent), warehoused for extended periods of time with only minimal custodial care, and, many believed, often physically abused. According to sociologist Erving Goffman (1961), mental hospitals are a classic example of a *total institution*—a place where **people are isolated from the rest of society for a period of time and come under the complete control of**

Although there are many causes of homelessness ranging from lack of affordable housing to drug dependency, some analysts believe that the deinstitutionalization of patients from mental hospitals has significantly increased the number of people living on the streets of our nation. What other alternatives can you suggest for dealing with mental illness?

the officials who run the institution. Patients in mental hospitals are stripped of their individual identities—or depersonalized—by being required to wear institutional clothing and to follow a strict regimen of activities, meals, and sleeping hours and sometimes by being referred to impersonally as "a CMI" (a person who is chronically mentally ill) (see Grobe, 1995). One goal of the deinstitutionalization movement was to release patients from the hospitals so that they could live at home and go about their daily activities. Professionals believed that the patients' mental disorders could be controlled with medication and treatment through community-based mental health services. Advocates of deinstitutionalization also believed that it would remove the stigma attached to hospitalization for mental illness. This stigma is described by Susanna Kaysen (1993:123–124), who, at age eighteen, was committed to a private mental hospital for two years:

The hospital had an address, 115 Mill Street. . . .
In Massachusetts, 115 Mill Street is a famous address. Applying for a job, leasing an apartment, getting a driver's license: all problematic. . . .

"You're living at One fifteen Mill Street?" asked [one prospective employer]. . . . "And how long have you been living there?"
"Oh, a while." I gestured at the past with one hand.
"And I guess you haven't been working for a while?" He leaned back, enjoying himself.
"No," I said. "I've been thinking things over."
I didn't get the job.
As I left the shop my glance met his, and he gave me a look of such terrible intimacy that I cringed. I know what you are, said his look. . . . In the world's terms . . . all of us [at the hospital] were tainted.

Although deinstitutionalization had worthwhile goals such as more humane and less costly treatment of mental disorders, many social analysts believe that the movement was actually triggered by changes in public health insurance. With the introduction of Medicare and Medicaid in 1965, states were more than willing to move patients from state-funded mental hospitals to nursing homes that would be paid for largely by federal government funding (Weitz, 1996). Critics of deinstitutionalization also argue that it exacerbated long-term problems associated with treating mental illness. In too many cases, deinstitutionalization simply moved people out of mental hospitals into the streets and jails; the mental problems were never successfully treated. As John A. Chiles, professor of psychiatry at the University of Texas Health Science Center in San Antonio, writes (quoted in Lawrence, 1996:20):

Some people [with schizophrenia] never find their way into the system. If they do, it's often into the legal system through petty crime. One local patient attempted a bank robbery while pointing a paintbrush at the teller. "Give me some money," he demanded. "How about $6.25?" asked the skeptical teller. "OK," he agreed. He was apprehended outside the bank and charged with armed robbery. There are more schizophrenics in the Bexar County Jail than there are in the San Antonio State Hospital. And this is similar to many cities across the country.

When schizophrenia and other serious mental illnesses do not lead to jail, they often result in homelessness. One study concluded that as many as 30 percent of homeless people were previously patients in mental hospitals and about 80 percent have some diagnosable mental disorder (Searight and Searight, 1988). However, it is difficult to determine which came first—the mental disorder or homelessness. If you or I were homeless, for instance, what are the chances that we might develop mental health problems in trying to survive on the streets or in-and-out of shelters and city jails? In any case, social scientists and homeless advocates agree that most homeless shelters and other community services cannot adequately meet the needs of people known as "the homeless mentally ill" (see Torrey, 1988).

Although involuntary commitment to mental hospitals has always been controversial, it remains the primary method by which police officers, judges, social workers, and other officials deal with people—particularly the homeless—whom they have reason to believe are mentally ill and imminently dangerous to themselves and others (Monahan, 1992). But involuntary commitment is a social control mechanism, used to keep people with a history of mental illness off the streets so that they cannot engage in violent crime. It does little—if anything—to treat the underlying medical and social conditions that contribute to mental disorders (Catalano and McConnell, 1996). State mental hospitals therefore tend to function as revolving doors to poverty-level board and care homes, nursing homes, or homelessness; patients who can pay private psychiatric facilities through private insurance coverage or Medicare are not part of this cycle (Brown, 1985).

Race, Class, Gender, and Mental Disorders

Studies of race, class, and gender-based differences in mental disorders show that some of these factors are more important than others. There are no significant differences in diagnosable mental illness between African Americans and white Americans (the two groups that are most often compared), but, interestingly, studies of racism show implications for mental health. For example, in studying the effects of racism on the everyday lives of middle-class African Americans, social scientists Joe R. Feagin and Melvin P. Sikes (1994) found that repeated per-

Contemporary high-tech medicine takes place in a wide variety of locales. Because of advanced technologies, this patient is receiving medical attention while being transported to a hospital in a helicopter. Does your city have "life flight" services such as this? Is it important to have such services, or do they merely run up the cost of medical care?

sonal encounters with racial hostility deeply affect the psychological well-being of most African Americans, regardless of their level of education or social class. In a subsequent study, Feagin and Hernán Vera (1995) found that white Americans also pay a high "psychic cost" for the prevalence of racism because it contradicts deeply held beliefs about the American dream and equality under the law. In earlier work on the effects of discrimination on mental well-being, social psychologist Thomas Pettigrew (1981) suggested that about 15 percent of whites have such high levels of racial prejudice that they tend to exhibit symptoms of serious mental illness. According to Pettigrew, racism in all its forms constitutes a "mentally unhealthy" situation in which people do not achieve their full potential.

Only a few studies have focused on mental disorders among racial-ethnic groups such as Mexican immigrants and Mexican Americans, and they have yielded contradictory results. One study found that strong extended (intergenerational) families—which are emphasized in Mexican culture—provide individuals with social support and sources of self-esteem, even if the individuals have low levels of education and income (Mirowsky and Ross, 1980). Another study found the opposite: that maintaining a strong connection to Mexican culture, rather than adopting an Anglo (white/non-Latino/a) culture, is not the primary consideration in whether or not Mexican Americans develop mental disorders (Burnham et al., 1987).

A more recent study from a national survey of people of Mexican origin shows that "dark and Indian-looking Chicano men" in the United States are more likely to develop depression than are "lighter, European-looking Chicanos and their dark-skinned female counterparts" (Codina and Montalvo, 1994). This study also found that women and men who lose their fluency in Spanish while living in the United States experience more depression than do those who remain fluent in the language and keep closer ties to their culture (Codina and Montalvo, 1994), findings that support the Mirowsky and Ross study.

One factor that researchers generally agree is related to mental illness is social class. For example, one study that examined the relationship between mental disorders, race, and class (as measured by *socioeconomic status*—a combined measure of income, occupation, and education) found that as social class increases for both white Americans and African Americans the rate of mental disorders decreases (Williams et al., 1992). However, though researchers agree that there is a relationship between class and mental disorders, they do not agree on whether lower social class status causes mental illness or mental illness causes lower social class (Weitz, 1996). Analysts using the *social stress framework* to examine schizophrenia—the disorder that is most consistently linked to class—believe that stresses associated with lower-class life lead to greater mental disorders. In contrast, analysts using the *social drift framework* argue that mental disorders cause people to drift downward in class position. To support their argument, they note that individuals who are diagnosed with schizophrenia typically hold lower-class jobs than would be expected on the basis of their family backgrounds (Eaton, 1980; Weitz, 1996).

As with class-based differences in mental illness, researchers have consistently found that the rate of diagnosable depression is about twice as high for women as for men, that this gender difference typically emerges in puberty (Cleary, 1987), and that the incident rate rises as women and men enter adulthood and live out their unequal statuses (Mirowsky,

1996). Although women have higher rates of minor depression and other disorders that cause psychological distress, men have higher rates of personality disorders such as compulsive gambling or drinking, as well as maladaptive personality traits such as antisocial behavior (Link and Dohrenwend, 1989; Weitz, 1996). Some analysts suggest that differences in mental disorders between women and men are linked to gender role socialization that instills aggressiveness in men and learned helplessness in women. According to the *learned helplessness theory*, people become depressed when they think they have no control over their lives (Seligman, 1975). This theory assumes a *subjective perception* of no control and therefore implies that women contribute to their own helplessness. But feminist analysts argue that the powerlessness that contributes to depression in many women's lives is an *objective condition* (Jack, 1993). Support for the feminist view comes from numerous studies indicating that women in high-income, high-status jobs usually have higher levels of psychological well-being and fewer symptoms of mental disorders, regardless of their marital status (Horowitz, 1982; Angel and Angel, 1993).

Numerous studies have been done on women with mild depression, but women with serious mental illnesses have been nearly ignored (Mowbray et al., 1992). Similarly, women's mental disorders have often been misdiagnosed, and on many occasions, physical illnesses have been confused with psychiatric problems (see Busfield, 1996; Lerman, 1996; Klonoff, 1997). It is generally agreed that additional studies of women's diversity across lines of race, class, age, religion, and other factors are necessary before we can accurately assess the relationship between gender and mental illness and how women are treated in the mental health care industry (Gatz, 1995).

THE CRISIS IN U.S. HEALTH CARE

The United States and the Union of South Africa are the only developed nations without some form of universal health coverage for all citizens. Considering the state of health care in this country, many professional and political advisors suggest that we look at government-subsidized medical services in countries such as Canada and Great Britain for models for providing basic medical care regardless of an individual's ability to pay (see Box 11.2).

SOCIAL PROBLEMS
AND SOCIAL POLICY

BOX 11.2

Health Care:
The Canadian Model

The United States faces a health care crisis: This country spends more on health care than does any other developed country, yet many people are going without health care because it is too expensive, and access to health care is often limited by race, class, or gender. But do people have a *right* to health care? No, say some; it is unfortunate that some people suffer illness or disability, but it is not up to society to make the world a fair place (Engelhardt, 1986). On the contrary, say others; health care *is* a right, not a privilege or a choice, because the choice is ultimately between life and death and every individual has inherent worth (Rawls, 1971). So far, the nays in the United States have it, but among developed nations, only the United States and the Union of South Africa stand together; all others—Canada, Great Britain, France, and Germany, to name only a few—provide universal coverage for their citizens. Should our system be reformed? How well, for example, does Canada's plan work?

A Canadian citizen never sees a medical bill or insurance form or pays for a prescription. Canada's national health insurance system pays all medical costs directly. Hospitals get a yearly budget, and doctors bill the provincial governments (equivalent to our state governments), which administrate the health care system, on a fee-for-service basis. Fees are negotiated annually between doctors and the provincial government. Individuals choose any primary care doctor they wish, but they do need a referral to a specialist.

But are Canadians actually healthier? What about those stories in the newspaper about people in Canada dying because they have to "wait in line" for surgery? First, those stories are not true. Across the board, Canadians have better access to health care than U.S.

citizens do. Canadians pay more visits to the doctor, are hospitalized more often and for longer times, and have higher immunization rates; 85 percent of one-year-olds in Canada are fully immunized compared to 45 percent in the United States (Himmelstein and Woolhandler, 1994). And, yes, Canadians are healthier; they have longer life expectancies and a lower infant mortality rate than do U.S. citizens.

Is there any fly in this ointment? Well, one. The cost of health care is skyrocketing, and Canada—like its neighbor to the south—must find ways to control costs. So far, that has mostly meant cutting services. For instance, the Ontario Health Insurance Plan no longer pays for a pre-employment physical or electrolysis (hair removal) and is reviewing other procedures, including vasectomies, circumcision of newborns, and psychoanalysis (Farnsworth, 1993). But the cost of medical care is still outstripping government funds, and the next step is to ask individuals and employers to pay a share of essential services.

Part of the reason for skyrocketing costs is, of course, new medical technology. The Canadian government also thinks that an oversupply of doctors is contributing to the problem. Since doctors charge on a fee-for-service basis, the more doctors there are, the more patients they see and the more the bills add up. There are no restrictions on doctor visits or types of treatment. Also, as in the United States, hospital stays are very expensive (Farnsworth, 1993).

What should the United States do? Is health care a right? Should we reform our health care system to provide universal coverage? Would the Canadian system be a good model? Would some modified version of the Canadian model be better? What do you think?

◢ Health Care Organization, Rising Costs, and Unequal Access

Throughout the twentieth century, medical care in the United States has been on a *fee-for-service* basis: Patients are billed individually for each service they receive, including treatment by doctors, laboratory work, hospital visits, prescriptions, and other health-related services. Fee-for-service is an expensive way of delivering health care because there are few restrictions on the fees charged by doctors, hospitals, and other medical providers.

PRIVATE HEALTH INSURANCE

Fee-for-service health care became even more costly with the expansion of medical insurance programs in the 1960s. At that time, third-party providers (public and private insurers) began pick-ing up large portions of doctor and hospital bills for insured patients. With third-party fee-for-service payment, patients pay premiums into a fund that in turn pays doctors and hospitals for each treatment the patient receives. According to medical sociologist Paul Starr (1982), third-party fee-for-service is the main reason for medical inflation in this country because it gives doctors and hospitals an incentive to increase medical services. That is, the more services they provide, the more fees they charge and the more money they make. Similarly, patients have no incentive to limit their visits to doctors or hospitals because they have already paid their premiums and feel entitled to medical care (Starr, 1982).

How did public and private insurers come to play such a large role in health care in this country? The health insurance industry arose during the Great Depression of the 1930s. Fearing that many

Drawing by Rini; © 1995 The New Yorker Magazine, Inc.

hospitals would go bankrupt because patients could not pay their hospital bills, the American Hospital Association founded Blue Cross—a nonprofit company—to sell health insurance to people so that they could pay their hospital bills. Shortly thereafter, the American Medical Association established Blue Shield to provide coverage for physicians' bills. Under Blue Cross/Blue Shield and other private insurance programs, patients go to doctors and hospitals that charge on a fee-for-service basis and are reimbursed for some portion of the cost of their medical bill as long as the services are covered and the patient has met the annual deductible.

Recently, in an effort to reduce the demand for health care services and medical costs, many insurance companies have established an option known as *preferred provider organizations (PPOs)*, with such names as HealthSelect (a Blue Cross/Blue Shield entity). In a PPO, doctors work out of their own offices on a fee-for-service basis but contract with an insurance company to provide care for insured patients. The doctors agree to charge set fees for particular services; these fees might be higher or lower than those for other patients who are not covered by the PPO. This model of health care delivery shares certain commonalities with the health maintenance organization and managed care models.

Like other private insurance plans, HMOs emerged during the Great Depression as a means of providing workers with health coverage at a reasonable rate by keeping costs down. A *health maintenance organization (HMO)* **provides, for a set monthly fee, total care with an emphasis on prevention to avoid costly treatment later.** The doctors do not work on a fee-for-service basis, and patients are encouraged to get regular checkups and to practice good health habits (exercise and eat right). As long as patients use only the doctors and hospitals that are affiliated with their HMO, they pay no fees, or only small copayments, beyond their insurance premium (Anders, 1996). Seeing HMOs as a potential source of high profits because of their emphasis on preventing serious illness, many for-profit corporations moved into the HMO business in the 1980s (Anders, 1996). However, research shows that preventive care is good for the individual's health but does not necessarily save money. Early detection of HIV infection, diabetes, or high cholesterol, for example, often means a lifetime of costly treatments and drugs. Some health experts therefore suggest

that for-profit HMOs are unlikely to provide top-notch early detection and prevention programs because of the costs—especially future costs—involved (Rosenthal, 1997). Some critics have even charged that some HMOs require their physicians to withhold vital information from their patients if it could cost the HMO money to provide the needed procedure or hospitalization (Gray, 1996).

Another approach to controlling health care costs is known as *managed care—***a term that is used to refer to any system of cost containment that closely monitors and controls health care providers' decisions about medical procedures, diagnostic tests, and other services that should be provided to patients** (Weitz, 1996). In most managed care programs, patients choose a primary-care physician from a list of participating doctors. When patients need medical services, they must first contact the primary-care physician; then, if a specialist is needed for treatment, the primary-care physician refers the patient to a specialist who participates in the program. Doctors must get approval before they perform certain procedures or admit a patient to the hospital, or the insurance company has the prerogative of not covering part of the cost. In one regard, managed care definitely contains medical care costs, but many physicians are opposed to managed care and HMOs. As one doctor explains (Williams, 1997:A19):

> I was a physician for more than 20 years. Now I am a provider. "Provider" is the term used by health maintenance organizations to refer to physicians and other health-care professionals. They attempt to suppress the very word "physician," and for good reason: It has connotations of expertise, authority and respect, which are incompatible with the managed-care agenda. . . . I have a busy and previously successful internal medicine practice. An hour of my time is now worth approximately 60 percent of its value several years ago. I work more than 60 hours a week. My current personal income, after office expenses, works out to less than $35 per hour. I know many internists who are doing no better. I find myself very discouraged and sometimes rather angry. . . . It is the apparent intent of those who drive managed care that medicine be reduced to a commodity, and a cheap commodity at that, to be bought, sold and manipulated sole-

ly for the financial benefit of their industry. I believe this portends very serious problems ahead, not only for the profession but for the future of patient care and the well-being of the population at large.

Not only are physicians' revenues reduced, but so are revenues to hospitals, which means that hospitals can no longer afford to treat uninsured patients who come through their doors seeking treatment for everything from flu to heart disease. In the past, hospitals passed on much of the cost of treating uninsured patients to paying patients, but managed care has cut out any margin for doing this (Preston, 1996). Finally, despite cost containment measures, health care continues to be a significant expenditure in the United States, partly because of the for-profit structure of much medical care and partly because of the fragmented health care provided by government-funded insurance programs.

PUBLIC HEALTH INSURANCE

Today, patients pay slightly less than 25 percent of their health care costs directly; insurance companies pay about 33 percent, and the government pays over 40 percent of the U.S. health care bill (Pear, 1996). Although private health insurance companies were well established by the 1950s and almost all working people and their immediate families had hospitalization insurance, federal legislation extending coverage to the elderly and the poor was not passed for another decade. From its inception in the 1960s, federally funded health care assistance was a two-tiered system: a medical entitlement program for older people (Medicare) and a medical welfare system for the poor (Medicaid). Medicare is a program that covers most people age 65 and over who are eligible for Social Security or who buy into the program by paying a monthly premium. The largest single insurance program in the country, Medicare is made up of two separate programs: Part A, a hospital insurance program, and Part B, a supplementary medical insurance program. Although Medicare provides coverage for many older people who otherwise would have no health insurance, there are large gaps in its coverage, and near-poor individuals often find it difficult to pay the required deductibles (an initial specified amount that the patient pays before the insurance company begins payments) and copayments (shared costs). Also, Medicare provides only limited coverage for costly and sometimes long-term expenses such as

post-hospital nursing services, home health care, nursing homes, and hospice services (Toner and Pear, 1995). Moreover, in 1996, 5 million of the 38 million Medicare recipients received their care through HMOs, but critics charge that some HMOs terminated stays in skilled nursing homes and certain medical procedures without patients having any voice in the decisions or any right to appeal decisions about their treatment (Pear, 1997b).

Unlike Medicare coverage, which is based primarily on age, Medicaid provides medical, hospital, and long-term care for people who are poor *and* either aged, blind, disabled, or pregnant. Also, whereas Medicare is funded by people's payments into the Social Security system, Medicaid is funded by federal and state governments. As a result, many people view Medicare as an entitlement program—people are assumed to have earned medical coverage through years of hard work and paying into the system—and Medicaid as a welfare program. Perceptions aside, both Medicare and Medicaid, like other forms of health insurance, dramatically expand the resources for supplying and financing medical services, especially for people with chronic disabling illnesses that extend over months or years. Analysts therefore suggest that these programs are extremely costly to the public because they provide no incentive for keeping costs down or managing resources. For example, many hospitals used Medicare funds to build new buildings, buy the latest high-tech equipment, and pay nonmedical personnel in marketing and fund-raising positions. Some physicians abuse the system by operating "Medicaid mills" that charge excessive fees for unnecessary tests and treatments.

During the 1990s the growing number of AIDS patients in the medical system has increased Medicaid costs, and Medicare costs will also increase in the future as more people over age fifty are being diagnosed with AIDS. In 1996, for example, AIDS was diagnosed in 56,000 people over age fifty (Gross, 1997). Further contributing to Medicaid costs are younger AIDS patients, who, on losing their jobs, also lose their company-provided private insurance coverage.

▲ The Uninsured and the Underinsured

Despite public and private insurance programs, about one-third of U.S. citizens are without health insurance or had difficulty getting or paying for medical care at some time in the last year. According to a study by the Harvard School of Public Health, 40 million adults were uninsured in 1995 or at some time in the prior year (Pear, 1996), though other analysts put the number as high as 43.4 million (Bradsher, 1995). Excluding the elderly and members of the military and their families—who are covered by the federal government—the majority of the uninsured are full-time workers (about 41 percent) (Toner, 1993). About 70 percent of the uninsured said that they had been employed some of the time they were without health insurance. Jobs in agriculture, personal services, construction, business and repair services, retail, self-employment, and recreation and entertainment have higher-than-average percentages of uninsured employees (Toner, 1993; Pear, 1996). Another study found that some corporations are cutting medical benefits for rank-and-file employees or moving them into managed care programs that strictly limit benefits but that executives continue to have health plans that provide full coverage for office visits and hospitalization for monthly premiums of less than $10 and no annual deductible or out-of-pocket expenses whatsoever (Myerson, 1996). The bitter reality of being uninsured was best expressed by Tommy Markham, who at age 48 was disabled by a stroke: "You could be damn near dying, and the first thing they ask is 'Do you have insurance?'" (Abraham, 1993:3).

Race, Class, Gender, and Health Care

Just as deinstitutionalization was initially seen as the solution to mental health care and is now viewed by many as the problem, health insurance plans were initially considered a solution but have now become a problem, especially when they perpetuate unequal access to health care because of race, class, or gender. According to a large federal study, even when people are covered by Medicare or Medicaid, the care they receive and their overall life expectations are influenced by their race and income. Among other things, people of color across class lines and low-income whites typically receive less preventive care and less optimal management of chronic diseases than others (Leary, 1996). Under Medicaid the poorest people sometimes receive the fewest services because of limitations placed on eligibility and the way payment of fees to doctors is structured. For example, many doctors are unwilling to work in a central city area for a Medicaid reimbursement of $13 a visit (Rosenthal, 1993). Regardless of their health insurance status, people living in central cities where there are high levels of poverty and crime or in remote rural areas generally have difficulty in getting health care because most doctors prefer to locate their practice in a "safe" area, particularly one with a patient base that will produce a high income.

Like race and class, gender is an important factor in health care. Numerous researchers have found pervasive gender inequality in health care in the United States (Nechas and Foley, 1994; Rosser, 1994). Women have historically been excluded from medicine in ways that continue to have a detrimental impact on their health. Women are underrepresented in the medical profession, representatively less research is done on health care issues specifically pertaining to women, and women have differential access to medical treatment.

Although more women have become physicians in recent years, about 80 percent of medical doctors in the United States today are men. The underrepresentation of women in medicine can be traced back to 1910 and the publication of the Flexner Report, a study commissioned by the American Medical Association and the Carnegie Foundation on the state of medical education in the United States. According to educator Abraham Flexner (1910), the only way to make the practice of medicine more scientific was to make medical education more rigorous, and the way to accomplish this was to close a number of medical schools. Flexner's plan was implemented, but not in an even-handed way: Only one of the three women's medical schools and two schools for African Americans survived. As a result, white women and people of color were largely excluded from medical education for the first half of the twentieth century. Until the civil rights movement and the women's movements of the 1960s and early 1970s, virtually all physicians were white, male, and upper- or upper-middle class. Today, however, women make up almost 42 percent of medical students, so the gender ratio in the profession will change rather dramatically early in the twenty-first century (Association of American Medical Colleges, 1996).

The more equitable gender enrollments in medical schools are welcome and long overdue, but in both medical school and medical practice there is still a male-centered focus on human health and health care delivery. Funding for research on women's health issues and diseases is lacking, and women have been excluded from most experimental drugs trials, which are conducted to determine the positive and negative effects that a specific drug has on a given category of patients (Laurence and Weinhouse, 1994). Many clinical studies also virtually ignore women. For example, although women are in the group with the most rapidly increasing incidence of AIDS, very little AIDS research relating to women is being conducted (Nechas and Foley, 1994). Similarly, in a widely reported study on the effects of aspirin on heart disease, all of the patients in the study were men, even though heart disease is the leading cause of death for both women and men (Steering Committee of the Physicians' Health Group Study, 1989).

Not including women in research contributes to their differential treatment for certain kinds of medical problems. Without adequate studies, disease in women may go unrecognized, be misdiagnosed, or be attributed to a nonphysical factor. For example, women with the same symptoms of kidney failure as men are much less likely to receive an organ transplant (Steingart et al., 1991). Similarly, far fewer women than men with an abnormal heart scan are referred for a procedure known as cardiac catheterization to remedy the problem. According to medical sociologists, both male and female doctors need more training in health issues pertaining to women so that they can treat the majority of the U.S. population (Rosser, 1994).

SOCIOLOGICAL EXPLANATIONS FOR HEALTH CARE PROBLEMS

What are the primary causes of health care problems in the United States? How can health care be improved? The answers that social scientists give to these questions depend on their theoretical framework. Analysts approaching these questions from a functionalist perspective focus on how illness affects the smooth operation of society and on the functions medicine serves as a social institution. Some sociologists using a conflict perspective focus on how a capitalist economy affects health and health care delivery; others look at inequalities of race, class, and gender. Finally, sociologists who use an interactionist framework look at social and cultural factors affecting communication between doctors and patients.

The Functionalist Perspective

The functionalist perspective considers illness a threat to a smoothly functioning society because it is necessary for all people to fulfill their appropriate social roles. When people become ill, they cannot fulfill their everyday responsibilities to family, employer, or the larger society and instead adopt the *sick role*—patterns of behavior expected from individuals who are ill. Sociologist Talcott Parsons (1951) identified four role expectations of the sick role: (1) sick people are not responsible for their incapacity; (2) they are exempted from their usual role and task obligations; (3) they must want to leave the sick role and get well; and (4) they are obligated to seek and comply with the advice of a medical professional. In other words, illness is a form of deviance that must be controlled, and according to Parsons, physicians are the logical agents of social control. By certifying that a person is physically or mentally ill and by specifying how the patient should behave, doctors use their professional authority to monitor people with illnesses, thereby granting them only a temporary reprieve from their usual social roles and responsibilities. Today, however, the dramatic increase in chronic illness and disorganization in the delivery system for medical services mean that sick people have less access to doctors and doctors have less control over aspects of patients' lives that increase their chances of becoming ill, such as exposure to occupational and environmental hazards and use of alcohol and tobacco. Patients thus end up incurring large medical bills and being generally unproductive in society.

Functionalists believe that the problems in U.S. health care are due to macrolevel changes, such as the development of high-tech medicine, overspecialization of doctors, erosion of health insurance, and increased demand for health care by consumers. Since World War II the rapid growth of medical knowledge has produced a glut of information, new technologies, and greatly improved surgical techniques. For example, several hospitals operating in the same city often purchase the same extremely expensive equipment that can be used only in specialized cases but that enables them to meet the demand for high-tech medicine and keep them competitive with other hospitals in their service area. The costs of the expensive equipment are passed on to consumers in the form of higher medical bills and insurance premiums. Similarly, most medical students believe that they have to specialize—rather than enter general or family practice—to build a large patient base and thereby increase their income and prestige. In the process, both doctors and hospitals begin to view health care as a commodity and to provide a far wider array of services—including treatment for alcohol and other substance abuse, day care for the mentally ill, and elective procedures such as cosmetic surgery—to sell to potential patients. At the same time, most individuals come to view health care as a right to which they are entitled. As both supply of and demand for medical treatment continue to grow, strong lobbying organizations such as the American Medical Association and the American Hospital Association and business, labor, consumer groups, and the elderly have entered into battle with Congress over the extent to which federal and state government should regulate health care in this country.

The disorganization in U.S. health care is clearly dysfunctional not only for individuals but also for society, but not all functionalists agree on what should be done. Some believe that the whole health care system needs to be reorganized; others think that managed care is the best answer. Most attempts at reorganization have ended up on the rocks like the Clinton health plan that was proposed in 1993. To control medical costs and provide secure coverage for all, the Clinton administration proposed a vast restructuring of the health care system, which would have been phased in over several years. Financial incentives would have encouraged consumers to join low-cost HMOs and pushed doctors, hospitals, and insurance companies to join together in networks. The plan would have made consumers conscious of the costs of their care and fostered competition among health plans in an effort to reduce costs and provide better services. However, since employers would have paid the bulk of the cost (because they would have paid the premiums for their workers), many small business owners and others who feared the financial impact adamantly opposed the proposal.

Without proper planning, the United States cannot have a fully functioning health care system. Instead, we have many individual components—ranging from doctors in private practice to for-profit HMOs, pharmaceutical companies, and insurance companies—each with its own agenda for health care delivery. Also, say the functionalists, health care must shift its focus from acute diseases to problems associated with chronic illness and disability.

The Conflict Perspective

The conflict approach typically is based on the assumption that problems in health care delivery are rooted in the capitalist economy, which views medicine as a commodity produced and sold by the medical-industrial complex. The *medical-industrial complex* **encompasses both local physicians and hospitals as well as global health-related industries such as pharmaceutical and medical supply companies that deliver health care today** (Relman, 1992). Although wealthy patients and patients with good insurance may receive high-quality care in the medical-industrial complex structure, low-income and poverty-level people often do without. Physicians—who hold a legal monopoly over medicine—benefit from the existing structure because they can charge inflated fees. Similarly, hospitals, clinics, and other medical facilities control how health care is delivered and what various services will cost patients. Conflict analysts therefore favor managed care and other cost containment strategies as a way of reducing the control of physicians and other players in the medical-industrial complex and thereby reducing inequalities in the system. At the same time, managed care is no more than a bandage on the hemorrhaging cost of health care because it does not deal with larger systemic problems with how health care is delivered.

Radical conflict theorists therefore say that only when race, class, and gender-based inequalities in society are reduced will inequalities in health care be reduced. To put it more specifically, as long as societal conditions such as environmental pollution, lack of affordable housing, high levels of stress associated with work conditions or unemployment, inadequate nutrition, and lack of early diagnosis for diseases such as breast cancer and heart disease affect people differently according to their race, class, and gender, health care will be unequal. Most conflict theorists believe that short of a dramatic change in the economic system, the primary way to deal with health care is to treat it as a common good that ought to be provided and regulated by the government like highways, schools, courts, and national defense (Shweder, 1997).

Some conflict theorists also suggest that the doctor–patient relationship should be demystified. If patients were given the information and resources they need for prevention, self-treatment, and home care, the need and demand for expensive medical care would be greatly reduced (Stewart, 1995). Some people now receive medical information on line; thousands of Internet sites are devoted to health and medical information, ranging from potentially life-saving research in top medical journals to alternative therapies such as herbal preparations and colonic irrigation (Fisher, 1996; Kolata, 1996c). Many computer bulletin boards, chat groups, and Usenet newsgroups have emerged to support people with diseases such as AIDS and multiple sclerosis (Kantrowitz, 1993). Capitalism also thrives on the Internet. Corporations that produce medical software now have on-line ventures that offer not only research on any health care topic but also information on physicians, nurses, hospitals, HMOs, and preferred provider organizations. In most cases, fees come from the providers, not from users viewing the pages (Fisher, 1996). Because of the proliferation of medical information on the Internet, the Food and Drug Administration is working to regulate promotion of drugs and medical devices to protect patients who may not be able to distinguish between science and quackery (Neergaard, 1996).

The Interactionist Perspective

Interactionists believe that many problems pertaining to health and illness in our society are linked to social and cultural factors that influence how people define physical illness and mental illness. According to interactionists, we socially construct "health" and "illness" and how both should be treated. As a result, both medical and nonmedical "experts" play a role in determining what constitutes physical and mental illnesses and how these illnesses should be treated by society. For example, in 1997 the Equal Employment Opportunity Commission established guidelines under the Americans with Disabilities Act requiring that employers take "reasonable steps" to accommodate employees with mental illnesses—the same requirement that previously applied only to people with physical disabilities (Stolberg, 1997a). What exactly does this mean? According to one analyst, "That could mean anything from a flexible

schedule for an anxious person, to a desk near a window for a person who grows depressed with too little light, to a quiet work space for a schizophrenic" (Stolberg, 1997a:E1).

Interactionists also examine how doctors and patients interact in health care settings. For example, medical schools provide future doctors with knowledge and skills that laypeople do not have. Given this competence gap, some physicians do not think it is necessary—or possible—to communicate certain kinds of medical information to patients. Some may hesitate to communicate the diagnosis of a fatal illness or, more often, may simply not explain why they are prescribing certain medications or what side-effects or drug interactions might occur.

One way to solve this communication problem, according to interactionists, is to increase the number of doctors in family practice who will focus on patient care and communication, not just the scientific and technological aspects of health care. Another way is to emphasize prevention and work with patients on behaviors to practice and avoid if they want to stay healthy. A third way to change health care is to limit the bureaucracies in mental hospitals where individuals are labeled by their diagnosis and not viewed as people with specific emotional and physical needs to be met. Finally, more public health campaigns are needed to make people aware of issues in health care and health care reform. The 1993 Clinton health reform proposal was debated by politicians and interest groups with very little input from everyday people whose lives would be affected by new health care policy—or the lack of one. Consider, for example, the Patten family, who, after decades of middle-class security, have dwindling savings and fear that another medical setback will drive them out of their $65,000 home and onto the welfare rolls. According to Elma Patten, "A person keeps their nose to the grindstone, works hard, pays their bills on time. Then when your health goes bad they kick you into a corner" (Kilborn, 1993:4A14). Some people might blame the Pattens' lifestyle for their problems. Leo Patten has emphysema from smoking and breathing foul air in the factories where he worked as a machinist. Elma Patten has had heart bypass surgery, a mastectomy, a hysterectomy, and two wrist operations for a repetitive motion injury related to her work (Kilborn, 1993). The Pattens wonder whether they will be able to pay their doctor, whom they like because she communicates with them. However, the Pattens' future—like that of many people with chronic illnesses—is caught up in political and economic issues about health care delivery that will apparently remain as we enter the twenty-first century.

Since Clinton withdrew his health care reform package, federal health officials have focused instead on reforming the Medicare/Medicaid system and on health coverage for children, particularly in families where parents are temporarily out of work. One plan would increase the cigarette tax to subsidize medical premiums for all children in families earning less than 185 percent of the poverty level. Another would offer refundable tax credits to low-income families. However, problems with access to health care will inevitably worsen as costs soar, increasing demands are placed on health care systems, and cuts are made in Medicaid and Medicare reimbursement rates for doctors and hospitals. Further cost-cutting by private insurers will squeeze out whatever is left of the financial slack that once paid for much charity health care.

Meanwhile, state and local governments are hard pressed to come up with money for health coverage as they try to deal with the side effects of welfare cuts in programs. Despite public policy decisions about health care delivery in this country, three factors will inevitably perpetuate inequalities of U.S. health care: (1) high health care costs due to advanced medical services and the use of expensive medications and technology; (2) abuse of existing systems by some health care professionals, particularly those who overcharge patients, provide unnecessary services, or charge for expensive services that were never rendered; and (3) the aging population that will continue to increase sharply and place greater strain on Medicare, Medicaid, and other health resources (Bagby, 1997). As one woman explained to her granddaughter, "Your generation is giving my generation a free ride and the sooner we stop it the better. There is no way on earth to eliminate the [federal] debt without touching entitlements" such as Medicare (Bagby, 1997:21).

SUMMARY

➤ *Why is health care a social problem?*

According to the World Health Organization, health is a state of complete physical, mental, and social well-being. In other words, health is not only a biological issue, it is also a social issue. Moreover, although people in the United States pay more for health services than people in other developed nations do, our expenditures do not translate into improved life expectancy for everyone.

➤ *What kinds of health problems cause most of today's high health care costs?*

Since acute illnesses (e.g., measles, polio) are largely under control with vaccinations and improved public health practices, most health problems today are chronic diseases (e.g., arthritis, diabetes, heart disease) or disabilities (e.g., back injuries, hearing or vision problems, mental retardation). Medical advances mean that many people born with serious disabilities survive, as do many who in earlier times would have died from acute illnesses or accidents. As more people survive and live longer, more are likely to experience chronic illnesses and disabilities.

➤ *Why is AIDS considered a health crisis in the United States and other nations?*

First, the number of cases is rising annually. Second, about 75 percent of people infected worldwide are infected through heterosexual intercourse—it is not a disease restricted to any single group. Third, there is no cure; once HIV develops into AIDS, it is fatal. Fourth, treatment is complex and costly and typically requires lengthy stays in a hospital or hospice. Finally, numerous ethical issues (e.g., issues relating to testing) have yet to be resolved.

➤ *Why is mental illness a social problem?*

Mental illness is a social problem because of the number of people it affects, the difficulty in defining and identifying mental disorders, and the ways mental illness is treated. Deinstitutionalization—discharging mental patients from hospitals into the community—was considered a solution to the problem of warehousing patients, but it has created new problems.

➤ *Historically, what kinds of health care have been available in the United States?*

Originally, there was fee-for-service care, with patients paying directly for treatment they receive from doctors and hospitals. With third-party fee-for-service care, patients pay premiums to private or public health insurance companies that in turn pay the doctors and hospitals. Both of these health care structures are very expensive because there are few restrictions on fees charged by health care providers.

➡ *What new types of health care are available in the United States?*

Some insurance companies now offer preferred provider organizations (PPOs), with doctors contracting to treat insured patients for set fees; these fees may be higher or lower than the fees for the doctor's other patients who are not enrolled in the PPO. For a set monthly fee a health maintenance organization (HMO) provides total care with an emphasis on prevention; patients must use the doctors and hospitals affiliated with the HMO. Managed care refers to any system of cost containment that closely monitors and controls health care providers' decisions about what medical tests, procedures, and other services should be provided to patients; a patient's primary care physician must get approval to send the patient to a specialist or order hospitalization and costly tests or procedures. Since many for-profit companies have entered health care, there is some concern that quality of care is sacrificed to cost containment.

➡ *What is the difference between Medicare and Medicaid?*

Medicare is public health insurance for people age 65 and over that is funded by Social Security payments. Medicaid is public health insurance for people who are poor and either aged, blind, disabled, or pregnant; it is funded by federal and state governments. Both programs are considered costly to the public because there are no incentives to keep costs down.

➡ *How do race, class, and gender affect health care?*

Research shows that people of color across class lines and low-income whites typically receive less preventive care and less optimal management of chronic diseases than others do. Women have been underrepresented in the medical profession (though that is changing); medical training, practice, and research are male-centered; and women receive differential treatment for certain kinds of medical problems.

➡ *What are the sociological explanations for health care problems?*

Functionalists consider the sick role a form of deviance that medicine as an institution could control until recently. Today, however, the supply of and demand for health care means that patients incur large medical bills and are unproductive to society. Some functionalists believe that the whole health system must be reorganized; others think that managed care is the best answer. Some conflict theorists believe that our health problems are rooted in capitalism and the medical-industrial complex; others believe that only when race-, class-, and gender-based inequalities are reduced will inequalities in health care be reduced. Interactionists believe that communication problems between doctors and patients create many of our health problems and that people must, among other things, become more involved in health care issues and health care reform.

KEY TERMS

acute diseases, pp. 228–229
chronic diseases, p. 229
deinstitutionalization, pp. 234–235
disability, p. 231
health maintenance organization (HMO), p. 241

infant mortality rate, p. 228
life expectancy, p. 228
managed care, p. 241
medical-industrial complex, p. 245
total institution, pp. 235–236

QUESTIONS FOR CRITICAL THINKING

1. Because the United States takes pride in its technological and social standing in the world, most people are usually surprised to learn that our infant mortality rate is higher than the rates in most other developed countries. Why is this and what do you think individuals can do at the community level to save these young lives?

2. In what ways are race, class, and gender intertwined with mental disorders? Consider causes and treatments.

3. Reread the doctor's statement on pages 241–242. Do you agree that managed care is detrimental to patient care, or do you side with conflict theorists who believe that doctors uphold the fee-for-service system because it allows them to inflate the cost of treatment? Is there a middle ground?

4. Do you think the U.S. health care system needs reforming? If so, what would you propose?

Chapter Twelve

The Changing Family

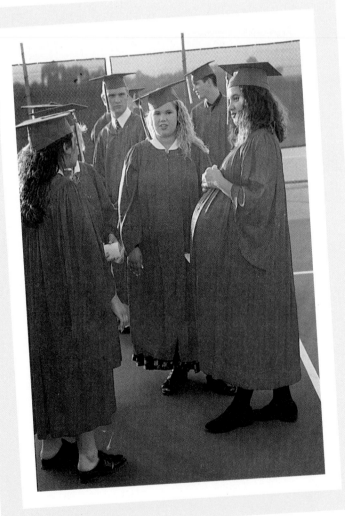

I was working from six-thirty in the morning to seven at night without breaks. I wasn't eating. I was irritable. I couldn't deal with anybody. I was fighting with my wife all the time. We were breaking apart. I wasn't communicating anymore. The job took control of me. I was possessed. I didn't feel patient with my daughter anymore. It was taking a big toll on me, and I didn't like it at all. I decided it wasn't worth it and the only way to stop it was to leave.

—Ernie, a physical therapist,
explaining that he resigned
from a managerial position in
a large corporation when he
discovered that his job was
damaging his family
relationships
(Gerson, 1993:145)

—A 35-year-old
white secretary,
who was married
for sixteen years
and had one child
(Kurz, 1995:90)

Since the divorce what's been hard is worrying about paying the bills—having enough money for food for my son. I don't even get to think about buying him new sneakers.

I wish my parents had had some time to spend with me when I was growing up. They were basically absentee parents. I'm not going to do that to my kids. I'm going to be there for them!

—A student in introductory
sociology discussing the
importance of early
childhood socialization
(Author's files, 1997)

—Renee, an
African American
woman, who was
considering
marriage to her
current companion
(Jarrett, 1997:353)

I could do bad by myself. . . . If we got married and he's working, then he lose his job. I'm going to stand by him and everything. I don't want to marry nobody that don't have nothing going for themselves . . . . I don't see no future . . . . I could do bad by myself.

Many people today experience the family-related problems described by these individuals: the family-work dilemma, economic hardship after divorce, lack of time for family life, and feelings of hopelessness brought about by unemployment and poverty. Although most sociologists believe that the family as a social institution is here to stay in one form or another, they also acknowledge that family-related problems are a challenge not only to individuals but to our entire society.

THE NATURE OF FAMILIES

What is a family? According to sociologist Robin Wolf (1996), that question generates heated debate: Some say that a definition of the family must emphasize tradition and stability; others argue that any useful definition must take into account diversity and social change. Traditionally, the *family* has been defined as a group of people who are related to one another by bonds of blood, marriage, or adoption and who live together, form an economic unit, and bear and raise children (Benokraitis, 1993). According to this definition, families are created through childbearing, and it is the parent–child relationship that links generations (Beutler, Burr, Bahr, and Herrin, 1989). Today, however, the traditional definition of family is often modified to incorporate diverse living arrangements and relationships such as single-parent households, cohabiting unmarried couples, domestic partnerships of lesbian or gay couples, and several generations of family members (grandparent, parent, and child) living under the same roof. Accordingly, *families* are defined as relationships in which people live together with commitment, form an economic unit and care for any young, and consider the group critical to their identity (Benokraitis, 1993; Lamanna and Riedmann, 1994). This is the definition we will use as we look at family-related social problems.

Changing Family Structure and Patterns

The basis of the traditional family structure is *kinship,* a social network of people based on common ancestry, marriage, or adoption. Kinship is very important in preindustrial societies because it serves as an efficient means of producing and distributing food and goods (clothing, materials for building shelter) and transferring property and power from one generation to the next. In many preindustrial societies the primary kinship unit is the *extended family*—a family unit composed of relatives in addition to parents and children who live in the same household. Extended families typically include grandparents, uncles, aunts, or other relatives in addition to parents and children. When growing and harvesting crops are the basis of economic production, extended families mean that larger numbers of people participate in food production, which can be essential to survival. Living together also enables family members to share other resources, such as shelter and transportation. Though extended families are not common in the United States, this pattern is found in some countries in Latin America, Africa, Asia, and parts of Eastern and Southern Europe (Busch, 1990).

With industrialization, other social institutions begin to fulfill kinship system functions. Production and distribution of goods and services, for example, largely shifts to the economic sector. The form of kinship that is most typical in industrialized nations is the *nuclear family*—a family unit composed of one or two parents and their dependent children who live apart from other relatives. The nuclear family in an industrialized society functions primarily to regulate sexual activity, socialize children, and provide family members with affection and companionship. Although many people view the two-parent nuclear family as the ideal family, only one out of four U.S. families is composed of a married couple and one or more children under age eighteen (U.S. Bureau of the Census, 1996b). This is a 15 percent decrease since 1970, when two out of five families were two-parent households. Sociologists attribute the decrease to a greater number of births among unmarried women, a trend toward postponing or forgoing marriage and childbearing, and high rates of separation and divorce.

Are U.S. Families in Decline?

Will the family as a social institution disappear in the future? Social analysts answer this question differently, depending on whether they adopt a traditional definition of the family or a modified definition. Sociologist David Popenoe (1988, 1996) uses a traditional definition and believes that three

"So how's the family? Still disintegrating?"

Drawing by M. Stevens; © 1995 The New Yorker Magazine, Inc.

trends mark the coming end of the traditional nuclear family:

♦ The divorce rate has increased sharply (it currently exceeds 50 percent), and parents increasingly decide to forgo marriage, so a sizable number of children are being raised in single-parent households, apart from other relatives.

♦ Large numbers of married women have left the role of full-time mother and housewife to go into the labor market, and not all the functions of their former role are being fulfilled.

♦ The focus of many families has shifted away from childbearing to the needs of the adult members. Increasingly, even when parents have young children to raise, they break up if their psychological and self-de-

velopment needs are unmet in the marriage relationship. (Popenoe, 1995:16)

Some sociologists go beyond Popenoe's analysis to suggest that if marriage and the family weaken enough and no satisfactory substitute for marriage emerges, industrial societies such as the United States will not survive (Davis and Grossbard-Shechtman, 1985). However, research shows that the structure of the family is undergoing profound changes around the world, in both rich and poor nations (see Box 12.1), giving rise to an alternative point of view on the survival of the American family.

Some analysts say the family isn't declining, it's simply changing. According to this social change perspective, families are becoming more complex and diverse—they are not in a state of irreversible decline (Skolnick, 1991; Cherlin, 1992). In fact, according to sociologist Andrew Cherlin (1992), the

SOCIAL PROBLEMS
IN GLOBAL PERSPECTIVE

BOX 12.1

The Changing Family around the World

Ms. Polyakovskaya lives with her 6-month-old baby, relying on friends and baby sitters to watch Aleksandr when she is at work. The father, an unmarried journalist, has never seen his child. Her 6-year-old son, Simeon, is being raised by his grandmother and great-grandmother in Kiev. Ms. Polyakovskaya says she hopes to bring him to Moscow, but cannot even afford train fare to visit him.

She loves her job covering music and ballet, but it is ill paid. In her bare one-room apartment, she sleeps on a tiny, fold-out couch next to the baby's crib. An ironing board serves as a desk. But like many women raising children alone, she said she does not want to marry again.

"My life is difficult," she said, "but God, if I had to come home from work and clean, cook and iron for a husband who keeps telling me I am doing it wrong, it would be even worse."

—Yelena Polyakovskaya, age 32,
a television reporter in Russia
(Stanley, 1995)

Yelena Polyakovskaya is one of a growing number of women in Russia raising her family without a husband. Approximately 15 to 20 percent of Russian families are single-parent households. This is a lower figure than in the United States (with about 27 percent single-parent households), but in Russia, single mothers span all social strata; in the United States, single-parent households are largely in the poorest urban areas (Stanley, 1995). In Japan, single-parenthood because of abandonment or divorce is rare, but a practice called *tanshin hunin* has the same effect. When middle-managers are transferred, they go without their families so that their children don't have to change schools. When possible, the fathers commute home on weekends, but the mothers are essentially single parents (O'Connell, 1994).

family will last as a social institution precisely because it can adapt to social change and modify its form. Cherlin goes on to say, though, that the best way to minimize the costs of change in the family unit is to modify the other social institutions of daily life—such as the economy and workplace.

Changing Views on Marriage and Families

The term *marriage* refers to a legally recognized and/or socially approved arrangement between two individuals that carries certain rights and obligations and usually involves sexual activity. In the United States the only legal form of marriage is *monogamy*—a marriage between one woman and one man. The marriage rate (number of marriages per 1,000 population) in the United States is about 9 percent annually.

Marriage was once a cultural imperative. There was "something wrong" with a person who didn't marry. But since the 1970s, people's attitudes toward marriage and the family have changed as other aspects of society have changed. Cultural guidelines on marriage and childbearing have grown weaker as our society has experienced a broader cultural shift toward autonomy and personal growth. According to Cherlin (1992:127), "Family life became a matter of personal choice in which individuals made decisions based on a calculus of self-inter-

Increasing single-parenthood is just one worldwide trend. According to Judith Bruce, author of a report recently published by the Population Council, a nonprofit group in New York, "trends like unwed motherhood, rising divorce rates, smaller households and the feminization of poverty are not unique to America, but are occurring worldwide" (Lewin, 1995). Among the report's findings are the following:

- Divorce rates are rising. In many developed countries, the divorce rates doubled between 1970 and 1990; in less developed countries, about one-fourth of first marriages end by the time women are in their forties.
- Unwed motherhood is increasing virtually everywhere.
- Children in single-parent households are more likely to be poor than are children in two-parent households, especially when the parent is the mother (often termed the *feminization of poverty*).
- Though the reason varies from country to country, more women are entering the work force and taking increasing economic responsibility for children. In

Bangladesh, for example, where older husbands take young wives, when a husband dies, the wife must find work to support their children. In Asia, if a father who migrates for better work opportunities stops sending money, the mother must support the family herself. In sub-Saharan Africa a woman's husband may go on to another polygamous marriage and support those children instead (Lewin, 1995).

The fact that families around the world are changing in similar ways shows that there is nothing inevitable about the form of the family or the roles of women and men even within a single society (O'Connell, 1994). The fact of so much change in the most basic unit of society also poses important questions for the twenty-first century. Is the basic problem really inequality between women and men? Would shared responsibilities in the home and equal opportunities in the workplace create better families? Can some general principles for social policies be developed, given vastly different societal conditions? What do you think?

est and self-fulfillment. Marriage was still desirable, but no one any longer had to be married to be a proper member of society." Beginning in the 1970s, too, marriage became much less of an economic necessity for women because of new job opportunities and rising incomes. Although women's wages remained low in comparison to men's, their wages rose in absolute terms (Cherlin, 1992).

Nevertheless, marriage is a persistent preference for most people today, especially those who plan to have children. More than 75 percent of high school seniors in a national survey conducted by sociologist Arland Thornton (1989) reported that marriage and family life were extremely important to them. Most also indicated that if they married, it was very like-

ly that they would stay married to the same person for life. Carrying out such intentions may not be easy, though. According to another national study, more than half the married people interviewed indicated that if they had it to do over again, they would marry the same person, but 20 percent said that they would definitely not marry their current partner again, and another 25 percent said that they weren't sure (Patterson and Kim, 1991).

The divorce rate (number of divorces per 1,000 population) in the United States during the twentieth century has varied from a low of 0.7 in 1900 to an all-time high of 5.3 in 1981; by 1994 it had stabilized at 4.6 (U.S. Bureau of the Census, 1996b). Though many believe marriage should last "until death do us part," for others, marriage is a commitment "for as long as love allows." Through a pattern of marriage, divorce, and remarriage, many people reaffirm their belief in the institution of marriage but not to the individual they initially married. This pattern of a succession of marriages, with a person having several spouses over a lifetime but being legally married to only one partner at a time, is referred to as *serial monogamy*. Some social analysts consider serial monogamy a natural adaptation to other social changes in society; others think it is detrimental to individuals and to society and further evidence of the decline of the family (see Popenoe, 1996). Who is right? As with other social problems we have examined, the causes, effects, and possible solutions for family-related problems depend on the theoretical framework the analyst uses.

SOCIOLOGICAL PERSPECTIVES ON FAMILY-RELATED PROBLEMS

What purposes do families serve in contemporary societies? Do families create problems for society or solve them? The latter, say functionalists, who believe that the family fulfills important functions at the microlevel for individuals and at the macrolevel for the entire society. Conflict and feminist theorists, however, consider families a primary source of inequality—and sometimes abuse and violence—in society. Interactionists, on the other hand, taking a microlevel approach, see problems in terms of socialization and social interactions among family members.

◢ Functionalist Perspectives

Functionalists emphasize the importance of the family in maintaining the stability of society and the well-being of individuals. According to Emile Durkheim, marriage is a microcosmic replica of the larger society; both marriage and society involve a mental and moral fusion of physically distinct individuals (Lehmann, 1994). Durkheim also believed that a division of labor contributed to greater efficiency in marriage and families (and all areas of life). In his study of family life in the United States, Talcott Parsons (1955) also saw the importance of a division of labor. He saw the husband in an ideal nuclear family as fulfilling an *instrumental role*—meeting the family's economic needs, making important decisions, and providing leadership—and the wife as fulfilling an *expressive role*—running the household, caring for children, and meeting family members' emotional needs.

Contemporary functionalists use Durkheim's and Parsons's work as a basis for their model of the family, believing that a division of labor makes it possible for families to fulfill a number of functions that no other social institution can perform as efficiently and effectively in developed nations:

1. *Regulate sexual behavior and reproduction.* Families are expected to regulate the sexual activity of their members and thus control reproduction so that it occurs within specific boundaries. Sexual regulation of family members by the family is supposed to protect the *principle of legitimacy*—the belief that all children should have a socially and legally recognized father (Malinowski, 1964).
2. *Socialize and educate children.* Parents and other relatives are responsible for teaching children the values and norms of their culture.
3. *Provide economic and psychological support.* Families are responsible for providing for their members' physical (food, shelter) and emotional needs.
4. *Provide social status.* Families confer social status on their members, including *ascribed statuses* such as race, ethnicity, nationality, class, and religious affiliation, although some of these statuses may change later in life.

Considering their view of the family, functionalists believe that problems in the family are a social crisis. The functional family provides both social order and economic stability by providing for the survival and development of children, the physical and emotional health of adults, and the care of the sick, injured, elderly, and disabled. The family is also the front line for reinforcing society's norms and values. Functionalists consider the family to be part of the solution to many problems faced by people in contemporary societies and dysfunctions in families to be problems that threaten the well-being of individuals, groups, and nations.

Functionalists believe that changes in other social institutions such as the economy, religion, education, law, medicine, and the government contribute to family-related problems. For example, changing the law to recognize no-fault divorce contributes to higher rates of divorce and dramatically increases single-parent households. Single-parenting, according to some social critics, does not provide children with the nurturance and guidance they get in a two-parent home (Popenoe, 1996).

Conflict and Feminist Perspectives

Most conflict and feminist analysts believe that functionalist views on family problems are idealized and inadequate. Rather than operating harmoniously and for the benefit of all members, families are sources of social inequality and conflict over values, goals, and access to resources and power.

Conflict theorists who focus on class relations in capitalist economies compare family members to workers in a factory. Women are dominated by men in the home just as workers are dominated by managers and capitalists in factories (Engels, 1972). As wives and mothers, women contribute to capitalism by producing the next generation of workers and providing the existing labor force with food, clean clothes, and emotional support. Not only does women's work in the family benefit the capitalist class, it reinforces women's subordination because their work is unpaid and often devalued. For example, women who work solely in their own homes for many years typically do not have health insurance or a retirement plan apart from sharing in their husbands' employment benefits.

Many feminist theorists, however, think that male dominance and female subordination began long before capitalism and the private ownership of property arose as an economic system (Mann, 1994). They see women's subordination as being rooted in patriarchy, particularly in men's control over women's labor power. At the same time that women's labor in the home is directed by men, it is undervalued, which allows men to benefit from their status as the family breadwinner (Firestone, 1970; Goode, 1982). In a recent study, sociologist Jane Riblett Wilkie (1993) found that most men are reluctant to relinquish their status as family breadwinner. Although only 15 percent of families in the United States are supported solely by a male breadwinner, many men continue to construct their ideal of masculinity on this role. It is acceptable for their wives to enter the paid work force if their role is simply to earn money; however, wives should not challenge the ideal roles of male breadwinner and female homemaker.

In sum, both conflict and feminist theorists think that family problems derive from inequality—not just within the family, but in the political, social, and economic arenas of the larger society as well (Aulette, 1994). In fact, pervasive societal inequality leads to one of the most tragic family problems: wife battering. Wife battering and other forms of domestic violence may even be conscious strategies that men use to control women and perpetuate gender inequality (Kurz, 1989). Forty percent of all female murder victims are killed by current or former husbands or boyfriends (see Chapter 10). In a study of women killed in New York City from 1990 through 1994, researchers found that one-third of the women killed by their husbands were married but not living with their spouses at the time of their death, a finding that suggests that these women were trying to leave the relationships at the time of their deaths (Belluck, 1997). In contrast, only 6 percent of all male murder victims are killed by current or former wives or girlfriends. According to conflict and feminist theorists, then, family-related problems, including domestic violence and wife battering, can be solved only if all social institutions work to eliminate the subordination of women in society.

Interactionist Perspectives

Some interactionists view the family communication process as being integral to understanding the diverse roles that family members play; therefore they primarily examine how husbands, wives, and children act out their own roles and react to the parts played by others. Although societies differ widely on rules and norms that shape family and kin relationships, people are socialized to accept their society's form of the family as the acceptable norm. According to sociologists Peter Berger and Hansfried Kellner (1964), marital partners develop a shared reality through their interactions with each other. Although newlyweds bring separate identities to a marriage, over time they construct a shared reality as a couple. In the process, the partners redefine their past identities to be consistent with their new realities. The process of developing a shared reality is continuous and occurs not only in the family but in any group in which the couple participates together. In case of separation and divorce, the process is reversed: Couples may start with a shared reality but once again become individuals with separate realities in the process of uncoupling their relationship.

How do interactionists explain problems in a family? Some look at the subjective meanings and interpretations people give to their everyday lives. According to sociologist Jessie Bernard (1982), women and men experience marriage differently. While the husband may see *his marriage* very positively, the wife may feel less positive about *her marriage*. The reverse may also be true. Evidence for the different realities of marriage comes from research that shows that husbands and wives often give very different accounts of the same event (Safilios-Rothschild, 1969).

Still other interactionists view family problems in terms of partners' unrealistic expectations about love and marriage that can lead to marital dissatisfaction and sometimes divorce. Our culture emphasizes *romantic love*—a deep and vital emotion based on significant need satisfaction, caring for and acceptance of another person, and development of an intimate relationship (Lamanna and Riedmann, 1994), and most couples in the United States get married because they are in love. But being a "nation of lovers" doesn't mean that men and women have the same ideas about what constitutes romantic love. According to sociologist Francesca Cancian (1990), women tend to express their feelings verbally, whereas men tend to express their love through nonverbal actions such as fixing dinner or doing household repairs. Women may not always interpret these actions as signs of love, as one man complained (Rubin, 1976:146): "What does she want? Proof? She's got it, hasn't she? Would I be knocking myself out to get things for her—like to keep up this house—if I didn't love her? Why does a man do things like that if not because he loves his wife and kids? I swear, I can't figure what she wants." His wife replied, "It's not enough that he supports us and takes care of us. I appreciate that, but I want him to share things with me. I need for him to tell me his feelings."

Whatever their different viewpoints on marriage and family, most social theorists agree on one fact:

Three decades ago, the nuclear family was the most common family form, and today it is only one of many patterns.

DIVERSITY IN INTIMATE RELATIONSHIPS AND FAMILIES

Greater diversity in intimate relationships and families in the United States has come about because of dramatic increases in (1) singlehood, (2) postponing marriage, (3) living together without marriage (cohabitation and domestic partnerships), (4) dual-earner marriages, and (5) one-parent families.

Singlehood

Although some will eventually marry, there are 42 million adults in the United States who have never been married. The proportion of the U.S. population that has never been married has continued to grow since the 1960s. Some people choose singlehood over marriage because it means greater freedom from commitments to another person. Other reasons include more career opportunities (especially for women), the availability of sexual partners without marriage, the belief that the single lifestyle is full of excitement, and the desire for self-sufficiency and freedom to change and experiment (Stein, 1976, 1981). Though some analysts think that individuals who prefer to remain single hold more individualistic values and are less family-oriented than are people who choose to marry, sociologist Peter Stein (1981) has found otherwise: Many singles still feel a strong need for intimacy, sharing, and continuity and, as a result, develop relationships with other singles, valuing friends and personal growth more highly than marriage and children (Cargan and Melko, 1982; Alwin, Converse, and Martin, 1985).

Some people are single not by choice but by necessity. Because of structural changes in the economy, many working-class young people cannot afford to marry and set up their own household. Even some college graduates have found that they cannot earn enough money to set up a household separate from that of their parents.

The proportion of never-married singles varies significantly by racial and ethnic group. Among males age eighteen and over, about 41 percent of African Americans have never been married, compared to about 32 percent of Latinos and 24 percent of whites. Among women age eighteen and over, about 35 percent of African Americans have never married, compared to almost 24 percent of Latinas and about 17 percent of whites (U.S. Bureau of the Census, 1996b). Lower marriage rates among African American women seem to be associated with these factors:

1. Young African American men have higher rates of mortality than young African American women.
2. More African American women are college-educated and tend to make more money than African American men.
3. Some African American men have less to offer in a marriage because they have experienced high levels of discrimination and limited educational opportunities.
4. Rates of homosexuality are higher among African American men than women.
5. More African American men than women marry members of other racial-ethnic groups (Staples, 1994).

There is a scarcity of research on singlehood among Latinos/as, Native Americans, and Asian Americans. Apparently the diverse experiences among Latinas/os, who may be Mexican Americans, Cuban Americans, or Puerto Ricans (among others), and Asian Americans, who may trace their roots to many parts of Asia and the Pacific Islands, is one of the primary reasons for the lack of research.

Postponing Marriage

Young people today are less eager to get married than they were two decades ago; many are remaining single into their late twenties. The median age at which men first get married is 26.7 years, and the median age for women is 24.5 years. (*Median* is a statistical midpoint; therefore half of all men who marry do so before age 26.7 and half marry after.) Although the age at which people marry for the first time has been rising steadily since the 1950s, it has been accelerating more rapidly since the 1970s. Between 1970 and today, the proportion of women aged 25 to 29 who have never married has tripled.

Why are more people postponing first marriages? Although some reasons are the same as those for staying single, sociologist Robin Wolf (1996) suggests four key factors: (1) economic uncertainty due to the changing job structure in the United States (see Chapter 1); (2) women's increasing participation in the labor force; (3) the sexual revolution of the 1970s that made sexual relationships outside marriage more socially acceptable; (4) the rising divorce rate—young people watching their parents divorce may be less anxious to jump into marriage themselves. Other analysts suggest that a significant increase in cohabitation and domestic partnerships also contributes to the percentage of people who are counted as single or postponing marriage.

Cohabitation and Domestic Partnerships

The popularity of cohabitation has increased in the past two decades. *Cohabitation* **is two unmarried adults living together in a sexual relationship without being legally married.** It is not known how many people actually cohabit because the U.S. Bureau of the Census refers to such couples simply as "unmarried couple households" and does not ask about emotional or sexual involvement. But on the basis of Census Bureau data, the heterosexual couples who are most likely to cohabit are under age forty-five and have been married before or are older individuals who do not want to lose financial benefits (such as retirement benefits) that are contingent on not remarrying. Among younger people, employed couples are more likely to cohabit than college students are.

For some couples, cohabitation is a form of trial marriage, constituting an intermediate stage between dating and marriage. According to anthropologist Margaret Mead (1966), dating patterns in the United States do not adequately prepare people for marriage and parenting responsibilities. Mead believed that marriage should occur in two stages, each with its own ceremony and responsibilities. In the first stage, the individual marriage, two people would make a serious commitment to each other but agree not to have children during this period. In the second stage, the parental marriage, the couple would decide to have children and to share responsibility for their upbringing. Mead's two stages of marriage would both be legally binding, unlike cohabitation. Also, cohabitation is not necessarily a first step toward marriage. In a recent study, researchers found that slightly more than 50 percent of cohabitation relationships eventually culminated in marriage, whereas 37 percent broke up and 10 percent were still ongoing at the time of the study (London, 1991).

Does cohabitation contribute to marital success? The evidence is mixed. Some studies show that cohabitation has little or no effect on marital adjustment, emotional closeness, satisfaction, and intimacy (Watson and DeMeo, 1987). But other studies indicate that couples who cohabit are more likely to divorce than those who do not (Bennett, Blanc, and Bloom, 1988). Apparently, partners who had cohabited were less satisfied with their marriage and less committed to the institution of marriage than were those who had not lived together before marrying. The researchers theorized that cohabitation may contribute to people's individualistic attitudes and values while making them more aware that alternatives to marriage exist (Axinn and Thornton, 1992; Thomson and Colella, 1992).

Many gay and lesbian couples establish *domestic partnerships*—household partnerships in which an unmarried couple lives together in a committed, sexually intimate relationship and is granted the same rights and benefits as married heterosexual couples (Aulette, 1994). Despite laws to the contrary, many lesbian and gay couples consider themselves married and living in a lifelong commitment. To make their commitment public, some couples exchange rings and vows under the auspices of churches such as the Metropolitan Community Church (the national gay church) and even some mainstream churches. At the time of this writing, the issue of legalizing same-sex marriage in Hawaii is winding its way through the court system and has not been resolved. If states begin to issue marriage licenses to same-sex couples, the number of domestic partnerships will no doubt decrease. One reason people prefer a legal marriage to a domestic partnership is that employee health insurance coverage and other benefits are offered to a legal spouse, although today some employers offer similar benefits to domestic partners.

▲ Dual-Earner Marriages

Over 50 percent of all marriages in the United States are *dual-earner marriages*—marriages in which both spouses are in the labor force. Over half of all employed women hold full-time, year-round jobs, and in a change from the past, more married women with young children are in the paid labor force. In 1995, 60.9 percent of all women with a child under age three were in the paid work force, and 77.3 percent of African American women with a child under age three were in the paid work force (U.S. Bureau of the Census, 1996b).

Many married women who are employed outside the household not only work at paid employment during the day but then go home to hours of domestic work and child care. Sociologist Arlie Hochschild (1989) refers to a women's dual workdays as the *second shift*—the domestic work that many employed women perform at home after completing their workday on the job. According to Hochschild, the unpaid housework that women do on the second shift amounts to an extra month of work each year. In households with small children or many children, the amount of housework increases (Hartmann, 1981). Across race and class, numerous studies confirm that domestic work remains primarily women's work (Gerstel and Gross, 1995).

In recent years, more husbands share some of the household and child-care responsibilities, espe-

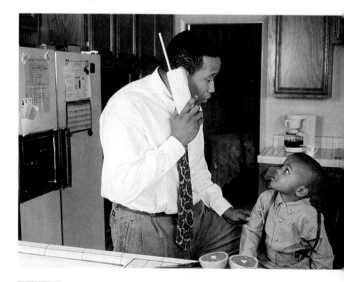

In the age of dual-earner marriages, it has become increasingly important for fathers to assume child care and household duties. How does this photo show the competing demands faced by many employed parents?

cially when the wife's earnings are essential to family finances (Perry-Jenkins and Crouter, 1990). But even when husbands assume some of the household responsibilities, they typically spend much less time in these activities than do their wives (see Coverman, 1989). Women and men perform different household tasks, and the deadlines for their work vary widely. Recurring tasks that have specific times for completion (such as bathing a child or cooking a meal) tend to be the women's responsibility, whereas men are more likely to do the periodic tasks that have no highly structured schedule (such as mowing the lawn or changing the oil in the car) (Hochschild, 1989).

Couples with more egalitarian ideas about women's and men's roles tend to share more equally in food preparation, housework, and child care (Wright, Shire, Hwang, Dolan, and Baxter, 1992). An *egalitarian family* is one in which the partners share power and authority equally. A trend toward more egalitarian relationships has been evident in the United States as some women gained new educational and employment opportunities. Some degree of economic independence makes it possible for women to delay marriage or to terminate a problematic marriage (O'Connell, 1994). For some men, the shift to a more egalitarian household occurs gradually, as Wesley, whose wife works full time, explains (quoted in Gerson, 1993:170):

> It was me taking the initiative, and also Connie pushing, saying, "Gee, there's so much that has to be done." At first I said, "But I'm supposed to be the breadwinner," not realizing she's also the breadwinner. I was being a little blind to what was going on, but I got tired of waiting for my wife to come home to start cooking, so one day I surprised the hell out [of] her and myself and the kids, and I had supper waiting on the table for her.

Problems associated with providing economic support for the family and rearing children are even more pressing in many one-parent households.

◣ Comparing Two-Parent and One-Parent Households

When the mother and father in a two-parent household truly share parenting, children have the benefit of two primary caregivers. Some researchers have found that when men take an active part in raising the children, the effect is beneficial not only for mothers and children but also for the fathers, whose increased contact with their children provides more opportunities for personal and emotional gratification (Coltrane, 1989).

However, living in a two-parent family does not guarantee children a happy childhood. Children whose parents argue constantly, are alcoholics, or abuse them have a worse family experience than do children in a single-parent family where there is a supportive environment. Women who are employed full-time and are single parents probably have the greatest burden of all; not only must they fulfill their paid employment duties and meet the needs of their children and the household, they often get very little help from ex-husbands or relatives.

How prevalent are one-parent households? The past two decades have seen a significant increase in one-parent households due to divorce, death of a parent, and births outside of marriage. Many more children under the age of eighteen are living with just one parent than was true a generation ago. In 1970, about 12 percent of all children lived with one parent; by 1995, 27 percent did (Seelye, 1997a). About 42 percent of all white children and 86 percent of all African American children spend part of their childhood in a household headed by a single mother who is divorced, separated, never-married, or widowed (Garfinkel and McLanahan, 1986).

Who heads most one-parent households? Today, 88 percent of one-parent families are headed by single mothers. Men are heads of about 17 percent of white one-parent families, 12 percent of Latino/a one-parent families, and 5 percent of African American one-parent families. Interestingly, a study of one-parent households headed by fathers after the mother died, left the family, or relinquished custody of the children found that most of the men had very positive relationships with their children (Risman, 1987).

What effect does a one-parent household have on children? According to one study based on six nationally representative data sets of over 25,000 children from various racial and social class backgrounds, children growing up with only one biological parent are at risk of serious problems, including poor academic achievement, high dropout rates, more drug and alcohol abuse, and higher rates of teen pregnancy, early marriage, and divorce

(McLanahan and Sandefur, 1994). Obviously, living in a one-parent family does not necessarily cause these problems. Factors such as poverty, discrimination, unsafe neighborhoods, and high crime rates must also be considered. In fact, other researchers have found some benefits to growing up in a one-parent family (Lauer and Lauer, 1991). For example, children in one-parent families are often less pressured to conform to rigid gender roles. Rather than having chores assigned by gender, as is common in two-parent families, single-parent children typically take on a wider variety of tasks and activities. Many single-parent children also show high levels of maturity and self-sufficiency earlier because they have to help out at a younger age than children in other families (Lauer and Lauer, 1991).

What about the fathers of children in one-parent households headed by women? Although some fathers remain involved in their children's lives, others become "Disneyland daddies," occasionally taking their children out for recreational activities or buying them presents on birthdays and holidays. Personal choice, workplace demands on time and energy, location of the ex-wife's residence, and limitations placed on visitation by custody arrangements are all factors that affect how often absentee fathers visit their children. As more parents are receiving joint custody of their children, it appears that joint custody can minimize the disruption of divorce in a child's life if the ex-spouses cooperate with each other and live in relatively close geographical proximity. Ex-spouses who constantly argue or live far apart from each other can create serious problems for "commuter" children, as author David Sheff (1995: 64) describes:

> My son began commuting between his two homes at age 4. . . . The commuter flights between San Francisco and Los Angeles were the only times a parent wasn't lording over him, so he was able to order Coca-Cola, verboten at home. . . . But such benefits were insignificant when contrasted with his preflight nightmares about plane crashes. . . . Like so many divorcing couples, we divided the china and art and our young son. . . . First he was ferried back and forth between our homes across town, and then, when his mother moved to Los Angeles, across the state. For the eight years since, he has been one of the thousands of American children with

two homes, two beds, two sets of clothes and toys, and two toothbrushes.

The transition from a two-parent to a one-parent family is only one of many child-related family issues that many people today must deal with, as we discuss in the next section.

CHILD-RELATED FAMILY ISSUES

One of the major issues facing many individuals and families today is reproductive freedom, which implies both the desire *to have* or *not to have* a child. As sociologists Leslie King and Madonna Harrington Meyer (1997:8) explain:

> The average woman is fertile, and therefore must attempt to control her reproductivity, for one-half of her life. For most women, it is the preoccupation with preventing births that consumes their health care dollars and energies; for a small minority, it is the preoccupation with achieving a birth that dominates. The ability to control fertility is, to a great extent, linked to access to various forms of reproductive health services, including contraceptives and infertility treatments. Yet, in the United States, insurance coverage of contraceptive and infertility treatments is fragmented.

Reproductive Freedom, Contraception, and Abortion

Reproductive freedom has been a controversial issue throughout much of U.S. history. In the nineteenth century, the government instituted formal, legal policies to ensure that some people would not produce children. By incarcerating "wayward girls" and limiting their right to marry and by passing laws to sterilize the poor, the criminal, or the "feeble-minded," political leaders attempted to prevent people who were thought to be "unfit" from reproducing (Luker, 1996). Now, say some researchers at the end of the twentieth century, the government discourages births among the poor by mandating coverage of contraceptives for women on Medicaid (King and Harrington Meyer, 1997).

Contraceptive devices such as condoms and diaphragms were widely available and relatively tech-

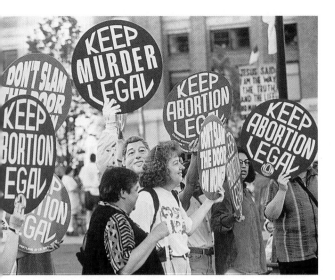

One of the most intense and ongoing public confrontations in the United States today is between abortion rights advocates and members of the anti-abortion movement. Look closely at this photo: Do you see anything unusual about the signs?

nologically sophisticated in the first half of the nineteenth century, but by the 1850s to 1860s, the government had established policies limiting their availability to prevent a drop in the birth rate among white Americans (Luker, 1996). These policies lasted into the twentieth century, but the introduction of the birth control pill in 1960 gave women almost complete control of their fertility. Within a few years, "the Pill" became the most popular contraceptive among married women in the United States. During the 1960s and early 1970s, public opinion about women's reproductive freedom also began to change somewhat. In 1971, the U.S. Supreme Court upheld women's right to privacy in reproductive matters in *Griswold* v. *Connecticut*. The Court ruled that laws prohibiting the use of contraception by married couples violated their constitutional right to privacy. In subsequent cases, the Court included unmarried adults and minors in this protection.

Today, many U.S. women spend about 90 percent of their fertile years trying to avoid pregnancy (Gold and Richards, 1994). An estimated 60 percent of women between the ages of fifteen and forty-four are using contraceptives at any specific time. The most effective forms of birth control, however, are the most expensive: Oral contraceptives cost about $300 a year, and five-year contraceptive implants average $500. In 1993, people in this country spent $1.5 billion for contraceptives (King and Harrington Meyer, 1997). Of the 6.4 million pregnancies in the United States each year, about 3.6 million (56 percent) are unintended, and about 2.8 million (44 percent) are intended (Gold and Richards, 1994). Unplanned pregnancies are usually the result of not using contraceptives or using contraceptives that do not work or are not used as intended.

As early as the nineteenth century, physicians—among others—crusaded to make abortion illegal because most procedures were done by people such as barbers who had no medical training. Some physicians believed that if these abortionists could be stopped, physicians would become the arbiters of whether or not women should have abortions. By 1900, most states had enacted laws forbidding abortion. Physicians continued to provide wealthy women with contraceptives and abortions, even though the ban was supposed to keep all women from practicing birth control or procuring an abortion (Luker, 1996).

Over the past three decades, the roles that government, religious organizations, physicians, and the legal establishment should play in these decisions continue to be highly controversial in this country. Perhaps the most significant legal action involving reproductive rights was the Supreme Court decision in *Roe* v. *Wade* (1973) that women have a constitutionally protected right to choose abortion and the state cannot unduly interfere with or prohibit that right. The court distinguished between trimesters of pregnancy in its ruling. During the first three months, decisions about the pregnancy are strictly private—made by women in consultation with their physicians; in the second trimester, the state may impose some restrictions but only to safeguard women's health; in the third trimester, the state may prohibit abortion—because of the viability of the fetus (the ability to survive outside a woman's womb)—except where necessary to preserve the woman's life or health.

Although the Court has not overturned *Roe* v. *Wade*, subsequent decisions have eroded some of women's reproductive rights and made abortion more difficult to obtain, particularly for poor women and unmarried pregnant teenagers. For example, in 1993 the Supreme Court ruled that requiring a minor to get written permission from both parents for an abortion did not constitute an "undue burden" for a fourteen- or fifteen-year-old girl. And as of this writing, members of Congress continue to argue over whether or not to ban partial birth (late term) abortions. Lack of consensus exists over how many partial birth abortions are actually performed and under what circumstances.

Opposition to abortion has also resulted in violence against physicians and personnel of clinics where abortions are performed, causing a number of facilities to close. But in 1993, Congress passed the Freedom of Access to Clinics Entrances Act, making it a federal offense to attack an abortion clinic or obstruct clients from going to one. In 1994, the Supreme Court ruled that organizers of violent protests against abortion clinics may be prosecuted under federal racketeering laws. Nevertheless, antiabortion activists continue to try to make it difficult for women to have abortions. The fear among some analysts is that if abortion is restricted, women will once again seek abortions in "back rooms" as they did in the era of illegal abortions when many women incurred life-threatening medical problems at the hands of illegal and often incompetent abortionists (see Miller, 1993; Messer and May, 1994). The Food and Drug Administration's recent approval of the drug RU-486, which is used for abortions in France, may reduce the number of direct confrontations between vocal—and sometimes violent—factions on all sides of the abortion debate (Rosser, 1994).

At the microlevel, abortion is a solution for some pregnant women and their families but a problem for others, particularly when they face religious or family opposition to their decision. At the macrolevel, abortion is both a problem and a solution when activists try to influence the making and enforcement of laws pertaining to women's reproductive rights and the control of new reproductive technologies.

Infertility and New Reproductive Technologies

Infertility is defined as an inability to conceive after a year of unprotected sexual relations. Today, infertility affects nearly 5 million U.S. couples, or one in twelve couples in which the wife is between the ages of fifteen and forty-four. In 40 percent of the cases, the woman is infertile, and in another 40 percent it is the man; 20 percent of the time, the cause is impossible to determine (Gabriel, 1996).

TABLE 12.1   FORMS OF ASSISTED REPRODUCTIVE TECHNOLOGY

Name	Description
In vitro fertilization (IVF)	Eggs that were produced as a result of administering fertility drugs are removed from the woman's body and fertilized by sperm in a laboratory dish. The embryos that result from this process are transferred to the woman's uterus.
Micromanipulation	Viewing the process through a microscope, a specialist manipulates egg and sperm in a laboratory dish to improve the chances of a pregnancy.
Cryopreserved embryo transfer (CPE)	Embryos that were frozen after a previous assisted reproductive technology procedure are thawed and then transferred to the uterus.
Egg donation	Eggs are removed from a donor's uterus, fertilized in a laboratory dish, and transferred to an infertile woman's uterus.
Surrogacy	An embryo is implanted in the uterus of a woman who is paid to carry the fetus until birth. The egg may come from either the legal or the surrogate mother, and the sperm may come either from the legal father or a donor.

Source: Gabriel, 1996.

Sexually transmitted diseases are a leading cause of infertility: Each year, 100,000 to150,000 women become infertile as a result of a sexually transmitted disease that develops into pelvic inflammatory disease (Gold and Richards, 1994). There are also some women—both married and unmarried—who would like to have a child but cannot because of disabilities. Still other women in lesbian relationships would like to be parents. Some analysts suggest that increasing demand for high-tech reproduction is driven partly by the large number of prospective parents who have delayed childbearing into their thirties and forties and partly by the recent advances in laboratory technologies.

About 50 percent of infertile couples who seek treatment can be helped by conventional, low-tech treatments such as fertility drugs, artificial insemination, and surgery to unblock fallopian tubes. The other 50 percent require advanced technology, sometimes called assisted reproductive technology (ART). Many middle- and upper-income couples, for example, receive in vitro fertilization (IVF), which costs between $8,000 and $11,000 per attempt (see Table 12.1). Despite the popularity of such treatments and the growth of fertility clinics (from 30 slightly over a decade ago to over 300 today), only one in five couples who receive ART actually become parents (Gabriel, 1996). For couples like Michael and Stephanie Plaut, who have spent three years and thousands of dollars trying to have a baby through IVF and other procedures, every unsuccessful attempt is traumatic. As journalist Felicia Lee (1996:A1) describes: "Michael Plaut answered the telephone . . . [and the] call confirmed his worst fear: the pregnancy test was negative. The Plauts sobbed, held each other and then had a glass of Scotch. 'It's like we're in a period of mourning,' Mrs. Plaut said. 'You just get to the point where you want this to be over.'" Couples like the Plauts, who have had their hopes raised by the new reproductive technologies only to find that they did not work in their case, often form support groups. Many couples finally decide to remain childless, but some adopt one or more children.

Adoption

Adoption is a legal process through which the rights and duties of parenting are transferred from a child's biological and/or legal parents to new legal parents.

Many parents who adopt one or more children also add to the racial and ethnic diversity of their household. What can children and adolescents learn from growing up with others whose background is not identical to their own?

The adopted child has all the rights of a biological child. In most adoptions, a new birth certificate is issued, and the child has no future contact with the biological parents, although some states have right-to-know laws under which adoptive parents must grant the biological parents visitation rights.

Matching children who are available for adoption with prospective adoptive parents can be difficult. The available children often have specific needs, and prospective parents often specify the kind of child they want to adopt. Consequently, although thousands of children are available for adoption each year in the United States, many move from foster home to foster home rather than being adopted because

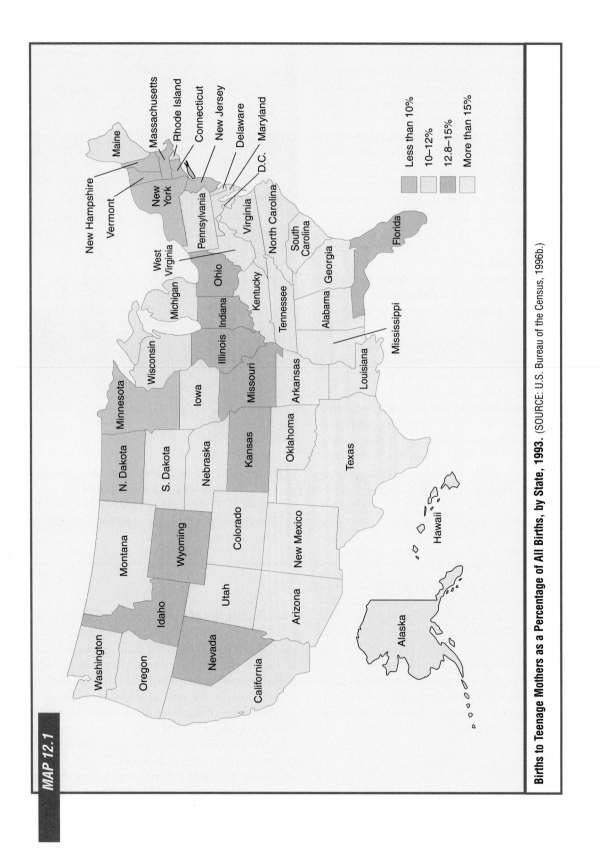

Births to Teenage Mothers as a Percentage of All Births, by State, 1993. (SOURCE: U.S. Bureau of the Census, 1996b.)

MAP 12.1

Less than 10%
10–12%
12.8–15%
More than 15%

prospective parents do not want to adopt children who are nonwhite (most prospective parents are white), older, or have disabilities or diseases (Zelizer, 1985). In addition, fewer infants are available for adoption today than in the past because better means of contraception exist, abortion is more readily available, and more unmarried teenage parents decide to keep their babies. Some teenagers, such as Christina, believe that adoption is the best way to solve the problem of early childbearing, however:

> I know I can't keep my baby. I can't give it all the things a baby needs and I sure can't dump it on my parents because they can't afford to take care of their own family. I've decided to give it up for adoption. I think it's better for the baby to give it up to parents who can't have a baby themselves. I think that I'm really doing a favor to my baby, although I'm always going to wonder what it looks like and what it's doing. (Luker, 1996:163)

Christina is one of many teenagers facing the realities of an early pregnancy and lack of resources to meet the child's needs.

Teen Pregnancies and Unmarried Motherhood

The teenage birth rate remains higher in the United States than in any other developed nation. Although the pregnancy rate among *all* female teenagers has actually decreased over the past three decades, the number of births among *unmarried* teenaged females has jumped from about 22 to 45 per 1,000 in the last two decades (U.S. Bureau of the Census, 1996b). About 500,000 children are born each year to girls aged thirteen to nineteen, three-fourths of whom are unmarried (Holmes, 1996a).

Despite the myth that most births to unmarried teenagers occur in the central cities of large urban areas, the greatest number of teen births occur in the South and in less urbanized areas (see Map 12.1). Similarly, although it is widely believed that teens from minority racial and ethnic groups are most likely to be unwed mothers, the majority of teen births occur among white teenagers. At the same time, given their relative numbers in the population, African American males and females are five times more likely than white teenagers to become unwed parents. One of the key factors behind this statistic is the poverty and lack of employment opportunity for African American males, as we discussed in Chapter 3.

According to social analysts, teen pregnancies are problematic because teenage mothers are typically unskilled at parenting, are likely to drop out of school, and have no social support other than relatives (Chase-Lansdale et al., 1992). Family support is extremely important to unmarried pregnant teens because spouse support is often lacking (Nath et al., 1991). Teen mothers rely on their own mothers and grandmothers to help with childrearing as well as to provide emotional and financial support for them and their children. As a result, many unmarried teenage mothers do not make the same transition from the family of orientation to the family of procreation that most people make when they become parents. The *family of orientation* **is the family into which a person is born and in which early socialization takes place.** When teenage mothers and their children live with their grandmother or another relative, they do not establish the separate family unit known as a *family of procreation*—**the family that a person forms by having or adopting children,** which married couples with young children create.

For teenage mothers without parental support, the picture is especially bleak because few have adequate parenting skills or knowledge of child development, and the long-term consequences for their children are grave. Children of unwed teenage mothers tend to have severely limited educational and employment opportunities and a high likelihood of living in poverty (Benokraitis, 1993). In addition, among teenagers who first give birth between the ages of fifteen and nineteen, about 43 percent have a second child within three years (Benokraitis, 1993). The future of these children is in even greater jeopardy today because of the 1996 welfare reform law that reduces assistance to single mothers with young children, especially unmarried mothers under age eighteen (see Chapter 2).

Teenagers are not the only ones having children without getting married these days. Since 1990 the birth rate for unmarried women between the ages of twenty and twenty-four increased to 68.5 births per 1,000, closely followed by that for women ages eighteen to nineteen (67.3 per 1,000). According to demographer Charles Westoff, these rates reflect "the declining significance of marriage as a social obligation or a social necessity for reproduction. Increasing proportions of white women who have not been married are deciding that having a child is more important than any kind of disapproval they might face" (quoted in Connell, 1995). With less of a social stigma attached to unmarried pregnancy, fewer women seem to be seeking abortion and are deciding instead to raise the child themselves whether the pregnancy was planned or not.

DIVORCE AND REMARRIAGE

Divorce is the legal process of dissolving a marriage that allows former spouses to remarry if they so choose. Have you heard such statements as "One out of every two marriages ends in divorce"? Statistics might initially appear to bear out this statement, but consider the following: Most sociologists use a statistic called the *refined divorce rate* to calculate the incidence of divorce. The number of divorces each year is divided by the total number of marriages in that year. According to the refined divorce rate, approximately 2.4 million marriages take place in the United States each year, and about 1.2 million divorces are granted. However, it is misleading to compare the number of marriages with the number of divorces from year to year because couples who divorce in any given year are very unlikely to come from the group that married that year. Also, some people go through several marriages and divorces, skewing the divorce rate because the likelihood of divorce goes up with each subsequent marriage.

Why do divorces occur? A number of factors contribute to a couple's statistical likelihood of becoming divorced, including the following:

◆ Getting married during the teenage years (Martin and Bumpass, 1989)
◆ Getting married after only a short acquaintanceship (Goode, 1976)
◆ Having relatives and friends disapprove of the marriage (Goode, 1976)
◆ Having limited economic resources and earning low wages (Spanier and Glick, 1981)

◆ Both partners having a high school education or less (Houseknecht et al., 1984)
◆ Having parents who were divorced or who had unhappy marriages (Goode, 1976)
◆ Having children present at the beginning of the marriage (Rankin and Maneker, 1985; Morgan et al., 1988; Martin and Bumpass, 1989)

These factors are, in turn, interrelated with such other factors as class, race, and age, so determining the likelihood of divorce is very complicated. For example, age is intertwined with economic resources because people from low-income families typically marry earlier than do people from more affluent families, raising the question of which factor is more closely associated with divorce—age or economic resources.

The relationship between race and divorce is also complex. Although African Americans are more likely than whites to get divorced, factors such as income level and the extent of racial discrimination in society must be taken into account. Latinos/as share some of the problems faced by African Americans, but their divorce rate is only slightly higher than the divorce rate among whites of European ancestry. Religion may affect the divorce rate of some Latinos/as who are Roman Catholic, although the divorce rate among Catholics is now approximately equal to the rate for Protestants (Lamanna and Riedmann, 1994).

Divorce law in many states once required that the partner seeking the divorce prove misconduct on the part of the other spouse. But under today's *no-fault divorce laws,* proof of blameworthiness is no longer necessary, and most divorces are granted on the grounds of *irreconcilable differences,* which means that a breakdown has occurred in the marital relationship and neither partner is to be specifically blamed.

Blame aside, divorce usually has a dramatic economic and emotional impact on family members. An estimated 60 percent of divorcing couples have one or more children. By age sixteen, about one out of every three white children and two out of every three African American children experience divorce in their families (Kurz, 1995). Furthermore, some children experience more than one divorce during their childhood because one or both of their parents may remarry and subsequently divorce again.

Divorce not only changes relationships for the couple and children involved but also for other relatives. Some grandparents feel that they are the big losers. To see their grandchildren, the grandparents have to keep in touch with the parent who has custody. In-laws are less likely to be welcomed and may be seen as taking the "other side" simply because they are the parents of the ex-spouse. Recently, some grandparents have sued for custody of minor grandchildren. They generally have not been successful except when there was some question about the emotional stability of the biological parents or the suitability of a foster care arrangement.

Most people who divorce remarry (Ihinger-Tallman and Pasley, 1987). In fact, in more than 40 percent of all marriages, either the bride, the groom, or both have previously been married. Among individuals who divorce before age thirty-five, about half remarry within three years of their first divorce (Bumpass, Sweet, and Martin, 1990). Most divorced people marry others who have been divorced (London and Wilson, 1988), though remarriage rates vary by gender and age. At all ages, a greater proportion of men than women remarry, often relatively soon after the divorce. Among women, the older a woman is at the time of divorce, the lower is her likelihood of remarrying (Wallerstein and Blakeslee, 1989). Women who have not graduated from high school and have young children tend to remarry relatively quickly. Women with a college degree and without children are less likely to remarry (Glick and Lin, 1986).

As a result of divorce and remarriage, complex family relationships often are created. **Blended families consist of a husband and wife, children from previous marriages, and children (if any) from the new marriage.** At least initially, stress in blended families may be fairly high because of rivalry among the children and hostilities directed toward stepparents or babies born into the family. In some cases, when parents divorce and marry other partners, the children become part of a *binuclear family,* living with one biological parent and a stepparent part of the time but with the other biological parent and another stepparent the rest of the time.

As sociologist Andrew Cherlin (1992) points out, the norms governing divorce and remarriage are ambiguous, so people must make decisions about family life (such as who should be invited to a birthday celebration or a wedding) on the basis of their own feelings about the people involved. But in spite of the problems, many blended families succeed.

FAMILY-RELATED PROBLEMS IN THE TWENTY-FIRST CENTURY

As we have seen, families and intimate relationships have changed dramatically during the twentieth century. Some people believe that the family as we know it is therefore doomed; others think that returning to traditional family values can save this important social institution and create a more stable society. Another point of view comes from sociologist Lillian Rubin (1994), who suggests that clinging to a traditional image of families is hypocritical in light of our society's failure to support the family, whether with family allowances or decent public-sponsored child care facilities (see Box 12.2). Some laws even hurt children whose families do not fit the traditional model. For example, welfare cuts affect children as well as the adults who are trying to provide for them.

Although many people demonstrate their faith in the future of the family as a social institution by choosing to have children, a macrolevel societal

Why is high-quality, affordable day care a pressing problem for parents and children in our society? How do other developed nations deal with this issue?

SOCIAL PROBLEMS
AND SOCIAL POLICY

BOX 12.2

Day Care: Jump-Starting the Stalled Revolution

- About 50 percent of all women with children under one year of age now work outside the home. (*New York Times,* 1997b)
- Sixty percent of women with children under six and 76 percent of women with school-age children are in the work force. (Hays, 1995b)
- Women make up 45 percent of the U.S. labor force. (Scarr, 1995)

In the 1960s, the women's movement sent women into the workplace, and in the 1970s, economic forces and changes in the family sent even more women looking for jobs. But, says sociologist Arlie Hochschild, we are in a "stalled revolution" (Smolowe, 1996). The need for good-quality child care far outdistances the availability, and most experts put that problem at the feet of government and business: "The workplace really hasn't changed much, and public policies haven't kept up with the social changes," says Paula Rayman, director of the Public Policy Institute at Radcliffe College.

The United States and Great Britain are the only two industrialized countries that do not provide tax-supported child care, and in recent elections in Britain, both parties have pledged reform (Scarr, 1995). Neither does the United States have national standards for child care; individual states set the ratio of children to caregiver, decide what job training (if any) is required, and regulate facilities.

As for business, with notable exceptions, most only talk a politically correct game. Several studies show that men with working wives are paid less and promoted less than are men with nonworking wives, apparently because they are not sufficiently visible at work (Mor-

ris, 1997). As companies try to do more with fewer people, the ideal employee is always available, not coming in late because of a sick child and unable to work through dinner and on weekends. According to Karen Nussbaum, Director of the Women's Bureau of the Labor Department, "We expect women and men to be at work, but we've made no provision for their children" (Hays, 1995b).

The problem is big, and it's not going to go away. In fact, it's going to get worse with increases in shift work and state and federal welfare reforms. According to the U.S. Department of Labor, one in five full-time workers works nonstandard hours in our increasingly twenty-four-hour, global economy (Hays, 1995b). At one time, only manufacturing and some service occupations required shift work, but today, banks and law offices routinely hire shift clerical help. Still, most day-care centers are open only 9 a.m. to 5 p.m., Monday through Friday. Parents—especially single parents—who work rotating schedules or on weekends are constantly scrambling among friends, relatives, home day care with extended hours, and standard day-care centers.

Moreover, the demand for odd-hour care will grow as more welfare parents enter the work force. According to Marianne Duddy, a child-care consultant in Boston, "If there's a job opening, it's going to be in that second shift in many communities, and that's going to force parents into the dilemma of 'What do I do with my children?'" (Hayes, 1995b).

What are we going to do about the work–family dilemma? What role should the government play in providing good-quality child care? What role should business play? What do you think?

commitment is needed, as sociologist Demie Kurz (1995:232) describes:

> As a society we should make a commitment to helping all families—traditional nuclear families, two-parent, two-earner families, and single-parent families—and to provide adequately for their members, particularly their children. To help families we must reduce female and male poverty, making special efforts to end institutionalized discrimination against minorities. We must also promote equality between men and women in the family. This includes creating new conceptions of what it means to be a father and what it means to be a partner in a marriage and share family life and household work. It also means taking decisive steps to end violence toward women and children. While the costs of creating humane and just social policies are high, the cost of failing to promote the welfare of family members is far higher.

SUMMARY

➡ *What is a family?*

A family is a relationship in which people live together with commitment, form an economic unit and care for any young, and consider the group critical to their identity. This definition modifies the traditional definition to account for today's greater diversity in living arrangements and relationships in families.

➡ *Are U.S. families in decline?*

Not at all, say analysts who take a social change perspective. Families are becoming more complex and diverse, adapting to other changes in society. For one thing, marriage is no longer a cultural imperative; for another, many people reaffirm their belief in the institution through serial monogamy, a succession of marriages over a lifetime.

➡ *What are the sociological perspectives on family-related problems?*

Functionalists believe that the family provides social order and economic stability; the family is the solution to many societal problems, and dysfunctional families threaten the well-being not only of individuals but of the whole society. Conflict and feminist theorists see the family as a problem in society, not a solution; they believe that the family is a major source of inequality in society. Interactionists view the family first in terms of socialization, and some speak of the shared reality of marriage. Some interactionists view family problems in terms of the subjective meanings that people give to their everyday lives; others cite partners' unrealistic expectations about love and marriage.

➡ *What characterizes singlehood in the United States today?*

The proportion of the U.S. population that has never married has continued to grow since the 1960s. Some people remain single by choice, others by necessity; many working-class young people cannot afford to marry and set up a household.

➡ *Why do young people postpone marriage today?*

Four factors are important: The changing job structure in the United States leads to economic uncertainty; more women are in the labor force; sexual relationships outside of marriage are more socially acceptable than before; and young people observing the rising divorce rate may be cautious about jumping into marriage.

➡ *Does cohabitation usually lead to a successful marriage? What is a domestic partnership?*

According to one recent study, only about 50 percent of cohabiting couples marry, and evidence on whether those marriages succeed is mixed. Some studies show little or no effect; others show that partners who cohabit are more likely to divorce than partners who do not. A domestic partnership is a household partnership in which an unmarried couple lives together in a committed, sexually intimate relationship and is granted the same rights and benefits as married heterosexual couples.

➤ *What does research show about dual-earner marriages?*

Over 50 percent of all marriages in the United States are dual-earner marriages, that is, marriages with both spouses in the labor force. Many women in these marriages do the domestic work at home after completing their workday jobs, a phenomenon known as the second shift, though there seems to be a trend toward more egalitarian families.

➤ *Is a two-parent family always preferable to a one-parent family?*

If the parents argue constantly, are alcoholics, or abuse the children, a supportive single-parent family is preferable. However, growing up in a single-parent household poses serious risks to a child that are complicated by other factors, such as poverty, discrimination, unsafe neighborhoods, and high crime rates. On the other hand, children in one-parent families are often more mature and feel less pressured to conform to rigid gender roles.

➤ *Why is reproductive freedom such a controversial issue?*

Reproductive freedom implies the desire to have or not to have a child, and the roles that religious organizations, physicians, and the legal establishment should play in controlling a woman's fertility continue to be debated. Contraception, abortion, and the new reproductive technologies all raise personal and—when activists on either side get involved—societal issues.

➤ *Are teen pregnancies increasing or declining?*

Teen pregnancies have decreased over the past thirty years, but the teenage birth rate is higher in the United States than in any other developed nation. Most unwed mothers are white teenagers, though given their relative numbers in the population, African American teens are five times more likely than white teens to become unwed parents.

➤ *Who gets divorced, and do most people remarry?*

Many factors affect who gets divorced (e.g., marrying during the teen years or having limited economic resources), and these factors are interrelated with class, race, and age, so it is very difficult to determine any kind of statistical likelihood of divorce. Most people do remarry, and divorce and remarriage leads to complex family relationships, such as blended families.

KEY TERMS

blended family, p. 269
cohabitation, p. 259
domestic partnership, p. 260
dual-earner marriages, p. 260
extended family, p. 252
family, p. 252

family of orientation, p. 267
family of procreation, p. 267
kinship, p. 252
monogamy, p. 254
nuclear family, p. 252
second shift, p. 260

QUESTIONS FOR CRITICAL THINKING

1. Sociologist Andrew Cherlin says that the family is a highly adaptable social institution, but we can minimize the costs of change in the family unit by modifying other social institutions of daily life, such as the economy and workplace. What specific suggestions can you give for modifications in these and other areas?

2. What do you think of Margaret Mead's proposal of a two-stage marriage? What problems might it forestall? Would it create any new ones?

3. What suggestions can you offer to help offset the potentially detrimental effects of single-parent households, especially when the parent is a woman who is employed full-time?

Chapter Thirteen

Problems in Education

One fateful day, in the second grade, my teacher decided to teach her class more efficiently by dividing it into six groups of five students each. Each group was assigned a geometric symbol to differentiate it from the others. There were the Circles. There were the Squares. There were the Triangles and Rectangles.

I remember being a Hexagon.

I remember something else, an odd coincidence. The Hexagons were the smartest kids in the class. These distinctions are not lost on a child of seven. . . . Even in the second grade, my classmates and I knew who was smarter than whom. And on the day on which we were assigned our respective shapes, we knew that our teacher knew, too. . . . We knew also that, along with our geometric shapes, our books were different and that each group had different amounts of work to do. . . . Not surprisingly, the Hexagons had the most difficult books of all, those with the biggest words and the fewest pictures, and we were expected to read the most pages. . . . What I had been exposed to, and in truth had benefited from, in that dusty elementary school was the educational practice of ability-grouping, or tracking. . . . it was tracking, along with the support of my family and my own effort and talent, that had ultimately carried me from a small farming town to [Harvard University]. . . . In essence, my ascension to the heights of academic privilege was orchestrated almost twenty years earlier by the well-intentioned grade school teachers and an assortment of odd geometric shapes. . . . Still, the more I learned about the insidious nature and harmful consequences of tracking, consequences even for its benefactors, the less I felt like thanking anyone.

—*Ruben Navarette, Jr.,
describes how he feels about
ability-grouping in his school*
(Navarette, 1997:275–276)

As Navarette explains, educational practices such as *tracking*—assigning students to specific courses and educational programs on the basis of their test scores, previous grades, or both—can have a positive effect on some students' educational achievements and aspirations but a negative effect on those of other students. Tracking benefited Navarette, but in racially integrated schools, it often harms Latinos/as, African Americans, and Native Americans. The harm isn't intentional. The United States and other industrialized nations highly value *education*—the social institution responsible for transmitting knowledge, skills, and cultural values in a formally organized structure. But a wide gap exists between the ideals of U.S. education and the realities of daily life in many schools. As a result, business and political leaders, parents, teachers, and everyday people tend to complain about the state of education in this country, even as many parents report feeling relatively positive about the particular schools their children attend. In this chapter, we examine problems in education, such as tracking, and analyze how issues in education are often intertwined with other social problems. We'll begin with an overview of sociological perspectives on problems in education.

SOCIOLOGICAL PERSPECTIVES ON EDUCATION

The way a sociologist studies education depends on the theoretical perspective he or she takes. Functionalists, for example, believe that schools should promote good citizenship and upward mobility and that problems in education are related to social disorganization, rapid social change, and the organizational structure of schools. Conflict theorists believe that schools perpetuate inequality and that problems in education are the result of bias based on race, class, and gender. Meanwhile, interactionists focus on microlevel problems in schools, such as how communication and teachers' expectations affect students' levels of achievement and dropout rates.

◢ Functionalist Perspectives

Functionalists believe that education is one of the most important social institutions because it con-

tributes to the smooth functioning of society and provides individuals with opportunities for personal fulfillment and upward social mobility. When problems occur, they can usually be traced to the failure of educational institutions—schools, colleges, universities—to fulfill one of their manifest functions. *Manifest functions* are open, stated, and intended goals or consequences of activities in an organization or institution. Probably the most obvious manifest function of education is teaching academic subjects, such as reading, writing, mathematics, science, and history. But education serves at least five major manifest functions in society:

1. *Socialization.* From kindergarten through college, schools teach students the student role, specific academic subjects, and political socialization. In kindergarten, children learn the appropriate attitudes and behavior for the student role (Ballantine, 1993). In primary and secondary schools, students are taught specific subject matter that is appropriate to their age, skill level, and previous educational experience. At the college level, students expand their knowledge and seek out new areas of study. Throughout, students learn the democratic process.

2. *Transmission of culture.* Schools transmit cultural norms and values to each new generation and play a major role in *assimilation,* the process whereby recent immigrants learn dominant cultural values, attitudes, and behavior so that they can be productive members of society.

3. *Social control.* Schools are responsible for teaching values such as discipline, respect, obedience, punctuality, and perseverance. Schools teach conformity by encouraging young people to be good students, conscientious future workers, and law-abiding citizens. However, controversy exists over whose values should be taught.

4. *Social placement.* Schools are responsible for identifying the most qualified people to fill available positions in society. Students are often channeled into programs on the basis of their individual ability and academic achievement. Graduates receive the appropriate credentials for entering the paid labor force.

5. *Change and innovation.* Schools are a source of change and innovation. To meet the needs of

student populations at particular times, new programs—such as AIDS education, computer education, and multicultural studies—are created. College and university faculty members are expected to conduct research and publish new knowledge that benefits the overall society. A major goal of change and innovation in education is to reduce social problems.

In addition to these manifest functions, education fulfills a number of *latent functions*—**hidden, unstated, and sometimes unintended consequences of activities in an organization or institution.** Consider, for example, these latent functions of education: Compulsory school attendance keeps children and teenagers off the streets (and, by implication, out of trouble) and out of the full-time job market for a number of years (controlling the flow of workers). High schools and colleges serve as matchmaking institutions where people often meet future marriage partners. By bringing people of similar ages, racial and ethnic groups, and social class backgrounds together, schools establish social networks.

Functionalists acknowledge many dysfunctions in education, but one seems overriding today: Our public schools are not adequately preparing students for jobs and global competition. In comparative rankings of students across countries on standardized reading, mathematics, and science tests, U.S. students are lagging. For example, in the 1996 International Mathematics and Science Study, a comprehensive study of science and math achievement by students in forty-one countries, U.S. students ranked slightly below average in math and slightly above average in science (Bagby, 1997). Countries that outperformed the United States in math included Singapore, where all students are tracked individually and expected to perform, and Japan, where teachers are generally better trained and prepared than their U.S. counterparts (see Box 13.1). Almost every top-ranked country has national educational standards set by the national government, unlike the largely decentralized educational system in the United States (Bagby, 1997).

▲ Conflict Perspectives

Sociologists using a conflict framework for analyzing problems in education believe that schools—which are supposed to reduce social inequality in so-

ciety—actually perpetuate inequalities based on class, race, and gender (Apple, 1982). In fact, conflict theorists such as Pierre Bourdieu argue that education *reproduces* existing class relationships (see Bourdieu and Passeron, 1990). According to Bourdieu, students have differing amounts of *cultural capital*—**social assets such as values, beliefs, attitudes, and competencies in language and culture that they learn at home and bring with them to the classroom.** Children from middle- and upper-income homes have considerable cultural capital because their parents have taught them about books, art, music, and other forms of culture. Children from low-income and poverty-level families have not had the same opportunities to acquire cultural capital. Some social analysts also think it is students' cultural capital—rather than their "natural" intelligence or aptitude—that is measured on the standardized tests used for tracking, and therefore some students' academic choices and career opportunities can be unfairly limited (Oakes, 1985).

Other sociologists using the conflict framework focus on problems associated with the hidden curriculum, a term coined by sociologist John C. Holt (1964) in his study of why children fail. The *hidden curriculum* **refers to the way certain cultural values and attitudes, such as conformity and obedience to authority, are transmitted through implied demands in the everyday rules and routines of schools** (Snyder, 1971). These conflict theorists suggest that elites manipulate the masses and maintain their power in society through a hidden curriculum that teaches students to be obedient and patriotic—values that uphold the status quo in society and turn students into compliant workers (Bowles and Gintis, 1976).

Although students from all social classes experience the hidden curriculum to some degree, working-class and poverty-level students are the most adversely affected (Ballantine, 1993). For example, when middle-class teachers teach students from lower-class backgrounds, their classrooms are very structured and they have low expectations about the students' academic achievement (Alexander et al., 1987). In one study of five elementary schools with students from different class backgrounds, researchers found significant differences in how knowledge was transmitted despite similar curricula (Anyon, 1980). Schools for working-class students emphasize procedures and rote memorization without much decision making, choice, or explanation of

SOCIAL PROBLEMS
IN GLOBAL PERSPECTIVE

BOX 13.1

Education in Japan: The Underside of Excellence

Everyone is still afraid of saying the truth: . . . that there are some things all students should know regardless of what state they live in.

—Bruce Alberts, president of the National Academy of Sciences (Applebome, 1996d)

Until recently, the education system was very uniform, producing children like manufactured goods.

—Michiro Iida, a teacher at Shingakai Educational Institute, a nationwide chain of cram schools in Japan (WuDunn, 1996)

In the United States, education is a local enterprise. States and local school districts decide on standards, set curricula, and assess— or do not assess—students' achievement. This system would seem to be just fine except that in international math and science tests, the United States ranks low in comparison to other modern, industrialized countries. Worse, some students graduate from high school barely able to read a menu or fill out a job application. Critics say that we need higher stan-

dards, which must be national standards backed up by a common nationwide curriculum that culminates in standardized achievement tests (Applebome, 1996d).

Countries that rank highest in international pupil achievement tests have national standards. Take Japan, which has nearly universal literacy and high school students who can solve complicated math problems. In Japan, at age three, sometimes earlier, children prepare for preschool entrance exams by entering their first of a series of cram schools—called *jukus*. Some jukus are national chains; others are held in small neighborhood apartments. The best are known only by word of mouth and charge more than $9,000 a year (WuDunn, 1996), but the discipline and thinking skills they teach set students on the path to a first-rate future. In Japan, the job you get depends on the university you attended, which depends on the high school you went to, which depends in turn on your elementary school, which, finally, depends on where you went to preschool. So to get into one of the best preschools, the sooner a child begins cramming, the better. Here's a scene from Keiokai Educational Institute, where three- and four-

why something is done a particular way. Schools for middle-class students, by contrast, stress the processes that are involved in getting the right answer. Elite schools develop students' analytical powers and critical thinking skills, teaching them how to apply abstract principles to problem solving. These schools also emphasize creative activities so that students can express their own ideas and apply them to different areas of study. Compare the following comments from students in high-track and low-track classes who were asked what they learned in a particular class (Oakes, 1985:86–89):

"I want to be a lawyer and debate has taught me to dig for answers and get involved. I can express myself." (High Track English).

"To understand concepts and ideas and experiment with them. Also to work independently." (High Track Science).

"To behave in class." (Low Track English).

"To be a better listener in class." (Low Track English).

"I have learned that I should do my questions for the book when he asks me to." (Low Track Science).

year-olds sit at little desks in a ninety-minute class designed to improve performance on IQ tests (WuDunn, 1996):

> The children followed the teacher's instructions: first, string as many colored beads as possible within two minutes; second, string only six beads or ten beads; third, string colored beads without letting two beads of the same color touch.
>
> Then the teacher pinned pictures of fruits on the blackboard, arranging them in a line. Which fruit is in the middle? Which is second from the left? Second from the right? Then the fruits were rearranged vertically and the exercise was repeated. To a U.S. student, a cram school for 3-year-olds may sound cruel, but many students enjoy the classes. That is not to say the system is perfect: Some Japanese parents and educators feel students become "trained seals"—mechanical thinkers—and there is a movement today to nurture more individuality and independent thinking.

Another problem comes from the competition for elite schools: "Preparation for entrance exams makes students turn everyone into rivals, so they come to find pleasure in another's failure," says one Japanese headmaster. "What is most important for human society [compassion] is not nurtured in Japan" (WuDunn, 1996).

Then there are the children who cannot function in the Japanese system: "school refusers"—children, as young as eight or nine, who will not go to school. They cannot handle the academic pressure, rigid dress and hairstyle codes, and corporal punishment during the day followed by cram school at night. Truancy is a growing problem, especially among junior high school students (Pollack, 1996b). Traditionally, truants have been considered psychologically ill and sent to strict private schools that taught discipline or to mental hospitals. With 210 beds, Tokyo Metropolitan Umegaoka Hospital is the world's largest psychiatric hospital devoted solely to treating truant students. Today, though, the Ministry of Education acknowledges that the school system itself may play a role in the problem, and one mother has even started an alternative school for truants (Pollack, 1996b).

Japan's educational system is admired throughout the world, but do Japan's children pay too high a price? On the other hand, how can the United States compete in the global economy of the twenty-first century without improving its children's academic performance? If state and local school districts don't seem able to accomplish the goal, should we adopt national standards? Is there, perhaps, a middle road—something between our current laissez-faire system and national tests—that would lead to academic excellence? What do you think?

As these comments show, the hidden curriculum makes working-class and poverty-level students aware that they will be expected to arrive at work on time, follow bureaucratic rules, take orders from others, and experience high levels of boredom without complaining (Ballantine, 1993). Furthermore, the limitations on what and how they are taught mean that many of these students do not get any higher education and therefore never receive the credentials to enter high-paying professions (Bowles and Gintis, 1976). Our society emphasizes *credentialism*—a process of social selection that gives class advantage and social status to people who possess academic qualifications (Collins, 1979). Credentialism is closely related to *meritocracy*—a social system in which status is assumed to be acquired through individual ability and effort (Young, 1994). People who acquire the appropriate credentials for a job are assumed to have gained the position through what they know, not who they are or who they know. According to conflict theorists, however, the hidden curriculum determines in advance that credentials will stay in the hands of the elites, so the United States is not a meritocracy even if it calls itself one.

◣ Interactionist Perspectives

Whereas functionalists examine the relationship between the functions of education and problems in schools and conflict theorists focus on how education perpetuates inequality, interactionists study classroom dynamics and how practices such as labeling affect students' self-concept and aspirations.

Interactionists believe that education is an integral part of the socialization process. Through the formal structure of schools and interpersonal relationships with peers and teachers, students develop a concept of self that lasts long beyond their schooling. Overall, social interactions in school can be either positive or negative. When students learn, develop, and function effectively, their experience is positive. For many students, however, the school environment and peer group interactions leave them discouraged and unhappy. When students who might do better with some assistance from teachers and peers are instead labeled "losers," they may come to view themselves as losers as well. **The process by which an unsubstantiated belief or prediction results in behavior that makes the originally false belief come true is termed a** *self-fulfilling prophecy.*

Not only can social interaction in the classroom lead to labeling, self-fulfilling prophecies, and low self-esteem, so can such taken-for-granted practices as standardized tests. In fact, say interactionists, standardized tests such as IQ (intelligence quotient) tests particularly disadvantage racial, ethnic, and language minorities in the United States (see Haney, 1993). IQ testing first became an issue in the United States in the early 1900s when immigrants from countries such as Italy, Poland, and Russia typically scored lower than immigrants from Northern Europe. When teachers therefore did not expect them to do as well as children from families with Northern European backgrounds and did not encourage them or help them overcome educational obstacles, some students from white ethnic groups did not do well in school (Feagin and Feagin, 1994). As a result, certain ethnic groups were stigmatized as less intelligent.

Today, the debate over intelligence continues, but the focus has shifted to African Americans. In their highly controversial book *The Bell Curve: Intelligence and Class Structure in American Life*, Richard J. Herrnstein and Charles Murray (1994) argue that intelligence is genetically inherited and people cannot be "smarter" than they are born to be, regardless of their environment or education. According to Herrnstein and Murray, certain racial-ethnic groups differ in average IQ and are likely to differ in "intelligence genes" as well. For example, they point out that on average, people living in Asia score higher on IQ tests than white Americans and that African Americans score 15 points lower on average than white Americans.

Many scholars have refuted Herrnstein and Murray's conclusions, but the idea of inherited mental inferiority tends to take on a life of its own when there are people who want to believe that such differences exist (Duster, 1995; Hauser, 1995; Taylor, 1995). Thus, on the basis of IQ testing and psychological evaluations, many minority students, particularly boys, are designated *learning disabled* and placed in special education programs. Nearly 75 percent of special education students are boys, and about 25 percent are African American (Bagby, 1997). Studies in California and Texas show that many African American and Mexican American children are placed in special education classes on the basis of IQ scores and other tests when their real problems are cultural influences and lack of English language skills and understanding (Brooks and South, 1996). Some analysts believe that 80 percent of students in special education classes are initially placed there because they do not know how to read (Bagby, 1997).

According to interactionists, labels such as *learning disabled* stigmatize students and *marginalize* them—put them at the lower or outer limits of a group—in their interactions with parents, teachers, and other students (Carrier, 1986; Coles, 1987). When educators label students, a self-fulfilling prophecy may take place if students believe that they are less intelligent and less capable than their peers. As a result, about 70 percent of special education students either drop out of school or are expelled (Bagby, 1997).

Labeling students *gifted and talented* may also result in a self-fulfilling prophecy. Students who are identified as having above average intellectual ability, academic aptitude, creative or productive thinking, or leadership skills may achieve at a higher level because of the label. This is not always the case, though. Girls who are identified as gifted may deny their intelligence because of cultural norms about the proper roles of women and men (see Eder, 1985; Eder and Parker, 1987). Afraid that their academic achievement will make them unpopular, high-achieving girls, and sometimes boys, can become victims of *anti-intellectualism*—hostility toward people who are assumed to have great mental ability or toward subject matter that is thought to require significant intellectual ability or knowledge. White students are overrepresented in gifted-and-talented programs, whereas students of color are underrepresented. For example, in Austin, Texas, African American students are five times less likely to be placed in gifted and talented programs than are whites (Brooks and South, 1996). As one social scientist put it, if students are not given equal opportunities for gifted education, it is "a mythology that schools represent the great equalizing force in society . . . [and] . . . every child has an equal chance at success and achievement" (Sapon-Shevin, 1993:43–44).

PROBLEMS IN U.S. EDUCATION

Although we have already identified a variety of problems in education, other issues must be addressed in planning for the future of this country. These issues include the problem of illiteracy; the impact of high rates of immigration on educational systems; race, class, and gender inequalities in educational opportunities; and growing concerns about violence in schools.

▲ What Can Be Done about Illiteracy?

In a book by Jonathan Kozol (1986:7), a mother described her reading problem: "Donny wanted me to read to him. I told Donny: 'I can't read.' He said, 'Mommy, you sit down. I'll read it to you.' I tried it one day, reading from the pictures. Donny looked at me. He said, 'Mommy, that's not right.' He's only five. He knew I couldn't read. . . . Oh, it matters. You *believe* it matters." Kozol uses this example to show how illiterate people make up a growing but largely invisible minority in our country. Today, one in four U.S. adults is *functionally illiterate*—**unable to read and/or write at the skill level necessary for carrying out everyday tasks.** Illiteracy is much higher for minority group members than for U.S.-born whites; 16 percent of white adults are illiterate, compared to 44 percent of adult African Americans and 56 percent of adult Latinos/as.

When functional literacy is measured not just in terms of reading words from a page but also in re-

Volunteers and trained professionals are an important link in reducing adult illiteracy. How can we make it easier for people to learn to read without experiencing embarrassment?

gard to such practical matters such as understanding a bus schedule, filling out a bank deposit slip, or computing the cost of having some work done, many more people qualify as illiterate. A 1993 U.S. Department of Education study concluded that nearly half (95 million people) of the adult population in this country was functionally illiterate when it came to tasks such as those just described (Kaplan, 1993). Astoundingly, many people who are functionally illiterate have graduated from high school. In the 1993 study, 50 percent of those who scored in the lowest 20 percent were high school graduates. Among urban high school graduates, 15 to 20 percent cannot read at the sixth-grade level (Kaplan, 1993).

Can illiteracy be reduced in the United States? In an effort to improve education and eliminate illiteracy in this country, Congress passed the Goals 2000: Educate America Act in 1994. One of the eight goals set forth was that every adult in this country be literate by the year 2000. Unfortunately, we have made little headway in reaching this goal—or the others (Bagby, 1997). Acknowledging that illiteracy is a social problem is an important first step in finding a solution, but so far, raising standards has been the primary approach. For example, the standards for high school dropouts seeking a high school equivalency certificate—known as General Equivalency Diploma (GED)—were raised in 1997 because current GED holders were not uniformly performing at the average literacy level. As one director at the American Council on Education, the Washington organization that oversees GED testing, explained: "With all the movement on higher standards and people in the workplace who were saying they were getting people who could not perform adequately, we could not make the claim that they could" (Arenson, 1997b:A18). Between 450,000 and 500,000 people take the GED exam annually, and individuals are allowed to take the test up to three times each year until they pass it (Arenson, 1997b). However, sociologists examining high dropout rates among Latino/a students found that some schools use the GED as a way to rid themselves of high-risk minority students who might instead graduate from high school if they were given the services and encouragement they need (Romo and Falbo, 1996).

Some social analysts believe that illiteracy will not be as big a problem in the future because new technologies will make reading and writing as we know it obsolete. That is, the information age increasingly depends on communication by computers, not on basic reading and math computation skills. Still other educators and community leaders believe that illiteracy can be overcome through televised instruction in basic skills and courses on the Internet. But not all social analysts believe that technology is the answer. As Jonathan Kozol (1986) points out, knowing how to read the printed word remains the access route to every other form of intellectual information. People need basic literacy skills before they can benefit from computers and other information technologies. Business and industry are playing a role in solving the problem; it is estimated that employers spend over $50 billion annually to educate functionally illiterate workers in the effort to increase their skill levels and productivity (Kaplan, 1993).

Some critics say that the illiteracy problem is largely an immigration problem. Recent immigrants to this country continue to speak their own languages rather than learn English. However, Kozol (1986) argues that high rates of illiteracy should not be blamed on U.S. immigration policies. According to Kozol, illiteracy is a home-grown problem that would exist even without immigration.

▲ Immigration and Increasing Diversity in Schools

Debates over the role of schools in educating immigrants for life in the United States are not new. In fact, high rates of immigration—along with the rapid growth of industrial capitalism and the factory system during the Industrial Revolution—brought about the free public school movement in the second half of the nineteenth century. Many immigrants arriving in U.S. cities spoke no English and could neither read nor write. Because of the belief that democracy requires an educated citizenry, schools were charged with the responsibility of "Americanizing" immigrants and their children. Workers also needed basic reading, writing, and arithmetic skills to get jobs in factories and offices. Initially, an eighth-grade education was considered sufficient for many jobs, but soon a high school diploma became a prerequisite for most jobs above the level of the manual laborer. Schooling during this era was designed primarily to give people the means to become self-supporting. Educational systems were supposed to turn out workers with the knowledge and skills needed to enter the labor market and produce profits for managers and owners.

In the second half of the twentieth century, this country is again experiencing high rates of immigration from many nations around the world, and many of the newcomers are school-age children (Portes and MacLeod, 1996). Though some of the recent groups of immigrants, including many Koreans and Asian Indians, are well educated, most people from other groups have limited formal education and few job skills. Moreover, about 14 percent of U.S. residents age five and older—or some 32 million people—speak a language other than English at home (see Table 13.1). Since we use language to communicate with others, develop a sense of personal identity, and acquire knowledge and skills necessary to survive, schools must cope with language differences among students.

Although most recent immigrants rely on public schools to educate their children, some also provide additional educational opportunities. For example, some Asian American parents have established weekend cram schools, which are similar to the *juku* in Japan, *buxiban* in China, and *hagwon* in Korea. Students spend a full day on subjects such as math and English and get specialized help in building

TABLE 13.1   PRINCIPAL LANGUAGES SPOKEN AT HOME (UNITED STATES)

Language Used at Home	Persons Five Years Old and over Who Speak It
English only	198,601,000
Spanish	17,339,000
French	1,702,000
German	1,547,000
Italian	1,309,000
Chinese	1,249,000
Tagalog	843,000
Polish	723,000
Korean	626,000
Vietnamese	507,000
Portuguese	430,000
Japanese	428,000
Greek	388,000
Arabic	355,000
Hindi (Urdu)	331,000
Russian	242,000
Yiddish	213,000
Thai (Laotian)	206,000
Persian	202,000
French Creole	188,000
Armenian	150,000
Navaho	149,000
Hungarian	148,000
Hebrew	144,000
Dutch	143,000
Mon-Khmer (Cambodian)	127,000
Gujarathi	102,000

Source: U.S. Bureau of the Census, 1996b.

study skills and learning test-taking strategies. The parents are willing to sacrifice so that their children will not experience the language and cultural barriers that limit their own opportunities (Dunn, 1995).

How best to educate children of recent immigrants with lower levels of education and income is a pressing problem in states that have high levels of immigration, such as California, Texas, Illinois, and New York. Some school districts establish transitional programs for newcomers, six months to four years of classes taught in English and in the student's native language (Belluck, 1995). Some schools offer bilingual education in as many as ten languages in major subjects such as math, science, and social studies. Preliminary studies of newcomer programs show that many children not only learn English and about U.S. culture, but also get help in overcoming traumatic experiences and educational deficits suffered in their country of origin.

Although some school officials believe that newcomer programs are the most efficient way to bring together students who speak the same language and teachers who can communicate with them, others consider them a form of segregation because recent immigrants are thus isolated from the mainstream (Belluck, 1995). Segregation is also still a problem for many students born in the United States.

Educational Opportunities and Race, Class, and Gender

Most research on access to educational opportunities for minority students has focused on how racially segregated schools affect student performance and self-esteem. Despite the 1954 Supreme Court ruling in Brown v. The Board of Education of Topeka, Kansas—which stated that "separate but equal" schools are unconstitutional because they are inherently unequal—some forty years later, racial segregation appears to be increasing in education rather than decreasing (Brooks and South, 1996). Progress in bringing about racial desegregation (the abolition of legally sanctioned racial-ethnic segregation) and integration (taking specific action to change the racial or class composition of the student body) has been extremely slow for African Americans because segregated schools mirror race- and class-based residential segregation. According to sociologists, racially segregated schools typically have high teacher–student ratios (more students per teacher), inexperienced teachers who are sometimes less qualified, lower expectations of students, and high dropout rates (Feagin and Feagin, 1994). Today, students of color comprise the vast majority of the student body in some urban school districts, whereas their middle- and upper-class white counterparts attend private urban schools or suburban public schools. For example, African Americans and Latinas/os make up 93 percent of the 24,000 public school students in Hartford, Connecticut, and 66 percent of these students come from families with incomes below poverty level (Gleick, 1995).

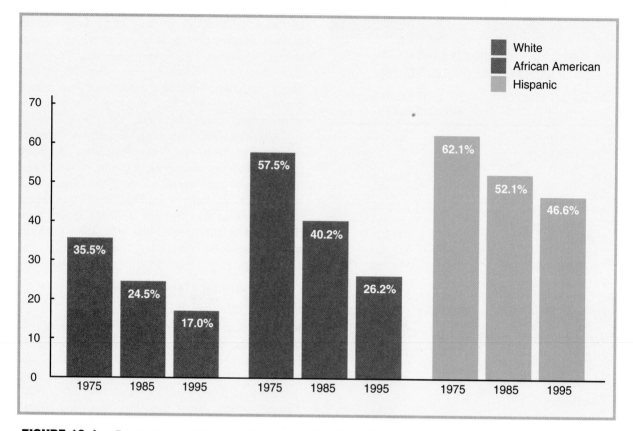

FIGURE 13.1 *Percentage of Persons Not Completing High School by Race and Hispanic Origin, 1975, 1985, and 1995*
(SOURCE: U.S. Bureau of the Census, 1996b.)

What are the future educational prospects for African Americans, Latinas/os, and other students of color? On the one hand, even with high levels of racial segregation in some areas of the country, the education gap between whites and African Americans appears to be narrowing; young African Americans are earning high school diplomas at about the same rate as their white counterparts (Holmes, 1996c). On the other hand, the President's Advisory Commission on Educational Excellence for Hispanic Americans recently concluded that segregation of Latina/o students in poorly funded schools contributes to Latino/a students' low educational attainment (Shannon, 1996). Latino/a students are more likely than white (Anglo) students to attend segregated schools where there are few Latino/a teachers to serve as role models and mentors. Although Lati-

na/o youth accounted for more than 12 percent of the public school population in 1994, fewer than 4 percent of public school teachers were Latinos/as. In fact, the faculty of most public schools does not reflect the racial-ethnic or gender composition of the student body. Both Latinas/os and African Americans are underrepresented among teachers, administrators, and school board members in most systems. About 85 percent of public school teachers are white (roughly the same proportion as twenty years ago), and nearly 75 percent are women.

Moreover, fewer Latina/o children have had the opportunity to attend preschool programs such as Head Start. The average Latino/a child has less well developed school-readiness skills—such as identifying colors and shapes—than do white (Anglo) children. As children move through high school and college, the dropout rate for Latinas/os between sixteen and twenty-four years of age grows dramatically: In 1993 it was 28 percent (Shannon, 1996). The percentage of Latinos/as who have not finished high school has been higher than have the white (Anglo) and African American rates over the past two decades (see Figure 13.1).

One explanation for the high dropout rate comes from a comprehensive study of Latino/a high school graduates in Texas. Researchers found that high dropout rates were more closely linked to practices in schools and attitudes within the community than to individual or family problems (Romo and Falbo, 1996). Across lines of race and ethnicity, students from poor families are three to four times more likely to become school dropouts than are students from affluent families.

Even racially integrated schools often recreate segregation in the classroom when they use tracking or ability grouping (Mickelson and Smith, 1995). Lower-level courses and special education classes are disproportionately filled with children of color, while gifted-and-talented programs and honors courses are more likely to be filled with white and Asian American students (McLarin, 1994). More-

over, even though roughly as many African Americans as whites are earning high school diplomas today, African American and white students do not achieve at the same level—and achievement differences increase with every year of schooling. The achievement gap between African American and white first-graders is less than the gap for twelfth-graders. According to some researchers, schools typically reinforce—rather than reduce—the effects of race and class inequalities in society (Mickelson and Smith, 1995).

In Chapter 4, we examined how gender bias in schools negatively affects female students. Contemporary gender bias has its roots in historical assumptions about the divergent roles of women and men in society, including the belief that males should be educated for the public sphere of work and civic involvement and females for the private sphere of home and childrearing. An extensive national survey on gender and self-esteem by the American Association of University Women (1992) found that young women and young men are treated differently in our educational system. First, teachers pay less attention to girls than to boys. For example, in scientifically observing thirty physical science and chemistry classes, researchers found that teachers encouraged boys to talk in class and to volunteer for demonstrations and experiments more often than girls; girls were more likely to be observers and to be self-conscious and quiet (Jones and Wheatley, 1990). Many teachers also encourage boys to be problem solvers by asking them more complicated questions than they ask girls. In these ways, and through reading materials, female students come to learn that they are less important than male students. Reading materials may use language in biased ways (e.g., using masculine pronouns throughout), or they may stereotype women or ignore them. Finally, since boys tend to be more boisterous than girls, classroom activities are geared to holding boys' interest and preventing boys from being disciplinary problems. Over time, differential treatment undermines females' self-esteem and discourages them from taking courses—such as mathematics and science—that are dominated by male teachers and students (Raffalli, 1994).

Some analysts believe that schools are "gender-sorting machines" that steer girls and young women into outdated female roles and contribute to permanently low self-esteem (Schrof, 1993). At best, low

To overcome gender bias in schools, some parents are now enrolling their children in same-sex schools such as this New York City public school that enrolls only girls.

self-esteem is associated with reduced expectations for the future and less self-confidence; at worst, it is associated with depression and sometimes even attempted suicide (American Association of University Women, 1992; Orenstein, 1994).

School Violence

According to the National School Safety Center, about fifty students are killed on school grounds during the school day during each academic year, and about 3 million felony or misdemeanor-level crimes are committed annually at school (Applebome, 1995a). Violence is a growing problem in schools throughout the country. In Washington, D.C., for example, a fourteen-year-old student was killed by two masked young people in the stairwell of one elementary school, a sixteen-year-old was killed just inside the entrance to another school, and two janitors were robbed by students at a third school (Janofsky, 1997a).

Not all school-related violence occurs in central city schools in large urban areas. Suburban and rural schools have experienced the same problems. Guns, knives, and other weapons have become more accessible to children and teens, while budget constraints limit supervision of students on school premises. Moreover, turf wars between rival gangs spill over into the schools in the form of drive-by shootings and other violence. Recent studies show that today's top high school students (with A and B averages) have a greater fear of unsafe schools than their counterparts of 25 years ago did (*New York Times*, 1995b).

Today, some school buildings look like fortresses or prisons with high fences, bright spotlights at night, and armed security guards. Many schools have installed metal detectors at entrances, and some search students for weapons, drugs, and other contraband as they enter. Consider this journalist's description of how one school district is attempting to reduce violence (Applebome, 1995a:A1):

> The sprawling new brick building next to the Dallas County Probation Department has 37 surveillance cameras, six metal detectors, five full-time police officers and a security-conscious configuration based on the principles of crime prevention through environmental design. It is not the Big

House. It is a schoolhouse: Dallas's $41 million state-of-the-art Townview Magnet Center.

Most educational analysts acknowledge that technology alone will not rid schools of violence and crime. Organizations such as the American Federation of Teachers have called for enhancing safety in schools by requiring higher student standards of conduct and achievement and giving teachers and administrators the authority to remove disruptive students from school. Some school districts now require students to wear uniforms in an effort to reduce violence, crime, and even truancy. The Clinton Administration advocates such a policy on the basis that young people are less likely to be killed for a pair of sneakers or for jewelry or designer clothes if all students are required to dress alike (Mathis, 1996). We do not know yet whether the positive effects of school uniforms outweigh the negative consequences—such as the embarrassment of poor families who cannot purchase the uniforms (Muto, 1995; Mathis, 1996).

Prison, airport, or school? Security guards and metal detectors have become an increasingly visible scene in many social institutions, including schools throughout the United States. Do such measures deter school violence? Why or why not?

Teachers, too, are the victims of violence on school premises. One study found that about 5,000 teachers are attacked or assaulted at schools each month; about 1,000 of the victims required medical attention (Applebome, 1995a). According to a spokesperson for one teacher's organization, "In the long run, we will not solve the problems of the schools by turning them into fortresses. But for the short term, we're going to have to cope with problems that are not immediately going away" (Applebome, 1995a:B8). Providing safety at school for students and teachers alike is only one crisis facing school districts that are burdened with shrinking budgets, decaying buildings, and heightened demands for services.

PROBLEMS IN SCHOOL FINANCING

Perhaps the biggest problem in education today is financial because that affects all other aspects of schooling. Although many people believe that the federal government makes significant contributions to public education, most funds come from state legislative appropriations and local property taxes. State and local governments contribute about 47 percent each toward total education expenses, and the federal government pays the remaining 6 percent, largely for special programs for students who are disadvantaged (e.g., the Head Start program) or have disabilities (Bagby, 1997). In recent years, however, local property taxes have been eroding in central cities as major industries have either gone out of business or relocated elsewhere. Similarly, many middle- and upper-income families choose to live in suburban areas that have a separate property tax base so that their children can attend relatively new schools that are equipped with the latest textbooks and computer technology, advantages that schools in central cities and poverty-ridden rural areas lack (see Kozol, 1991; Ballantine, 1993). However, in what many see as a controversial move, some corporations are now providing supplies and media technology to some schools (see Box 13.2).

At the same time that educational funds are growing more scarce, a record number of students are entering the nation's schools—51.7 million in 1996. According to the Department of Education, enrollment increases will continue through 2006, when 3 million more students than today will enter the public school system annually. But many schools are already overcrowded and in need of major repairs. A report on New York City's public schools, for example, noted that one school in the borough of Queens was so overcrowded that science classes were held in a boys' shower room off the gymnasium (Applebome, 1996c). This same report found that many buildings had crumbling brickwork, rotting window frames, and rusted steel beams that were about as resistant to stress as a chocolate chip cookie (Applebome, 1995b). According to the U.S. General Accounting Office, at least $112 billion is needed immediately for building repairs and upgrades in the nation's 80,000 schools (Bagby, 1997).

Is there a way to resolve problems of unequal funding among the states, among school districts within states, and among schools within school districts? In recent years, the federal courts have held some states accountable for the unequal funding that has resulted in "rich" and "poor" school districts. However, most proposals to improve educational funding have been limited in scope and seemed to benefit some groups at the expense of others. One plan—a voucher system—would give students and their families a specified sum of government money to purchase education at the school of their choice. Advocates of the voucher system say that the U.S. Department of Education should be eliminated and federal funds should be given to the states in the form of block grants that would then be dispersed as vouchers, approximately $1,000 per student regardless of family income. Schools would have to provide better-quality instruction at lower costs because they would be competing for students. However, critics argue that the voucher system would offer only a limited number of students better opportunities and would not resolve the larger problem of underfunded schools. Moreover, a fully operational voucher system might mark the end of public education in this country. As a result, some parents have formed organizations, such as Parents for Public Schools, to support public education and build alliances among parents from different races and economic backgrounds. Some of these groups focus on raising bond issues; others organize public rallies to call attention to problems in education (Applebome, 1997).

SOCIAL PROBLEMS

IN THE MEDIA

BOX 13.2

Channel One: Commercialism in the Classroom

The TV set is mounted atop the front chalk-board. Seated at desks facing the center of the classroom, most of the eighth graders peer sideways and upwards in the semidarkness. . . . [The Channel One logo appears.]. . . . Next, a few moments of rock music and music-video-style graphics. . . . Dissolve to Lisa Ling and Rawley Valverde, two casually dressed young anchors, in the game room–like Channel One news set. Mr. Valverde, talking forcefully and seriously—the Channel One anchor style—reports briefly on President Clinton's trip to an Asian Pacific economic summit in Manila. Cut to: commercials for M&M candies and Nintendo video games. . . . Then back to Ms. Ling, who introduces a mini-documentary [on] China.

> —Channel One at Pliny Haskell Junior High, Cerritos, California (Meisler, 1995)

Channel One is a television network that broadcasts ten minutes of news and two minutes of commercials daily to 8 million students in 12,000 public, private, and parochial schools—approximately 40 percent of the twelve-to-eighteen-year-olds in the country (Jayson, 1997). It was founded by Whittle Communications in 1989 and sold in 1994 to K-III Communications Corporation, which still owns it, for $300 million. The arrangement is simple: Schools agree to broadcast the twlelve-minute segment daily; in return they get a satellite dish and closed-circuit television system with a nineteen-inch TV for every classroom in grades six through twelve (paid for by the advertisers).

Since the beginning, though, Channel One has been controversial. Proponents say that two minutes of advertising is a small price to pay for bringing news and public affairs programming to students who often don't read newspapers or watch TV newscasts. Then, of course, there's the $25,000 worth of free equipment that most schools couldn't otherwise afford. Paulette Fuller, principal at Haskell Junior High, which no longer has sports teams or after-school activities because of budget cuts, says firmly, "We

Some analysts believe that the problem of underfunding could be solved by significantly reducing expenditures for administration and other noninstructional activities and using that money in the classroom. For example, spending on administration and other noninstructional functions grew by 107 percent between 1960 and 1984, but teachers' salaries dropped over 56 percent during the same period (Bagby, 1997). Problems in education are not limited to the elementary and secondary levels; higher education has its problems, too.

PROBLEMS IN HIGHER EDUCATION

Higher education serves several important functions in society: the transmission of specialized knowledge and skills, production of new information and technologies, and preparation of the next generation of professionals and scholars. But over the past decade, many public colleges and universities have become increasingly financially strapped as appropriations by state legislatures and federal funding have been like Channel One. The benefits greatly out-weigh the disadvantages" (Meisler, 1995).

What are the disadvantages? Are those two minutes of advertising really so awful? Yes, says social analyst Ellen Wartella. Business leaders may say they're becoming partners in education, but in actuality, they're becoming "partners in the increasing commercialization of American youth" (Wartella, 1995:451). Wartella isn't alone in her views. Edward Miller, former editor of the *Harvard Education Newsletter,* says that advertising to a captive audience of sixth- through twelfth-graders is an ethical issue: "By and large, educators are aware of these ethical issues, but . . . they are incredibly squeezed when it comes to resources and materials, and they'll take help where they can get it" (Stead, 1997).

Commercials are only part of the problem with Channel One. The media watchdog group Fairness & Accuracy in Reporting (FAIR) hired sociologist William Hoynes, an expert in analyzing news programs, to evaluate Channel One. Here are some of Hoynes's findings (Jayson, 1997):

◆ News is presented as drama, not reportage. The style is quick-cutting, like MTV, and, says Hoynes, "The news is filtered through youthful and very hip and attractive anchors. It becomes kind of a news drama that focuses on their lives and feelings."

◆ Racial and ethnic diversity is largely limited to the anchors. The news sources are not diverse. For example, Hoynes found that 69 percent of the sources were government officials or politicians, and they were primarily white males. Over half the African American sources were athletes or prisoners.

◆ Only one minute of every four is about breaking news. Political coverage is shallow, and economic coverage amounts to promoting consumption.

When Channel One was for sale in 1994, many parents, teachers, and social analysts hoped that the federal government would buy it and provide commercial-free news coverage. Unfortunately, that didn't happen, and the controversy continues. Is it immoral to sell tennis shoes and soda in the classroom? Or is two minutes of advertising a good trade-off for an educational tool that many schools couldn't otherwise provide? What about the other content problems—dramatization instead of reportage, bias in the news sources, and poor or slanted coverage? What do you think?

cut. In response, some schools have intensified their fund-raising efforts, pursuing corporations, non-profit foundations, and alumni. Many of these institutions have also had to increase tuition and student fees to remain financially solvent.

◢ The Soaring Cost of a College Education

A recent study by the College Board found that the increases in average yearly tuition for four-year colleges in 1996–1997 were higher than the rate of inflation (Bagby, 1997). Although public community colleges and state colleges and universities typically have lower overall costs than private colleges have, because they are funded primarily by tax dollars, some have grown too expensive for low-income students, particularly with the decline in scholarship funds and grants during the 1990s. Many students today must take out student loans and go into debt to attend college. Although some find part-time jobs, their earnings make only a small dent in the

Reprinted by permission.

cost of tuition and books. Students from more affluent families with two parents present are more likely to attend private colleges, where annual costs range from an average of $12,823 annually to more than $30,000.

Some social analysts maintain that a college education is still a bargain at about $90 a day for private schools and $35 for public schools, because students receive instruction, a room, and three meals a day, as well as athletic facilities, counseling, job placement help, and other services. But social scientists applying a conflict framework to the problem of soaring college costs say that the high cost of a college education reproduces the existing class system. Some students lack access to higher education because they do not have adequate resources, and those who attend college are stratified according to their ability to pay. Among people of color from lower-income families, Latina/o enrollment as a percentage of total college attendance increased from about 3.5 percent to 6.0 percent between 1976 and

1990. However, for African American men, college enrollment decreased from 9 percent in 1976 to 8.4 percent in 1990; for African American women, enrollment decreased from 11.5 percent to 10.6 percent. Also discouraging is the fact that Native American college enrollment rates have stagnated at about 0.8 percent between 1976 and 1990. The disproportionately low number of people of color enrolled in colleges is also reflected in later educational achievement. The underrepresentation of people of color among those receiving doctorate degrees is even more striking.

What can be done about the cost of higher education? Some colleges have tried to reduce tuition, but most say they cannot do this and provide the same level of instruction and services. Since most federal aid is in the form of loans, not outright grants, recent proposals have included a two-year, $1,500 annual tax credit for families with students in college and a cash grant for families with insufficient taxable income (Bagby, 1997).

The Continuing Debate over Affirmative Action

Affirmative action programs in higher education are the subject of much controversy among academics and nonacademics alike (see Chapter 3). These debates have continued in the court system and in public life since the 1978 U.S. Supreme Court decision in *Bakke* v. *The University of California at Davis*. In that case, Allan Bakke, a white male, was denied admission to the University of California, Davis, medical school even though he had a higher grade point average and Medical College Admissions Test score than some minority applicants who were admitted under a special program; 16 of 100 places in the first year class had been allocated to members of underrepresented minority groups. Despite the ruling that Bakke should be admitted, the Supreme Court left the door open for schools to increase diversity in their student population. But there is widespread ambivalence toward programs that take race, ethnicity, and gender into consideration for admissions, financial aid, scholarships and fellowships, and faculty hiring.

The affirmative action controversy intensified with the 1995 decision of the Regents of the University of California to discontinue any special consideration of "race, religion, sex, color, ethnicity, or national origin" as a criterion for admission; the passage of Proposition 209 in California, which is an even more sweeping prohibition of affirmative action; and the 1996 U.S. Fifth Circuit Court of Appeals ruling in *Hopwood* v. *State of Texas*. This case is named for Cheryl Hopwood, one of four white students rejected by the University of Texas law school who claimed that they were more qualified than some minority students who were admitted. According to the Circuit Court's ruling, the school's affirmative action policies discriminated against whites. The court also ruled that colleges and universities in Texas, Louisiana, and Mississippi (the states in the jurisdiction of the Fifth Circuit) could not use race as a factor in deciding which applicants to admit, even if the intention is to (1) achieve a diverse student body, (2) combat the perceived effects of a hostile environment, (3) alleviate a school's poor reputation in the minority community, or (4) eliminate any present effects of past discrimination by actors other than the school (*Texas Lawyer*,

1997). The U.S. Supreme Court refused to overrule the Fifth Circuit's decision that the school's affirmative action policies unconstitutionally discriminated against whites (Brooks, 1997).

Whether affirmative action policies will continue to apply to college and university admissions is uncertain. What does seem clear, however, is that minority enrollments have dropped in many schools that have reduced or eliminated affirmative action programs either voluntarily or on the basis of a court order. For example, after the *Hopwood* ruling, the University of Texas's admissions procedures changed, and minority applicants and enrollment dropped sharply. African Americans showed a 21 percent decrease, and Latinos/as showed a 17 percent decrease (Brooks, 1997). As a result, presidents and chancellors of major research universities who belong to the Association of American Universities issued a statement strongly supporting diversity in university admissions (*New York Times*, 1997a:A17). The statement reads, in part:

> We believe that our students benefit significantly from education that takes place within a diverse setting. In the course of their university education, our students encounter and learn from others who have backgrounds and characteristics very different from their own. . . . [A] very substantial portion of our curriculum is enhanced by the discourse made possible by the heterogeneous backgrounds of our students. . . . a significant part of education in our institutions takes place outside the classroom, in extracurricular activities where students learn how to work together, as well as to compete; how to exercise leadership, as well as build consensus. If our institutional capacity to bring together a genuinely diverse group of students is removed—or severely reduced—then the quality and texture of the education we provide will be significantly diminished.

According to spokespeople for the Association of American Universities, applicants for college admission cannot be evaluated solely on statistical definitions of merit such as academic grades and standardized test scores. They must also be assessed on the basis of unquantifiable human qualities and capacities such as their potential to become leaders in a diverse society (Arenson, 1997a).

What is the future of affirmative action in higher education? Some say that we must explicitly address problems of racial inequality in university admissions (Takagi, 1992). The areas to be examined include (1) minimum qualifications, (2) racial differences in academic achievement, and (3) race relations in campus academic, social, and political life. Admissions officers at some schools believe that minimum qualifications can be easily determined, but others—including elite private schools such as Brown, Harvard, Princeton, Stanford, and Yale—argue that minimum standards are not clear-cut and depend on other factors such as academic promise, motivation, and ability to grasp concepts and ideas. Even when schools decide to eliminate affirmative action in admissions, they usually do not dismantle "special talents" categories such as athletics, which is a crucial money-maker for many universities. Student athletes get special academic advising and help, whereas academic services for nonathlete members of racial minorities are very limited on many campuses (Takagi, 1992).

Racial differences in academic achievement should also be taken into account. For example, sociologist Dana Takagi (1992:203) points out differences in Asian Americans' achievement compared to that of other students:

How should admissions officers evaluate an Asian American with a below-average SAT verbal score, an above-average SAT math score, outstanding grades, and strong extracurriculars against others? Because grade point average is a better predictor of Asian American undergraduate grades than test scores, should the admissions officer weigh the high school grade point averages of Asian Americans more heavily than those of whites? The important issue underlying racial differences in academic achievement is whether selection decisions are based on a universal set of criteria or are keyed to the indicators of success for different racial groups.

Takagi believes that a social policy dealing with differences in the performance of students of different racial categories is preferable to simply ignoring the problem or denying its existence.

Finally, students of different races often self-segregate in academic, social, and political life, a tendency that some people view as symbolic of resentment among various groups. However, Takagi (1992:204) believes that such self-segregation is more accurately viewed as "the loss of language and hope necessary to talk and act on racial differences." If problems of racial inequality were dealt with more specifically, affirmative action might eventually cease to be a problem in higher education.

EDUCATIONAL PROBLEMS IN THE TWENTY-FIRST CENTURY

Many problems remain unsolved in U.S. education. Rising rates of illiteracy are so worrisome that some members of Congress are proposing plans to expand spending on literacy programs. Still, some analysts believe that the best models for fighting illiteracy can be found in local programs, such as Literacy Austin, that use volunteers to teach basic reading skills to adults (*Austin American-Statesman*, 1997b). Perhaps the best way to give the greatest number of people the opportunity to learn how to read and hence have more opportunities in society is to address illiteracy at both the national and local levels.

What about the problem of U.S. students who are not achieving at the levels of students in other developed nations? Initially, political leaders and educators sought to address the problem by developing Goals 2000, which included these eight education goals to be met by the year 2000:

◆ All children in the United States will start school ready to learn.
◆ The high school graduation rate will be 90 percent or higher.
◆ Students will leave grades four, eight, and twelve showing competency in challenging subject matter.
◆ American students will be the best in the world in mathematics and science.
◆ Every American adult will be literate.
◆ Schools will be free of drugs, guns, and violence.
◆ Schools will promote partnerships with parents.

◆ Teachers will have the means for professional development.

Progress has been limited, and in the case of two goals, we've lost ground: Drug activity and classroom disruptions have increased, and reading achievement among twelfth graders has declined. Some state governors, corporate leaders, and educators believe that these national goals are too broad and they should be implemented at the state and local levels. States and local school districts could jointly develop rigorous, concrete standards in basic subject areas, such as English, mathematics, and science. Then the local districts would be responsible for implementing plans that would bring students up to the standards (Applebome, 1996f). However, critics of both positions, national and local, point out that being first in the world in mathematics or science achievement does little for African American children in underfunded, drug- and crime-plagued central city schools or Native American children in substandard classrooms on U.S. government–run reservations.

Some parents are avoiding the problems of school safety and quality by home schooling their children. By the mid-1990s, home schooling was legal in every state, and the number of children being taught at home exceeded 500,000 (Gibbs, 1994). Some children seem to like home schooling or not know the difference because they have never attended school with other children. Others, such as Lydia Kiefer, age six, have mixed feelings about it: "Sometimes I like playing school. I'll get up in the morning, get my backpack, put some books in it, come downstairs, and sit down at my little brown table and pretend I have a teacher and other kids next to me. But I'm not so sure it would be so much fun in real life" (Gibbs, 1994).

Parents and children in a dozen states have become involved in the charter school movement, creating autonomous public schools. A charter school has full authority and is freed from the bureaucracy of a larger school district. Some charter schools have a special emphasis, such as science or special education; others offer the same curricula as other public schools but in an "improved," more creative version. However, many people believe charter schools create more problems than they solve because they take money away from already financially strapped, conventional public schools (Wallis, 1994).

In some cases, for-profit companies have been hired to operate public schools on a contract basis. For example, the Edison Project took over management of schools in Boston; Mount Clemens, Michigan; Sherman, Texas; and Wichita, Kansas. Initially, the project was hailed as a rousing success because academic performance improved and students received such extras as home computers. But now there is some question about for-profit corporations delivering the same quality of instruction over time. Demands from investors that profits increase are likely to result in cost-cutting measures and lack of public accountability (Applebome, 1996e).

Innovative approaches to improving the quality of public schools are being tried by individuals and groups across the country. For example, two professors at San Francisco State University became co-principals of an elementary school that educated needy urban children; they recruited minority students who were education majors at their university to serve as interns at the elementary school while earning their teaching credentials. Not only did the college students gain experience, the children's test scores went up and discipline problems went down as they were exposed to minority role models and given an improved curriculum and instruction (Nicklin, 1996).

What should education be like in the future? According to one analyst, the education we need for the future is different from what was needed in the past (Fenstermacher, 1994):

> For this education [in the future] is not bent on assimilation, to . . . melting . . . different cultures and languages into some common American pot, or to merely readying today's children for tomorrow's workforce. In contrast, the education that must engage us today and in the future is how to form common space and common speech and common commitment while respecting and preserving our differences in heritage, race, language, culture, gender, sexual orientation, spiritual values, and political ideologies. It is a new challenge for America.

As we approach the twenty-first century, we must not underestimate the importance of education as a social institution. It is a powerful and influential force that imparts the values, beliefs, and knowledge necessary for the social reproduction of individual personalities and entire cultures (Bourdieu and Passeron, 1990). But in what direction should this tremendous social force move? Some educators, parents, and political leaders believe that we should continue to focus on a core curriculum and instilling discipline in students. We must also provide safety and order in our public schools (Loury, 1997).

Others argue that education must prepare students for high-tech living in the next century. Learning to use the computer and learning to access information on the Internet and the World Wide Web are perhaps the most important skills schools can teach contemporary students (MacFarquhar, 1996). However, some experts strongly disagree that technology should be emphasized in education. Here is what author Clifford Stoll (1996:E15) says:

What's most important in a classroom? A good teacher interacting with motivated students. Anything that separates them—filmstrips, instructional videos, multimedia displays, E-mail, TV sets, interactive computers—is of questionable education value. . . . Yes, kids love these high-tech devices and play happily with them for hours. But just because children do something willingly doesn't mean that it engages their minds. Indeed, most software for children turns lessons into games. The popular arithmetic program Math Blaster simulates an arcade shoot-'em-down, complete with enemy flying saucers. Such instant gratification keeps the kids clicking icons while discouraging any sense of studiousness or sustained mental effort. . . . For decades, we've welcomed each new technology . . . as a way to improve teaching. Each has promised better students and easier learning. None has succeeded. Except that it is even more expensive, I suspect that classroom computing isn't much different.

Stoll—and others, no doubt—would endorse the following statement from Ennis Cosby, the late son of actor Bill Cosby, writing on why he was becoming a teacher (Cosby, 1997:E13):

First, I have a natural love for children, and children get along with me very well. It is one of those nonobservable variables that exists between me and children. I am far from being perfect, but I get along very well with most children.

Second, I believe in chances, so I do not give up on people or children. I know that if I have a class full of kids, I would want all of them to be successful students. I believe in finding solutions to any and every problem. I don't believe in quitting because of my academic experiences [with dyslexia]. With all of the chances I was given, I am going to give all of my students as many chances as they need to find themselves as students.

Third, I believe teachers need to bond with students. When I reflect on my favorite teachers in my life, they were teachers who were my friends, too. I see teachers wearing many titles besides TEACHER. I see psychologist, mother, father, friend and adviser. I believe students react to my behavior. The more I give of myself, the more they will give back to me. Fourth, I believe in a saying one of my favorite teachers told me: "Whatever you teach a child, it will not be digested completely by that student until they leave your classroom." I feel that learning is a slow process, and patience is a very crucial quality to have as a teacher.

Lastly, my best quality is that I am very personal with all students. I work with kids and try to make them feel that I understand them. I am very stern on good morals and manners. I am not old-fashioned. I just believe in respect, honesty and truthfulness. I feel that children will be better students if they become better people. . . . I believe in fairness within the [school] system. I just want all students to have an equal opportunity. I have a lifetime to devote to making the school system more balanced any way I can.

Unfortunately, we will never know what kind of teacher Ennis Cosby would have become; he was murdered as he changed a tire late one night on the side of a Los Angeles freeway. But perhaps other future teachers will pursue similar goals, helping individual students to succeed and thereby remedying problems in U.S. schools.

SUMMARY

➡ *What is education?*

Education is the social institution responsible for transmitting knowledge, skills, and cultural values in a formally organized structure.

➡ *What is the functionalist perspective on education?*

Functionalists believe that education contributes to the smooth functioning of society when it fulfills its manifest functions as an institution—the open, stated, and intended goals or consequences of its activities. Education serves at least five major manifest functions: socialization, transmission of culture, social control, social placement, and change and innovation. Schools also fulfill a number of latent functions—hidden, unstated, and sometimes unintended consequences of its activities.

➡ *What is the conflict perspective on education?*

Conflict theorists believe that schools, which are supposed to reduce inequality in society, actually perpetuate inequalities based on class, race, and gender. The sociologist Pierre Bourdieu, for example, says that children from low-income and poverty-level families come to school with less cultural capital—social assets such as values, beliefs, attitudes, and competencies in language and culture that they learn at home—than middle- and upper-income children. Conflict theorists also think elites manipulate the masses and maintain their power in society through a hidden curriculum that teaches students to be obedient and patriotic and thus perpetuates the status quo in society.

➡ *What is the interactionist perspective on education?*

Interactionists study classroom dynamics and how practices such as labeling affect students' self-concept and aspirations. If students are labeled "learning disabled" for example, the label may become a self-fulfilling prophecy, that is, an unsubstantiated or erroneous belief results in behavior that makes the false belief come true. A student who is erroneously labeled "learning disabled" may stop trying and teachers may lower their expectations, with the result that the student doesn't succeed in the long run.

➡ *What is illiteracy and what can be done about it?*

Functional illiteracy is being unable to read and/or write at the skill level necessary for carrying out everyday tasks. Today, one in four adults in the United States is illiterate; the problem is greatest among minorities. On the national level, the United States took action toward solving the illiteracy problem by passing the Goals 2000: Educate America Act in 1994, though progress in achieving the goals has been slow. At the local level, business and industry are taking a leading role, spending over $50 billion annually to educate functionally illiterate workers. Volunteer organizations that teach adults basic reading skills have been very successful.

➡ *Why are high rates of immigration a problem for U.S. schools?*

Though some immigrants are well educated, most have limited formal education and few job skills. Also, many immigrants are children, so schools must cope with language differences among students. Some school districts offer transitional newcomer programs with bilingual instruction, but critics say that these programs are a form of segregation.

➡ *How do race, class, and gender affect educational opportunities?*

The Supreme Court outlawed segregation in 1954, but segregated schools still exist because segregated schools mirror race- and class-based residential segregation. Racially segregated schools typically have high teacher–student ratios, less qualified teachers, lower expectations of students, and high dropout rates. Despite such disadvantages, young African Americans are earning high school diplomas at the same rate as white Americans. Latino/a students face many educational obstacles, including few school-readiness programs (like Head Start), few Latino/a teachers as role models, and high dropout rates. An extensive survey on gender shows that teachers treat boys and girls differently in the classroom, so females' self-esteem and life expectations suffer.

➤ *Why is violence a growing problem in our schools?*

This is a complex question, but one reason is that guns, knives, and other weapons are more accessible to children and teens than they used to be. Also, gang wars sometimes spill over into the schools. At the same time, schools have limited budgets for supervision of students on school premises. In response, many schools look like fortresses and use metal detectors and security guards to screen entering students.

➤ *What is the crisis in school financing?*

Most educational funds come from state legislative appropriations and local property taxes, but the eroding tax base in central cities leaves schools underfunded. At the same time, record numbers of students are entering the public school system, and many schools are overcrowded and need major repairs. One proposed solution is the voucher system, whereby families are given vouchers to "buy" edu-

cation at the school of their choice. But critics say that this plan would offer only a limited number of students better opportunities and still wouldn't solve the funding problem.

➤ *What are the major problems in higher education?*

The soaring cost of a college education is a major problem because, say conflict theorists, it reproduces the existing class system: Those who attend college are stratified according to their ability to pay. There is also the question of affirmative action. Should race, ethnicity, and gender be taken into consideration for admissions, financial aid, scholarships, and faculty hiring? While the debate continues, one thing is certain: Minority enrollments have dropped in many schools that have reduced or eliminated affirmative action programs either voluntarily or on the basis of a court order.

➤ *What are the urgent educational problems of the twenty-first century?*

To compete in the global economy, we must come to terms with illiteracy in our adult population and we must provide *all* children with safe, high-quality education. Some experts say that the best way to achieve both goals is to reframe the Goals 2000 program so that it can be implemented at the local level. Some parents, though, deal with issues of school safety and quality by home schooling their children or starting a charter school, an autonomous public school. Other innovative approaches are being tried by individuals and groups across the country.

KEY TERMS

cultural capital, p. 277
education, p. 276
functionally illiterate, p. 281
hidden curriculum, p. 277

latent functions, p. 277
manifest functions, p. 276
self-fulfilling prophecy, p. 280
tracking, p. 276

QUESTIONS FOR CRITICAL THINKING

1. Are you for or against school uniforms? What psychological effects of uniforms might improve student behavior and academic performance? What are the drawbacks to school uniforms?

2. What do you think of the Goals 2000 program? Is it realistic? Do you agree with all the goals? Are there others that should be added? Do you agree with the critics who say the goals are too broad? How do you reconcile this viewpoint with the fact that almost every top-ranked country in the 1996 International Mathematics and Science Study has national educational standards?

3. What creative solutions can you propose for the school financial crisis? That is, if the federal government doesn't increase its contribution and voters resist increased taxes, where can the state legislature find more money for education?

Chapter Fourteen

Problems in Politics and the Economy

I voted, although I know most in my generation didn't. I don't think it's from lethargy, but more so a general distrust of Washington.

—Amy Gwiazda,
screenwriter, New York,
New York
(quoted in Bagby, 1997:73)

—Nineteen-year-old
woman in author's
Introduction to
Sociology class,
Spring 1997
(author's files)

I voted because my mother told me to. Of course, I brush my teeth and go to church because my mother tells me to. But, I don't know what I'll be like when I move away from home.

I didn't vote in the [1996] election. . . . I've never voted. And, you know what? I was more excited about being old enough to drive or buy beer than I've ever been about being old enough to vote. [Pause] Especially for some old . . . in a fancy suit who rides in a limousine and is on the dole in Washington. You think those guys care about me? Hell, no! Well, I don't care about them either—as long as they don't do away with student loans until I get out of this place.

—Twenty-one-year-old
man in author's Introduction
to Sociology class, Spring
1997
(author's files)

What causes voter apathy? The answers are varied and complex, but some indications come from national opinion surveys that show that most people in the United States feel ambivalent about government. On the one hand, they think the federal government is too big, too powerful, and too unresponsive to their needs. At the same time, they look to the government to protect them from outside intervention, reduce crime and poverty, create jobs, and even provide student loans for college (Golay and Rollyson, 1996).

Why do we tend to hold contradictory views about the government? Is government the *cause* of our social problems or the *solution* to them? How does the economy figure into government policy and practice? What is the military-industrial complex, and where does it fit into the picture? These are the questions we examine in this chapter. We'll begin by making an important distinction between government and politics.

PROBLEMS IN U.S. POLITICS

Social scientists distinguish between politics and government: *Politics* **is the social institution through which power is acquired and exercised by some people and groups.** The essential component of politics is *power*—the ability of people to achieve their goals despite opposition from others (see Chapter 2). People who hold positions of power achieve their goals because they have control over other people; those who lack power carry out the wishes of others. Powerful people get others to acquiesce to their demands by using persuasion, authority, or force.

In contemporary societies, the primary political system is the *government*—**a formal organization that has the legal and political authority to regulate relationships among people in a society and between the society and others outside its borders.** The government (sometimes called *the state*) includes all levels of bureaucratized political activity such as the executive, central, and local administrations, the legislature, the courts, and the armed forces and police (Perdue, 1993).

The United States has a democratic political system. In a *democracy,* **the people hold the ruling power either directly or through elected representatives.** In a *direct participatory democracy,* citizens meet regularly to debate and decide issues of the day. Ancient Athens was a direct democracy, as was colonial New England with its town meetings. Even today, many New England towns use the town meeting. However, the United States has never been a direct democracy. From the beginning, the framers of the Constitution believed that decisions should be made by representatives of the people. To ensure that no single group could control the government, they established a *separation of powers* among the legislative, executive, and judicial branches of gov-

ernment and a *system of checks and balances*, giving each branch some degree of involvement in the activities of the others.

In a *representative democracy*, such as the United States (and other countries, such as Canada, Great Britain, and Australia), citizens elect representatives who are responsible for conveying the concerns and interests of those they represent. That is not to say that representative democracy is equally accessible to all people in a nation. The framers of the U.S. Constitution gave the right to vote only to white males who owned property. Eventually, nonlandowners were given the vote, then African American men, and finally, in 1920, women. Today, democratic participation is at least theoretically available to all U.S. citizens age eighteen and over.

In a representative democracy, if the government is not responsive to the wishes of the people, voters can unseat their representatives through elections. But today, voter apathy threatens to undermine the principles on which our government is based. Another problem facing the U.S. political system at the end of the twentieth century is influence-buying through campaign contributions. We'll look at voter apathy first.

▲ Voter Apathy and the Gender Gap

In 1996, fewer than 50 percent of eligible voters participated in electing the president and filling all 435 seats in the House of Representatives and 34 of the 100 seats in the Senate. Overall voter turnout was lower in 1996 than in the 1992 presidential election, even though the Motor Voter Law of 1995 had made it possible for 15 million people to register to vote when they applied for a driver's license (Bagby, 1997). What causes such voter apathy?

According to studies by the Pew Research Center for the People and the Press, many people did not vote in the election because of the strong economy (so they saw no reason to change their representation, though, of course, this is spurious reasoning), excessive polling by media and other groups (people saw no point to voting if the outcomes were predictable), negative advertising by candidates and parties, and issues that didn't seem as important as those in previous elections. On this last point, for example, a nationwide telephone poll conducted before the 1996 election by media analysts found that the U.S. economy and jobs were the top-priority issue of 11 percent of respondents; in a similar poll conducted before the 1992 election, the economy and jobs were the top-priority issue for 52 percent of respondents (*New York Times,* 1997c).

Along with voter apathy, the emergence and persistence of the *gender gap*—**the difference between a candidate's number of votes from women and men**—is a dominant feature of U.S. politics in the 1980s and 1990s. Political analysts first noticed a gender gap in the early 1980s, but it grew wider in the 1996 election. In 1980, the gender gap was about eight points (men were 8 percent more likely than women to support Ronald Reagan for president). In 1996, the gap increased to eleven points (women were eleven percent more likely than men to vote for Bill Clinton). For voters under age thirty, the gap was even wider: Women were 17 percent more likely than men to vote for Clinton. However, the gender gap narrowed in the forty-five to fifty-nine age category; women were only 8 percent more likely than men to vote for Clinton (Bagby, 1997).

Why is there a gender gap? Most analysts agree that the gap is rooted in how women and men view economic and social issues such as welfare reform, abortion, child care, and education—and what they believe the nation's priorities should be.

Voter apathy and an increase in the gender gap received attention after the 1996 election, but nothing like the scrutiny given to allegations of political influence-buying by large campaign contributors. We turn to this issue now.

▲ Politics and Money in Political Campaigns

Candidates for president and Congress and their supporters raised and spent more than $2 billion in 1996—almost double what was spent in the 1992 national elections (Rosenbaum, 1996). Where does all the money go? The cost of running for political office has skyrocketed. Advertising and media time, staff, direct-mail operations, telephone banks, computers, consultants, travel expenses, office rentals, and many other campaign expenses have increased dramatically over the past two decades. Unless a candidate has private resources, contributions greatly determine the success or failure of a candidate's bid for election or reelection.

Certain kinds of campaign contributions are specifically prohibited by law: Corporate contributions to candidates for president and Congress have been illegal since 1907, and contributions from labor unions were outlawed in 1943. In 1974 (in the Watergate scandal era), Congress passed a law limiting an individual's total contribution to federal candidates to $25,000 a year and no more than $2,000 per candidate. However, these individual limits can be sidestepped by *bundling,* which occurs when a donor collects contributions from family members, business associates, and others and then "bundles" them together and sends them to a candidate. For example, Steve Wynn, a major contributor to Bob Dole's 1996 presidential campaign, bundled money from family members and ninety-nine employees of firms he owns to give Dole a contribution of $78,300 (Gup, 1996).

Federal law also limits individual contributions to a political action committee to a maximum of $5,000. *Political action committees (PACs)* **are special-interest groups that fund campaigns to help elect (or defeat) candidates based on their positions on specific issues.** PACs were originally organized by unions to get around the laws that prohibited union gifts. Today, thousands of PACs represent businesses, labor unions, and various single-issue groups (such as gays and lesbians and environmental groups).

Finally, federal law limits contributions to political parties for campaigning to $25,000, but there is no limit on contributions to political parties for purposes of party-building, such as distributing "vote Democratic" or "vote Republican" bumper stickers or organizing get-out-the-vote drives (Rosenbaum, 1996). What happens in practice, however, is that the Democratic and Republican parties use these contributions to pay for administrative expenses and overhead, freeing up other party money to support candidates. This *soft money loophole*—contributing to a political party instead of to a specific candidate—was a particular issue in the 1996 election. In fact, most of the money donated to campaigns in the 1996 election came through the soft money loophole (Bagby, 1997). Table 14.1 shows how much money the twenty-five largest contributors donated to political parties and federal candidates in 1996. No doubt a large proportion of this money was given through the soft money loophole.

The Federal Election Commission—the enforcement agency that monitors campaign contributions—

◀ TABLE 14.1 THE 25 LARGEST POLITICAL CONTRIBUTORS

CONTRIBUTIONS TO REPUBLICAN AND DEMOCRATIC CAMPAIGNS OF ALL FEDERAL CANDIDATES, JANUARY 1, 1995, TO JUNE 30, 1996

Contributor[1]	Amount Donated[2]
Phillip Morris	2,741,659
AT&T	2,130,045
Association of Trial Lawyers of America	2,106,325
Teamsters Union	2,097,410
Laborers Union	1,938,250
International Brotherhood of Electrical Workers	1,821,710
RJR Nabisco	1,765,306
National Education Association	1,661,960
American Medical Association	1,633,530
American Federation of State, County, and Municipal Employees	1,616,125
United Auto Workers	1,592,298
Ernst & Young	1,590,215
National Auto Dealers Association	1,563,175
Food and Commercial Workers Union	1,510,395
United Parcel Service	1,479,581
National Association of Realtors	1,408,233
Machinists/Aerospace Workers Union	1,396,375
National Association of Home Builders	1,338,049
Marine Engineers Union	1,317,165
Atlantic Richfield	1,278,678
Lockheed Martin	1,272,153
Communication Workers of America	1,201,380
Goldman, Sachs & Co.	1,191,962
Joseph E. Seagram & Sons	1,190,200
American Bankers Association	1,122,909

[1] Includes contributions made by affiliates and subsidiaries.

[2] Includes "soft money."

Source: Data from Rosenbaum, 1996.

is considered "one of the most toothless agencies in Washington" (Cohn, 1997). Violations, when discovered, are typically not punished until some time after an election is over. As a result, a very small percentage of the U.S. population contributes extraordinarily large amounts to get their candidates elected:

> The Federal Election Commission's records indicate that in the first 21 months of the Presidential race, both parties took in nearly $470 million in "soft dollars." Republicans raised $274 million in soft money, significantly more than the Democrats, who raised only $195 million. These 21-month totals amount to more than double what was raised in the entire two years of the 1992 Presidential race. . . . To put things in perspective, 99.97% of Americans do not make political contributions over $200. In other words, .03% of the population has the strongest political influence. (Bagby, 1997:76)

During the 1990s, allegations arose that the Republican and Democratic national parties had accepted unethical and/or illegal campaign contributions. It was alleged that a Hong Kong businessman helped the Republican party raise money to take over Congress in 1994, but the most widely reported allegations of influence-buying by foreign governments, lobbyists, or interests involved the Democratic National Committee. According to media accounts, in the days and weeks prior to the 1996 election, President Bill Clinton and more than twenty-four members of Congress may have received donations from individuals associated with the Lippo Group, a powerful Indonesian banking group formerly headed by James Riady, a longtime friend and supporter of Clinton. The reports stated that the Lippo Group was hoping to buy influence with a number of government agencies and regulators that could help the group invest millions of dollars in a California bank (*Austin American-Statesman*, 1997a). Through the fund-raising activities of John Huang, a Commerce Department official who formerly worked for the Lippo Group, other foreign contributors also allegedly gave money to the Democratic National Committee, though the Committee returned the donations after information about them became public (*Austin American-Statesman*, 1997a). Also, an FBI investigation found that top Chinese officials may have approved financial contributions to U.S. politicians in an effort to influence votes on decisions affecting Chinese interests in this country and elsewhere (Woodward, 1997). But as one analyst recently noted, the Senate inquiry into campaign funding abuses merely proves "the dictum that politics stops at the water's edge" (Clines, 1997: A9). Because the Senate committee's authority stops at the Pacific Ocean, the trail of money from Asian contributors and others is lost when it reaches beyond the jurisdiction of U.S. officials. For example, senators cannot search foreign bank accounts or interview crucial witnesses who are not in the United States or who claim a constitutional right against self-incrimination (Clines, 1997: A9).

Are influence-buying and unethical campaign contributions recent phenomena? According to journalist Kevin Phillips (1995), influence-buying, particularly by representatives of foreign interests, has been taking place for some time in this country. Most political candidates and elected officials do not refuse such contributions or suggest campaign finance reform:

Were most senators and presidential candidates to refuse contributions from foreign lobbyists or interests, and then further refuse to let lobbyists for foreign interests raise money for them or serve on their campaign committees, the Washington lobbying community would receive a powerful message. This, however, was not an idea anyone ever wanted to discuss. Striking at an accepted culture is not how things are done. . . . A significant overhaul of campaign finance, unlikely through federal legislation, could also come, if it can come at all, from a broader uncorking of populist politics. . . . But attempts to change campaign finance and regulation of lobbyists too often resemble shooting paper clips at a tank because the system is so resistant. Massive infusions of direct democracy and blistering public discussion are the most plausible flamethrowers of change. (Phillips, 1995:247–248)

As Phillips notes, special-interest groups and lobbyists often have undue influence on political decisions and the outcome of elections. Though the general public largely realizes this is the case, people believe that they are powerless to do anything about it. When respondents in a recent Gallup Poll survey were asked, "Would you say the government is pretty much run by a few big interests looking out for themselves or that it is run for the benefit of all the people?," 76 percent of the respondents said they believed "big interests" ran the country, whereas only 18 percent believed the government operates for the "benefit of all," and 6 percent had no opinion (Golay and Rollyson, 1996). Although campaign finance reform appears unlikely at the federal level, voters across the country have passed state-level reform initiatives (see Box 14.1).

Government by Special-Interest Groups

What happens when special-interest groups have a major influence on how the government is run? Some special-interest groups focus on single issues such as the environment, gun control, abortion, or legislation that affects a particular occupation (e.g., the American Medical Association) or business (e.g., the National Restaurant Association). The Christian Coalition (which placed political pressure on Republican candidates to stay "right" on issues such as

SOCIAL PROBLEMS

AND SOCIAL POLICY

BOX 14.1

Campaign Reform: The States Take the Initiative

[T]he money flowing into the coffers of political candidates and political parties is staggering. It comes from corporations, wealthy individuals, political action committees and other interest groups—all with agendas that often are at odds with what is good for average Americans.

—Donald L. Barlett and James B. Steele of the *Philadelphia Inquirer* (1996)

It's a real movement that's beginning. People are just tired of money buying influence.

—Ben Senturia of the Missouri Alliance for Campaign Reform (Weiss, 1996)

In the wake of the 1996 elections, several campaign finance reform bills have been put before the U. S. House and Senate. The bipartisan McCain-Feingold bill, for example, seeks to close the soft money loophole, but not many believe that a Republican Congress will pass a bill that would limit their resources in the next presidential election.

Instead, say some reformers, we should strengthen the Federal Election Commission (FEC), the agency that is responsible for enforcing campaign laws. The six commissioners, who must approve all investigations and prosecutions, are "in perpetual deadlock" because each party appoints three commissioners (Cohn, 1997). Nonpartisan watchdogs would make more sense. So would electronic reporting of contributions. Currently, campaign contributions need be reported only monthly for presidential campaigns and quarterly for congressional campaigns; instantaneous electronic reporting would be much easier to monitor.

Other critics say that the only hope for campaign finance reform comes from the state level, where some progress is already evident (Weiss, 1996):

- In Florida, Minnesota, and Rhode Island, candidates who voluntarily agree to spending limits in a campaign receive public financing and media discounts.
- In California, candidates are allowed to receive larger individual gifts if they agree to spending caps.
- Oregon passed a law eliminating contributions from outside a candidate's district.
- Oregon, Missouri, and Montana passed legislation reducing the $2,000 federal limit per federal candidate to $100 to $500.

But even when campaign finance reform passes at the state level, it can be a matter of two steps forward, one back. Both of the Oregon laws and the Missouri law are being challenged in court.

Campaign finance reform is a difficult issue. Must we make sweeping national reforms to have any impact? For example, should PAC contributions to candidates be banned? Or should we cut out corporate welfare subsidies and use that money to publicly finance campaigns? The $60 billion a year in subsidies would more than cover the $2.7 billion spent in 1996 federal campaigns (Cohn, 1997). Or is it unrealistic to think that campaign reform can be legislated by campaigners—the same representatives and senators who will be out campaigning for reelection? Must we begin with average citizens at the state level? What do you think?

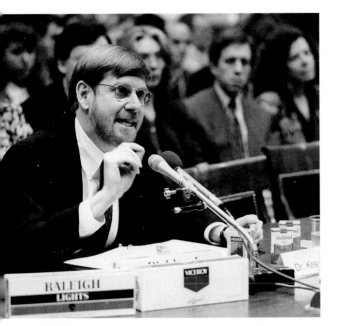

In one of the most intense political debates in U.S. history, cigarette manufacturers and anti-smoking advocates continue to debate regulation of the tobacco industry. Here, Commissioner David Kessler of the Food and Drug Administration discusses the nicotine content of various products and calls for full government regulation of nicotine as a drug. Why is this a major political issue in the United States?

abortion) and the AFL-CIO (a labor union that sought to influence candidates to take a prolabor stance on relevant issues) were among the best-funded and most politically active special-interest groups in the 1996 election (Bagby, 1997).

Other special-interest groups represent specific industries and make contributions to candidates who will protect their interests and profits. For example, representatives of the tobacco industry make significant contributions to members of Congress in states where tobacco is grown, including Virginia, North Carolina, Kentucky, Missouri, and Mississipi (Fisher, 1995). Officials from tobacco companies and their lobbyists also testify before congressional committees and attend administrative hearings conducted by various federal agencies, such as the Food and Drug Administration (about the effects of nicotine on health) and the Federal Trade Commission,

which polices advertising by tobacco companies (Kluger, 1996). The power of tobacco company lawyers, lobbyists, and other representatives was evident in 1997 when a federal judge in North Carolina ruled that the Food and Drug Administration could regulate nicotine as a drug but a spokesperson for the FDA said that the agency was not going to regulate the ingredients in cigarettes because so many people were already addicted to the product. In other words, as one journalist put it, "So officials are charting a delicate course. . . . the agency is keeping a watchful distance, focusing instead on how to negotiate the political minefield of tobacco regulation" (Stolberg, 1997b:A1). Although as this book goes to press it appears possible that some nationwide agreement may be reached regarding tobacco, some analysts have suggested that issues pertaining to the FDA and the tobacco industry will be tied up in the courts for years to come (Stolberg, 1997b).

Another strong lobby is the sugar industry, which makes major contributions to members of Congress in hopes of maintaining price supports, special loans, and protective restrictions on imports that help to prop up the price of sugar. The price of raw sugar in this country is about 21 cents a pound, roughly double the world price (*New York Times*, 1997d). Higher raw sugar prices translate into higher retail prices for U.S. consumers. Although the price support program may have kept some marginal sugar producers in business, its primary beneficiaries are corporations such as Flo-Sun, which is controlled by José and Alfonso Fanjul (Boller, 1997). The Fanjuls are major contributors to political candidates and to both the Democratic and Republican parties, though it is difficult to determine the amount they give because they bundle contributions from family members and company executives, give through PACs, and make large soft money contributions through companies they own or control (*New York Times*, 1997c). Estimates place their overall 1996 contributions at $902,580 (Boller, 1997), but according to the General Accounting Office, the sugar subsidy adds about 65 million dollars in annual profits to the Fanjuls' bottom line (*New York Times*, 1997d).

Of course, not everyone is represented by a special-interest group or a PAC. As one Senator pointed out, "There aren't any Poor PACs or Food Stamp PACs or Nutrition PACs or Medicare PACs" (quoted in Greenberg and Page, 1993: 240). Conversely, "big business" interest groups wield disproportionate power in U.S. politics, undermining the democratic process (Lindblom, 1977; Domhoff, 1978).

◤ Government by Bureaucracy

Special-interest groups wield tremendous political power, but so does the federal bureaucracy. The federal bureaucracy, or *permanent government,* **refers to the top-tier civil service bureaucrats who have a strong power base and play a major role in developing and implementing government policies and procedures.** Sociologists point out that bureaucratic power, in any sphere, tends to take on a life of its own over time, and this is evident in the U.S. government. The federal government played a relatively limited role in everyday life in the nineteenth century, but it expanded greatly during the Great Depression in the 1930s. Faced with high rates of unemployment and persistent poverty, people demanded that the government do something. Public welfare was instituted, security markets were regulated, and programs for labor–management relations were set in place. With better technology and people's demands that the government "do something" about problems facing society, government has continued to grow. In fact, since 1960, the federal government has grown faster than any other segment of the U.S. economy. Today, more than 3 million people are employed by the federal bureaucracy, in which much of the actual functioning of the government takes place.

Despite efforts by presidents, White House staffs, and various presidential cabinets, neither Republican nor Democratic administrations have been able to establish control over the federal bureaucracy (Dye and Zeigler, 1993). In fact, many federal bureaucrats have seen a number of presidents come and go. The vast majority of top-echelon positions in the permanent government have been held by white men for many years. Rising to the top of the bureaucracy may take as much as twenty years, and fewer white women and people of color have reached these positions in the federal government (Weiner, 1994).

The government bureaucracy is able to perpetuate itself and expand because many of its employees possess highly specialized knowledge and skills and cannot easily be replaced. In addition, as the United States has grown in size and complexity, public policy is increasingly made by bureaucrats rather than

elected officials. Offices and agencies have been established to create rules, policies, and procedures for dealing with complex issues such as nuclear power, environmental protection, and drug safety. These government bureaucracies announce about twenty rules or regulations for every one law passed by Congress (Dye and Zeigler, 1993). Government agencies receive little direction from Congress or the president, and while their actions are subject to challenge in the courts, most are highly autonomous.

The federal budget is the central ingredient in the bureaucracy. Preparing the annual federal budget is a major undertaking for the president and the Office of Management and Budget, one of the most important agencies in Washington. Getting the budget approved by Congress is an even more monumental task. However, as Dye and Zeigler (1993) point out, even with the highly publicized wrangling over the budget by the president and Congress, the final congressional appropriations usually are within 2 to 3 percent of the budget originally proposed by the president.

What role do special-interest groups play in influencing the federal bureaucracy? Special-interest groups can help an agency to get more operating money. Even though the president has budgetary authority over the bureaucracy, any agency that believes that it did not get its fair share can raise a public outcry by contacting friendly interest groups and congressional subcommittees. This outcry can force the president to restore funding to the agency or prod Congress to appropriate money that was not requested by the president, who may then go along with the appropriation to avoid a confrontation. Special-interest groups also influence the bureaucracy through the military-industrial complex.

THE MILITARY-INDUSTRIAL COMPLEX

The term *military-industrial complex* **refers to the interdependence of the military establishment and private military contractors.** The complex is actually a three-way arrangement involving one or more private interest groups (usually corporations that manufacture weapons or other military-related goods), members of Congress who serve on congressional committees or subcommittees that appro-

The U.S. Air Force F-117 stealth fighter has played a key role in the destruction of targets in nations such as Iraq. What are the benefits of having advanced military technologies such as this? What are the costs?

priate money for military programs, and a bureaucratic agency (such as the Defense Department). Often, a revolving door of money, influence, and jobs is involved: Military contractors who receive contracts from the Defense Department also serve on advisory committees that recommend what weapons should be ordered. Many people move from job to job, serving in the military, then in the Defense Department, then in military industries (Feagin and Feagin, 1994).

In the 1970s, sociologist C. Wright Mills (1976) stated that the relationship between the military and private industry was problematic and could result in a "permanent war economy" or "military economy" in this country. But economist John Kenneth Galbraith (1985) disagreed, believing that the threat of war is good for the economy. Government expenditures for weapons and jet fighters stimulates the private sector of the economy, creates jobs, and encourages spending. In other words, military spending by Congress is not an economic burden but a source of economic development because it provides jobs and contributes to the economy. It also enriches corporations such as McDonnell Douglas, Lockheed Martin, and Boeing that build jet fighters and other warplanes. According to one ex-

ecutive who has spent much of his career building jet fighters for the U.S. military, getting a 1 trillion dollar Pentagon contract for a new generation of jet fighters is of utmost important to his company: "It's the Super Bowl. It's winner takes all. It's the huge plum. It's the airplane program of the century. If you don't win this program, you're a has-been in tactical aircraft" (quoted in Shenon, 1996b:A1).

The 1997 federal budget allocated $244 billion for military programs, including $44 billion for weapons procurement and $800 million for two attack submarines and other major military systems. This budget also included funding for ongoing military operations in Bosnia and southern Iraq (Bagby, 1997). In budget negotiations, President Clinton and the Republican-controlled Congress agreed to $85 billion in military cuts over the five-year period from 1997 through 2002 (Stevenson, 1997). But many members of Congress actively support military spending, particularly if it benefits their local constituencies economically in the form of defense contracts or support for military bases or space centers. When members of Congress secure government funding for projects that will bring jobs and tax money to their home districts, it is called *pork barreling* (Greenberg and Page, 1993).

Despite the large sums in the federal budget for defense spending, the overall amount that we spend on defense is lower than it was in the 1980s. For example, the United States will spend only 3.6 percent of its gross domestic product—the total value of the nation's annual output of goods and services—on the military, compared to 6.3 percent in 1986 (Bagby, 1997). When the Cold War ended in the 1980s, the United States downsized its defense industries and found new markets for arms made by U.S. manufacturers. We are now the major supplier of weapons to the developing nations of the world; in fact, the United States and Western Europe combined provide over 75 percent of all arms transfers to developing nations.

From one point of view, the United States will always have an active military-industrial complex because of our emphasis on *militarism*—a societal focus on military ideals and an aggressive preparedness for war. The belief in militarism is maintained and reinforced by values such as patriotism, courage, reverence, loyalty, obedience, and faith in authority, as sociologist Cynthia H. Enloe (1987: 542–543) explains:

Military expenditures, militaristic values, and military authority now influence the flow of foreign trade and determine which countries will or will not receive agricultural assistance. They shape the design and marketing of children's toys and games and of adult fashions and entertainment. Military definitions of progress and security dominate the economic fate of entire geographic regions. The military's ways of doing business open or shut access to information and technology for entire social groups. Finally, military mythologies of valor and safety influence the sense of self-esteem and well-being of millions of people.

Problems with the military-industrial complex are intricately linked to problems in the overall U.S. economy, which we will examine now.

PROBLEMS IN THE U.S. ECONOMY

Like the political system, the U.S. economy has both strengths and problems. The *economy* **is the social institution responsible for producing and distributing goods and services.** *Goods* are tangible objects that people need (such as food and clothing) or want (such as high-definition television sets); *services* are intangible activities that people pay for (such as medical treatment or dry cleaning).

▲ Types of Economic Systems

To set the stage for our discussion of the U. S. economy, we need to look briefly at the three main types of modern economic systems: capitalism, socialism, and mixed economies. The U.S. economy is a form of *capitalism,* **which is characterized by private ownership of the means of production so that personal profits are derived through market competition and without government intervention.** Unlike capitalist economies, in which the primary motivation for economic activity is personal profit, the primary motivation in a socialist economy is the collective good of all citizens. *Socialism* **is characterized by public ownership of the means of production, the pursuit of collective goals, and centralized decision making.** For Karl Marx, socialism was only an intermediate stage to an ideal communist society in which the means of

production and all goods would be owned by everyone. Under communism, people would contribute according to their abilities and receive according to their needs. Moreover, the government would no longer be necessary, since it had previously existed to serve the interests of the capitalist class.

No economy is purely capitalist or socialist; most are mixtures of both. A *mixed economy* **combines elements of both capitalism (a market economy) and socialism (a command economy).** For example, Sweden, Great Britain, and France have mixed economies known as *democratic socialism*— an economic and political system that combines private ownership of some of the means of production with governmental distribution of some essential goods and services and free elections. Although most industry in mixed economies is privately owned, there is considerable government involvement in setting rules, policies, and objectives. The government is also heavily involved in providing services such as medical care, child care, and transportation. Debates about problems in the U.S. economy often involve comparisons of capitalism with other types of economic systems.

As we discuss problems associated with the U.S. economy, keep in mind the four distinctive features of "ideal" capitalism: private ownership of the means of production, pursuit of personal profit, competition, and lack of government intervention. First, capitalism is based on the right of individuals to own various kinds of property, including those that produce an income (e.g, factories and businesses). Second, capitalism is based on the belief that people should be able to maximize their individual gain through personal profit, which is supposed to benefit everyone, not just capitalists. Third, capitalism is based on competition, which is supposed to prevent excessive profits. For example, when companies are competing for customers, they must offer innovative goods and services at competitive prices. Finally, capitalism is based on a lack of government intervention in the marketplace. According to this *laissez-faire* (meaning "leave alone") policy, also called *free enterprise,* competition in a free marketplace—not the government—should be the force that regulates prices and establishes workers' wages. How do these "ideal" characteristics of capitalism compare with the realities of our economic system today? Let's look first at problems that arise from the concentration of wealth in the United States.

▲ Capitalism and the Concentration of Wealth

At the end of the twentieth century, corporate wealth has become increasingly concentrated. *Economic concentration* refers to the extent to which a few individuals or corporations control the vast majority of all economic resources in a country. Concentration of wealth is a social problem when it works to society's detriment, particularly when people are unable to use the democratic process to control the actions of the corporations.

The concentration of wealth in the United States can be traced through several stages. In the earliest stage (1850–1890), most investment capital was individually owned. Before the Civil War, about 200 families controlled all major trade and financial organizations. By the 1890s, even fewer capitalists—including such notables as Andrew Carnegie, Cornelius Vanderbilt, and John D. Rockefeller—controlled most of the investment capital in this country (Feagin and Feagin, 1994).

In early monopoly capitalism (1890–1940), ownership and control of capital shifted from individuals to *corporations*—**large-scale organizations that have the legal power (separate from individual owners or shareholders) to enter into contracts, buy and sell property, and engage in other business activity.** Because individual shareholders owning corporate stock cannot be held liable for the actions of the corporation, they are in a position to benefit from what the corporation does without losing personal assets. As monopoly capitalism grew, a few corporations gained control over major U.S. industries, including the oil, sugar, and grain industries. For example, John D. Rockefeller held a virtual monopoly on oil with his Standard Oil Company (Lundberg, 1988). A *monopoly* **exists when a single firm controls an industry and accounts for all sales in a specific market.** In early monopoly capitalism, some stockholders derived massive profits from such companies as American Tobacco Company, Westinghouse Electric Corporation, F. W. Woolworth, and Sears, which held near-monopolies on specific goods and services (Hodson and Sullivan, 1995).

In advanced monopoly capitalism (1940–present), ownership and control of major industrial and business sectors have become increasingly concentrated. After World War II, there was a dramatic increase in *oligopolies*—**overwhelming control of an** entire industry or service by a small number of companies or suppliers. Although over 300,000 corporations are headquartered in the United States, about fifty of them control over half of all corporate assets. These few large corporations use their economic resources—through campaign contributions, PACs, and lobbying—to influence the outcome of government decisions affecting their operations. Smaller corporations have only limited power and resources to bring about political change or keep the largest corporations from dominating the economy.

In advanced monopoly capitalism, mergers often occur *across* industries. That is, corporations gain near-monopoly control over all aspects of the production and distribution of a product by acquiring both the companies that supply the raw materials and the companies that are the outlets for their products. For example, an oil company may hold leases on the land where the oil is pumped out of the ground, own the refineries that convert the oil into gasoline, and own the individual gasoline stations that sell the product to the public.

Corporations with control both within and across industries often are formed by a series of mergers and acquisitions across industries. These corporations are referred to as *conglomerates*—combinations of businesses in different commercial areas, all of which are owned by one holding company. Media ownership is a case in point. Companies such as Time Warner and Viacom have extensive holdings in radio and television stations, cable television companies, book-publishing firms, and film production and distribution companies, to name only a few.

Competition is further reduced by *interlocking corporate directorates*—members of the board of directors of one corporation who also sit on the board of one or more other corporations. For example, former Defense Secretary Frank C. Carlucci sat on the corporate boards of fourteen Fortune 1,000 companies in 1996; Ann D. McLaughlin, the former Labor Secretary, sat on eleven; and Joseph A. Califano, Jr., former Secretary of Health, Education and Welfare sat on nine boards (Dobrzynski, 1996b). As these examples show, it isn't uncommon to sit on multiple corporate boards and have previously held a high government position.

Is it legal to sit on the boards of so many corporations at the same time? Although the Clayton Antitrust Act of 1914 made it illegal for a person to sit simultaneously on the boards of directors of two corporations that are in direct competition with each other, a person may serve simultaneously on the board of a financial institution (a bank, for example) and the board of a commercial corporation (a computer-manufacturing company or a furniture store chain, for example) that borrows money from the bank. Directors of competing corporations also may serve together on the board of a third corporation that is not in direct competition with the other two. The problem with such interlocking directorates is that they diminish competition by producing interdependence. People serving on multiple boards are in a position to forge cooperative arrangements that benefit their corporations but not necessarily the general public. When several corporations are controlled by the same financial interests, they are more likely to cooperate with one another than to compete (Mintz and Schwartz, 1985). Compensation for board members of top corporations ranges from $15,000 to $50,000 annually, plus stock, stock options, and pensions in the $100,000 to $400,000 range, making the total compensation package as high as $400,000 to $500,000 per board position (Dobrzynski, 1996b).

Although "ideal" capitalism is characterized by lack of government interference in the everyday operations of businesses, government has stepped in at times to keep individuals and companies from running roughshod over weaker competitors, workers, and the environment as they pursued higher profits. However, government regulations have had little impact on most transnational corporations.

Advertisements for U.S. products dot the global landscape. Today, Coca-Cola and Pepsi-Cola are waging a "cola war" in Vietnam and many other nations.

Transnational Corporations and the Lack of Accountability

Today, the most important corporate structure is the *transnational corporation*—a large-scale business organization that is headquartered in one country but operates in many countries. Some transnational corporations constitute a type of international monopoly capitalism that transcends the boundaries and legal controls of any one nation. The largest transnationals are headquartered in the United States, Japan, Korea, other industrializing Asian nations, and Germany. In the late 1990s, transnational corporations account for more than 25 percent of total world production. Not all large U.S. corporations that do business abroad are transnational; for example, General Mo-

tors doesn't qualify because only about one-third of its assets and one-third of its sales are outside the United States, and most of these are in other developed nations such as Canada, Europe, and Australia. Examples of true transnational corporations are Asea Brown Boveri, a Swiss-Swedish engineering group, and Philips, a Dutch electronics firm. Both have 85 percent of their sales outside the country where they are headquartered (Waters, 1995). Transnationals dominate in petrochemicals, motor vehicles, consumer electronics, tires, pharmaceuticals, tobacco, soft drinks, fast food, financial consulting, and luxury hotels (Waters, 1995).

Transnational corporations' shareholders live throughout the world; some have homes in four or five different countries. A large number of other people may own some stock, but they do not own control and so cannot participate in making decisions such as where to locate plants, how much to pay employees, or how to protect the environment (see Chapter 16).

Transnational corporations have grown in power and wealth over the past two to three decades, but analysts predict that future growth will be in the form of alliances between transnationals, not more transnational corporations. These alliances will include equity swaps, technology transfers, production licensing, and division of labor in manufacturing, assembling, marketing, and distribution of products and services. Some large corporations that specialize in information technology prefer global cooperation so that they will not be left behind. For example, over 100 semiconductor firms have international interfirm agreements to cooperate in research (Waters, 1995).

Transnational corporations raise some serious concerns. As big and powerful as they are, they play a significant role in the economies and governments of many countries. At the same time, by their very nature, they lack accountability to any government or any regulatory agency. Another concern is that transnationals do not depend on any one country for labor, capital, or technology. In the interest of greater profitability, they can locate their operations in countries where political and business leaders accept their practices and few other employment opportunities exist. For example, when Nike workers went on strike in Indonesia, Nike subcontracted to Korean entrepreneurs operating assembly plants in Vietnam, where employees work for bare-bones wages and, according to media coverage, plant managers physically abuse some of the women. Although many workers in developing nations earn less than a living wage from transnational corporations, the products they make are often sold for hundreds of times the cost of raw materials and labor. Designer clothing and athletic shoes are two examples of this kind of exploitation. Young women working in Nike factories in Indonesia and Vietnam, for example, go barefoot and cannot afford to buy the shoes they assemble (Goodman, 1996).

Still another concern is that transnational corporations foster global consumerism through advertising and strategic placement of their business operations around the world. McDonald's golden arches and Coca-Cola signs can be seen from Times Square in New York to Red Square in Moscow and in many other locations around the world (see Box 14.2). Both companies are conquering other nations as aggressively as they have the United States. Coca-Cola has 33,000 employees on its payroll, 70 percent of whom work outside the United States (Hardy, 1996).

The National Debt and Consumer Debt

Although a booming economy in the late 1990s helped to shrink the national debt, as of January 1997 it was still at $5.3 trillion. The *national debt* is the total amount of money the federal government has borrowed over the years from U.S. citizens and foreign lenders to finance overspending by the government. How much is the national debt in everyday language? According to political analysts, "If you laid the debt out in dollars from end to end, it would reach out into space four times the distance between the earth and the sun" (Bagby, 1997:47). What would it take to pay off the debt? Consider this: "If Congress paid down the deficit at a dollar every second, it would take 130,000 years, or roughly the amount of time that has passed since the Ice Age, to pay down the present debt" (Bagby, 1997:47).

But the United States isn't paying down the national debt; generally speaking, it becomes more indebted each year. For example, at the time of this writing, the projected 1997 federal budget deficit is 75 billion dollars, which amounts to about 1 percent of the gross domestic product (Sanger, 1997). Increases in the national debt actually mean that we are borrowing from future generations, which will leave them with higher taxes, fewer benefits, and a lower rate of economic growth. However, in 1997, Congress and the president took a step in the right direction by agreeing on a budget that will reduce annual deficits and move toward a balanced federal budget by 2002, meaning that the government will no longer spend more money than it brings in (Mitchell, 1997). The United States is not the only country borrowing from future generations with its deficit: Sweden, Italy, Germany, and Japan face similar problems (Bagby, 1997).

Like the federal government, many individuals and families in the United States are deeply in debt. Consumer debt rose significantly during the 1980s

SOCIAL PROBLEMS
IN GLOBAL PERSPECTIVE

BOX 14.2

Global Consumerism: Something for Everyone?

Chen Jingwen has a symbol of China's rising affluence tucked away near the dinner table in his two-bedroom apartment just outside Beijing.

It is an Ab-Rotor, a stomach exerciser he bought in September through a new television home shopping program for about $24, more than one-fifth of his monthly salary.

Mr. Chen, 33, a Communist Party member who works as a youth league organizer, reported just one glitch on his path to a trimmer stomach: he did not have a telephone to order the contraption. So instead of buying the product on impulse from home, he had to wait a day and make the call from his office.

"My next plan is I want to buy a jogging machine or a stationary bicycle, if the price is fair," said Mr. Chen, dressed in a new yellow warm-up suit and running shoes as he headed home after work to do some stomach crunches.

—From a report on China's new home shopping networks, which sell primarily Western goods (Hilsenrath, 1996)

The Chinese consumer market is largely undeveloped—but it won't be for long. With the demise of heavy industry in the United States, our major export is our consumer culture and its products (Ritzer, 1995:170). At the same time, economic success in any country—or even a hint of it—prompts consumption, which is fed by U.S. advertising. In Russia, for example, where Christmas has returned after seventy years, a twelve-foot Christmas tree in front of Moscow's biggest toy store "glimmers with unsubliminal advertising. It is trimmed with huge fake boxes of Nesquik, the Nestle chocolate powder" (Stan-

---

and 1990s; even more worrisome is that the ratio of consumer debt to income increased. According to a definitive study of bankruptcy, "the most distinguishing characteristic of bankrupt debtors is their high debts in relation to their incomes" (Sullivan et al., 1989:331). Although the increase in consumer debt may benefit the U.S. and global economies, it is detrimental to individuals who cannot pay their bills and must declare bankruptcy (Sullivan et al., 1989).

One factor contributing to high rates of consumer debt is the instability of economic life; especially problematic are unemployment and underemployment (see Chapter 1). Another factor is the extent to which credit card companies and other lenders extend credit beyond people's ability to repay

and the fact that people use this credit. For example, one study of credit card debt found that about 15 percent of wage earners owe more than half a year's income on credit card debt alone (Sullivan et al., 1989). Some people run up large credit card debts that are greatly out of proportion to their income; others cannot pay off the debts they initially believed they could afford when their income is interrupted or drops. For example, "Sally Bowman" (a pseudonym) explains how she ran up $20,000 in debt, a sum that is more than half her total yearly income:

It all started when I graduated from college and took a low-paying job. . . . I didn't want to live like a student so I used credit cards to buy myley, 1996). At Christmastime, billboards all over the city show Santa drinking Coca-Cola, and parents can buy their children nonalcoholic champagne in bottles decorated with Disney's Pocahontas and the Lion King.

Sometimes, though, U.S. business has to really work for its market share. In the 1960s, when Mattel, Inc., the world's largest toy company, introduced the Barbie doll to Japan, the world's second largest toy market, it was a crashing failure (Pollack, 1996a). Barbie was simply too threatening to Japanese girls and their mothers. So instead of a toothy smile, Mattel gave Barbie a closed mouth because, in Japan, many women still cover their mouths when they laugh. And instead of presenting her as a fashionable professional woman, Barbie was given a stroller for pushing baby sister Kelly, a more nurturing look that fit with Japan's family-oriented values. These changes helped to make Barbie a success, but not nearly as much as another factor: the simple passage of time and, with it, massive U.S. marketing of *everything*—from Levi's to Holiday Inn to Visa to Friskies cat food. Over time, as Japanese tastes became Americanized in general, Barbie became more popular (Pollack,

1996a). Today, in fact, Barbie has a cult following, young women can buy Barbie clothing, and the most popular weight-loss diet is "the Barbie diet."

Some critics see global consumerism in strictly negative terms, leading to global homogenization—the loss of cultural practices and distinctive features of a society (Ritzer, 1995: 173). But others say that along with homogenizing comes differentiating: If something can be sold in one locale, it can be sold in any locale (Waters, 1995:142). In other words, we're all enriched by global consumerism. Britishers may eat Big Macs instead of fish and chips, but Americans now eat fish and chips—and we drink Perrier mineral water, buy Chanel perfume, and drive Volvos, Toyotas, Volkswagens, and Hyundais. We import from other cultures just as other countries import American culture.

Where do you stand on the global consumerism debate? Do you think global consumerism leads to more homogenization or more differentiation? Is there any going back? That is, can global consumerism be stopped? If it can't be stopped, can it be controlled? Should it be controlled? What do you think?

---

self furniture and eat dinners out. I wasn't extravagant, I just didn't want to deprive myself. . . . When I got a new card with a $5,000 credit limit, it felt like someone just handed me $5,000. . . . The reality has been that I got in the hole financially. (Tyson, 1993:E1; cited in Ritzer, 1995:67)

Having a high level of consumer debt is a personal problem for people like "Sally Bowman," but it is also a public issue, particularly when credit card issuers negligently give fifth, sixth, or seventh credit cards to people who are already so far in debt that they cannot pay the interest on their other cards, much less pay off the principal they owe (Sullivan et

al., 1989). For example, one businessman had accumulated a total debt of $183,000 on forty-one cards when he received an unsolicited application for still another card, which he accepted and quickly "maxed out" at $5,000 (Ritzer, 1995). According to sociologist George Ritzer, both consumers and credit card companies must become more responsible if consumer debt is to be reduced so that fewer people end up in financial ruin. Ritzer (1995:71) is particularly critical of banks and credit card companies that entice students in high school or college to become accustomed to buying on credit, saying that it lures many people into a "lifetime of imprudence and indebtedness." He believes that the government should restrain credit card companies by limiting the

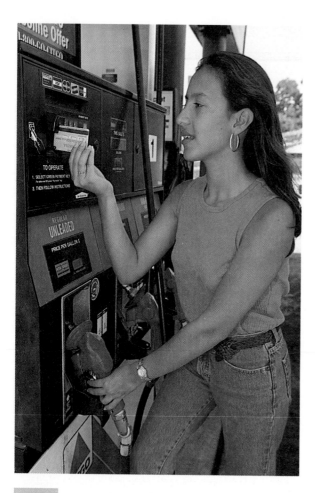

This photo shows an important irony in our consumer society. Just as credit cards and automated gasoline pumps make it easier for consumers to purchase gasoline, these same factors also have significant downside risks. One risk is a substantial increase in consumer debt. What are other risks affecting U.S. workers and the overall economy?

▲ Corporate Welfare

Corporate welfare occurs when the government helps industries and private corporations in their economic pursuits (see Chapter 2). Corporate welfare is not new in the United States. Between 1850 and 1900, corporations received government assistance in the form of public subsidies and protection from competition by tariffs, patents, and trademarks. The federal government also gave large tracts of land to the privately owned railroads to encourage westward expansion, and antitrust laws that were originally intended to break up monopolies were used instead against labor unions that supported workers' interests (Parenti, 1988).

Today, government intervention includes billions of dollars in subsidies to farmers, tax credits for corporations, and large subsidies or loan guarantees to auto makers, aircraft companies, railroads, and others. Overall, most corporations have gained much more than they have lost as a result of government involvement in the economy. For example, U.S. taxpayers have spent $1 million promoting Uncle Ben's rice in Poland, Turkey, and Saudi Arabia and $2 billion to help keep electric power a bargain in resort communities like Aspen, Colorado, and Hilton Head, South Carolina (Tumulty, 1996). In 1996, government subsidies included $1.1 million to Campbell Soup for product promotion, $2.6 million to E & J Gallo Winery for product promotion, and $3 million to a cargo ship owner for making his vessel available to the United States during wartime even though the Pentagon no longer wants to use it (Tumulty, 1996).

Why do we have corporate welfare programs today? Some can be traced back to the Great Depression in the 1930s, when programs were initiated to bail out companies and stabilize the U.S. economy. Today, for example, federal subsidies in the billions are given to the shipbuilding industry to protect it from foreign competition and appease maritime unions that want to salvage high-paying jobs for workers. But even existing ships have difficulty making a profit, so it hardly makes sense to build new ones. Some analysts say that the subsidies continue because of labor union lobbies and because PACs representing the shipbuilding industry have contributed more than $17 million to congressional campaigns (Tumulty, 1996). As a result, many members of

profits they can make and by restricting mail and telephone campaigns offering incentives to accept new credit cards (Ritzer, 1995). But many people are adamantly opposed to any kind of government intervention in the marketplace, whether it relates to credit cards or anything else. Of course, what some refer to as "government intervention" is considered corporate welfare for businesses by others.

Congress find it is easier to cut back on domestic spending and medical programs such as Medicare and Medicaid than to cut corporate handouts totaling as much as $75 billion a year, or almost half the federal deficit (Tumulty, 1996).

SOCIOLOGICAL PERSPECTIVES ON THE POLITICAL ECONOMY

Politics and the economy are so intertwined in the United States that many social scientists speak of the two as a single entity, the *political economy*. At issue for most social scientists is whether political and economic power are concentrated in the hands of the few or distributed among the many in this country. On the one hand, functionalists adopt a pluralistic model of power, while conflict theorists adopt an elitist model.

The Functionalist Perspective

Pluralism is rooted in the functionalist perspective, which assumes that people generally agree on the most important societal concerns, including freedom and security, and that the government fulfills important functions in these two regards that no other institution can fulfill. According to the early functionalists, government serves to socialize people to be good citizens, regulate the economy so that it operates effectively, and provide necessary services for citizens (Durkheim, 1933/1893). Contemporary functionalists identify four similar functions: A government maintains law and order, plans society and coordinates other institutions, meets social needs, and handles international relations, including warfare.

But what happens when people do not agree on specific issues or concerns? Functionalists say that divergent viewpoints lead to political pluralism; that is, when competing interests or viewpoints arise, government arbitrates. Thus, according to the *pluralist model*, **power is widely dispersed throughout many competing interest groups in our political system** (Dahl, 1961). In the pluralist model, (1) political leaders make decisions on behalf of the people through a process of bargaining, accommodation, and compromise; (2) leadership groups (such as business, labor, law, and consumer organizations) serve as watchdogs to protect ordinary people from the abuses of any one group; (3) ordinary people influence public policy through voting and participating in special-interest groups; (4) power is widely dispersed in society (the same groups aren't equally influential in all arenas); and (5) public policy reflects a balance among competing interest groups, not the majority group's view (Dye and Zeigler, 1993).

How might social analysts who use a functionalist framework address problems in politics and the economy? First, since dysfunctions are inevitable in any social institution, it is important to sort out and remedy the specific elements of the system that are creating the problems. It should not be necessary to restructure or replace the entire system. Consider, for example, government regulations: Some regulations are good, and some are bad. The trick is to keep the good ones and get rid of the bad (Barlett and Steele, 1996). Too often, the U.S. government moves between two extremes: overregulation of business and society or seeking to end most, if not all, regulation. As social analysts Donald L. Barlett and James B. Steele (1996:214) suggest, "We must preserve the rules that assure the quality of American life: the food you eat, the medicines you take, the air you breathe and the water you drink. They have evolved over a century." Barlett and Steele go on to say, however, that demanding that U.S.-owned companies comply with regulations that are not required of their competitors in foreign countries creates an uneven playing field. Hence a tariff should be imposed on imported products equal to the amount of money that U.S. businesses must spend to comply with government regulations (Barlett and Steele, 1996). This perspective is based on the belief that a certain amount of government intervention in the economy is appropriate but that too much—or the wrong kind—is detrimental.

The Conflict Perspective

Most conflict theorists believe democracy is an ideal, not a reality, in our society today because the government primarily benefits the wealthy and the politically powerful, especially business elites. In fact, economic and political elites use the powers of the government to impose their will on the masses. According to the *elite model,* **power in political systems is concentrated in the hands of a small group,** whereas the masses are relatively powerless. In the elite model, (1) elites possess the greatest wealth, education, status, and other resources and make the most important decisions in society; (2) elites generally agree on the basic values and goals for the society; (3) power is highly concentrated at the top of a pyramid-shaped social hierarchy, and those at the top set public policy for everyone; (4) public policy reflects the values and preferences of the elite, not of ordinary people; and (5) elites use the media to shape the political attitudes of ordinary people (Dye and Zeigler, 1993).

According to sociologist C. Wright Mills (1959a), the United States is ruled by a *power elite,* which is composed of leaders at the top of business, the executive branch of the federal government, and the military (especially the "top brass" at the Pentagon). The corporate rich—the highest-paid CEOs of major corporations—are the most powerful because they have the unique ability to parlay their vast economic resources into political power. The next most powerful level is occupied by Congress, special-interest groups, and local opinion leaders. The lowest (and widest) level of the pyramid is occupied by ordinary people, the unorganized masses who are relatively powerless and vulnerable to economic and political exploitation.

Individuals in the power elite have similar class backgrounds and interests and interact on a regular basis. Through a revolving door of influence, they tend to shift back and forth between and among the business, government, and military sectors. It is not unusual for people who have served in the president's cabinet to become directors of major corporations that do business with the government, for powerful businesspeople to serve in the cabinet, or for former military leaders to become important businesspeople. Through such political and economic alliances, people in the power elite can influence many important decisions, including how federal tax money will be spent and to whom lucrative subsidies and government contracts are awarded.

Similarly, sociologist G. William Domhoff (1978) speaks of a *ruling class,* which is made up of the corporate rich, a relatively fixed group of privileged people who wield sufficient power over political processes and serve capitalist interests. The corporate rich influence the political process in three ways: (1) financing campaigns of candidates who favor their causes; (2) using PACs and loophole contributions to obtain favors, tax breaks, and favorable regulatory rulings; and (3) gaining appointment to governmental advisory committees, presidential commissions, and other governmental positions. For example, some members of the ruling class influence international politics through their involvement in banking, business services, and law firms that have a strong interest in overseas sales, investments, or raw materials extraction (Domhoff, 1990).

Some analysts who take a conflict perspective say that the only way to overcome problems in politics and the economy is to change the entire system. Our present system exploits poor whites, people of color, women of all colors, people with disabilities, and others who consider themselves disenfranchised from the political and economic mainstream of society.

Other conflict theorists think that we can solve many problems by curbing the abuses of capitalism and the market economy and thereby reduce the power of political and economic elites. Political scientist Benjamin R. Barber believes that we cannot rely on the capitalist (market) economy to look after common interests:

It is the job of civil society and democratic government and not of the market to look after common interests and make sure that those who profit from the common planet pay its common proprietors their fair share. When governments abdicate in favor of markets, they are declaring *nolo contendere* [no contest] in an arena in which they are supposed to be primary challengers, bartering away the rights of their people along the way. . . .

Markets simply are not designed to do the things democratic polities do. They enjoin private rather than public modes of discourse, allowing us as consumers to speak via our currencies of consumption to producers of material goods, but ignoring us as citizens speaking to one another about such things as the social consequences of our private market choices. . . . They advance individualistic rather than social goals. . . . Having created the conditions that make markets possible, democracy must also do all the things that markets undo or cannot do. It must educate citizens so that they can use their markets wisely and contain market abuses well. (Barber, 1996:242)

PROBLEMS IN POLITICS AND THE ECONOMY IN THE TWENTY-FIRST CENTURY

What will U.S. politics and the economy be like in the twenty-first century? There is no single vision, of course, but many social analysts think that *digital democracy*—the use of information technologies such as the Internet and the World Wide Web—will dramatically change not only economic relationships but also the way in which politics and government are conducted. For example, digital democracy can be used to inform people about political candidates and issues. As a case in point, the office staff of 1996 presidential candidate Bob Dole created a Web site that recruited more than 12,000 volunteers to work states with early election primaries. In addition, tens of thousands of customized e-mail messages were sent to voters who indicated an interest in a specific topic. The entire cost of these activities was less than purchasing the average amount of television advertising in one major market such as Houston or New York (Fineman, 1997).

Most analysts agree that the 1996 election was just the beginning of digital grass-roots activism in U.S. politics. Access to political information is being radically democratized by the World Wide Web, cable access channels, and other new information technologies. However, critics point out that there are some major problems with trying to maintain a pluralist democracy through digital democracy:

The ultimate threats to American democracy in the digital age aren't the rise of splinter groups, or new tycoons, or government-imposed limits on speech. The dangers are more subtle and insidious. One is the lack of a common starting point for discussion. . . . If anyone can see the world from any angle—if everything is relative and the dominant reality virtual—where's the place called America?. . . . The other danger is that leadership as we knew it . . . will disappear as politicians become all too connected to the voters. . . . What if our presidents become nothing more than the sum of our whims and misinformation? The netizens of the future will have to take their jobs seriously. Are we ready for this much democracy? Let's hope so. (Fineman, 1997:52)

Will the U.S. economy and democratic politics become obsolete in the twenty-first century? Despite digital democracy and the transnational nature of politics and the economy, scholars such as Paul Kennedy (1993: 134) argue that individual nations will remain the primary locus of identity for most people. Regardless of who their employer is and what they do for a living, individuals pay taxes to a specific government, are subject to its laws, serve in its armed forces, and can travel only by having its passport. Therefore as new challenges arise, most people in democracies will turn to their own governments and demand solutions.

SUMMARY

➡ *What is the difference between politics and government?*

Politics is the social institution through which power is acquired and exercised by some people and groups. Government is a formal organization that has the legal and political authority to regulate relationships among people in a society and between the society and others outside the borders.

➡ *Why is voter apathy a problem? What is the gender gap?*

Voter apathy undermines the basis on which representative democracy is built; if large numbers of people don't vote, the interests of only a few are represented. The gender gap is the difference between a candidate's number of votes from women and men. More than ever today, women and men seem to view economic and social issues differently.

➡ *Why have campaign contributions become an issue in recent elections?*

Campaign contributions are regulated, but individuals, unions, and corporations circumvent the law through the soft money loophole—contributing to a political party instead of to a specific candidate—and through political action committees. Political action committees (PACs) are special-interest groups that fund campaigns to help elect (or defeat) candidates on the basis of their positions on specific issues. Because running for office is so expensive, contributions can make the difference between a candidate's success or defeat, but the risk is that special-interest groups make campaign contributions for the purpose of buying political influence, as has been alleged with the tobacco and sugar industries.

➡ *What is the permanent government, and why does it pose a risk?*

The permanent government refers to the top tier of civil service bureaucrats who possess a strong power base and play a major role in developing and implementing government policies and procedures. The problem is that bureaucratic power—in government, as in any sphere—tends to take on a life of its own over time. Since 1960, the federal government has grown faster than any other segment of the U.S. economy. Government agencies and special-interest groups can develop a symbiotic relationship that allows the agency to perpetuate itself, but at the risk of owing special-interest groups.

➡ *What is the military-industrial complex?*

The military-industrial complex refers to the interdependence of the military establishment and private military contractors. The military-industrial complex can be a revolving door of money, influence, and jobs.

➡ *What is the economy? What kind of economic system does the United States have?*

The economy is the social institution responsible for producing and distributing goods and services. The United States has a capitalist economy. Ideally, capitalism is characterized by private ownership of the means of production, pursuit of personal profit, competition, and lack of government intervention.

➡ *How did wealth become concentrated in the hands of a few in the United States?*

In early monopoly capitalism, ownership of cap-ital shifted from individuals to corporations. After World War II, the number of oligopolies—entire industries or services controlled by a small number of companies or suppliers—increased. These large corporations could use their economic resources, through campaign contributions, to influence government decisions affecting their operations.

➡ *What are transnational corporations, and why do they pose social problems?*

Transnational corporations are large-scale business organizations headquartered in one country but operating in many countries. Transnationals lack accountability to any government or regulatory agency. Nor do they depend on any one country for labor, capital, or technology. They can play important roles in the economies and governments of countries that need them as employers and accept their practices.

➡ *Why is the national debt a serious problem? How is consumer debt a public issue?*

When we increase the national debt, we are borrowing from future generations, which will leave them with higher taxes, fewer benefits, and a lower rate of economic growth. Consumer debt becomes a public issue when people cannot repay their credit card loans.

➡ *What is corporate welfare?*

Corporate welfare occurs when the government helps industries and private corporations in their economic pursuits. Many subsidies that were originally put in place to help stabilize the economy continue unnecessarily because of labor union and PAC lobbying and campaign contributions.

➡ *What are the sociological perspectives on the political economy?*

The functionalists use a pluralist model, believing that power is widely dispersed through many competing interest groups in our political system. Functionalists therefore believe that problems can be solved by identifying the dysfunctional element and correcting it. Conflict theorists use an elite model, believing that power in political systems is concentrated in the hands of a small group, whereas the masses are relatively powerless. Sociologist C. Wright Mills used the term *power elite* for this small group of top business leaders, the executive branch of the federal government, and the "top brass" of the military.

KEY TERMS

capitalism, p. 308
corporation, p. 309
democracy, p. 300
economy, p. 308
elite model, pp. 315–316
gender gap, p. 301
government, p. 300
military-industrial complex, p. 306
mixed economy, p. 308

monopoly, p. 309
oligopoly, p. 309
permanent government, p. 306
pluralist model, p. 315
political action committees (PACs), p. 301
politics, p. 300
power elite, p. 316
socialism, p. 308
transnational corporation, p. 310

QUESTIONS FOR CRITICAL THINKING

1. Imagine that you are given unlimited funds and resources to reverse the trend in voter apathy. What would you do at the local level? What would you do at the state and national levels?

2. How would you respond to the Gallup Poll survey question: "Would you say the government is pretty much run by a few big interests looking out for themselves or that it is run for the benefit of all the people?" Explain your answer.

3. Do you favor or oppose sociologist George Ritzer's proposal that the government restrain credit card companies? Do you agree with his means—limiting profit and restricting incentives for accepting new credit cards? Would you propose other means?

Chapter Fifteen

Problems in the Workplace

I was seven years old the first time I ever set foot inside an automobile factory. The occasion was Family Night at the old Fisher Body plant in Flint where my father worked the second shift. General Motors provided this yearly intrusion as an opportunity for the kin of the work force to funnel in and view their fathers, husbands, and granddads as they toiled away on the assembly line. . . . we found my old man down on the trim line. His job was to install windshields using this goofy apparatus with large suction cups that resembled an octopus being crucified. . . . Car, windshield. Car, windshield. Car, windshield. No wonder my father preferred playin' hopscotch with barmaids. This kind of repetition didn't look like any fun at all. . . . Thank God that, even at age seven, I knew what I was going to be when I grew up. There wouldn't be any car windshield cha-cha awaiting me. I was going to be an ambulance driver, the most glamorous calling in the world.

—Ben Hamper, a former assembly line riveter at GM's truck and bus division, tells why, as a child, he believed that he would never work on an assembly line as his father did
(Hamper, 1991:1–3)

To a kid growing up, the fruit tramp life meant changing schools three to five times a year, some years more. Among my earliest memories are leaving, in early morning, the Imperial Valley, or the lower San Joaquin, and moving north, winding up one job and heading for another. I was the youngest of three, and my position in the car . . . was the ledge in front of the back window, where I would lie crosswise, staring out at the receding highway. . . . I started working rather young, mostly in summer and, until I achieved some growth, always in the fields or orchards. No self-respecting fruit tramp of the old blood would pick anything for a living
continued

—Reg Theriault, a dock worker in San Francisco, describes how he and his family traveled across the western United States harvesting apple crops (Theriault, 1995:23–24)

once he had made it up to a job on the shed [where the apples are washed, sorted, and packed for shipping]. I was no exception. When I finally made it I felt as if I had successfully completed a rite of passage. I had arrived.

Like Ben and Reg, many people become aware of the problems of work at an early age, though their understanding is incomplete. As children, we hardly realize that our economic position, lifestyle, and self-image are associated with our parents' employment. Nor do we realize that our future work opportunities and experiences are intricately linked to our families and to the larger society in which we live. Moreover, the kind of labor that a society values changes with time. In other eras, for example, athletes—no matter how outstanding—didn't make millions of dollars in playing contracts and endorsement fees; society did not hold sports competition and celebrity athletes in such high esteem, and the media were not the pervasive influence they are today.

In this chapter, we examine problems associated with paid employment in the United States today and some of the special concerns of individuals who do certain types of *labor*—the physical and intellectual services that workers contribute to the economic production process. As we discussed in Chapter 1, at the end of the twentieth century, many people have personal problems as a result of the changing nature of work in the United States. Sociologists Randy Hodson and Teresa A. Sullivan note (1995:3–4), "The changing nature of work has had important implications for personal satisfaction, for the cohesion of society, for relations between men and women, and for our ideas about the meaning of work and its place in our social life." As we examine these implications, you will see that many work-related problems—including the replacement of permanent jobs with temporary jobs, high levels of worker stress and alienation, hazardous working conditions, structural unemployment, and discrimination—are not just personal problems of individuals but threats to the economic and social well-being of society.

THE CHANGING NATURE OF WORK

Are the disruptions in people's lives that are brought about by the changing nature of work a new phenomenon? Not at all, say social scientists: The social organization of work and technology has gone through a series of historical transformations. These transformations have largely determined the nature of many societies—including the division of labor between men and women and the degree of social inequality—at specific points in time (Hodson and Sullivan, 1995). Before examining how people are affected by the changing nature of jobs as we approach the twenty-first century, let's briefly look at how societies in the past were transformed as the nature of economic production changed. Depending on its major type of production, a society can be classified as having a preindustrial, industrial, or postindustrial economy.

Preindustrial Economies

Hunting and gathering societies, horticultural societies, and agrarian societies are all preindustrial economies. Most workers engage in *primary sector production—the extraction of raw materials and natural resources from the environment.* In this type of production, materials and resources are used without much processing. Today, extracting gold and silver from mines in Indonesia is an example of primary sector production. Since families in early hunting and gathering societies produced the goods they consumed, the division of labor typically was based on age and gender, and inequality was minimal. But in horticultural societies, in which production shifts somewhat away from the family unit, the division of labor becomes more complex. For the first time, more than enough food is produced to feed everyone, and some people can engage solely in work-related activities other than food production. In agrarian societies, people can assume even more specialized tasks—becoming warriors and priests, for example—in addition to working in food production. At each stage in preindustrial economies, inequality grows more distinct as some people are more able than others to put the surplus to their own use.

▲ Industrial Economies

Social inequality grows more pronounced in industrial economies where most workers are engaged in *secondary sector production*—**the processing of raw materials (from the primary sector) into finished products.** Work in industrial economies is much more specialized, repetitious, and bureaucratically organized than in preindustrial economies. Consider, for example, Ben Hamper's first day on the rivet line at the General Motors' truck and bus division in Flint, Michigan (Hamper, 1991:88–89):

> The Rivet Line was the starting point for all that went on during the three-day snake trail needed to assemble a truck. The complex birth procedure began right here. It started with a couple of long black rails. As the rails were hoisted onto crawling pedestals, the workers began riveting them together and affixing them with various attachments. There weren't any screws or bolts to be seen. Just rivets. Thousands upon thousands of dull gray rivets. They resembled mushrooms. . . . For the next couple of hours I stood back and studied the routine. You were given three days to learn your assignment. I didn't plan on jumpin' in until absolutely necessary. I looked around at those who would soon be my neighbors. I'd seen happier faces on burn victims.

Hamper describes the work in the General Motors factory as not only specialized and repetitious, but also highly bureaucratic. There are rules to follow, and workers are assigned to check that everyone obeys, as in Hamper's following description (Hamper, 1991:46–47):

> The Plant Manager introduced the man in charge of overseeing worker attendance. . . . The attendance man unveiled a large chart illustrating the trends in absenteeism. With a long pointer, he traced the roller-coaster tendencies of the unexcused absence. He pointed to Monday, which slung low to the bottom of the chart. Monday was an unpopular day attendance-wise. He moved the pointer over to Tuesday and Wednesday which showed a significant gain in attendance. The chart peaked way up high on Thursday. Thursday was pay night. Everybody showed up on Thursday. . . . "Then we arrive at Friday," the attendance man announced. A guilty wave of laughter spread through the workers. None of the bossmen appeared at all amused. Friday was an unspoken Sabbath for many of the workers. Paychecks in their pockets, the leash was temporarily loosened. To get a jump on the weekend was often a temptation too difficult to resist. The Corporation saw it quite differently. . . . [The attendance man said,] "Each time you take an unexcused absence, you damage the company along with the security of your own job!" (Hamper, 1991:46-47)

Although many workers are involved in the production process in industrial economies, people primarily get their jobs done by working with machines and other "things" rather than through workers interacting.

Two of the chief characteristics of contemporary industrial production—scientific management (Taylorism) and mass production (Fordism)—first emerged in the late nineteenth and early twentieth centuries. The assembly line that Hamper describes was originally developed according to principles of *scientific management*—breaking every task in a process into its most minute components, determining the best way to do each of them, and then teaching workers to perform the tasks in a concise series of steps. Scientific management is associated with the work of industrial engineer Frederick Taylor, who believed that productivity could be increased if individual thinking and decision making were removed and workers were simply taught to perform the tasks in the most efficient way. Ultimately, however, breaking work into specialized tasks and minute operations contributes to *job deskilling,* which, as defined in Chapter 1, is the process by which technological innovations reduce the skills needed to perform a job, leading to lower wages for that job (Braverman, 1974). Scientific management also shifts much of the control of knowledge and skills from workers to managers, which can lead to feelings of powerlessness and frustration among workers (Westrum, 1991). As a result, scientific management increases the social inequality between managers and workers because it increases the gap between managers' and workers' interests and rewards (Zuboff, 1988). That is, management is interested in increased productivity because it means increased profits; however, workers do not get the personal satisfaction of a job well done because they do only a small part of the job (e.g., riveting the frame of a truck) and they don't share in the profits.

Inequalities between managers and workers are further intensified by mass production. Mass production through automation is often referred to as *Fordism* because Henry Ford, the founder of Ford Motor Company, revolutionized the automobile industry with the automated assembly line, which produced large numbers of standardized products using product-specific equipment (Collier and Horowitz, 1987). The automated assembly line allows workers to perform a specialized operation on an unfinished product as it moves by conveyor past their work stations, greatly enhancing efficiency and productivity. With the automated assembly line, a Model T Ford could be assembled in one-eighth the time it took to put a car together manually. But even more important, Fordism gave managers technical control over the work process, especially the pace at which work was done, because they controlled the speed of the assembly line (Edwards, 1979). A faster assembly line means more product, which means increased profits—always the end goal of management. Mass production through automation thus contributes to social inequality because it creates a large surplus that benefits stockholders, owners, and upper-level managers who are given shares of stock in the corporation. Meanwhile, the workers who produce the surplus are mere cogs in the wheels of production, and many feel dehumanized and alienated. However, their alienation can be reduced somewhat by two factors: growth in their purchasing power and, until the 1970s, unionization, which we will discuss later in the chapter.

Over the last two decades, some sectors of the industrial economy have undergone *deindustrialization*—the process by which capital is diverted from investment in basic industries (in the form of economic resources, plants, and equipment) to business practices such as mergers and acquisitions and foreign investment (Bluestone and Harrison, 1982). According to some social analysts, deindustrialization has brought about "shuttered factories, displaced workers, and a newly emerging group of ghost towns" (Bluestone and Harrison, 1982:6). Although it might seem natural that deindustrialization would transform the United States into a postindustrial economy, this has not yet been the case.

▲ Postindustrial Economies

Postindustrial economies are characterized by *tertiary sector production*—providing services rather than goods as the primary source of livelihood. Tertiary sector production includes work in such areas as fast-food service, transportation, communication, education, real estate, advertising, sports, and entertainment. Some tertiary sector jobs are personally fulfilling and economically rewarding, but certainly not all of them are. Here's what one college student had to say about working her way through college in fast-food service (Loeb, 1994:289):

> I came here . . . as a freshman. I didn't know about the previous tuition hikes. I didn't care. I thought it wouldn't affect me. Then I started hearing rumors and I freaked. I'm the youngest of seven children trying to get a degree. Right now I work at Roy Rogers flipping chicken and baking biscuits for $4.25 an hour—[then] minimum wage. Is my career being a biscuit babe for the rest of my life?

In highly paid, primary tier jobs in postindustrial economies, people may work at home, connecting to employers' or clients' offices via computer and modem from anywhere in the world, or network with business contacts virtually anywhere, as this chief executive officer of a major corporation describes (Akasie, 1997:18):

> There's nothing like a goose blind. It's just you and the other person or two other people, and you're in that blind for six or eight hours and there's nowhere to go. It's a camouflaged, tight

tiny fraction of workers is producing manufactured goods.

In postindustrial economies, work may become more flexible and more demanding at the same time. Working at home has both its pleasures and its frustrations for this woman. What do you think the office of the future will look like?

According to Hodson and Sullivan, the United States is best characterized as an *advanced industrial society* that has a small sector of primary production, a larger manufacturing sector, and a growing service sector. Although some people have good-paying, postindustrial-type jobs (as discussed in Chapter 1), many others work in manufacturing, sometimes in sweatshop conditions, or in agricultural settings, harvesting crops for domestic and international consumption. Daniel Bell predicted that workers in the postindustrial society would primarily be well-educated professionals, scientists, and technicians. But the trend is toward a growing number of lower-paying, second tier service positions—such as counter help in fast-food restaurants—rather than higher-paying, primary tier positions (Ritzer, 1996). Some highly compensated chief executive officers do not have many years of formal education either. Bill Gates of Microsoft, Larry Ellison of Oracle, and Michael Dell of Dell Computer, for example, did not earn college degrees (Pappas, 1997a).

An advanced industrial society is characterized by greater dependence on an international division of labor. For example, when U.S. manufacturers are faced with stiff international competition, they use foreign assembly plants such as the ones in nations such as Indonesia, China, and Vietnam where labor costs are low. Some manufacturers have set up *maquiladora* plants—factories in Mexico where components manufactured in the United States are assembled into finished goods and shipped back to the United States for sale. Of course, when U.S. manufacturing workers are displaced by workers in other nations, their earnings are diminished. At the same time, technological innovations have led to considerable deskilling in work that is available. The result is a decrease in the absolute number of well-paid workers in the United States (Wilson, 1992).

Another characteristic of the United States as an advanced industrial society is a shift toward flexible production. *Flexible production* involves small batch production rather than mass production, product innovation rather than product standardization, and responsiveness to rapid changes in market opportunities rather than dependence on mass markets (Wilson, 1992). Flexible production is sometimes referred to as "post-Fordism" and differs from mass production, or Fordism, in three important ways:

little place built of wood, out in the middle of the water or buried in the ground. You just hunker down and wait for the geese to come. [Mergers and acquisitions] work is really good in a goose blind because you can sit and talk about the company if you're representing the buyer or the seller. You're uninterrupted if the shooting's poor. If the shooting's good, the guy's so happy that nothing else matters.

Over two decades ago, sociologist Daniel Bell (1973) predicted that the United States would eventually become a postindustrial economy characterized by service and information processing. That may be, but Hodson and Sullivan (1995:206) do not think we are there now and may never be:

The current economy, with a large share of the labor force in services, has not gone *beyond* being an industrial society. Rather, it is based on a highly productive industrial base in which it is possible to produce more goods with fewer workers. Because the need for manufactured goods can be expanded to a greater extent than the need for agricultural products, the economy will probably never reach a state in which only a

(1) Technology is based on programmable automated machines that allow a variety of products or models to be produced without downtime or retooling; (2) factories are organized so that workers are rotated through a variety of tasks, usually as a team; and (3) firms subcontract activities that they cannot easily or cheaply perform to other firms that can. In *subcontracting,* a larger corporation hires other (usually smaller) firms to provide specialized components, products, or services. Many companies—ranging from manufacturers of athletic shoes to high-tech industries—find that it is more cost efficient (and therefore profitable) to subcontract certain work to small contractors than to do it in-house.

PROBLEMS IN THE WORKPLACE

These two trends—toward an international division of labor and flexible production with subcontracting—create or add to such work problems as increasing contingent work, worker stress and alienation, hazardous working conditions, and unemployment. We now look at these problems and at discrimination in the workplace.

Contingent Work

In recent years, there has been a dramatic increase in *contingent work*—**part-time work, temporary work, and subcontracted work that offers advantages to employers but can be detrimental to workers' welfare.** Unlike permanent jobs that have good pay, health and pension benefits, some degree of job security, and the possibility of future advancement, contingent jobs typically are lower-paying, have few (if any) benefits, and offer very little job security or possibility for future advancement (see Bonacich, 1972). Early in the 1990s, the contingent work force consisted of 25 to 33 percent of all U.S. workers. In the late 1990s, temporary workers (temps) are the fastest-growing segment of the contingent work force, and the number of agencies placing temps has grown rapidly in the last decade. Most temp agencies provide workers on a contract basis to employers for an hourly fee, and workers are paid a portion of this fee (Bassi and Chasanov, 1996). Besides temporary workers sent by agencies, the contingent work force includes part-time employees; leased,

contracted, or subcontracted workers; some of the self-employed; and day laborers (Parker, 1994).

Contingent workers can be found in virtually every segment of the U.S. work force, including accounting, law, health care, computers, and all levels of government. For example, many colleges and universities hire contingent instructors (known as part-time or adjunct faculty) on a course-by-course or semester-by-semester basis. In recent years, as older faculty members have retired, their tenure-track positions have not been filled, and administrators have hired adjunct faculty. As a result, many more college instructors in the late 1990s are "academic gypsies" who move through a series of one-year, non-tenure-track appointments at the lecturer or instructor level (Mydans, 1995). Many adjunct faculty members are employed by several schools during a semester and travel from location to location—sometimes many miles apart—to teach classes each week.

Why has contingent work increased so much in recent years? Employers benefit financially by hiring workers on a part-time or temporary basis. A contingent work force makes it possible to cut costs, maximize profits, and still have workers available when they are needed. As some companies have cut their work force, or *downsized,* they have replaced employees who had higher salaries and full benefit packages with part-time and hourly employees who receive lower wages and no benefits.

Although some people voluntarily work part time, many part-time workers would like to be employed full time but don't have the option (see Table 15.1). Most part-time workers are teenagers, older people, and women, who constitute about 75 percent of all part-time workers (Applebaum and Schettkat, 1989). All contingent workers are more vulnerable than full-time, permanent employees, but low-skilled workers are particularly vulnerable because they can be easily replaced if they demand better wages, benefits, or working conditions (Costello et al., 1996).

A large number of contingent workers are subcontracted workers. Rather than employing a large work force, a company can reduce its payroll and benefit plans but get the requisite work done by subcontracted workers, who are often hired through an industry known as *business services* (Parker, 1994). Business services actually includes a wide range of companies that specialize in services ranging from janitorial services and security services to computer

TABLE 15.1 REASONS FOR WORKING PART TIME, 1995

PEOPLE AGE SIXTEEN AND OVER, IN THE CIVILIAN NONINSTITUTIONAL POPULATION,
GAVE THE FOLLOWING REASONS FOR WORKING PART TIME (1–34 HOURS PER WEEK)

Reason	Total
ECONOMIC REASONS	
Slack work or business conditions	2,471,000
Could find only part-time work	1,702,000
Seasonal work	120,000
NONECONOMIC REASONS	
Child-care problems	774,000
Other family or personal obligations	5,585,000
Health or medical limitations	699,000
In school or training	5,986,000
Retired or Social Security limitation on earnings	1,848,000
Weather-related curtailment	439,000

Source: U.S. Bureau of the Census, 1996b.

and data processing services and collection agencies. Sociologist Robert Parker, who conducted an in-depth study of temporary workers, describes sub-contracted workers this way (Parker, 1994:60):

> They tend to be paid less than permanent work-ers, they have minimal access to fringe benefits, they are unlikely to stay with a particular busi-ness service firm for any significant duration, and they are almost never unionized. And like other contingent workers, subcontracted workers de-press wages and working conditions for the working class as a whole. In particular, unionized workers . . . and minority workers . . . are suffer-ing significant occupational losses in the trend toward the increasing use of subcontracting.

Some companies have their own in-house tem-porary personnel division, so they do not have to rely on business service agencies. Companies that have their own temporary help division include Travelers and Union Fidelity insurance companies, Lockheed, and Motorola (Parker, 1994).

In his study of temporary work, Parker con-cluded that the temporary help industry has grown in prominence and profitability in the 1990s because of the progressive deskilling of occupations and the

benefit to employers of using temporary workers. According to Parker (1994:153), "Temporary work-ers can be a highly sophisticated instrument for em-ployers, part of an overall staffing strategy that fa-cilitates management's control over the labor process and maximizes the potential output of every hour of paid labor." Obviously, as the use of contin-gent workers undermines the pay and working con-ditions of full-time workers, job satisfaction is likely to decrease while worker alienation increases.

Job Satisfaction and Worker Alienation

Job satisfaction involves people's attitudes toward their work based on their job responsibilities, the or-ganizational structure in which they work, and their individual needs and values (Hodson and Sullivan, 1995). For most people, work is an important source of self-identity. It can help people to feel positive about themselves, or it can cause them to feel alien-ated. Studies have found that worker satisfaction is highest when employees have some degree of control over their work, when they are involved in decision making, when they are not too closely supervised, and when they feel that they play an important part in the outcome (Kohn et al., 1990). People in management and supervisory positions may even have a sense of ownership toward their organization's products or services. For example, Deborah Kent, the first African American woman to head a vehicle assembly plant at the Ford Motor Company, feels such a strong sense of ownership that she sometimes asks strangers on the street how they like their vehicle if it was produced in her plant (L. Williams, 1995: F7): "I feel this sense of ownership, responsibility and pride about every Econoline, Villager, and Quest on the road. Particularly since I know we're the only manufacturing plant producing those vehicles. And if something's wrong, I want to know about it."

Job satisfaction is often related to both intrinsic and extrinsic factors. Intrinsic factors pertain to the nature of the work itself; extrinsic factors include such things as vacation and holiday policies, parking privileges, on-site day-care centers, and other amenities that contribute to workers' overall perception that their employer cares about them. Many people have mixed feelings about intrinsic and extrinsic factors in their work. In a recent study, sociologist Ruth Milkman (1997) found that auto workers were ambivalent about their jobs. Although they hated the chronic stress and humiliation of factory work, they liked the high pay and good benefits.

On the other hand, *alienation* occurs when **workers' needs for self-identity and meaning are not met and when work is done strictly for material gain, not a sense of personal satisfaction.** Workers and supervisors or owners are engaged in an ongoing struggle because workers lack control over their work and over the goods and services that they produce. Usually, the struggle stays below the surface, but sometimes it erupts. Here, for example, is how John Pierce, a worker at the GM automobile assembly plant in Linden, New Jersey, reacted to a control issue he had with a supervisor (Milkman, 1997:44):

I had a supervisor once; we had a beef about something. And he told me, "I'm your boss, and you do what I tell you to do." I said, "Sir, that's the wrong answer." I said, "I can make you or break you, because I'm the worker. So therefore if I want to give you good work, I can give you good work, but don't harass me. It's not going to get you good work. Only thing that's going to do is make me angry and [not] want to work for you. 'Cause to me, people is the resources you have in business."

Job segmentation, isolation on the job, and the discouraging of any type of proworker organizations (such as unions) further contribute to feelings of helplessness and frustration among workers. However, not all people are dissatisfied and alienated. Some occupations have high levels of job satisfaction.

Job satisfaction among professionals tends to be relatively high. *Professions* are high-status, knowledge-based occupations that have five major characteristics: (1) abstract, specialized knowledge based on formal education and interaction with colleagues; (2) autonomy in decision making; (3) self-regulation through licensing, accreditation, and regulatory associations; (4) authority over clients and subordinate occupational groups, based on the professional's mastery of a body of specialized knowledge; and (5) altruism toward others, whereby professionals go beyond their self-interest or personal comfort to help a patient or client (Freidson, 1970, 1986; Larson, 1977). Most social analysts agree that these occupational specialties have the characteristics of a profession: lawyers, doctors, ministers, university professors, military officers, and scientists (Hodson and Sullivan, 1995). But people in many other occupational categories—ranging from dog groomers and hair stylists to real estate agents and paid fundraisers—consider themselves professionals today.

Professionals have higher levels of job satisfaction than do people in other careers for several reasons. First, professionals have control over their own work lives. Unlike people in some other occupations, professionals typically are able to determine what they will do, how other workers should perform tasks, and how to prevent people in other occupations from taking over aspects of their professional work (e.g., physicians preventing midwives from delivering babies in hospitals). In addition to control over their work, many professionals have economic power because of their high fees and political power that allows them to influence political decisions affecting their profession and their livelihood.

That is not to say that all professionals have high levels of job satisfaction. Today, many professionals practice in, or are employed by, bureaucratic organizations—large corporations or government agencies. For example, physicians employed by health maintenance organizations or for-profit hospital chains typically must adhere to cost-containment policies established by the corporation. Even physicians who practice on their own are constrained by managed care plans, hospital policies and procedures, insurance company guidelines, and governmental rules and regulations governing their conduct (see Chapter 11). Moreover, some professions are undergoing *deprofessionalization*—the process by which some of the characteristics of a profession are eliminated (Hodson and Sullivan, 1995). Deprofessionalization is a form of deskilling. As pharmacist Nino Guidici explains (quoted in Terkel, 1990/1972):

In the old days [people] took druggists as doctors. . . . All we do [now] is count pills. Count out twelve on the counter, put 'em in here, count out twelve more. . . . Doctors used to write out their own formulas and we made most of these things. Most of the work is now done in the laboratory. The real druggist is found in the manufacturing firms. They're the factory workers and they're the pharmacists. We just get the name of the drugs and the number and the directions. It's a lot easier.

Like professionals, *semiprofessionals*—workers in occupational categories that have some (but not all) attributes of a profession—often believe that they are more satisfied with their jobs than do workers in some other occupational categories. However, semiprofessionals may have lower levels of satisfaction than professionals, at least partly because of their subordinate roles in relation to professionals. For example, large law firms often hire paralegals or legal assistants to perform many tasks that were previously done by lawyers but at less cost to the firm. Like many other semiprofessional positions, the paralegal field is dominated by women. In contrast, the field of law remains dominated by men who oversee the work of the paralegals and secretaries in the law firm hierarchy (Pierce, 1995). In a study of emotional lives in contemporary law firms, sociologist Jennifer L. Pierce (1995:102) found that paralegals feel that they must be deferential to the male attorneys for whom they work:

Paralegals are expected to utilize certain feminized components of emotional labor: deference and caretaking. . . . the paralegal defers to the attorney's authority and affirms his status by submitting to and smoothing over his angry outbursts, being non-critical vis-à-vis his written

work and professional habits, submitting to constant interruptions, and being treated as if she were invisible. And like the "perfect mother" who tends to the needs of the family while suppressing her own, the legal assistant is expected to be pleasant, cheerful, and reassuring, to express gratitude to others for her boss, and to serve as an arbiter of his feelings to others. . . . It is male litigators who can expect to receive nurturing and support from women paralegals and not the reverse.

As Pierce shows, job satisfaction may vary from person to person, but occupational categories do have specific characteristics. For example, virtually all high-paying professions continue to be dominated by men, whereas most semiprofessions are dominated by women. Even when men are employed in semiprofessional occupations, they are more likely to receive higher salaries and be promoted to managerial positions more quickly than their female colleagues (C. L. Williams, 1992).

Another group that tends to have relatively high levels of job satisfaction is *managers,* people who have responsibility for workers, physical plants, equipment, and/or the financial aspects of a bureaucratic organization. One reason is that, like professionals, they have control in the workplace. Managers control workers by applying organizational rules, and workers are required to take orders from their immediate superiors. Some social analysts believe that work must be hierarchically arranged so that managers can coordinate and control the activities of a large number of people; but others believe that a hierarchical authority pattern produces alienation in mid- and lower-level workers (Blauner, 1964).

Among middle-level managers, however, alienation can occur because of job deskilling through technology. For example, in fast-food restaurants, where hamburgers and other foods are produced in assembly line fashion, what do managers do? Not too much other than keep an eye on the computer, according to Jon DeAngelo, a McDonald's manager (Garson, 1989:36):

You have to trust the computer to do a lot of the job. These computers . . . calculate the payrolls, because they're hooked into the time clocks. My payroll is paid out of a bank in Chicago. . . . It's so fast that the manager hasn't got time to think about it. He has to follow the procedures like the crew. And if he follows the procedures everything is going to come out more or less as it's supposed to. So basically the computer manages the store.

Managers do hire workers and take care of other tasks, but automation has dramatically deskilled their jobs and intensified feelings of alienation (Garson, 1989; Ritzer, 1996).

If managers in service-sector jobs sometimes feel alienated, individuals who occupy positions in the lower tier of the service sector—such as janitors, waitpersons, messengers, sales clerks, typists, file clerks, migrant laborers, and textile workers—fit the classic "factory" model of alienation. As a waitress in one study of a New Jersey restaurant explained (Paules, 1991:110):

> Some of the food you even serve is disgusting. . . . and you have no choice but to serve it, unless you want to get into a fight with Bennett [a cook]. . . . So you have to basically go along with the system. . . . You can't go to [the manager] and say, "Well, listen. Bennett's giving me these really lousy orders," cause . . . who's he going to fire first? You or Bennett? You. Because it's harder for him to get a cook. . . . I mean, if a cook assaulted a waitress, the cook should have been dismissed. Instead, Tess [another waitress] was fired.

One important finding from this study was that the waitresses were far from passive; they looked out for their own interests. In other words, not all workers simply give up and accept an alienated lot in life. Many resist oppressive or hazardous working conditions, and some even demand changes in the nature and conditions of their work (Paules, 1991). Let's turn now to hazardous working conditions, another problem that some workers face at their job site.

Hazardous Working Conditions

Occupational accidents and illnesses are a significant problem in some workplaces. In 1994, 3.5 million workers sustained injuries or illnesses that were serious enough to temporarily or permanently disable them or even kill them (U.S. Bureau of the Census, 1996b). The true figure may be even higher because many workplace injuries go unreported. Some companies, for example, may give injured workers light duty and not report the injury to government authorities or insurance companies to keep lower insurance premiums and a reputation as a safe company (Hodson and Sullivan, 1995). Fatal occupational injuries result from (1) transportation-related accidents on highways, streets, or the industrial premises, aircraft accidents, and workers struck by a vehicle; (2) assaults and violent acts, including homicides (primarily shootings and stabbings) and suicides that occur at the work site; (3) contact with objects and equipment (including being struck by falling or flying objects or being caught in or compressed by equipment or objects), falls, exposure to harmful materials such as electric current or hazardous chemicals, or environmental situations including oxygen deprivation or drowning; and (4) fires and explosions (U.S. Department of Labor, 1995).

New technologies often introduce new safety hazards. For example, robots on automobile assembly lines may be efficient, but according to workers, "If you don't take the right precautions, you can get seriously hurt. . . . A robot has no conscience. If it goes into working mode and you're there, it's going to hurt you" (Milkman, 1997:152–153). Max Funk, another worker at the same plant, described the hazards of working alongside robots (Milkman, 1997:153):

> I got three stitches in my head. A robot came down on top of me. And I almost lost a finger another time. Some other people really got hurt badly; they were out maybe six, seven weeks. We had one guy in there who got fifty-two stitches in his hands. But nobody got killed. . . . There's one machine, the lay-down side frame, that has twenty-eight robots on it. . . . That machine is the most feared piece of equipment in the plant. . . . We've thought about bringing in a live chicken, maybe once a week, and just throwing it into the machine, you know, to satisfy the side-frame god.

Employees in manufacturing plants have the highest rate of nonfatal occupational injuries and illnesses each year. Meat-packing and shipbuilding industries also have high rates of injuries and illnesses, whereas finance, insurance, and real estate typically have the lowest rates (U.S. Department of Labor, 1996).

Other frequent workplace hazards include chronic stress injuries, occupational diseases from chemicals and asbestos (an inorganic fiber), and illnesses associated with high-tech industries and "sick buildings" (indoor air pollution that contains dust, chemicals, molds, and/or radiation). Chronic stress injuries occur as a result of using improper equipment, assuming unnatural positions or poor posture, and performing repetitious tasks with too few breaks and too little variation. The most common stress injuries are to the back, hands, arms, and hearing. Agricultural workers and employees in sweatshop industries such as garment factories typically experience repetitive motion injuries and respiratory problems due to chemicals or fibers, but they are often excluded from reports of occupational accidents and injuries because it can be difficult to pinpoint the source of their health problems as the workplace (Hodson and Sullivan, 1995). "Sick buildings" affect many thousands of office workers each year, some of whom may simply think they have colds or allergies (M. Williams, 1993).

Occupational diseases brought about by industrial chemicals, asbestos, and other harmful materials are also difficult to track because of the time lag between cause and symptoms. As many as twenty years may pass before a worker who is exposed to carcinogenic chemicals in the workplace is diagnosed with cancer. By that time, it's difficult to separate the effects of exposure to chemicals from the effects of smoking, drinking, or diet (Hodson and Sullivan, 1995). Although health hazards associated with exposure to asbestos have been known for many years, it is still used in many products, including car brakes, building materials, and insulation. Workers in the textile industry, shipbuilding, and the building and construction trades are at high risk for asbestos-related illnesses.

In 1970, Congress created a federal agency, the Occupational Safety and Health Administration (OSHA), to reduce or eliminate risks to workers' health, but enforcing OSHA regulations is difficult because of the agency's limited budget. Unless employees work at large unionized factories or workers file official complaints with OSHA, most workplaces are never inspected. Even when workers file complaints, follow-up by OSHA or a state agency typically takes months or years. Meanwhile, the workers who filed the original complaint have either given up or taken jobs elsewhere, rendering the issue somewhat moot as far as some inspectors are concerned. In recent years, some workers have pushed for "right-to-know" legislation that would require companies to share information about the potential health hazards of chemicals at specific work sites. But companies that use hazardous chemicals have actively fought such initiatives at the state and local level, and lobbyists have suppressed such legislation at the federal level. Often, too, workers don't press their claims or demand change because they fear that their employer might be put out of business, leaving them unemployed, and they fear the corresponding loss of wages and health and pension benefits more than they fear occupational accidents and illnesses, which somehow seem remote until they happen to them or someone they know.

▲ Unemployment

The unemployment rate in the 1990s has been lower than it was in the 1970s and 1980s (see Figure 15.1). At the end of 1996, unemployment was at 5.3 percent. Employment growth in the 1990s was primarily in service and retail; two-thirds of the new jobs created were in these areas. Manufacturing ac-

Although being laid off at work is a problem for many people, white women and people of color who have limited amounts of education and work experience often are uniquely affected by unemployment.

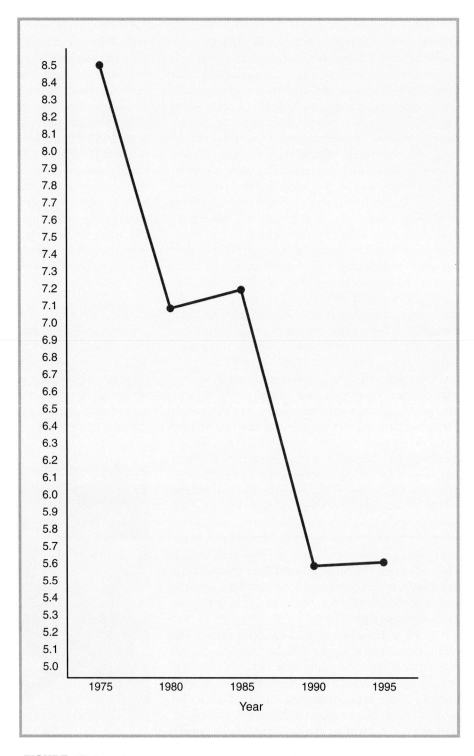

FIGURE 15.1 *Unemployment Rates, 1975–1995*

(SOURCE: U.S. Bureau of the Census, 1996b.)

counted for less than 2 percent of employment growth in 1996 (Bagby, 1997).

How are unemployment statistics calculated, and how accurate are they? The unemployment rate reflects the percentage of unemployed people who are *actively* seeking jobs. But as with other official statistics, unemployment rates may be misleading. For example, government unemployment statistics do not include all workers. Rather, they are based on a monthly sample survey of about 60,000 households, and *discouraged workers*, people who are no longer actively seeking work, are not counted as unemployed. Nor do unemployment statistics include the *underemployed*—people who are working at low-wage temporary or part-time jobs for which they may be overqualified until they can find more suitable full-time employment (Hodson and Sullivan, 1995).

The official unemployment rate also masks different rates of unemployment among various racial and ethnic groups. Although the national unemployment rate was between 5 and 7 percent during the 1990s, the unemployment rate for African Americans was between 10 and 14 percent, reaching as high as 40 percent for sixteen- to nineteen-year-old African Americans (U.S. Bureau of the Census, 1996b). Regardless of race or ethnicity, people with less than four years of high school have much higher rates of unemployment (between 10 and 14 percent) than do those with a college degree (between 2.8 and 3 percent) (U.S. Bureau of the Census, 1996b).

Not all unemployment is long-term. Cyclical and seasonal employment are typically temporary, whereas structural employment is permanent. *Cyclical unemployment* occurs as a result of lower rates of production during recessions in the business cycle. Although massive layoffs may initially take place, workers are rehired as the economy improves and plants get new, large orders. *Seasonal unemployment* results from periodic shifts in worker demand based on such factors as the weather (in agriculture, the construction industry, and tourism) or seasons (holidays and summer vacations). In contrast, **structural unemployment occurs when workers' skills and educational levels do not match employers' requirements, or when unemployed workers do not live where jobs they could perform are located** (McEachern, 1994). Structural unemployment often occurs when several plants in the same industry are closed or certain categories of jobs are rendered obsolete by new technologies. For example, workers in the Appalachian coal

industry and Midwestern steel industry faced structural unemployment when their mines and factories shut down and their job skills did not transfer to other types of industries. Business leaders and politicians often use the term *job displacement* or *job dislocation* to describe structural unemployment, but these terms just sidestep the real problem: **capital flight—investing U.S. money and other resources in facilities located in other nations where indigenous workers do the work previously done by U.S. workers.** Capital flight is a complex phenomenon because at the same time it creates unemployment in one country, it brings employment (at least temporarily) to another country (see Box 15.1 on pages 334–335).

In the United States, unemployment compensation provides workers with short-term income while they look for other jobs, but not everyone is eligible. Workers who quit a job without "good cause," go on strike in a labor dispute, or are fired for misconduct are not usually eligible for unemployment benefits. Furthermore, eligibility requirements and benefits vary from state to state. During the 1990s, worries about unemployment and fear that unemployment compensation might run out before displaced workers found other jobs received priority coverage in the media and political debates, taking the spotlight off other important workplace issues, such as race- and gender-based discrimination.

◢ Discrimination

As you know from your earlier reading, *discrimination*—actions or practices of dominant group members that harm members of subordinate groups—is a significant problem in the workplace (Feagin and Feagin, 1996). Discrimination creates a hostile work environment and costs corporations millions of dollars in wasted time, energy, and sometimes lawsuits (Feagin and Vera, 1995).

Racial stereotyping and discrimination occurs in initial hiring practices; in decisions regarding salaries, evaluations, and promotions; and in everyday interactions between people of color and white supervisors, coworkers, and associates (Feagin and Sikes, 1994). Sexism is another factor in discrimination; it affects both men and women in the workplace but is most harmful to women. For example, **sexual harassment—unwanted sexual advances, requests for sexual favors, or other verbal or physical conduct of a sexual nature**—is a form of intentional, institution-

SOCIAL PROBLEMS
IN GLOBAL PERSPECTIVE

BOX 15.1

Capital Flight: Can Workers on Both Sides Benefit?

I lost my job, my other benefits . . . It's an injustice. . . . I have 30 years of living in the United States, and I have never asked for welfare or food stamps. But right now, what am I going to do? All I want is a job.
　—Romana Melendez, speaking at a
　　labor rally in El Paso, April 1997
　　(Myerson, 1997:C1)

To keep the jobless quiet, the government supports them with high benefits. With at least one child, the unemployed can collect 57% of their former income indefinitely, tax free, with more for the first six months on the dole.
　—From a report in Forbes Magazine on
　　German industry (Banks, 1997:132)

On the surface, it would seem preferable to be an unemployed German worker than an unemployed American worker. Of course, most preferable would be to have a job. But

today, capital flight is a worldwide problem. It's the reason Romana Melendez is out of a job and the reason for high unemployment in Germany.

Romana Melendez is unemployed because Sun Apparel, where she stitched Polo and Sassoon jeans, shut down in El Paso and moved its operations to a maquiladora plant across the border in Mexico. Why pay U.S. workers the $4.75 minimum wage when garment workers in Mexico get less than $1 an hour? While the United States has almost full employment nationwide, the Texas border economy—El Paso, Laredo, McAllen, and Brownsville—has unemployment rates ranging from 11.7% (El Paso) to 19.1% (McAllen) (Myerson, 1997). Many observers trace the problem to the North American Free Trade Agreement (NAFTA), which lowered trade barriers with Mexico and Canada in 1994. In evidence, they point not only to closed factories and unemployment here, but also to new factories and new jobs in Mexico. The Department of Labor estimates

alized gender discrimination that creates a hostile work environment for women. Many working women of color experience *gendered racism*—**the interactive effect of both racism and sexism.** According to sociologists Nijole V. Benokraitis and Joe R. Feagin (1995:39), "Women are more likely than men to face many layers of sex-related obstacles. They often encounter a double, triple, or even quadruple 'whammy' because of their race or ethnicity, age, social

What constitutes sexual harassment is sometimes viewed differently by women and men in the workplace. However, certain kinds of conduct do create a hostile work environment for many people. How would you feel if you were the woman in this photo?

that 124,000 jobs have been lost to Mexico (and to some degree Canada) since 1994. In this same period, over 500 maquiladora plants—mostly producing apparel, auto parts, and electronics—have arisen along the Mexican border (Myerson, 1997). Maquiladora payrolls have expanded by 300,000 in the last two years, to a total of approximately 800,000 workers (Myerson, 1997).

NAFTA supporters argue that U.S. capital flight to Mexico is due not to the lowered trade barriers, but to a devalued peso and low labor rates. Whatever the reason, unemployed workers in the Texas border towns are not mollified by the fact that U.S. unemployment is at an all-time low. And they aren't heartened by knowing that Mexican workers benefit from the new maquiladora plants. If there is any solace, it is in the government's promise to provide retraining. So far, however, the training has been left to states, and workers complain that it has been of no benefit—they have no new skills and no new jobs (Myerson, 1997).

How does Germany fit into this picture? While the United States is investing in Mexico, Germany is investing in the United States and thus contributing to our overall rosy employment picture. Industrial labor costs in Germany are $31.76 an hour in western Germany and $20.82 in the eastern region, compared to $20.26 in France, $14.63 in Britain, and $17.50 in the United States (Banks, 1997). It makes much better business sense to hire workers in other countries. In May 1997, for example, the German Bayer Group announced that it would invest an additional $6 billion in the United States by 2000 (Banks, 1997). The industrial labor costs are extremely high for several reasons, including strong unions and a tightly regulated business establishment (Banks, 1997). But as in the Texas border towns, the upshot of capital flight from Germany is lost jobs—on a nationwide scale. The official unemployment rate in Germany is 12 percent, but most experts say that the real figure is closer to 16–17 percent (Banks, 1997). Worse, with such high labor rates, there is no capital flight *into* Germany to offset the flow out.

What can be done about problems created by capital flight? Is there a general solution that will ensure a flow of capital into a country even as capital goes out? Or must each case be considered separately? What can be done to help workers whose jobs are lost? What do you think?

---

class, *and* sex." As Benokraitis and Feagin point out, other factors such as ageism, classism, and ableism (bias against people with disabilities) can also contribute to a hostile work environment.

Discrimination can be blatant or subtle. Derogatory remarks and jokes are examples of blatant discrimination. If the target of a comment or joke feels intimidated, insulted, or humiliated and does not laugh, the person is considered "uptight" and a bad sport for not having a sense of humor. Subtle discrimination is less obvious, sometimes to the point that the target of such action denies that it even occurred. Consider, for example, this statement by Marleen McDaniel, CEO of Wire Networks, Inc., about her experiences in a male-dominated work environment (Pappas, 1997b):

When in Rome, do as the Romans. When you're in a male-oriented culture, men expect behavior that is more like their own. . . . When I was at Sun Microsystems, I remember being at a sales meeting. There had to be 200 guys and me. At the break we all went downstairs to the rest rooms, and one of the guys opened the door to the men's room for me—being the gentleman that he was. They realized what they had done so they all started slapping me on the back, you know, "Marleen, you've really made it to the men's club." I probably should have gone into the bathroom with them, but I didn't. I turned beet red and went into the ladies' room. . . . I really felt welcomed. I had been working more than 20 years, and that level of acceptance was fabulous.

Although some people might see this incident as just a joke among peers, many social analysts believe that supposedly inadvertent behavior such as that described above is used by dominant group members—in this case males—to point out that subordinate group members—in this case females—are "outsiders," even when their accomplishments are equal to or greater than those of dominant group members (Kanter, 1977).

As with individual discrimination, some forms of institutional discrimination are more obvious than others. *Direct institutionalized discrimination* is an organizationally or community-prescribed action that intentionally has a differential and negative impact on members of subordinate groups (Feagin and Feagin, 1996). Historical examples include policies and procedures in schools and businesses that categorically excluded African Americans or Jewish Americans on the basis of their race, ethnicity, or religion. *Indirect institutionalized discrimination* refers to practices that have a harmful impact on subordinate group members even though the organizationally or community-prescribed norms or regulations guiding these actions initially intended no harm. For example, job interviews have a negative and differential impact on central-city African American applicants because they are biased in favor of people who share common understandings of interaction and conversational style (i.e., a shared culture) with prospective employers (Neckerman and Kirschenman, 1997). In contrast, employers who use skills tests have on average a higher proportion of African American workers in the same job than do employers who interview but do not test (Neckerman and Kirschenman, 1997). Research also shows that recruitment and hiring practices are a factor in the underrepresentation of Jewish Americans in the top managerial and executive positions (the corporate elite) of most Fortune 500 Companies (Korman, 1988). Underrepresentation is particularly evident in the largest, most powerful industries—including petroleum, chemicals, food, glass and building materials, mining, and pharmaceuticals—in corporate America. Contributing to this underrepresentation are recruiting practices on college and university campuses. College recruiters from major corporations are far more likely to go to schools where there are few Jewish American undergraduates than they are to go to schools with a significant number of Jewish American students (Korman, 1988).

As all of these examples show, workplace discrimination involves actions by employers and employees. Some actions may be unintentional, while others are intentional. Some dominant group members are acutely aware of racism, sexism, and other kinds of bias in the workplace, but others think such problems no longer exist. From time to time, though, the public gets a wake-up call signaling that changes are needed in the workplace.

WORKER ACTIVISM

Many workers do not passively accept everything that happens to them in the workplace. Throughout the twentieth century, workers have organized to fight low wages, poor working conditions, and alienation in the workplace. To have more clout, many people have joined a *labor union*—a group of employees who join together to bargain with an employer or a group of employers over wages, benefits, and working conditions. For example, as automobile and steel plants converted to mass production earlier in this century, skilled and unskilled workers joined unions such as the Congress of Industrial Organizations (CIO) to enhance their bargaining power with management. Labor unions were instrumental in bringing about the eight-hour work day, the five-day work week, health and pension benefits, sick leave and unemployment insurance, and workplace health and safety standards for workers in some economic sectors. Most gains resulted from *collective bargaining*—negotiations between employers and labor union leaders on behalf of workers—and *strikes*, work stoppages to force employers to accept the union's position on wages, benefits, or some other work issue. Few strikes have been called in recent years. Only 31 strikes involving more than 1,000 workers were reported in 1995—down from a high of 424 in 1974 (see Table 15.2). However, in 1997, a strike by 185,000 members of the Teamsters Union against United Parcel Service (UPS), the nation's largest package-shipping company, virtually closed UPS down until a settlement was reached under which the union gained many of the concessions it had sought from the company. The proportion of all U.S. workers who are union members also has declined, although the overall number of union mem-

TABLE 15.2   WORK STOPPAGES, 1960–1995

EXCLUDES WORK STOPPAGES INVOLVING FEWER THAN 1,000 WORKERS AND LASTING LESS THAN 1 DAY

Year	Number of Stoppages	Workers Involved (thousands)
1960	222	896
1965	268	999
1970	381	2,468
1971	298	2,516
1972	250	975
1973	317	1,400
1974	424	1,796
1975	235	965
1976	231	1,519
1977	298	1,212
1978	219	1,006
1979	235	1,021
1980	187	795
1981	145	729
1982	96	656
1983	81	909
1984	62	376
1985	54	324
1986	69	533
1987	46	174
1988	40	118
1989	51	452
1990	44	185
1991	40	392
1992	35	364
1993	35	182
1994	45	322
1995	31	192

Source: U.S. Bureau of the Census, 1996b.

Some workers resist what they perceive to be unjust or oppressive behavior by supervisors and employers. Domestic workers, for example, often try to maintain their personal dignity when they interact with their employers. A Korean-American woman, interviewed by sociologist Esther Ngan-Ling Chow (1994:214) in her study of Asian American women in low-status occupations such as hotel housekeepers, put it this way: "Many of us depend on this job to support our families. When I am blamed for the things that I do not do and have no part of it, I will yell my guts out to protest. At most I will lose this job. I want my dignity, to be an honorable person, which my parents taught me."

In general, workplace resistance helps employees to cope with low-tier service jobs (Chow, 1994; Dill, 1988). Scholars have documented acts of resistance by African American domestic workers (Rollins, 1985; Dill, 1988), Chicana private housekeepers (Romero, 1992), and Japanese domestic helpers (Glenn, 1986). According to Chow, many Asian American women become "active agents and goal-oriented actors, capable of taking charge of their own lives," in interactions with supervisors and coworkers (Chow, 1994:218). Workers who believe that they control their own lives and work conditions are less likely to experience high levels of alienation than are workers who feel powerless.

Until fairly recently, workers (especially women) have been portrayed as passive victims of their work environment. But this is not always the case; many workers—both men and women—resist oppressive situations and demand better wages and work conditions. Studies of worker resistance are very important to our understanding of how people deal with the social organization of work.

bers has increased because of the rise in public employee unions (such as the American Federation of Teachers). Today, about 17 percent of all U.S. employees belong to unions or employee associations. Part of the decline in union participation and strikes is attributed to the shift away from manufacturing to service jobs, where employees typically have been less able to unionize. Some labor organizers, however, think more service sector jobs in the United States and Canada will be unionized in the future (see Box 15.2 on pages 338–339).

SOCIOLOGICAL PERSPECTIVES ON WORK

Social scientists who try to understand what causes social problems in the workplace and how these problems might be reduced or eliminated arrive at different answers depending upon their frame of reference. Functionalists see the problems—and therefore the solutions—differently from the conflict theorists, who, in turn, see things differently from the interactionists.

SOCIAL PROBLEMS
AND SOCIAL POLICY

BOX 15.2

Unionizing the Service Sector: Turning McJobs into Real Jobs

"Limité (which is not connected with The Limited chain in the U.S.) is a retailer with 47 stores in . . . Canada. Like The Gap or Contempo Casuals in the U.S., Limité is composed primarily of look-alike mall stores that blend into each other. . . . electronic music wafts into the mall promenade. . . . Upon entering Limité, a shopper is greeted by a pleasant, attractive, accessorized young woman like Nancy MacLean. . . . MacLean's job was her sole support and allowed her to pay tuition for courses at a local college. She basically liked the work, until the day in April 1994 that Christine Carter, a brand-new 22-year-old manager, posted a notice at the store: 'Anyone not averaging at least $50 an hour (in sales) is out of a job!' In the store's back room, the employees, all women, huddled around Carter's note. None had sold $50 an hour and some had sold as little as $6."

—The inciting incident for unionizing at Limité (Klein, 1996:32–33).

To the Limité clerks, the $50 quota meant management wanted to bring in a new crew of "girls" who were desperate for work and therefore willing to work without breaks, without overtime pay, and without vacations. Nancy MacLean, however, expected some security and respect in a job, so she called a meeting of the Limité clerks at the mall food court. "We're in a lot of trouble," Nancy said to the group. "We can all walk out of here and go our own ways or we can stick together and fight for our jobs" (Klein, 1996:35). Nine of the eleven women decided in favor of forming a union, and on June 13, 1994, Canada's first fashion retail union was formed as part of the International Ladies' Garment Workers' Union.

The service sector is growing, and what used to be considered throwaway jobs at the

The Functionalist Perspective

Functionalists believe that work and the economy are essential elements of social organization. If our society were operating under ideal conditions, the economy would run smoothly and the supply of workers would match the available jobs. However, today, dysfunctions arise in the system as a result of fluctuations in the global economy, rapid technological change, and the growth of transnational corporations, creating an imbalance between the supply of and demand for workers. When the U.S. economy does not adapt quickly enough to social change, work-related problems—including high rates of unemployment—typically occur. According to some

functionalists, the economy will take care of everyone if it is left to itself—that is, if the government doesn't intervene. From this viewpoint, peaks (expansion periods) in the U.S. business cycle produce large profits for owners and corporate shareholders and new job opportunities, higher wages, and upward mobility for workers. During peaks, the economy grows rapidly, and corporations grow in size as more people are employed and production increases. However, once the peak is reached, *inflation*—a sustained and continuous increase in prices—erodes the value of money, and consumers can no longer purchase as many products, a situation that sets off a chain reaction. When consumers do not purchase products, manufacturers produce fewer goods. Then

Gap, Limité, McDonald's, or Dunkin' Donuts are viewed very differently today. With many fewer jobs in industry, increasing numbers of young people, especially women, work in retail fashion and food to support themselves, and they want some security. For years, though, service sector employers have relied on a ready supply of young workers who didn't know their rights or were too afraid to demand them, and the employers prefer not to lose this advantage (Klein, 1997). The stage is therefore set for service-sector revolution. Nancy MacLean and workers like her want to turn their "McJobs"—minimum wage, low-security service sector jobs—into jobs that provide a living wage and good benefits (Klein, 1997). They've decided that the way to do this is to organize.

After MacLean organized her store, nineteen-year-old Tammy Gulati organized a Limité shop at another mall. Limité fired both women, but firing a union organizer is against Canadian law, so both were reinstated and were paid back wages. Limité then tried to bribe MacLean and Gulati to break with the union (Klein, 1996). When this tactic also failed, Limité agreed to talk. But in early 1995, in a surprise move, Limité sold the two stores that had been organized, putting everyone out of work.

Still, the message was out. Soon afterward, Kimberly Watt, age twenty-five, organized a Levi's 1850 shop in Toronto. Fast-food restaurants—Pizza Hut, KFC, and Tim Horton's Donut Shop—have also organized, and Canada has a growing labor movement in the service sector. Today, 18 percent of Canadian workers age seventeen to twenty-four are union members. The dwindling, aging union membership that resulted from downsizing, plant closings, and a shrinking industrial sector has gained new life from the struggle for mall workers' rights.

What is happening in the United States? Not much. Mall workers in the United States are no better off than in Canada, and neither are unions. Perhaps Canada's revolution in the service sector will inspire its U.S. counterparts. What has been your experience with McJobs and workers' rights? Are you in favor of unionizing? Is there a downside to unionizing? What do you think?

workers, who are also consumers, either are laid off or live in fear of losing their jobs, so they purchase even fewer products.

How do functionalists see these workplace problems being resolved? Some believe that the loss of jobs and the increase in contingent work can be overcome through the coordinated efforts of social institutions such as schools and the economy. For example, if schools provide students with the knowledge and job skills necessary for employment in the contemporary workplace, problems of structural unemployment and underemployment might be reduced. Similarly, training programs that address technological change, job satisfaction, hazardous working conditions, and discrimination can make workers and managers aware of these issues and thereby reduce the problems. Some functionalists believe that *limited* government intervention in the form of tax breaks (which may benefit the wealthy more than the poor and the working class) should be given to companies that establish job training programs that target the chronically unemployed. In a nutshell, functionalists believe that workplace problems can be reduced or eliminated if social institutions such as education do their jobs effectively.

The Conflict Perspective

Many conflict analysts think problems in the workplace are side effects of the capitalist economy, in

To many conflict analysts, these Nepalese rug makers are an example of the global exploitation of workers—men, women, and children alike—by wealthy capitalists who not only derive economic benefits from the workers' labor but also gain personal pleasure from ownership of the items the workers produce.

which workers are exploited by owners, high-level managers, and other powerful elites. Moreover, as capitalists seek to maximize profits, they contribute to high rates of unemployment in the United States through such practices as moving their plants to developing nations where workers can be paid lower wages and governments ignore environmental pollution and hazardous working conditions. Because of their economic clout, capitalists have privileged access to the nation's political hierarchy. According to political sociologist Michael Parenti (1988), the intertwining relationships between corporate and political elites is so complete in the United States that politicians treat the health of the capitalist economy as a necessary condition for the health of the nation (see Chapter 14). In fact, the goals of large corporations—including rapid growth, high profits, and expanding markets at home and abroad—become the goals of government (Parenti, 1988). For example, some analysts think the North American Free Trade Agreement (NAFTA) has left the Texas border economy more depressed because hundreds of new factories have opened in Mexican border states with a corresponding rise in unemployment in U.S. border cities such as El Paso. The hardest hit by such government policies are the U.S. workers who are already at the bottom in pay and skills, as a one journalist explains (Myerson, 1997:C1):

> Even after 15 years of work, Maria Consuelo García made only slightly more than $4.75 minimum wage stitching together Polo, Fila and Sassoon jeans in the Sun Apparel Inc. factory [in El Paso]. Seeing friends laid off at her plant and others, she kept her sewing machine whirring to beat her quotas. But that was not good enough. Company managers said their costs were still too high. Early in April, Ms. García and 297 others were let go. . . . the Labor Department said that these workers, and 320 others about two years ago, lost their jobs because the company is bringing in more goods from Mexico, where garment workers usually get less than $1 an hour.

Government efforts, such as the Texas Workforce Commission's retraining programs for workers displaced by the NAFTA agreement, have been of little assistance because workers say they mostly learn English or skills (e.g., basic electronics) that don't help them to find other jobs (Myerson, 1997).

How do conflict theorists suggest that problems related to work should be reduced? Most believe that workers must first develop *class consciousness*—**a feeling of unity based on an awareness of their shared exploitation by members of the capitalist class.** Then they can work together to get control of the workplace through activism, unionization, and worker-controlled organizations, such as this one described by sociologists Barbara Reskin and Irene Padavic (1994:178):

> Women workers in U.S.-owned factories just over the border in Mexico have organized the *Comite Fronterizo de Obreras* (Border Committee of Women Workers), which has fought successfully to gain higher pay, to protect workers from industrial chemicals, and to force employers to obey Mexican labor laws. These workers have broadened their influence by forming alliances with churches and sympathetic unions in

"Hello, and welcome to another edition of 'Sweatshops of the Rich and Famous.'"

Drawing by Maslin; © 1996 The New Yorker Magazine, Inc.

the United States. They are now investigating ways to permanently change their factories.

However, an important question remains unanswered: If workers are successful in their activism, will capitalists move their operations to other nations where workers are more compliant and labor costs are lower? Will worker activism lead to a larger *global assembly line*—workers, usually girls and young women, in developing nations, who are hired by transnational corporations to work for very low wages, often under hazardous conditions (Ehrenreich and Fuentes, 1981)? As long as the global assembly line exists, workers around the world will be suffering inequitable pay and oppressive working conditions.

▲ The Interactionist Perspective

Unlike the functionalist and conflict models, which look at how macrolevel economic changes affect workers and the workplace, interactionists focus on how people view their jobs and the conditions under which they work. Interactionists believe that work is

a source of self-identity that can make people feel either good or bad about themselves.

Jobs that bring little intrinsic or extrinsic satisfaction become a source of frustration and alienation that affect all aspects of a person's life, including time with family members. Lack of job satisfaction often comes from lack of control—little power in the workplace and no opportunities to make workplace decisions, and this lack of control produces feelings of isolation and alienation, which discourage workers from becoming involved in unions or other proworker organizations. It is a downward spiral. Just as bad as—or perhaps worse than—an unfulfilling job, however, is unemployment. Individuals who lose their jobs experience not only loss of wages but also feelings of isolation, boredom, and uselessness.

How do interactionists propose reducing workplace problems that produce negative self-identities? Solving problems of frustration, alienation, and unemployment is not easy. For example, sociologist Steven P. Dandaneau (1996) studied a variety of public service efforts to make people feel better about themselves after losing well-paying factory jobs in the GM plant in Flint, Michigan, when it was closed.

But according to Dandaneau, policy solutions to Flint's problems failed to reduce the social psychological trauma of workers and their families because they were, in essence, public relations solutions.

Recent research by sociologist Arlie Hochschild (1997) points to a new problem. Hochschild found that workers in Fortune 500 companies are choosing to spend more hours at work because their self-identities are better served in the workplace than in their own homes. Women employees in particular found that friendship groups and shared social occasions such as birthdays were more rewarding than their harried experiences at home with overworked spouses, housework stacking up, and children demanding attention because they have been left in child-care centers for eight to ten hours a day. However, the constant time bind that leaves people feeling guilty about home life and family relationships may be a solution to the problem. Some individuals start their own new businesses or take jobs at companies that make fewer demands on their time. Other people voluntarily simplify their lives by moving to a smaller home, having only one car, taking inexpensive vacations, and practicing other economies that allow them to work less and accept lower pay. However, Hochschild believes that workplace problems such as the time bind ultimately require collective, rather than individual, action. Workers must directly challenge organizations to offer shorter or more flexible hours. A collective movement would also need to encourage family-friendly programs and bring about a national dialogue on the importance of emotional investment in family life, asking such questions as these (Hochschild, 1997:250):

> How many hours a day, a week, a year should people work? How can we press for better work environments without inadvertently making them havens from life at home? How can both partners in a relationship achieve a stable and compatible work-family balance? In an era of growing income inequality, how can more time be made available to the working poor as well as to the better off?

Will the workplace of the future come to grips with such issues? It is difficult to say, but new technologies such as computers, the Internet, and the World Wide Web are dramatically changing the relationship between work life and home life for many people.

WORK-RELATED PROBLEMS IN THE TWENTY-FIRST CENTURY

Many of the trends—such as increasing contingent work, job deskilling, a growing service sector, and an increasing international division of labor—that we examined in this chapter will produce dramatic changes in the organization of work in the next century. The labor market may increasingly become divided into those who hold high-paying, full-time jobs with good benefits and those who hold low-paying jobs with few benefits and little job security. In the latter category, alienation will grow as temporary workers, sometimes professionals, look for avenues of upward mobility or at least a chance to make their work life more tolerable. Labor unions will be unable to help workers unless the unions develop innovative programs to recruit new members, improve their image, and recover their former political clout (Hodson and Sullivan, 1995). And even as the gender and racial-ethnic composition of the labor force continues to diversify, some workers will continue to face discrimination and alienation due to race- and/or gender-segregated occupations.

Despite these problems, workers in the United States will continue to have opportunities in the high-tech fields, as we discussed in Chapter 1. A global workplace is emerging in which telecommunications networks will link workers in distant locations, and the skills of some professions will transcend the borders of their countries. The demand for international law specialists, engineers, and software designers across countries is already great. Most social analysts predict that the United States will remain a major player in the world economy (see P. Kennedy, 1993).

SUMMARY

➡️ *How are societies classified by their predominant type of work?*

Societies can be classified as preindustrial, industrial, or postindustrial. Preindustrial societies engage in primary sector production—the extraction of raw materials and natural resources from the environment. Industrial societies engage in secondary sector production—the processing of raw materials (from the primary sector). Two major problems in industrial societies are job deskilling (doing a job with fewer skills) and deindustrialization (diverting capital from investment in basic industries to mergers and acquisitions and foreign investment). Postindustrial societies engage in tertiary sector production—providing services rather than goods.

➡️ *What type of society is the United States?*

Some social analysts say that the United States is an advanced industrial society because it has a small sector of primary production, a larger manufacturing sector, and a growing service sector. As an advanced industrial society, the United States increasingly depends on an international division of labor and flexible production (also called small batch production—the opposite of mass production).

➡️ *What is contingent work and why is it a problem?*

Contingent work is an umbrella term for part-time work, temporary work, and subcontracted work that offers advantages to employers but can be detrimental to workers' welfare. When companies downsize, or cut their work force, they often replace employees who had high salaries and full benefit packages with part-time and hourly employees who receive lower wages and no benefits. Many contingent workers would like to be employed full-time.

➡️ *Why are job satisfaction and alienation problems in the 1990s?*

Job satisfaction, which involves people's attitudes toward their work, has traditionally been highest among professionals and managers because they have considerable decision-making power. When workers' needs for self-identity and meaning are not met and work is done strictly for material gain, they become alienated. Today, deprofessionalization (when characteristics of a profession are eliminated and the job becomes semiprofessional) and job deskilling through technology at the middle-manager level have led to increased alienation.

➡️ *What kinds of hazardous working conditions exist and what action has the government taken?*

Occupational accidents can be transportation-related or can occur as a result of contact with equipment. Fires and explosions cause some injuries, as do assaults and violence. Occupational illnesses can result from exposure to dangerous chemicals or environmental situations. In 1970, a federal agency called the Occupational Safety and Health Administration (OSHA) was created to eliminate risks to workers' health, but OSHA's small budget limits its effectiveness.

➡️ *Is unemployment much of a problem in the United States today?*

Unemployment in the 1990s is much lower than it was in the 1970s and 1980s, but the statistics are not entirely accurate because they do not include discouraged workers—people who are no longer seeking work—or the underemployed, people with temporary or low-wage work because they can't find more suitable full-time employment. Structural employment, which occurs when workers' skills and educational levels do not match employers' requirements or when unemployed workers do not live where jobs they could perform are located, is a particular problem. One cause of structural unemployment is capital flight, the investing of U.S. money and other resources in facilities located in other countries where indigenous workers do the work that was previously done by U.S. workers.

➤ *Is discrimination still a problem in the workplace?*

Discrimination as a result of racism and sexism is very much a problem in the workplace. It can be blatant (derogatory remarks) or subtle; sometimes the target of discrimination may not even realize that discrimination has occurred. Many working women of color experience gendered racism—the interactive effect of both racism and sexism. And, of course, ageism, classism, and ableism (bias against persons with disabilities) can also cause discrimination.

➤ *What has happened to worker activism through labor unions?*

Unions were instrumental in bringing about many improvements for workers, including the eight-hour work day and five-day work week, but unions have less political clout today. One reason is the shift from manufacturing to service jobs, in which employees typically have been less able to unionize.

➤ *What is the functionalist perspective on work?*

Functionalists believe that dysfunctions in the economy occur today because of fluctuations in the global economy, rapid technological change, and the growth of transnational corporations. The result is an imbalance between the supply of and demand for workers. Functionalists believe that workplace problems can be reduced or eliminated if the social institutions in society cooperate.

➤ *What is the conflict perspective on work?*

Most conflict theorists believe that problems in the workplace are side effects of the capitalist economy wherein workers are exploited by power elites. Only when workers develop class consciousness—a feeling of unity based on an awareness of their shared exploitation by the capitalist class—can they get control of the workplace through activism.

➤ *What is the interactionist perspective on work?*

Interactionists focus on how people view their jobs and the conditions under which they work; work is a source of self-identity. Solving workplace problems is not easy. One sociologist, Arlie Hochschild, recently proposed that workers challenge the premises of the work culture in the United States and initiate a national dialogue asking such basic questions as "How many hours a day, a week, a year should people work?"

➤ *What will work in the twenty-first century look like?*

Today's trends may divide the labor market into two segments: those who hold high-paying, full-time jobs with good benefits and those who hold low-paying jobs with few benefits and little job security. At the same time, opportunities in the high-tech fields will ensure that the United States will remain a major player in the global economy.

KEY TERMS

alienation, p. 328
capital flight, p. 333
class consciousness, p. 340
contingent work, p. 326
deindustrialization, p. 324
gendered racism, p. 334

primary sector production, p. 322
secondary sector production, p. 323
sexual harassment, pp. 333–334
structural unemployment, p. 333
tertiary sector production, p. 324

QUESTIONS FOR CRITICAL THINKING

1. Think back over the jobs you have held and perhaps currently hold. Did you ever experience worker alienation? What were the causes? What could have been done to create more job satisfaction?

2. Analyze your local newspaper for evidence of problems in the workplace. What do you find in the business section about capital flight, for example, or hazardous work conditions? Look at the employment want ads. How many of the available jobs are in the service sector? How many are contingent jobs?

3. If you had to single out one workplace problem as the most serious facing the United States in the next century, what would it be and how would you propose solving it?

Chapter Sixteen

Population and the Environmental Crisis

You see, there are only nine cabins in the steamer launch which comes from Dhaka to Patuakhali. In the nine cabins only 18 people can travel. The ticket is expensive, so only the rich people travel in the cabins. The rest of the common passengers travel in the deck. The latrine facility [restroom] is provided only for the cabin passengers. But sometimes the passengers from the deck want to use the latrines. The cabin passengers allow them to use the latrine because they are afraid that if the poor deck passengers get angry then they might go down and make a hole in the launch. Then the launch will sink; they will die no doubt but the rich cabin passengers will not survive either. So, my dear sisters, do not give birth to more children as they cause a problem for the cabin passengers.

—*Writer Farida Ahkter*
recalls the story she heard
one family planning officer
tell a group of poor and
illiterate women in a remote
village in Bangladesh
(*The Ecologist,* 1993:143)

Global population control policies are the subject of international controversy. Although some people believe that government policies are essential to curbing overpopulation, others argue that government policies are a means by which dominant group members decide "*who* will be born, *how* many will be born, and of *what* race, class, sex and 'quality' they will be" (*The Ecologist,* 1993: 143). In this chapter, we examine the problem of global overpopulation, including its impact on the environment.

GLOBAL OVERPOPULATION

During the past fifty years, the world's population has more than doubled—from 2.5 billion in 1950 to almost 5.8 billion in 1996—and it is increasing by about 94 million people each year (U.S. Bureau of the Census, 1996b). At this rate, the world population will be over 6 billion by the year 2000, and it will double again in the following 50 years (Hauchler and Kennedy, 1994). Can the earth's resources support this growing population? Population experts answer this question in different ways, but it is an urgent question, and we need answers. Even today, more than 1 billion of the world's people do not have enough food and lack basic health care (Hauchler and Kennedy, 1994).

Rapid Population Growth

Growth rate varies among nations, more developed nations (including the United States) having lower population growth than less developed nations, especially those in Africa, Asia, and Latin America. In some nations, the population growth rate is negative, meaning that fewer people are added to the population through birth and immigration than are lost through death and emigration. A *population* is all the people living in a specified geographic area.

The area of sociology that studies the size, composition, and distribution of populations, among other things, is *demography*. Global population changes are important because they have a powerful influence on social, economic, and political structures in societies. For example, the population growth imbalance between developed and developing nations is a potential source of global conflict, particularly if world hunger and environmental destruction increase. Three primary factors affect the rate of population growth in any nation or area: fertility (births), mortality (deaths), and migration (movement between geographic areas). We'll look at each in turn.

Fertility

Fertility refers to the actual number of children born to an individual or a population. The most basic measure of fertility is the *crude birth rate*—the number of live births per 1,000 people in a population in a given year. In 1995, there were 4 million live births in the United States, yielding a crude birth rate of 15.2 per 1,000, down slightly from 16 per 1,000 in 1993 (U.S. Bureau of the Census, 1996b). The crude birth rate is used to gauge fertility because it is based on the entire population and does not take into account the variables that affect fertility, such as age, marital status, and race/ethnicity.

The level of fertility in a society is associated with social as well as biological factors. Countries that have high rates of infant and child mortality often have high birth rates. By having many children, parents in developing nations are more likely to see a few of them survive to adulthood. In nations

without social security systems to provide old-age insurance, children may be viewed as an "insurance plan" for the parents' old age, and in patriarchal societies, having many children—especially sons—is proof of manliness. Finally, in cultures in which religion dictates that children are God-given and family planning is forbidden because it "interferes with God's will," many more children are usually born (Hauchler and Kennedy, 1994).

Although men obviously are important in the reproductive process, the measure of fertility focuses on women because pregnancy and childbirth are more easily quantified than biological fatherhood. The number of women of childbearing age (usually between the ages of fifteen and forty-five) who live in the society is one factor in determining how many children will be born in a given year. Other biological factors that affect fertility include the general health and nutrition level of women of childbearing age. However, on the basis of biological capability alone, most women could produce twenty or more children during their childbearing years. In industrialized nations, therefore, many people limit their biological capabilities by practicing abstinence, refraining from sexual intercourse until an older age, using contraceptives, being sterilized, or having one or more abortions over the course of their reproductive years. Fertility rates also are affected by the number of available partners for sex and/or marriage, the number of women of childbearing age in the work force, and government policies regarding families. For example, China has a one-child policy, so abortion or sterilization can be required when there is an unauthorized pregnancy (Mosher, 1994).

Mortality

Birth rates are one factor in population growth; another is a decline in *mortality*—**the number of deaths that occur in a specific population.** The simplest measure of mortality is the *crude death rate*—the number of deaths per 1,000 people in a population in a given year. In 1995, there were 2.3 million deaths in the U.S. population, yielding a crude death rate of 8.8 per 1,000 (U.S. Bureau of the Census, 1996b). In many nations, mortality rates have declined dramatically as diseases such as malaria, polio, cholera, tetanus, typhoid, and measles have been virtually eliminated by vaccinations and improved sanitation and personal hygiene (Weeks, 1992).

In addition to measuring the crude death rate, demographers often measure the *infant mortality rate*—the number of deaths of infants under one year of age per 1,000 live births in a given year. In general, infant mortality has declined worldwide over the past two decades because many major childhood and communicable diseases are now under control. But infant mortality rates vary widely between nations. In developed nations, the average was 10 per 1,000 live births in 1995 (Japan having a low of 5 per 1,000), in sharp contrast to 89 per 1,000 live births in southern Asia and 95 per 1,000 live births in sub-Saharan Africa (United Nations, 1995).

In any nation, the infant mortality rate is an important reflection of a society's level of preventive (prenatal) medical care, maternal nutrition, childbirth procedures, and neonatal care for infants. In the United States, differential levels of access to these services are reflected in the gap between infant mortality rates for African Americans and whites. In 1995, for example, mortality for African American infants was 16 per 1,000 live births, compared to 7 per 1,000 live births for white infants (U.S. Bureau of the Census, 1996b).

Demographers also study *life expectancy*, the estimated average lifetime of people born in a specific year. For example, in 1995, the life expectancy at birth was 76.3 years for a person born in the United States, compared to 79.6 years in Japan and less than 50 years in the African nations of Burundi, Chad, Rwanda, and Uganda (U.S. Bureau of the Census, 1996b). In fact, the estimated life expectancy for people in Uganda and Zambia has dropped significantly over the past two decades. In Uganda, life expectancy dropped from 48 to 43 years for women and from 45 to 41 years for men (United Nations, 1995). Life expectancy varies not only by nation, but also by sex. Females born in the United States in 1995 have a life expectancy of about 79 years, whereas males born that year have a life expectancy of about 73 years. Life expectancy also varies by race. African American men, for example, have a life expectancy at birth of about 64 years, compared to 73 years for white males (U.S. Bureau of the Census, 1996b).

▲ Migration

Migration **is the movement of people from one geographic area to another for the purpose of changing residency.** Migration takes two forms: *immigra-* *tion*—the movement of people into a geographic area to take up residency—and *emigration*—the movement of people out of a geographic area to take up residency elsewhere. Today, over 23 million people live outside their countries of origin (Kane, 1995).

In the early 1990s, about 1 million people were entering the United States each year, but this number has decreased to about 800,000 annually because of more restrictive U.S. immigration policies and stricter enforcement. However, official immigration statistics do not reflect the actual number of immigrants who arrive in this country. The U.S. Immigration and Naturalization Service records only legal immigration based on entry visas and change-of-immigration-status forms. Some people enter the country as temporary visitors, coming for pleasure or business, as students, or as temporary workers or trainees but then do not leave when their stated purpose has been achieved and their permit expires.

Approximately 121,000 refugees are also admitted to this country annually as permanent residents. According to the 1951 United Nations Convention on Refugees, *refugees* are identified solely in terms of persecution for reasons of race, religion, nationality, membership in a particular social group, or political opinion (Kane, 1995). People who leave home to escape famine, for example, do not officially qualify as refugees.

The largest proportion of immigrants entering the United States each year arrive illegally. Many come from Mexico, El Salvador, Guatemala, Poland, Haiti, the Bahamas, and Nicaragua (U. S. Bureau of the Census, 1996b). Government officials estimate that between 3.5 million and 4 million people annually enter this country illegally (U.S. Bureau of the Census, 1996b). Of course, it is not known how many of them return to their countries of origin or how many people enter, leave, and reenter the United States, as is often done by undocumented workers coming and going between the United States and Mexico or Canada (Weeks, 1992).

Many immigrants come to the United States because it offers them greater job opportunities and freedom from the political, religious, sexual, or racial/ethnic oppression of their home country. For example, researchers found that many women migrate from the Dominican Republic to this country to improve their economic position and escape a repressive patriarchal environment. When both husband

SOCIAL PROBLEMS
IN GLOBAL PERSPECTIVE

BOX 16.1

Immigration and Anti-Immigrant Sentiment: A Growing Problem

In the still midnight air, only the coils of razor wire glinting in the harsh yellow floodlights hinted at the divide between the vast poverty of China and the compact neon glitter of Hong Kong.

Along the fence, in green camouflage fatigues and with a pistol strapped to his waist, the Hong Kong immigration inspector whispered into his radio to his ambush team ahead in the darkness. The inspector, Jeff Eng, turned to a visitor in his police van and explained, "Our job is to catch I.I.'s,"—illegal immigrants. The van crawled next to the border fence. He peered into China. "It's very quiet tonight," he said. "Very quiet."

—A routine border patrol to keep Chinese mainlanders from illegally entering Hong Kong (Gargan, 1997:A3)

For years, both Hong Kong and China have strictly limited immigration to Hong Kong—only 150 mainlanders a day. But in the year before Hong Kong was returned to China, mainlanders began illegally entering Hong Kong in droves, to reunite families and to better their opportunities. They hoped that Beijing would declare an amnesty on all illegal immigrants. But Beijing was adamant: Illegal immigrants would be returned, forcibly, if necessary. As it is, Hong Kong's population is expected to grow from 6.3 million to 8.2 million in the next 10 years, and Hong Kong residents are alarmed (Gargan, 1997).

In Hong Kong, controlling immigration is a means of controlling population. France and Germany also have tightened immigration laws, but for a different reason. Chronic double-digit unemployment and a history of mak-

---

and wife migrate from the Dominican Republic, the women are more likely to remain in this country because they find that working gives them more economic security and power at home, whereas many of the men save their money and return to the Dominican Republic (Grasmuck and Pessar, 1991). However, some people leave their countries of origin for various social, economic, and political reasons, only to learn that they are not welcomed or even tolerated when they arrive in the new country (see Box 16.1).

To determine the effects of immigration and emigration, demographers compute the *crude net migration rate*—the net number of migrants (total in-migrants minus total out-migrants) per 1,000 people in a population in a given year. Currently, the net migration rate in the United States is about 2.4 per 1,000 population, which means that between two

and three more people per 1,000 population enter this country than leave it each year (based on U.S. Bureau of the Census, 1996b).

The Impact of Population Growth

What is the effect of population growth on a society? Population growth affects *population composition*—**the biological and social characteristics of a population, including such attributes as age, sex, race, marital status, education, occupation, income, and size of household.** In the United States, for example, the age distribution of the population is associated with people's demands for community resources such as elementary and secondary schools, libraries, health care and recreational facilities, employment opportunities, and age-appropriate housing.

ing immigrants into scapegoats underlie the anti-immigrant mood in these countries (Whitney, 1996b). Both countries have also redefined citizenship. It used to be that children born to foreign parents on French soil were automatically citizens, but now they must apply for citizenship before their eighteenth birthday (Whitney, 1996a). In Germany, descendants of German workers who went to Russia 200 years ago to farm the Volga River Valley can return to Germany as full citizens, while children of Turkish workers who were born in Germany and schooled in Germany—who speak no Turkish and may have never set foot in Turkey—might find it easier to pass through the eye of a needle than to acquire German citizenship (Whitney, 1996a).

An anti-immigrant mood also pervades parts of the United States. Citizen groups in California, Texas, and Washington, D.C., lobby to reduce immigration quotas and cut welfare aid to immigrants. "They seem to forget that, in an earlier generation, their relatives were newcomers, too" (Kane, 1995, p. 18). The concern is rising taxes. But research shows that since 1970, immigrants have paid a total of $70 bil-lion in taxes, which is $25–30 billion more than they used in public services (Kane, 1995).

The anti-immigrant sentiment that we see in Western countries doesn't bode well for the future. According to the United Nations, we can expect 46 million refugees by the year 2000—double the number in 1995 (Kane, 1995). We can also expect large migrations due to inequality between the rich and the poor in the world. Already, 900,000 Turks have moved to Germany and the Scandinavian countries for work; 2.5 million Mexicans live in the United States; and 1.2 million foreigners work in Saudi Arabia (Kane, 1995). Then there are the disasters that no one can predict: A reactor blows up in Chernobyl; floods ravage Bangladesh; famine strikes Ethiopia and Somalia.

How do you see the problem of anti-immigrant sentiment and growing immigration? Are we facing a crisis in the near future? Can we overcome intolerance? Knowing that the number of refugees is rapidly increasing, do you think there is anything we can do in advance to plan for relief for the victims? What do you think?

What are the consequences of global population growth? Not all social analysts agree on the answer to this question. As discussed below, some analysts warn that the earth is a finite system that cannot support its rapidly growing population. But others believe that capitalism—if freed from government intervention—could develop innovative solutions to such problems as hunger and pollution. Still others argue that capitalism is part of the problem, not part of the solution.

What about the effects of rapid population growth on individuals? According to Population Action International's Human Suffering Index (HSI), the countries that have the highest rates of growth also have the most human suffering. For example, twenty of the twenty-seven countries listed in the "extreme human suffering" category are in Africa, the fastest-growing region in the world (*Human Suffering Index*, 1992). The HSI also shows that while many people in poverty-stricken regions die from hunger and malnutrition each year, people in the most developed nations spend billions of dollars annually on diet products and exercise gear because they think they are overfed and overweight.

Rapid population growth and overpopulation are not new problems. Causes and solutions have been debated for nearly two centuries.

THE MALTHUSIAN PERSPECTIVE

In 1798, Thomas Malthus, an English clergyman and economist, published *An Essay on Population*. Malthus (1965/1798) argued that the global population, if left unchecked, would exceed the available food supply. The population would increase in a geo-

Starving children in nations such as Somalia raise important questions about Malthusian and neo-Malthusian perspectives. Is world hunger primarily a consequence of overpopulation or are other political and economic factors also important?

metric (exponential) progression (2, 4, 8, 16, . . .), but the food supply would increase only by an arithmetic progression (1, 2, 3, 4, . . .). The population would surpass the food supply, thus ending population growth and perhaps eliminating the world population (Weeks, 1992). Disaster could be averted only by positive checks (e.g., famine, disease, and war) or preventive checks (e.g., sexual abstinence before marriage and postponement of marriage for as long as possible) to limit people's fertility.

THE NEO-MALTHUSIAN PERSPECTIVE

Today, *neo-Malthusians* (or "new Malthusians") speak of the "population explosion" and "population bomb" to emphasize the urgent need to reduce global population growth. Among the best known neo-Malthusians are biologists Paul Ehrlich and Anne H. Ehrlich, who believe that world population growth is following the exponential growth pattern that Malthus described (Ehrlich and Ehrlich, 1991:15):

> Exponential growth occurs in populations because children . . . remain in the population and themselves have children. A key feature of exponential growth is that it often seems to start slow and finish fast. A classic example . . . is the pond weed that doubles each day . . . to cover the entire pond in thirty days. The question is, how much of the pond will be covered in twenty-nine days? The answer, of course, is that just half of the pond will be covered in twenty-nine days. The weed will then double once more and cover the entire pond the next day. As this example indicates, exponential growth contains the potential for big surprises.

To neo-Malthusians, the earth is a dying planet with too many people in relation to the available food supply. Overpopulation and rapid population growth exacerbate global environmental problems, ranging from global warming and rainforest destruction to famine and epidemics such as AIDS. However, some analysts offer another explanation of global population patterns, known as demographic transition theory.

DEMOGRAPHIC TRANSITION THEORY

According to *demographic transition theory,* societies move from high birth and death rates to relatively low birth and death rates as a result of technological development. The demographic transition takes place in four stages: The *preindustrial stage* is characterized by little population growth: High birth rates are offset by high death rates. This period is followed by the *transitional* or *early industrial stage,* which is characterized by significant population growth as the birth rate remains high but death rates decline because of new technologies that improve health, sanitation, and nutrition. Today, large parts of Africa, Asia, and Latin America are in this second stage. The third stage is *advanced industrialization and urbanization*: The birth rate declines as people control their fertility with various forms of contraception, and the death rate likewise declines as medicine and other health care technologies control acute and chronic diseases. Finally, in the *postindustrial stage*, the population grows very slowly, if at all. In this stage, a decreasing birth rate is coupled with a stable death rate.

Proponents of demographic transition theory believe that technology can overcome the dire predictions of Malthus and the neo-Malthusians. But critics point out that not all nations go through all the stages or as outlined. They think that demographic transition theory explains development in Western societies but not necessarily in others. For example, China is in the process of significantly reducing its birth rate, but this change is a result of the government's mandated one-child-per-family policy, not technological advances or urbanization (Weeks, 1992).

◣ World Hunger

Food shortages, chronic hunger, and malnutrition are the consequences of rapid population growth, particularly in developing nations. Approximately 800 million people in developing nations experience continuous hunger or *chronic malnourishment*—inadequate food to provide the minimum energy necessary for doing light work over a period of time (FAO, 1995). Chronic malnutrition contributes to childhood health problems such as anemia (a blood condition that produces weakness and a lack of energy that can result in child mortality or impaired mental functioning), stunting (impaired physical growth or development), and being underweight (United Nations, 1995). In pregnant women, malnutrition increases the risk of anemia, infection, birth complications, and lack of breast milk (see Figure 16.1). In contrast, improvements in nutrition significantly reduce health risks and the spread of some communicable illnesses (Hauchler and Kennedy, 1994).

What efforts are being made to reduce global food shortages and world hunger? Organizations such as the United Nations, the World Health Organization, and the International Red Cross have programs in place, but the most far-reaching initiatives are known as the green revolution and the biotechnological revolution.

THE GREEN REVOLUTION

The *green revolution* refers to dramatic increases in agricultural production made possible by high-yield "miracle" crops. In the 1940s, researchers at the International Maize and Wheat Improvement Center started the green revolution by developing high-yield varieties of wheat that increased world grain production. The new dwarf-type wheat, which produces more stalks, has dramatically increased the wheat yield in countries such as India and Pakistan since the 1960s. Researchers have also developed a high-yield dwarf rice with twice as many grains per plant, greatly improving the rice output in India, Pakistan, the Philippines, Indonesia, and Vietnam (Weeks, 1992).

How successful has the green revolution been in reducing world hunger? During the 1970s, the green revolution helped to increase the global food supply at a somewhat faster pace than the global population grew, but in the 1980s and 1990s, agricultural production slowed considerably. Also, while the new miracle crops have increased food production in Latin American and Asia, they have not really benefited Africa (Kennedy, 1993).

A major problem is that costly fertilizers, pesticides, and irrigation systems are needed to produce the high-yield crops. Not only are the supplies and equipment beyond the budgets of most developing nations, but the fertilizers and pesticides often constitute health hazards and become a source of surface water and groundwater pollution (Weeks, 1992). Moreover, for the green revolution to eliminate hunger and malnutrition, the social organization of life in many developing nations would have to change significantly. For example, people would have to adopt the Western methods of farming on which the green revolution was built and be willing to produce a single crop in very high volume. But single-crop production can lead to nutritional deficiencies if other varieties of food are not available. Nevertheless, researchers recently developed high-yield sorghum, yams, and other crops that can be grown successfully in the nations of Africa where some of the greatest food shortages exist (Weeks, 1992).

THE BIOTECHNOLOGICAL REVOLUTION

A second approach to reducing global food shortages, known as the *biotechnological revolution*, encompasses any technique for "improving"

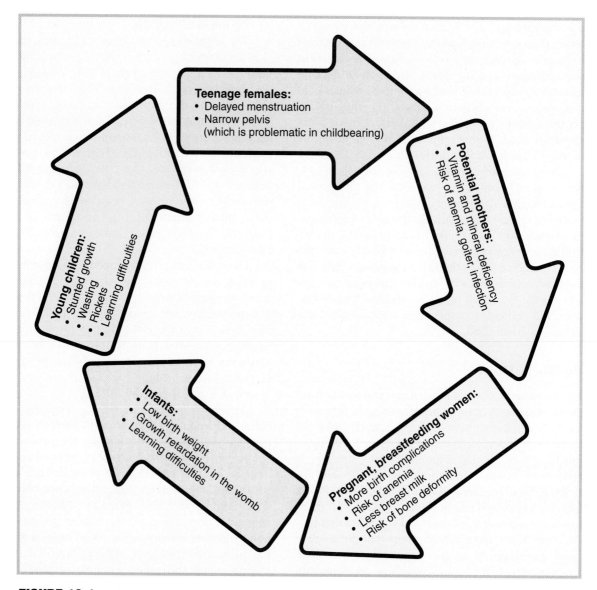

Teenage females:
• Delayed menstruation
• Narrow pelvis
  (which is problematic in childbearing)

Potential mothers:
• Vitamin and mineral deficiency
• Risk of anemia, goiter, infection

Young children:
• Stunted growth
• Wasting
• Rickets
• Learning difficulties

Infants:
• Low birth weight
• Growth retardation in the womb
• Learning difficulties

Pregnant, breastfeeding women:
• More birth complications
• Risk of anemia
• Less breast milk
• Risk of bone deformity

FIGURE 16.1 *The Circle of Malnutrition*
(SOURCE: Based on United Nations, 1995.)

plants or animals or using microorganisms in innovative ways. Using growth hormone to increase milk output in cows is one possibility. Scientists are also exploring ways to genetically alter the reproductive cells of fish, poultry, sheep, and pigs to speed up conventional breeding times (Kennedy, 1993). Scientists have already genetically altered microorganisms in several ways. Soon, for example, it should be possible to spray frost-sensitive plants, such as strawberries, with a strain of bacteria that will protect crops against up to 95 percent of frost damage.

Some scientists believe that the biotechnological revolution can close the gap between worldwide food production and rapid population growth, but the new technology is not without problems of its own. First, giving growth hormones to animals can make their meat unfit for human consumption. Hogs that get growth hormones are prone to gastric ulcers, arthritis, dermatitis, and other diseases (Kennedy, 1993). Second, the cost of biotechnological innovations is beyond the budgets of most developing nations. Third, the new biotechnologies are developed for use with conventional (Western) farming methods (Hauchler and Kennedy, 1994). Fourth, genetic erosion (by breeding or gene manipulation) could eventually make the people of the world reliant on only a few varieties of plants and animals for their entire food supply and thus vulnerable to famine as the result of a single pest or disease. Finally, environmental accidents, such as the unintentional release of genetically manipulated microorganisms, pose a potential hazard.

Increasing the food supply is one way of coping with a rapidly growing world population, but hardly the only way. Some people believe that we can forestall the problem by controlling fertility.

CONTROLLING FERTILITY

The global population increase in the twentieth century has been unprecedented, and an additional 3 billion young people around the globe will soon enter their reproductive years (United Nations, 1995). Although demographers suggest that limiting fertility is the best way to slow down population growth, they acknowledge that the issue is fraught with controversy. Consider the three preconditions that demographer Ansley Coale (1973) believes are necessary before there can be a sustained decline in a society's fertility:

◆ *People must accept calculated choice as a valid element in marital fertility.* If a supernatural power is believed to control human reproduction, it is unlikely that people will risk offending that deity by trying to limit fertility. On the other hand, the more worldly-wise people are, the more likely they are to believe they have the right to control reproduction.

◆ *People must see advantages to reduced fertility.* People must have some reason to want to limit fertility. Otherwise, natural attraction will lead to unprotected sexual intercourse and perhaps numerous children.

◆ *People must know about and master effective techniques of birth control.* The means for limiting family size must be available, and people must know how to use them successfully.

Although Coale believes that all three preconditions must be met to limit fertility effectively, most government policies focus only on the third: family planning measures (Weeks, 1992).

▲ Family Planning

Family planning programs provide birth control information, contraceptive devices, sometimes sterilization and abortion procedures, and health services. The earliest programs were based on the assumption that women have large families because they do not know how to prevent pregnancy or they lack access to birth control devices. Though we know today that other issues are involved, most programs still follow the early pattern. They do little,

Some analysts believe that China's one-child policy has further devalued female infants. What long-term effects might such a policy have on the sex ratio (number of males in relation to number of females) in that country? Could this influence the number of females and males available for marriage and parenting in the future?

for example, to influence a couple's desire to have children, and in some developing nations, women are not free to make their own decisions about reproduction. There is overwhelming evidence that women want only the number of children that they can care for adequately (United Nations, 1995); an estimated 120 million women want to postpone the next birth or avoid further childbearing altogether (Westoff, 1995). At the same time, many women are socialized to accept the ideal of the perfect mother, so motherhood confers social status and a sense of personal achievement. Children are considered a gift and a blessing, providing women with affection that they might not otherwise receive and securing the mother's position in the kinship group and the larger society (O'Connell, 1994).

Critics of family planning programs argue that most policies are developed by political leaders in developed nations who are motivated by race and class issues, not a genuine concern about world hunger or overpopulation. They say that developed nations—such as England, France, and the United States—encourage births among middle- and upper-income white women in their own countries but advocate depopulation policies in developing regions such as sub-Saharan Africa, where most residents are people of color who live in poverty (O'Connell, 1994). For example, the French government is promoting larger families because of a rapidly aging population, a low fertility rate, and a national concern that the country is losing its identity because of high immigration rates (Weeks, 1992).

▲ Zero Population Growth

With *zero population growth,* there is a totally stable population, one that neither grows nor decreases from year to year because births, deaths, and migration are in perfect balance (Weeks, 1992). For example, if a nation had no immigration or emigration and the birth rate and the death rate were the same, the population growth rate would be zero (Ehrlich and Ehrlich, 1991).

The United States is nearing zero population growth because of several factors: (1) A high proportion of women and men in the labor force find satisfaction and rewards outside of family life; (2) birth control is inexpensive and readily available; (3) the trend is toward later marriage (see Chapter 12); (4) the cost of raising a child from birth to adulthood is

rising rapidly; and (5) schools and public service campaigns make teenagers more aware of how to control fertility (United Nations, 1995). Near-zero population growth is one characteristic of the U.S. population; another is a rapidly changing population.

IMMIGRATION AND ITS CONSEQUENCES

High rates of immigration are changing the composition of the U.S. population. Today, approximately 20 million people—or 8 percent of the total U.S. population—came here from other nations. In fact, the proportion of U.S. immigrants is at its highest point since the early 1940s, when people born in other countries accounted for 9 percent of the population. In 1944, immigration accounted for 30 percent of that year's increase in the U.S. population and contributed to the growth of large urban centers such as New York, Los Angeles, and Miami. On a global basis, immigration and internal migration are causing urban populations to grow faster than the total population (see Map 16.1). The consequences often are patterns of urban squalor and high levels of stress in daily living because most cities do not have the capacity to deal with existing residents, much less significant increases in the number of people with limited education and economic wherewithal.

What are the consequences of today's high rate of immigration to the United States? Not all social analysts agree on the answer to this question. Some believe that immigrants cost U.S. taxpayers billions of dollars each year (see Huddle, 1993), although the cost varies widely from state to state. One study estimated that households in California pay about $1,200 a year in state and local taxes to cover services such as education, welfare, public health, and police protection for immigrants, whereas New Jersey residents pay about $230 a year for immigrant services (Serrin, 1997). But a recent study conducted by the National Academy of Sciences found that immigration produces substantial economic benefits for the United States (Pear, 1997a). In fact, immigrants may contribute as much as $10 billion a year to the economic output of this country. This same study also pointed out that low-skilled, U.S.-born workers can lose jobs because of competition from

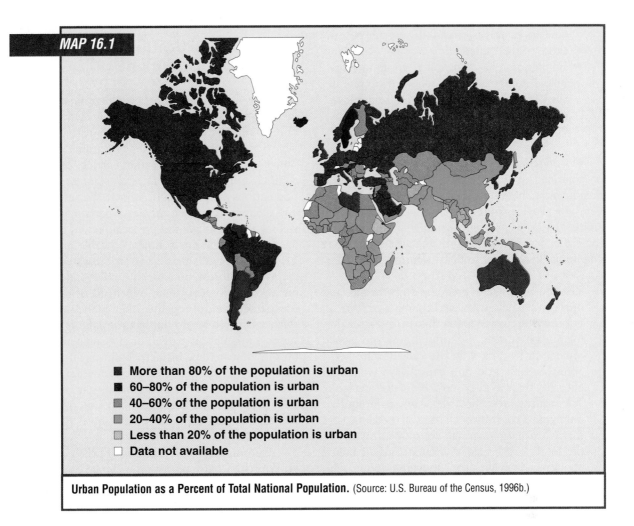

MAP 16.1

■ More than 80% of the population is urban
■ 60–80% of the population is urban
■ 40–60% of the population is urban
■ 20–40% of the population is urban
□ Less than 20% of the population is urban
□ Data not available

Urban Population as a Percent of Total National Population. (Source: U.S. Bureau of the Census, 1996b.)

immigrant workers (Pear, 1997a). Economist James P. Smith sums up this way (Pear, 1997a:1, 15):

> It's true that some Americans are now paying more taxes because of immigration, and native-born Americans without a high school education have seen their wages fall slightly because of the competition sparked by lower-skilled, newly arrived immigrants. But the vast majority of Americans are enjoying a healthier economy as a result of the increased supply of labor and lower prices that result from immigration.

The National Academy of Sciences study also found that, despite a widespread belief to the contrary, African Americans are not universally hurt by immigration or competition with immigrants. It ap-

pears that only in big cities where many recent immigrants have settled, such as New York and Los Angeles, are African Americans likely to lose jobs directly because of the large concentration of immigrants (Pear, 1997a).

Other findings from the National Academy of Sciences report provide important insights (Pear, 1997a:1, 15):

♦ If immigration to the United States continues at the present rate, it will account for nearly two-thirds of the expected population growth in the next 50 years.
♦ The wage gap between immigrants and U.S.-born workers will grow wider because many recent immigrants are arriving from poorer nations where the average levels of

education, wages, and skills are far below those of the United States.

◆ Immigration has contributed to an increase in the number of high school dropouts in the United States, and this increase has lowered the wages of high school dropouts by about 5 percent.

One more consequence of immigration needs to be examined: immigrant-bashing. It is not a new phenomenon, but the recent influx of immigrants seems to provide more opportunities for such behavior. Here is what a representative of an immigration rights organization found when she spent a day with some high school students (Duran, 1997:A7):

> The students were predominantly white and upper-middle-class. I went in hoping to have an informed discussion about this divisive issue [immigration]. Instead, I glimpsed how entrenched immigrant-bashing is in the United States. . . . Some students said you can always tell illegal aliens by the way they look. How do they look? The students described Mexicans, ignoring that immigrants come from all parts of the globe, and that Mexican immigrants are only a fraction of the total. . . . I tried a different tack. I talked about people in Mexico who were starving, who needed to find work or join their families. Their need is so great that they endure desperate conditions on the journey. . . . I told of a women who drowned attempting to swim the crossing [from Mexico] with her baby. Her last act was to hand over her baby to a companion, saving its life. The response was dismaying, "Why didn't they just use a boat?" a student asked. "If they're so stupid that they can't use a boat, what do they expect?" The class erupted into laughter. . . . As I continue to promote immigrant rights, my job will be to open those closed [hearts and minds], and to remind people that their fate is connected to the fate of others, including immigrants.

Most population-related policies in the United States focus on immigration, particularly undocumented workers or illegal immigrants. But stemming the flow of immigrants appears to be a virtually impossible task for any one nation, as does alleviating the problem of environmental degradation.

POPULATION AND THE ENVIRONMENT

Although it is popularly believed that most environmental problems arise from rapid growth in developing nations, this isn't the case. Many scientists believe that the richest developed nations present a much greater threat to the earth's ecosystems (Ehrlich and Ehrlich, 1991). An *ecosystem* is "all the populations of plants and animal species that live and interact in a given area at a particular time, as well as the chemical and physical factors that make up the nonliving environment" (Cable and Cable, 1995:124). Thus an ocean is an ecosystem, as is a tropical rainforest; on a much smaller scale, a house on a lot is an ecosystem. When all of the earth's ecosystems are put together, they make up the *biosphere*. Ecosystems do not have an infinite ability to support population growth or environmental depletion or destruction. In fact, some scientists believe that many of the world's ecosystems have already exceeded their *carrying capacity*—the maximum population that an ecosystem can support without eventually being degraded or destroyed (Cable and Cable, 1995).

According to biologists Paul Ehrlich and Anne H. Ehrlich, a baby born in the United States represents twice the destructive impact on the earth's ecosystems and services as a baby born in Sweden, 140 times the impact of a baby born in Bangladesh or Kenya, and 280 times the impact of a baby born in Chad, Rwanda, Haiti, or Nepal. How did the Ehrlichs reach such a conclusion? They developed a formula for determining the impact that human beings have on their environment: $I = P \times A \times T$, or Impact = Population × Affluence × Technology. Thus the size of the population, its level of affluence, and the technology available in the society are major contributing factors to **environmental degradation—disruptions to the environment that have negative consequences for ecosystems** (Cable and Cable, 1995). Environmental degradation involves both removing natural resources from the environment and adding to environmental problems through pollution.

In the United States, environmental degradation increases as people try to maintain the high levels of wealth and material comfort to which they have be-

"I'm rather fortunate. I have no parents, so Medicare is no problem, and I have no children, so the environment is no problem."

Drawing by Handelsman; © 1995 The New Yorker Magazine, Inc.

come accustomed. They consume the earth's resources and pollute its environment with automobiles, airplanes, speedboats, computers, television sets and VCRs, year-around air conditioning and heating, and other amenities that are far beyond the grasp of most of the world's people. Although these products are made possible by high levels of industrial production and economic growth, economic growth often depletes and destroys the environment. Let's look briefly at how this can happen.

▲ Economic Growth and Environmental Degradation

During most of the twentieth century, economic growth in the United States has been based on in-creased output in the manufacturing sector. The environment is affected at all phases of the manufacturing process, from mining and transportation to manufacturing and waste disposal. As we discussed in Chapter 15, industrial production involves extracting raw materials—natural resources—from the environment, usually through mining. The process depletes mineral resources and fossil fuel reserves—the coal, oil, and natural gas on which industry currently depends. Mining also disturbs ecosystems through pollution, particularly surface mining that strips bare the land, destroying natural vegetation and wildlife habitats. Other problems typically follow, including erosion of the land by wind and water; runoff of acids, silt, and toxic substances into nearby surface water and groundwater; and pollution of rivers and streams with toxic compounds that kill fish and other aquatic life (Cable and Cable, 1995).

But the environmental impact of mining doesn't stop when the raw materials have been mined. Now the raw materials must be transported to a plant or factory, where workers transform the resources into manufactured products. Transporting requires the use of energy—particularly the burning of fossil fuels—that contributes to air pollution. Motor vehicles produce carbon monoxide, nitrogen oxides, and photochemical pollutants. Each of these is associated with various illnesses, including heart and respiratory disease and cancer. The manufacturing process further depletes fossil fuels and contributes to air pollution. People who work in or live near facilities that pollute the environment are often most harmed by the manufacturing process, because of the solid or toxic wastes.

Many analysts believe that we cannot continue this pattern of environmental degradation. Future economic development—in the United States and globally—will require drastic changes in the structure of industry, especially in the energy, transportation, chemical, and agricultural sectors of the economy (Hauchler and Kennedy, 1994). If we don't make changes, environmental degradation consti-

tutes a major threat to the well-being of all human beings and ecosystems on the earth. Let's look now at some specific kinds of environmental degradation: air pollution; problems with water, soil, and forests; and solid, toxic, and nuclear waste.

▲ Air Pollution

Air pollution involves several related problems. One problem is a drastic increase in carbon dioxide and other gases that pollute the air we breathe and keep the sun's heat from radiating back into space, thereby causing the earth to heat up (the greenhouse effect, discussed below). Another problem is depletion of the upper atmosphere ozone that shields the earth from ultraviolet radiation. The ozone layer, located thirty miles above our planet's surface, protects us from the sun's ultraviolet rays (Petersen, 1994). Ozone depletion can kill the organic life that produces food and oxygen, making life unsustainable. In fact, nature performs many *ecosystem services*, which are valuable, practical functions. For example, if the atmosphere is not overburdened, it can maintain a proper balance between carbon dioxide and oxygen, as well as providing ozone for protection against ultraviolet radiation (see Table 16.1).

▲ TABLE 16.1   WHAT THE NATURAL WORLD DOES FOR US (IF WE DON'T MESS IT UP TOO MUCH)

FOOD PRODUCTION	Produces fish, game, and crops—even without our help.
RAW MATERIALS	Produces (without our help) the raw materials from which humans create things.
GENETIC RESOURCES	On its own, creates the ability for crops, vegetation, and animals to survive.
POLLINATION	Without our help, plants and animals naturally reproduce.
BIOLOGICAL CONTROL	Somehow, most species of plants and animals survive for millions of years without our help.
CLIMATE REGULATION	Unless we mess it up, nature has created an ozone layer that protects all plant and animal life from the sun's ultraviolet radiation.
WATER REGULATION	If we don't mess with it, the world's water supply keeps reproducing and distributing itself.
GAS REGULATION	If we don't mess it up too badly, nature keeps carbon dioxide and oxygen in balance—a balance necessary for life.
RECREATION	Just think of the wonderful sights and recreation that nature has created.

Source: Stevens, 1997.

Air pollution is a pressing problem in many nations, but nowhere more so than in Mexico City, where daylight hours often look like this photo. How is air pollution related to people's health and life expectancy?

The drastic increase in air pollution during this century has placed an undue burden on the atmosphere's ecosystem services (Stevens, 1997). Beginning with the Industrial Revolution in the late nineteenth and early twentieth centuries, households, industries, and automobile traffic have emitted more and more pollutants into the atmosphere. The result is constantly increasing amounts of carbon dioxide, carbon monoxide, nitrogen oxide, and sulfur oxide, as well as heavy metals such as lead, zinc, and copper in our air (Hauchler and Kennedy, 1994). Today, 85 percent of the air pollution in urban areas is attributed to the internal combustion engine used in automobiles and other vehicles (U.S. Bureau of the Census, 1996b). Although laws have reduced the amount of pollution from automobiles and industries in the United States, over 40 percent of the population resides in areas where air pollutants exceed acceptable levels (Hauchler and Kennedy, 1994).

Not only does air pollution affect human beings, it also affects all life and ecosystems on the planet. Air pollution in the form of acid rain destroys forests, streams and lakes, and other ecosystems. *Acid rain* is rainfall containing large concentrations of sulfuric and nitric acids (primarily from the burn-ing of fuel and car and truck exhausts). In Germany, for example, acid rain is believed to have damaged more than half the trees—up to 80 percent in some regions (Hauchler and Kennedy, 1994). Efforts to reduce acid rain in the United States have been blocked by the automobile industry; companies that mine, haul, and sell high-sulfur coal; and coal miners. Fortunately, new industries are less dependent on burning coal than are older factories in the industrial Northeast and Midwest states (Petersen, 1994).

In the past, air pollution in developing nations was attributed mainly to fighting for survival and economic development, whereas most air pollution in developed nations was linked to automobiles and maintaining a relatively luxurious lifestyle. Although the United States and other Western industrial nations account for about 68 percent of the carbon monoxide in the atmosphere, distinctions between air pollution in developed and developing nations are otherwise growing weaker (World Resources Institute, 1992). Automobile ownership is rising rapidly in urban centers in developing nations such as Mexico, Brazil, Taiwan, Indonesia, and China (Bradsher, 1997). In 1997, for example, São Paulo, Brazil, had approximately 4.5 million cars on its streets—more than twice the 2.1 million cars in New York City, which has about the same population (Bradsher, 1997). Mexico City, known as the smog capital of the world, has only thirty-seven days a year when the air quality measures as "satisfactory" (Walker, 1994). Affluent Mexican residents buy bottled oxygen at the drug store; the less affluent buy quick shots of oxygen at street-corner kiosks (Cleeland, 1991). Cities such as Bombay, Lagos, Shanghai, and Jakarta have also seen a significant increase in the number of automobiles, bringing a corresponding rise in air pollution and traffic problems (Bradsher, 1997).

But there are some hopeful signs that we are curbing fossil fuel pollution. In the United States, antipollution laws have brought about changes in how automobiles are made and the fuels they consume. Cars are now equipped with catalytic converters and other antipollution devices, and leaded gasoline (a major offender) has been phased out. However, while some developing nations are requiring antipollution devices on new vehicles, many leaded gas–burning cars—often used cars from the United States—are still a significant source of air pollution.

Industrial air pollution has been reduced in some regions of the United States, but pollution controls are often expensive, and many corporations try to find ways to get around making costly plant conversions. Some move their plants to developing nations that have less stringent environmental regulations; others try to avoid antipollution guidelines through government waivers, sometimes known as pollution credits. These credits were initially created by the federal Clean Air Act of 1990 to reward state agencies and companies that keep their emissions below federal governmental limits. Recently, however, New York State used its accumulated credits to lure heavily polluting corporations to the state. Essentially, then, the pollution credits that were earned by the state for reducing its own pollution emissions would allow these corporations to pollute in return for moving to the state and paying New York taxes (Hernandez, 1997). Environmental activists ask why the state should subsidize polluters in the name of economic development and at the expense of people's health and the environment (Hernandez, 1997).

THE GREENHOUSE EFFECT

Emissions from traffic and industry not only add to general air pollution but also contribute to the *greenhouse effect*—**an environmental condition caused by excessive quantities of carbon dioxide, water vapor, methane, and nitrous oxide in the atmosphere.** When carbon dioxide molecules build up in the earth's atmosphere, they act like the glass roof of a greenhouse, allowing sunlight to reach the earth's surface but preventing the escape of solar infrared radiation (heat) back into space. The heat that cannot escape is reflected, causing the earth's surface temperature to rise (Weiner, 1990). Some scientists believe that the earth will have a temperature increase of as much as five degrees over the next hundred years. In fact, if current rates of emission into the atmosphere remain unchanged, temperature increases might eventually bring about catastrophic consequences.

One consequence of global warming could be significant changes in weather patterns and climate. Changes in weather patterns could bring increased evaporation, creating new deserts and decreasing regional water reserves. Changes in air circulation and climatic conditions could result in more frequent hurricanes, flooding, tidal waves, and droughts. Vegetation zones could shift, and forests in the northern hemisphere might die off.

Not all scientists believe that the greenhouse effect exists or that its effects will be this disastrous

(Hauchler and Kennedy, 1994). But studies show a marked retreat of glaciers and the beginning of a shift in vegetation, and one possible cause is the greenhouse effect (Hauchler and Kennedy, 1994).

To reduce greenhouse gases, political and economic leaders in developed nations want less-developed nations to lower their birth rates so that the total number of people contributing to the problem does not rise. But leaders in developing nations think that developed nations should institute stringent restrictions on consumption and pollution in their own countries and use some of their resources to help other countries with economic development and alleviating poverty. Then, they say, it may be possible to significantly reduce their birth rates (Hauchler and Kennedy, 1994).

DEPLETION OF THE OZONE LAYER

But the air pollution problem gets worse yet. There is some indication that the ozone layer of the atmosphere is endangered. Ozone is vital to life on earth because it is the only gas in the atmosphere that can absorb the sun's dangerous ultraviolet radiation. Yet in 1992, a hole in the ozone layer the size of North America was reported over Antarctica, and scientists have concluded that the ozone layer has been thinning out at a rate of 6 percent a year in the 1990s (Hauchler and Kennedy, 1994). It is important to note that the ozone shrinkage that scientists are currently measuring is the result of emissions in the early 1980s; the emissions we produce in the late 1990s will exert their destructive effects in the twenty-first century (Hauchler and Kennedy, 1994). A thinning ozone layer increases risks of skin cancer, damages marine life, and lowers crop yields. Past damage cannot be undone, but many countries are now phasing out products that contain chemicals that damage the ozone layer, hoping to control damage to this delicate ecosystem in the future.

▲ Problems with Water, Soil, and Forests

Water, soil, and forests (vegetation) are interdependent resources that are increasingly being degraded or destroyed. Both the existence and quality of soil, water, and vegetation are crucial for sustaining life. Yet as a result of climate changes, waste, pollution, and rapid depletion, the earth's drinking water is endangered and its fertile land is being lost.

WATER SHORTAGES AND POLLUTION

The United States is described as stretching "from sea to shining sea," but water depletion and pollution are serious problems in this country. The western United States already suffers from chronic water scarcity, and other regions are periodically affected by drought and other weather-related conditions. Although approximately 70 percent of the earth's surface is covered by water, most water is not drinkable: 97 percent is saltwater, 2 percent is in ice caps and glaciers, and most of the remaining 1 percent is so far underground that it is beyond human reach (Petersen, 1994). The primary sources of water for use and consumption are rainfall, streams, lakes, rivers, and aquifers (accessible underground water supplies).

Because of the current rate of world population growth and existing climatic conditions, water scarcity is increasing on a global basis. It is estimated that by the year 2000, many countries will have only half as much water available per person as was available in 1975. If the greenhouse effect brings about changes in the climate, as many as twenty-one countries in Africa could experience serious water shortages that will be further exacerbated by the growing problem of water pollution (Hauchler and Kennedy, 1994).

Where does the water go? The largest amount (about 70 percent) is used for crop irrigation; in some African and Asian countries, as much as 85 percent of the water is used in agriculture. The second largest use of water is in industry (23 to 25 percent). Industrial use of water depends on the level of development in a country and the structure of its economy. For example, developed nations use as much as 60 percent of their water for industry, whereas a developing nation may use less than 10 percent. A mere 8 percent of all water is used for domestic or private household use. Affluent people in developed nations use far more water (up to 1,000 quarts per person per day) than do families living in African villages, where water must often be carried several miles (about 2 to 5 quarts is the physical minimum). Medical analysts believe that about 80 percent of all illnesses in developing nations are partly due to insufficient water supplies (Petersen, 1994).

Water pollution seriously diminishes the available supply of water. Water may be polluted in a variety of ways. Most often, though, the cause is unpurified or insufficiently treated sewage from households and industry that is discharged into groundwater or surface water or pesticides and mineral fertilizers that leach from farmland into ground and surface water (Hauchler and Kennedy, 1994). The pollutants range from nitrates and phosphates to metals, salts, and pathogenic microorganisms.

The paper-manufacturing industry is one of the major water polluters. Dioxin and other chlorinated organic compounds used in manufacturing paper products are emitted into streams below the paper mills. People can become seriously ill from drinking the polluted water or eating contaminated fish. Environmental activists believe that paper mills should be required to convert to a totally closed system in which there would be no chemical discharges into nearby water. Converting is costly, but a few paper mills are leading the way in the United States. Mills in Canada and Europe are required to be closed systems (Cushman, 1997). But not all water pollution comes from industry. Agriculture, especially transnational corporations that are engaged in agribusiness, extensively uses fertilizers and pesticides containing hazardous toxic chemicals that seriously impair water quality.

SOIL DEPLETION AND DESERTIFICATION

About 11 percent of the earth's surface is used for growing crops, 32 percent is forest, and 24 percent is used to graze animals. Each year, however, many acres of usable land are lost through erosion

In our delicate ecosystem, water pollution has a disastrous effect on all forms of life—not just on human life. What measures might we implement to reduce water pollution such as this?

SOCIAL PROBLEMS
AND SOCIAL POLICY

BOX 16.2

Extended Producer Responsibility (EPR): Can It Be Voluntary?

◆ Fresh Kills on Staten Island is the world's largest landfill, providing a repository for the garbage of New York city. Covering 4 square miles and more than 100 feet deep, it contains 2.9 billion cubic feet of trash, including 100 million tons of newspaper, paint cans, potato peels, cigarette butts, chicken bones, dryer lint, and an occasional corpse. . . . But as massive as Fresh Kills is, it takes in just .02 percent of the waste generated in the United States.

◆ Our annual shopping spree generates 6 billion pounds of polystyrene, 28 billion bounds of discarded food, and 300 billion pounds of chemicals.

◆ We are far better at making waste than at making products. For every 100 pounds of product we manufacture in the United States, we create at least 3,200 pounds of waste.

—Statistics on the U.S. waste problem (Hawken, 1997:44)

When the United States was first industrializing, there were few people and abundant natural resources. Today, we still act as if this were the case. The problem is that, eventually, we will have to pay the price. As environmentalist Paul Hawken (1997:40) puts it, "Decades from now, we may look back at the end of the 20th century and ponder . . . how politics, the media, economics, and commerce created an industrial regime that wasted our social and natural environment and called it growth."

Now contrast the picture painted above with this scene (Montavalli, 1997:36):

On a drugstore's shelves in downtown Stuttgart, Germany, the toothpaste tubes are flat caps like rows of little soldiers. Each tube is

and contamination. Some of the loss is due to climatic factors, but an increasing amount is due to *desertification*—the process by which usable land is turned into desert because of overgrazing, harmful agricultural practices, or deforestation. It is estimated that desertification destroys as much as 15 million acres of land a year. An additional 50 million acres of crop and pasture land become inefficient each year because of excessive application of herbicides and pesticides, insufficient crop rotation, and intensified agricultural production (United Nations Environmental Program, 1992).

Deforestation—excessive removal of trees—also depletes usable land. Since the 1992 Earth Summit in Rio de Janeiro, developed nations have made an effort to protect forests. Unfortunately, prior industrialization in the United States and other developed nations had already taken a serious toll on forests, and the pattern is continuing in some developing na-

tions as they become more industrialized. In the United States, logging in the National Forest System, especially in the Pacific Northwest, is currently an issue. Environmentalists say that logging increases landslides, floods, and changes in rivers and streams that have devastated fish stocks (Goldberg, 1997). Furthermore, when road building, which is necessary to get to the trees in the forest, is combined with cutting all the timber in an area (clear-cutting), the effect on the ecosystem is even more damaging. More water flows down slopes, and when roads wash out, they dump rocks and soil onto lower slopes and into streambeds (Goldberg, 1997).

Although desertification takes place in both developed and developing nations, it is more prevalent in developing nations. When a country is already hard hit by rapid population growth, virtually any loss of land or crops is potentially devastating to large numbers of people (United Nations Environdecorated with a tiny green dot, meaning it's in compliance with the world's most stringent packaging law. In Germany, reducing waste paper and plastic isn't just a nice idea or good public relations, it's mandated.

In 1991, Germany passed the Ordinance on the Avoidance of Packaging Waste in response to shrinking landfill space and a nationwide recognition that resources are scare (Montavalli, 1997). The policy is based on extended producer responsibility (EPR) or the "polluter pays" principle, which means, essentially, that the company that makes the package has to take it back. Needless to say, smaller and fewer packages are being made in Germany these days.

The German program has been overwhelmingly successful. In fact, the excess that's collected—what German companies can't recycle—is shipped to China, Pakistan, Indonesia, and Rumania, where the waste is recycled for use in those countries (Montavalli, 1997). And Germany isn't the only country making inroads on waste as a social problem. Nine other European countries and Japan and Canada have passed EPR laws (Rembert, 1997).

In the United States, however, efforts to pass EPR laws have been blocked by the packaging industry lobby and individual companies that use packaging to sell their products at the point of purchase (Montavalli, 1997). Our best hope, according to Clare Lindsay of the Environmental Protection Agency, is "to work with industry to make it [EPR] happen voluntarily, because there are a lot of business opportunities in EPR. We don't have the political will—or the landfill crisis—that would lead to mandates, but we can do a lot incrementally" (Montavalli, 1997). Lindsay cites some promising examples of voluntary action by such companies as DuPont, Xerox, and Duracell, but these are admittedly the exception, not the rule.

How do you think the United States should tackle its waste problem? Can we do it incrementally—company by company or, as is usually the case today, product by product? What are the incentives for companies to take voluntary action? Or do we need federal policy mandating EPR? What do you think?

---

mental Program, 1992). The United Nations and other international organizations have therefore tried to make protection of the environment an integral part of all economic development policy. However, environmental protection specialists say that to translate policy into action, conservation programs must be supported by the people, and the major sources of the problem must also be addressed: overpopulation and poverty (United Nations Environmental Program, 1992).

Solid, Toxic, and Nuclear Wastes

Even with a rapidly growing world population and ongoing economic development in industrialized nations, the planet might be able to sustain life for a longer time if it weren't for all the solid and toxic chemical waste that is dumped into the environment.

SOLID WASTE

In the United States and some other developed nations, people consume a vast array of products and—in these *disposable societies*—throw away huge quantities of paper, plastic, metal, and other materials. The typical North American creates over 1,500 pounds of municipal solid waste per year, compared to slightly over 700 pounds produced by the average Western European (Petersen, 1994). *Solid waste* is any and all unwanted and discarded materials that are not liquids or gases, including sewage solids. For example, each year people in the United States throw away:

- 16 billion disposable diapers
- 2 billion razors and razor blades
- 220 million tires
- more glass and aluminum than existed

in the entire world before World War II (Petersen, 1994:107)

One partial solution is *recycling*—reusing resources that would otherwise be discarded. Some governments are also taking a hard look at packaging waste and making manufacturers bear the cost of its disposal (see Box 16.2 on pages 364–365).

TOXIC WASTE

At the same time that technology has brought about improvements in the quality and length of life, it has created the potential for new disaster. One of these is *toxic waste*, the hazardous chemical by-products of industrial processes. Perhaps the most widely known U.S. case of toxic waste is Love Canal. In the late 1970s, residents of Niagara Falls, New York, learned that their children were attending a school built on top of what was formerly a toxic landfill (Gibbs, 1982). After large numbers of children became ill and the smell and appearance of the chemicals made it difficult for the residents to overlook the problem, many mobilized against Hooker Chemical Company, which had dumped tons of chemicals into the area (Gibbs, 1982). Eventually, the federal government bought many of the houses, moved the residents out, and removed as much of the toxic waste as possible. Today, families once again live in the area, but they have a highly visible neighbor: a forty-acre grassy landfill, thirty feet high at the center, with an eight-foot-high chain-link fence surrounding it, that covers 21,000 tons of toxic chemical waste and the remains of 239 contaminated houses (Hoffman, 1994).

Today, government regulations exist for the disposal of toxic wastes, but some hazardous wastes are not covered by the regulations, and some corporations get around U.S. government regulations by locating their factories in other countries (see Chapters 2 and 15). In addition, there is often nowhere to safely dispose of the chemicals. Many people take a "not in my backyard" attitude about having a toxic chemical waste dump nearby (Dunlap, 1992; Freudenberg and Steinsapir, 1992).

What is it like to suddenly find that your neighborhood is polluted by toxic waste? A resident of the East Swallow Road neighborhood in Fort Collins, Colorado, where pools of petroleum leaked out of a service station's underground tanks and contaminated the area, describes the uncertainty and worry (Erikson, 1994:115):

you just sort of live your life on hold. I'm always saying, "God, will it ever end so we can get on with our lives?" You can't really make any plans, you just sort of live your life in limbo. Sometimes it's almost unbearable. It's like you really don't live, you just sort of exist, and you wait and you wait and you wait for it to end. But it doesn't, so you just struggle through each day and you worry. You know, it's really, really a pretty sad way to have to live.

NUCLEAR WASTE

Nuclear, or radioactive, wastes are the most dangerous of all toxic wastes. Radioactive waste comes primarily from manufacturers of nuclear weapons and nuclear power plants; small amounts are by-products of certain medical procedures. Weapons-manufacturing plants in Washington, South Carolina, and Colorado store huge amounts of radioactive waste and chemicals in underground tanks. But some of the older tanks leak, and others have been found empty. When tanks leak, they contaminate groundwater and thousands of cubic feet of soil (Petersen, 1994),

One of the reasons nuclear waste is so hazardous is the length of time it remains deadly. For example, uranium waste from nuclear power plants (an estimated 50,000 tons by the year 2000) will remain dangerously radioactive for the next 10,000 years, and plutonium waste for the next 240,000 years (Petersen, 1994).

TECHNOLOGICAL DISASTERS

Technological disasters such as the 1986 meltdown and radiation leak at the Chernobyl nuclear power plant in Ukraine have increased global awareness of the problems associated with radioactive waste. Despite the disaster, the former Soviet Union was still using nineteen similar reactors in 1994 (Petersen, 1994). According to sociologist Kai Erikson (1991:15), the world faces a new species of trouble today:

[Environmental problems that] contaminate rather than merely damage . . . they pollute, befoul, taint, rather than just create wreckage . . .

they penetrate human tissue indirectly rather than just wound the surfaces by assaults of a more straightforward kind. . . . And the evidence is growing that they scare human beings in new and special ways, that they elicit an uncanny fear in us.

The chaos that Erikson (1994:141) describes is the result of *technological disasters*—"meaning everything that can go wrong when systems fail, humans err, designs prove faulty, engines misfire, and so on." Chernobyl and Love Canal were technological disasters, as were radiation leakage at the Three Mile Island nuclear power plant in Pennsylvania in 1979 and the leakage of lethal gases at the pesticide plant in Bhopal, India, in 1984. In the worst-case scenario, technological disasters kill tens of thousands of people; in the best-case scenario, they place tremendous stress on the world's ecosystems and greatly diminish the quality of life for everyone.

SOCIOLOGICAL PERSPECTIVES ON POPULATION AND THE ENVIRONMENT

As sociologists have examined how human behavior affects population and environmental problems, the subdiscipline of environmental sociology has emerged. According to Cable and Cable (1995:5), "*environmental sociology* examines people's beliefs about their environment, their behavior toward it, and the ways in which the structure of society influences them and contributes to the persistent abuse of the environment." Like all sociologists, environmental sociologists—as well as demographers—approach their study from one or another perspective.

▲ The Functionalist Perspective

Some functionalists focus on the relationship between social structure, technological change, and environmental problems. On the one hand, technological innovation serves important functions in society. For example, automation and mass production have made a wide array of goods—ranging

from automobiles and computers to McDonald's burgers—available to many people. But technological innovation also has latent dysfunctions; automation and mass production, for example, create air pollution, overuse and depletion of natural resources, and excessive solid waste. From this point of view, some environmental problems are the price a society pays for technological progress. If this is true, the best way to alleviate the problem is to develop new technologies. This is what happened when the catalytic converter and other antipollution devices were developed for automobiles.

Other functionalists take a neo-Malthusian perspective, believing that to reduce food shortages and environmental problems, population must be controlled. In other words, the more people there are alive, the greater are the overuse of finite resources and degradation of soil, water, and land.

Functionalists believe that solutions to overpopulation and environmental degradation lie in social institutions such as education and the government. Educators can encourage population control by teaching people about the limits to agriculture and the difficulty of feeding rapidly increasing populations. Government leaders and international organizations such as the United Nations can cooperate to find far-reaching and innovative solutions and develop understandings about more equitable use of the world's resources (Ehrlich and Ehrlich, 1991).

▲ The Conflict Perspective

Analysts using a conflict framework believe that population and environmental problems have less to do with overpopulation and shortages of resources than with power differentials in societies and in the larger global economy. For example, early conflict theorists such as Karl Marx and Friedrich Engels (1976/1848) did not think that the food supply was threatened by overpopulation because agricultural technology (even in their era) could meet the food needs of the growing world population if it were not for poverty. According to Marx and Engels (1976/1848), the main cause of poverty is exploitation of workers by capitalists. They argued, for example, that poverty existed in England because the capitalists skimmed off some of the workers' wages as profits. The labor of the working classes was used by capitalists to earn profits, which, in turn, were used to purchase machinery that could replace the workers rather than supply food for all. From this classical Marxist point of view, population growth is encouraged by capitalists who use unemployed workers (the industrial reserve army) to keep other workers from demanding higher wages or better working conditions.

According to contemporary conflict theorists, corporations and the government are the two main power institutions in society. As a result, when economic decisions made by members of the capitalist class and elite political leaders result in environmental problems, the costs are externalized, or passed along to the people (Cable and Cable, 1995:13):

> [The externalization of environmental costs of production] . . . means that the costs of production's negative impact on the environment (for example, the expense of cleaning polluted water to make it suitable for drinking) are not included in the price of the product. The company neither pays for the privilege of polluting the water nor cleans it; it saves the cost of proper waste disposal and makes environmentally conscious competition impossible. Not even the consumer of the product pays the environmental costs of production directly. Rather, the public at large essentially subsidizes the company, by either paying for the cleanup of the environment or enduring degraded environmental quality.

Although most conflict approaches to studying the environment focus on the relationship between members of the capitalist class and political elites, there is also an approach known as *ecofeminism*—the belief that patriarchy is a root cause of environmental problems. According to ecofeminists, patriarchy results in not only the domination of women by men, but also the belief that nature is to be possessed and dominated rather than treated as a partner (Ortner, 1974; Merchant, 1983, 1992; Mies and Shiva, 1993).

Another conflict approach uses an *environmental justice framework*—examining how race and class intersect in the struggle for scarce environmental resources. Of particular interest to these theorists is *environmental racism*—**the belief that a disproportionate number of hazardous facilities are placed in areas populated primarily by poor people and people of color** (Bullard and Wright, 1992). Haz-

ardous facilities include waste disposal and treatment plants and chemical plants (Schneider, 1993). A 1987 study by the Commission for Racial Justice concluded, "Race was the most potent variable in predicting the location of uncontrolled (abandoned) and commercial toxic waste sites in the United States" (Bullard and Wright, 1992:41). For example, the Carver Terrace housing subdivision in Texarkana, Texas, which is composed of 100 African American households, was built over an area that had been previously contaminated by a creosote wood treatment facility (Capek, 1993). The federal government eventually bought out some of the homeowners and relocated the subdivision, but not until a number of years after it was determined that toxins in the neighborhood had caused the deaths of twenty-six people and the illnesses of many others (Capek, 1993).

The Interactionist Perspective

Since interactionists take a microlevel approach, viewing society as the sum of all people's interactions, they look at environmental problems in terms of individuals. Specifically, they think environmental problems are exacerbated by people's subjective assessment of reality. Through socialization, children learn core values that are considered important in the United States, but some of these values can be detrimental to the environment. Consider the following widely held beliefs (Cable and Cable, 1995:11–12):

- *A free market system provides the greatest good for the greatest number of people:* Economic decision making works best in private hands.
- *The natural world is inexhaustible:* There will always be more natural resources.
- *Faith in technology:* Any challenge can be met through technology.
- *The growth ethic:* Growth equals progress; bigger is better.
- *Materialism:* Success can be measured in terms of consumption.
- *Individualism:* Individual rights and personal achievement are most important.
- *An anthropocentric world view:* Human beings are at the center of the world, and humans are superior to other species. Standing

apart from nature rather than recognizing that we are *part of* nature, we attempt to conquer and subdue the environment.

It may be, however, that as people become aware of the effects of environmental degradation, concern for the environment will emerge as a core value in the United States. According to sociologist Alan Scott (1990), quality-of-life issues, such as concern for the environment, have become an impetus for new social movements. It may be, too, that concern will spread in the twenty-first century, resulting in global environmental movements.

POPULATION AND THE ENVIRONMENT IN THE TWENTY-FIRST CENTURY

As we look toward the twenty-first century, the problems that we have discussed in this chapter present some of the greatest challenges that humans face. Global overpopulation and environmental depletion and devastation have irreversible consequences, and actions taken—or not taken—today will be with us far into the future. Futurists believe that we must use a wide-angle lens to examine population and environmental concerns (Peterson, 1994). We must see the world and our role in it in a much different way than we did in the past. We must understand that environmental issues are *security* issues—as much so as a terrorist threat or a missile or bomb (Peterson, 1994). Once we understand that, we will think of environmental problems in a completely different light. For example, to eliminate the global threats posed by overpopulation and the environmental degradation, all societies can make the following changes (based on Petersen, 1994:109):

◆ Reduce the use of energy.
◆ Shift from fossil fuels to solar-based energy systems or other energy-efficient systems such as water power, wind power, or geothermal energy.
◆ Develop new transportation networks and city designs that reduce automobile use.
◆ Work for redistribution of land and wealth so that the poor in all nations can make a positive contribution.
◆ Push for equality between women and men in all nations, emphasizing literacy training, educational opportunities, and health care (including reproduction and contraception information) for women.
◆ Effect a rapid transition to smaller families.
◆ Cooperate internationally to reduce the consumption of resources by the wealthy nations and bring higher living standards to poorer nations.

Are these changes likely to occur? Probably not if people in developing and developed nations adhere to their current belief systems. Some social analysts think that it will take a threatening event—such as a drastic change in the earth's weather patterns or a sudden increase in natural disasters—to capture the attention of enough of the earth's people and convince political leaders that a serious change in direction is required if the planet is to continue to support human life (Petersen, 1994). Vice President Al Gore describes this change in mindset in his book *Earth in Balance* (cited in Petersen, 1994:111):

> I have come to believe that we must take bold and unequivocal action: We must make the rescue of the environment the central organizing principle for civilization. Whether we realize it or not, we are now engaged in an epic battle to right the balance of our earth, and the tide of this battle will turn only when the majority of people in the world become sufficiently aroused by a shared sense of urgent danger to join an all-out effort.

We can only hope that people will not wait until it's too late.

SUMMARY

➡ *What is the global population and why is population growth a problem?*

The world's population was almost 5.8 billion in 1996; it doubled in the last 50 years and is expected to double again in the next 50 years. The concern is whether the earth's resources can support this rapid population growth.

➡ *What are the primary factors that affect population growth?*

Three factors affect population growth: fertility, the actual number of children born to an individual or a population; mortality, the number of deaths that occur in a specific population; and migration, the movement of people from one geographic area to another for the purpose of changing residency.

➡ *How does population growth affect a society?*

Population growth affects population composition, the biological and social characteristics of a population, including such attributes as age, sex, race, marital status, education, occupation, income, and size of household. In the United States, for example, the age distribution of the population affects the need for schools, employment opportunities, health care, and age-appropriate housing.

➡ *What are the major theoretical perspectives on overpopulation?*

According to the Malthusian perspective, population expands geometrically while the food supply increases only arithmetically; disaster can only be averted through positive checks (e.g., famine, disease, war) or preventive checks (e.g., sexual abstinence, delayed marriage). The neo-Malthusians believe that the earth is a ticking bomb because population problems exacerbate environmental problems. The third perspective is more hopeful. According to demographic transition theory, societies move from high birth and death rates to low birth and death rates as a result of technological development. However, critics say that demographic transition theory applies chiefly to Western societies.

➡ *What solutions do we have to world hunger?*

Two of the most far-reaching initiatives are the green revolution (the growing of high-yield "miracle" crops) and the biotechnological revolution, which involves "improving" plants or animals or using microorganisms in innovative ways. However, some social analysts believe that the solution is not to produce more food but to control fertility.

➡ *How is immigration changing the population composition of the United States?*

Today, the proportion of U.S. immigrants in the population is the highest since 1940. If immigration continues at the present rate, it will account for two-thirds of the expected population growth in the next fifty years. (The United States is otherwise almost at zero population growth—a stable population.) Immigration leads to higher taxes, but it also brings substantial economic benefits.

➡ *What is environmental degradation and what are its causes?*

Environmental degradation is caused by disruptions to the environment that have negative consequences for ecosystems. Human beings, particularly as they pursue economic development and growth, cause environmental degradation.

➡ *What is the major source of air pollution and what are its effects?*

The major source is fossil fuel pollution, especially from vehicles but somewhat from industry. One of the most serious consequences of air pollution is the greenhouse effect, an environmental condition caused by excessive quantities of carbon dioxide, water vapor, methane, and nitrous oxide in the atmosphere that leads to global warming. Another is depletion of the ozone layer, the part of the earth's atmosphere that absorbs dangerous ultraviolet radiation from the sun.

➡ *What water, soil, and forest problems do we face?*

Water scarcity is increasing on a global basis, and water pollution further diminishes the available water supply. One of the major water polluters in the United States is the paper-manufacturing industry. About 15 million acres of soil are lost each year to desertification (the process by which usable land is turned into desert because of overgrazing, harmful agricultural practices) and deforestation (excessive removal of trees). Desertification is greatest in developing nations.

➡ *Why are solid, toxic, and nuclear wastes a problem?*

Solid waste is particularly a problem in developed nations because they are "disposable societies." Toxic waste (hazardous chemical by-products of industry) causes death and disease if it is not disposed of properly. Nuclear, or radioactive, waste is a problem because of the length of time it remains deadly.

➡ *What is the functionalist perspective on population and the environment?*

On the subject of environment, functionalists say that the latent dysfunctions of technology cause problems but that new technologies can solve these problems. Most functionalists take a neo-Malthusian perspective on population but believe that social institutions, especially education and the government, can cooperate to solve population and environmental problems.

➡ *What is the conflict perspective on population and the environment?*

In the classical Marxist view, there would be enough food for all people if poverty were alleviated, and poverty exists because capitalists skim workers' wages for profits. Contemporary conflict theorists believe that the two main power institutions in society—corporations and the government—make economic decisions that result in environmental problems. An approach known as ecofeminism says that patriarchy is a root cause of environmental problems: Nature is viewed as something to be possessed and dominated.

➡ *What is the interactionist perspective on population and environment?*

Interactionists see population and environment problems in microlevel—individual—terms. Through socialization, children learn core values that are often detrimental to the environment. However, there is some indication that concern for the environment is becoming a core value in the United States.

KEY TERMS

acid rain, p. 361
demographic transition theory, p. 352
demography, p. 348
desertification, p. 364
environmental degradation, p. 358
environmental racism, p. 368

fertility, p. 348
greenhouse effect, p. 362
migration, p. 349
mortality, p. 348
population composition, p. 350
zero population growth, p. 356

QUESTIONS FOR CRITICAL THINKING

1. Which perspective on population growth do you favor—neo-Malthusian or demographic transition theory—and why?

2. Reread the excerpt on p. 358 describing immigrant-bashing, and develop an action plan for opening the "closed hearts and minds" of these high school students.

3. If you had to focus on a single aspect of environmental degradation—air pollution; water, soil, or forest problems; solid, toxic, or nuclear waste disposal—which would it be and why? What would you do to make people aware of the seriousness of the problem? What new solutions could you propose?

Chapter Seventeen

Urban Problems

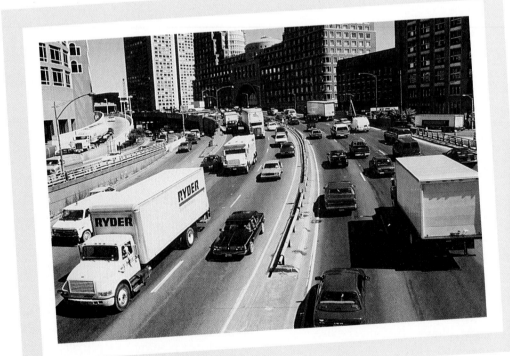

The Number 6 [subway] train from Manhattan to the South Bronx makes nine stops in the 18-minute ride between East 59th Street [the Upper East Side] and Brook Avenue. When you enter the train, you are in the seventh richest congressional district in the nation. When you leave, you are in the poorest. . . . In 1991, the median household income of the [Brook Avenue] area . . . was $7,600. . . . The houses in which these children live, two-thirds of which are owned by the City of New York, are often as squalid as the houses of the poorest children I have visited in rural Mississippi, but there is none of the greenness and the healing sweetness of the Mississippi countryside outside their windows, which are often barred and bolted as protection against thieves. Some of these houses are freezing in the winter. In dangerously cold weather, the city sometimes distributes electric blankets and space heaters to its tenants. . . . In humid summer weather, roaches crawl on virtually every surface of the houses in which many of the children live. Rats emerge from holes in bedroom walls, terrorizing the infants in their cribs. In the streets outside, the restlessness and anger that are present in all seasons frequently intensify under the stress of heat. . . . If there is a deadlier place in the United States, I don't know where it is.

*—Social analyst
Jonathan Kozol
describes life in one
part of New York City*
(Kozol, 1995:3–5)

"[Upper Fifth Avenue is] . . . the closest thing to heaven. When I close my eyes I can hear the seals [in Central Park] honking for their food in the children's zoo and the horses' hoofs as the carriages pass under my window. 'Where am I?' I think. It's wonderful. . . ." The Metropolitan Museum is my children's best babysitter. We lived here so the children would be near the museum and the park. My children grew up knowing every animal in the zoo by name."

*—Two women
describing life on
Upper Fifth Avenue in
New York City*
(Moonan, 1989:199)

Can these people be describing life in the same city? Yes, most definitely. People living in the same city have very divergent experiences because of their positions in the social structure and particularly as their position is affected by race, class, gender, and age. Although the rich and the poor may live near one another in many cities, they are worlds apart in lifestyles and life chances. As the two examples above show, African American children living in poverty in the South Bronx do not have the same opportunities as affluent white children who live on Upper Fifth Avenue in Manhattan. Differences in lifestyle and life chances can partly be attributed to the fact that most U.S. cities are enclaves of geographic, socioeconomic, and racial-ethnic isolation (Higley, 1995).

In this chapter, we examine some of the most pressing urban problems in the United States and other nations. Many social problems discussed in this book—including the wide gap between the rich and the poor, racial and ethnic strife, inadequate educational opportunities, and homelessness—are found in urban areas, of course, but they are much more pronounced than in less densely populated rural areas. For example, crime rates typically are higher, and schools tend to be dilapidated. City governments also seem to face a fiscal crisis periodically, and inadequate resources lead to drastic reductions in such vital services as public sanitation and police and fire protection. As a framework for examining urban problems today, let's briefly look at the changes in U.S. cities that have led to these problems.

CHANGES IN U.S. CITIES

Urban problems in the United States are closely associated with profound socioeconomic, political, and spatial changes that have taken place since the Industrial Revolution. Two hundred years ago, most people (about 94 out of 100) lived in sparsely populated rural areas, where they farmed. In the 1990s, about 78 percent of the U.S. population lives in urban areas, and many of these people live in cities that did not exist two hundred years ago (U.S. Bureau of the Census, 1996b).

▲ Early Urban Growth and Social Problems

Industrialization and urbanization bring about profound changes in societies and frequently spawn new social problems such as housing shortages, overcrowding, unsanitary living and working conditions, environmental pollution, and crime (see Chapter 1). By definition, a city involves population density. According to sociologists, a *city* is the relatively dense and permanent settlement of people who secure their livelihood primarily through nonagricultural activities (Weeks, 1992). Although cities existed long before the Industrial Revolution, the birth of the factory system brought about rapid *urbanization*—the **process by which an increasing proportion of a population lives in cities rather than in rural areas.** For example, the population of New York City swelled by 500 percent between 1870 and 1910 as rural dwellers and newly arrived immigrants from Ireland, Italy, Germany, Poland, and other nations arrived in massive numbers, seeking jobs in factories and offices.

Early cities were a composite of commercial, residential, and manufacturing activities located in close proximity. But rapidly growing cities such as New York always had a few blocks (e.g., Upper Fifth Avenue) of houses where the wealthy lived (Palen, 1995). These residences were located near the center of the city, and the address was considered a sign of social and economic success (Baltzell, 1958; Birmingham, 1967). With the introduction of horse-drawn streetcar lines in the 1850s and electric streetcars in the 1880s, people were able to move more easily from place to place within the core city and to commute between the core city and outlying suburban areas. As a result, many middle-class families moved out of the central areas (Palen, 1995).

City leaders established municipal governments for building and repairing streets, fire protection, crime control, sewage disposal, lighting, and other general needs. In the late nineteenth and early in the twentieth century, improved transportation and new technologies for supplying water and disposing of waste enabled cities to grow even faster. However, municipal governments had trouble keeping pace with the negative side effects of "progress," including urban slums, traffic congestion, and high crime rates. Despite these problems, people continued to move to northeastern and midwestern cities in unprecedented numbers, looking for jobs, educational opportunities, and such new amenities as big department stores, parks, libraries, and theaters.

Contemporary Urban Growth

The growth of suburbs and outlying areas forever changed the nature of city life in this country. Suburban areas existed immediately adjacent to many central cities as early as the nineteenth century, but in the 1920s, these communities began to grow in earnest because of the automobile. They were referred to as "bedroom communities" because most of the residents were there on nights and weekends but went into the central city for jobs, entertainment, and major shopping. During the 1930s, about 17 million people lived in suburban areas (Palen, 1995). With the exception of a few cities, such as New York and Chicago, that built subways or other forms of mass transit, most suburban dwellers drove to work each day, establishing a pattern that would result, decades later, in traffic congestion and air pollution, problems that have drastically worsened in the past two decades (Palen, 1995).

Between the end of World War II (1945) and 1970, mass suburbanization brought about a dramatic shift in the distribution of the U.S. population. During the war, construction of apartments and single-family dwellings had halted as industry produced war-related goods. When the war ended, many veterans returned home, got married, and had children (the "baby boom" generation). Consequently, in the late 1940s, as many as 6 million families were unable to find housing to rent or buy; many had to live with relatives or friends until they could find a place of their own (Palen, 1995).

To reduce the housing shortage, the federal government subsidized what became a mass exodus from the central city to outlying suburbs. Congress passed the Housing Act of 1949, giving incentives to builders to develop affordable housing. In addition, federal agencies such as the Veterans Administration (VA) and the Federal Housing Authority (FHA) established more lenient lending policies so that war veterans could qualify to buy homes for their families (Palen, 1995). Other factors also contributed to the postwar suburban boom, including the availability of inexpensive land, low-cost mass construction methods for building tract houses, new federally financed freeway systems, inexpensive gasoline, racial tension in central cities, and consumers' pent-up demands for single-family homes on individually owned lots (Jackson, 1985). The most widely known, and perhaps the most successful, suburban developer of this era was Abraham Levitt and Sons, the company that developed Levittown (on Long Island, New York). Levittown was the first large-scale, mass-produced housing development in this country (see Map 17.1). Eventually, more than 17,000 single-family residences—occupied by more than 82,000 people—were located in Levittown. Sometimes referred to as "cracker boxes" because of their simple, square construction, these were typically two-bedroom, one-

MAP 17.1

Levittown, New York

bath Cape Cod–style houses built on a concrete slab; the driveway was unpaved, and there was a small lawn with a couple of small bushes (Nieves, 1995).

Early suburbanization provided many families with affordable housing, good schools and parks, and other amenities not found in the central city. However, the shift away from central cities set up an ongoing economic and racial division of interests between cities and suburbs that remains today, at the end of the century (Flanagan, 1995). Although many people in the suburbs still rely on the central city for employment, entertainment, or other services, suburbanites pay their taxes to their local government and school district. As a result, suburban police and fire departments, schools, libraries, and recreational facilities are usually well funded and well staffed, with up-to-date facilities. Suburbs also have a newer infrastructure (such as roads, sewers, and water treatment plants) and money to maintain it. In contrast, many central cities have aging and dilapidated schools and typically lack funds for essential government services (see Chapter 13). According to national estimates, for example, fewer than 40 percent of African American students who attend school in predominantly minority central city districts have access to computers at school, compared with nearly 60 percent of white schoolchildren in suburban schools (Gardy, 1995).

Since 1970, cities in the South, Southwest, and West have been considered postindustrial cities because their economic production largely consists of information-processing or service jobs (Orum, 1995). Whereas the older, northeastern and midwestern cities initially grew up around heavy manufacturing, the newer Sunbelt cities have grown through light industry, such as computer software manufacturing; information-processing services, such as airline and hotel reservation services; educational complexes; medical centers; convention and entertainment centers; and retail trade centers and shopping malls (Sawers and Tabb, 1984). In these postindustrial cities, most families do not live near the central business district.

Today, edge cities are springing up beyond the central cities and existing suburbs. An *edge city* is a **middle- to upper-middle-class area that has complete living, working, shopping, and leisure activities so that it is not dependent on the central city or other suburbs** (Garreau, 1991). The Massachusetts Turnpike Corridor west of Boston and the Perimeter Area north of Atlanta are examples. Initially, edge cities develop as residential areas, then retail establishments and office parks move into the adjacent area, creating an unincorporated edge city. Automobiles are the primary source of transportation in many edge cities, and pedestrian traffic is discouraged—and dangerous—because streets are laid out to facilitate high-volume automobile traffic, not walkers or bicyclists. Edge cities may not have a governing body, so they drain taxes from central cities and older suburbs. Many businesses and industries move their physical plants—and tax dollars—to these areas because land is cheaper, workers are better educated, and utility rates and property taxes are lower than those in the city. As a result, many jobs have moved away from the growing proportion of poor, minority workers in central cities, creating structural employment (see Chapter 15). In Dallas, Texas, for example, most new jobs have been created in the northern and northwestern parts of the metropolitan area, which is far removed from where most low-income African American and Latina/o workers reside (Leinberger, 1992).

Over time, large-scale metropolitan growth produces a *megalopolis*—**a continuous concentration of two or more cities and their suburbs that have grown until they form an interconnected urban area.** The East Coast, for example, is a megalopolis, with Boston, Providence, Hartford, and their suburbs merging into New York City and its suburbs, which in turn, merge southward into Newark, Philadelphia, Baltimore, and Washington, D.C., and their suburbs. It is almost impossible to tell where one metropolitan area ends and another begins. When metropolitan areas merge into a megalopolis, there are big population changes that can bring about or exacerbate social problems and inequalities based on race, class, and gender.

URBAN PROBLEMS IN THE UNITED STATES

Even the most optimistic of observers tends to agree that cities in the United States have problems brought on by years of neglect and deterioration. As we saw in previous chapters, poverty, crime, racism, homelessness, inadequate public school systems, alcoholism and other drug abuse, and other social problems are most visible and acute in urban settings. Intertwined with these problems in many older central cities are periodic fiscal crises.

Fiscal Crisis in Cities

Not all U.S. cities are in a state of fiscal crisis and decline, but over the past three decades, some have been in such trouble as to be on the brink of bankruptcy. New York City was on the edge of financial collapse in 1975 until the federal government provided an elaborate bailout plan; Cleveland actually went into financial default in 1978. When federal aid to cities was slashed during the recession of the early 1980s, some state governments provided additional monies to cities, but most did not have the means to do so (Clark and Walter, 1994). As a result, the governments of Detroit, Boston, and New York had to drastically reduce services; they closed some public hospitals and other facilities, laid off employees, significantly cut public transit, and all but stopped maintaining the cities' infrastructure.

Finding a solution to the fiscal crises of the 1980s was a real dilemma, and the situation hasn't gotten much better. Not only have middle- and upper-income people moved out of the central city to the suburbs, but retail businesses and corporations have also gone to the suburbs or moved their operations to other countries. The shrinking central cities are left with greatly reduced sources of revenue, and municipal governments can't very well increase taxes when their taxes are already much higher than those in the more affluent suburbs or in Sunbelt cities such as Las Vegas, Phoenix, and Arlington and Austin, Texas (Moore and Stansel, 1992). Many of the remaining central city residents are poor, unemployed, or older people living on fixed incomes, who cannot pay additional taxes but still need city services such as hospitals, police and fire departments, and public transportation.

Joblessness and declining wages among central city residents further diminish the tax base in many cities and create tremendous social dislocation. For example, sociologist William J. Wilson (1996:34–35) describes the extent of job loss in the predominantly African American community of North Lawndale in central Chicago:

> After more than a quarter century of continuous deterioration, North Lawndale resembles a war zone. . . . Two large factories anchored the economy of this West Side neighborhood in its good days—the Hawthorne plant of Western Electric, which employed over 43,000 workers and an International Harvester plant with 14,000 workers. The world headquarters for Sears, Roebuck and Company was located there, providing another 10,000 jobs. The neighborhood also had a Copenhagen snuff plant, a Sunbeam factory, and a Zenith factory, a Dell Farm food market, an Alden's catalog store, and a U.S. Post Office bulk station. But conditions rapidly changed. Harvester closed its doors in the late 1960s. Sears moved most of its offices to the Loop in downtown Chicago in 1973; a catalogue distribution center with a workforce of 3,000 initially remained in the neighborhood but was relocated outside the state of Illinois in 1987. The Hawthorne plant gradually phased out its operations and finally shut down in 1984. The departure of the big plants triggered the demise or exodus of the smaller stores, the banks, and other businesses that relied on the wages paid by the large employers. . . . In 1986, North Lawndale, with a population of over 66,000, had only one bank and one supermarket; but it was also home to forty-eight state lottery agencies, fifty currency exchanges, and ninety-nine licensed liquor stores and bars.

Similar examples can be given for Detroit and Flint, Michigan, among other cities, because of deindustrialization and plant closings (see Dandaneau, 1996).

The fiscal crisis of cities is extremely visible in the decaying infrastructure. For example, downtown Chicago suffered more than 1 billion dollars in damage and lost revenues in the 1990s because an old water main burst and flooded office buildings, department stores, and other retail businesses. In many cities, roads are scarred with potholes, and sections of highways have fallen in. Railroad overpasses are buckled, and 40 percent of all bridges in the United States today are rated structurally deficient or functionally obsolete by the Department of Transportation (Eitzen and Baca Zinn, 1994). Given the acute shortage of funds, these problems will not be solved any time soon. Many cities have also experienced natural disasters such as floods, brushfires, earthquakes, hurricanes, or tornados—all of which add to the cities' financial burdens by creating

Signe Wilkinson/Cartoonists & Writers Syndicate

new infrastructure problems at the same time that relief must be provided for the hardest-hit residents.

To what extent are cities' financial problems brought on by suburbanites? On the one hand, city governments bear the economic burden for municipal services (e.g., street maintenance, fire and police departments) and amenities such as parks and other recreational facilities that are used by suburban residents. On the other hand, some suburban dwellers believe that they do their fair share of helping cities to finance necessary services. Consider this recent editorial, in which the writer argues that although he and his family live in a suburban community outside the taxing authority of the city of Austin, they contribute significantly to the central city's sales tax, which helps to pay for the city's transit system (Barry, 1997:A13).

> You hear a lot of demonizing of suburban dwellers. . . . We use the city streets but don't pay for them; we work in town but pay property taxes to some other entity. . . . Of all the suburban-bashing mantras, the one that irks me most is the one that says we don't pay taxes. . . . We're still paying Austin taxes, and we still support Austin businesses. . . . Practically everything we buy, we buy in Austin. My sport utility vehicle and [my wife's] car were bought at Austin dealerships. . . . Although there's a grocery store two

minutes from the house, we still do much of our grocery shopping in Austin. I eat at least five meals a week at Austin restaurants. . . . We gas up from Austin dealer's pumps. We buy clothes at Austin clothiers. We shop at Austin malls. My barber is in Austin, as is [my wife's] beauty shop of choice. . . . Ninety percent of the [metropolitan transit authority] sales tax may be collected in Austin, but a lot of it is collected from people like us. . . . Austin is a city in a region, not a fortress. We're friends, neighbors and coworkers, not barbarians at the gate.

According to this point of view, cities benefit from suburban residents more than critics think. Still, the federal government programs that subsidized private housing and contributed to the mass exodus to the suburbs after World War II, combined with years of government neglect, have greatly intensified urban problems. Moreover, the financial crises that we've seen so far in the Northeast and Midwest are expected to spread to Sunbelt cities early in the twenty-first century (Lazare, 1991).

The Crisis in Health Care

Health care is a problem throughout the United States, but it is a bigger problem in the nation's largest cities (see Chapter 11). Not only are hospitals and other medical facilities in cities subject to cutbacks and closings because of cities' economic problems, but people who live in central cities are more likely to become ill or injured than are people in more affluent suburbs. Poverty is associated with many medical problems. Poor people are more likely to contract certain diseases (such as tuberculosis) and suffer from problems associated with inadequate nutrition and lack of preventive care (many children are not immunized against the basic childhood diseases). Moreover, drug-related problems and HIV/AIDS have placed tremendous financial burdens on already overworked and underfunded community clinics, hospitals, and other medical facilities in the central cities. According to the National Centers for Disease Control in Atlanta, both the number of AIDS patients and the costs of caring for AIDS patients are highest in central cities (Eitzen and Baca Zinn, 1994).

Finding affordable health care is a major problem for city residents as community clinics and publicly financed hospitals have closed because of lack of funding. Essential services have also been cut back in many metropolitan hospitals. And as managed care plans and large hospital chains have taken over ownership of privately funded hospitals in large urban centers, more hospitals now claim that they cannot afford to provide uncompensated care, and some refuse to admit uninsured patients except in life-threatening circumstances (see Chapter 11). Although public hospitals cannot legally deny patients care, a patient may have to wait many hours (sometimes even days) to see a physician or other medical personnel, who must deal with one life-and-death medical emergency after another. Today, many poor people use emergency rooms for all medical services because they do not have—and cannot afford to pay—a private physician. Consequently, the cost of providing medical services for patients continues to be driven higher at a time when public hospitals in large urban centers have greatly diminished resources. The growing homeless population in major urban areas has added to the cost of providing health care.

Housing Problems

Many regions in the United States lack affordable housing for low-income individuals and families (see Chapter 2). Consequently, over the last ten years, there has been a significant increase in homelessness, especially among families with children. Each year, we are made aware of the plight of homeless people through extensive media coverage during the Thanksgiving to Christmas holiday season. During the rest of the year, many people view the homeless with less compassion (see Box 17.1 on pages 380–381).

THE HOUSING SHORTAGE

The U.S. housing shortage has grown worse over recent decades as city neighborhoods have become blighted and houses have been abandoned. It may seem surprising that landlords will abandon rental property that they own. But single-room-occupancy (SRO) hotels and inexpensive apartments for lower-income residents may become so great an economic liability that landlords decide they're better off simply abandoning the properties. Landlords are most likely to give up their property when they find themselves caught between increasing property taxes, demands from the city to maintain or upgrade the property so that it complies with safety standards or building codes, and tenants who demand services but do not pay their rent or severely damage the units so that extensive repair is needed before another tenant can move in and start paying rent.

Often, landlords have let the properties become substandard through years of neglect, as one journalist describes (Golden, 1992:27):

> Many SRO tenants . . . had long lost whatever human connections they might have had, and amid the brutal life of the hotel their mental and emotional condition deteriorated through sheer fear and isolation. These hotels were dirty, cold, depressing, and dangerous. The way landlords made a profit from the low rents charged was by not maintaining the buildings. Toilets and faucets did not work; heat was often nonexistent; locks were insecure; and the shared bathrooms in the hallways were particularly dangerous because men tried to break in while women were in the shower.

Abandoned buildings increase fear and isolation in the residents of adjoining properties. The empty buildings often become hiding places for drug dealers or fugitives, and some are dangerous places for children to play. In some cities, however, *urban squatters*—people who occupy land or property without any legal title to it—have moved into abandoned apartment buildings and fixed them up. As people take up unofficial residence in the buildings, they create a sense of community by watching out for each

SOCIAL PROBLEMS

IN THE MEDIA

BOX 17.1

Homelessness and the Holidays

The charity of the holiday season is traditional—and welcome. The problem is that so much is seasonal. . . . Come January, when people go back to their normal routines, the hunger and homelessness recognized in the holiday season will remain. It would be nice if most of the spirit of giving remained, too.
—From a *Los Angeles Times* editorial, December 25, 1988

Not only does charity towards the homeless wax and wane during the year, so does media coverage. Research shows that the media, especially newspapers, give steady, fairly minimal coverage to the homeless until late fall (around Thanksgiving), when the amount increases. Coverage peaks in December (at Christmas), and then in January it diminishes again until it returns to its standard plateau in April (Bunis, Yancik, and Snow, 1996; Snow and Anderson, 1991). Why does this happen?

For one thing, homeless people are human interest stories for the holiday season. At Thanksgiving, the nightly news team shows up with its camera crews at one of the city soup kitchens and interviews volunteers serving turkey and trimmings to people still wearing their overcoats. A month later, around Christmastime, the press appears at homeless shelters to interview "Jimmy G." and "Sherry P.," and their stories are all the more poignant because, by now, in many parts of the country, the weather is pretty raw.

For another thing, people are in a giving mood during the holidays, so if the media make us aware of the plight of the homeless, people are likely to help. It is true that an important function of the media is to make the public aware of social problems. One billboard poster, for example, showed a drawing of Jesus above the head, "How can you worship a homeless man on Sunday and ignore one on Monday?"

---

other's possessions. But most of these projects have been short-lived. Developers who recognize potential in the area demand that the buildings be razed to make way for new hotels and office towers.

In recent years, some cities have instituted programs to provide low-cost owner-occupied housing, but some social analysts believe that these programs promote the interests of the housing industry and protect property values more than they actually help people to acquire housing (Flanagan, 1995). Similarly, one of the best-known federal government housing initiatives, the urban homesteading program, has been fraught with problems. The urban homesteading program was designed to allow low-income families to purchase—for a nominal fee—properties that had been abandoned by their previous owners. In return,

the purchasers had to agree that they would live in the property and make improvements to it for a period of time, after which they could resell the property and derive a profit from it. But apparently, the government did not provide sufficient housing units in a given area to meet the demand and offset the urban deterioration that was already in progress (Flanagan, 1995). In addition, the Federal Housing Administration (FHA) flooded central city neighborhoods with federally insured loans that were attractive to lenders and real estate agents, who often arranged for families to purchase homes that they were then unable to maintain when repairs became necessary. As a result, massive foreclosures occurred, causing people to lose their homes and bringing about further deterioration of central city neighborhoods (Squires, 1994).

Sociologists, though, dig deeper. Why do the media increase coverage at *this* time of year—during the holidays? Part of the reason may come from sociologist Lewis A. Coser, who says "we have only so much emotional energy and yet we live in a world filled with inhumanity and suffering" (1969:104). Thus, sympathy for the afflicted in a society fluctuates over time. Otherwise, we would be emotionally overwhelmed.

Another reason, more to the point of the holidays as the time that most people express sympathy for the homeless, comes from Emile Durkheim (1995): Holidays are times of ritual, opportunities to affirm shared values. But, of course, the values that are affirmed by any particular holiday ritual derive from the culture. In the United States, where individualism is highly valued but people believe, at the same time, that they are responsive to social problems, the holidays function to reassert community solidarity by redistributing goods in the community (Barnett, 1954).

Along these same lines, researchers William K. Bunis, Angela Yancik, and David Snow (1996) cite the work of Thomas J. Scheff (1977:71–73), who sees sympathy as catharsis (emotional release) for guilt:

> Insofar as Americans have imbibed this heady drink of socially induced ambition, they tend to ignore or slight the precepts of brotherhood, kindness, and cooperation in favor of those related to attaining individual success. However, many persons experience a sharp conflict of values because, though the ideals of brotherhood and kindness are relegated to a secondary place, they retain their normative quality. Therefore, widespread feelings of guilt develop into this clash of divergent social norms and furnish some of the motivation for Christmas charity.

What have you observed in the media's coverage of social problems and particularly homelessness? Are you aware of the November-to-January pattern that Bunis, Yancik, and Snow document in their work? Can you cite personal experience to support or negate Coser's concept of limited emotional energy? Does "charity as catharsis" make sense to you? What do you think?

Although the Department of Housing and Urban Development (HUD) has continued in the 1990s to explore ways to provide affordable housing for low-income and poverty-level people, it hasn't been successful. Federal housing policy continues to reinforce the patterns and practices of private housing industries, as sociologist Gregory D. Squires (1994:51) explains:

> Working through their trade associations like the National Association of Homebuilders, the National Association of Realtors, the Associated General Contractors, the American Bankers Association, the U.S. League of Savings Institutions, and many others, housing-related industries have for over fifty years secured federal housing policies that focus on the provision of low-interest loans, mortgage interest subsidies, rent supplements, and other market-based inducements. Lobbyists have successfully kept public housing to a minimum in the United States (approximately 3% of all housing), labeling it as "socialistic" and, therefore, un-American. Again, it is the winners in the competitive market that have been the primary beneficiaries of housing policy.

The federal government's involvement in housing has been criticized on several fronts. Some critics believe that federal housing aid, which is supposed to provide decent housing for the poor, has done a better job of providing housing for more affluent people. Beginning in the 1950s, federally funded urban renewal projects were supposed to replace housing units in slums with better-quality, affordable housing for the poor. However, what actually happened, some analysts say, is that once the slums were cleared, more expensive housing or commercial properties were built (Jacobs, 1961). Moreover, sometimes the worst, most dilapidated housing units sometimes were not chosen for redevelopment because they were not in a strategic location for economic development. Because the power of *eminent domain* gives governmental officials the authority to condemn certain properties, individual owners' wishes regarding their property were not always taken into consideration (Flanagan, 1995). The most successful recent initiatives for replacing substandard housing and building lower-cost housing for poor and lower-income families have come from community groups and voluntary organizations. One of the best known of these is Habitat for Humanity, which has received extensive press coverage because of former President Jimmy Carter's participation

A second major criticism of federal housing initiatives has been directed at public housing. Most federal and state housing projects have been huge, high-rise constructions that intensified many problems and

Habitat for Humanity and other community groups and voluntary organizations have sought to provide lower-cost housing for poor and lower-income families. Do you think that the federal government should play a more active role in providing affordable housing? Why or why not?

created new ones. Perhaps the Pruitt-Igoe project in St. Louis is the all-time bad example of public housing projects. Built as a monolithic high-rise, the building immediately had structural problems, high rates of crime, inadequate maintenance, and poor management. Pruitt-Igoe received media attention and was the subject of sociological research, but finding a solution to the building's many problems was virtually impossible, and it was demolished in the 1970s.

Most urban sociologists agree that public housing works best when it is situated in less densely populated areas with a small number of families in any one housing project. In Charleston, South Carolina, for example, one public housing project is located in a neighborhood of historic residences that tourists visit on horse-drawn carriage tours. Tour guides even point to the housing unit as a sign that their community has overcome housing segregation. But when some communities have placed federally funded housing projects in neighborhoods of middle-income apartments and housing, adjoining property owners object, fearing that the value of their property and their personal safety will be diminished.

Since the 1970s, some middle- and upper-middle-class families have reentered central city areas and gentrified properties. **Gentrification is the process by which people renovate or restore properties in central cities.** Centrally located, naturally attractive areas are the most likely candidates for gentrification (Palen and London, 1984). Some people view gentrification as the way to revitalize the central city. Others think that it further depletes the stock of affordable housing for the poor and pushes low-income people out of an area where they had previously lived (Palen and London, 1984; Flanagan, 1995). The worst outcome of the housing shortage has been a significant increase in the number of homeless people in the United States.

HOMELESSNESS

Accurate data about the actual number of homeless people in the United States is unavailable. The total is probably somewhere between the Bureau of the Census's figure of roughly 250,000 and the 3 million estimated by advocates for the homeless (Mathews, 1992). It is extremely difficult to count the number of homeless people because most avoid interviews with census takers and social scientists. But each year, the U.S. Conference of Mayors conducts a survey on urban homelessness, and some consistent patterns have emerged during the 1990s. Who are the homeless? People of color are overrepresented; African Americans make up the largest part of the homeless population (about 50 percent), compared to whites (33 percent), Latinas/os (11 percent), Native Americans (3 percent), and Asian Americans (1 percent) (U.S. Conference of Mayors, 1995). Families and children are the fastest-growing segment of the homeless population in both urban and rural areas of this country. Today, infants, preschoolers, school-age children, and their parents account for almost half of the homeless (Vissing, 1996).

Many people think that "the homeless" are all alike, but homeless people come from all walks of life, including Vietnam war veterans; people with mental illnesses, physical disabilities, or AIDS; the elderly; runaway children and teenagers; alcoholics and other substance abusers; recent immigrants; and families with young children (Torrey, 1988; Snow and Anderson, 1993; Vissing, 1996). According to social scientists, studies that focus exclusively on personal problems of the homeless, such as mental illness or substance abuse, may result in *specialism*—the assumption that individual characteristics of poor people cause their homeless condition and therefore the only way to alleviate homelessness is to cure the individual's personal problems (Wagner, 1993). But this approach downplays the significance of structural factors such as the unavailability of low-income housing and of mental health care, which are the most important determinants of homelessness. According to sociologists Marta Elliott and Lauren J. Krivo (1991:128), solutions to the problem of homelessness must take into account these two structural factors:

> attempts to lower levels of homelessness in U.S. metropolitan areas must address the structural conditions which underlie this phenomenon. More specifically, mental health care services for the indigent mentally ill must be made more available to those who are or would become homeless without them. Furthermore, the structure of the housing market must be altered in order to have the greatest effects on reducing homelessness. This means that more low-cost rental housing needs to be made available to reach the most marginal and disadvantaged members of society. Such a restructuring of the housing market is unquestionably one of the primary means by which people will avoid or overcome homelessness. Without this basic resource of cheap housing in an area, some individuals fall

out of the housing market completely, a problem exacerbated by an economic environment with proportionately higher numbers of unskilled jobs. Stable well-paid employment must replace this segment of the economy to reduce current levels of homelessness.

Racial and Ethnic Segregation

Problems in housing are closely intertwined with racial and ethnic segregation in the United States. Despite passage of the Federal Fair Housing Act in 1968, segregation of African Americans and whites in major metropolitan areas declined only slightly between 1970 and 1990 (see Squires, 1994). According to sociologists Douglas S. Massey and Nancy A. Denton (1993), no other racial or ethnic group in the history of this country has ever experienced the sustained high levels of residential segregation that African Americans have experienced in central cities. Moreover, residential segregation not only affects living conditions, but is also associated with other problems (Massey and Denton, 1993:2):

> Residential segregation is not a neutral fact; it systematically undermines the social and economic well-being of blacks in the United States. Because of racial segregation, a significant share of black America is condemned to experience a social environment where poverty and joblessness are the norm, where a majority of children are born out of wedlock, where most families are on welfare, where educational failure prevails, and where social and physical deterioration abound. Through prolonged exposure to such an environment, black chances for social and economic success are drastically reduced.

Although African Americans may have experienced the longest and most harmful effects of housing segregation in the United States, other groups have also suffered a history of housing discrimination (Santiago and Wilder, 1991; Menchaca, 1995; Santiago and Galster, 1995). For example, a number of studies have documented that restrictive covenants prohibited Mexican Americans from living in white (Anglo) areas and that they were supported by racial harassment and violence (see Menchaca, 1995). In some cases, local custom dictated residential segregation patterns that continue into the present. In one recent study of Mexican American segregation, one woman recalls that Twelfth Street was the dividing line between the white (Anglo) American and Mexican American neighborhoods in Santa Paula, California (Menchaca, 1995:27):

La calle doce was the main division. The ranchers owned the homes in the northeast, and that was for the people whose parents worked in agriculture—which would be the lemon or the orange. . . . If you worked for them in the packing house or picking lemons, that's where you would live. . . . They used to tell us, You live in that side and we live in this side. . . . The rednecks used to tell us that.

Vestiges of similar patterns of residential segregation based on race or ethnicity remain in many cities. In Austin, Texas, the historic geographic and political divide between Mexican Americans and white (Anglo) Americans is an interstate highway. In other communities the divide is a river or some other geographic or social boundary that is well known to local residents, whether or not they acknowledge its existence. Although there is less overt discrimination, and courts have ruled that racial and ethnic restrictive covenants on property are unenforceable, housing segregation continues through custom.

Some analysts argue that residence is a personal choice, and people voluntarily segregate themselves on the basis of who they want to live near. But many people are involuntarily segregated because of certain attributes—such as race, religion, age, or disability—that others devalue. Some landlords, homeowners, and white realtors perpetuate residential segregation based on race or ethnicity through a discriminatory practice known as *steering*—guiding people of color to different neighborhoods than those shown to their white counterparts. Banks sometimes engage in another discriminatory (and illegal) practice, *redlining*, refusing loans to people of color for properties in certain areas. The behavior of neighbors can also perpetuate residential segregation (see Feagin and Sikes, 1994; Squires, 1994).

Unequal property taxation is another kind of residential segregation problem. In a study of suburban property taxes, social scientist Andrew A. Beveridge found that African American homeowners are taxed more than whites on comparable homes in 58 percent of the suburbs and 30 percent of the cities (cited in Schemo, 1994). The reason may be that African Americans are more likely to move to suburbs with declining tax bases because they have limited finances or are steered there by real estate agents or because white flight occurs as African American homeowners move in. Since houses are often reassessed when they're sold, newcomers face a heavier tax burden than longer-term residents, whose taxes may not go up for some period of time or until they sell their own houses (Schemo, 1994).

The continual influx of immigrants into urban areas is changing the population composition in many of the nation's largest cities, including Los Angeles, Houston, Miami, Chicago, and New York. For example, Monterey Park, California, which is about a ten-minute drive east of Los Angeles during non-rush-hour traffic, has been slowly transformed from a white (Anglo) community in the 1960s to a predominantly Asian community. And younger Chinese newcomers are replacing older U.S.-born Japanese Americans as the largest Asian group (Horton, 1995).

The 1990 Census showed that for the first time, minorities had experienced a higher percentage of growth in the nation's suburbs than in its central cities. However, only 27 percent of all African Americans lived in suburbs (U.S. Bureau of the Census, 1996b). Overall, 41 percent of central city residents were African Americans and other people of color, although all minority groups combined constituted only 19.3 percent of the nation's population. As more African Americans have moved to the suburbs, some social analysts have suggested that we now have greater residential integration and minority social mobility in this country. This may be true for middle-class African Americans who have moved to suburbs near Atlanta, Dallas, or Washington, D.C., but it is certainly not true for all African Americans, as urban sociologist William G. Flanagan (1995:271) explains:

Increase in the black suburban population cannot be taken to represent either dramatic improvements in residential integration or minority social mobility. In general analysts agree that suburban blacks are found disproportionately in areas that share many features with poorer central city locations: low income, poor-quality older housing, and strained municipal finances. . . . Black residential areas tend to be suburban only in a technical, locational sense. That is, they are "sub-urban," located adjacent to, but not in, central city areas. For their residents these areas represent neither the political nor economic liberation from the problems of the city that the white suburbs do. The black suburban movement is overwhelmingly to suburbs that are already inhabited by blacks, locations from which whites are moving away.

Despite an increased minority presence, most suburbs are predominantly white, and many upper-middle-class and upper-class suburbs remain virtually all white. For example, only 5 percent of the population in northern Fulton County (adjoining Atlanta, Georgia) is African American. In Plano (adjoining Dallas, Texas), nearly nine out of ten students in the public schools are white, whereas the majority of students in the Dallas Independent School District are African American, Latina/o, or Asian American (Roberts, 1993). Suburban Latinas/os are highly concentrated in eight metropolitan areas in California, Texas, and Florida. By far the largest such racial-ethnic concentration is found in the Los Angeles–Long Beach metropolitan area, with over 1.7 million Latinas/os. Like other groups, affluent Latinas/os live in affluent suburbs, while poorer Latinas/os remain segregated in less desirable central city areas (Palen, 1995).

In the suburbs, people of color (especially African Americans) often become resegregated (see Feagin and Sikes, 1994). Chicago, for example, remains one of the most segregated metropolitan areas in the country in spite of its fair-housing ordinance. Most of the African Americans who have fled the high crime of Chicago's South Side live in nearby suburbs such as Country Club Hill and Chicago Heights; suburban Asian Americans are most likely to live in Skokie and Naperville; and suburban Latinos/as live in Maywood, Hillside, and Bellwood (De Witt, 1994).

What will be the future of racial and ethnic relations in the cities and suburbs of this country? Sociologist John Horton is optimistic and uses Monterey Park as an example of a community that has moved gradually and peacefully toward a culture of diversity (Horton, 1995:225):

> Although the pressure to be American without "foreign" influence is increasing in California, in places like Monterey Park, where the world has already imploded, an Anglo or Eurocentric American identity is giving way to greater openness. The transformation happens unconsciously and on an incremental basis through compro-

mise and accommodation in the pragmatic process of getting things done. It is also undertaken consciously at public events and festivals where diversity and patriotism come together, using a formula that varies with the ethnicity and politics of those who plan the events. . . . The results may be small and seemingly trivial, but in an era of virulent nationalism and ethnic genocide, these local experiments in multiculturalism are advances to be celebrated.

At the same time, we must acknowledge that some dominant group members, especially those in the upper classes, strive to perpetuate their position at the top of the societal pyramid not only by living in certain areas of the city, but also by isolating themselves from the "Other"—the poor and many minority group members (see Baltzell, 1958; Birmingham, 1967; Domhoff, 1983). Thus, in the United States at the end of the twentieth century, racial segregation remains interlocked with class-based residential segregation (Santiago and Galster, 1995), as the vignettes at the beginning of the chapter show.

PROBLEMS IN GLOBAL CITIES

Although people have lived in cities for thousands of years, the time is rapidly approaching when more people worldwide will live in or near a city than in a rural area. In 1900, only one person out of ten lived in a city; by 2005, one person out of two will live in a city (Crossette, 1996c). Moreover, two-thirds of the world's expected population of 8 to 9 billion people will live in cities by 2025 (Crossette, 1996c). Of all developing regions, Latin America is becoming the most urbanized: Four megacities—Mexico City (20 million), Buenos Aires (12 million), Lima (7 million), and Santiago (5 million)—already contain more than half of the region's population and continue to grow rapidly. By 2010, Rio de Janeiro and São Paulo are expected to have a combined population of about 40 million people living in a 350-mile-long megalopolis (Petersen, 1994). By 2015, no U.S. city will be among the ten most populous in the world (see Table 17.1).

Rapid global population growth is producing a wide variety of urban problems, including overcrowding, environmental pollution, and the disappearance of farmland (see Chapter 16). In fact,

◢ TABLE 17.1   POPULATIONS OF THE WORLD'S TEN LARGEST CITIES
(IN MILLIONS, ESTIMATED)

1996		2015	
Tokyo, Japan	26.8	Tokyo, Japan	28.7
São Paulo, Brazil	16.4	Bombay, India	27.4
New York City, U.S.A.	16.3	Lagos, Nigeria	24.4
Mexico City, Mexico	15.6	Shanghai, China	23.4
Bombay, India	15.1	Jakarta, Indonesia	21.2
Shanghai, China	15.1	São Paulo, Brazil	20.8
Los Angeles, U.S.A.	12.4	Karachi, Pakistan	20.6
Beijing, China	12.4	Beijing, China	19.4
Calcutta, India	11.7	Dhaka, Bangladesh	19.0
Seoul, South Korea	11.6	Mexico City, Mexico	18.8

Source: *New York Times,* 1996c.

many cities in developing nations are quickly reaching the point at which food, housing, and basic public services are available to only a limited segment of the population (Crossette, 1996c). With urban populations growing at a rate of 170,000 people a day, cities such as Cairo, Lagos, Dhaka, Beijing, and São Paulo are likely to soon have acute water shortages; Mexico City is already experiencing a chronic water shortage (*New York Times,* 1996c).

Overcrowded living conditions are a way of life for people residing in this area of Bombay. How will rapid population growth in the future affect urban areas in global cities?

Natural increases in population (higher birth rates than death rates) account for two-thirds of new urban growth, and rural-to-urban migration accounts for the rest. Migration has caused rapid growth in cities in sub-Saharan Africa, India, Algeria, and Egypt. At the same time that the population is growing rapidly, the amount of available farmland for growing crops to feed people is decreasing. In Egypt, for example, land that was previously used for growing crops is now the site of petroleum refineries, food-processing plants, and other factories (Kaplan, 1996). One reason for the high rates of migration from rural areas is that people who are displaced from their land move to the cities to find jobs, but farmers leave, too, looking for a better life. Some analysts believe the United Nations should encourage governments to concentrate on rural development; otherwise, acute food shortages brought about by unchecked rural-to-urban migration could lead to riots (Kaplan, 1996).

As global urbanization has increased over the past three decades, differences in urban areas based on economic development at the national level have become apparent. According to sociologist Immanuel Wallerstein (1979, 1984), nations occupy one of three positions in the global economy: core, semiperipheral, and peripheral. *Core nations* are **dominant capitalist centers characterized by high levels of industrialization and urbanization.** The United States, Japan, and Germany, among others, are core nations. Some cities in core nations are referred to as *global cities*—interconnected urban areas that are centers of political, economic, and cultural activity. New York, Tokyo, and

London are generally considered the largest global cities. They are also considered postindustrial cities because their economic base has largely shifted from heavy manufacturing to information technologies and services such as accounting, marketing, finance, mergers and acquisitions, telecommunications, and other highly specialized fields (Friedmann, 1995). Global cities are the sites of new and innovative product development and marketing, and they often are the "command posts" for the world economy (Sassen, 1995). But economic prosperity is not shared equally by all people in the core nation global cities. Growing numbers of poor people work in low-wage service sector jobs or in assembly production, in which they are paid by the item (piecework) for what they produce but they have no employment benefits or job security. In fact, the living arrangements of some of these workers more closely resemble the living conditions of workers in semiperipheral nations than those of middle-class workers in their own country.

Most African countries and many countries in South America and the Caribbean are **peripheral nations—nations that depend on core nations for capital, have little or no industrialization (other than what may be brought in by core nations), and have uneven patterns of urbanization.** According to Wallerstein (1979, 1984), the wealthy in peripheral nations support the exploitation of poor workers by core nation capitalists in return for maintaining their own wealth and position. Poverty is thus perpetuated, and the problems worsen because of the unprecedented population growth in these countries.

Between the core and the peripheral nations are the *semiperipheral nations,* **which are more developed than peripheral nations but less developed than core nations.** Only two global cities are located in semiperipheral nations: São Paulo, Brazil, the center of the Brazilian economy, and Singapore, the economic center for a multicountry region in Southeast Asia (Friedmann, 1995). Like the peripheral nations, the semiperipheral nations—such as India, Iran, and Mexico—are confronted with unprecedented population growth. In addition, a steady flow of rural migrants to large cities is creating enormous urban problems. Semiperipheral nations exploit peripheral nations, just as the core nations exploit both the semiperipheral and the peripheral nations.

According to Wallerstein, it is very difficult—if not impossible—for peripheral and semiperipheral nations to ever occupy anything but their marginal positions in the classlike structure of the world economy directly because of their exploitation by the core nations (Wallerstein, 1979, 1984). Capital investment by core nations results in uneven economic growth, and in the process, the disparity between the rich and the poor in the major cities increases. Such economic disparity and urban growth is obvious at the U.S.–Mexican border, where transnational corporations have built *maquiladora plants,* factories where goods are assembled by low-wage workers to keep production costs down, on the Mexican side. The demand for workers in these plants has caused thousands of people to move from the rural areas of Mexico to urban areas along the border in hope of earning a higher wage. The influx has pushed already overcrowded cities far beyond their capacity. Many people live in central city slums or at the edge of cities in *shantytowns,* where houses are made from discarded materials, because their wages are low and affordable housing is nonexistent. Squatters are the most rapidly growing segment of the population in many Mexican cities (Flanagan, 1995).

Social analysts are just beginning to develop comprehensive perspectives on the position of cities in the contemporary world economy, and not all analysts agree with Wallerstein's hierarchy (1979, 1984). But most scholars acknowledge that nations throughout the world are influenced by a relatively small number of cities (e.g., New York) and transnational corporations that have brought about a shift from an international to a more global economy (see Knox and Taylor, 1995; Wilson, 1997). In developing nations, all social problems are "incubated and magnified in cities" (Crossette, 1996c:A3).

SOCIOLOGICAL PERSPECTIVES ON URBAN PROBLEMS

Throughout the twentieth century, sociologists have analyzed urban problems to determine the causes and consequences of rapid industrialization and urbanization on people's daily lives and the structure of society. The conclusions they reach about the underlying problems and possible solutions depend on the framework they apply.

▲ The Functionalist Perspective

In examining urban problems, most functionalists focus on three processes that contributed to social

SOCIAL PROBLEMS
AND SOCIAL POLICY

BOX 17.2

Urban Empowerment Zones: A New Initiative

For three generations, an enormous Cadillac factory stretched across eight blocks on the southwest side of the Motor City, providing a path to the middle class for tens of thousands of workers. It closed a decade ago, becoming a vast, derelict monument to the decay of a great manufacturing center. The surrounding neighborhood deteriorated almost as fast as the weeds grew up around the factory. The only high-paying job nearby was drug-dealing.

But for the last two years, the inner city where the factory is situated—an endless sprawl of blocks so bleak that rundown houses can sell for less than used cars—has been a magnet for business.

—"Before" and "after" in the Detroit urban empowerment zone (Meredith, 1997:C1)

The United States has never had a national urban development policy, and many urban sociologists believe that we have suffered for it with "a chronically underemployed and underhoused inner-city population" (Flanagan, 1995:345). Instead, our urban policy has been program after program, in response to economic shifts. Sometimes that approach has worked, as during the Great Depression of the 1930s when so many people lost their homes and the Roosevelt administration responded with New Deal policies that created work. But at other times, the "go with the flow" approach has not worked (Flanagan, 1995:351). In the recession of the early 1980s, for example, there were almost as many homeless people as there had been during the Depression (Flanagan, 1995:346). In fact, the great number of homeless people could not be accounted for with the usual category, "vagrants," and

a new category appeared in the *New York Times:* "homeless persons" (Bunis, Yancik, and Snow, 1996:393). But this time, the federal government did not respond, and homelessness is now an even bigger problem.

Today, in keeping with the program-by-program approach, the federal government has developed an initiative based on urban empowerment zones. Since 1994, six urban empowerment zones have been designated: Atlanta, Baltimore, Chicago, New York, Philadelphia–Camden, N.J., and Detroit. Cities receive development grants and businesses get tax breaks. New York and Philadelphia–Camden have had problems, but Detroit has been a real success story.

Detroit's empowerment zone is an 18.35-square-mile area where twenty-nine companies have pledged to invest 2.17 billion dollars. The two core companies are General Motors and Chrysler. Most of the other businesses make automotive products to supply the GM and Chrysler plants. The new jobs are "the first ray of hope in years" for an area where unemployment was at 50 percent and most of the 101,000 residents lived below the poverty line (Meredith, 1997). Detroit's City Council and business leaders believe that the empowerment zone has also been a catalyst for change in the downtown area, where plans are underway for a new football stadium. Still, according to City Council member Sheila M. Cockrel, "There is more that can and should and must be done" (Meredith, 1997).

What do you suppose Cockrel is referring to? How would you build on the success of Detroit's empowerment zone? Would you like to see the United States develop a national urban development policy to set plans in advance? Or are there advantages to "going with the flow"? What do you think?

disorganization and disruption of social institutions. First, mass migration from rural areas to urban areas during the Industrial Revolution contributed to social disorganization by weakening personal ties in the family, religion, education, and other institutions. Second, the large-scale immigration in the late nineteenth and early twentieth centuries was more than most cities could absorb, and many individuals were never fully assimilated into the cultural mainstream. With larger numbers of strangers living close together in central cities, symptoms of social disorganization, such as high rates of crime, mental illness, and suicide, grew more pronounced. According to Emile Durkheim, urban life changes people's relationships. Rural areas are characterized by *mechanical solidarity*—social bonds based on shared religious beliefs and a simple division of labor—but these bonds are changed with urbanization. Urban areas are characterized by *organic solidarity*—social bonds based on interdependence and an elaborate division of labor (specialization). Although Durkheim was optimistic that urbanization could be positive, he also thought that some things were lost in the process. Third, mass suburbanization created additional social disorganization, and most central cities have been unable to reach an equilibrium since the mass exodus to the suburbs following World War II. According to urban ecologist Amos Hawley (1950, 1981), new technologies such as commuter railways and automobiles led to the decentralization of city life and the movement of industry from the central city to the suburbs, and the results were disastrous for some people. Although urbanization, mass immigration, and suburbanization have had functional consequences for many people—including U.S. citizenship, job opportunities, and home ownership—they have also created problems, particularly for people who are left behind in rapidly declining central cities and people who experienced discrimination.

How do functionalists suggest that urban problems might be reduced? To alleviate the fiscal crisis facing many cities and level the inequality in services provided in cities and suburbs, sociologist Anthony M. Orum (1995) suggests establishing metropolitan or regional governments. Problems such as water supply, pollution, and traffic congestion, which are not confined to one geographic area, could be dealt with more effectively through metropolitan or regional planning. However, as Orum acknowledges, it is unlikely that officials of cities and suburban municipalities would willingly give up some of their power, and people living in the more affluent suburbs are unlikely to be willing to take on the problems of central cities.

Another option for alleviating urban problems is expanding the urban tax base by creating urban enterprise zones. Cities could offer tax incentives for industries to open plants in central cities and provide job training for workers, so a match could be made between jobs and workers. But critics of enterprise zones argue that business tax incentives alone won't improve conditions in central cities (see Cozic, 1993). Some U.S. cities are finding that another program—urban empowerment zones—can be a catalyst for jobs and development in areas of high unemployment (see Box 17.2).

▲ The Conflict Perspective

Conflict analysts do not believe that cities grow or decline by chance. Members of the capitalist class and political elites make far-reaching decisions about land use and urban development that benefit some people at the expense of others (Castells, 1977; Feagin and Parker, 1990). The upper classes have successfully maintained class-based and sometimes racially based segregation through political control and legal strategies such as municipal incorporation, defensive annexation, restrictive covenants, and zoning regulations (Feagin and Parker, 1990; Higley, 1995). But where do these practices leave everyone else? Karl Marx suggested that cities are the arenas in which the intertwined processes of class conflict and capital accumulation take place; class consciousness and worker revolt were more likely to develop when workers were concentrated in urban areas (Flanagan, 1995).

Contemporary conflict theorists Joe E. Feagin and Robert Parker (1990) speak of a *political economy model*, believing that both economic *and* political factors affect patterns of urban growth and decline. Urban growth is influenced by capital investment decisions, power and resource inequality, class and class conflict, and government subsidy programs. Members of the capitalist class choose corporate locations, decide on sites for shopping centers and factories, and spread the population that can afford to purchase homes into sprawling suburbs located exactly where the capitalists think they should be located (Feagin and Parker, 1990). Today, a few hundred financial institutions and developers finance and construct most major and many smaller urban development projects, including skyscrapers, shopping malls, and suburban housing projects. These decision makers set limits on the real estate choices of ordinary citizens (Feagin and Parker, 1990). They can make housing more affordable or totally unaffordable for many people. Ultimately, their motivation rests not in benefiting the community, but rather in making a profit, and the cities they produce reflect this mindset.

One of the major results of the political economy model of urban development is *uneven development*—the tendency of some neighborhoods, cities, or regions to grow and prosper while others stagnate and decline (Perry and Watkins, 1977). Conflict theorists argue that uneven development reflects inequalities of wealth and power in society. Uneven development not only affects areas in decline, but also produces external costs that are paid by the entire community. Among these costs are increased pollution, traffic congestion, and rising rates of crime and violence. According to sociologist Mark Gottdiener (1985:214), these costs are "intrinsic to the very core of capitalism, and those who profit the most from development are not called upon to remedy its side effects." One advantage of the political economy framework is that it can be used to study cities in developing as well as developed nations (see Jaffee, 1990; Knox and Taylor, 1995; D. Wilson, 1997).

Short of major changes in the political economy, most analysts who take a conflict perspective believe that urban problems can be reduced only through political activism and organized resistance to oppressive conditions. Some believe that central cities are powder kegs of urban unrest that periodically threaten to explode because of massive job loss and economic hardship, racial tensions, allegations of police brutality, controversial court cases, and similar issues. These analysts cite the Los Angeles civil unrest of 1992 as an example of what happens when people are cut off from mainstream social and economic institutions and have little, if any, hope of providing for themselves and their families. Although in the years since 1992, most of South-Central Los Angeles has been physically restored, many of the old tensions remain. According to scholar Michael Dear, the 1992 violence proved that Los Angeles "didn't learn the lessons of the Watts riots [in the 1960s] too well, because the same basic underlying structural tensions which we experienced in

Demonstrators outside the Los Angeles police headquarters helped fuel one of many fires that ensued in the civil unrest following the acquittal of police officers charged in the brutal attack on Rodney King, an African American in police custody. How are issues of race, class, and gender inequality intertwined with concerns about political unrest in the United States?

the region hadn't been addressed. It really took another economic downturn to bring them to the fore again" (cited in Purdum, 1997:16).

The Interactionist Perspective

Interactionists examine urban problems from the standpoint of people's *experience* of urban life and how they subjectively define the reality of city living. How does city life affect the people who live in a city? According to early German sociologist Georg Simmel (1950), urban life is so highly stimulating that people have no choice but to become somewhat insensitive to events and individuals around them. Urban residents generally avoid emotional involvement with one another and try to ignore events—including violence and crime—that take place nearby. They are wary of other people, looking at others as strangers; some people act reserved to cloak deeper feelings of distrust or dislike toward others. At the same time, Simmel thought that urban living could be liberating because it gives people opportunities for individualism and autonomy (Flanagan, 1995).

On the basis of Simmel's observations of social relations in the city, early University of Chicago sociologist Louis Wirth (1938) suggested that urbanism is a "way of life" that increases the incidence of both social and personality disorders in individuals. *Urbanism* refers to the distinctive social and psychological patterns of life that are typically found in the city. According to Wirth, the size, density, and heterogeneity of urban populations result in an elaborate division of labor and in spatial segregation of people by race/ethnicity, social class, religion, and/or lifestyle. The division of labor and spatial segregation produce feelings of alienation, powerlessness, and loneliness.

In contrast to Wirth's gloomy analysis of urban life, sociologist Herbert Gans (1982/1962) believed that not everyone experiences the city in the same way. On the basis of research in the West End of Boston in the late 1950s, Gans concluded that many residents develop strong loyalties and a sense of community in central city areas that outsiders often view negatively. According to Gans, personal behavior is shaped by the type of neighborhood a person lives in within the larger urban area. For example, *cosmopolites*—students, artists, writers, musicians, entertainers, and professionals—view the city as a place where they can be close to cultural facilities and people with whom they share common interests. *Unmarried people and childless couples* live in the city because they want to be close to work and entertainment. *Ethnic villagers* live in ethnically segregated neighborhoods because they feel most comfortable within their own group. But the *deprived* and the *trapped* live in the city because they believe they have no other alternatives. Gans concluded that the city is a pleasure and a challenge for some urban dwellers and an urban nightmare for others.

According to interactionists, the deprived and the trapped contribute to a social construction of reality that stereotypes city dwellers as poor, down-and-out, and sometimes dangerous, whereas many people living in the city are not this way at all. But an antiurban bias remains strong among many nonurban dwellers because movies, television shows, and, particularly, extensive media coverage of crime or racial unrest in the nation's largest metropolitan areas present a very negative image of cities.

To reduce problems of loneliness and alienation in city life, some interactionists propose that people who live in large metropolitan areas develop subcultural ties to help them feel a sense of community and identity. A *subculture* is a group of people who share a distinctive set of cultural beliefs and behaviors that set them apart from the larger society. Joining an interest group—from bowling with friends from the office to volunteering in a literacy program—is one way of feeling connected. Ethnic neighborhoods are an example of subcultures; some are tightly knit, whereas others have little influence on residents' daily lives. Members of subcultures, especially those based on race, ethnicity, or religion, sometimes come into conflict with each other. These conflicts can result in verbal exchanges, hate crimes, or other physical violence, or they can cause the individuals to withdraw almost entirely from the larger community and become more intensely involved with the subculture.

URBAN PROBLEMS IN THE TWENTY-FIRST CENTURY

In a best-case scenario, the United States might convert to regional governments to provide water, wastewater (sewage), transportation, schools, parks, hospitals, and other public services. Revenues would be shared among central cities, affluent suburbs, and edge cities, since everyone would benefit from the improved quality of life. Admittedly, this may be an overly optimistic view. Still, although we may not be able to do anything about urbanization at the macrolevel, we can more likely exercise some degree of control over our communities and our own lives. There is increasing impetus to take control because one thing is certain: As the world population continues to grow in the twenty-first century, race-, class-, and age-related demographics will change globally, and these demographic changes will intensify urban problems and affect us all.

SUMMARY

How did urbanization come about?

Urbanization is the process by which an increasing proportion of a population lives in cities rather than rural areas. Before the Industrial Revolution, most people lived in sparsely populated rural areas, where they farmed. Industrialization led to the growth of cities, and urbanization brought about profound changes in societies and spawned new social problems such as housing shortages, overcrowding, unsanitary conditions, environmental pollution, and crime.

How did mass suburbanization occur and what were the results?

Mass suburbanization began with government efforts to correct the housing shortage that followed World War II. The Housing Act of 1949 gave incentives to builders to develop affordable housing, while government agencies made it possible for returning veterans to qualify for home mortgages. Other factors included the availability of inexpensive land, low-cost mass construction methods, new federally financed highway systems, inexpensive gasoline, racial tension in central cities, and consumers' pent-up demands for single-family homes on individually owned lots. Mass suburbanization brought about a dramatic shift in the distribution of the U.S. population and set up an ongoing economic and racial division of interests between cities and suburbs that still exists today.

Why are many cities in fiscal crisis?

Large numbers of middle- and upper-income people moved out of the central city to the suburbs, and more recently, many retail businesses and corporations have also exited for the suburbs or moved their operations abroad. The shrinking central cities are left with greatly reduced sources of revenue. Many of the remaining central city residents are poor, unemployed, or older people living on fixed incomes who cannot afford to pay higher taxes. At the same time, city governments must still provide city services for them. Moreover, suburbanites who regularly use city services do not pay taxes to the city to keep up these services.

Why is health care a crisis in U.S. cities?

Health care is a big problem in big cities because hospitals and other medical facilities are subject to cutbacks and closings when cities face economic problems. Also, people in impoverished sections of central cities are more likely to become ill or injured because poverty is associated with many medical problems. Drug-related problems and HIV/AIDS put an added burden on facilities. All of these problems are exacerbated when managed care plans and large hospital chains take over urban hospitals and streamline services to turn a profit.

Why is there a housing shortage in the United States and what is being done about it?

When city agencies demand that a landlord comply with safety standards and building codes, many landlords abandon their buildings rather than make the investment. A bigger reason, however, is that the United States has yet to find a way to provide safe, livable, low-income housing. The urban homesteading program, for example, has been criticized for promoting the interests of the building industry instead of actually helping people to get good housing. Federal housing projects have characteristically been monolithic high-rises that intensified many problems and created new ones. One of the most successful initiatives for creating affordable housing is the voluntary organization Habitat for Humanity.

How great a problem is homelessness? Are there any solutions?

Accurate data on the actual number of the homeless are extremely difficult to get because homeless people avoid interviews with census takers and social researchers. But the U.S. Conference of Mayors survey shows that people of color are overrepresented in the homeless population, and the fastest-growing segment of the homeless population is families and children. Most experts agree that any long-term, successful solution to homelessness must take structural factors into account, especially low-income housing and mental health care.

Why does residential segregation exist even if it is illegal?

In some cases, housing segregation continues through custom. Sometimes landlords, homeowners, and white realtors perpetuate residential segregation through steering—guiding people of color to different neighborhoods than those shown to their white counterparts. Unequal property taxation is another kind of residential segregation problem.

→ *What are the major problems in global cities?*

By 2005, one out of every two people in the world will live in a city. Increasing population accounts for two-thirds of the new urban growth, and rural-to-urban migration accounts for the rest. Rapid urban growth brings a wide variety of problems, including overcrowding, environmental pollution, and the disappearance of farmland. In addition, semiperipheral nations are exploited by core nations, and peripheral nations are exploited by both semiperipheral and core nations. Core nations are dominant capitalist centers characterized by high levels of industrialization and urbanization. Peripheral nations depend on core nations for capital, have little or no industrialization (other than what is brought in by core nations), and have uneven patterns of urbanization. Semiperipheral nations are more developed than peripheral nations but less developed than core nations.

→ *What are the functionalist and conflict perspectives on urban problems?*

Functionalists believe that today's urban problems are the result of mass migration from rural areas during the Industrial Revolution, large-scale immigration in the late nineteenth and early twentieth centuries, and mass suburbanization. One solution is to create metropolitan governments. Conflict theorists believe that cities grow or decline according to decisions made by capitalists and the political elite. In other words, they use a political economy model. The resulting urban problems can be reduced through political activism and organized resistance to oppressive conditions.

→ *What is the interactionist perspective on urban problems?*

Interactionists look at how people subjectively experience urban life. According to German sociologist Georg Simmel, urban life is so stimulating that people have no choice but to become somewhat insensitive to people and events around them. On the other hand, urban living gives people opportunities for individualism and autonomy. Sociologist Louis Wirth expanded on Simmel's ideas, saying that urbanism produces feelings of alienation and powerlessness. Herbert Gans concluded from his research that city life is a pleasure for some and a nightmare for others. The way to avoid alienation is to develop subcultural ties.

KEY TERMS

core nations, p. 386
edge city, p. 376
gentrification, p. 382
mechanical solidarity, p. 389
megalopolis, p. 376

organic solidarity, p. 389
peripheral nations, p. 387
semiperipheral nations, p. 387
subculture, p. 391
urbanization, p. 374

QUESTIONS FOR CRITICAL THINKING

1. Where do you live—in the core central city, an edge city, a suburb, a megalopolis? What examples from your everyday life can you give that relate to the problems described in this chapter? Which sociological perspective do you think best explains the urban problems you observe?

2. The government has so far failed to provide adequate low-income and poverty-level housing. What new initiatives can you suggest?

3. Why do you think families with children are the fastest-growing segment of the homeless population in both urban and rural areas of this country? What can be done about the problem?

Global Social Problems

War and Terrorism

It's hard to judge a generation by its statistics. Five years ago, my generation was a group of overstuffed slackers; today we're Gordon Gekkos [the greedy, corporate-raider of the 1987 movie *Wall Street*]. An unlikely transformation. But there's at least one statistic that resonates: more of us are taking a full five years to get through college. Most of the country's parents look at this as a sort of slacker ritual. . . . But there's another way to regard that extra year: as a peace dividend. A generation ago, in the midst of the Vietnam War, the idea of a year off from college was dangerously ridiculous. Leaving school meant a one-way ticket to Saigon. Two generations ago it was Korea. Three generations ago, war-torn Europe or the inferno of the Pacific. My generation has had the blessing of growing up in peaceful times, and it has made all the difference. . . . It is premature (also probably unlucky) to call Generation X the peace generation, but the evidence is mounting. No generation in American history has had less traffic with war or its brutally congruent demands for sacrifice and faith. And because we haven't had to fight, we've been free from the conformist pressures of a nation at war. We've found our own, unique identity as a generation that thinks and does at it pleases. . . . But this peaceful outlook has brought with it a mouthful of unanswerably hard questions. Is an innocence of war a blessing or curse? Will our naiveté make us dangerously curious about the tools of violent power? Or is this the start of a thousand years of peace, secured by a certainty that what we have now is forever worth having?

—*Author Joshua Cooper Ramo describes life in the absence of war for "Generation X'ers."*
(Ramo, 1997:69)

Thankfully, as Ramo describes, a whole generation has grown up in the United States without having war and preparedness for war a part of their lives. They see the United States as a peaceful country, even though some social analysts believe that history shows us as one of the most war-prone nations in the world (Fussell, 1992; Maass, 1996). With the collapse of the former Soviet Union and the end of the Cold War between the United States and the former Soviet bloc countries in the 1980s, prospects for world peace were bright. But today, the Congo (the former Zaïre), Rwanda, and the Balkans are at war, and Bahrain, Cameroon, the Central African Republic, Cyprus, Ireland, and the United Kingdom are in conflict (Briscoe, 1997). There are also state-versus-state conflicts in China and North Korea, and the threat of a global nuclear arsenal that could destroy all life on this planet (Daley, 1997).

The twentieth century has seen the development of advanced technologies that provide new potential for wars that are far more deadly and remote than in the past. For example, the U.S. military has long-range, hypersonic munitions that strike from the air, making it unnecessary to send aircraft into the theater of war (Friedman and Friedman, 1996). Moreover, the stockpile of nuclear weapons left over from the arms race between the former Soviet Union and the West vastly increases the potential for waging warfare on a massive scale. But with the capability of war comes resistance to war, as social critic Barbara Ehrenreich (1997:239) explains, "If the twentieth century brought the steady advance of war and war-related enterprises, it also brought the beginnings of organized resistance to war. . . . in the situation where everyone is expected to participate in one way or another, and where anyone can become a victim whether they participate or not, opposition could at last develop to the institution of war itself." In this chapter, we examine war, terrorism, resistance to war and terrorism, and prospects for peace.

Unlike some U.S. residents who do not go to the polls to vote, Bosnians were so anxious to vote in the presidential election in that country—and angry over delays—that some of them kicked in doors and smashed windows at a polling station in Sarajevo. Why might voting be considered more important by people in war-torn nations than by people in the United States?

WAR AS A SOCIAL PROBLEM

What is war? Most people think of war as armed conflict between two countries or two factions within a country, such as the North and the South in the U.S. Civil War. But social scientists define war more broadly, including not only declared wars between nations or parties, but also undeclared wars, civil and guerrilla wars, covert operations, and some forms of terrorism (Wright, 1964). To social scientists, *general warfare* refers to violent armed conflict between nations, whereas *regional warfare* refers to conflict between rival factions located within a specific geographic area. Also, societies that are prepared at all times for war have a *war system*—components of social institutions (e.g., the economy, government, and education) and cultural beliefs and practices that promote the development of warriors, weapons, and war as a normal part of the society and its foreign policy (Cancian and Gibson, 1990).

How, then, do social scientists define *peace*? Sociologists Francesca M. Cancian and James William Gibson (1990) believe that peace is a less clearly defined concept than war. People generally agree that peace is highly desirable, but they often have different ideas of what constitutes peace. Some equate peace with harmonious relations in a world where there is no bloodshed between groups; but some nations equate peace with prevailing in battle (Gibson and Cancian, 1990). Despite the problems associated with distinguishing between war and peace, we can conclude that both consist of actions and beliefs held by people like ourselves and that these actions and beliefs have serious consequences for individuals, groups, and nations.

The Nature of War

First and foremost, war is an institution that involves *violence*—behavior intended to bring pain, physical injury, and/or psychological stress to people or to harm or destroy property (Sullivan, 1997). Violence is a component of many social problems, including violent crime and domestic violence. Both of these forms of *interpersonal violence* typically involve a relatively small number of people who are responding to a particular situation or pursuing their own personal goals. In contrast, war is a form of **collective violence that involves organized violence by people seeking to promote their cause or resist social policies or practices that they consider oppressive** (Sullivan, 1997).

Except for media coverage and for those who go into combat or are friends or relatives of those who do, war is very remote to most people in the United States. Early in our country's history, just the opposite was true: War took place very close to home, in the Civil War and war with Mexico. But in the twentieth century, the two world wars transformed the nature of U.S. military action. First, those wars were fought on foreign soil; second, vastly more U. S. military personnel were involved. In World War I, for example, about 5 million people served in the U.S. armed forces, and over 16 million men and women served in World War II (Ehrenreich, 1997).

The two world wars were different from each other in a very significant way, too. In World War I, killing civilians was considered unduly violent, but the nations fighting in World War II intentionally killed civilians. Bombing cities in Europe and Asia during World War II added a different dimension to war: Now war was waged against civilians (Hynes, 1997). This is how social critic Barbara Ehrenreich (1997:206–207) describes the shift to civilians as the targets of war-related violence:

> By World War II, the destruction (and exploitation) of civilians was deliberate policy on all sides. The British used air power to "de-house" the German population; the U.S. bombed the civilian populations of Hiroshima, Nagasaki, and Dresden; the Germans and Japanese destroyed cities and exploited defeated populations as slave labor. . . . Air power made the mass bombings of civilians possible, but it was the huge involvement of civilians in the industrial side of war that made it seem strategically necessary. . . . In this situation, there were no "innocent" civilians, except possibly children, and the war took on a genocidal character unknown to the more gentlemanly conflict of [World War I].

One of the most significant characteristics of war is its persistence. According to Ehrenreich, World War II not only provided the United States with the opportunity to declare itself the "leader of the free world," but also gave political and economic leaders the impetus to perpetuate this nation's position as the world's military superpower. Accordingly, Congress established defense spending as a top national priority, and the U.S. military–industrial complex that initially emerged during World War II became a massive industrial infrastructure that produces an array of war-related goods such as uniforms, tanks, airplanes, and warships. The military–industrial complex flourished during the 1950s, when the international arms race brought about the *Cold War*—a conflict between nations based on military preparedness and the threat of war but not actual warfare. Between 1950 and the mid-1990s, the U.S. government responded to the perceived Soviet threat by spending approximately $10.2 trillion for its arms buildup. In 1991 alone, the defense industry received more than $121 billion in government contracts, giving some corporations a virtual monopoly over an entire market in which there was only one buyer (the U.S. government) and very few (if any) competitors.

The Consequences of War

The major direct effects of war are loss of human life and serious physical and psychological effects on war's survivors (see Box 18.1). It is impossible to determine how many human lives have been lost in wars throughout human history. Not only would we need a more more precise definition of what constitutes war, but we would also have to assume that survivors were always available to count the dead in

SOCIAL PROBLEMS
IN GLOBAL PERSPECTIVE

BOX 18.1

Surviving the War in Bosnia

The quiet life on Gavrilo Princip Street . . . died four years ago with the torture of several Muslims and the expulsion of them all, residents said. It came at the hands of what were sometimes close Serb acquaintances from down the street.

Few here saw the war coming in late 1991, even as their childhood friends took sides and some Serbian neighbors began to parade under their nationalist flag. And of those that finally fled to Sarajevo, most only packed enough for a weekend.

And now many of the original Muslim owners return here in their spare time to work at putting their homes back in order, splicing cables for electricity and replacing plumbing taken by the squatters.

—A scene in Ilidza, a suburb of
Sarajevo, in Bosnia and
Herzegovina (Roane, 1996)

The people in Ilidza are the lucky ones. Their town was taken over by the Bosnian Serbs during the war, but it has since been transferred to the Muslim-Croat federation, so they were able to return. What they returned to, though, was devastation—no electricity or plumbing, burned buildings, graffiti and litter everywhere. The psychological loss is no less than the physical loss, and it is compounded by knowing that one-time friends and neighbors are responsible. Says twenty-four-year-old Jasna Hadzimehmedovic, "I had so many friends who I never thought would expel us, or kill us, and they did. Everything is different now. So when we rebuild here, it will all be different. Nothing can be like it was before the war" (Roane, 1996).

If these are the lucky ones, who are the unlucky? Tens of thousands of refugees on both sides. Some of the worst-off are the Muslim widows from Srebrenica. When Bosnian Serbs

the aftermath of every war that has taken place (Hynes, 1997).

Nonetheless, social analyst Ruth Sivard (1991, 1993) tackled the problem in a limited way. She determined that 589 wars had been fought by 142 countries since 1500 and that approximately 142 million lives were lost. But according to Sivard, more lives were lost in wars during the twentieth

◤ TABLE 18.1 **U.S. ARMED FORCES PERSONNEL CASUALTIES IN WARS**

War	Battle Deaths (In Thousands)	Wounds, Not Mortal (In Thousands)
Spanish-American War	*	2
World War I	53	204
World War II	292	671
Korean conflict	34	103
Vietnam conflict	47	153

* Fewer than 500 total.

Source: U.S. Bureau of the Census, 1996b.

took Srebrenica in July 1995, they killed almost the entire male Muslim population from the town and surrounding villages. The 30,000 survivors, mostly women and children, live in refugee camps, though some, like Mila Ahmetovic, age twenty-five, have left the camps to move into abandoned houses. There is not one man left in Mrs. Ahmetovic's extended family, and for women who were brought up to depend on men for everything, the future is terrifying: "I used to be afraid of the nightmares. . . . Now I am afraid of reality. I don't know how my family will survive. . . . Inside of me, way inside, I don't think I can do very much for my family because my man is gone and I can't be strong enough as only a woman," said Mrs. Ahmetovic (O'Connor, 1996).

In rural Bosnian society, women view themselves not as individuals, but as part of their family, extended family, and village. According to Irfanka Pasagic, one of the therapists who were brought in to counsel the Srebrenica widows, "From the time she could speak, the woman was told in words and examples that her value was based on what a man thought of her" (O'Connor, 1996). Men were educated and dealt with the outside world; girls went to school only until the fourth grade, married at about age fifteen, and never left their villages. These women, who were never psychologically prepared to be independent—let alone as survivors of war—are understandably frightened and depressed. As Mrs. Ahmetovic says, "I have trouble seeing as far as tomorrow. My children and I think about little things, like making a meal, but everything else is empty" (O'Connor, 1996).

Even the smallest attempts to resume day-to-day life during peacetime carry reminders of the war. Soccer games are being played again in Grbavica Stadium in Sarajevo even though there are bomb craters near one goalpost and a quarter of the stands are missing because Muslim and Bosnian Serb troops fought there (Associated Press, 1996). And along with the usual police and ambulance on the sidelines, there is a mine sweeper.

Do these stories give you a sense of what it is like to be a survivor of war? Will these people ever get over their war experience? What do you think?

century than in all the other centuries combined. World War I took the lives of approximately 8 million combatants and 1 million civilians, and the toll was even higher in World War II, when over 50 million people (17 million combatants and 35 million civilians) lost their lives. During World War II, U.S. casualties alone totaled almost 300,000 deaths and over 600,000 wounded (see Table 18.1).

These numbers would pale, though, compared to an all-out nuclear war. The devastation would be beyond description. Although the development of nuclear weapons may have contributed to peace among the major world powers since the late 1940s, we can see the potentially destructive effects of nuclear war in the U.S. attacks on Hiroshima and Nagasaki, Japan. In an attempt to end World War II, a U.S. aircraft flew over Hiroshima and dropped a 1.5-kiloton atomic bomb, killing 130,000 people either instantly or over the next few months as a result of deadly radiation that rained on the city (Erikson, 1994). Today, some nuclear warheads held by governments throughout the world are over 4,000 times more powerful than the bombs that were dropped on Japan. In fact, scientists estimate that a nuclear war would kill more than 160 million people outright, and over 1 billion people would die in the first few hours as a result of radiation poisoning, environmental contamination and destruction, and massive social unrest (Friedman and Friedman, 1996).

Even though an international treaty bans underground nuclear tests, nations may still be developing and stockpiling nuclear weapons. In 1997, the U.S. government became concerned that China was purchasing U.S.-made supercomputers to design lighter, more efficient nuclear warheads that could be put on missiles capable of reaching the United States (Gerth, 1997). These high-performance supercomputers operate at ten times the speed of the fastest personal computer available and can process huge amounts of data. They would allow China to do very small underground nuclear weapons tests that outsiders would be unable to detect. U.S. government officials and military experts disagree over whether or not selling such technology to other nations, especially those not considered allies of the U.S. government, should be strictly monitored or even banned (Gerth, 1997).

Since World War II, two factors—how wars are fought and where they are fought—have changed the numbers and types of war casualties. Today, military strategy calls for deploying bombs and long-range missiles to eliminate the enemy's weapon production plants and supply centers. Because these plants are located in major cities, civilians are more likely to be killed than they were in the past. And whereas Europe was the primary battleground for most wars from 1500 through World War II, developing nations are now the primary sites.

Before World War II, soldiers were the primary casualties of war. But in World War II and subsequent wars, including the Vietnam War and the Gulf War, civilians make up the greater percentage of injured and dead (Ehrenreich, 1997). Some analysts believe that civilians accounted for 75 percent of all war-related deaths in the 1980s and nearly 90 percent in the 1990s (Renner, 1993). But social analysts don't agree on the number of civilian casualties in recent wars. On the one hand, in their recent book *The Future of War* (1996), George Friedman and Meredith Friedman argue that the use of precision-guided munitions ("smart weapons") in Desert Storm (another name for the Gulf War) made it possible for the United States to strike particular parts of particular buildings without striking any noncombatants, hence keeping the civilian death count low. On the other hand, a demographer employed by the U.S. Bureau of the Census calculated that 40,000 Iraqi soldiers were killed during the war but more than 80,000 Iraqi civilians, mostly women and children, were killed in air strikes—13,000 in precision bombing and 70,000 as a result of disease associated with the systematic destruction of water purification and sewage treatment systems in their country (Colhoun, 1992). Moreover, many hospitals were damaged or destroyed. In some cases, when nearby power plants were hit, hospitals could no longer operate basic equipment or provide emergency medical care to people injured by bombs (Burleigh, 1991).

At home in the United States, however, one immediate consequence of the Gulf War was a national festivity that analyst Barbara Ehrenreich (1997:223) believes was manipulated by television coverage of the war:

> Flags appeared everywhere, along with bumper stickers, T-shirts, and buttons urging Americans to SUPPORT OUR TROOPS. As if flags were not a sufficient proof of loyalty, they were joined by yellow ribbons. . . . In my town the Boy Scouts affixed yellow ribbons to every tree and bush lining the main street, and similar outbreaks of nationalistic fetishism occurred all over the country. Sports teams and public employees insisted on the right to wear American-flag patches on their uniforms; dissenters (and those deemed to look like Iraqis) were in some cases attacked or threatened with attack.

As Ehrenreich points out, most wars at least temporarily create a strong sense of patriotism. In this way, war is functional because it provides an external enemy for people to hate. In the Gulf War, this enemy was Iraqi leader Saddam Hussein (Ehrenreich, 1997). A dysfunctional aspect of war, however, is that the enemy is dehumanized, that is, seen as an object to obliterate rather than as another human being. Also, according to sociologist Tamotsu Shibutani (1970), prolonged conflicts such as wars tend to be turned into a struggle between good and evil; one's own side is, of course, righteous and just, while the other side has no redeeming social or moral value.

In 1994, over 2 million U.S. veterans were receiving compensation from the government for injuries they sustained in war-related activities; about 138,000 of these veterans were totally disabled (U.S. Bureau of the Census, 1996b). But not all injuries sustained in wars are physical. We have no accurate count of the soldiers and civilians—of all nations involved—who experience psychological trauma that affects them the remainder of their lives. Here, for example, is a description by Vietnam War veteran Rod Kane, who was asked by a nurse whether he was having trouble with his concentration (Hynes, 1997: 219–220):

> "Trouble with concentration?" I stare at her defensively. I forgot her name already. "Not neces-

sarily. I concentrate on the war, or drinking . . . but I'm not here because of my concentration problems, or my memory. I will say that if I've had trouble with anything since Nam, it's been sleeping. . . . One reason I drink so much, so I could pass out and not have to worry about nightmares. Of course, after a while, all the booze in the world couldn't keep them down . . . I mean, there are booby-trap nightmares that speak for themselves. Instant replay nightmares where, asleep or awake, I play the same scene over and over again. There are nightmares that combine Viet Nam action with stateside stuff. . . . Do I have to get into all this right away?"

Rod Kane was diagnosed with a disorder known as post-traumatic stress disorder (PTSD). Symptoms include difficulty sleeping and concentrating, anxiety, and recurring flashbacks or nightmares, many of which are triggered by loud, sudden noises such as thunder, automobiles backfiring, or something that sounds like a gunshot blast or an explosion. When some stimulus triggers a flashback, the individual re-experiences the horror of some deeply traumatic wartime event. Some medical specialists link high rates of drug abuse and suicide among Vietnam War veterans with PTSD. According to one congressional study, more than 475,000 of the 3.5 million Vietnam veterans have severe symptoms of PTSD, and another 350,000 have moderate symptoms (Witteman, 1991).

We cannot put a price tag on loss of life, physical disability, or psychological trauma associated with war, but we know that the direct economic costs of war are astronomical. Consider, for example, the cost of forty F-117A stealth fighters that were deployed with laser-guided bombs during the Gulf War—over 4 billion dollars. These fighters, which are capable of penetrating enemy air defenses without being seen by radar or infrared or acoustical sensors, destroyed critical Iraqi air defense command posts and communication centers (Friedman and Friedman, 1996). We have no way of knowing the exact dollar amount of the property damage inflicted on Iraqi buildings, power plants, and communications centers. The cost for the F-117A stealth fighters is only a minuscule part of our nation's approximately 250-billion-dollar annual defense budget. To put defense and war-related expenditures in perspective, one analyst calculated that a single aircraft carrier would build 12,000 high schools and

the cost of developing one new bomber would pay the annual salaries of 250,000 teachers to staff the schools, and this was nearly 20 years ago, in 1980 (de Silva, 1980).

More developing nations are involved in defense buildups than in the past. Map 18.1 (on page 402) shows the nations that purchase military equipment and supplies from this country. In 1993, the nations of the world spent about 689 billion dollars on their military (U.S. Bureau of the Census, 1996b). About 15 percent of the total amount was spent by developing nations. In the United States, even in time of peace, 16 cents of every dollar of taxpayers' money goes to defense, compared to 3 cents for education (Bagby, 1997).

MILITARY TECHNOLOGY AND WAR

War is conducted on the basis of the technology that is available in given societies at a specific point in time. However, wars are not necessarily won or lost on the basis of military technology alone. In the Vietnam War, for example, many factors contributed to the inability of the United States to declare a victory. Among these factors were conflicting ideologies and war strategies set forth by government officials and the fact that U.S. troops could not distinguish the Viet Cong ("the enemy") from the South Vietnamese ("the ally") (Hynes, 1997).

The most significant military technology is referred to as the *weapons system*, **which comprises a weapons platform (e.g., a ship, aircraft, or tank), a weapon (e.g. a gun, missile, or torpedo), and the means of command and communication** (Kaldor, 1981). The importance of the weapons system is pointed out by Friedman and Friedman (1996:25): "The rise and fall of strategically significant weapons systems is the history of the rise and fall of nations and epochs. **The strategically significant weapon is the one that brings force to bear in such a way that it decisively erodes the war-making capability of the enemy**" [bold in original]. According to Friedman and Friedman (1996:25–26), the use of strategically significant weapons determines the "winners" and "losers" in war:

> let us assume that the greatest threat presented by the enemy is the ability to move weapons

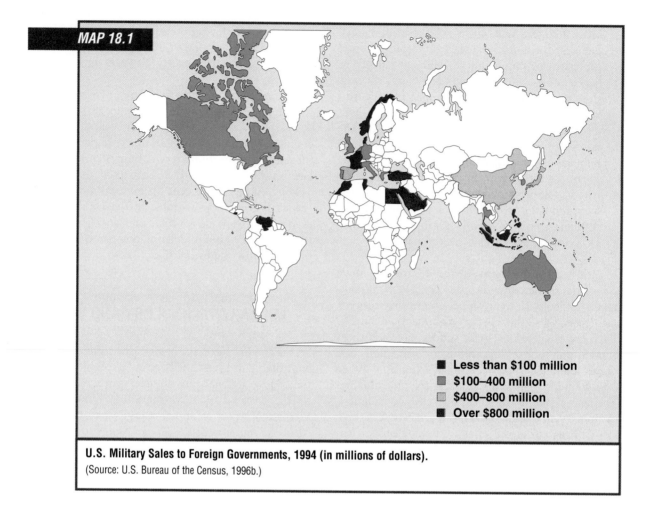

MAP 18.1

- ■ Less than $100 million
- ■ $100–400 million
- ▫ $400–800 million
- ■ Over $800 million

U.S. Military Sales to Foreign Governments, 1994 (in millions of dollars).
(Source: U.S. Bureau of the Census, 1996b.)

platforms around quickly, and that by destroying his petrochemical production facilities we could impede his mobility. Strategically significant weapons would be those that would destroy petrochemical plants. So, in World War II, bombers with the range to reach these targets were such weapons. In Vietnam, the enemy's war-making ability could not be decisively crippled by the same sort of long-range bombers. There, the strategic weapon was North Vietnamese infantry, able to move stealthily and impose a rate of attrition on American troops that was politically unacceptable to the United States. The failure to recognize strategically decisive weapons is catastrophic. The Soviet Union's illusion that intercontinental ballistic missiles and swarms of tanks were strategically decisive led it to disaster.

In other words, though other factors than military technology may determine a nation's ability to win or lose a war, military technology is a dominant factor. For example, in the fourteenth century, Europeans used a simple new technology—black powder, an explosive made from charcoal, sulfur, and saltpeter—to overwhelm larger armies. Black powder could destroy the enemy's walls and other fortifications. Then, when it was discovered that black powder could be exploded at the base of a metal tube and propel a projectile to a target, the gun became the basis of European and Western military power. Gunpowder made it possible for a small number of troops to overwhelm a much larger army that had only nonexplosive weapons (Friedman and Friedman, 1996).

Although black powder weapons remained the primary type of weaponry for many years, the platform that was used for carrying the weapons changed over time. With the development of weapons platforms such as coal-powered ships, petroleum-driven ships, and railroad locomotives, it became possible to move explosive-based technology virtually anywhere to destroy enemy forces. Between the early 1900s and the end of World War II, the battleship, the tank, and the bomber were the primary weapons platforms. Today, the battleship has been replaced by the aircraft carrier, but the tank and the bomber continue to be important sources of weapons transportation (Friedman and Friedman, 1996).

As the U.S. military sought to enhance traditional weapons platforms and deal with enemy threats, new precision-guided munitions were developed, rendering many of the older ideologies and technologies obsolete. For example, the concept of the battlefield has changed. For war to take place, foot soldiers no longer have to engage in skirmishes; missiles can be fired from sites located ten thousand miles away from the target (Friedman and Friedman, 1996). Unfortunately, the same technology that makes possible the expanded battlefield brings with it a new system of intelligence that makes global warfare possible. According to Friedman and Friedman (1996:37–38), sensors, guidance systems, satellite communications, and other technologies that make it possible to hit a target ten thousand miles away also make it possible for weapons fired from one continent to guide themselves to targets on other continents very quickly and relatively inexpensively:

> The hyperintelligent, hypersonic, long-range projectile is almost here. Born of the air age, it will destroy the old way of making war, while securing the new geopolitical system for generations. Where guns were inaccurate, these projectiles are extraordinarily precise. Where guns must travel to within miles of a target before firing, precision munitions can devastate an enemy from any distance. Where gun/petrochemical technology requires total commitment of resources and mass production, precision munitions require technical skill. The new weaponry places inherent limits on war, both in terms of scope and in terms of damage to unintended targets. The age of total war is at an end and a more limited type of war is at hand. . . . [A]s the new weapons culture [has] slowly emerged, the United States has been at war with itself over the na-

ture of its military power and the principles that ought to guide that power. At its core, this has been a struggle to define the proper place of technology—and of technologies—in American military doctrine. More precisely, it has been an agonizing search for a doctrine that could define and control the overwhelming claims that technology makes on all aspects of American life—a search for principles of waging war that transcend mere weaponry.

Although the high-technology weaponry that is used in warfare has received widespread media coverage, less attention has been paid to the potential significance of poison gas manufacturing and the use of chemical and biological toxic agents by international and domestic terrorists (Vetter and Perlstein, 1991).

GLOBAL TERRORISM

Terrorism refers the use of calculated, unlawful physical force or threats of violence against a government, organization, or individual to gain some political, religious, economic, or social objective. Terrorist tactics include bombing, kidnapping, hostage taking, hijacking, assassination, and extortion (Vetter and Perlstein, 1991). Although terrorists sometimes attack government officials and members of the military, they more often target civilians as a way of pressuring the government.

As collective violence, terrorism shares certain commonalities with war. Both terrorism and war are major threats to world stability and domestic safety. Terrorism and war also extract a massive toll on individuals and societies by producing rampant fear, widespread loss of human life, and extensive destruction of property.

One form of terrorism—political terrorism—is actually considered a form of unconventional warfare. *Political terrorism* uses intimidation, coercion, threats of harm, and other violent attempts to bring about a significant change in or overthrow an existing government. There are three types of political terrorism: revolutionary terrorism, repressive terrorism, and state-sponsored terrorism.

Revolutionary terrorism refers to acts of violence against civilians that are carried out by internal ene-

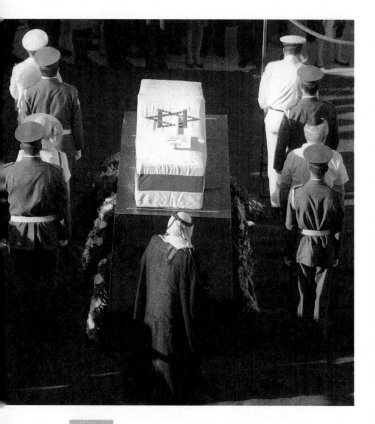

The assassination of Israeli Prime Minister Yitzhak Rabin posed new problems for the peace process in the Middle East. How does the potential for terrorist acts influence the behavior of political leaders on a global basis?

mies of the government who want to bring about political change. Some groups believe that if they perpetrate enough random terrorist acts, they will achieve a political goal. In Lebanon and Jordan, for example, members of revolutionary movements engage in terrorist activities such as car bombings and assassinations of leading officials. On occasion, they also are the victims of such actions. In 1994, for example, a car bomb killed one of the officials of the Party of God, a militant Shiite group battling Israeli troops in southern Lebanon. At the time of the killing, the Party of God was suspected in the kidnappings of U.S. citizens (including a newspaper correspondent) who were living in Lebanon (*New York Times*, 1994a). In Jordan, members of a militant Muslim movement were accused of bombing two theaters that showed adult films and attempting to bomb a supermarket that sold alco-

hol; pornography and alcohol both represent decadent Western values that the Muslim movement adamantly opposes (*New York Times*, 1994c). In 1995, the Aum Shinri Kyo (Japanese for "sublime truth") religious sect allegedly set off a nerve gas attack in a Tokyo subway, killing ten people, making thousands more ill, and raising the specter of a new and even deadlier form of terrorism (WuDunn, 1995b). In some circumstances, revolutionary terrorists receive economic help from other governments that support their objectives (Vetter and Perlstein, 1991).

Unlike revolutionary terrorism, *repressive terrorism* is conducted by a government against its own citizens for the purpose of protecting an existing political order. Repressive terrorism has taken place in many countries around the world, including Haiti, the People's Republic of China, and Cambodia, where the Pol Pot regime killed more than 1 million people in the four years between 1975 and 1979. In 1975, for example, Cambodia's Khmer Rouge, a Communist faction, forced the evacuation of all city dwellers into the countryside, where many died of disease or starvation. Teachers, civil servants, Buddhist monks, and other "enemies of the revolution" were killed in mass executions (Mydans, 1997). According to a recent book, *Children of Cambodia's Killing Fields* by Teeda Butt Mam (1997), everyone was a potential victim: The rebellious, the kind-hearted, the brave, the clever, the individuals, the people who wore glasses, the literate, the popular, the complainers, the lazy, those with talent, those with trouble getting along with others, those with soft hands (Mam, 1997; cited in Mydans, 1997:5). After a Vietnamese invasion in 1979, the Khmer Rouge was driven into the mountains and jungles, where they tried to regain power through guerrilla warfare (Mydans, 1997).

In the third type of political terrorism, *state-sponsored terrorism*, a government provides financial resources, weapons, and training for terrorists who conduct their activities in other nations. In Libya, for example, Colonel Muammar Qaddafi has provided money and training for terrorist groups such as the Arab National Youth Organization, which was responsible for skyjacking a Lufthansa airplane over Turkey and forcing the Bonn government to free the surviving members of Black September. Black September is the terrorist group responsible for killing the Israeli Olympic athletes in the 1970s (Parry, 1976). Other countries that have been charged with using terrorism as a form of surrogate warfare include Iran,

Syria, Yugoslavia, Bulgaria, Israel, and the United States (Vetter and Perlstein, 1991). The United States conducted surrogate warfare when it supported the Contras, who waged war against the Sandinista government of Nicaragua, until the Sandanistas were defeated in a 1990 election (Vetter and Perlstein, 1991).

How widespread is terrorism? In 1995, terrorist attacks killed 311 people worldwide, one of the highest terrorist death tolls recorded (Weiner, 1997). Nearly 200 of the deaths are attributed to the Tamil Tigers, a separatist group in Sri Lanka. In 1996, there were 296 international terrorist incidents; however, most attacks did not kill anyone. Once again, the most deadly attack was carried out by the Tamil Tigers of Sri Lanka, who bombed a section of downtown Colombo (the capital), killing 90 people, and blew up a commuter train, killing 70 people (Weiner, 1997). Today, Iran, Iraq, Libya, North Korea, the Sudan, Syria, and Cuba are on the U.S. State Department's list of nations that are suspected of engaging in state-sponsored terrorism. According to the State Department report, however, no terrorist attack anywhere in the world during 1995 or 1996 equaled the April 1995 explosion in Oklahoma City. In fact, domestic terrorism is a greater problem in most nations—including the United States—than international terrorism is (Weiner, 1997).

Human faces tell an important and often forgotten story about the effects of domestic terrorism on the survivors of horrendous events such as the bombing of the federal building in Oklahoma City.

DOMESTIC TERRORISM IN THE UNITED STATES

Domestic terrorism is sometimes referred to as "home-grown terrorism" by the media because the perpetrator is usually a resident of the country where the incident occurs or has other strong ties to the country, such as relatives or acquaintances who live there. Like international terrorism, domestic terrorism typically is used to reach some political goal.

The worst act of domestic terrorism in the United States took place in 1995 when a bomb destroyed the Alfred P. Murrah Federal Building in Oklahoma City, taking 168 lives and injuring 850 other people. The horror of this act—and its similarities to war—are brought home in this statement from police officer Jerry Flowers: "I saw a body in a blanket. When I opened up the blanket, there was a five-year-old boy. His face was gone" (cited in Collins, 1997:28). A Denver jury found Timothy McVeigh guilty of

bombing the federal building and sentenced him to death on charges ranging from conspiracy to use a weapon of mass destruction to the murder of eight federal law-enforcement agents (Thomas, 1997). Among the survivors of the bomb blast, many lost limbs or their vision or hearing or incurred other physical or psychological scars that will remain with them throughout their lives. One victim, Cliff Cagle, whose face was mangled by the bomb, testified in the McVeigh trial, saying "I lost my job, my honor, and my grandsons have to see me like this!" (cited in Collins, 1997:28). The relatives and friends of those who died in the bomb blast realize that executing McVeigh will not bring back their loved ones (Bragg, 1997), and McVeigh is appealing his sentence, a process that takes years. But for some people, knowing that McVeigh was sentenced to death allows them to cope, and survivors must find a way to cope, as Bud Welch, a father whose daughter Julie-Marie was a Spanish interpreter in the federal building, explains (Welch, 1997:36):

I now go to the fence [surrounding the vacant lot where the Murrah building once stood] about twice a week. . . . This place has a lot of meaning for me, especially the elm tree in the parking lot. We call it the Survivor Tree. Julie always liked to park her little red Grand Am on the east side of that tree, in the shade. Now it's the only living thing left in this place. When I go there, sometimes I lean against the trunk, close my eyes, listen to the leaves and think about the way it used to be. Then I go down to the fence, and strangers will sometimes ask me questions: "Where was the front door of the building?" or "Where was the truck [loaded with explosives] parked?" Then I tell them who I am, and they share their deepest thoughts with me. That's a very positive thing—to touch and see and talk and visit. And to continue to tell the story of who my Julie-Marie was.

The Oklahoma City bombing may be the worst case of domestic terrorism, but it is not the only recent case. In 1993, the World Trade Center in New York City was the target of a bombing allegedly carried out by some followers of Sheik Omar Abdel Rahman. Six people were killed, more than a thousand were injured, and business at the Trade Center was disrupted for an extended period of time. Companies that stored important data on desktop computer systems spent weeks trying to recreate valuable records that were lost in the bombing, since—unlike mainframe computers—desktop computers often are not backed up regularly (Holusha, 1993).

The longest series of terrorists acts in the United States was carried out by the "Unabomber," later identified as Theodore Kaczynski. Between 1978 and 1995, Kaczynski allegedly mailed sixteen bombs that caused three deaths and twenty-two injuries. Primary targets for the self-described anarchist's bombs were business executives and university researchers. Kaczynski also allegedly threatened to blow up an airliner flying out of Los Angeles International Airport but did not follow through (Weiner, 1995). In a letter to the *New York Times,* the Unabomber stated that the terrorist group FC was conducting terrorist actions "to promote social instability in industrial society" (cited in Weiner, 1995:A1). But in a 35,000-word manifesto on the Internet, he gave a different reason, speaking of how difficult it is for some people to fit into society (cited in McFadden, 1996:12):

The moral code of our society is so demanding that no one can think, feel and act in a completely moral way. For example, we are not supposed to hate anyone, yet almost everyone hates somebody at some time or other, whether he admits it to himself or not. In order to avoid feelings of guilt, they continually have to deceive themselves about their own motives and find moral explanations for feelings and actions that in reality have a non-moral origin. We use the term oversocialized to describe such people. Oversocialization can lead to low self-esteem, a sense of powerlessness, defeatism, guilt, etc. If a particular child is especially susceptible to such feelings, he ends by feeling ashamed of HIMSELF. . . .

The oversocialized person is kept on a psychological leash and spends his life running on rails society has laid down for him. In many oversocialized people this results in a sense of constraint and powerlessness that can be a severe hardship. We suggest that oversocialization is among the most serious cruelties that human beings inflict on one another.

Apparently having similar feelings about his own life, Kaczynski moved to the Montana wilderness, where he lived in a one-room wooden cabin until he was arrested. We will probably never know whether he would have been apprehended if his brother hadn't notified authorities of Kaczynski's whereabouts in hopes of preventing more lives from being lost (Johnston and Scott, 1996).

In recent years, great potential for domestic terrorism has arisen in the form of militias opposed to the U.S. government. In 1996, an eighty-one-day standoff between the Montana Freemen and the Federal Bureau of Investigation was resolved peacefully. However, a series of events leading up to that event were very violent. There was, first, the 1992 siege of white separatist Randy Weaver's farmhouse in Ruby Ridge, Idaho; Weaver's wife and son were killed by federal agents during the siege. There was also the 1993 standoff between armed Branch Davidian cult members and U.S. agents near Waco, Texas, and the subsequent fire that killed eighty cult members. Militia members consider both events to be evidence that the U.S. government is determined to take away their freedom. The Brady Bill, which established a mandatory waiting period for handgun purchases, is viewed as another form of government oppression.

Some militias are part of the far-right Patriot movement, which also includes white supremacists, neo-Nazis, and skinheads. The Patriot movement has established "common-law courts" in as many as forty states whereby adherents reject all state and federal laws and all constitutional amendments except the Bill of Rights. They base their authority instead on selected passages of English common law, the Bible, U.S. case law, and the Constitution (Janofsky, 1996a). As a result, groups such as the Militia of Montana have threatened violence against court officials. For example, when municipal judge Martha A. Bethel summoned a Freeman who had not paid three parking tickets, she was "charged" with treason by the group and received numerous threats of kidnapping and death. According to Bethel (1995, A13), "This has been a living nightmare. As judges, we all expect to deal with disgruntled people who refuse to take responsibility for their actions. But who in their right mind would choose to serve their community when the community becomes defenseless in the face of such terrorism." As isolated as such threats may appear, experts believe that this kind of antigovernment militia ideology is what provoked the Oklahoma City bombing. If they are right, Timothy McVeigh and others like him may become martyrs for militia members, some of whom already believe that the government carried out the Oklahoma City bombing so that it could justify a crackdown on freedom in this country (*New York Times*, 1997e).

How can we stop domestic terrorism? According to some social analysts, acts of domestic terrorism will continue in this country as long as such behavior remains unchecked. However, they are not optimistic that Congress will tighten U.S. policies on terrorism. Some members of Congress lack expertise on terrorism; others are sympathetic to some militias or organizations such as the National Rifle Association, which holds views on gun control and individual liberty similar to those of the militias (Dreyfuss, 1996; *New York Times*, 1997e). Moreover, shortwave radio broadcasts and the Internet provide militia members with a communication network whereby offensive action can be called for against the government (Noble, 1995). Although some members of militias shun media coverage of their activities, others—along with many domestic and international terrorists—realize the importance of the media to their goals (see Box 18.2 on pages 408–409).

EXPLANATIONS OF WAR AND TERRORISM

What causes collective violence such as war and terrorism? Can war and acts of terrorism be reduced? Despite centuries of war and terrorism, we still know little about the origins of violence or how to reduce such acts (Turpin and Kurtz, 1997). In Chapter 10, we discussed biological, psychological, and sociological explanations for violence. We will now examine these approaches as they relate to war and terrorism.

Biological Perspectives

Analysts who use a biological framework for explaining war and terrorism emphasize that people inherit a tendency (or predisposition) toward aggressive behavior, which may culminate in warfare or terrorist acts. Contemporary policy makers who trace violent behavior to chemical or physical abnormalities such as a brain lesion, brain dysfunction, endocrine disorder, hormonal imbalance, or other genetic factors are taking such an approach (Turpin and Kurtz, 1997).

Perhaps the most widely known advocate for biological explanations of war and terrorism is anthropologist Konrad Lorenz (1966:261), who stated, "To the humble seeker of biological truth there cannot be the slightest doubt that human militant enthusiasm evolved out of a communal defense response of our prehuman ancestors." According to Lorenz, just as our hominid ancestors confronted and repelled predatory animals, we have an almost instinctive desire to protect ourselves from our perceived enemies. Therefore people engage in terrorism or fight wars when stimuli trigger their predisposition toward aggression. Lorenz believes that although the predisposition toward violence was functional at one time because it ensured that the most "fit" would survive, this instinct is a problem in contemporary societies. Similarly, philosopher William James suggested that the kind of courage and altruism people bring to war could better be directed toward some more worthy enterprise (cited in Ehrenreich, 1997).

SOCIAL PROBLEMS

IN THE MEDIA

BOX 18.2

Media and Terrorism:
Partners in Crime?

We have said a hundred times or more that when modern revolutionaries carry out actions, what is important is not solely these actions themselves but also the propagandistic effect they are able to achieve. Hence we preach not only action in and for itself, but also action as propaganda.

— John Most, American anarchist, in
1880 (Laqueur, 1978:105, quoted in
Vetter and Perlstein, 1991)

Even though news traveled slowly in 1880, John Most understood the importance of publicizing terrorist acts. Today, terrorists are equally aware of the importance of the media to accomplishing their goals, especially since coverage is often live by satellite. At the same time, terrorism is news, and the public wants information. The media, then, play a

pivotal role. How do they do? Do they provide objective, complete, noninflammatory coverage of terrorist events? Or are they "crossing the line from portrayal into advocacy," as some analysts charge (Vetter and Perlstein, 1991)? In other words, do terrorists manipulate the media?

As a case study, consider what happened when TWA Flight 847 was hijacked in Beirut in June 1985 by militant Muslim Shiite terrorists. In exchange for releasing the TWA hostages, including 39 Americans, the Shiites demanded (1) the release of 700 Lebanese being detained in Israel, (2) the release of 17 Shiite prisoners in Kuwait and 2 prisoners in Spain, (3) the overthrow of King Hussein of Jordan and President Hosni Mubarak of Egypt, and (4) U.S. support for Arab states in the Middle East and an end to all support for Israel. But the media reported only one of the conditions—the release of the 700 Lebanese—

Some scholars have sought to identify genetic influences on violence and warfare. Among the earliest was sociobiologist Edward O. Wilson (1975), who believed that aggressive tendencies are part of human nature but that people can learn not to engage in violent behavior. More recently, anthropologists Richard Wrangham and Dale Peterson, who study aggression in animals and humans, published their findings in *Demonic Males: Apes and the Origins of Human Violence* (1996). According to Wrangham and Peterson, both human and nonhuman animals, such as chimpanzees, have the inherent capacity to commit premeditated assaults. Premeditated violence is used by humans (especially males) and lower animals to intimidate enemies, beat them up, and destroy their abil-

ity to bring future challenges. Female chimps and humans, however, are less apt to murder or take part in war. Women were deliberately excluded from participating in war-related activities in fifty-eight of the sixty-seven human societies that Wrangham and Peterson studied (Wheeler, 1997). But this brings up another question: Do women not participate in war by choice, or are they categorically excluded by social norms and customs? More research is needed to answer this and other questions about the biological origins of warfare and terrorism. Thus far, no scientific evidence conclusively demonstrates than humans are innately violent or that biological factors are more important than social factors in producing violent behavior (Turpin and Kurtz, 1997).

so eventually, the terrorists limited their demands to that one (Vetter and Perlstein, 1991).

At this point it may appear that the media manipulated the terrorists, but the Shiites' reduced demands were, at best, an incidental outcome or, more probably, an opportunistic move. At first coverage was incomplete, but then, with only one demand to focus on, the media could dramatize the event. Barbara Rosen (1985, quoted in Vetter and Perlstein, 1991:92), wife of one of the TWA hostages, put it this way: "Television journalists see 'stories' as dramas. Being employees of a medium whose prime time products are soap operas, sitcoms and cop shows, reporters focus on the feelings of the hostages and their families. To the medium, it's all emotion, which must be restructured as entertainment."

The particular drama that television reporters fashioned made the terrorists the "good guys" and the Israelis the "bad guys"—exactly the picture the terrorists wanted portrayed. Shortly before, the media reported, Israel had freed 1,150 convicted murderers for the return of 3 Israeli soldiers, but now it would not free innocent Lebanese to save the lives of 39 U.S. tourists. Furthermore, the media set up a moral symmetry between the terrorists trying to free their Lebanese relatives being held hostage in Israel (who were all men, incidentally, of military age) and the families of the U.S. hostages (Vetter and Perlstein, 1991). That is, the media suggested that the Shiites, like Americans, just wanted their families safe and together at home again. If the Israelis would just release the Lebanese, the Americans could, in turn, be released. In fact, though, "The comparison between the Israeli prisoners and the hostages in Beirut was wrong—factually, as well as morally. Presenting Lebanese families in juxtaposition to American families only served to cloud and confuse the primary issue—the hijacking, murder and terrorism of American citizens" (Rosen, 1985, quoted in Vetter and Perlstein, 1991:92).

Were the media manipulated by the terrorists? Did the media act unethically at any point? Does media coverage of terrorist acts lead to more terrorism? Should media coverage of terrorist acts be regulated or censored? What do you think?

Psychological Perspectives

Psychologists have provided significant insights into violence, but they do not focus on collective violence such as war and terrorism. In fact, most psychological explanations emphasize individualistic sources of violence, resulting from such causes as abnormal psychological development. For example, Sigmund Freud contended that violent behavior occurs when the three aspects of the human personality come into conflict with one another. If the individual's id (unconscious drives and instincts) conflicts with the superego (internalized social values), and the ego (the mediator between the id and superego) is unable to resolve the conflict, violent behavior may ensue, particularly if the individual has an overdeveloped id, which contains the aggressive drive, or an underdeveloped superego (Turpin and Kurtz, 1997).

Contemporary social psychologists generally believe that both individual and cultural factors must be considered in explaining why people go to war or engage in terrorism. Some focus primarily on the processes by which cultural influences make some individuals, but not others, behave violently. From these studies, they conclude that it is easier to harm enemies when they have been depersonalized (Milgram, 1974). People also are more likely to behave violently when they are placed in positions in which they have a great deal of power and authority over others (Haney, Banks, and Zimbardo, 1984).

Do human beings have biological predispositions toward aggressive behavior? How do analysts using a biological perspective differ in their answers to this question as compared to those using a sociological perspective?

An interesting insight into the psychological processes that are involved in violence comes from the work of Robert Jay Lifton (1997), who studied violence inflicted by Nazi doctors at Auschwitz. According to Lifton, these doctors—who had previously been committed to saving lives—were able to commit horrible atrocities because of the psychological principle of *doubling*—"the division of the self into two functioning wholes, so that a part-self acts as an entire self" (Lifton, 1997:30). Through the process of doubling, the doctors could embrace evil without restraint and, at the same time, not feel remorse or guilt and be loving parents and normal members of society. According to Lifton (1997), not only can doubling save the life of a soldier in combat who is confronted with the enemy, but it also can contribute to extreme wartime brutalities and the embracing of evil without restraint.

If social psychologists are correct in believing that individual personality factors contribute to war and terrorism, then how can such behavior be reduced? The answer is to emphasize social and cultur-

al factors that head off violence and deadly conflict. In other words, societies should deemphasize violence and encourage peaceful behavior in daily life. However, social critic Barbara Ehrenreich (1977:76) believes that our impulse to make war resides in deep ancestral memory of our role as prey and that we live in a society that still glorifies such impulses:

> Why . . . would human beings want to reenact . . . the terror of predation? Probably for the same reason that "civilized" people today pay to see movies in which their fellow humans are stalked and devoured by flesh-eating ghouls, vampires, and extraterrestrial monsters. Nothing gets our attention like the prospect of being ripped apart, sucked dry, and transformed into another creature's meal.

Although she concedes that people enjoy such fictional encounters because they are "fun," Ehrenreich also thinks that today's films and television programming pose interesting questions about why many people enjoy watching acts of violence and terrorism.

Ehrenreich's analysis brings up a larger question: Why are many people relatively positive about war, and why do they seemingly condone the violence associated with war? According to sociologists Jennifer Turpin and Lester R. Kurtz (1997:1), many people are deeply ambivalent about war because they believe that the only way to fight violence is with more violence:

> Since most people believe they can be secure only by repelling violence with violence, they simultaneously deplore and condone it. The use of violence is considered taboo almost universally in modern society except under certain conditions. It is widely abhorred yet widely used to promote social control in settings ranging from the household to the global socioeconomic order. Because of that ambivalence, elaborate social mechanisms have been institutionalized to distinguish between legitimate and illegitimate violence. Not only are individuals threatened by violence, but so are whole societies, and now—in the nuclear age—the species itself. Ironically, the very structures supposedly created to provide security against violence instead threaten everyone.

▲ Sociological Explanations

Sociological explanations use a functionalist, conflict, or interactionist perspective. We'll look at all three, starting with the functionalist.

THE FUNCTIONALIST PERSPECTIVE

Some functionalist explanations focus on the relationship between social disorganization and warfare or terrorism. The rise of militias in this country is an example of how disorganization in social institutions such as the government contributes to overall political instability. Militia members believe that the U.S. government no longer serves the purpose for which it was intended, namely, to protect the individual's rights and freedom. In other words, in their eyes, the U.S. government has become dysfunctional, and they engage in acts of terrorism to undermine the government so that it will radically change or be abolished.

Other functionalists focus on the functions that war serves. War can settle disputes between nations. However, in the age of nuclear weaponry, many nations now seek other means to deal with their disagreements. For example, the United States has increasingly used *economic sanctions,* cutting off all trade—rather than war or military action—to promote its goals and punish nations. The United States has imposed economic sanctions against countries engaging in terrorism, environmental violations, abuse of workers' rights, regional strife, drug trafficking, human and political rights abuses, and nuclear proliferation (Myers, 1997). However, some political analysts argue that we are cutting off our nose to spite our face when we impose economic sanctions against other governments: Economic sanctions are dysfunctional for another of our social institutions—the economy. Also, even though this country has used sanctions against other nations from its earliest days, corporations are concerned that the sanctions deny them access to the world's markets and the profits in those markets (Myers, 1997).

Some functionalists believe that we will always have wars because of other important functions that they serve in societies. First, war demonstrates that one nation or group has power over another. Historically, conquering forces acquire the "spoils of war," including more territory and material possessions. Second, war functions as a means of punishment in much the same manner that the U.S. government uses sanctions against other nations to force them to comply with our viewpoint on certain issues. Third, war is a way to disseminate ideologies, usually political or religious. For example, the United States has fought its largest wars in defense of a democratic form of government, under the slogan "making the world safe for democracy" (Crossette, 1997). According to sociologist Seymour Martin Lipset, "We are a revolutionary country with a revolutionary tradition. We want everyone to be democrats" (cited in Crossette, 1997:E3). But not even other democracies are automatically friends of the United States. Larry Diamond, a scholar who has examined new democracies in other nations, explains (cited in Crossette, 1997:E3):

> Political freedom has deteriorated in several of the longest-surviving democracies of the developing world, including India, Sri Lanka, Colombia, and Venezuela. . . . It isn't enough to have elections. . . . Democracy is not something that is simply present or absent. It's not like a light switch that you flip on or off. It emerges in different fragments in different sequences in different countries and in different historical periods.

Finally, many functionalists point out the economic function of war. War benefits society because it stimulates the economy through increased war-related production and provides jobs for civilians who otherwise might not be able to find employment. In 1994, for example, the United States sold more than 10.3 billion dollars in military equipment and supplies to other countries (see Map 18.1 on page 402). Conflict analysts also see an economic side to war, but they are not so optimistic.

THE CONFLICT AND INTERACTIONIST PERSPECTIVES

Conflict theorists view war from the standpoint of how militarism and aggressive preparedness for war contribute to the economic well-being of some, but not all, people in a society. According to sociologist Cynthia Enloe (1987:527), people who consider capitalism the moving force behind the military's influence "believe that government officials enhance the status, resources, and authority of the military in order to protect the interests of private enterprises at home and overseas." In other words, the origins of war can be traced to corporate boardrooms, not the U.S. government's war room. In addition, workers come to rely on military spending for jobs. Labor unions, for example, support defense spending because it provides well-paid, stable employment for union members.

A second conflict explanation focuses on the role of the nation and its inclination toward coercion in response to perceived threats. From this perspective, nations inevitably use force to ensure compliance within their society and to protect themselves from outside attacks.

A third conflict explanation is based on patriarchy and the relationship between militarism and masculinity. Across cultures and over time, the military has been a male institution, and the "meanings attached to masculinity appear to be so firmly linked to compliance with military roles that it is often impossible to disentangle the two" (Enloe, 1987:531).

Interactionists would call this last perspective the *social construction of masculinity*. That is, certain assumptions, teachings, and expectations that serve as the standard for appropriate male behavior—in this case, values of dominance, power, aggression, and violence—are created and recreated. Presumably, such values are learned through gender socialization, particularly in military training. Historically, the development of manhood and male superiority has been linked to militarism and combat—the ultimate test of a man's masculinity (Enloe, 1987; Cock, 1994).

WAR AND TERRORISM IN THE TWENTY-FIRST CENTURY

What will happen in the twenty-first century? How will nations deal with the proliferation of arms and nuclear weapons? Will some of the missiles and warheads fall into the hands of terrorists? What should be done with the masses of nuclear waste being produced? No easy answers are forthcoming, as Ehrenreich explains (1997:239):

> War . . . is a more formidable adversary than it has ever been. . . . war has dug itself into economic systems, where it offers a livelihood to millions. . . . It has lodged in our souls as a kind of religion, a quick tonic for political malaise

and a bracing antidote to the moral torpor of consumerist, market-driven cultures. In addition, our incestuous fixation on combat with our own kind has left us ill-prepared to face many of the larger perils of the situation in which we find ourselves: the possibility of drastic climatic changes, the depletion of natural resources, the relentless predations of the microbial world. The wealth that flows ceaselessly to the project of war is wealth lost, for the most part, to the battle against these threats.

But Ehrenreich, like most other social analysts, is not totally pessimistic about the future. She believes that human resistance to war could still provide a means to spare this nation and the world from future calamities. According to Ehrenreich, the antiwar movements of the late twentieth century show that "the passions we bring to war can be brought just as well to the struggle *against* war." But people must be willing to educate, inspire, and rally others to the cause. Like other forms of warfare, the people fighting for peace must be willing to continue the struggle even when the odds seem hopeless. Ehrenreich's point is supported by sociologists James William Gibson and Francesca M. Cancian (1990:9), who believe that making peace can be more difficult than making war:

> making peace requires democratic relationships: soldiers who refuse to fight in a war they do not support; citizens who claim the right to participate in making decisions instead of accepting rule by elites who make decisions in secret; newspaper reporters, magazine editors, movie makers, and others in the mass media who question the necessity of casting another nation as an "enemy" and instead look for ways to communicate with other human beings who are potentially our friends.

Why does this book end with a discussion of war and terrorism? They are the ultimate category of social problems. When class, race, ethnicity, or any of the other dominant/subordinate categories discussed in this book escalate to a level of "doing something about it" regardless of the consequences, terrorism or war may be the result. Redressing inequality is an admirable goal, but perhaps the goal should be the one stated by Tim O'Brien, who wrote about his tour of duty in Vietnam (quoted in Hynes, 1997:283–284): "I would wish this book could take the form of a plea for everlasting peace, a plea from one who knows, from one who's been there and come back, an old soldier looking back at a dying war. . . . That would be good. It would be fine to integrate it all to persuade my younger brother and perhaps some others to say "No" to wars and other battles.

The international society—the community of all of the nations of the world—must work to alleviate inequalities and create a better—peaceful—world for future generations. What role will you and I play in the twenty-first century? Will we be part of the problem or part of the solution? The answer is up to us.

SUMMARY

➡️ *How do social scientists define war?*

Social scientists define war more broadly than the average person. The term *war* means not only armed conflict between two countries, but also undeclared wars, civil and guerrilla wars, covert operations, and some forms of terrorism. War is a form of collective violence that involves organized violence by people seeking to promote their cause or resist social policies or practices that they consider oppressive.

➡️ *What are the consequences of war?*

The major direct effect of war is loss of human life. In World War I and before, it was mostly military personnel who lost their lives, but in World War II and thereafter, war was waged against civilians. If a nuclear war took place, the devastation would be beyond description. Wars temporarily create a strong sense of patriotism. War survivors are left with serious physical and psychological effects, including post-traumatic stress syndrome. Finally, the economic costs of war and war preparedness are astronomical.

➡️ *How important is military technology to winning a war?*

Military technology is a dominant factor, as military history shows. In the fourteenth century, smaller European and Western armies defeated bigger armies by using the newly discovered black powder. Today, precision-guided munitions render old technologies obsolete and global warfare possible. But wars can be won on the basis of factors other than military technology, too, as the U.S. experience in Vietnam shows.

➡️ *What is terrorism?*

Terrorism is the use of calculated unlawful physical force or threats of violence against a government, organization, or individual to gain some political, religious, economic, or social objective. Its tactics include bombing, kidnapping, hostage taking, hijacking, assassination, and extortion.

➡️ *What are the three types of political terrorism?*

Revolutionary terrorism involves acts of violence against civilians that are carried out by internal enemies of the government who want to bring about political change. Repressive terrorism is conducted by a government against its own citizens for the purpose of protecting an existing political order. In state-sponsored terrorism, a government provides financial resources, weapons, and training for terrorists who conduct their activities in other nations.

➡️ *How extensive is domestic terrorism in the United States and what can be done about it?*

The Oklahoma City bombing in 1995 was the worst act of domestic terrorism in our country's history but hardly the only recent example (there were also the World Trade Center bombing and the Unabomber's terrorist activities). The major current threat of domestic terrorism comes from militia members and the far-right Patriot movement, which reject the U.S. government. According to experts, one of the major obstacles to stopping domestic terrorism is that some members of Congress are sympathetic to some militias and organizations such as the National Rifle Association, which hold views on gun control similar to those of militias.

➡ *What are the biological perspectives on war and terrorism?*

Some biological proponents say that humans, especially males, are innately violent, but there is no conclusive scientific evidence to support this view or the view that biological factors are more important than social factors.

➡ *What are the psychological perspectives on war and terrorism?*

Most strictly psychological perspectives focus on individualistic sources of violence, but social psychologists take both individual and cultural factors into account. Their research findings show that it is easier to harm enemies when they are depersonalized and that people are more likely to act violently when they are in positions of power. Some individuals can commit horrible atrocities without feeling guilt through the process of doubling. Social psychologists say that, to reduce war and terrorism, society must emphasize peace, not glorify violent impulses.

➡ *What is the functionalist perspective on war and terrorism?*

Some functionalists focus on the relationship between social disorganization and warfare or terrorism, and they cite the growth of militias as an example. Other functionalists say that war serves certain functions. War settles disputes; war demonstrates that one nation or group has power over another; war can punish; war is one way to disseminate religious and political ideologies; and, finally, war stimulates the economy.

➡ *What are the conflict and interactionist perspectives on war and terrorism?*

Some conflict theorists say that militarism and preparedness for war contribute to the economic well-being of some—not all—people. Another conflict perspective says that nations inevitably use force to ensure compliance within their society and to protect themselves from outside attacks. A third conflict perspective is based in patriarchy: Across cultures and over time, the military is a male institution; it is almost impossible to untangle masculinity from militarism. Interactionists call this last perspective the *social construction of masculinity*—the connection between manhood and militarism is historically created and recreated through gender socialization.

KEY TERMS

collective violence, p. 397
repressive terrorism, p. 404
revolutionary terrorism, pp. 403–404
state-sponsored terrorism, p. 404

terrorism, p. 403
war system, p. 396
weapons system, p. 401

QUESTIONS FOR CRITICAL THINKING

1. In World War II and every war since, more civilians than military personnel have died. Given the military technology available, how can we safeguard civilians?
2. How do you perceive the problem of domestic terrorism in the United States? Do you think militias pose a growing threat? What solutions can you suggest?
3. Consider the question posed in the last paragraph of this chapter and this book: What can you yourself do to make the world a better—peaceful—place in the twenty-first century?

Glossary

absolute poverty a condition that exists when people do not have the means to secure the most basic necessities of life.

acid rain rainfall containing large concentrations of sulfuric and nitric acids (primarily from the burning of fuel and car and truck exhausts).

acquaintance rape forcible sexual activity that meets the legal definition of rape and involves people who first meet in a social setting.

acute diseases illnesses that strike suddenly and cause dramatic incapacitation and death.

ageism prejudice and discrimination against people on the basis of age.

alienation occurs when workers' needs for identity and meaning are not met and when work is done strictly for material gain, not for a sense of personal satisfaction.

amalgamation (the melting pot model) a process whereby the cultural attributes of diverse racial-ethnic groups are blended together to form a new society incorporating the unique contributions of each group.

Anglo-conformity model a pattern of assimilation whereby members of subordinate racial-ethnic groups are expected to conform to the culture of the dominant (white) Anglo-Saxon population.

anti-Semitism prejudice and discriminatory behavior directed toward Jews.

assimilation the process by which members of subordinate racial and ethnic groups become absorbed into the dominant culture.

blaming the victim a practice engaged in by people who view a social problem as emanating from within the individual who suffers from the problem.

blended family a family that consists of a husband and wife, children from previous marriages, and children (if any) from the new marriage.

capital flight investing U.S. money and other resources in facilities located in other nations where indigenous workers do the work previously done by U.S. workers.

capitalism an economic system characterized by private ownership of the means of production so that personal profits are derived through market competition and without government intervention.

chronic diseases illnesses that are long term or lifelong and that develop gradually or are present from birth.

class consciousness a feeling of unity workers have based on an awareness of their shared exploitation by members of the capitalist class.

class system a system of social inequality based on the ownership and control of resources and on the type of work people do.

codependency a reciprocal relationship between the alcoholic and one or more nonalcoholics who unwittingly aid and abet the alcoholic's excessive drinking and resulting behavior.

cohabitation two unmarried adults living together in a sexual relationship without being legally married.

collective violence organized violence by people seeking to promote their cause or resist social policies or practices that they consider oppressive.

comparable worth the belief that wages ought to reflect the worth of a job, not the gender or race of the worker.

conflict perspective a framework for viewing society that is based on the assumption that groups in society are engaged in a continuous power struggle for control of scarce resources.

conglomerates combinations of businesses in different commercial areas, all of which are owned by one holding company.

contingent work part-time work, temporary work, and subcontracted work that offers advantages to employers but can be detrimental to workers' welfare.

core nations dominant capitalist centers characterized by high levels of industrialization and urbanization.

corporate crime illegal acts committed by corporate employees on behalf of the corporation and with its support.

corporations large-scale organizations that have the legal power (separate from individual owners or shareholders) to enter into contracts, buy and sell property, and engage in other business activity.

crime a behavior that violates criminal law and is punishable by a fine, a jail term, or other negative sanctions.

criminal justice system the network of organizations involved in law enforcement and the administration of justice.

cultural capital social assets such as values, beliefs, attitudes, and competencies in language and culture that are learned at home and required for success and social advancement.

cultural lag a situation in which changes in ideas, values, and moral and legal institutions trail behind changes in material technology.

deindustrialization the process by which capital is diverted from investment in basic industries (in the form of economic resources, plants, and equipment) to business practices such as mergers and acquisitions and foreign investment.

deinstitutionalization the practice of discharging patients from mental hospitals into the community.

democracy a political system in which the people hold the ruling power either directly or through elected representatives.

demographic transition theory the process by which some societies move from high birth and death rates to relatively low birth and death rates as a result of technological development.

demography the area of sociology that studies the size, composition, and distribution of populations, among other things.

dependency ratio the number of workers necessary to support people under age fifteen and over age sixty-three.

desertification the process through which once usable land is turned into desert because of overgrazing, harmful agricultural practices, or deforestation.

developed nations countries with highly industrialized economies; technologically advanced industrial, administrative, and service occupations; and relatively high levels of national and per capita (per person) income.

developing nations countries undergoing transformation from agrarian to industrial economies.

deviance a behavior, belief, or condition that violates social norms.

differential association theory the belief that individuals have a greater tendency to deviate from societal norms when they frequently associate with people who tend toward deviance rather than conformity.

disability a restricted ability or total lack of ability to perform certain activities as a result of physical limitations or the interplay of these limitations, social responses, and the social environment.

discrimination actions or practices of dominant group members (or their representatives) that have a harmful impact on members of subordinate groups.

domestic partnerships household partnerships in which an unmarried couple lives together in a committed, sexually intimate relationship and is granted the same rights and benefits accorded to heterosexual couples.

drug any substance—other than food or water—that, when taken into the body, alters its functioning in some way.

drug addiction (or drug dependency) a psychological and/or physiological need for a drug to maintain a sense of well-being and avoid withdrawal symptoms.

drug subculture a group of people whose attitudes, beliefs, and behaviors pertaining to drug use differ significantly from those of most people in the larger society.

dual-earner marriages marriages in which both spouses are in the labor force.

economy the social institution that is responsible for producing and distributing goods and services.

edge city an area of middle- to upper-middle-class residences with complete working, shopping, and leisure activities that make the area independent of the central city or other suburbs.

education the social institution that is responsible for transmitting knowledge, skills, and cultural values in a formally organized structure.

elite model a view of society in which power in political systems is concentrated in the hands of a small group, while the masses are relatively powerless.

environmental degradation disruptions to the environment that have negative consequences for ecosystems.

environmental racism the practice of placing a disproportionate number of hazardous facilities in areas populated primarily by poor people and people of color.

environmental tobacco smoke   the smoke in the air that nonsmokers inhale as a result of other people's tobacco smoking.

erotica   materials that depict consensual sexual activities that are sought by and pleasurable to all parties involved.

ethnic group   a category of people who are distinguished, by others or by themselves, as inferior or superior, primarily on the basis of cultural or nationality characteristics.

ethnic pluralism   a situation in which diverse racial-ethnic groups coexist in society but have separate identities and cultures.

ethnocentrism   the assumption that one's own group and way of life are superior to all others.

experiments   carefully designed situations in which the researcher studies the impact of certain factors on subjects' attitudes or behavior.

extended family   a family unit composed of relatives in addition to parents and children who live in the same household.

families   relationships in which people live together with commitment, form an economic unit and care for any young, and consider their identity to be significantly attached to the group.

family of orientation   the family into which a person is born and in which early socialization takes place.

family of procreation   the family that a person forms by having or adopting children.

felony   a serious crime, such as murder, rape, or aggravated assault, that is punishable by more than a year's imprisonment or even death.

feminization of poverty   the trend whereby women are disproportionately represented among individuals living in poverty.

fertility rate   the ratio between births and individuals in a population.

fetal alcohol syndrome (FAS)   a condition characterized by mental retardation and craniofacial malformations in the child of an alcoholic mother.

field research   the study of social life in its natural setting—observing and interviewing people where they live, work, and play.

forcible rape   the act of forcing sexual intercourse on an adult of legal age against her or his will.

functionalist perspective   a framework for viewing society that views society as a stable, orderly system composed of a number of interrelated parts, each of which performs a function that contributes to the overall stability of society.

functionally illiterate   being unable to read and/or write at the skill level necessary for carrying out everyday tasks.

gender   culturally and socially constructed differences between females and males that are based on meanings, beliefs, and practices that a group or society associates with "femininity" or "masculinity."

gender bias   a situation in which favoritism is shown toward one gender.

gender gap   the difference between a candidate's number of votes from women and men.

gendered division of labor   the process whereby productive tasks are separated on the basis of gender.

gendered racism   the interactive effect of racism and sexism in exploiting women of color.

genocide   the deliberate, systematic killing of an entire people or nation.

gentrification   the process by which people renovate or restore properties in central cities.

glass ceiling   an invisible institutional barrier constructed by male management that prevents women from reaching top positions in major corporations and other large-scale organizations.

government   a formal organization that has the legal and political authority to regulate relationships among people in a society and between the society and others outside its borders.

greenhouse effect   an environmental condition caused by excessive quantities of carbon dioxide, water vapor, methane, and nitrous oxide in the atmosphere.

hate crimes   attacks against people because of their race, religion, skin color, disability, sexual orientation, national origin, or ancestry.

health maintenance organization (HMO)   an organization that provides, for a fixed monthly fee, total health care with an emphasis on prevention to avoid costly treatment later.

hidden curriculum   the way certain cultural values and attitudes, such as conformity and obedience to authority, are transmitted through implied demands in the everyday rules and routines of schools.

homophobia   excessive fear or intolerance of homosexuality.

hospices   organizations that provide a homelike facility or home-based care (or both) for persons who are terminally ill.

illegitimate opportunity structures   circumstances that allow people to acquire through illegitimate activities what they cannot achieve legitimately.

income the economic gain derived from wages, salaries, income transfers (governmental aid such as Aid to Families with Dependent Children), or ownership of property.

individual discrimination one-on-one acts by members of the dominant group that harm members of the subordinate group or their property.

industrialization the process by which societies are transformed from a dependence on agriculture and handmade products to an emphasis on manufacturing and related industries.

infant mortality rate the number of deaths of infants under one year of age per 1,000 live births in a given year.

institutional discrimination the day-to-day practices of organizations and institutions that have a harmful impact on members of subordinate groups.

interactionist perspective a framework that views society as the sum of the interactions of individuals and groups.

internal colonialism a process that occurs when members of a racial-ethnic group are conquered or colonized and forcibly placed under the economic and political control of the dominant group.

job deskilling the process by which technological innovations reduce the proficiency needed to perform a specific job, leading to correspondingly lower wages for that job.

juvenile delinquency a violation of law or the commission of a status offense by a young person under a specific age.

kinship a social network of people based on common ancestry, marriage, or adoption.

labeling theory the proposition that delinquents and criminals are those people who have been successfully labeled as such by others.

latent functions hidden, unstated, and sometimes unintended consequences of activities in an organization or institution.

life chances the extent to which individuals have access to important societal resources such as food, clothing, shelter, education, and health care.

life expectancy an estimate of the average lifetime of people born in a specific year.

lifestyle–routine activity approach the belief that the patterns and timing of people's daily movements and activities as they go about obtaining the necessities of life—such as food, shelter, companionship, and entertainment—are the keys to understanding violent personal crimes and other types of crime in our society.

macrolevel analysis focuses on social processes occurring at the societal level, especially in large-scale organizations and major social institutions such as politics, government, and the economy.

majority (or dominant) group the group that is advantaged and has superior resources and rights in a society.

managed care any system of cost containment that closely monitors and controls health care providers' decisions about medical procedures, diagnostic tests, and other services that should be provided to patients.

manifest functions open, stated, and intended goals or consequences of activities within an organization or institution.

mass murder the killing of four or more people at one time and in one place by the same person.

master status the most significant status a person possesses because it largely determines how individuals view themselves and how they are treated by others.

mechanical solidarity social bonds based on shared religious beliefs and a simple division of labor.

medical-industrial complex a term that encompasses local physicians and hospitals as well as global health-related industries such as pharmaceutical and medical supply companies that deliver health care today.

megalopolis a continuous concentration of two or more cities and their suburbs that have grown until they form an interconnected urban area.

melting pot see **amalgamation.**

microlevel analysis focuses on small group relations and social interaction among individuals.

migration the movement of people from one geographic area to another for the purpose of changing residency.

military-industrial complex the interdependence of the military establishment and private military contractors.

minority (or subordinate) group a group whose members, because of physical or cultural characteristics, are disadvantaged and subjected to unequal treatment by the dominant group and regard themselves as objects of collective discrimination.

misdemeanor a relatively minor crime that is punishable by a fine or less than a year in jail.

mixed economy an economic system that combines elements of both capitalism (a market economy) and socialism (a command economy).

monogamy a marriage between one woman and one man.

monopoly a situation that exists when a single firm controls an industry and accounts for all sales in a specific market.

mortality the number of deaths that occur in a specific population.

murder the unlawful, intentional killing of one person by another.

norms established rules of behavior or standards of conduct.

nuclear family a family unit composed of one or two parents and their dependent children who live apart from other relatives.

obscenity the legal term for pornographic materials that are offensive by generally accepted standards of decency.

occupational (white-collar) crime illegal activities committed by people in the course of their employment or normal business activity.

oligopoly a situation that exists when overwhelming control of an entire industry or service is held by a small number of companies or suppliers.

organic solidarity social bonds based on interdependence and an elaborate division of labor.

organized crime a business operation that supplies illegal goods and services for profit.

patriarchy a hierarchical system of social organization in which cultural, political, and economic structures are controlled by men.

peripheral nations nations that depend on core nations for capital, have little or no industrialization (other than what may be brought in by core nations), and have uneven patterns of urbanization.

permanent government the top-tier civil service bureaucrats who have a strong power base and play a major role in developing and implementing government policies and procedures.

perspective an overall approach or viewpoint toward some subject.

pink-collar occupations the relatively low-paying, non-manual, semiskilled positions that are held primarily by women.

plea bargaining a process in a criminal case whereby the prosecution negotiates a reduced sentence in exchange for a guilty plea.

pluralist model the view that power is widely dispersed throughout many competing interest groups in a political system.

political action committees (PACs) special-interest groups that fund campaigns to help elect (or defeat) candidates on the basis of their positions on specific issues.

politics the social institution through which power is acquired and exercised by some people and groups.

population composition the biological and social characteristics of a population, including such attributes as age, sex, race, marital status, education, occupation, income, and size of household.

pornography the graphic depiction of sexual behavior though pictures and/or words—including by electronic or other data retrieval systems—in a manner that is intended to be sexually arousing.

poverty rate the proportion of the population whose income falls below the government's official poverty line—the level of income below which a family of a given size is considered to be poor.

power the ability to achieve goals despite opposition from others.

power elite the leaders at the top of business, the federal government, and the military (especially the "top brass" at the Pentagon).

prejudice a negative attitude about people based on such characteristics as race, age, religion, or sexual orientation.

prestige the respect, esteem, or regard accorded to an individual or group by others.

primary deviance the initial act of rule breaking.

primary prevention programs that seek to prevent drug problems before they begin.

primary sector production the extraction of raw materials and natural resources from the environment.

property crime taking money or property from another without force, the threat of force, or the destruction of property.

prostitution the sale of sexual services (of oneself or another) for money or goods and without emotional attachment.

punishment any action designed to deprive a person of things of value (including liberty) because of an offense the person is thought to have committed.

racial group a category of people who have been singled out, by others or themselves, as inferior or superior on the basis of subjectively selected physical characteristics such as skin color, hair texture, and eye shape.

racism a set of attitudes, beliefs, and practices that are used to justify the superior treatment of one racial or ethnic group and the inferior treatment of another racial or ethnic group.

relative poverty a condition that exists when people may be able to afford basic necessities such as food, clothing, and shelter but cannot maintain an average standard of living for members of their society or group.

repressive terrorism terrorism conducted by a government against its own citizens for the purpose of protecting an existing political order.

revolutionary terrorism acts of violence against civilians that are carried out by internal enemies of the government who want to bring about political change.

scapegoat a person or group that is blamed for some problem and is therefore subjected to hostility or aggression by others.

second shift the domestic work that many employed women perform at home after completing their work day on the job.

secondary analysis of existing data a research design in which investigators analyze data that originally were collected by others for some other purpose.

secondary deviance the process that occurs when a person who has been labeled a deviant accepts that new identity and continues the deviant behavior.

secondary sector production the processing of raw materials (from the primary sector) into finished products.

segregation the spatial and social separation of categories of people by race/ethnicity, class, gender, religion, or other social characteristics.

self-fulfilling prophecy the process by which an unsubstantiated belief or prediction results in behavior that makes the originally false belief come true.

semiperipheral nations nations that are more developed than peripheral nations but less developed than core nations.

serial murder the killing of three or more people over more than a month by the same person.

sex the biological differences between females and males.

sexism the subordination of one sex, usually female, on the basis of the assumed superiority of the other sex.

sexual harassment unwanted sexual advances, requests for sexual favors, or other verbal or physical conduct of a sexual nature.

sexual orientation a preference for emotional-sexual relationships with individuals of the same sex (homosexuality), the opposite sex (heterosexuality), or both (bisexuality).

sexuality sexual attraction and intimate relationships with others.

situational approach the belief that violence results from a specific interaction process, termed a "situational transaction."

social bond theory the proposition that criminal behavior is most likely to occur when a person's ties to society are weakened or broken.

social control the systematic practices that social groups develop to encourage conformity and discourage deviance.

social disorganization the conditions in society that undermine the ability of traditional social institutions to govern human behavior.

social gerontology the study of the social (nonphysical) aspects of aging.

social problem a social condition (such as poverty) or a pattern of behavior (such as substance abuse) that people believe warrants public concern and collective action to bring about change.

social stratification the hierarchical arrangement of large social groups on the basis of their control over basic resources.

socialism an economic system characterized by public ownership of the means of production, the pursuit of collective goals, and centralized decision making.

society a large social grouping that shares the same geographical territory and is subject to the same political authority and dominant cultural expectations.

sociological imagination the ability to see the relationship between individual experiences and the larger society.

sociology the academic and scholarly discipline that engages in systematic study of human society and social interactions.

state the political entity that possesses a legitimate monopoly over the use of force within its territory to achieve its goals.

state-sponsored terrorism political terrorism resulting from a government providing financial resources, weapons, and training for terrorists who conduct their activities in other countries.

statutory rape the act of having sexual intercourse with a person who is under the legal age of consent as established by state law.

stereotypes overgeneralizations about the appearance, behavior, or other characteristics of all members of a group.

strain theory the proposition that people feel strain when they are exposed to cultural goals that they cannot reach because they do not have access to culturally approved means of achieving those goals.

strategically significant weapon one that brings force to bear in such a way that it decisively erodes the enemy's war-making capability.

structural unemployment unemployment that occurs when workers' skills and educational levels do not match employers' requirements or when unemployed workers do not live where jobs they could perform are located.

subculture a group of people who share a distinctive set of cultural beliefs and behaviors that sets them apart from the larger society.

subculture of violence hypothesis the belief that violence is part of the normative expectations governing everyday behavior among young males in the lower classes.

survey research a poll in which researchers ask respondents a series of questions about a specific topic and record their responses.

technology both the knowledge, techniques, and tools that allow people to transform resources into usable form and the knowledge and skills required to use what is developed.

terrorism the use of calculated, unlawful physical force or threats of violence against a government, organization, or individual to gain some political, religious, economic, or social objective.

tertiary sector production providing services rather than goods as the primary source of livelihood.

theory a set of logically related statements that attempt to describe, explain, or predict social events.

theory of racial formation a theory based on the assumption that the government substantially defines racial and ethnic relations.

tolerance a condition that occurs when larger doses of a drug are required over time to produce the same physical or psychological effect that was originally achieved by a smaller dose.

total institution a place where people are isolated from the rest of society for a period of time and come under the complete control of the officials who run the institution.

tracking assigning students to specific courses and educational programs on the basis of their test scores, previous grades, or both.

transnational corporation a large-scale business organization that is headquartered in one country but operates in many countries.

urbanization the process by which an increasing proportion of a population lives in cities rather than in rural areas.

values collective ideas about what is right or wrong, good or bad, and desirable or undesirable in a specific society.

victimless crime a crime that many people believe has no real victim because it involves willing participants in an economic exchange.

violence the use of physical force to cause pain, injury, or death to another or to damage another's property.

violent crime actions involving force or the threat of force against others.

wage gap the disparity between women's and men's earnings.

war system components of social institutions (e.g., the economy, government, and education) and cultural beliefs and practices that promote the development of warriors, weapons, and war as a normal part of the society and its foreign policy.

wealth the value of all economic assets, including income, personal property, and income-producing property.

weapons system military technology comprised of a weapons platform (i.e., a ship, aircraft, or tank), a weapon (i.e., a gun, missile, or torpedo), and the means of command and communication.

welfare state a situation in which a government takes responsibility for specific categories of citizens by offering them certain services and benefits, such as employment, housing, health, education, or guaranteed income.

withdrawal a variety of physical and/or psychological symptoms that habitual drug users experience when they stop using a specific drug.

zero population growth a situation in which a population is totally stable, neither growing nor decreasing from year to year, because births, deaths, and migration are in total balance.

References

AAUW Educational Foundation. 1992. *The AAUW Report: How Schools Shortchange Girls.* Developed by the Wellesley College Center for Research on Women. Washington, DC: American Association of University Women Educational Foundation.

Abraham, Laurie Kaye. 1993. *Mama Might Be Better Off Dead: The Failure of Health Care in Urban America.* Chicago, IL: University of Chicago Press.

Acuna, Rodolfo. 1984. *A Community under Siege: A Chronicle of Chicanos in East of the Los Angeles River, 1945–1975.* Los Angeles: Chicano Studies Research Center, University of California at Los Angeles.

Adams, Karen L., and Norma C. Ware. 1995. "Sexism and the English Language: The Linguistic Implications of Being a Woman." In Jo Freeman (Ed.), *Women: A Feminist Perspective* (5th ed.). Mountain View, CA: Mayfield Publishing, pp. 331–346.

Adams, Scott. 1996. *The Dilbert Principle: A Cubicle's-Eye View of Bosses, Meetings, Management Fads and Other Workplace Afflictions.* New York: Harper-Business.

Aday, David P., Jr. 1990. *Social Control at the Margins: Toward a General Understanding of Deviance.* Belmont, CA: Wadsworth.

Adorno, Theodor W., Else Frenkel-Brunswick, Daniel J. Levinson, and R. Nevitt Sanford. 1950. *The Authoritarian Personality.* New York: Harper & Row.

Akasie, Jay. 1997. "The Fine Art of Networking." *Forbes* (May 19):18.

Akers, Ronald L. 1992. *Drugs, Alcohol, and Society: Social Structure, Process, and Policy.* Belmont, CA: Wadsworth.

Albert, Steven M., and Maria G. Cattell. 1994. *Old Age in Global Perspective: Cross-Cultural and Cross-National Views.* New York: G.K. Hall.

Albrecht, Gary L. 1992. *The Disability Business: Rehabilitation in America.* Newbury Park, CA: Sage.

Alexander, Karl L., Doris Entwisle, and Maxine Thompson. 1987. "School Performance, Status Relations, and the Structure of Sentiment: Bringing the Teacher Back In." *American Sociological Review,* 52:665–682.

Allen, Michael Patrick. 1987. *The Founding Fortunes: A New Anatomy of the Super-Rich Families in America.* New York: Dutton.

Allen, Robert L. 1974. *Reluctant Reformers.* Washington, DC: Howard University Press.

Allport, Gordon. 1958. *The Nature of Prejudice* (abridged ed.). New York: Doubleday/Anchor.

Almaguer, Tomás. 1995. "Chicano Men: A Cartography of Homosexual Identity and Behavior." In Michael S. Kimmel and Michael A. Messner (Eds.), *Men's Lives* (3rd ed.). Boston: Allyn and Bacon, pp. 418–431.

Alston, Maude H., Sharon H. Rankin, and Carol A. Harris. 1995. "Suicide in African American Elderly." *Journal of Black Studies,* 26(1):31–35.

Altman, Lawrence K. 1996a. "AIDS Meeting: Signs of Hope and Obstacles." *New York Times* (July 7):A1.

Altman, Lawrence K. 1996b. "India Quickly Leads in H.I.V. Cases, AIDS Meeting Hears." *New York Times* (July 8):A8.

Altman, Lawrence K. 1996c. "U.N. Reports 3 Million New H.I.V. Cases Worldwide for '96." *New York Times* (November 28):A6.

Alwin, Duane, Philip Converse, and Steven Martin. 1985. "Living Arrangements and Social Integration." *Journal of Marriage and the Family,* 47:319–334.

American Association of University Women. 1992. *The AAUW Report: How Schools Short-Change Girls.* Washington, DC: The AAUW Educational Foundation and National Educational Association.

American Psychiatric Association. 1994. *Diagnostic and Statistical Manual of Mental Disorders IV.* Washington, DC: American Psychiatric Association.

Amott, Teresa, and Julie Matthaei. 1991. *Race, Gender, and Work: A Multicultural Economic History of Women in the United States.* Boston: South End Press.

Anders, George. 1996. *Health against Wealth: HMOs and the Breakdown of Medical Trust.* Boston: Houghton Mifflin.

Andersen, Margaret L., and Patricia Hill Collins (Eds.). 1995. *Race, Class, and Gender: An Anthology* (2nd ed.). Belmont, CA: Wadsworth.

Anderson, Elijah. 1990. *Streetwise: Race, Class, and Change in an Urban Community*. Chicago, IL: University of Chicago Press.

Andrews, Alice C., and James W. Fonseca. 1995. *The Atlas of American Society*. New York: New York University Press.

Angel, Ronald J., and Jacqueline L. Angel. 1993. *Painful Inheritance: Health and the New Generation of Fatherless Families*. Madison, WI: University of Wisconsin Press.

Angier, Natalie. 1990. "New Antidepressant Is Acclaimed but Not Perfect." *New York Times* (March 29):B9.

Angier, Natalie. 1993. "Report Suggests Homosexuality Is Linked to Genes." *New York Times* (July 16):A1, C18.

Angier, Natalie. 1995a. "Disputed Meeting to Ask if Crime Has Genetic Roots." *New York Times* (September 19):B5, B9.

Angier, Natalie. 1995b. "If You're Really Ancient, You May Be Better Off: The Rise of the 'Oldest Old.'" *New York Times* (June 11):E1.

Anyon, Jean. 1980. "Social Class and the Hidden Curriculum of Work." *Journal of Education*, 162:67–92.

Apple, Michael W. 1982. *Education and Power: Reproduction and Contradiction in Education*. London: Routledge & Kegan Paul.

Applebaum, Eileen R., and Ronald Schettkat. 1989. "Employment and Industrial Restructuring: A Comparison of the U.S. and West Germany." In E. Matzner (Ed.), *No Way to Full Employment?* Research Unit Labor Market and Employment, Discussion Paper FSI 89–16 (July):394–448.

Applebome, Peter. 1995a. "For the Ultimate Safe School, Official Eyes Turn to Dallas." *New York Times* (September 20):A1, B8.

Applebome, Peter. 1995b. "Record Cost Cited to Fix or Rebuild Nation's Schools." *New York Times* (December 26):A1, A11.

Applebome, Peter. 1996a. "Blacks Show Gains in Getting College Degrees." *New York Times* (June 12):B8.

Applebome, Peter. 1996b. "Crime Fear Is Seen Forcing Changes in Youth Behavior." *New York Times* (January 12):A6.

Applebome, Peter. 1996c. "Dilapidated Schools Are Busting at Frayed Seams." *New York Times* (August 25):8.

Applebome, Peter. 1996d. "Education Summit Calls for Tough Standards to Be Set by States and Local School Districts." *New York Times* (March 27):B7.

Applebome, Peter. 1996e. "Grading For-Profit Schools: So Far, So Good." *New York Times* (June 26):A1, A13.

Applebome, Peter. 1996f. "Building Better Schools: One Size Doesn't Fit." *New York Times* (December 18):E4.

Applebome, Peter. 1997. "Mixed Results for Public School Proponents." *New York Times* (April 16):A17.

Arenson, Karen W. 1996. "CUNY Says Workfare Hurts Enrollment." *New York Times* (June 1):9.

Arenson, Karen W. 1997a. "62 Top Colleges Endorse Bias in Admissions." *New York Times* (April 24):A17.

Arenson, Karen W. 1997b. "Standard for Equivalency Degree Is Raised." *New York Times* (April 9):A18.

Arnold, Regina A. 1990. "Processes of Victimization and Criminalization of Black Women." *Social Justice*, 17 (3):153–166.

Associated Press. 1996. "Soccer in Sarajevo: More Than a Game." *New York Times International* (May 3):A3.

Association of American Medical Colleges. 1996. *Medical School Admission Requirements 1997–98*. (47th ed.). Washington, DC: Association of American Medical Colleges.

Atchley, Robert C. 1994. *Social Forces and Aging: An Introduction to Social Gerontology* (7th ed.). Belmont, CA: Wadsworth.

Atlas, James. 1995. "Here's the Future. Look Familiar?" *New York Times* (December 31):EI, E5.

Aulette, Judy Root. 1994. *Changing Families*. Belmont, CA: Wadsworth.

Austin American-Statesman. 1995. "Abuse of Elderly Is Increasing, Report Says." (May 2):A6.

Austin American-Statesman. 1997a. "Indonesia's Riady Family Wants into U.S. Banking." (April 27):A30.

Austin American-Statesman. 1997b. "Nation Needs Readers." (April 21):A6.

Axinn, William G., and Arland Thornton. 1992. "The Relationship between Cohabitation and Divorce: Selectivity or Casual Influence?" *Demography*, 29(3):357–374.

Bachman, Ronet. 1992. *Death and Violence on the Reservation: Homicide, Family Violence, and Suicide in American Indian Populations*. New York: Auburn House.

Bagby, Meredith (Ed.). 1997. *Annual Report of the United States of America 1997*. New York: McGraw-Hill.

Bailey, J. Michael, and D. S. Benishay. 1993. "Familial Aggregation of Female Sexual Orientation." *American Journal of Psychiatry*, 150 (February):272–277.

Bailey, J. Michael, and Richard C. Pillard. 1991. "A Genetic Study of Male Sexual Orientation." *Archives of General Psychiatry*, 48 (December):1089–1098.

Baldwin, James. 1963. *The Fire Next Time*. New York: Dial Press.

Ballantine, Jeanne H. 1993. *The Sociology of Education: A Systematic Analysis* (3rd ed.). Englewood Cliffs, NJ: Prentice-Hall.

Baltzell, E. Digby. 1958. *Philadelphia Gentlemen: The Making of a National Upper Class*. New York: Free Press.

Bandura, Albert. 1973. *Aggression: A Social Learning Analysis*. Englewood Cliffs, NJ: Prentice-Hall.

Bane, Mary Jo. 1986. "Household Composition and Poverty: Which Comes First?" In Sheldon H. Danziger and Daniel H. Weinberg (Eds.), *Fighting Poverty: What Works and What Doesn't*. Cambridge, MA: Harvard University Press.

Bane, Mary Jo, and David T. Ellwood. 1994. *Welfare Realities: From Rhetoric to Reform*. Cambridge, MA: Harvard University Press.

Banks, Howard. 1997. "Deutsche Hegira." *Forbes* (May 5):130–133.

Banta, Bob. 1996. "Hyde Hopes to Be Example to Drivers." *Austin American-Statesman* (September 27):A1, A11.

Barber, Benjamin R. 1996. *Jihad vs. McWorld: How Globalism and Tribalism Are Reshaping the World*. New York: Ballantine Books.

Barlett, Donald L., and James B. Steele. 1996. *America: Who Stole the Dream?* Kansas City, KS: Andrews and McMeel.

Barlow, Hugh D. 1996. *Introduction to Criminology* (7th ed.). New York: HarperCollins.

Barnett, James H. 1954. *The American Christmas: A Study in National Culture*. New York: Macmillan.

Baron, Harold M. 1969. "The Web of Urban Racism." In Louis L. Knowles and Kenneth Prewitt (Eds.), *Institutional Racism in America*. Englewood Cliffs, NJ: Prentice-Hall, pp. 134–176.

Barrows, Sydney Biddle, with William Novak. 1986. *Mayflower Madam: The Secret Life of Sydney Biddle Barrows*. New York: Ivy Books.

Barry, Kathleen. 1995. *The Prostitution of Sexuality*. New York: New York University Press.

Barry, Tom. 1997. "'Burb-arians Pay Share of Austin's Sales Tax." *Austin American-Statesman* (May 27):A13.

Basow, Susan A. 1992. *Gender Stereotypes and Roles* (3rd ed.). Pacific Grove, CA: Brooks/Cole.

Bassi, Laurie J., and Amy B. Chasanov. 1996. "Women and the Unemployment Insurance System." In Cynthia Costello and Barbara Kivimae Krimgold (Eds.) for the Women's Research and Education Institute, *The American Woman 1996–97: Women and Work*. New York: W.W. Norton, pp. 104-126.

Bauerlein, Monika. 1995. "The Borderless Bordello." *Utne Reader* (November–December):30–32.

Bawer, Bruce. 1994. *A Place at the Table: The Gay Individual in American Society*. New York: Touchstone.

Becker, Gary S. 1964. *Human Capital*. New York: Columbia University Press.

Becker, Howard S. 1963. *Outsiders: Studies in the Sociology of Deviance*. New York: Free Press.

Beeghley, Leonard. 1989. *The Structure of Social Stratification in the United States*. Boston: Allyn and Bacon.

Belknap, Joanne. 1996. *The Invisible Woman: Gender, Crime, and Justice*. Belmont, CA: Wadsworth.

Bell, Daniel. 1973. *The Coming of Post-Industrial Society: A Venture in Social Forecasting*. New York: Basic Books.

Belluck, Pam. 1995. "Educators Divided on Immigrant Schools." *New York Times* (March 26):13.

Belluck, Pam. 1997. "A Woman's Killer Is Likely to Be Her Partner, a Study Finds." *New York Times* (March 31):A12.

Belsky, Janet. 1990. *The Psychology of Aging: Theory, Research, and Interventions* (2nd ed.). Pacific Grove, CA: Brooks/Cole.

Bennett, Colin J. 1996. "The Public Surveillance of Personal Data: A Cross-National Analysis." In David Lyon and Elia Zureik (Eds.), *Computers, Surveillance, and Privacy*. Minneapolis, MN: University of Minnesota Press, pp. 237–259.

Bennett, Niel G., Ann Klimas Blanc, and David E. Bloom. 1988. "Commitment and the Modern Union: Assessing the Link between Premarital Cohabitation and Subsequent Marital Stability." *American Sociological Review*, 53:127–138.

Benokraitis, Nijole V. 1993. *Marriage and Families: Changes, Choices, and Constraints*. Englewood Cliffs, NJ: Prentice-Hall.

Benokraitis, Nijole V., and Joe R. Feagin. 1995. *Modern Sexism: Blatant, Subtle, and Covert Discrimination*. Englewood Cliffs, NJ: Prentice-Hall.

Bensley, L. S., and R. Wu. 1991. "The Role of Psychological Reactance in Drinking Following Alcohol Prevention Messages." *Journal of Applied Social Psychology*, 21:1111–1124.

Berg, John C. 1994. *Unequal Struggle: Class, Gender, Race, and Power in the U.S. Congress*. Boulder, CO: Westview.

Berger, Peter. 1963. *Invitation to Sociology: A Humanistic Perspective*. New York: Anchor.

Berger, Peter, and Hansfried Kellner. 1964. "Marriage and the Construction of Reality." *Diogenes*, 46:1–32.

Berger, Peter, and Thomas Luckmann. 1967. *The Social Construction of Reality: A Treatise in the Sociology of Knowledge*. Garden City, NY: Anchor Books.

Berger, Ronald J., Patricia Searles, and Charles E. Cottle. 1991. *Feminism and Pornography*. Westport, CT: Praeger.

Bergmann, Barbara R. 1986. *The Economic Emergence of Women*. New York: Basic Books.

Berke, Richard L. 1996. "Is Age-Bashing Any Way to Beat Bob Dole?" *New York Times* (May 5):E1, E6.

Berkowitz, Leonard (Ed.). 1969. *Roots of Aggression: A Reexamination of the Frustration-Aggression Hypothesis*. New York: Atherton.

Bernard, Jessie. 1982. *The Future of Marriage*. New Haven, CT: Yale University Press.

Bertram, Eva, Morris Blachman, Kenneth Sharpe, and Peter Andreas. 1996. *Drug War Politics: The Price of Denial*. Berkeley, CA: University of California Press.

Bethel, Martha A. 1995. "Terror in Montana." *New York Times* (July 20):A13.

Beutler, Ivan F., Wesley R. Burr, Kathleen S. Bahr, and Donald A. Herrin. 1989. "The Family Realm: Theoretical Contributions for Understanding Its Uniqueness." *Journal of Marriage and the Family*, 51:805–815.

Bieber, Irving, and the Society of Medical Psychoanalysts. 1962. *Homosexuality: A Psychoanalytic Study*. New York: Basic Books.

Birmingham, Stephen. 1967. *The Right Places*. Boston: Little, Brown.

Blauner, Robert. 1964. *Alienation and Freedom*. Chicago: University of Chicago Press.

Blauner, Robert. 1972. *Racial Oppression in America*. New York: Harper & Row.

Block, Carolyn Rebecca, and Richard Block. 1993. "Street Gang Crime in Chicago." *NIJ* [National Institute of Justice] *Research in Brief* (December):1–11.

Blount, Jeb. 1996. "Saltwater Spirituals and Deeper Blues." *Houston Chronicle* (February 25):24A.

Bluestone, Barry, and Bennett Harrison. 1982. *The Deindustrialization of America: Plant Closings, Community Abandonment, and the Dismantling of Basic Industry*. New York: Basic Books.

Boller, Gregory. 1997. "Sugar Daddies." *Mother Jones* (May–June, 1997):45.

Bonacich, Edna. 1972. "A Theory of Ethnic Antagonism: The Split Labor Market." *American Sociological Review*, 37:547–549.

Bonacich, Edna. 1976. "Advanced Capitalism and Black-White Relations in the United States: A Split Labor Market Interpretation." *American Sociological Review*, 41:34–51.

Bonger, Willem. 1969. *Criminality and Economic Conditions* (abridged ed.). Bloomington, IN: Indiana University Press (orig. pub. 1916).

Bonnin, Julie. 1997. "Knockout Drugs." *Austin American-Statesman* (February 2):E1, E12.

Borosage, Robert L. 1996. "The Politics of Austerity." *The Nation* (May 27):22–24.

Botvin, Gilbert, and Stephanie Tortu. 1988. "Preventing Adolescent Substance Abuse through Life Skills Training." In Richard M. Price, Emory L. Cowen, Raymond P. Lorion, and Julia Ramos-McKay (Eds.), *Fourteen Ounces of Prevention: A Casebook for Practitioners*. Washington, DC: American Psychological Association, pp. 98–110.

Bourdieu, Pierre, and Jean-Claude Passeron. 1990. *Reproduction in Education, Society, and Culture*. Newbury Park, CA: Sage.

Bourdon, Karen H., Donald S. Rae, Ben Z. Locke, William E. Narrow, and Darrel A. Regier. 1992. "Estimating the Prevalence of Mental Disorders in U.S. Adults from the Epidemiological Catchment Area Survey." *Public Health Reports*, 107:663–668.

Bourgeois, Philippe. 1995. *In Search of Respect: Selling Crack in el Barrio*. New York: Cambridge University Press.

Bowers, William J. 1984. *Legal Homicide: Death as Punishment in America, 1864–1982*. Boston: Northeastern University Press.

Bowles, Samuel, and Herbert Gintis. 1976. *Schooling in Capitalist America: Education and the Contradictions of Economic Life*. New York: Basic Books.

Bradsher, Keith. 1995. "As One Million Leave Ranks of Insured, Debate Heats Up." *New York Times* (August 27):1, 10.

Bradsher, Keith. 1996. "Rich Control More of U.S. Wealth Study Says, as Debts Grow for Poor." *New York Times* (June 23):17–18.

Bradsher, Keith. 1997. "In the Biggest, Booming Cities, a Car Population Problem." *New York Times* (May 11):E4.

Bragg, Rick. 1997. "Many Find Satisfaction, but Few Find Any Joy." *New York Times* (June 14):8.

Braverman, Harry. 1974. *Labor and Monopoly Capital*. New York: Monthly Review Press.

Brinton, Mary C. 1988. "The Social-Institutional Bases of Gender Stratification: Japan as an Illustrative Case." *American Journal of Sociology*, 94(2):300–334.

Brinton, Mary C. 1989. "Gender Stratification in Contemporary Japan." *American Sociological Review*, 54:549–564.

Briscoe, David. 1997. "Groups Differ on War Count." *Austin American-Statesman* (January 1):A29.

Brody, Jane E. 1996. "Good Habits Outweigh Genes as Key to a Healthy Old Age." *New York Times* (February 28):B9.

Brooks, A. Phillips. 1997. "UT Minority Applicants Drop Sharply." *Austin American-Statesman* (February 27): B1, B7.

Brooks, A. Phillips, and Jeff South. 1996. "In Town after Town, Minorities Fill Programs." *Austin American-Statesman* (December 1):A1, A14.

Brown, Phil. 1985. *The Transfer of Care: Psychiatric Deinstitutionalization and Its Aftermath*. Boston: Routledge & Kegan Paul.

Browne, Jan, and Victor Minichiello. 1995. "The Social Meanings behind Male Sex Work: Implications for Sexual Interactions." *British Journal of Sociology*, 46(4): 598–623.

Browne, Jan, and Kirk R. Williams. 1987. "Gender Specific Effects on Patterns of Homicide Perpetration." Presented to the American Psychological Association, cited in Barlow, 1996.

Bruni, Frank. 1996. "Gay Couples Cheer Adoption Ruling, Saying It Lets Law Reflect Reality." *New York Times* (November 5):16.

Buckley, William F., Jr. 1995. "Thou Shalt Not . . . What?" *National Review* (July 31):71.

Bullard, Robert D., and Beverly H. Wright. 1992. "The Quest for Environmental Equity: Mobilizing the African-American Community for Social Change." In Riley E. Dunlap and Angela G. Mertig (Eds.), *American Environmentalism: The U.S. Environmental Movement, 1970–1990*. New York: Taylor & Francis, pp. 39–50.

Bullough, Vern, and Bonnie Bullough. 1987. *Women and Prostitution: A Social History*. Buffalo, NY: Prometheus.

Bumpass, Larry, James E. Sweet, and Teresa Castro Martin. 1990. "Changing Patterns of Remarriage." *Journal of Marriage and the Family*, 52:747–756.

Bunis, William K., Angela Yancik, and David Snow. 1996. "The Cultural Patterning of Sympathy toward the Homeless and Other Victims of Misfortune," *Social Problems* (November):387–402.

Burleigh, Nina. 1991. "Watching Children Starve to Death." *Time* (June 10):56–58.

Burnham, M. Audrey, Richard L. Hough, Marvin Karno, Javier I. Escobar, and Cynthia A. Telles. 1987. "Acculturation and Lifetime Prevalence of Psychiatric Disorders among Mexican Americans in Los Angeles." *Journal of Health and Social Behavior*, 28:89–102.

Burns, John F. 1996. "Denial and Taboo Blinding India to the Horror of Its AIDS Scourge." *New York Times* (September 22):A1.

Busch, Ruth C. 1990. *Family Systems: Comparative Study of the Family*. New York: P. Lang.

Busfield, Joan. 1996. *Men, Women and Madness: Understanding Gender and Mental Disorder*. Houndmills, Basingstoke, Hampshire, England: MacMillan Press.

Butler, Robert N. 1969. "Ageism: Another Form of Bigotry." *The Gerontologist*, 9:243–246.

Butler, Sandra, and Barbara Rosenblum. 1991. *Cancer in Two Voices*. San Francisco, CA: Spinsters.

Butterfield, Fox. 1996. "Crimes of Violence among Juveniles Decline Slightly." *New York Times* (August 9):A1, A9.

Butterfield, Fox. 1997. "Serious Crime Decreased for Fifth Year in a Row." *New York Times* (January 5):8.

Bynum, Jack E., and William E. Thompson. 1996. *Juvenile Delinquency: A Sociological Approach*. Boston: Allyn and Bacon.

Cable, Sherry, and Charles Cable. 1995. *Environmental Problems, Grassroots Solutions: The Politics of Grassroots Environmental Conflict*. New York: St. Martin's Press.

Camp, Camille G., and George M. Camp. 1994. *The Corrections Yearbook, 1994*. Washington, DC: U.S. Department of Justice, Bureau of Justice Statistics.

Cancian, Francesca M. 1990. "The Feminization of Love." In C. Carlson (Ed.), *Perspectives on the Family: History, Class, and Feminism*. Belmont, CA: Wadsworth, pp. 171–185.

Cancian, Francesca M., and James William Gibson. 1990. *Making War, Making Peace: The Social Foundations of Violent Conflict*. Belmont, CA: Wadsworth.

Cannon, Margaret. 1995. *The Invisible Empire: Racism in Canada*. Toronto: Random House of Canada.

Capek, Stella M. 1993. "The 'Environmental Justice' Frame: A Conceptual Discussion and an Application." *Social Problems*, 40:5–24.

Cargan, Leonard, and Matthew Melko. 1982. *Singles: Myths and Realities*. Newbury Park, CA: Sage.

Carmichael, Stokely, and Charles V. Hamilton. 1967. *Black Power: The Politics of Liberation in America*. New York: Vintage.

Carrier, James G. 1986. *Social Class and the Construction of Inequality in American Education*. New York: Greenwood Press.

Carter, Bill. 1995. "After Killing, Hard Questions for Talk Shows." *New York Times* (March 14):A1, A8.

Cass, Vivien C. 1984. "Homosexual Identity Formation: Testing a Theoretical Model." *Journal of Sex Research*, 20:143–167.

Castells, Manuel. 1977. *The Urban Question*. London: Edward Arnold.

Catalano, Ralph A., and William McConnell. 1996. "A Time-Series Test of the Quarantine Theory of Involuntary Commitment." *Journal of Health and Social Behavior*, 37:381–387.

Cavender, Gray. 1995. "Alternative Approaches: Labeling and Critical Perspectives." In Joseph F. Sheley (Ed.), *Criminology: A Contemporary Handbook* (2nd ed.). Belmont, CA: Wadsworth, pp. 349–367.

Chambliss, William J. 1988. *Exploring Criminology*. New York: Macmillan.

Chan, Sucheng (Ed.). 1991. *Entry Denied: Exclusion and the Chinese Community in America, 1882–1943*. Philadelphia: Temple University Press.

Chase-Lansdale, P. Lindsay, Jeanne Brooks-Gunn, and Roberta L. Palkoff. 1992. "Research and Programs for Adolescent Mothers: Missing Links and Future Promises." *Family Relations*, 40(4):396–403.

Chavez, Leo R. and Rebecca Martinez. 1996. "Mexican Immigration in the 1980s and Beyond: Implications for Chicanas/os." In David R. Maciel and Isidro D. Ortiz (Eds.), *Chicanas/Chicanos at the Crossroads: Social Economic, and Political Change*. Tucson, AZ: University of Arizona Press, pp. 25–41.

Chavez, Linda. 1991. *Out of the Barrio: Toward a New Politics of Hispanic Assimilation*. New York: Basic Books.

Chen, Hsiang-shui. 1992. *Chinatown No More: Taiwan Immigrants in Contemporary New York*. Ithaca: Cornell University Press.

Cherlin, Andrew J. 1992. *Marriage, Divorce, and Remarriage* (rev. and enlarged ed.). Cambridge, MA: Harvard University Press.

Chermak, Steven M. 1995. *Victims in the News: Crime and the American News Media*. Boulder, CO: Westview.

Chilcoat, Howard D., and Naomi Breslau. 1996. "Alcohol Disorders in Young Adulthood: Effects of Transitions into Adult Roles." *Journal of Health and Social Behavior*, 37(4):339–349.

Children's Defense Fund. 1995. *The State of America's Children Yearbook 1995*. Washington, DC: Children's Defense Fund.

Children's Express. 1993. Voices from the Future: Our Children Tell Us about Violence in America. Edited by Susan Goodwillie. New York: Crown.

Chow, Esther Ngan-Ling. 1994. "Asian American Women at Work." In Maxine Baca Zinn and Bonnie Thornton Dill (Eds.), *Women of Color in U.S. Society*. Philadelphia: Temple University Press, pp. 203–227.

Chronicle of Higher Education. 1996. "Attitudes and Characteristics of Freshman, Fall 1995." Almanac Issue (September 2):19.

Chudacoff, Howard P. 1989. *How Old Are You? Age Consciousness in American Culture*. Princeton, NJ: Princeton University Press.

Churchill, Ward. 1992. *Fantasies of the Master Race*. Monroe, ME: Common Courage Press.

Churchill, Ward. 1994. *Indians Are Us? Culture and Genocide in Native North America*. Monroe, ME: Common Courage Press.

City of Austin. 1996. Internal communication from Information Systems Department (October 23).

Clark, Cal, and Oliver Walter. 1994. "Cuts, Cultures, and City Limits in Reagan's New Federalism." In Terry Nichols Clark (Ed.), *Urban Innovation: Creative Strategies for Turbulent Times*. Thousand Oaks, CA: Sage, pp. 169–196.

Cleary, Paul D. 1987. "Gender Differences in Stress-Related Disorders." In Rosalind C. Barnett, Lois Biener, and Grace K. Baruch (Eds.), *Gender and Stress*. New York: Free Press, pp. 39–72.

Cleeland, N. 1991. "Gasping in Smoggy Mexico City Oxygen Kiosk May Prove Helpful." *San Diego Union* (March 9). (Cited in Michael P. Soroka and George J. Bryjak. 1995. *Social Problems: A World at Risk*. Boston: Allyn and Bacon, p. 116.)

Clinard, Marshall B., and R. F. Meier. 1989. *Sociology of Deviant Behavior* (7th ed.). Fort Worth, TX: Holt, Rinehart and Winston.

Clines, Francis X. 1997. "'Soft' Money Source Proves Hard to Find." *New York Times* (July 31):A9.

Cloward, Richard A., and Lloyd E. Ohlin. 1960. *Delinquency and Opportunity: A Theory of Delinquent Gangs*. New York: Free Press.

Coale, Ansley. 1973. "The Demographic Transition." Proceedings of the International Population Conference, Liege. Vol. 1, pp. 53–72. (Cited in Weeks, 1992.)

Cock, Jacklyn. 1994. "Women and the Military: Implications for Demilitarization in the 1990s in South Africa. *Gender and Society*, 8(2):152–169.

Codina, G. Edward, and Frank F. Montalvo. 1994. "Chicano Phenotype and Depression." *Hispanic Journal of Behavioral Sciences*, 16 (August):296–307.

Cohen, Lawrence E., and Marcus Felson. 1979. "Social Change and Crime Rate Trends: A Routine Activity Approach." *American Sociological Review*, 44:588–608.

Cohn, Jonathan. 1997. "Reform School." *Mother Jones* (May–June): 62.

Coleman, Eli. 1981/2. "Developmental Stages of the Coming Out Process." *Journal of Homosexuality*, 7:31–43.

Coleman, James S. 1966. *Equality of Educational Opportunity*. Washington, DC: U.S. Government Printing Office.

Coleman, James W. 1995. "Respectable Crime." In Joseph F. Sheley (Ed.), *Criminology: A Contemporary Handbook* (2nd ed.). Belmont, CA: Wadsworth, pp. 249–269.

Coles, Gerald. 1987. *The Learning Mystique: A Critical Look at "Learning Disabilities."* New York: Pantheon.

Colhoun, J. 1992. "Census Fails to Quash Report on Iraqi Deaths." *The Guardian* (April 22):5.

Collier, Peter, and David Horowitz. 1987. *The Fords: An American Epic*. New York: Summit Books.

Collins, James. 1997. "Day of Reckoning." *Time* (June 16): 27–29.

Collins, Patricia Hill. 1990. *Black Feminist Thought: Knowledge, Consciousness, and the Politics of Entitlement*. London: HarperCollins Academic.

Collins, Patricia Hill. 1991. *Black Feminist Thought: Knowledge, Consciousness, and the Politics of Empowerment*. New York: Routledge.

Collins, Patricia Hill. 1995. "Symposium: On West and Fenstermaker's 'Doing Difference,'" *Gender and Society*, 9(4) (August):491–494.

Collins, Randall. 1979. *The Credential Society: An Historical Sociology of Education*. New York: Academic Press.

Coltrane, Scott. 1989. "Household Labor and the Routine Production of Gender." *Social Problems*, 36:473–490.

Community Childhood Hunger Identification Project. 1995. *A Survey of Childhood Hunger in the United States*. Washington, DC: Food Research and Action Committee (July).

Comstock, Gary David. 1991. *Violence against Lesbians and Gay Men*. New York: Columbia University Press.

Conant, Marcus. 1997. "This Is Smart Medicine." *Newsweek* (February 3):26.

Connell, Christopher. 1995. "Birth Rate for Unmarried Women Surges." *Austin American-Statesman* (June 7):A18.

Corelli, Rae. 1995. "A Tolerant Nation's Hidden Shame." *Maclean's* (August 14):38–43.

Corr, Charles A., Clyde M. Nabe, and Donna M. Corr. 1994. *Death and Dying, Life and Living*. Pacific Grove, CA: Brooks/Cole.

Cosby, Ennis. 1997. "Teaching from the Heart." *New York Times* (January 26):E13.

Cose, Ellis. 1993. *The Rage of a Privileged Class*. New York: HarperCollins.

Coser, Lewis A. 1969. "The Visibility of Evil." *Journal of Social Issues*, 25:101–109. In Bunis, William K., Angela Yancik, and David Snow. 1996. "The Cultural Patterning of Sympathy toward the Homeless and Other Victims of Misfortune." *Social Problems* (November):387–402.

Costello, Cynthia, Anne J. Stone, and Betty Dooley. 1996. "A Perspective on America's Working Women." In Cynthia Costello and Barbara Kivimae Krimgold (Eds.) for the Women's Research and Education Institute, *The American Woman 1996–97: Women and Work.* New York: W.W. Norton, pp. 23–32.

Cottle, Charles E., Patricia Searles, Ronald J. Berger, and Beth Ann Pierce. 1989. "Conflicting Ideologies and the Politics of Pornography." *Gender and Society,* 3:303–333.

Court TV. 1996. "Prime Time Justice." Ruth Harlow interview by anchor Terry Moran (November 21).

Coverman, Shelley. 1989. "Women's Work Is Never Done: The Division of Domestic Labor." In Jo Freeman (Ed.), *Women: A Feminist Perspective* (4th ed.). Mountain View, CA: Mayfield, pp. 356–368.

Cowan, Gloria, C. Lee, D. Levy, and D. Snyder. 1988. "Domination and Inequality in X-Rated Videocassettes." *Psychology of Women Quarterly,* 12:299–311.

Cowan, Gloria, and Margaret O'Brien. 1990. "Gender and Survival vs. Death in Slasher Films: A Content Analysis." *Sex Roles,* 23:187–196.

Cowgill, Donald O. 1986. *Aging around the World.* Belmont, CA: Wadsworth.

Cowley, Geoffrey. 1997. "Can Marijuana Be Medicine?" *Newsweek* (February 3):22–27.

Cox, Oliver C. 1948. *Caste, Class, and Race.* Garden City, NY: Doubleday.

Cozic, Charles P. (Ed.). 1993. *America's Cities: Opposing Viewpoints.* San Diego, CA: Greenhaven Press.

Crossette, Barbara. 1996a. "Agency Sees Risk in Drug to Temper Child Behavior: Worldwide Survey Cites Overuse of Ritalin." *New York Times* (February 29):A7.

Crossette, Barbara. 1996b. "U.N. Survey Finds World Rich-Poor Gap Widening." *New York Times* (July 15):A3.

Crossette, Barbara. 1996c. "Hope, and Pragmatism, for U.S. Cities Conference." *New York Times* (June 3):A3.

Crossette, Barbara. 1997. "Democracies Love Peace, Don't They?" *New York Times* (June 1):E3.

Cumming, Elaine C., and William E. Henry. 1961. *Growing Old: The Process of Disengagement.* New York: Basic Books.

Curatolo, Peter W., and David Robertson. 1983. "The Health Consequences of Caffeine." *Annals of Internal Medicine,* 98:641–653. (Cited in Levinthal, 1996.)

Cushman, John H., Jr. 1997. "E.P.A. Seeks Cut, Not End, to Pollution by Paper Mills." *New York Times* (May 21):A10.

Dahl, Robert A. 1961. *Who Governs?* New Haven, CT: Yale University Press.

Daley, Suzanne. 1997. "Zaïre's Fall Jolts Neighboring Angola's Frail Peace." *New York Times* (June 8):3.

Daly, Kathleen, and Meda Chesney-Lind. 1988. "Feminism and Criminology." *Justice Quarterly,* 5:497–533.

Dandaneau, Steven P. 1996. *A Town Abandoned: Flint, Michigan, Confronts Deindustrialization.* Albany, NY: State University of New York Press.

Danziger, Sheldon, and Peter Gottschalk. 1995. *America Unequal.* Cambridge, MA: Harvard University Press.

Darling, Lynn. 1994. "As Customers Age, Marketers Discover New Notions of Beauty." *New York Times* (January 24):B1.

Davidson, Julia O'Connell. 1996. "Sex Tourism in Cuba." *Race and Class,* 38(1):39–49.

Davis, F. James. 1991. *Who Is Black? One Nation's Definition.* University Park, PA: Pennsylvania State University Press.

Davis, Kingsley. 1937. "The Sociology of Prostitution." *American Sociological Review,* 2:744–755.

Davis, Kingsley, and Amyra Grossbard-Shechtman (Eds.). 1985. *Contemporary Marriage: Comparative Perspectives on a Changing Institution.* New York: Russell Sage Foundation.

Davis, Nancy J., and Robert V. Robinson. 1988. "Class Identification of Men and Women in the 1970s and 1980s." *American Sociological Review,* 53(February):103–112.

Dawes, Amy. 1995. "Latinos Keep Pounding on Network Doors." *Austin American-Statesman* (October 22):4.

Deans, Bob. 1995. "Women in Japan Still Face Family vs. Career Conflict." *Austin American-Statesman* (September 3):E4.

De Castro, Steven. 1994. "Identity in Action: A Filipino American's Perspective." In Karin Aguilar-San Juan (Ed.), *The State of Asian America: Activism and Resistance in the 1990s.* Boston: South End Press, pp. 295–320.

Dell'Angela, Tracy, and Jon Anderson. 1995. "Trash TV Has Its Fans, Critics." *Austin American-Statesman* (November 19):7.

DeParle, Jason. 1994. "Despising Welfare, Pitying Its Young." *New York Times* (December 18):E5.

de Silva, Rex. 1980. "Developing the Third World." *World Press Review* (May):48.

Devereaux, Anna. 1987. "Diary of a Prostitute." *Cosmopolitan* (October 1987):164, 166.

DeWitt, Karen. 1992. "The Nation's Schools Learn a 4th R: Resegregation." *New York Times* (January 19):A5.

DeWitt, Karen. 1994. "Wave of Suburban Growth Is Being Fed by Minorities." *New York Times* (August 15):A1, A12.

Dews, Peter B. 1984. "Behavioral Effects of Caffeine." In Peter B. Dews (Ed.), *Caffeine: Perspectives from Recent Research.* Berlin: Springer-Verlag, pp. 86–103. (Cited in Levinthal, 1996.)

Diamond, Timothy. 1992. *Making Gray Gold: Narratives of Nursing Home Care.* Chicago: University of Chicago Press.

Dietz, P. 1986. "Mass, Serial and Sensational Homicide." *Bulletin of the New England Medical Society,* 62: 477–491.

DiFranza, Joseph R., and Robert A. Lew. 1995. "Effect of Maternal Cigarette Smoking on Pregnancy Complications and Sudden Infant Death Syndrome." *The Journal of Family Practice,* 40:385–394.

DiFranza, Joseph R., John W. Richards, Jr., Paul M. Paulman, Nancy Wolf-Gillespie, Christopher Fletcher, Robert D. Jaffe, and David Murray. 1991. "RJR Nabisco's Cartoon Camel Promotes Camel Cigarettes to Children." *Journal of the American Medical Association,* 266 (22):3149–3153.

Dill, Bonnie Thornton. 1988. "'Making Your Job Good Yourself': Domestic Service and the Construction of Personal Dignity." In Ann Bookman and Sandra Morgen (Eds.), *Women and the Politics of Empowerment.* Philadelphia: Temple University Press, pp. 33–52.

Dines, Gail. 1995. "'I Buy It for the Articles': *Playboy* Magazine and the Sexualization of Consumerism." In Gail Dines and Jean M. Humez (Eds.), *Gender, Race and Class in Media: A Text-Reader.* Thousand Oaks, CA: Sage, pp. 254–262.

Dobrzynski, Judith H. 1996a. "Study Finds Few Women in 5 Highest Company Jobs." *New York Times* (October 16):C3.

Dobrzynski, Judith H. 1996b. "When Directors Play Musical Chairs." *New York Times* (November 17):F1, F8, F9.

Dollard, John, Neal E. Miller, Leonard W. Doob, O. H. Mowrer, and Robert R. Sears. 1939. *Frustration and Aggression.* New Haven, CT: Yale University Press.

Domhoff, G. William. 1978. *The Powers That Be: Processes of Ruling Class Domination in America.* New York: Random House.

Domhoff, G. William. 1983. *Who Rules America Now?* New York: Touchstone.

Domhoff, G. William. 1990. *The Power Elite and the State: How Policy Is Made in America.* New York: Aldine De Gruyter.

Donziger, Steven R. (Ed.). 1996. *The Real War on Crime: The Report of the National Criminal Justice Commission.* New York: HarperPerennial.

Dougherty, Robin. 1996. "Hispanic Actor Worries about Sitcom Politics." *Austin American-Statesman* (August 4):6.

Doyle, James A. 1995. *The Male Experience* (3rd ed.). Madison, WI: Brown and Benchmark.

Dreyfuss, Robert. 1996. "Good Morning, Gun Lobby!" *Mother Jones* (July–August):38–47.

Du Phuoc Long, Patrick (with Laura Ricard). 1996. *The Dream Shattered: Vietnamese Gangs in America.* Boston: Northeastern University Press.

Dull, Diana, and Candace West. 1991. "Accounting for Cosmetic Surgery: The Accomplishments of Gender." *Social Problems,* 38(1):54–70.

Duncan, David F. 1991. "Violence and Degradation as Themes in 'Adult' Videos." *Psychology Reports,* 69(1): 239–240.

Dunlap, David W. 1995. "Court Upholds Anti-Homosexual Initiative." *New York Times* (May 14):10.

Dunlap, David W. 1996. "Role of Openly Gay Episcopalians Causes a Rift in the Church." *New York Times* (March 21):A8.

Dunlap, Riley E. 1992. "Trends in Public Opinion toward Environmental Issues: 1965–1990." In Riley E. Dunlap and Angela G. Mertig (Eds.), *American Environmentalism: The U.S. Environmental Movement, 1970–1990.* New York: Taylor & Francis, pp. 89–113.

Dunn, Ashley. 1995. "Cram Schools: Immigrants' Tools for Success." *New York Times* (January 28):1, 9.

Duran, Lisa. 1997. "Ignorance about Immigrants." *Austin American-Statesman* (May 19):A7.

Durkheim, Emile. [1915] 1965. *The Elementary Forms of the Religious Life,* translated by J.W. Swain. New York: The Free Press. In Bunis, William K., Angela Yancik, and David Snow. 1996. "The Cultural Patterning of Sympathy toward the Homeless and Other Victims of Misfortune." *Social Problems* (November):387–402.

Durkheim, Emile. 1933. *Division of Labor in Society.* Trans. George Simpson. New York: Free Press (orig. published in 1893).

Durkheim, Emile. 1964. *The Rules of Sociological Method.* Trans. Sarah A. Solovay and John H. Mueller. New York: Free Press (orig. pub. 1895).

Duster, Troy. 1995. "Symposium: The Bell Curve." *Contemporary Sociology: A Journal of Reviews,* 24(2): 158–161.

Dworkin, Andrea. 1988. *Letters to a War Zone.* New York: Dutton/New America Library.

Dye, Thomas R., and Harmon Zeigler. 1993. *The Irony of Democracy: An Uncommon Introduction to American Politics* (9th ed.). Belmont, CA: Wadsworth.

Dynes, Wayne R. (Ed.). 1990. *Encyclopedia of Homosexuality.* New York: Garland.

Eaton, William W. 1980. "A Formal Theory of Selection for Schizophrenia." *American Journal of Sociology,* 86:149–158.

Eberstadt, Nicholas. 1992. "America's Infant Mortality Problem: Parents." *Wall Street Journal* (January 20):A12.

The Ecologist. 1993. *Whose Common Future? Reclaiming the Commons.* Philadelphia, PA: New Society Publishers.

The Economist. 1995. "Size of the Internet" (April 15):102.

Eder, Donna. 1985. "The Cycle of Popularity: Interpersonal Relations among Female Adolescents." *Sociology of Education,* 58(July):154–165.

Eder, Donna, and Stephen Parker. 1987. "The Cultural Production and Reproduction of Gender: The Effect of Extracurricular Activities on Peer Group Culture." *Sociology of Education,* 60:200–213.

Edwards, Richard. 1979. *Contested Terrain*. New York: Basic Books.

Egan, Timothy. 1996. "Back From Everest, Haunted by Death and Doubt." *New York Times* (May 23):B1, B4.

Ehrenreich, Barbara. 1997. *Blood Rites: Origins and History of the Passions of War*. New York: Metropolitan Books.

Ehrenreich, Barbara, and Annette Fuentes. 1981. "Life on the Global Assembly Line." *Ms.* (January):52–59.

Ehrlich, Paul R., and Anne H. Ehrlich. 1991. *The Population Explosion*. New York: Touchstone/Simon & Schuster.

Eitzen, D. Stanley, and Maxine Baca Zinn. 1994. *Social Problems* (6th ed.). Boston: Allyn and Bacon.

Elliott, Marta, and Lauren J. Krivo. 1991. "Structural Determinants of Homelessness in the United States." *Social Problems*, 38(1):113–131.

Ellis, Lee. 1989. *Theories of Rape: Inquiries into the Causes of Sexual Aggression*. New York: Hemisphere.

Elmer-Dewitt, Philip. 1995. "Snuff Porn on the Net." *Time* (February 20):69.

Engelhardt, H. Tristan, Jr. 1996. *Foundations of Bioethics*. New York: Oxford University Press.

Engels, Friedrich. 1972. *The Origins of the Family, Private Property, and the State*. (Ed. Eleanor Burke Leacock). New York: International.

Enloe, Cynthia H. 1987. "Feminists Thinking about War, Militarism, and Peace." In Beth Hess and Myra Marx Ferree (Eds.), *Analyzing Gender: A Handbook of Social Science Research*. Newbury Park, CA: Sage, pp. 526–547.

Epstein, Cynthia Fuchs. 1988. *Deceptive Distinctions: Sex, Gender, and the Social Order*. New Haven, CT: Yale University Press.

Epstein, Cynthia Fuchs. 1993. *Women in Law* (3rd ed.). Urbana, IL: University of Illinois Press.

Erikson, Kai T. 1962. "Notes on the Sociology of Deviance." *Social Problems*, 9:307–314.

Erikson, Kai T. 1991. "A New Species of Trouble." In Stephen Robert Crouch and J. Stephen Kroll-Smith (Eds.), *Communities at Risk: Collective Responses to Technological Hazards*. New York: Peter Land, pp. 11–29.

Erikson, Kai T. 1994. *A New Species of Trouble: Explorations in Disaster, Trauma, and Community*. New York: Norton.

Espiritu, Yen Le. 1995. *Filipino American Lives*. Philadelphia: Temple University Press.

Essed, Philomena. 1991. *Understanding Everyday Racism*. Newbury Park, CA: Sage.

Estrich, Susan. 1987. *Real Rape*. Cambridge, MA: Harvard University Press.

Facts on File. 1995. "Divine Brown." 55 (October 19):792.

Fagot, Beverly I. 1984. "Teacher and Peer Reactions to Boys' and Girls' Play Styles." *Sex Roles*, 11:691–702.

Fairstein, Linda A. 1995. *Sexual Violence: Our War against Rape*. New York: Berkley.

Faludi, Susan. 1991. *Backlash: The Undeclared War against American Women*. New York: Crown.

FAO. 1995. *FAO Yearbook 1995*. Rome, Italy: Food and Agricultural Organization of the United Nations.

Farnsworth, Clyde H. 1993. "Soaring Costs for Health Care Touch Off Service Cuts and Fees." *New York Times* (November 14):HD9.

Feagin, Joe R. 1975. *Subordinating the Poor: Welfare and American Beliefs*. Englewood Cliffs, NJ: Prentice-Hall.

Feagin, Joe R., and Clairece Booher Feagin. 1994. *Social Problems: A Critical Power-Conflict Perspective* (4th ed.). Englewood Cliffs, NJ: Prentice-Hall.

Feagin, Joe R., and Clairece Booher Feagin. 1996. *Racial and Ethnic Relations* (5th ed.). Upper Saddle River, NJ: Prentice-Hall.

Feagin, Joe R., and Robert Parker. 1990. *Building American Cities: The Urban Real Estate Game* (2nd ed.). Englewood Cliffs, NJ: Prentice-Hall.

Feagin, Joe R., and Melvin P. Sikes. 1994. *Living with Racism: The Black Middle-Class Experience*. Boston: Beacon Press.

Feagin, Joe R., and Hernán Vera. 1995. *White Racism: The Basics*. New York: Routledge.

Fedders, Charlotte, and Laura Elliott. 1987. *Shattered Dreams*. New York: Dell.

Federal Bureau of Investigation (FBI). 1995a. *Crime in the United States, 1994*. Washington, DC: U.S. Government Printing Office.

Federal Bureau of Investigation (FBI). 1995b. *Uniform Crime Reports for the United States: 1994*. Washington, DC: U.S. Department of Justice.

Federal Bureau of Investigation (FBI). 1996. *Crime in the United States, 1995*. Washington, DC: U.S. Government Printing Office.

Fenstermacher, Gary D. 1994. "The Absence of Democratic and Educational Ideals from Contemporary Educational Reform Initiatives." The Elam Lecture, presented to the Educational Press Association of America. Chicago, June 10.

Fernandez, Joseph M. 1991. "Bringing Hate Crime into Focus." *Harvard Civil Rights–Civil Liberties Law Review*, 26(1):261–293.

Findlen, Barbara. 1995. "Is Marriage the Answer? Domestic Partnership Activists Don't Think So." *Ms.* (May–June):86–91.

Fine, Gary Alan. 1987. *With the Boys: Little League Baseball and Preadolescent Culture*. Chicago: University of Chicago Press.

Fine, Michelle. 1991. *Framing Dropouts: Notes on the Politics of an Urban Public High School*. Albany, NY: State University Press of New York.

Fineman, Howard. 1997. "Who Needs Washington?" *Newsweek* (January 27):50–52.

Finkelhor, David. 1984. *Child Abuse: New Theory and Research*. New York: Free Press.

Finkelhor, David, and Kersti Yllo. 1985. *License to Rape: Sexual Abuse of Wives.* New York: Free Press.

Firestone, Shulamith. 1970. *The Dialectic of Sex.* New York: Morrow.

Fish, Stanley. 1996. "Professor Sokal's Bad Joke." *New York Times* (May 21):A11.

Fishbein, Diana H., and Susan E. Pease. 1996. *The Dynamics of Drug Abuse.* Boston: Allyn and Bacon.

Fisher, Ian. 1995. "Tobacco Funds Go to Black Officials." *New York Times* (November 19):21.

Fisher, Lawrence M. 1996. "Health on Line: Doctor Is In, and His Disk Is Full." *New York Times* (June 14):C1, C8.

Flanagan, William G. 1995. *Urban Sociology: Images and Structure* (2nd ed.). Boston: Allyn and Bacon.

Flexner, Abraham. 1910. *Medical Education in the United States and Canada.* New York: Carnegie Foundation.

Foreman, Judy. 1993. "Older Adults May Face Obstacles on Job." *San Antonio Express-News* (December 15):B7.

Foreman, Judy. 1996. "Caring for Parents Long-Distance Is a Baby Boomer's Nightmare." *Austin American-Statesman* (November 3):E1, E14.

Fox, Mary Frank. 1995. "Women and Higher Education: Gender Differences in the Status of Students and Scholars." In Jo Freeman (Ed.), *Women: A Feminist Perspective* (5th ed.). Mountain View, CA: Mayfield, pp. 220–237.

Frankenberg, Ruth. 1993. *White Women, Race Matters: The Social Construction of Whiteness.* Minneapolis, MN: University of Minnesota Press.

Franklin, John Hope. 1980. *From Slavery to Freedom* (3rd ed.). New York: Knopf.

Freidson, Eliot. 1970. *Profession of Medicine.* New York: Dodd, Mead.

Freidson, Eliot. 1986. *Professional Powers.* Chicago, IL: University of Chicago Press.

French, Dolores, with Linda Lee. 1988. *Working: My Life As A Prostitute.* New York: E.P. Dutton.

French, Howard W. 1995. "On the Internet, Africa Is Far Behind." *New York Times* (November 17):A8.

Freudenberg, Nicholas, and Carl Steinsapir. 1992. "Not in Our Backyards: The Grassroots Environmental Movement." In Riley E. Dunlap and Angela G. Mertig (Eds.), *American Environmentalism: The U.S. Environmental Movement, 1970–1990.* New York: Taylor & Francis, pp. 27–37.

Freund, Matthew, Nancy Lee, and Terri Leonard. 1991. "Sexual Behavior of Clients with Street Prostitutes in Camden, New Jersey." *Journal of Sex Research,* 28(4) (November):579–591.

Friedan, Betty. 1993. *The Fountain of Age.* New York: Simon & Schuster.

Friedman, George, and Meredith Friedman. 1996. *The Future of War: Power, Technology, and American World Dominance in the 21st Century.* New York: Crown.

Friedman, Robert I. 1996. "The Money Plane." *New York* (January 22):24–33.

Friedmann, John. 1995. "The World City Hypothesis." In Paul L. Knox and Peter J. Taylor (Eds.), *World Cities in a World-System.* Cambridge, England: Cambridge University Press, pp. 317–331.

Friedrichs, David O. 1996. *Trusted Criminals: White Collar Crime in Contemporary Society.* Belmont, CA: Wadsworth.

Friend, Tim. 1996. "Teens and Drugs: Today's Youth Just Don't See the Dangers." *USA Today* (August 21):1A, 2A.

Frohmann, Lisa. 1991. "Discrediting Victims' Allegations of Sexual Assault: Prosecutorial Accounts of Case Rejections." *Social Problems,* 38(2):213–228.

Fugh-Berman, Adriane. 1992. "Tales out of Medical School." In Amber Coverdale Sumrall and Dena Taylor (Eds.), *Sexual Harassment: Women Speak Out.* Freedom, CA: The Crossing Press, pp. 80–84.

Fullilove, Mindy Thompson, E. Anne Lown, and Robert E. Fullilove. 1992. "Crack 'Hos and Skeezers: Traumatic Experiences of Women Crack Users." *Journal of Sex Research,* 29(2):275–288.

Funderburg, Lise. 1994. *Black, White, Other: Biracial Americans Talk about Race and Identity.* New York: William Morrow.

Fussell, Paul. 1992. *Wartime: Understanding and Behavior in the Second World War.* New York: Oxford University Press.

Gabriel, Trip. 1995a. "A New Generation Seems Ready to Give Bisexuality a Place in the Spectrum." *New York Times* (June 12):C10.

Gabriel, Trip. 1995b. "Some On-Line Discoveries Give Gay Youths a Path to Themselves." *New York Times* (July 2):1, 9.

Gabriel, Trip. 1996. "High-Tech Pregnancies Test Hope's Limit." *New York Times* (January 7):1, 10–11.

Gailey, Christine Ward. 1987. "Evolutionary Perspectives on Gender Hierarchy." In Beth B. Hess and Myra Marx Ferree (Eds.), *Analyzing Gender: A Handbook of Social Science Research.* Newbury Park, CA: Sage, pp. 32–67.

Galbraith, John Kenneth. 1985. *The New Industrial State* (4th ed.). Boston: Houghton Mifflin.

Gamson, Joshua. 1996. "Do Tell." *Utne Reader* (January–February):79–83.

Gandy, Oscar H., Jr. 1996. "Coming to Terms with the Panoptic Sort." In David Lyon and Elia Zureik (Eds.), *Computers, Surveillance, and Privacy.* Minneapolis, MN: University of Minnesota Press, pp. 121–155.

Gans, Herbert. 1982. *The Urban Villagers: Group and Class in the Life of Italian Americans* (updated and expanded ed.; orig. pub. 1962). New York: Free Press.

Gardner, Carol Brooks. 1995. *Passing By: Gender and Public Harassment.* Berkeley, CA: University of California Press.

Gardner, Tracey A. 1994. "Racism in Pornography and the Women's Movement." In Alison M. Jaggar (Ed.), *Liv-*

ing with Contradictions: Controversies in Feminist Social Ethics. Boulder, CO: Westview, pp. 171–176.

Gardy, Alison. 1995. "Forging Links between Inner Cities and the Internet." *New York Times* (March 12):F10.

Garfinkel, Irwin, and Sara S. McLanahan. 1986. *Single Mothers and Their Children: A New American Dilemma.* Washington, DC: Urban Institute Press.

Gargan, Edward A. 1997. "Illegal Chinese Race to Get Toehold in Hong Kong." *New York Times International Edition* (May 23, 1997):A3.

Garreau, Joel. 1991. *Edge City: Life on the New Frontier.* New York: Doubleday.

Garson, Barbara. 1989. *The Electronic Sweatshop: How Computers Are Transforming the Office of the Future into the Factory of the Past.* New York: Penguin.

Garson, Barbara. 1994. *All the Livelong Day: The Meaning and Demeaning of Routine Work* (rev. and updated). New York: Penguin.

Gastil, Raymond. 1971. "Homicide and a Regional Culture of Violence." *American Sociological Review,* 36:412–427.

Gatz, Margaret (Ed.). 1995. *Emerging Issues in Mental Health and Aging.* Washington, DC: American Psychological Association.

Gawin, F. H., and E. H. Ellinwood, Jr. 1988. Cocaine and Other Stimulants: Actions, Abuse, and Treatment. *New England Journal of Medicine,* 318:1173–1182.

Gelfand, Donald E. 1994. *Aging and Ethnicity: Knowledge and Services.* New York: Springer.

Gentry, Cynthia. 1995. "Crime Control through Drug Control." In Joseph F. Sheley (Ed.), *Criminology: A Contemporary Handbook* (2nd ed.). Belmont, CA: Wadsworth, pp. 477–493.

Gerbner, George, 1995. "Television Violence: The Power and the Peril." In Gail Dines and Jean M. Humez (Eds.), *Gender, Face, and Class in Media: A Text-Reader.* Thousand Oaks, CA: Sage, pp. 547–557.

Geronimus, Arline T., and Sanders Korenman. 1992. "The Socioeconomic Consequences of Teen Childbearing Reconsidered." *Quarterly Journal of Economics,* 107(4):1187–1214.

Gerson, Kathleen. 1993. *No Man's Land: Men's Changing Commitments to Family and Work.* New York: Basic Books.

Gerstel, Naomi, and Harriet Engel Gross. 1995. "Gender and Families in the United States: The Reality of Economic Dependence." In Jo Freeman (Ed.), *Women: A Feminist Perspective* (5th ed.). Mountain View, CA: Mayfield, pp. 92–127.

Gerth, Jeff. 1997. "China Buying U.S. Computers, Raising Arms Fears." *New York Times* (June 10):A1, A8.

Gessen, Masha. 1993. "Lesbians and Breast Cancer." *The Advocate* (February 9):22–23.

Gibbs, Lois Marie, as told to Murray Levine. 1982. *Love Canal: My Story.* Albany, NY: State University of New York Press.

Gibbs, Nancy. 1994. "Home Sweet School." *Time* (October 31):62–63.

Gibbs, Nancy. 1996. "Cause Celeb: Two High-Profile Entertainers Are Props in a Worldwide Debate over Sweatshops and the Use of Child Labor." *Time* (June 17):28–30.

Gibson, James William, and Francesca M. Cancian. 1990. "Is War Inevitable?" In Francesca M. Cancian and James William Gibson (Eds.), *Making War, Making Peace: The Social Foundations of Violent Conflict.* Belmont, CA: Wadsworth, pp. 1–10.

Gil, Vincent E., Marco S. Wang, Allen F. Anderson, Guo Matthew Lin, and Zongjian Oliver Wu. 1996. "Prostitutes, Prostitution and STD/HIV Transmission in Mainland China." *Social Science and Medicine,* 42(1): 141–153.

Gilbert, Richard J. 1986. *Caffeine: The Most Popular Stimulant.* New York: Chelsea House.

Gilder, George. 1981. *Wealth and Poverty.* New York: Basic Books.

Giobbe, Evelina. 1993. "Surviving Commercial Sexual Exploitation." In Diana E. H. Russell (Ed.), *Making Violence Sexy: Feminist Views on Pornography.* New York: Teachers College Press, pp. 37–41.

Giobbe, Evelina. 1994. "Confronting the Liberal Lies about Prostitution." In Alison M. Jaggar (Ed.), *Living with Contradictions: Controversies in Feminist Social Ethics.* Boulder, CO: Westview, pp. 120–136.

Gladwell, Malcolm. 1997. "Damaged: Why Do Some People Turn into Violent Criminals?" *The New Yorker* (February 24–March 3):132–147.

Glaser, Barney, and Anselm Strauss. 1968. *Time for Dying.* Chicago: Aldine.

Glass Ceiling Commission. 1995. *Good for Business: Making Full Use of the Nation's Human Capital.* Washington, DC: Glass Ceiling Commission.

Gleick, Elizabeth. 1995. "Segregation Anxiety." *Time* (April 24):63.

Gleick, Elizabeth. 1996. "The Children's Crusade." *Time* (June 3):30–35.

Glenn, Evelyn Nakano. 1986. *Issie, Nisei, War Bride: Three Generations of Japanese American Women in Domestic Service.* Philadelphia: Temple University Press.

Glick, Paul C., and Sung-Ling Lin. 1986. "More Young Adults Are Living with Their Parents: Who Are They?" *Journal of Marriage and the Family,* 48:107–112.

Goffman, Erving. 1961. *Asylums: Essays on the Social Situation of Mental Patients and Other Inmates.* Chicago, IL: Aldine.

Golay, Michael, and Carl Rollyson. 1996. *Where America Stands: 1996.* New York: John Wiley.

Gold, Rachel Benson, and Cory L. Richards. 1994. "Securing American Women's Reproductive Health." In Cynthia Costello and Anne J. Stone (Eds.), *The American Woman, 1994–1995.* New York: W.W. Norton, pp. 197–222.

Goldberg, Carey, 1996a. "A Victory for Same-Sex Parenting, at Least." *New York Times* (December 5):A20.

Goldberg, Carey, 1996b. "Brutal Case Illustrates Trend of Guns' Replacing Toys." *New York Times* (August 3):6.

Goldberg, Carey. 1997. "Quiet Roads Bringing Thundering Protests." *New York Times* (May 23):A8.

Golden, Stephanie. 1992. *The Women Outside: Meanings and Myths of Homelessness.* Berkeley, CA: University of California Press.

Gonzalez, David. 1995. "After Infinite Practice at Grief, a Mother Acts." *New York Times* (August 30):A16.

Goode, Erich. 1989. *Drugs in American Society* (3rd ed.). New York: McGraw-Hill.

Goode, Erich. 1996. "Deviance, Norms, and Social Reaction." In Erich Goode (Ed.), *Social Deviance.* Boston: Allyn and Bacon, pp. 36–40.

Goode, William J. 1976. "Family Disorganization." In Robert K. Merton and Robert Nisbet (Eds.), *Contemporary Social Problems* (4th ed). New York: Harcourt Brace Jovanovich, pp. 511–554.

Goode, William J. 1982. "Why Men Resist." In Barrie Thorne with Marilyn Yalom (Eds.), *Rethinking the Family: Some Feminist Questions.* New York: Longman, pp. 131–150.

Goodman, Peter S. 1996. "The High Cost of Sneakers." *Austin American-Statesman* (July 7):F1, F6.

Gordon, David M. 1996. Fat and Mean: The Corporate Squeeze of Working Americans and the Myth of Managerial "Downsizing." New York: Martin Kessler Books/The Free Press.

Gordon, Linda. 1994. *Pitied but Not Entitled: Single Mothers and the History of Welfare.* Cambridge, MA: Harvard University Press.

Gordon, Milton M. 1964. *Assimilation in American Life: The Role of Race, Religion, and National Origins.* New York: Oxford University Press.

Gotlieb, Calvin C. 1996. "Privacy: A Concept Whose Time Has Come and Gone." In David Lyon and Elia Zureik (Eds.), *Computers, Surveillance, and Privacy.* Minneapolis, MN: University of Minnesota Press, pp. 156–171.

Gottdiener, Mark. 1985. *The Social Production of Urban Space.* Austin, TX: University of Texas Press.

Gover, Tzivia. 1996a. "Fighting for Our Children." *The Advocate* (November 26):22–30.

Gover, Tzivia. 1996b. "Occupational Hazards." *The Advocate* (November 26):36–38.

Gover, Tzivia. 1996c. "The Other Mothers." *The Advocate* (November 26):31.

Graham, Lawrence Otis. 1995. "It's No Longer the Back of the Bus, but . . . " *New York Times* (May 21):F13.

Grasmuck, Sherri, and Patricia R. Pessar. 1991. *Between Two Islands: Dominican International Migration.* Berkeley, CA: University of California Press.

Gray, Herman. 1995. *Watching Race: Television and the Struggle for "Blackness."* Minneapolis, MN: University of Minnesota Press.

Gray, Paul. 1996. "Gagging the Doctors." *Time* (January 8):50.

Green, Donald E. 1977. *The Politics of Indian Removal: Creek Government and Society in Crisis.* Lincoln, NE: University of Nebraska Press.

Green, Michelle. 1995. "Fatal Attraction." *People* (March 27):40–44.

Greenberg, Edward S., and Benjamin I. Page. 1993. *The Struggle for Democracy.* New York: HarperCollins.

Greene, Vernon L., and J. I. Ondrich. 1990. "Risk Factors for Nursing Home Admissions and Exits." *Journal of Gerontology,* 45:S250–S258.

Grobe, Jeanine (Ed.). 1995. *Beyond Bedlam: Contemporary Women Psychiatric Survivors Speak Out.* Chicago, IL: Third Side Press.

Gross, Jane. 1994. "Simpson Case Is Galvanizing U.S. About Domestic Abuse." *New York Times* (July 4):1, 9.

Gross, Jane. 1997. "More AIDS Is Seen in People over 50." *New York Times* (March 16):23.

Gross, Leonard. 1983. *How Much Is Too Much: The Effects of Social Drinking.* New York: Random House.

Gubernick, Lisa, with Luisa Kroll. 1996. "Gray Hair Is Cool." *Forbes* (May 6):116.

Guerra, Carlos. 1996. "Education Paves Way to Lifelong Dream." *Austin American-Statesman* (May 15):A11.

Gup, Ted. 1996. "The Mother Jones 400." *Mother Jones* (March–April):39–59, 74–77.

Hacker, Andrew. 1995. *Two Nations: Black and White, Separate, Hostile, Unequal* (rev. ed.). New York: Ballantine Books.

Hagedorn, John M. 1988. *People and Folks: Gangs, Crime, and the Underclass in a Rustbelt City.* Chicago: Lake View Press.

Hall, Roberta M., with Bernice R. Sandler. 1982. *The Classroom Climate: A Chilly One for Women?* Washington, DC: Association of American Colleges, Project on the Status and Education of Women.

Hall, Roberta M. 1984. *Out of the Classroom: A Chilly Campus Climate for Women.* Washington, DC: Association of American Colleges, Project on the Status and Education of Women.

Hamper, Ben. 1991. *Rivethead: Tales from the Assembly Line.* New York: Warner Books.

Haney, Craig, Curtis Banks, and Philip Zimbardo. 1984. "A Study of Prisoners and Guards in a Simulated Prison." In E. Aronson (Ed.)., *Readings about the Social Animal.* New York: W.H. Freeman.

Haney, Walter. 1993. "Testing and Minorities." In Lois Weis and Michelle Fine (Eds.), *Beyond Silenced Voices: Class, Race, and Gender in United States Schools.* Albany, NY: State University of New York Press, pp. 45–73.

Hansell, Saul. 1996. "Identity Crisis: When a Criminal's Got Your Number." *New York Times* (June 16):E1, E5.

Hardy, Eric S. 1996. "Annual Report on American Industry." *Forbes* (January 1):76–79.

Harlow, C. W. 1991. *Female Victims of Violent Crime*. Washington, DC: U.S. Department of Justice, Bureau of Justice Statistics.

Harrington Meyer, Madonna. 1990. "Family Status and Poverty among Older Women: The Gendered Distribution of Retirement Income in the United States." *Social Problems,* 37:551–563.

Harrington Meyer, Madonna. 1994. "Gender, Race, and the Distribution of Social Assistance: Medicaid Use among the Frail Elderly," *Gender and Society,* 8(1):8–28.

Harris, Anthony R., and Lisa R. Meidlinger. 1995. "Criminal Behavior: Race and Class." In Joseph F. Sheley (Ed.), *Criminology: A Contemporary Handbook* (2nd ed.). Belmont, CA: Wadsworth, pp. 115–143.

Hartley, Nina. 1994. "Confessions of a Feminist Porno Star." In Alison M. Jaggar (Ed.), *Living with Contradictions: Controversies in Feminist Social Ethics*. Boulder, CO: Westview, pp. 176–178.

Hartmann, Heidi. 1976. "Capitalism, Patriarchy, and Job Segregation by Sex." *Signs: Journal of Women in Culture and Society,* 1(Spring):137–169.

Hartmann, Heidi. 1981. "The Family as the Locus of Gender, Class, and Political Struggle: The Example of Housework." *Signs,* 6:366–394.

Harvard Medicare Project. 1986. "Special Report: The Future of Medicare." *New England Journal of Medicine,* 314:722–728.

Hauchler, Ingomar, and Paul M. Kennedy (Eds.). 1994. *Global Trends: The World Almanac of Development and Peace*. New York: Continuum.

Hauser, Robert M. 1995. "Symposium: The Bell Curve." *Contemporary Sociology: A Journal of Reviews,* 24(2):149–153.

Havighurst, Robert J., Bernice L. Neugarten, and Sheldon S. Tobin. 1968. "Disengagement and Patterns of Aging." In Bernice L. Neugarten (Ed.), *Middle Age and Aging*. Chicago: University of Chicago Press, pp. 161–172.

Hawken, Paul. 1997. "Resource Waste." *Mother Jones* (March–April):40–53.

Hawley, Amos. 1950. *Human Ecology*. New York: Ronald Press.

Hawley, Amos. 1981. *Urban Society* (2nd ed.). New York: Wiley.

Hays, Constance L. 1995a. "If the Hair Is Gray, Con Artists See Green: The Elderly Are Prime Targets." *New York Times* (May 21):F1, F5.

Hays, Constance L. 1995b. "Increasing Shift Work Challenges Child Care." *New York Times* (June 8):B5.

Hendriks, Aart, Rob Tielman, and Evert van der Veen. 1993. *The Third Pink Book: A Global View of Lesbian and Gay Liberation and Oppression*. Buffalo, NY: Prometheus.

Henry, William A., III. 1990. "Beyond the Melting Pot." *Time* (April 9):28–35.

Herbert, Bob. 1995. "Not a Living Wage." *New York Times* (October 9):A11.

Herbert, Bob. 1996. "In the Mouths of Babes." *New York Times* (October 21):A15.

Herd, D. 1988. "Drinking by Black and White Women: Results from a National Survey." *Social Problems,* 35(5):493–520.

Herek, Gregory M. 1995. "Psychological Heterosexism and Anti-Gay Violence: The Social Psychology of Bigotry and Bashing." In Michael S. Kimmel and Michael A. Messner (Eds.), *Men's Lives* (3rd ed.). Boston: Allyn and Bacon, pp. 341–353.

Hernandez, Raymond. 1997. "New York Offers Pollution Permits to Lure Companies." *New York Times* (May 19):A1, B8.

Herring, Cedric, and Sharon M. Collins. 1995. "Retreat from Equal Opportunity? The Case of Affirmative Action." In Michael Peter Smith and Joe R. Feagin (Eds.), *The Bubbling Cauldron: Race, Ethnicity, and the Urban Crisis*. Minneapolis, MN: University of Minnesota Press, pp. 163–181.

Herrnstein, Richard J., and Charles Murray. 1994. *The Bell Curve: Intelligence and Class Structure in American Life*. New York: Free Press.

Herz, Diane E., and Barbara H. Wootton. 1996. "Women in the Workforce: An Overview." In Cynthia Costello and Barbara Kivimae Krimgold (Eds.) for the Women's Research and Education Institute, *The American Woman 1996–97: Women and Work*. New York: W.W. Norton, pp. 44–78.

Higginbotham, Elizabeth. 1994. "Black Professional Women: Job Ceilings and Employment Sectors." In Maxine Baca Zinn and Bonnie Thornton Dill (Eds.), *Women of Color in U.S. Society*. Philadelphia: Temple University Press, pp. 113–131.

Higley, Stephen Richard. 1995. *Privilege, Power and Place: The Geography of the American Upper Class*. Lanham, MD: Rowman & Littlefield.

Hilden, Patricia Penn. 1995. *When Nickels Were Indians: An Urban, Mixed-Blood Story*. Washington, DC: Smithsonian Institution Press.

Hills, Stuart L. 1971. *Crime, Power, and Morality*. Scranton, PA: Chandler.

Hilsenrath, Jon. 1996. "In China, a Taste of Buy-Me TV." *New York Times* (November 17):F1.

Himmelstein, David U., and Steffie Woolhandler. 1994. *The National Health Program Book: A Source Guide for Advocates*. Monroe, ME: Common Courage.

Hirschi, Travis. 1969. *Causes of Delinquency*. Berkeley: University of California Press.

Hirschi, Travis, and Michael J. Hindelang. 1977. "Intelligence and Delinquency: A Revisionist Review." *American Sociological Review,* 42:571–586.

Hochschild, Arlie Russell. 1997. *The Time Bind: When Work Becomes Home and Home Becomes Work.* New York: Metropolitan Books/Henry Holt.

Hochschild, Arlie Russell, with Ann Machung. 1989. *The Second Shift: Working Parents and the Revolution at Home.* New York: Viking/Penguin.

Hochschild, Jennifer L. 1995. *Facing Up to the American Dream: Race, Class, and the Soul of the Nation.* Princeton, NJ: Princeton University Press.

Hodson, Randy, and Teresa A. Sullivan. 1995. *The Social Organization of Work* (2nd ed.). Belmont, CA: Wadsworth.

Hoffman, Andrew J. 1994. "Love Canal Lives." *E Magazine* (November–December):19–22.

Hoffman, Jan. 1997. "Crime and Punishment: Shame Gains Popularity." *New York Times* (January 16):A1, A11.

Holden, Stephen. 1997. "Pornography as a Way of Life." *New York Times* (January 10):B22.

Holmes, Ronald M. 1983. *The Sex Offender and the Criminal Justice System.* Springfield, IL: Charles C. Thomas.

Holmes, Robert M. 1988. *Serial Murder.* Beverly Hills, CA: Sage.

Holmes, Robert M., and Stephen T. Holmes. 1993. *Murder in America.* Newbury Park, CA: Sage.

Holmes, Steven A. 1996a. "1996 Cost of Teen Pregnancy Is Put at $7 Billion." *New York Times* (June 13):A11.

Holmes, Steven A. 1996b. "Children of Working Poor Are Up Sharply, Study Says." *New York Times* (June 4):C19.

Holmes, Steven A. 1996c. "Education Gap Between Races Closes." *New York Times* (September 6):A8.

Holt, J. 1964. *How Children Fail.* New York: Dell.

Holusha, John. 1993. "The Painful Lessons of Disruption." *New York Times* (March 17):C1, C5.

Hooker, Evelyn. 1957. "The Adjustment of the Male Overt Homosexual." *Journal of Projective Techniques,* 21:18–31.

Hooker, Evelyn. 1958. "Male Homosexuality and the Rorschach." *Journal of Projective Techniques,* 22:33–54.

Hooyman, Nancy R., and H. Asuman Kiyak. 1996. *Social Gerontology: A Multidisciplinary Perspective.* Boston: Allyn and Bacon.

Hopkins, Evans D. 1997. "Lockdown: Life Inside Is Getting Harder." *The New Yorker* (February 24/March 3):66–71.

Horowitz, Allan V. 1982. *Social Control of Mental Illness.* New York: Academic.

Horton, John. 1995. *The Politics of Diversity: Immigration, Resistance, and Change in Monterey Park, California.* Philadelphia, PA: Temple University Press.

Hostetler, A. J. 1995. "Joe Camel Blamed for Rise in Teen Smoking." *Austin American-Statesman* (July 21):A2.

Hounsell, Cindy. 1996. "Women and Pensions: A Policy Agenda." In Cynthia Costello and Barbara Kivimae Krimgold (Eds.) for the Women's Research and Education Institute, *The American Woman 1996–97: Women and Work.* New York: W.W. Norton, pp. 166–173.

Houseknecht, Sharon, Suzanne Vaughn, and Anne Macke. 1984. "Marital Disruption among Professional Women: The Timing of Career and Family Events." *Social Problems,* 31(1):273–284.

Huddle, Donald. 1993. *The Net National Cost of Immigration.* Washington, DC: Carrying Capacity Network.

Human Suffering Index. 1992. Washington, DC: Population Crisis Committee (now Population Action International).

Huston, Aletha C. 1985. "The Development of Sex Typing: Themes from Recent Research." *Developmental Review,* 5:2–17.

Hutchison, Ray, and Charles Kyle. 1993. "Hispanic Street Gangs in Chicago's Public Schools." In Scott Cummings and Daniel J. Monti (Eds.), *Gangs: The Origins and Impact of Contemporary Youth Gangs in the United States.* Albany, NY: State University of New York Press, pp. 113–136.

Hynes, Samuel. 1997. *The Soldiers' Tale: Bearing Witness to Modern War.* New York: Allen Lane/Penguin.

Ignico, Arlene A., and Barbara J. Mead. 1990. "Children's Perceptions of Gender-Appropriate Physical Activities." *Perceptual and Motor Skills,* 71:1275–1281.

Ihinger-Tallman, Marilyn, and Kay Pasley. 1987. *Remarriage.* Newbury Park, CA: Sage.

Inciardi, James A., Ruth Horowitz, and Anne E. Pottieger. 1993. *Street Kids, Street Drugs, Street Crime: An Examination of Drug Use and Serious Delinquency in Miami.* Belmont, CA: Wadsworth.

Inciardi, James, Dorothy Lockwood, and Anne E. Pottieger. 1993. *Women and Crack-Cocaine.* New York: Macmillan.

Jack, Dana Crowley. 1993. *Silencing the Self: Women and Depression.* New York: HarperPerennial.

Jackson, James O. 1995. "It's a Wired, Wired World." *Time: Special Issue: Welcome to Cyberspace* (Spring):80–82.

Jackson, Kenneth T. 1985. *Crabgrass Frontier: The Suburbanization of the United States.* New York: Oxford University Press.

Jacobs, Jane. 1961. *The Death and Life of Great American Cities.* New York: Random House.

Jaffee, David. 1990. *Levels of Socio-economic Development Theory.* Westport, CT: Praeger.

JAMA: The Journal of the American Medical Association. 1996. "Health Care Needs of Gay Men and Lesbians in the United States" (May 1):1354–1360.

James, William H., and Stephen L. Johnson. 1996. *Doin' Drugs: Patterns of African American Addiction.* Austin, TX: University of Texas Press.

Jameson, Sam. 1993. "Sailor on Gay Killing: 'I Would Do It Again.'" *Austin American-Statesman* (May 26):A6.

Jankowski, Martín Sánchez. 1991. *Islands in the Street: Gangs and American Urban Society.* Berkeley, CA: University of California Press.

Janofsky, Michael. 1996a. "Home-Grown Courts Spring Up as Judicial Arm of the Far Right." *New York Times* (April 17):A1, A13.

Janofsky, Michael. 1996b. "Shooting at Johns Hopkins Results in Student's Death." *New York Times* (April 12):A8.

Janofsky, Michael. 1997a. "Money Is Just Part of Woes Facing Washington Schools." *New York Times* (April 16):A17.

Janofsky, Michael. 1997b. "Old Friends, Once Felons, Regroup to Fight Crime." *New York Times* (March 10):A1, A10.

Jarrett, Robin L. 1997. "Living Poor: Family Life among Single Parent, African-American Women." In Diana Kendall (Ed.), *Race, Class, and Gender in a Diverse Society: A Text-Reader.* Boston: Allyn and Bacon, pp. 344–365.

Jayson, Sharon. 1997. "Case of Channel One." *Austin American-Statesman* (January 22):B1, B6.

Jencks, Christopher, Marshall Smith, Henry Acland, Mary J. Bane, David Cohen, Herbert Gintis, Barbara Heyns, and Stephan Michelson. 1972. *Inequality: A Reassessment of the Effect of Family and Schooling in America.* New York: Basic Books.

Johnson, Bruce D., Paul J. Goldstein, Edward Preble, James Schmeidler, Douglas S. Lipton, Barry Spunt, and Thomas Miller. 1985. *Taking Care of Business: The Economics of Crime by Heroin Abusers.* Lexington, MA: Lexington Books.

Johnson, Dirk. 1996. "A Celebration of the Urge to Unplug." *New York Times* (April 15):A8.

Johnston, David, and Janny Scott. 1996. "The Tortured Genius of Theodore Kaczynski." *New York Times* (May 26):1, 15.

Johnston, Lloyd D., Patrick M. O'Malley, and Jerald G. Bachman. 1994. *National Survey Results on Drug Use from the Monitoring the Future Study, 1975–1993,* Vol. 1. Rockville, MD: National Institute on Drug Abuse.

Jolin, Annette. 1994. "On the Backs of Working Prostitutes: Feminist Theory and Prostitution Policy." *Crime and Delinquency,* 40(1):69–83.

Jones, M. Gail, and Jack Wheatley. 1990. "Gender Differences in Teacher-Student Interactions in Science Classrooms." *Journal of Research in Science Teaching,* 27(9):861–874.

Jung, John. 1994. *Under the Influence: Alcohol and Human Behavior.* Pacific Grove, CA: Brooks/Cole.

Kaldor, Mary. 1981. *The Baroque Arsenal.* New York: Hill and Wang.

Kalish, Richard A. 1985. *Death, Grief, and Caring Relationships* (2nd ed.). Monterey, CA: Brooks/Cole.

Kalish, Richard A., and D. K. Reynolds. 1981. *Death and Ethnicity: A Psychocultural Study.* Farmingdale, NY: Baywood.

Kalof, Linda, and Timothy Cargill. 1991. "Fraternity and Sorority Membership and Gender Dominance Attitudes." *Sex Roles,* 25(7–8):417–423.

Kaminer, Wendy. 1990. *A Fearful Freedom: Women's Flight from Equality.* Reading, MA: Addison-Wesley.

Kane, Hal. 1995. "Leaving Home." *Transaction: Social Science and Modern Society* (May–June):16–25.

Kanter, Rosabeth Moss. 1977. *Men and Women of the Corporation.* New York: Basic Books.

Kantrowitz, Barbara. 1993. "Live Wires." *Newsweek* (September 6):42–48.

Kaplan, David A. 1993. "Dumber Than We Thought." *Newsweek* (September 20):44–45.

Kaplan, Robert D. 1996. "Cities of Despair." *New York Times* (June 6):A19.

Karmen, Andrew A. 1995. "Crime Victims." In Joseph F. Sheley (Ed.), *Criminology: A Contemporary Handbook* (2nd ed.). Belmont, CA: Wadsworth, pp. 145–164.

Kasindorf, Jeanie. 1988. "Hustling: Working Girl." *New York* (April 18):56.

Katz, Janet, and William J. Chambliss. 1995. In Joseph F. Sheley (Ed.), *Criminology: A Contemporary Handbook* (2nd ed.). Belmont, CA: Wadsworth, pp. 275–303.

Katz, Michael B. 1989. *The Undeserving Poor: From the War on Poverty to the War on Welfare.* New York: Pantheon Books.

Kayal, Philip M. 1993. *Bearing Witness: Gay Men's Health Crisis and the Politics of AIDS.* Boulder, CO: Westview.

Kaysen, Susanna. 1993. *Girl, Interrupted.* New York: Vintage.

Kellner, Douglas. 1989. *Critical Theory, Marxism and Modernity.* Baltimore: Johns Hopkins University Press.

Kelso, William A. 1994. *Poverty and the Underclass: Changing Perceptions of the Poor in America.* New York: New York University Press.

Kemp, Alice Abel. 1994. *Women's Work: Degraded and Devalued.* Englewood Cliffs, NJ: Prentice-Hall.

Kempe, C. Henry, F. Silverman, B. Steele, W. Droegemueller, and H. Silver. 1962. "The Battered-Child Syndrome." *Journal of the American Medical Association,* 181:17–24.

Kempe, Ruth S., and C. Henry Kempe. 1978. *Child Abuse.* Cambridge, MA: Harvard University Press.

Kennedy, Paul. 1993. *Preparing for the Twenty-First Century.* New York: Random House.

Kessler, Ronald C. 1994. "Lifetime and 12-Month Prevalence of DSM-III-R Psychiatric Disorders in the United States: Results of the National Comorbidity Survey." *JAMA, The Journal of the American Medical Association*, 271 (March 2):654D.

Kessler-Harris, Alice. 1990. *A Woman's Wage: Historical Meanings and Social Consequences.* Lexington, KY: University Press of Kentucky.

Kidron, Michael, and Ronald Segal. 1995. *The State of the World Atlas.* New York: Penguin.

Kiel, Douglas P., David T. Felson, Marian T. Hanna, Jennifer J. Anderson, and Peter W. F. Wilson. 1990. "Caffeine and the Risk of Hip Fracture: The Framington Study." *American Journal of Epidemiology,* 132:675–684.

Kilborn, Peter T. 1993. "Voices of the People: Struggle, Hope and Fear." *New York Times* (November 14):4A1, 4A14.

Kilborn, Peter T. 1996. "With Welfare Overhaul Now Law, States Grapple with the Consequences." *New York Times* (August 23):A1, A10.

Kim, Elaine H., and Eui-Young Yu. 1996. *East to America: Korean American Life Stories.* New York: New Press.

Kimmel, Michael S. 1987. "The Contemporary 'Crisis' in Masculinity in Historical Perspective." In Harry Brod (Ed.), *The Making of Masculinities.* Boston: Allen and Unwin, pp. 121–153.

Kimmel, Michael S. (Ed.). 1990. *Men Confront Pornography.* New York: Crown Books.

King, Leslie, and Madonna Harrington Meyer. 1997. "The Politics of Reproductive Benefits: U.S. Insurance Coverage of Contraceptive and Infertility Treatments." *Gender and Society*, 11(1):8–30.

Kipnis, Laura. 1996. *Bound and Gagged: Pornography and the Politics of Fantasy in America.* New York: Grove Press.

Kitano, Harry H. L., and Roger Daniels. 1995. *Asian Americans: Emerging Minorities* (2nd ed.). Englewood Cliffs, NJ: Prentice-Hall.

Kivel, Paul. 1996. *Uprooting Racism: How White People Can Work for Racial Justice.* Philadelphia: New Society Publishers.

Klein, Naomi. 1996. "Can a McJob Provide a Living Wage?" *Ms.* (May–June):32–38.

Klein, Robert. 1996. "This Funny Business about Comedy and Politics." *New York Times* (November 3):H1, H41.

Kleinfield, N. R. 1996. "The Company as Family, No More." *New York Times* (March 4):Al, A8–A10.

Kling, Rob, and Jonathan P. Allen. 1996. "How the Marriage of Management and Computing Intensifies the Struggle for Personal Privacy." In David Lyon and Elia Zureik (Eds.). *Computers, Surveillance, and Privacy.* Minneapolis, MN: University of Minnesota Press, pp. 104–131.

Klockars, Carl B. 1979. "The Contemporary Crises of Marxist Criminology." *Criminology,* 16:477–515.

Klonoff, Elizabeth A. 1997. *Preventing Misdiagnosis of Women: A Guide to Physical Disorders That Have Psychiatric Symptoms.* Thousand Oaks, CA: Sage.

Kluger, Richard. 1996. *Ashes to Ashes: America's Hundred-Year Cigarette War, the Public Health and the Unabashed Triumph of Philip Morris.* New York: Alfred A. Knopf.

Knapp, Caroline. 1996. *Drinking: A Love Story.* New York: Dial.

Knox, Paul L., and Peter J. Taylor (Eds.). 1995. *World Cities in a World-System.* Cambridge, England: Cambridge University Press.

Knudsen, Dean D. 1992. *Child Maltreatment: Emerging Perspectives.* Dix Hills, NY: General Hall.

Kohn, Melvin L., Atsushi Naoi, Carrie Schoenbach, Carmi Schooler, and Kazimierz M. Slomczynski. 1990. "Positions in the Class Structure and Psychological Functioning in the United States, Japan, and Poland." *American Journal of Sociology*, 95:964–1008.

Kolata, Gina. 1995. "New Picture of Who Will Get AIDS Is Crammed with Addicts." *New York Times* (February 28):A16.

Kolata, Gina. 1996a. "Experts Are at Odds on How Best to Tackle Rise in Teen-Agers' Drug Use." *New York Times* (September 18):A17.

Kolata, Gina. 1996b. "New Era of Robust Elderly Belies the Fears of Scientists." *New York Times* (February 27):A1, B10.

Kolata, Gina. 1996c. "On Fringes of Health Care, Untested Therapies Thrive." *New York Times* (June 17):A1, C11.

Kolbert, Elizabeth. 1995. "Wages of Deceit: Untrue Confessions." *New York Times* (June 11):H1, H29.

Korman, Abraham K. 1988. *The Outsiders: Jews and Corporate America.* Lexington, MA: Lexington Books.

Kosmin, Barry A., and Seymour P. Lachman. 1993. *One Nation under God: Religion in Contemporary American Society.* New York: Crown Trade Paperbacks.

Koss, Mary P. 1988. "Hidden Rape: Sexual Aggression and Victimization in a National Sample of Students in Higher Education." In Ann W. Burgess (Ed.), *Rape and Sexual Assault II.* New York: Garland, pp. 3–25.

Kozol, Jonathan. 1986. *Illiterate America.* New York: Plume/Penguin.

Kozol, Jonathan. 1991. *Savage Inequalities: Children in America's Schools.* New York: HarperPerennial.

Kozol, Jonathan. 1995. *Amazing Grace: The Lives of Children and the Conscience of a Nation.* New York: Crown.

Kramer, Peter D. 1993. *Listening to Prozac.* New York: Viking.

Kristof, Nicholas D. 1996a. "Aging World, New Wrinkles." *New York Times* (September 22):E1, E5.

Kristof, Nicholas D. 1996b. "Asian Childhoods Sacrificed to Prosperity's Lust." *New York Times* (April 14):1, 6.

Kristof, Nicholas D. 1996c. "Guns: One Nation Bars, The Other Requires." *New York Times* (March 10):E3.

Krohn, Marvin. 1995. "Control and Deterrence Theories of Criminality." In Joseph F. Sheley (Ed.), *Criminology: A Contemporary Handbook* (2nd ed.). Belmont, CA: Wadsworth, pp. 329–347.

Kübler-Ross, Elisabeth. 1969. *On Death and Dying.* New York: Macmillan.

Kurz, Demie. 1989. "Social Science Perspectives on Wife Abuse: Current Debates and Future Directions." *Gender and Society*, 3(4):489–505.

Kurz, Demie. 1995. *For Richer, for Poorer: Mothers Confront Divorce.* New York: Routledge.

LaFree, Gary D. 1980. "The Effect of Sexual Stratification by Race on Official Reactions to Rape." *American Sociological Review,* 45:824–854.

LaFree, Gary D. 1989. *Race and Criminal Justice: The Social Construction of Sexual Assault.* Belmont, CA: Wadsworth.

Lamanna, Marianne, and Agnes Riedmann. 1994. *Marriages and Families: Making Choices and Facing Change* (5th ed.). Belmont, CA: Wadsworth.

Landers, Peter. 1996. "Women in Japan Covet Flight Positions." *Austin American-Statesman* (April 28):G5.

Langelan, Martha J. 1993. *Back Off! How to Confront and Stop Sexual Harassment and Harassers.* New York: Fireside/Simon & Schuster.

Langford, Terri. 1996. "Welfare Recipients Must Make Job Promise Today." *Austin American-Statesman* (June 1):B6.

Lantos, T. 1992. "The Silence of the Kids: Children at Risk in the Workplace." *Labor Law Journal,* 43:67–70.

Laqueur, W. 1978. *The Terrorism Reader: A Historical Anthology.* New York: New American Library.

Larson, Magali Sarfatti. 1977. *The Rise of Professionalism: A Sociological Analysis.* Berkeley, CA: University of California Press.

Lauber, Almon W. 1913. *Indian Slavery in Colonial Times within the Present Limits of the United States.* New York: Columbia University Press.

Lauderback, David, and Dan Waldorf. 1993. "Whatever Happened to ICE: The Latest Drug Scare." *Journal of Drug Issues,* 23:597–613.

Lauer, Robert H. 1995. *Social Problems and the Quality of Life* (6th ed.). Madison, WI: Brown.

Lauer, Robert H., and Jeannette C. Lauer. 1991. "The Long-Term Relational Consequences of Problematic Family Backgrounds." *Family Relations,* 40:286–290.

Laurence, Leslie, and Beth Weinhouse. 1994. *Outrageous Practices: The Alarming Truth About How Medicine Mistreats Women.* New York: Fawcett Columbine.

Lawrence, Mike. 1996. "Prisoners of Another Reality." *The Mission,* 23 (Spring). San Antonio, TX: The University of Texas Health Science Center at San Antonio.

Lazare, Daniel. 1991. "Urbacide!" *The Village Voice* (December 10). Reprinted in Charles P. Cozic (Ed.), *America's Cities: Opposing Viewpoints.* San Diego, CA: Greenhaven Press, 1993, pp. 17–24.

Leaper, Campbell. 1994. *Childhood Gender Segregation: Causes and Consequences.* San Francisco: Jossey-Bass.

Leary, Warren E. 1996. "Even When Covered by Insurance, Black and Poor People Receive Less Health Care." *New York Times* (September 12):A10.

Leary, Warren E. 1997. "Researchers Investigate (Horrors!) Nicotine's Potential Benefits." *New York Times* (January 14):B11.

Lederman, Douglas. 1992. "NCAA Officials Try to Counter Charges of Sex Bias in Sports," *The Chronicle of Higher Education* (April 15):A43–A44.

Lee, D. J., and Kyriakos S. Markides. 1990. "Activity and Mortality among Aged Persons over an Eight Year Period." *Journal of Gerontology,* 45:S39–S42.

Lee, Felicia R. 1996. "Infertile Couples Forge Ties within Society of Their Own." *New York Times* (January 9):A1, A7.

Lefrançois, Guy R. 1993. *The Lifespan* (4th ed.). Belmont, CA: Wadsworth.

Lehmann, Jennifer M. 1994. *Durkheim and Women.* Lincoln, NE: University of Nebraska Press.

Lehne, Gregory K. 1995. "Homophobia among Men: Supporting and Defining the Male Role." In Michael S. Kimmel and Michael A. Messner (Eds.), *Men's Lives* (3rd ed.). Boston: Allyn and Bacon, pp. 325–336.

Leidner, Robin. 1993. *Fast Food, Fast Talk: Service Work and the Routinization of Everyday Life.* Berkeley, CA: University of California Press.

Leinberger, Christopher B. 1992. "Business Flees to the Urban Fringe." *The Nation* (July 6):10–14.

Leinen, Stephen. 1993. *Gay Cops.* New Brunswick, NJ: Rutgers University Press.

Leland, John. 1995. "Bisexuality." *Newsweek* (July 17): 44–50.

Lemert, Edwin. 1951. *Social Pathology.* New York: McGraw-Hill.

Lemert, Edwin. 1953. "An Isolation and Closure Theory of Naive Check Forgery." *Journal of Criminal Law and Police Science,* 44:297–298.

Leong, Russell (Ed.). 1996. *Asian American Sexualities: Dimensions of the Gay and Lesbian Experience.* New York: Routledge.

Leong, Wai-Teng. 1991. "The Pornography 'Problem': Disciplining Women and Young Girls." *Media, Culture, and Society,* 13:91–117.

Lerman, Hannah. 1996. *Pigeonholing Women's Misery: A History and Critical Analysis of the Psychodiagnosis of Women in the Twentieth Century.* New York: Basic Books.

Lester, David. 1992. *Why People Kill Themselves: A 1990s Summary of Research Findings of Suicidal Behavior* (3rd ed.). Springfield, IL: Thomas.

LeVay, Simon, and Dean H. Hamer. 1994. "Evidence for a Biological Influence in Male Homosexuality." *Scientific American* (May):45–49.

Lever, Janet. 1978. "Sex Differences in the Complexity of Children's Play and Games." *American Sociological Review,* 43:471–483.

Levin, Jack, and Jack McDevitt. 1993. *Hate Crimes: The Rising Tide of Bigotry and Bloodshed.* New York: Plenum.

Levin, William C. 1988. "Age Stereotyping: College Student Evaluations." *Research on Aging,* 10(1): 134–148.

Levine, Peter. 1992. *Ellis Island to Ebbets Field: Sport and the American Jewish Experience.* New York: Oxford University Press.

Levinthal, Charles F. 1996. *Drugs, Behavior, and Modern Society.* Boston: Allyn and Bacon.

Lewin, Tamar. 1995. "The Decay of Families Is Global, Study Says." *New York Times* (May 30):A5.

Lewis, Neil A. 1995a. "Administration Won't Join Attack on Gay Rights Ban." *New York Times* (June 9):A11.

Lewis, Neil A. 1995b. "At the Bar." *New York Times* (May 5):A11.

Lewis, Oscar. 1966. *La Vida: A Puerto Rican Family in the Culture of Poverty—San Juan and New York.* New York: Random House.

Lichter, S. Robert, Linda S. Lichter, and Stanley Rothman. 1991. *Watching America.* New York: Prentice-Hall.

Liebow, Elliot. 1993. *Tell Them Who I Am: The Lives of Homeless Women.* New York: Free Press.

Lifton, Robert Jay. 1997. "Doubling: The Faustian Bargain." In Jennifer Turpin and Lester R. Kurtz (Eds.), *The Web of Violence: From Interpersonal to Global.* Urbana and Chicago: University of Illinois, pp. 31–44.

Lindblom, Charles. 1977. *Politics and Markets.* New York: Basic Books.

Lindsey, Linda L. 1994. *Gender Roles: A Sociological Perspective* (2nd ed.). Englewood Cliffs, NJ: Prentice-Hall.

Link, Bruce G., and Bruce P. Dohrenwend. 1989. "The Epidemiology of Mental Disorders." In Howard E. Freeman and Sol Levine (Eds.), *Handbook of Medical Sociology* (4th ed.). Englewood Cliffs, NJ: Prentice-Hall, pp. 102–127.

Lips, Hilary M. 1993. *Sex and Gender: An Introduction* (2nd ed.). Mountain View, CA: Mayfield.

Littlefield, Kinney. 1995. "Gray: TV's Least Favorite Color." *Austin American-Statesman* (May 28):5.

Loeb, Paul Rogat. 1994. *Generation at the Crossroads: Apathy and Action on the American Campus.* New Brunswick, NJ: Rutgers University Press.

Loftin, Colin, and Robert H. Hill. 1974. "Regional Subculture and Homicide: An Examination of the Gastil-Hackney Thesis." *American Sociological Review,* 39:714–724.

London, Kathryn A. 1991. "Advance Data Number 194: Cohabitation, Marriage, Marital Dissolution, and Remarriage: United States 1988." U.S. Department of Health and Human Services. Vital and Health Statistics of the National Center, January 4.

London, Kathryn A., and Barbara Foley Wilson. 1988. "Divorce." *American Demographics,* 10(10):23–26.

Lorber, Judith. 1994. *Paradoxes of Gender.* New Haven, CT: Yale University Press.

Lorenz, Konrad. 1996. *On Aggression.* New York: Bantam.

Los Angeles Times. 1988. "If Only the Spirit of Giving Could Continue." (December 25).

Lottes, Ilsa. 1993. "Reactions to Pornography on a College Campus: For or Against?" *Sex Roles: A Journal of Research,* 29(1–2):69–90.

Loury, Glenn C. 1997. "Integration Has Had Its Day." *New York Times* (April 23):A21.

Luckenbill, David F. 1977. "Criminal Homicide as a Situated Transaction." *Social Problems,* 25:176–186.

Luker, Kristin. 1996. *Dubious Conceptions: The Politics of Teenage Pregnancy.* Cambridge, MA: Harvard University Press.

Lundberg, Ferdinand. 1988. *The Rich and the Super-Rich: A Study in the Power of Money Today.* Secaucus, NJ: Lyle Stuart.

Lundy, Katherine Coleman. 1995. *Sidewalk Talk: A Naturalistic Study of Street Kids.* New York: Garland Publishing.

Lyon, David. 1994. *The Electronic Eye: The Rise of Surveillance Society.* Minneapolis, MN: University of Minnesota Press.

Lyon, David, and Elia Zureik (Eds.). 1996. *Computers, Surveillance, and Privacy.* Minneapolis, MN: University of Minnesota Press.

Maas, Peter. 1996. *Love Thy Neighbor: A Story of War.* New York: Vintage.

Maccoby, Eleanor E., and Carol Nagy Jacklin. 1987. "Gender Segregation in Childhood." *Advances in Child Development and Behavior,* 20:239–287.

MacCorquodale, Patricia, and Gary Jensen. 1993. "Women in the Law: Partners or Tokens?" *Gender and Society,* 7(4):582–593.

MacDonald, Kevin, and Ross D. Parke. 1986. "Parental-Child Physical Play: The Effects of Sex and Age of Children and Parents." *Sex Roles,* 15:367–378.

Macdonald, Scott. 1995. "The Role of Drugs in Workplace Injuries: Is Drug Testing Appropriate?" *Journal of Drug Issues,* 25(4):703–723.

MacFarquhar, Neil. 1996. "The Internet Goes to School, and Educators Debate." *New York Times* (March 7):C3.

MacKinnon, Catharine. 1987. *Feminism Unmodified: Discourses on Life and Law*. Cambridge, MA: Harvard University Press.

MacLeod, Jay. 1995. *Ain't No Makin' It: Aspirations and Attainment in a Low-Income Neighborhood*. Boulder, CO: Westview Press.

Macy, Marianne. 1996. *Working Sex: An Odyssey into Our Cultural Underworld*. New York: Carroll & Graf.

Madden, Patricia A., and Joel W. Grube. 1994. "The Frequency and Nature of Alcohol and Tobacco Advertising in Televised Sports, 1990 through 1992." *The American Journal of Public Health*, 84(2):297–300.

Malinowski, Bronislaw. 1964. "The Principle of Legitimacy: Parenthood, the Basis of Social Structure." In Rose Laub Coser (Ed.), *The Family: Its Structure and Functions*. New York: St Martin's Press.

Malthus, Thomas R. 1965. *An Essay on Population*. New York: Augustus Kelley, Bookseller (orig. pub. 1798).

Mam, Teeda Butt. 1997. *Children of Cambodia's Killing Fields*. New Haven, CT: Yale University Press.

Mandel, Ruth B. 1981. *In the Running: The New Woman Candidate*. New Haven, CT: Ticknor & Fields.

Mann, Coramae Richey. 1993. *Unequal Justice: A Question of Color*. Bloomington, IN: Indiana University Press.

Mann, Patricia S. 1994. *Micro-Politics: Agency in a Post-Feminist Era*. Minneapolis, MN: University of Minnesota Press.

Marable, Manning. 1995. *Beyond Black and White: Transforming African-American Politics*. New York: Verso.

Marcus, Eric. 1992. *Making History: The Struggle for Gay and Lesbian Equal Rights*. New York: HarperCollins.

Marger, Martin N. 1994. *Race and Ethnic Relations: American and Global Perspectives*. Belmont, CA: Wadsworth.

Marine, William M., and Tracy Jack. 1994. "Analysis of Toxology Reports from the 1992 Census of Fatal Occupational Injuries." *Compensation and Working Conditions*, 46(10):1–7.

Marquart, James W., Sheldon Ekland-Olson, and Jonathan R. Sorensen. 1994. *The Rope, The Chair, and the Needle*. Austin, TX: University of Texas Press.

Marshall, Victor W. 1980. *Last Chapters: A Sociology of Aging and Dying*. Monterey, CA: Brooks/Cole.

Marshall, Victor W., and Judith Levy. 1990. "Aging and Dying." In Robert H. Binstock and Linda George (Eds.), *Handbook of Aging and the Social Sciences* (3rd ed). New York: Academic Press.

Martin, Carol L. 1989. "Children's Use of Gender-Related Information in Making Social Judgments." *Developmental Psychology*, 25:80–88.

Martin, Laura. 1992. *A Life without Fear*. Nashville, TN: Rutledge Hill Press.

Martin, Teresa Castro, and Larry L. Bumpass. 1989. "Recent Trends in Marital Disruption." *Demography*, 26:37–51.

Marx, Karl, and Friedrich Engels. 1971. "The Communist Manifesto." [orig. pub. 1847]. In Dirk Struik (Ed.), *The Birth of the Communist Manifesto*. New York: International.

Marx, Karl, and Friedrich Engels. 1976. *The Communist Manifesto*. New York: Pantheon (orig. pub. 1848).

Massey, Douglas S., and Nancy A. Denton. 1992. *American Apartheid: Segregation and the Making of the Underclass*. Cambridge, MA: Harvard University Press.

Massey, James L., and Marvin D. Krohn. 1986. "A Longitudinal Examination of an Integrated Social Process Model of Deviant Behavior." *Social Forces*, 65:106–134.

Mastrofski, Stephen D. 1995. "The Police." In Joseph F. Sheley (Ed.), *Criminology: A Contemporary Handbook* (2nd ed.). Belmont, CA: Wadsworth, pp. 373–405.

Mathews, Jay. 1992. "Rethinking Homeless Myths." *Newsweek* (April 6):29.

Mathis, Nancy. 1996. "Clinton Urges Student Uniforms." *Houston Chronicle* (February 25):6A.

Mayall, Alice, and Diana E. H. Russell. 1993. "Racism in Pornography." In Diana E. H. Russell (Ed.), *Making Violence Sexy: Feminist Views on Pornography*. New York: Teachers College Press, pp. 167–177.

Maynard, Joyce. 1994. "To Tell the Truth." In Jay David (Ed.), *The Family Secret: An Anthology*. New York: William Morrow, pp. 79–85.

McCaffrey, Barry R. 1997. "We're on a Perilous Path." *Newsweek* (February 3):27.

McCall, Nathan. 1994. *Makes Me Wanna Holler: A Young Black Man in America*. New York: Random House.

McDonnell, Janet A. 1991. *The Dispossession of the American Indian, 1887–1934*. Bloomington, IN: Indiana University Press.

McEachern, William A. 1994. *Economics: A Contemporary Introduction*. Cincinnati, OH: South-Western.

McFadden, Robert D. 1996. "From a Child of Promise to the Unabom Suspect." *New York Times* (May 26):1, 12–15.

McIntosh, Peggy. 1995. "White Privilege and Male Privilege: A Personal Account of Coming to See Correspondences through Work in Women's Studies." In Margaret A. Andersen and Patricia Hill Collins (Eds.), *Race, Class, and Gender: An Anthology*. Belmont, CA: Wadsworth, pp. 76–87.

McKinlay, John B. 1994. "A Case for Refocussing Upstream: The Political Economy of Illness." In Peter Conrad and Rochelle Kern (Eds.), *The Sociology of Health and Illness*. New York: St. Martin's, pp. 509–530.

McLanahan, Sara, and Gary D. Sandefur. 1994. *Growing Up with a Single Parent: What Hurts, What Helps*. Cambridge, MA: Harvard University Press.

McLarin, Kimberly J. 1994. "A New Jersey Town Is Troubled by Racial Imbalance between Classrooms: Would End to Tracking Harm Quality?" *New York Times* (August 11):A12.

McNamara, Robert P. 1994. *The Times Square Hustler: Male Prostitution in New York City.* Westport, CT: Praeger.

McWilliams, Carey. 1968. *North from Mexico: The Spanish-Speaking People of the United States.* New York: Greenwood (orig. pub. 1948).

McWilliams, Peter. 1996. *Ain't Nobody's Business if You Do: The Absurdity of Consensual Crimes in Our Free Country.* Los Angeles, CA: Prelude Press.

Mead, Margaret. 1966. "Marriage in Two Steps." *Redbook*, 127:48–49, 85–86.

Mead, Rebecca. 1994. "Playing It Straight: In and out of the Closet." *New York* (June 20):40–46.

Mechanic, David, and David A. Rochefort. 1990. "Deinstitutionalization: An Appraisal of Reform." *Annual Review of Sociology*, 16:301–350.

Mednick, Sarnoff A., W. F. Gabrielli, and B. Hutchings. 1984. "Genetic Influences in Criminal Convictions: Evidence from an Adoption Cohort." *Science,* 224: 891–894.

Meers, Erik Ashok. 1996. "Murder, He Wrote." *The Advocate* (March 5):49–52.

Meisler, Andy. 1995. "The World According to Channel One." *New York Times* (January 8):4A.

Melendez, Edgardo. 1993. "Colonialism, Citizenship, and Contemporary Statehood." In Edwin Melendez and Edgardo Melendez (Eds.), *Colonial Dilemma: Critical Perspectives on Contemporary Puerto Rico.* Boston: South End Press, pp. 41–52.

Menchaca, Martha. 1995. *The Mexican Outsiders: A Community History of Marginalization and Discrimination in California.* Austin, TX: University of Texas Press.

Mendels, Pamela. 1996. "Judges Visit Cyberspace Sites in Suit over an Indecency Law." *New York Times* (May 12):10.

Mendoza, Manuel. 1995. "Minority Actors Scarce on TV." *Austin American-Statesman* (June 12): B12.

Merchant, Carolyn. 1983. *The Death of Nature: Women, Ecology, and the Scientific Revolution.* San Francisco: Harper and Row.

Merchant, Carolyn. 1992. *Radical Ecology: The Search for a Livable World.* New York: Routledge.

Mercy, James A., and Linda E. Saltzman. 1989. "Fatal Violence among Spouses in the United States, 1976–1985." *The American Journal of Public Health,* 79: 595–599.

Meredith, Robyn. 1997. "Motown Enters the Zone." *New York Times* (April 11):C1.

Merton, Robert. 1938. "Social Structure and Anomie." *American Sociological Review,* 3(6):672–682.

Merton, Robert King. 1968. *Social Theory and Social Structure* (enlarged ed.). New York: Free Press.

Merzer, Martin. 1997. "Free to Be Flynt." *Austin American-Statesman* (January 11):C1, C6.

Messer, Ellen, and Kathryn E. May. 1994. *Back Rooms: Voices from the Illegal Abortion Era.* Buffalo, NY: Prometheus.

Michael, Robert T., John H. Gagnon, Edward O. Laumann, and Gina Kolata. 1994. *Sex in America: A Definitive Survey.* New York: Warner Books.

Michigan Department of Education. 1990. *The Influence of Gender Role Socialization on Student Perceptions.* Lansing, MI: Michigan Department of Education, Office of Sex Equity in Education.

Mickelson, Roslyn Arlin, and Stephen Samuel Smith. 1995. "Education and the Struggle Against Race, Class, and Gender Inequality." In Margaret L. Andersen and Patricia Hill Collins (Eds.), *Race, Class, and Gender* (2nd ed.). Belmont, CA: Wadsworth, pp. 289–304.

Mies, Maria, and Vandana Shiva. 1993. *Ecofeminism.* Atlantic Highlands, NJ: Zed Books.

Milgram, Stanley. 1974. *Obedience to Authority.* New York: Harper & Row.

Milkman, Harvey, and Stanley Sunderwirth. 1987. *Craving for Ecstasy: The Consciousness and Chemistry of Escape.* Lexington, MA: Heath.

Milkman, Ruth. 1997. *Farewell to the Factory: Auto Workers in the Late Twentieth Century.* Berkeley, CA: University of California Press.

Miller, Casey, and Kate Swift. 1991. *Words and Women: New Language in New Times* (updated). New York: HarperCollins.

Miller, Eleanor M. 1986. *Street Woman.* Philadelphia, PA: Temple University Press.

Miller, Michael W. 1994. "Quality Stuff: Firm Is Peddling Cocaine, and Deals Are Legit." *Wall Street Journal* (October 17):A1, A14.

Miller, Patricia G. 1993. *The Worst of Times.* New York: HarperCollins.

Miller, Walter B. 1958. "Lower Class Culture as a Generating Milieu of Gang Delinquency." *Journal of Social Issues* 14:5–19.

Mills, C. Wright. 1959a. *The Power Elite.* Fair Lawn, NJ: Oxford University Press.

Mills, C. Wright. 1959b. *The Sociological Imagination.* London: Oxford University Press.

Mills, C. Wright. 1976. *The Causes of World War Three.* Westport, CT: Greenwood Press

Mintz, Beth, and Michael Schwartz. 1985. *The Power Structure of American Business.* Chicago: University of Chicago Press.

Mirowsky, John. 1996. "Age and the Gender Gap in Depression." *Journal of Health and Social Behavior,* 37 (December):362–380.

Mirowsky, John, and Catherine E. Ross. 1980. "Minority Status, Ethnic Culture, and Distress: A Comparison of Blacks, Whites, Mexicans, and Mexican Americans." *American Journal of Sociology,* 86:479–495.

Mitchell, Alison. 1997. "Despite Angry Colleagues, Clinton Unites His Party." *New York Times* (May 3):9.

Mohawk, John. 1992. "Looking for Columbus: Thoughts on the Past, Present, and Future of Humanity." In M. Annette Jaimes (Ed.), *The State of Native America: Genocide, Colonization, and Resistance.* Boston: South End Press, pp. 439–444.

Monahan, John. 1992. "Mental Disorder and Violent Behavior: Perceptions and Evidence." *American Psychologist,* 47:511–521.

Montavalli, Jim. 1997. "The Producer Pays." *E Magazine* (May–April):36–41.

Moonan, W. L. 1989. "At Home on Fifth." *Town and Country Magazine* (September):199–207.

Moore, Joan. 1993. "Gangs, Drugs, and Violence." In Scott Cummings and Daniel J. Monti (Eds.), *Gangs: The Origins and Impact of Contemporary Youth Gangs in the United States.* Albany, NY: State University of New York Press, pp. 27–46.

Moore, Joan W. (with Harry Pachon). 1976. *Mexican Americans* (2nd ed.). Englewood Cliffs, NJ: Prentice-Hall.

Moore, Stephen, and Dean Stansel. 1992. "The Myth of America's Under-Funded Cities." *Cato Policy Analysis* (December). (Reprinted in Charles P. Cozic (Ed.), *America's Cities: Opposing Viewpoints.* San Diego, CA: Greenhaven Press, 1993, pp. 25–32.)

Moraga, Cherrie. 1995. "Art in America Con Acento." In Lillian Castillo-Speed (Ed.), *Latina: Women's Voices from the Borderlands.* New York: Touchstone, pp. 211–220.

Morales, Ed. 1996. "The Last Blackface." *Si Magazine* (Summer 1996):44–47, 85.

Morgan, S. Philip, Diane N. Lye, and Gretchen A. Condran. 1988. "Sons, Daughters, and the Risk of Marital Disruption." *American Journal of Sociology,* 94(1):110–129.

Morganthau, Tom. 1995. "What Color Is Black?" *Newsweek* (February 13):63–65.

Morris, Betsy. 1997. "Is Your Family Wrecking Your Career (and Vice Versa)?" *Fortune* (March 17):71–90.

Mosher, Steven W. 1994. *A Mother's Ordeal: One Woman's Fight against China's One-Child Policy.* New York: HarperPerennial.

Moss, J. Jennings. 1996. "Blaming the Victim." *The Advocate* (November 26):39.

Mowbray, Carol T., Sandra E. Herman, and Kelly L. Hazel. 1992. "Gender and Serious Mental Illness." *Psychology of Women Quarterly,* 16(March):107–127.

Murphy-Milano, Susan. 1996. *Defending Our Lives: Getting Away from Domestic Violence and Staying Safe.* New York: Anchor.

Muto, Sheila. 1995. "Student Uniforms Pay Off, One School District Says." *New York Times* (September 20):B6.

Mydans, Seth. 1995. "Part-Time College Teaching Rises, as Do Worries." *New York Times* (January 4):B6.

Mydans, Seth. 1997. "Brutal End for an Architect of Cambodian Brutality." *New York Times* (June 14):5.

Myers, Daniel J., and Kimberly B. Dugan. 1996. "Sexism in Graduate School Classrooms: Consequences for Students and Faculty." *Gender and Society,* 10(3): 330–350.

Myers, Steven Lee. 1997. "Converting the Dollar into a Bludgeon." *New York Times* (April 20):E5.

Myerson, Allen R. 1996. "A Double Standard in Health Coverage." *New York Times* (March 17):F1, F13.

Myerson, Allen R. 1997. "Borderline Working Class: In Texas, Labor Is Feeling Trade Accord's Pinch." *New York Times* (May 8):C1, C22.

Nagourney, Adam. 1996. "Affirmed by the Supreme Court." *New York Times* (May 26):E4.

Nath, Pamela S., John G. Borkowski, Thomas L. Whitman, and Cynthia J. Schellenbach. 1991. "Understanding Adolescent Parenting: The Dimensions and Functions of Social Support." *Family Relations,* 40:411–420.

National Council on Crime and Delinquency. 1969. *The Infiltration into Legitimate Business by Organized Crime.* Washington, DC: National Council on Crime and Delinquency

National Victim Center. 1992. *Rape in America: A Report to the Nation.* Arlington, VA/Charleston, SC: National Victim Center.

National Victims Resource Center. 1991. *Juvenile Prostitution: Fact Sheet.* Rockville, MD: Victims Resource Center.

Nava, Michael, and Robert Dawidoff. 1994. *Created Equal: Why Gay Rights Matter to America.* New York: St. Martin's Press.

Navarette, Ruben, Jr. 1997. "A Darker Shade of Crimson." In Diana Kendall (Ed.), *Race, Class, and Gender in a Diverse Society.* Boston: Allyn and Bacon, 1997: 274–279. (Reprinted from Ruben Navarette, Jr., *A Darker Shade of Crimson.* New York: Bantam, 1993.)

Navarro, Mireya. 1996. "Marijuana Farms Are Flourishing Indoors, Producing a More Potent Drug." *New York Times* (November 24):13.

Nechas, Eileen, and Denise Foley. 1994. *Unequal Treatment: What You Don't Know about How Women Are Mistreated by the Medical Community.* New York: Simon & Schuster.

Neckerman, Kathryn M., and Joleen Kirschenman. 1991. "Hiring Strategies, Racial Bias, and Inner-City Workers." In Diana Kendall (Ed.), *Race, Class, and Gender in a Diverse Society.* Boston: Allyn and Bacon, pp. 388–404.

Neergaard, Lauran. 1996. "FDA Prepares to Regulate Medical Info on the Internet." *Austin American-Statesman* (October 20):A7.

Neill, Monty. 1995. "Computers, Thinking, and Schools in 'the New World Economic Order.'" In James Brook and Iain A. Boal (Eds.), *Resisting the Virtual Life: The Culture and Politics of Information*. San Francisco: City Lights, pp. 181–194.

Nelkin, Dorothy. 1994. "Ironies in the Public Response to Information Technology." *National Forum: The Phi Kappa Phi Journal* (Spring):7–10.

Nelkin, Dorothy. 1995. "Biology Is Not Destiny." *New York Times* (September 28):A17.

Neuman, Elena. 1992. "Cancer: The Issue Feminists Forgot." *Insight* (February 24):7–11, 32–43.

New York Times. 1993. "Despite 6-Year U.S. Campaign, Pornography Industry Thrives" (July 4):10.

New York Times. 1994a. "Car Bomb Kills 3 in Beirut; Arabs Accuse Israel." (December 22):A5.

New York Times. 1994b. "Educating Elderly on AIDS." (August 9):A8.

New York Times. 1994c. "Jordan Dooms 11 Militants." (December 22):A5.

New York Times. 1995a. "Malnutrition Hits Many Elderly." (July 3):A7.

New York Times. 1995b. "More Students, in a Study, See Unsafe Schools." (June 15):A13.

New York Times. 1996a. "Aging World, New Wrinkles." (September 22):E1.

New York Times. 1996b. "Guns Are No. 2 Cause of Death among the Young, Data Show." (April 9):A8.

New York Times. 1996c. "The Megacity Summit." (April 8):A14.

New York Times. 1996d. "Where the Drugs Come from." (March 2):5.

New York Times. 1997a. [Advertisement] "On the Importance of Diversity in University Admissions." (April 24):A17.

New York Times. 1997b. "A New Study of Day Care Shows Benefit of Attention." (April 5):A10.

New York Times. 1997c. "Public's Assessment of Presidents and Problems." (January 20):A10.

New York Times. 1997d. "Sugar's Sweet Deal." (April 27):E14.

New York Times. 1997e. "The Militia Threat." (June 14):18.

Nicklin, Julie L. 1996. "Elementary Partnership." *Chronicle of Higher Education* (July 5):A13.

Niebuhr, Gustav. 1996. "Bishop Who Ordained Gay Deacon Is Accused of Heresy." *New York Times* (February 28):A8.

Nieves, Evelyn. 1995. "Wanted in Levittown: One Little Box, with Ticky Tacky Intact." *New York Times* (November 3):A12.

Noble, Kenneth B. 1995. "U.S. Studies Wave of Violence in Nevada." *New York Times* (December 22):A10.

Noriega, Chon A. 1992. *Chicanos and Film: Representation and Resistance*. Minneapolis, MN: University of Minnesota Press.

Noriega, Chon A., and Ana M. Lopez. 1996. *The Ethnic Eye: Latino Media Arts*. Minneapolis, MN: University of Minnesota Press.

Norman, Michael. 1993. "One Cop, Eight Square Blocks." *New York Times Magazine* (December 12):62–90, 96.

Oakes, Jeannie. 1985. *Keeping Track: How Schools Structure Inequality*. New Haven, CT: Yale University Press.

O'Connell, Helen. 1994. *Women and the Family*. Prepared for the UN-NGO Group on Women and Development. Atlantic Highlands, NJ: Zed Books.

O'Connor, Mike. 1996. "Muslim Widows in Bosnia Try to Rebuild Lives without Men." *New York Times* (July 13):A4.

Ogburn, William F. 1966. *Social Change with Respect to Culture and Original Nature*. New York: Dell (orig. pub. 1922).

O'Hare, William P., and Margaret Usdansky. 1992. "What the 1990 Census Tells Us About Segregation in 25 Large Metros." *Population Today*, 20(9). Washington, DC: Population Reference Bureau.

Oliver, Melvin L., and Thomas M. Shapiro. 1995. *Black Wealth/White Wealth: A New Perspective on Racial Inequality*. New York: Routledge.

Olzak, Susan, Suzanne Shanahan, and Elizabeth H. McEneaney. 1996. "Poverty, Segregation, and Race Riots: 1960 to 1993." *American Sociological Review*, 61(August):590–613.

Omi, Michael, and Howard Winant. 1994. *Racial Formation in the United States: From the 1960s to the 1990s* (2nd ed.). New York: Routledge.

Orenstein, Peggy (in association with the American Association of University Women). 1994. *School Girls: Young Women, Self-Esteem, and the Confidence Gap*. New York: Anchor/Doubleday.

Orenstein, Peggy. 1996. "For Too Many Schoolgirls, Sexual Harassment Is Real." *Austin American-Statesman* (October 4):A15.

Ortner, Sherry B. 1974. "Is Female to Male As Nature Is to Culture?" In Michelle Rosaldo and Louise Lamphere (Eds.), *Women, Culture, and Society*. Stanford, CA: Stanford University Press.

Orum, Anthony M. 1995. *City-Building in America*. Boulder, CO: Westview.

Otis, Leah. 1985. *Prostitution in Medieval Society*. Chicago: University of Chicago Press.

Oxendine, Joseph B. 1995. *American Indian Sports Heritage*. Lincoln, NE: University of Nebraska Press (originally published in 1988).

Padilla, Felix M. 1993. *The Gang as an American Enterprise*. New Brunswick, NJ: Rutgers University Press.

Palen, J. John. 1995. *The Suburbs*. New York: McGraw-Hill.

Palen, J. John, and Bruce London. 1984. *Gentrification, Displacement, and Neighborhood Revitalization*. Albany, NY: State University of New York Press.

Pappas, Ben. 1997a. "Dropouts Are Okay." *Forbes* (May 19):206.

Pappas, Ben. 1997b. "Princessa." *Forbes* (May 5):20.

Parenti, Michael. 1988. *Democracy for the Few* (5th ed.). New York: St. Martin's Press.

Parker, Keith D., Greg Weaver, and Thomas Calhoun. 1995. "Predictors of Alcohol and Drug Use: A Multiethnic Comparison." *Journal of Social Psychology*, 135(5): 581–591.

Parker, Robert E. 1994. *Flesh Peddlers and Warm Bodies: The Temporary Help Industry and Its Workers*. New Brunswick, NJ: Rutgers University Press.

Parker, Robert Nash. 1989. "Poverty, Subculture of Violence, and Type of Homicide." *Social Forces*, 67:983–1007.

Parker, Robert Nash. 1995. "Violent Crime." In Joseph F. Sheley (Ed.), *Criminology: A Contemporary Handbook* (2nd ed.). Belmont, CA: Wadsworth, pp. 169–185.

Parry, A. 1976. *Terrorism: From Robespierre to Arafat*. New York: Vanguard Press.

Parsons, Talcott. 1951. *The Social System*. New York: Free Press.

Parsons, Talcott. 1955. "The American Family: Its Relations to Personality and to the Social Structure." In Talcott Parsons and Robert F. Bales (Eds.), *Family, Socialization, and Interaction Process*. Glencoe, IL: Free Press, pp. 3–33.

Pateman, Carole. 1994. "What's Wrong with Prostitution?" In Alison M. Jaggar (Ed.), *Living with Contradictions: Controversies in Feminist Social Ethics*. Boulder, CO: Westview, pp. 127–132.

Patterson, Charlotte J. 1992. "Children of Lesbian and Gay Parents." *Child Development*, 63:1025–1042.

Patterson, James, and Peter Kim. 1991. *The Day America Told the Truth*. New York: Prentice-Hall.

Patterson, Martha Priddy. 1996. "Women's Employment Patterns, Pension Coverage, and Retirement Planning." In Cynthia Costello and Barbara Kivimae Krimgold (Eds.) for the Women's Research and Education Institute, *The American Woman 1996–97: Women and Work*. New York: W.W. Norton, pp. 148–165.

Paules, Greta Foff. 1991. *Dishing It Out: Power and Resistance among Waitresses in a New Jersey Restaurant*. Philadelphia, PA: Temple University Press.

Pear, Robert, 1994. "Health Advisers See Peril in Plan to Cut Medicare." *New York Times* (August 31):A1, A10.

Pear, Robert. 1996. "Health Costs Pose Problems for Millions, a Study Finds." *New York Times* (October 23):A14.

Pear, Robert. 1997a. "Academy's Report Says Immigration Benefits the U.S." *New York Times* (May 18):1, 15.

Pear, Robert. 1997b. "H.M.O.'s Limiting Medicare Appeals, U.S. Inquiry Finds." *New York Times* (March 18):A1, A11.

Pearce, Diana M. 1978. *The Feminization of Poverty: Women, Work, and Welfare*. Chicago: University of Illinois Press.

Pedersen-Pietersen, Laura. 1997. "You're Sober at Last. Now Prove It to the Boss." *New York Times* (January 12):F10.

Perdue, William Dan. 1993. *Systemic Crisis: Problems in Society, Politics, and World Order*. Fort Worth, TX: Harcourt Brace Jovanovich.

Perrolle, Judith A. 1996. "Privacy and Surveillance in Computer-Supported Cooperative Work." In David Lyon and Elia Zureik (Eds.), *Computers, Surveillance, and Privacy*. Minneapolis, MN: University of Minnesota Press, pp. 47–65.

Perry, David C., and Alfred J. Watkins (Eds.). 1977. *The Rise of the Sunbelt Cities*. Beverly Hills, CA: Sage.

Perry-Jenkins, Maureen, and Ann C. Crouter. 1990. "Men's Provider Role Attitudes: Implications for Household Work and Marital Satisfaction." *Journal of Family Issues*, 11:136–156.

Petersen, John L. 1994. *The Road to 2015: Profiles of the Future*. Corte Madera, CA: Waite Group Press.

Peterson, V. Spike, and Anne Sisson Runyan. 1993. *Global Gender Issues*. Boulder, CO: Westview Press.

Petras, James F. 1983. *Capitalist and Socialist Crises in the Late Twentieth Century*. Totowa, NJ: Rowman and Allenheld.

Pettigrew, Thomas. 1981. "The Mental Health Impact." In Benjamin Bowser and Raymond G. Hunt (Eds.), *Impacts of Racism on White Americans*. Beverly Hills, CA: Sage, p. 117.

Phillips, Kevin. 1995. *Arrogant Capital: Washington, Wall Street, and the Frustration of American Politics*. Boston: Little, Brown.

Pierce, Jennifer L. 1995. *Gender Trials: Emotional Lives in Contemporary Law Firms*. Berkeley, CA: University of California Press.

Pizzo, Steve, M. Fricker, and P. Muolo. 1991. *Insider Job: The Looting of America's Savings and Loans*. New York: Harper Perennial.

Polakow, Valerie. 1993. *Lives on the Edge: Single Mothers and Their Children in the Other America*. Chicago: University of Chicago Press.

Pollack, Andrew. 1996a. "Barbie's Journey in Japan." *New York Times* (December 22):E3. (Ch14)

Pollack, Andrew. 1996b. "Square Pegs Stay Home from Japan's Schools." *New York Times* (September 15):A4.

Ponse, Barbara. 1978. *Identities in the Lesbian World: The Social Construction of Self*. Westport, CT: Greenwood Press.

Pontell, Henry N., and Kitty Calavita. 1992. "Bilking Bankers and Bad Debts: White-Collar Crime and the

Savings and Loan Crisis." In K. Schlegel and David Weisburd (Eds.), *White-Collar Crime Reconsidered*. Boston: Northeastern University Press, pp. 195–213.

Popenoe, David. 1988. *Disturbing the Nest: Family Change and Decline in Modern Societies*. New York: Aldine de Gruyter.

Popenoe, David. 1995. "The American Family Crisis." *National Forum: The Phi Kappa Phi Journal,* 73(Summer 1995):15–19.

Popenoe, David. 1996. *Life without Father: Compelling New Evidence That Fatherhood and Marriage Are Indispensable for the Good of Children and Society*. New York: Martin Kessler/Free Press.

Portes, Alejandro, and Dag MacLeod. 1996. "Educational Progress of Children of Immigrants: The Roles of Class, Ethnicity, and School Context." *Sociology of Education*, 69(4):255–276.

Poster, Mark. 1996. "Databases as Discourse; or, Electronic Interpellations." In David Lyon and Elia Zureik (Eds.), *Computers, Surveillance, and Privacy*. Minneapolis, MN: University of Minnesota Press, pp. 175–192.

Potterat, John J., Donald E. Woodhouse, John B. Muth, and Stephen Q. Muth. 1990. "Estimating the Prevalence and Career Longevity of Prostitute Women." *Journal of Sex Research*, 27(May):233–243.

Preston, Jennifer. 1996. "Hospitals Look on Charity Care As Unaffordable Option of Past." *New York Times* (April 14):1, 15.

Purdum, Todd S. 1997. "Legacy of Riots in Los Angeles: Fears and Hope." *New York Times* (April 27):1, 16.

Pursell, Carroll. 1994. *White Heat: People and Technology*. Berkeley, CA: University of California Press.

Purvis, Andrew. 1996. "The Global Epidemic: AIDS Is Tightening Its Grip on the Developing World." *Time* (December 30):76–78.

Quadagno, Jill. 1994. *The Color of Welfare: How Racism Undermined the War on Poverty*. New York: Oxford University Press.

Quadagno, Jill, and Catherine Fobes. 1995. "The Welfare State and the Cultural Reproduction of Gender." *Social Problems*, 42(2):171–190.

Raffalli, Mary. 1994. "Why So Few Women Physicists?" *New York Times Supplement* (January):Sect. 4A, 26–28.

Ramo, Joshua Cooper. 1997. "Peace is an Xcellent Adventure." *Time* (June 9):69.

Rank, Mark Robert. 1994. *Living on the Edge: The Realities of Welfare in America*. New York: Columbia University Press.

Rankin, Robert P., and Jerry S. Maneker. 1985. "The Duration of Marriage in a Divorcing Population: The Impact of Children." *Journal of Marriage and the Family*, 47(February):43–52.

Raphael, Ray. 1988. *The Men From the Boys: Rites of Passage in Male America*. Lincoln, NE: University of Nebraska Press.

Ratan, Suneel. 1995. "A New Divide between Haves and Have-Nots?" *Time: Special Issue: Welcome to Cyberspace* (Spring):25–26.

Rawlings, Steve W. 1995. "Households and Families." *Population Profile of the United States: 1995*. Washington, DC: U.S. Department of Commerce, Bureau of the Census.

Rawls, John. 1971. *A Theory of Justice*. Cambridge, MA: Harvard University Press.

Reckless, Walter C. 1967. *The Crime Problem*. New York: Meredith.

Reid, Sue Titus. 1987. *Criminal Justice*. St. Paul, MN: West.

Reiss, I. L. 1986. *Journey into Sexuality: An Exploratory Voyage*. Englewood Cliffs, NJ: Prentice-Hall.

Relman, Arnold S. 1992. "Self-Referral—What's at Stake?" *New England Journal of Medicine,* 327 (November 19):1522–1524.

Rembert, Tracy. 1997. "Package Deal: Europeans and the War on Waste." *E Magazine* (May–June):41.

Renner, Michael. 1993. *Critical Juncture: The Future of Peacekeeping*. Washington, DC: Worldwatch Institute.

Renzetti, Claire M., and Daniel J. Curran. 1995. *Women, Men, and Society* (3rd ed.). Boston: Allyn and Bacon.

Reskin, Barbara F., and Heidi Hartmann. 1986. *Women's Work, Men's Work: Sex Segregation on the Job*. Washington, DC: National Academy Press.

Reskin, Barbara F., and Irene Padavic. 1994. *Women and Men at Work*. Thousand Oaks, CA: Pine Forge.

Reynolds, Helen. 1986. *The Economics of Prostitution*. Springfield, IL: Charles C. Thomas.

Richardson, Laurel. 1993. "Inequalities of Power, Property, and Prestige." In Virginia Cyrus (Ed.), *Experiencing Race, Class, and Gender in the United States*. Mountain View, CA: Mayfield, pp. 229–236.

Rifkin, Glenn. 1996. "Yikes! Computers in the Comics." *Forbes ASAP* (June 3):114–119.

Risman, Barbara J. 1987. "Intimate Relationships from a Microstructural Perspective: Men Who Mother." *Gender and Society*, 1:6–32.

Ritzer, George. 1995. *Expressing America: A Critique of the Global Credit Card Society*. Thousand Oaks, CA: Pine Forge.

Ritzer, George. 1996. *The McDonaldization of Society: An Investigation into the Changing Character of Contemporary Social Life* (rev. ed.). Thousand Oaks, CA: Pine Forge Press.

Roane, Kit R. 1996. "In Bosnia, Paint and Plumbing Alone Cannot Heal." *New York Times International* (May 5):A4.

Roberts, Nickie. 1992. *Whores in History: Prostitution in Western Society*. London: HarperCollins.

Roberts, Sam. 1993. *Who We Are: A Portrait of America Based on the Latest U.S. Census*. New York: Times Books.

Rogers, Deborah D. 1995. "Daze of Our Lives: The Soap Opera as Feminine Text." In Gail Dines and Jean M. Humez (Eds.), *Gender, Race and Class in Media: A Text-Reader.* Thousand Oaks, CA: Sage, pp. 325–331.

Rogg, E. 1974. *The Assimilation of Cuban Exiles: The Role of Community and Class.* New York: Aberdeen.

Rollins, Judith. 1985. *Between Women: Domestics and Their Employers.* Philadelphia: Temple University Press.

Romero, Mary. 1992. *Maid in the U.S.A.* New York: Routledge.

Romo, Harriett D., and Toni Falbo. 1996. *Latino High School Graduation.* Austin, TX: University of Texas Press.

Roos, Patricia A., and Barbara F. Reskin. 1992. "Occupational Desegregation in the 1970s: Integration and Economic Equity?" *Sociological Perspectives,* 35:69.

Ropers, Richard H. 1991. *Persistent Poverty: The American Dream Turned Nightmare.* New York: Plenum.

Rose, Arnold. 1951. *The Roots of Prejudice.* Paris: UNESCO.

Rosen, Barbara. 1985. *The Wall Street Journal* (September 12).

Rosenbaum, David E. 1996. "In Political Money Game, the Year of Big Loopholes." *New York Times* (December 26):A1, A10.

Rosenberg, Janet, Harry Perlstadt, and William Phillips. 1993. "Now That We Are Here: Discrimination, Disparagement and Harassment at Work and the Experience of Women Lawyers." *Gender and Society,* 7(3): 415–433.

Rosenthal, Elisabeth. 1993. "The Inner City: Lack of Doctors for the Poor Is Obstacle to Health Plans." *New York Times* (November 14):HD6.

Rosenthal, Elisabeth. 1997. "The H.M.O. Catch: When Healthier Isn't Cheaper." *New York Times* (March 16):E1, E4.

Rosser, Sue V. 1994. *Women's Health—Missing from U.S. Medicine.* Bloomington, IN: Indiana University Press.

Rossi, Peter H. 1989. *Down and Out in America: The Origins of Homelessness.* Chicago: University of Chicago Press.

Rothchild, John. 1995. "Wealth: Static Wages, Except for the Rich." *Time* (January 30):60–61.

Rothman, Robert A. 1993. *Inequality and Stratification: Class, Color, and Gender* (2nd ed.). Englewood Cliffs, NJ: Prentice-Hall.

Rubin, Beth A. 1996. *Shifts in the Social Contract: Understanding Change in American Society.* Thousand Oaks, CA.: Pine Forge Press.

Rubin, Lillian B. 1976. *Worlds of Pain: Life in the Working-Class Family.* New York: Basic Books.

Rubin, Lillian B. 1994. *Families on the Fault Line.* New York: HarperCollins.

Rubington, Earl, and Martin S. Weinberg (Eds.). 1996. *Deviance: The Interactionist Perspective* (6th ed.). Boston: Allyn and Bacon.

Ruggles, Patricia. 1990. *Drawing the Line: Alternative Policy Measures and Their Implications for Public Policy.* Washington, DC: Urban Institute Press.

Ruggles, Patricia. 1992. "Measuring Poverty." *Focus,* 14(1):1–5.

Rule, James B. 1996. "High-Tech Workplace Surveillance: What's Really New?" In David Lyon and Elia Zureik (Eds.), *Computers, Surveillance, and Privacy.* Minneapolis, MN: University of Minnesota Press, pp. 66–76.

Russell, Diana E. H. 1993. "Introduction." In Diana E. H. Russell (Ed.), *Making Violence Sexy: Feminist Views on Pornography.* New York: Teachers College Press, pp. 1–20.

Ryan, William. 1976. *Blaming the Victim* (rev. ed.). New York: Vintage.

Sachs, Aaron. 1994. "The Last Commodity: Child Prostitution in the Developing World." *World Watch,* 7(4) (July–August):24–31.

Sadker, Myra. 1994. *Families on the Fault Line.* New York: HarperCollins.

Sadker, Myra, and David Sadker. 1994. *Failing at Fairness: How America's Schools Cheat Girls.* New York: Scribner.

Safilios-Rothschild, Constantina. 1969. "Family Sociology or Wives' Family Sociology? A Cross-Cultural Examination of Decision-Making." *Journal of Marriage and the Family,* 31(2):290–301.

Sale, Kirkpatrick. 1990. *The Conquest of Paradise.* New York: Knopf.

Sampson, Robert J. 1986. "Effects of Socioeconomic Context on Official Reactions to Juvenile Delinquency." *American Sociological Review,* 51(December):876–885.

Sanday, Peggy Reeves. 1990. *Fraternity Gang Rape: Sex, Brotherhood, and Privilege on Campus.* New York: New York University Press.

Sanday, Peggy Reeves. 1996. *A Woman Scorned: Acquaintance Rape on Trial.* New York: Doubleday.

Sanger, David E. 1997. "A Booming Economy Made It All Much Easier." *New York Times* (May 2):A12.

Santiago, Anna M., and George Galster. 1995. "Puerto Rican Segregation in the United States: Cause or Consequence of Economic Status?" *Social Problems,* 42: 361–389.

Santiago, Anna M., and Margaret G. Wilder. 1991. "Residential Segregation and Links to Minority Poverty: The Case of Latinos in the United States." *Social Problems,* 38:701–723.

Sapon-Shevin, Mara. 1993. "Gifted Education and the Protection of Privilege: Breaking the Silence, Opening the Discourse." In Lois Weis and Michelle Fine (Eds.), *Beyond Silenced Voices: Class, Race, and Gender in United States Schools.* Albany, NY: State University of New York Press, pp. 25–44.

Sassen, Saskia. 1991. *The Global City: New York, London, Tokyo*. Princeton, NJ: Princeton University Press.

Sassen, Saskia. 1995. "On Concentration and Centrality in the Global City." In Paul L. Knox and Peter J. Taylor (Eds.), *World Cities in a World-System*. Cambridge, England: Cambridge University Press, pp. 63–75.

Sawers, Larry, and William K. Tabb (Eds.). 1984. *Sunbelt/Snowbelt: Urban Development and Regional Restructuring*. New York: Oxford University Press.

Scarr, Sandra. 1995. "The Two Worlds of Child Care." *National Forum: The Phi Kappa Phi Journal*, 75 (3):39–41.

Scheff, Thomas J. 1977. "The Distancing of Emotion in Ritual." *Current Anthropology*. 18:483–505. In Bunis, William K., Angela Yancik, and David Snow. 1996. "The Cultural Patterning of Sympathy toward the Homeless and Other Victims of Misfortune." *Social Problems* (November):387–402.

Schemo, Diana Jean. 1994. "Suburban Taxes Are Higher for Blacks, Analysis Shows." *New York Times* (August 17):A1, A16.

Schiller, Herbert I. 1996. *Information Inequality: The Deepening Social Crisis in America*. New York: Routledge.

Schneider, Keith. 1993. "The Regulatory Thickets of Environmental Racism." *New York Times* (December 19):E5.

Schreuder, Cindy. 1996. "What Kindergartners Can Teach Us about Living in a Multicultural World." *Austin American-Statesman* (July 7):F1, F5.

Schrof, Joanne M. 1993. "The Gender Machine." *U.S. News and World Report* (August 2):42–44.

Schur, Edwin M. 1965. *Crimes without Victims: Deviant Behavior and Public Policy*. Englewood Cliffs, NJ: Prentice-Hall.

Scott, Alan. 1990. *Ideology and the New Social Movements*. Boston: Unwin & Hyman.

Scott, Denise Benoit. 1996. "Shattering the Instrumental-Expressive Myth: The Power of Women's Networks in Corporate-Government Affairs." *Gender and Society*, 10(3):232–247.

Scott, Joseph E. 1993. "Violence and Sexual Violence in Pornography: Is It Really Increasing?" *Archives of Sexual Behavior*, 22(4):357–372.

Scott, Joseph E., and Steven J. Cuvelier. 1987. "Sexual Violence in Playboy Magazine: A Longitudinal Content Analysis." *Journal of Sex Research*, 23:534–539.

Scully, Diana. 1990. *Understanding Sexual Violence: A Study of Convicted Rapists*. Boston: Unwin Hyman.

Searight, H. Russell, and Priscilla R. Searight. 1988. "The Homeless Mentally Ill: Overview, Policy Implications, and Adult Foster Care as a Neglected Resource." *Adult Foster Care Journal*, 2:235–259.

Seavor, Jim. 1996. "Closing the Books on Homophobia." *Austin American-Statesman* (November 24):E11.

Seelye, Katharine Q. 1997a. "Future U.S.: Grayer and More Hispanic." *New York Times* (March 27):A18.

Seelye, Katharine Q. 1997b. "Trickle of Television Liquor Ads Releases Torrent of Regulatory Uncertainty." *New York Times* (January 12):8.

Segal, Lynn. 1990. "Pornography and Violence: What the 'Experts' Really Say." *Feminist Review*, 36:29–41.

Seidman, Steven A. 1992. "An Investigation of Sex-Role Stereotyping in Music Videos." *Journal of Broadcasting & Electronic Media* (Spring):212.

Seligman, Martin E. P. 1975. *Helplessness: On Depression, Development and Death*. San Francisco, CA: Freeman.

Serrill, Michael S. 1992. "Struggling to Be Themselves." *Time* (November 9):52–54.

Serrin, Judith. 1997. "Immigration Helps Economy, Analysis Shows." *Austin American-Statesman* (May 18):A7.

Shah, Sonia. 1994. "Presenting the Blue Goddess: Toward a National Pan-Asian Feminist Agenda." In Karin Aguilar-San Juan (Ed.), *The State of Asian America: Activism and Resistance in the 1990s*. Boston: South End Press, pp. 147–158.

Shannon, Kelley. 1996. "Allocations, Segregation Hurt Latinos' Schooling." *Austin American-Statesman* (September 13):A11.

Shea, Christopher. 1996. "A Scholar Links Sexual Orientation to Gender Roles in Childhood." *Chronicle of Higher Education* (November 22):A11, A12.

Shedler, J., and J. Block. 1990. "Adolescent Drug Users and Psychological Health." *American Psychologist*, 45:612–630.

Sheff, David. 1995. "If It's Tuesday, It Must Be Dad's House." *New York Times Magazine* (March 26):64–65.

Sheldon, William H. 1949. *Varieties of Delinquent Youth: An Introduction to Constitutional Psychiatry*. New York: Harper.

Sheley, Joseph F. (Ed.). 1995. *Criminology* (2nd ed.) Belmont, CA: Wadsworth.

Shelton, Beth Ann. 1992. *Women, Men and Time: Gender Differences in Paid Work, Housework and Leisure*. Westport, CT: Greenwood.

Shenon, Philip. 1996a. "AIDS Epidemic, Late to Arrive, Now Explodes in Populous Asia." *New York Times* (January 21):A1.

Shenon, Philip. 1996b. "Jet Makers Preparing Bids for a Rich Pentagon Prize." *New York Times* (March 12):A1, C4.

Shenon, Philip. 1996c. "When 'Don't Ask, Don't Tell' Means Do Ask and Do Tell All." *New York Times* (March 3):E7.

Sher, Kenneth J. 1991. *Children of Alcoholics: A Critical Appraisal of Theory and Research*. Chicago, IL: University of Chicago Press.

Shibutani, Tamotsu. 1970. "On the Personification of Adversaries." In Tamotsu Shibutani (Ed.), *Human Nature and Collective Behavior*. Englewood Cliffs, NJ: Prentice-Hall, pp. 223–233.

Shilts, Randy. 1988. *And the Band Played On: Politics, People, and the AIDS Epidemic.* New York: Penguin.

Shilts, Randy. 1993. *Conduct Unbecoming: Lesbians and Gays in the U.S. Military, Vietnam to the Persian Gulf.* New York: St. Martin's Press.

Shweder, Richard A. 1997. "It's Called Poor Health for a Reason." *New York Times* (March 9):E5.

Sidel, Ruth. 1996. *Keeping Women and Children Last: America's War on the Poor.* New York: Penguin.

Simmel, Georg. 1950. *The Sociology of Georg Simmel.* Trans. Kurt Wolff. Glencoe, IL: Free Press (orig. written in 1902–1917).

Simon, David R. 1996. *Elite Deviance* (5th ed.) Boston: Allyn and Bacon.

Singer, Bennett L., and David Deschamps. 1994. *Gay and Lesbian Stats.* New York: New Press.

Sivard, Ruth L. 1991. *World Military and Social Expenditures—1991.* Washington, DC: World Priorities.

Sivard, Ruth L. 1993. *World Military and Social Expenditures—1993.* Washington, DC: World Priorities.

Skolnick, Arlene. 1991. *Embattled Paradise: The American Family in an Age of Uncertainty.* New York: HarperCollins.

Skolnick, Jerome H. 1975. *Justice without Trial* (2nd ed.). New York: Wiley.

Skolnick, Jerome H., and James J. Fyfe. 1993. *Above the Law: Police and the Excessive Use of Force.* New York: Free Press.

Sleeter, Christine E. 1996. "White Silence, White Solidarity." In Noel Ignatiev and John Garvey (Eds.), *Race Traitor.* New York: Routledge, pp. 257–265.

Smith, Alexander B., and Harriet Pollack. 1994. "Deviance as Crime, Sin, and Poor Taste." In Patricia A. Adler and Peter Adler (Eds.), *Constructions of Deviance: Social Power, Context, and Interaction.* Belmont, CA: Wadsworth.

Smith, M. Dwayne. 1995. "The Death Penalty in America." In Joseph F. Sheley (Ed.), *Criminology: A Contemporary Handbook* (2nd ed.). Belmont, CA: Wadsworth, pp. 557–572.

Smolowe, Jill. 1996. "The Stalled Revolution." *Time* (May 6):63.

Snell, Cudore L. 1995. *Young Men in the Street: Help-Seeking Behavior of Young Male Prostitutes.* Westport, CT: Praeger.

Snitow, Ann Barr. 1994. "Mass Market Romance: Pornography for Women is Different." In Alison M. Jaggar (Ed.), *Living with Contradictions: Controversies in Feminist Social Ethics.* Boulder, CO: Westview, pp. 181–188.

Snow, David A., and Leon Anderson. 1991. "Researching the Homeless: The Characteristic Features and Virtues of the Case Study." In Joe R. Feagin, Anthony M. Orum, and Gideon Sjoberg (Eds.), *A Case for the Case Study.* Chapel Hill: University of North Carolina Press, pp. 148–173.

Snow, David A., and Leon Anderson. 1993. *Down on Their Luck: A Study of Homeless Street People.* Berkeley, CA: University of California Press.

Snyder, Benson R. 1971. *The Hidden Curriculum.* New York: Knopf.

Soble, Alan. 1986. "Pornography in Capitalism: Powerlessness." In Alan Soble, *Pornography: Marxism, Feminism and the Future of Sexuality.* New Haven, CT: Yale University Press, pp. 78–84.

Spanier, Graham, and Paul Glick. 1981. "Marital Instability in the U.S.: Some Correlates and Recent Changes." *Family Relations,* 30(July):329–338.

Squires, Gregory D. 1994. *Capital and Communities in Black and White: The Intersections of Race, Class, and Uneven Development.* Albany, NY: State University of New York Press.

Stanko, Elizabeth. 1990. *Everyday Violence: How Women and Men Experience Sexual and Physical Danger.* London: HarperCollins.

Stanley, Alessandra. 1995. "Russian Mothers, from All Walks, Walk Alone." *New York Times* (October 21): A1.

Stanley, Alessandra. 1996. "Dec. 25 in Russia: The Adoration of the Monetary." *The New York Times International* (December 24):A4.

Stanley, Julia P. 1972. "Paradigmatic Woman: The Prostitute." Paper presented at South Atlantic Modern Language Association, Jacksonville, FL, cited in Jessie Bernard, *The Female World.* New York: Free Press, 1981.

Staples, Robert. 1994. *The Black Family: Essays and Studies* (5th ed.). Belmont, CA: Wadsworth.

Stares, Paul B. 1996. *Global Habit: The Drug Problem in a Borderless World.* Washington, DC: Brookings Institution.

Starr, Paul. 1982. *The Social Transformation of American Medicine.* New York: Basic.

Stead, Deborah. 1997. "Corporations, Classrooms, and Commercialism." *New York Times Education Supplement* (January 5):30–33.

Steering Committee of the Physicians' Health Study Group. 1989. "Final Report on the Aspirin Component of the Ongoing Physician's Health Study." *New England Journal of Medicine,* 321:129–135.

Stefanac, Suzanne. 1993. "Sex and the New Media." *New Media* (April):38–45.

Steffensmeier, Darrell, and Emilie Allan. 1995. "Criminal Behavior: Gender and Age." In Joseph F. Sheley (Ed.), *Criminology: A Contemporary Handbook* (2nd ed.). Belmont, CA: Wadsworth, pp. 83–143.

Stein, Peter J. 1976. *Single.* Englewood Cliffs, NJ: Prentice-Hall.

Stein, Peter J. (Ed.). 1981. *Single Life: Unmarried Adults in Social Context.* New York: St. Martin's Press.

Steinem, Gloria. 1997. "Hollywood Cleans Up Hustler." *New York Times* (January 7):A13.

Steingart, R. M., M. Packer, P. Hamm, and others. 1991. "Sex Differences in the Management of Coronary Artery Disease." *New England Journal of Medicine,* 325:226–230.

Sterngold, James. 1993. "Killer Gets Life as Navy Says He Hunted Down Gay Sailor." *New York Times* (May 28):A1, A11.

Stevens, Patricia E. 1992. "Lesbian Health Care Research: A Review of the Literature from 1970 to 1990." *Health Care for Women International,* 13.

Stevens, William K. 1997. "How Much Is Nature Worth? For You, $33 Trillion." *New York Times* (May 20):B7, B9.

Stevenson, Richard W. 1997. "Clinton and Congress in Accord on Budget, Except for Tax Cuts." *New York Times* (May 2):A1, A12.

Stewart, Charles T., Jr. 1995. *Healthy, Wealthy, or Wise? Issues in American Health Care Policy.* Armonk, NY: M.E. Sharpe.

Stock, Robert W. 1995. "Balancing the Needs and Risks of Older Drivers." *New York Times* (July 13):B5.

Stolberg, Sheryl Gay. 1997a. "Breaks for Mental Illness: Just What the Government Ordered." *New York Times* (May 4):E1, E5.

Stolberg, Sheryl Gay. 1997b. "Wary of Big Steps, U.S. Isn't Moving to Curb Tobacco." *New York Times* (May 2):A1, A16.

Stoll, Clifford. 1996. "Invest in Humanware." *New York Times* (May 19):E15.

Stoller, Robert J. 1991. *Porn: Myths for the Twentieth Century.* New Haven, CT: Yale University Press.

Story, Paula. 1997. "L.A. Police Assess Robbers' Greater Firepower." *Austin American-Statesman* (March 2):A5.

Straus, Murray A., Richard J. Gelles, and Suzanne K. Steinmetz. 1980. *Behind Closed Doors: Violence in the American Family.* New York: Anchor.

Substance Abuse and Mental Health Services Administration. 1996. *National Household Survey on Drug Abuse: Population Estimates 1995.* Rockville, MD: U.S. Department of Health and Human Services.

Sullivan, Maureen. 1996. "Rozzie and Harriet? Gender and Family Patterns of Lesbian Coparents." *Gender and Society,* 10(6):747–767.

Sullivan, Mercer L. 1993. "Puerto Ricans in Sunset Park, Brooklyn: Poverty amidst Ethnic and Economic Diversity." In Joan Moore and Raquel Pinderhughes (Eds.), *In the Barrios: Latinos and the Underclass Debate.* New York: Russell Sage Foundation, pp. 1–24.

Sullivan, Teresa A., Elizabeth Warren, and Jay Lawrence Westbrook. 1989. *As We Forgive Our Debtors: Bankruptcy and Consumer Credit in America.* New York: Oxford University Press.

Sullivan, Thomas J. 1997. *Introduction to Social Problems* (4th ed.). Boston: Allyn and Bacon.

Sutherland, Edwin H. 1939. *Principles of Criminology.* Philadelphia: Lippincott.

Sutherland, Edwin H. 1949. *White Collar Crime.* New York: Dryden.

Takagi, Dana Y. 1992. *The Retreat from Race: Asian-American Admissions and Racial Politics.* New Brunswick, NJ: Rutgers.

Takaki, Ronald. 1993. *A Different Mirror: A History of Multicultural America.* Boston: Little, Brown.

Tannen, Deborah. 1990. *You Just Don't Understand: Women and Men in Conversation.* New York: William Morrow.

Tannen, Deborah. 1994. *Gender and Discourse.* New York: Oxford University Press.

Taylor, Howard F. 1995. "Symposium: The Bell Curve." *Contemporary Sociology: A Journal of Reviews,* 24(2):153–157.

Taylor, J., and B. Jackson. 1990. "Factors Affecting Alcohol Consumption in Black Women." *International Journal of the Addictions,* 25(12):1415–1427.

Taylor, Verta, and Nicole C. Raeburn. 1995. "Identity Politics as High-Risk Activism: Career Consequences for Lesbian, Gay, and Bisexual Sociologists." *Social Problems,* 42(2):252–273.

Terkel, Studs. 1990. *Working: People Talk about What They Do All Day and How They Feel about What They Do.* New York: Ballantine (orig. pub. 1972).

Terkel, Studs. 1996. *Coming of Age: The Story of Our Century by Those Who've Lived It.* New York: St. Martin's Griffin.

Terry, Don. 1996. "Suit Says Schools Failed to Protect a Gay Student." *New York Times* (March 29):A8.

Texas Lawyer. 1997. "A.G.'s Opinions: Hopwood/Scholarship Programs/Equal Protection." (February 17):24–25.

Theriault, Reg. 1995. *How to Tell When You're Tired: A Brief Examination of Work.* New York: W.W. Norton.

Thomas, Cal. 1996. "Overrule Same-Sex Marriage." *Austin American-Statesman* (December 6):A15.

Thomas, Gale E. 1995. "Conclusion: Healthy Communities as a Basis for Healthy Race and Ethnic Relations." In Gail E. Thomas (Ed.), *Race and Ethnicity in America: Meeting the Challenge in the 21st Century.* Bristol, PA: Taylor & Francis, pp. 335–342.

Thomas, Jo. 1997. "McVeigh Jury Decides on Sentence of Death in Oklahoma Bombing." *New York Times* (June 14):1, 8.

Thomson, Elizabeth, and Ugo Colella. 1992. "Cohabitation and Marital Stability: Quality or Commitment?" *Journal of Marriage and the Family,* 54:259–267.

Thornberry, Terence P., Marvin D. Krohn, Alan J. Lizotte, and Deborah Chard-Wierschem. 1993. "The Role of Juvenile Gangs in Facilitating Delinquent Behavior. *Journal of Research in Crime and Delinquency,* 30(1):55–87.

Thorne, Barrie. 1995. "Girls and Boys Together . . . But Mostly Apart: Gender Arrangements in Elementary School." In Michael S. Kimmel and Michael A. Messner (Eds.), *Men's Lives* (3rd ed.). Boston: Allyn and Bacon, pp. 61–73.

Thornton, Arland. 1989. "Changing Attitudes toward Family Issues in the United States." *Journal of Marriage and the Family,* 51 (November):873–893.

Thornton, Michael C., Linda M. Chatters, Robert Joseph Taylor, and Walter R. Allen. 1990. "Sociodemographic and Environmental Correlates of Racial Socialization by Black Parents." *Child Development,* 61:401–409.

Thornton, Russell. 1984. "Cherokee Population Losses during the Trail of Tears: A New Perspective and a New Estimate." *Ethnohistory,* 31:289–300.

Thornton, Russell. 1987. *American Indian Holocaust and Survival.* Norman: University of Oklahoma Press.

Thurow, Lester C. 1996. *The Future of Capitalism: How Today's Economic Forces Shape Tomorrow's World.* New York: William Morrow.

Tienda, Marta, and Haya Stier. 1996. "Generating Labor Market Inequality: Employment Opportunities and the Accumulation of Disadvantage." *Social Problems,* 43(2):147–165.

Tierney, John. 1994. "Porn, the Low-Slung Engine of Progress." *New York Times* (January 9):H1, H18.

Time. 1996a. "A Journey of 10,000 Miles Begins with the Shoes." *Time* (June 17):78.

Time. 1996b. "Pulling the Plug on Porn." *Time* (January 8):62.

Toner, Robin. 1993. "People without Health Insurance." *New York Times* (November 14):HD16.

Toner, Robin. 1995. "No Free Rides: Generational Push Has Not Come to Shove." *New York Times* (December 31):E1, E4.

Toner, Robin, and Robert Pear. 1995. "Medicare, Turning 30, Won't Be What It Was." *New York Times* (July 23):1, 12.

Torrey, E. Fuller. 1988. *Nowhere to Go: The Tragic Odyssey of the Homeless Mentally Ill.* New York: Harper and Row.

Tower, Cynthia Crosson. 1996. *Child Abuse and Neglect* (3rd ed.). Boston: Allyn and Bacon.

Trattner, Walter I. 1989. *From Poor Law to Welfare State: A History of Social Welfare in America.* New York: The Free Press.

Travis, John. 1995. "X Chromosome Again Linked to Homosexuality." *Science News,* 148 (November 4):295.

Tribe, Laurence H. 1996. "Toward a Less Perfect Union." *New York Times* (May 26):E11.

Trice, Harrison M., and Paul Michael Roman. 1970. "Delabeling, Relabeling, and Alcoholics Anonymous." *Social Problems,* 17(4):538–546.

Tumulty, Karen. 1996. "Why Subsidies Survive." *Time* (March 25):46–47.

Turk, Austin T. 1966. "Conflict and Criminality." *American Sociological Review,* 31:338–352.

Turk, Austin T. 1971. *Criminality and Legal Order.* Chicago: Rand McNally.

Turkle, Sherry. 1995. *Life on the Screen: Identity in the Age of the Internet.* New York: Simon & Schuster.

Turpin, Jennifer, and Lester R. Kurtz. 1997. "Introduction: Violence The Micro/Macro Link." In Jennifer Turpin and Lester R. Kurtz (Eds.), *The Web of Violence: From Interpersonal to Global.* Urbana and Chicago: University of Illinois, pp. 1–27.

Tyson, Eric K. 1993. "Credit Crackdown: Control Your Spending Before It Controls You." *San Francisco Examiner* (November 28):E1. (Cited in Ritzer, 1995.)

Uchitelle, Louis. 1995. "Retirement's Worried Face: For Many, the Crisis Is Now." *New York Times* (July 30):F1, F4.

Uchitelle, Louis, and N. R. Kleinfield. 1996. "On the Battlefields of Business, Millions of Casualties." *New York Times* (March 3):1, 14–17, 28.

United Nations. 1995. *The World's Women 1995: Trends and Statistics.* New York: United Nations.

United Nations. 1996. *Human Development Report 1996.* New York: Oxford University Press.

United Nations Environmental Program. 1992. *Status of Desertification and Implementation of the United Nations Plan of Action to Combat Desertification.* Nairobi, Egypt: United Nations.

U.S. Bureau of the Census. 1995a. *Employment and Earnings.* Washington, DC: U.S. Government Printing Office.

U.S. Bureau of the Census. 1995b. *Population Profile of the United States, 1995.* Current Population Reports, Series P23–189. Washington, DC: U.S. Government Printing Office.

U.S. Bureau of the Census. 1995c. *Statistical Abstract of the United States, 1995* (115th ed.). Washington, DC: U.S. Government Printing Office.

U.S. Bureau of the Census. 1996a. *Current Population Reports: A Brief Look at Postwar U.S. Income Inequality.* Washington, DC: U.S. Government Printing Office.

U.S. Bureau of the Census. 1996b. *Statistical Abstract of the United States, 1996.* (116th ed.). Washington, DC: U.S. Government Printing Office.

U.S. Bureau of Labor Statistics. 1995. *Current Population Survey.* Washington, DC: U.S. Government Printing Office, January 1995.

U.S. Bureau of Labor Statistics, 1996. *Current Population Survey.* Washington, DC: U.S. Government Printing Office, January 1996.

U.S. Conference of Mayors. 1995. *A Status Report on Hunger and Homelessness in America's Cities.* Washington, DC: United States Conference of Mayors.

U.S. Department of Labor, Bureau of Labor Statistics. 1995. *USDL News,* Bulletin 95–288 (August 3). Washington, DC: U.S. Government Printing Office.

U.S. Department of Labor, Bureau of Labor Statistics. 1996. *Occupational Injuries and Illnesses in the United States by Industry*. Washington, DC: U.S. Government Printing Office.

U.S. Department of State. 1996. *International Narcotics Control Strategy Report*. Washington, DC: U.S. Department of State.

U.S. House of Representatives, Committee on Ways and Means. 1994. *1994 Green Book*. Washington, DC: U.S. Government Printing Office.

Urschel, Joe. 1996. "How Girls Get Scared Away from Computers." *USA Today* (June 26):1D–2D.

Valdez, Avelardo. 1993. "Persistent Poverty, Crime, and Drugs: U.S.-Mexican Border Region." In Joan Moore and Raquel Pinderhughes (Eds.), *In the Barrios: Latinos and the Underclass Debate*. New York: Russell Sage Foundation, pp. 173–194.

Vanneman, Reeve, and Lynn Weber Cannon. 1987. *The American Perception of Class*. Philadelphia: Temple University Press.

Vetter, Harold J., and Gary R. Perlstein. 1991. *Perspectives on Terrorism*. Pacific Grove, CA: Brooks/Cole.

Vick, Karl. 1997. "Intoxicated N.C. Driver Handed Life Sentence." *Washington Post* (May 7):A9.

Vissing, Yvonne M. 1996. *Out of Sight, out of Mind: Homeless Children and Families in Small-Town America*. Lexington, KY: University Press of Kentucky.

Vito, Gennaro F., and Ronald M. Holmes. 1994. *Criminology: Theory, Research and Policy*. Belmont, CA: Wadsworth.

Viviano, Frank. 1995. "The New Mafia Order." *Mother Jones* (May–June):45–55.

Wagner, David. 1993. *Checkerboard Square: Culture and Resistance in a Homeless Community*. Boulder, CO: Westview.

Wajcman, Judy. 1991. *Feminism Confronts Technology*. University Park, PA: Pennsylvania State University Press.

Wald, Matthew L. 1996a. "A Fading Drumbeat against Drunken Driving." *New York Times* (December 15):E5.

Wald, Matthew L. 1996b. "Group Says Alcohol-Related Traffic Deaths Are Rising." *New York Times* (November 27):A11.

Walker, S. L. 1994. "Critics Fume at Mayor of World Smog Capital. *San Diego Union-Tribune* (April 22). (Cited in Michael P. Soroka and George J. Bryjak, *Social Problems: A World at Risk*. 1995. Boston: Allyn and Bacon, p. 115.)

Wallace, Jonathan, and Mark Mangan. 1996. *Sex, Laws, and Cyberspace*. New York: M&T Books/Holt.

Wallerstein, Immanuel. 1984. *The Politics of the World Economy*. Cambridge, England: Cambridge University Press.

Wallerstein, Judith, and Sandra Blakeslee. 1989. *Second Chances: Men, Women and Children a Decade after Divorce*. New York: Ticknor & Field.

Wallis, Claudia. 1994. "A Class of Their Own." *Time* (October 31):53–61.

Warner, W. Lloyd, with Marchia Meeker and Kenneth Eells. 1960. *Social Class in America: The Evaluation of Status*. New York: Harper and Row (orig. pub. 1949).

Warr, Mark. 1995. "Public Perceptions of Crime and Punishment." In Joseph F. Sheley (Ed.), *Criminology: A Contemporary Handbook* (2nd ed.). Belmont, CA: Wadsworth, pp. 15–31.

Warshaw, Robin. 1994. *I Never Called It Rape*. New York: HarperPerennial.

Wartella, Ellen. 1995. "The Commercialization of Youth: Channel One in Context." *Phi Delta Kappan*, 76 (February):448–451.

Waters, Malcolm. 1995. *Globalization*. New York: Routledge.

Watson, Roy E. L., and Peter W. DeMeo. 1987. "Premarital Cohabitation Versus Traditional Courtship and Subsequent Marital Adjustment: A Replication and a Follow-Up." *Family Relations*, 36:193–197.

Webster, Frank. 1995. *Theories of the Information Society*. London and New York: Routledge.

Weeks, John R. 1992. *Population: An Introduction to Concepts and Issues* (5th ed.). Belmont, CA: Wadsworth.

Weinberg, Martin S., and Colin Williams. 1975. *Male Homosexuals*. New York: Penguin.

Weinberg, Martin S., Colin J. Williams, and Douglas W. Pryor. 1994. *Dual Attraction: Understanding Bisexuality*. New York: Oxford University Press.

Weiner, Jonathan. 1990. *The Next One Hundred Years: Shaping the Fate of Our Living Earth*. New York: Bantam.

Weiner, Tim. 1994. "The Men in the Gray Federal Bureaucracy." *New York Times* (April 10):E4.

Weiner, Tim. 1995. "Serial Bomber Threatens Blast aboard a Los Angeles Airliner." *New York Times* (June 29):A1, A6.

Weiner, Tim. 1997. "Terrorism's Worldwide Toll Was High in 1996, U.S. Report Says." *New York Times* (May 1):A10.

Weise, Elizabeth. 1996. "Two Computer Hackers Serving Prison Time." *Austin American-Statesman* (April 8):D1, D6.

Weisner, Thomas S., Helen Garnier, and James Loucky. 1994. "Domestic Tasks, Gender Egalitarian Values, and Children's Gender Typing in Conventional and Nonconventional Families." *Sex Roles*, 30:23–54.

Weiss, Leslie. 1996. "Tightening the Beltway." *Mother Jones* (March–April):57.

Weiten, Wayne, and Margaret A. Lloyd. 1994. *Psychology Applied to Modern Life: Adjustment in the 90s*. Pacific Grove, CA: Brooks/Cole.

Weitz, Rose. 1996. *The Sociology of Health, Illness, and Health Care: A Critical Approach*. Belmont, CA: Wadsworth.

Weitzman, Lenore J. 1985. *The Divorce Revolution.* New York: Free Press.

Welch, Bud. 1997. "A Father's Urge to Forgive." *Time* (June 16):36.

Wellman, David T. 1993. *Portraits of White Racism* (2nd ed.). New York: Cambridge University Press.

Westoff, Charles F. 1995. "International Population Policy." *Society* (May–June):11–15.

Westrum, Ron. 1991. *Technologies and Society: The Shaping of People and Things.* Belmont, CA: Wadsworth.

Wheeler, David L. 1997. "The Animal Origins of Male Violence." *Chronicle of Higher Education* (March 28):A15–A16.

Whitney, Craig R. 1996a. "Europeans Redefine What Makes a Citizen." *New York Times* (January 7, 1996):E6.

Whitney, Craig R. 1996b. "African Immigrants Refusing to Leave France." *New York Times International Edition* (April 4, 1996):A3.

Wilhelm, Anthony. 1996. *Latinos and Information Technology: Perspectives on the 21st Century.* Claremont, CA: The Tomás River Center.

Wilkie, Jane Riblett. 1993. "Changes in U.S. Men's Attitudes toward the Family Provider Role, 1972–1989." *Gender and Society,* 7(2):261–279.

Williams, Christine L. 1992. "The Glass Escalator: Hidden Advantages for Men in the 'Female' Professions." *Social Problems,* 39(3):253–268.

Williams, Christine L. 1995. *Still a Man's World: Men Who Do Women's Work.* Berkeley, CA: University of California Press.

Williams, David R., David T. Takeuchi, and Russell K. Adair. 1992. "Socioeconomic Status and Psychiatric Disorders among Blacks and Whites." *Social Forces,* 71:179–195.

Williams, Gregory Howard. 1996. *Life on the Color Line: The True Story of a White Boy Who Discovered He Was Black.* New York: Plume/Penguin.

Williams, Lena. 1995. "A Silk Blouse on the Assembly Line? (Yes, the Boss's)." *New York Times* (February 5):F7.

Williams, Mike. 1993. "'Sick Building' Epidemic Silently Sweeps the Workplace." *Houston Chronicle* (February 21):A1.

Williams, Richard G. 1997. "Once a Doctor, Now a 'Provider.'" *Austin American-Statesman* (March 19): A19.

Williams, Robin M., Jr. 1970. *American Society: A Sociological Interpretation* (3rd ed.). New York: Knopf.

Williamson, Robert C., Alice Duffy Rinehart, and Thomas O. Blank. 1992. *Early Retirement: Promises and Pitfalls.* New York: Plenum Press.

Willis, Ellen. 1981. *Beginning to See the Light.* New York: Alfred Knopf.

Willis, Ellen. 1983. "Feminism, Moralism, and Pornography." In Ann Snitow, Christine Stansell, and Sharon Thompson (Eds.), *Powers of Desire: The Politics of Sexuality.* New York: Monthly Review Press, pp. 460–466.

Wilson, David (Ed.). 1997. "Globalization and the Changing U.S. City." *The Annals of the American Academy of Political and Social Science,* 551(May). Special Issue. Thousand Oaks, CA: Sage.

Wilson, Edward O. 1975. *Sociobiology: A New Synthesis.* Cambridge, MA: Harvard University Press.

Wilson, Patricia A. 1992. *Exports and Local Development: Mexico's New Maquiladoras.* Austin, TX: University of Texas Press.

Wilson, Wayne. 1991. *Good Murders and Bad Murders: A Consumer's Guide to the Age of Information.* New York: University Press of America.

Wilson, William Julius. 1996. *When Work Disappears: The World of the New Urban Poor.* New York: Knopf.

Wirth, Louis. 1938. "Urbanism as a Way of Life." *American Journal of Sociology,* 40:1–24.

Wirth, Louis. 1945. "The Problem of Minority Groups." In Ralph Linton (Ed.), *The Science of Man in the World Crisis.* New York: Columbia University Press, p. 38.

Witteman, P. 1991. "Lost in America." *Time* (February 11):76-77.

Wolf, Robin. 1996. *Marriages and Families in a Diverse Society.* New York: HarperCollins.

Wolfgang, Marvin E., and Franco Ferracuti. 1967. *The Subculture of Violence: Towards an Integrated Theory in Criminology.* Beverly Hills, CA: Sage.

Women's International Network. 1995a. "Sex Trade Flourishing in Japan." *WIN News* 21(1) (Winter):42.

Women's International Network. 1995b. "Women in Medicine and Health Face Discrimination." *WIN News* 21(4):43.

Women's Research and Education Institute. 1994. *The American Woman 1994–95: Women and Health.* Edited by Cynthia Costello and Anne J. Stone. New York: W.W. Norton.

Women's Research and Education Institute. 1996. *The American Woman 1996–97: Women and Work.* Edited by Cynthia Costello and Barbara Kivimae Krimgold. New York: W.W. Norton.

Women's Sports Foundation. 1989. *The Women's Sports Foundation Report, Minorities in Sports: The Effect of Varsity Sports Participation on the Social, Educational, and Career Mobility of Minority Students.* New York: Women's Sports Foundation.

Woods, James D., with Jay H. Lucas. 1993. *The Corporate Closet: The Professional Lives of Gay Men in America.* New York: Free Press.

Woodward, Bob. 1997. "Chinese Officials Linked to Influence-Buying Plan." *Austin American-Statesman* (April 27):A3.

Woog, Dan. 1995. *School's Out: The Impact of Gay and Lesbian Issues on America's Schools.* Boston: Alyson Publications.

The World Almanac and Book of Facts, 1996. Mahwah, NJ: World Almanac Books.

World Health Organization. 1946. *Constitution of the World Health Organization.* New York: World Health Organization Interim Commission, 1946.

World Resources Institute. 1992. *World Resources 1992–93.* New York: Oxford.

Wrangham, Richard, and Dale Peterson. 1996. *Demonic Males: Apes and the Origins of Human Violence.* New York: Houghton Mifflin.

Wren, Christopher. 1996a. "Clinton Declares That Columbia Has Failed to Curb Drug Trade." *New York Times* (March 2):1, 5.

Wren, Christopher. 1996b. "Teen-Agers Find Drugs Easy to Obtain and Warnings Easy to Ignore." *New York Times* (October 10):A12.

Wright, Erik Olin. 1979. *Class Structure and Income Determination.* New York: Academic Press.

Wright, Erik Olin. 1985. *Class.* London: Verso.

Wright, Erik Olin, Karen Shire, Shu-Ling Hwang, Maureen Dolan, and Janeen Baxter. 1992. "The Non-Effects of Class on the Gender Division of Labor in the Home: A Comparative Study of Sweden and the U.S." *Gender and Society,* 6(2):252–282.

Wright, Quincy. 1964. *A Study of War.* Chicago: University of Chicago Press.

Wright, Richard T., and Scott Decker. 1994. *Burglars on the Job: Streetlife and Residential Break-ins.* Boston: Northeastern University Press.

WuDunn, Sheryl. 1995a. "In Japan, Still Getting Tea and No Sympathy." *New York Times* (August 27):E3.

WuDunn, Sheryl. 1995b. "Japanese Cult: A Strong Lure and a Danger to Challenge." *New York Times* (March 24):A1.

WuDunn, Sheryl. 1995c. "Japanese Women Fight Servility." *New York Times* (July 9):6.

WuDunn, Sheryl. 1996. "In Japan, Even Toddlers Feel the Pressure to Excel." *New York Times* (January 23):A3.

Young, J. H. 1961. *The Toadstool Millionnaires: A Social History of Patent Medicine in America before Federal Regulation.* Princeton, NJ: Princeton University Press.

Young, Jeffrey R. 1996a. "'Indecency' on the Internet." *The Chronicle of Higher Education* (April 26):A21, A25.

Young, Jeffrey. 1996b. "Spies Like Us." *Forbes ASAP* (June 3):71–76.

Young, Michael Dunlap. 1994. *The Rise of the Meritocracy.* New Brunswick, NJ: Transaction.

Zate, Maria. 1996. "Hispanics Struggle for Corporate Stature." *Austin American-Statesman* (August 11): H1, H3.

Zatz, Marjorie S., and William J. Chambliss (Ed.). 1993. *Making Law: The State, the Law, and Structural Contradictions.* Bloomington, IN: Indiana University Press.

Zelizer, Viviana. 1985. *Pricing the Priceless Child: The Changing Social Value of Children.* New Haven, CT: Yale University Press.

Zuboff, Shoshana. 1988. *In the Age of the Smart Machine: The Future of Work and Power.* New York: Basic Books.

Name Index

Subject Index

Note: Italicized letters *f, m,* and *t* following page numbers indicate figures, maps, and tables, respectively.

PHOTO CREDITS

Page xviii, Andrew Lichtenstein/The Image Works; Page 3, Michael Dwyer/Stock, Boston; Page 12, Dorothy Littell Greco/Stock, Boston; Page 13, Bob Strong/The Image Works; Page 17, Stephen Ferry/Gamma Liaison; Page 22, Reuters/Corbis-Bettmann; Page 30 Left, A. Ramey/ Woodfin Camp & Associates; Page 30 Right, Joe Sohm/The Image Works; Page 37, Donna Binder/Impact Visuals; Page 39, AP/Wide World Photos; Page 44, Will Faller; Page 48, AP/ Wide World Photos; Page 56, Library of Congress; Page 59, Steven Rubin/The Image Works; Page 61, Will Faller; Page 66, Bob Daemmrich/Stock, Boston; Page 70, Lawrence Migdale/ Stock, Boston; Page 73, AP/Wide World Photos; Page 82, Bob Daemmrich/Stock, Boston; Page 85, Dennis Brack/Black Star; Page 90, Les Todd/Duke University Photo; Page 98, Michael A. Schwarz/The Image Works; Page 102, Stacy Pick/Stock, Boston; Page 105, Herb Snitzer/Stock, Boston; Page 107, Bob Daemmrich/Stock, Boston; Page 112, Donna Binder/Impact Visuals; Page 118, Ilkka Uimonen/Sygma; Page 126 Top, Paula Lerner/Woodfin Camp & Associates; Page 126 Bottom, Tom McKitterick/Impact Visuals; Page 132, John Maher/ Stock, Boston; Page 137, Gary Way/Sygma; Page 146, Robert Harbison; Page 148, AP/Wide World Photos; Page 152, Larry Kolvoord/The Image Works; Page 160, Charles Gupton/Stock, Boston; Page 167, Kim Kulish/L.A. Daily News/Sygma; Page 171, Allan Clear/Impact Visuals; Page 180, Ed Lallo (TCSS)/The Picture Cube; Page 184, Chet Seymour/The Picture Cube; Page 187, A. Ramey/Woodfin Camp & Associates; Page 195, Lester Sloan/Woodfin Camp & Associates; Page 199, A. Ramey/Woodfin Camp & Associates; Page 204, Abbas/Magnum Photos; Page 209, Mark Peters/Gamma Liaison; Page 217, Sygma; Page 218, Rick Hunter/SA Express News/Sygma; Page 223, Courtesy of The National Association of Midnight Basketball Leagues, Inc.; Page 226, Mikki Ansin/The Picture Cube; Page 236, Gabe Kirchheimer/Impact Visuals; Page 237, William Campbell/Sygma; Page 250, Spencer Grant/The Picture Cube; Page 260, Esbin-Anderson/The Image Works; Page 263, Robert Harbison; Page 265, James Wilson/Woodfin Camp & Associates; Page 269, Rob Crandal/The Image Works; Page 274, Brian Smith; Page 281, Jim Pickerell; Page 285, Armen Kachaturian/Gamma Liaison; Page 286, Jon Levy/Gamma Liaison; Page 298, AP/Wide World Photos; Page 305, Reuters/Mike Theiler/Archive Photos; Page 307, Reuters/Corbis-Bettmann; Page 310, Reuters/Corbis-Bettmann; Page 314, Bob Daemmrich/Stock, Boston; Page 320, Frank Pedrick/The Image Works; Page 325, Richard Shock/Gamma Liaison; Page 331, Bob Daemmrich/The Image Works; Page 334, John Coletti; Page 340, Jon Burbank/The Image Works; Page 346, Kim Newton/Woodfin Camp & Associates; Page 352, Les Stone/Sygma; Page 355, A. Ramey/Woodfin Camp & Associates; Page 361, Stephanie Maze/Woodfin Camp & Associates; Page 363, Jack Rosen/Impact Visuals; Page 372, Robert Harbison; Page 382, AP/Wide World Photos; Page 386, Dinodia/Impact Visuals; Page 390, Gene Blevins/Los Angeles Daily News/Sygma; Page 394, Reuters/Grigory Tambulov/Archive Photos; Page 396, Reuters/ Oleg Popov/Archive Photos; Page 404, AP/Wide World Photos; Page 405, AP/Wide World Photos; Page 410, Tom Walker/Stock, Boston.